The

NORTON MIX

NORTON CUSTOM

W · W · NORTON & COMPANY · *New York* · *London*

The
NORTON MIX

A CUSTOM PUBLICATION

BLINN COLLEGE

COMPOSITION I

W. W. Norton & Company has been independent since its founding in 1923, when William Warder Norton and Mary D. Herter Norton first published lectures delivered at the People's Institute, the adult education division of New York City's Cooper Union. The firm soon expanded its program beyond the Institute, publishing books by celebrated academics from America and abroad. By mid-century, the two major pillars of Norton's publishing program— trade books and college texts—were firmly established. In the 1950s, the Norton family transferred control of the company to its employees, and today—with a staff of four hundred and a comparable number of trade, college, and professional titles published each year— W. W. Norton & Company stands as the largest and oldest publishing house owned wholly by its employees.

Editor: Katie Hannah
Developmental editors: Mike Fleming and Erin Granville
Managing editor: Marian Johnson
Project editor: Melissa Atkin
Editorial assistant: Sophie Hagen
Production managers: Eric Pier-Hocking and Ashley Horna
Permissions editor: Nancy Rodwan
Photo permissions editor: Trish Marx, Stephanie Romeo
Designer: Toni Krass
Cover designs: Debra Morton-Hoyt
Emedia editor: Eileen Connell
Marketing manager: Scott Berzon
Proofreaders: Paulette McGee, Ben Reynolds
Composition: RR Donnelley
Manufacturing: RR Donnelley

ISBN-13 978-0-393-52069-9

W. W. Norton & Company, Inc., 500 Fifth Avenue, New York, N.Y. 10110
www.wwnorton.com
W. W. Norton & Company Ltd., Castle House, 75/76 Wells Street, London W1T 3QT

GENERAL EDITORS

ELIZABETH RODRIGUEZ KESSLER
COORDINATING EDITOR
University of Houston

JEFFREY ANDELORA
Mesa Community College

MELISSA GOLDTHWAITE
St. Joseph's University

CHARLES HOOD
Antelope Valley College

KATHARINE N. INGS
Manchester College

ANGELA L. JONES
Western Kentucky University

CHRISTOPHER KELLER
University of Texas–Pan American

WITH CONTRIBUTIONS FROM

CEDRIC BURROWS
University of Kansas

LORI CHASTAINE
Boise State University

MICHELLE L. CHESTER
Towson University

DENNIS McGLOTHIN
*University of North Carolina
at Pembroke*

WANDA FRIES
Somerset Community College

HOLLY HASSEL
*University of Wisconsin–
Marathon County*

BETH DINATALE JOHNSON
Ursuline College

Contents

Analysis

MALCOLM GLADWELL
from The Tipping Point   *1*

STEPHEN JAY GOULD
Sex, Drugs, Disasters, and the Extinction of Dinosaurs   *12*

ELISABETH KÜBLER-ROSS
On the Fear of Death   *23*

PLATO
Allegory of the Cave   *33*

NEIL POSTMAN, STEVE POWERS
The Bias of Language, the Bias of Pictures   *40*

MOTOKO RICH
Literacy Debate: Online, R U Reading?   *54*

PAUL CHAAT SMITH
The Big Movie (from Everything You Know About Indians Is Wrong)   *66*

Argument

ROBERT APPLEBAUM
Cancel Student Loan Debt to Stimulate the Economy   *78*

Contents

JUDY BRADY
I Want a Wife   85

PAUL GOODMAN
A Proposal to Abolish Grading   89

MICHAEL LEVIN
The Case for Torture   94

JONATHAN SWIFT
A Modest Proposal   99

ELIE WIESEL
The Perils of Indifference: Lessons Learned from a Violent Century   110

Cause and Effect

DIANE ACKERMAN
Why Leaves Turn Color in the Fall (from A Natural History of the Senses)   117

HUSSEIN AGHA, ROBERT MALLEY
The Arab Counterrevolution   123

WILLIAM F. BUCKLEY JR.
Why Don't We Complain?   137

NICHOLAS CARR
Hal and Me   145

TERRELL F. DIXON, LISA SLAPPEY
The Bayou and the Ship Channel: Finding Place and Building Community in Houston, Texas   159

MAXINE HONG KINGSTON
No Name Woman   174

JONATHAN RAUCH
What Is Marriage For?   189

Contents

ERIC SCHLOSSER
Why McDonald's French Fries Taste So Good 196

KATINA R. STAPLETON
*From the Margins to the Mainstream: The Political Power of
Hip-Hop* 211

Classification and Division

NATALIE ANGIER
Men, Women, Sex, and Darwin 233

RUSSELL BAKER
The Plot Against People 248

JAMAICA KINCAID
Girl 252

WILLIAM LUTZ
The World of Doublespeak 256

GEORGE ORWELL
Politics and the English Language 272

AMY TAN
Two Kinds 288

DEBORAH TANNEN
*Sex, Lies, and Conversation: Why Is It So Hard for Men and
Women to Talk to Each Other?* 302

Comparison and Contrast

DAVE BARRY
A GPS Helps a Guy Always Know Where His Couch Is 310

SUZANNE BRITT
Neat People vs. Sloppy People 314

Contents

BRUCE CATTON
Grant and Lee: A Study in Contrasts   318

SANDRA CISNEROS
Only Daughter   324

JUDITH ORTIZ COFER
The Myth of the Latin Woman; I Just Met a Girl Named María   329

T. ALLEN CULPEPPER
The Myth of Inferiority   338

JOAN DIDION
On Going Home   344

JOAN DIDION
On Keeping a Notebook   349

SOJOURNER TRUTH
Ar'n't I a Woman?   359

Definition

MARGARET ATWOOD
The Female Body   362

ROB FISHMAN
The Generation of Generation Q   368

THOMAS FRIEDMAN
Generation Q   373

GLORIA NAYLOR
A Word's Meaning Can Often Depend on Who Says It   378

JO GOODWIN PARKER
What Is Poverty?   383

Contents

Description

JAMES BALDWIN
Stranger in the Village   389

EDWARD HOAGLAND
The Football Game in My Head   404

NANCY MAIRS
On Being a Cripple   410

JOYCE CAROL OATES
Where Are You Going, Where Have You Been?   426

RICHARD RODRIGUEZ
Aria   446

SARAH VOWELL
Shooting Dad   456

ALICE WALKER
Everyday Use   465

Exemplification

BARBARA EHRENREICH
Cultural Baggage   476

LINDA M. HASSELSTROM
Why One Peaceful Woman Carries a Pistol   482

MARTIN LUTHER KING JR.
I Have a Dream   491

HORACE MINER
Body Ritual Among the Nacirema   498

ANNA QUINDLEN
Homeless   506

Contents

BRENT STAPLES
Just Walk on By: Black Men and Public Space   511

Exposition

FRANCIS BACON
Of Studies   516

TANYA BARRIENTOS
Se Habla Espanol   520

RACHEL CARSON
A Fable for Tomorrow   525

SHELBY STEELE
I'm Black, You're White, Who's Innocent?   529

E. B. WHITE
Once More to the Lake   547

Narration

PAULA GUNN ALLEN
Deer Woman   556

MAYA ANGELOU
Champion of the World   568

CECILIA BALLÍ
Ciudad de la Muerte   573

ANTHONY BOURDAIN
Food Is Good   596

SHIRLEY JACKSON
The Lottery   606

Contents

RANDY PAUSCH
I Never Made It to the NFL   617

Audrey Wick
The Siren Call of the Bingo Hall   622

Process Analysis

MORTIMER J. ADLER
How to Mark a Book   628

FREDERICK DOUGLASS
Learning to Read   635

LARS EIGHNER
On Dumpster Diving   643

TEMPLE GRANDIN
My Mind Is a Web Browser: How People with Autism Think   658

JON KRAKAUER
The Alaska Interior   669

JOSEPH WOOD KRUTCH
The Most Dangerous Predator   685

JESSICA MITFORD
Behind the Formaldehyde Curtain   698

SAMUEL H. SCUDDER
Look at Your Fish: In the Laboratory with Agassiz   709

MALCOLM GLADWELL { *from* The Tipping Point

MALCOLM GLADWELL (b. 1963) was born in England and grew up in Elmira, Ontario, Canada. He graduated from the University of Toronto's Trinity College in 1984 with a BA in history and became a reporter for the *Washington Post* and later the *Post*'s New York bureau chief. Since 1996 he has been a staff writer at the *New Yorker*. He is the author of three best-selling books: *The Tipping Point: How Little Things Make a Big Difference* (2000), *Blink: The Power of Thinking without Thinking* (2005), and *Outliers: The Story of Success* (2008). In 2005 *Time* magazine named Gladwell one of its 100 Most Influential People.

In this selection from *The Tipping Point*, Gladwell explains how a "Tipping Point" works in an epidemic, whether of Hush Puppies shoes or crime, and analyzes the causes and effects of tipping points. As you read, consider some trends you are familiar with—an online text or video going "viral," for instance. Can you pinpoint the Tipping Point of any trends with which you are familiar?

FOR HUSH PUPPIES—THE CLASSIC American brushed-suede shoes with the lightweight crepe sole—the Tipping Point came somewhere between late 1994 and early 1995. The brand had been all but dead until that point. Sales were down to 30,000 pairs a year, mostly to backwoods outlets and small-town family stores. Wolverine, the company that makes Hush Puppies, was thinking of phasing out the shoes that made them famous. But then something strange happened. At a fashion shoot, two Hush Puppies executives—Owen Baxter and Geoffrey Lewis—ran into a stylist from New York who told them that the classic Hush Puppies had suddenly become hip in the clubs and bars of downtown Manhattan. "We were being told," Baxter recalls, "that there were resale shops in the Village, in Soho, where the shoes were being sold. People were going to the Ma and Pa stores, the little stores that still carried them, and buying them up." Baxter and Lewis were baffled at first. It made no sense to them that shoes that were so obviously out of fashion could make a comeback. "We were told that Isaac Mizrahi[1] was wearing the shoes himself," Lewis says. "I think it's fair to say that at the time we had no idea who Isaac Mizrahi was."

By the fall of 1995, things began to happen in a rush. First the designer John Bartlett called. He wanted to use Hush Puppies in his spring collection. Then another Manhattan designer, Anna Sui, called, wanting shoes for her show as well. In Los Angeles, the designer Joel Fitzgerald put a twenty-five-foot inflatable basset hound—the symbol of the Hush Puppies brand—on the roof of his Hollywood store and gutted an adjoining art gallery to turn it into a Hush Puppies boutique. While he was still painting and putting up shelves, the actor Pee-wee Herman walked in and asked for a couple of pairs. "It was total word of mouth," Fitzgerald remembers.

In 1995, the company sold 430,000 pairs of the classic Hush Puppies, and the next year it sold four times that, and the year after that still more, until Hush Puppies were once again a staple of the wardrobe of the young American male. In 1996, Hush Puppies won the prize for best accessory at the Council of Fashion Designers awards dinner at Lincoln Center, and the president of the firm stood up on the stage with Calvin Klein and Donna Karan and accepted an award for an achievement that—as he would be the first to admit—his company had almost nothing to do with. Hush Puppies had suddenly exploded, and it all started with a handful of kids in the East Village and Soho.

How did that happen? Those first few kids, whoever they were, weren't deliberately trying to promote Hush Puppies. They were wearing them precisely because no one else would wear them. Then the fad spread to two fashion designers who used the shoes to peddle something else—haute couture. The shoes were an incidental touch. No one

[1]American fashion designer (b. 1961). [Ed.]

was trying to make Hush Puppies a trend. Yet, somehow, that's exactly what happened. The shoes passed a certain point in popularity and they tipped. How does a thirty-dollar pair of shoes go from a handful of downtown Manhattan hipsters and designers to every mall in America in the space of two years?

1.

There was a time, not very long ago, in the desperately poor New York City neighborhoods of Brownsville and East New York, when the streets would turn into ghost towns at dusk. Ordinary working people wouldn't walk on the sidewalks. Children wouldn't ride their bicycles on the streets. Old folks wouldn't sit on stoops and park benches. The drug trade ran so rampant and gang warfare was so ubiquitous in that part of Brooklyn that most people would take to the safety of their apartment at nightfall. Police officers who served in Brownsville in the 1980s and early 1990s say that, in those years, as soon as the sun went down their radios exploded with chatter between beat officers and their dispatchers over every conceivable kind of violent and dangerous crime. In 1992, there were 2,154 murders in New York City and 626,182 serious crimes, with the weight of those crimes falling hardest in places like Brownsville and East New York.[2] But then something strange happened. At some mysterious and critical point, the crime rate began to turn. It tipped. Within five years, murders had dropped 64.3 percent to 770 and total crimes had fallen by almost half to 355,893. In Brownsville and East New York, the sidewalks filled up again, the bicycles came back, and old folks reappeared on the stoops. "There was a time when it wasn't uncommon to hear rapid fire, like you would hear somewhere in the jungle in Vietnam," says Inspector Edward Messadri, who commands the police precinct in Brownsville. "I don't hear the gunfire anymore."

[2]For a good summary of New York City crime statistics, see: Michael Massing, "The Blue Revolution," in the *New York Review of Books*, November 19, 1998, pp. 32–34. There is another good discussion of the anomalous nature of the New York crime drop in William Bratton and William Andrews, "What We've Learned About Policing," in *City Journal*, Spring 1999, p. 25. [Unless otherwise indicated, all notes are those of the author.]

The New York City police will tell you that what happened in New York was that the city's policing strategies dramatically improved. Criminologists point to the decline of the crack trade and the aging of the population. Economists, meanwhile, say that the gradual improvement in the city's economy over the course of the 1990s had the effect of employing those who might otherwise have become criminals. These are the conventional explanations for the rise and fall of social problems, but in the end none is any more satisfying than the statement that kids in the East Village caused the Hush Puppies revival. The changes in the drug trade, the population, and the economy are all long-term trends, happening all over the country. They don't explain why crime plunged in New York City so much more than in other cities around the country, and they don't explain why it all happened in such an extraordinarily short time. As for the improvements made by the police, they are important too. But there is a puzzling gap between the scale of the changes in policing and the size of the effect on places like Brownsville and East New York. After all, crime didn't just slowly ebb in New York as conditions gradually improved. It plummeted. How can a change in a handful of economic and social indices cause murder rates to fall by two-thirds in five years?

2.

The Tipping Point is the biography of an idea, and the idea is very simple. It is that the best way to understand the emergence of fashion trends, the ebb and flow of crime waves, or, for that matter, the transformation of unknown books into bestsellers, or the rise of teenage smoking, or the phenomena of word of mouth, or any number of the other mysterious changes that mark everyday life is to think of them as epidemics. Ideas and products and messages and behaviors spread just like viruses do.

The rise of Hush Puppies and the fall of New York's crime rate are textbook examples of epidemics in action. Although they may sound as if they don't have very much in common, they share a basic, underlying pattern. First of all, they are clear examples of contagious behavior. No one took out an advertisement and told people that the traditional Hush Puppies were cool and they should start wearing them. Those kids simply wore the shoes when they went to clubs or cafes or walked the streets of downtown New York, and in so doing exposed other people to their fashion sense. They infected them with the Hush Puppies "virus."

The crime decline in New York surely happened the same way. It wasn't that some huge percentage of would-be murderers suddenly sat up in 1993 and decided not to commit any more crimes. Nor was it that the police managed magically to intervene in a huge percentage of situations that would otherwise have turned deadly. What happened is that the small number of people in the small number of situations in which the police or the new social forces had some impact started behaving very differently, and that behavior somehow spread to other would-be criminals in similar situations. Somehow a large number of people in New York got "infected" with an anti-crime virus in a short time.

The second distinguishing characteristic of these two examples is 10 that in both cases little changes had big effects. All of the possible reasons for why New York's crime rate dropped are changes that happened at the margin; they were incremental changes. The crack trade leveled off. The population got a little older. The police force got a little better. Yet the effect was dramatic. So too with Hush Puppies. How many kids are we talking about who began wearing the shoes in downtown Manhattan? Twenty? Fifty? One hundred—at the most? Yet their actions seem to have single-handedly started an international fashion trend.

Finally, both changes happened in a hurry. They didn't build steadily and slowly. It is instructive to look at a chart of the crime rate in New York City from, say, the mid-1960s to the late 1990s. It looks like a giant arch. In 1965, there were 200,000 crimes in the city and from that point on the number begins a sharp rise, doubling in two years and continuing almost unbroken until it hits 650,000 crimes a year in the mid-1970s. It stays steady at that level for the next two decades, before plunging downward in 1992 as sharply as it rose thirty years earlier. Crime did not taper off. It didn't gently decelerate. It hit a certain point and jammed on the brakes.

These three characteristics—one, contagiousness; two, the fact that little causes can have big effects; and three, that change happens not gradually but at one dramatic moment—are the same three principles that define how measles moves through a grade-school classroom or the flu attacks every winter. Of the three, the third trait—the idea that epidemics can rise or fall in one dramatic moment—is the most important, because it is the principle that makes sense of the first two and that permits the greatest insight into why modern change happens the way it does. The name given to that one dramatic moment in an epidemic when everything can change all at once is the Tipping Point.

3.

A world that follows the rules of epidemics is a very different place from the world we think we live in now. Think, for a moment, about the concept of contagiousness. If I say that word to you, you think of colds and the flu or perhaps something very dangerous like HIV or Ebola. We have, in our minds, a very specific, biological notion of what contagiousness means. But if there can be epidemics of crime or epidemics of fashion, there must be all kinds of things just as contagious as viruses. Have you ever thought about yawning, for instance? Yawning is a surprisingly powerful act. Just because you read the word "yawning" in the previous two sentences—and the two additional "yawns" in this sentence—a good number of you will probably yawn within the next few minutes. Even as I'm writing this, I've yawned twice. If you're reading this in a public place, and you've just yawned, chances are that a good proportion of everyone who saw you yawn is now yawning too, and a good proportion of the people watching the people who watched you yawn are now yawning as well, and on and on, in an ever-widening, yawning circle.[3]

Yawning is incredibly contagious. I made some of you reading this

---

[3]The leader in research on yawning is Robert Provine, a psychologist at the University of Maryland. Among his papers on the subject are:

Robert Provine, "Yawning as a Stereotyped Action Pattern and Releasing Stimulus," *Ethology* (1983), vol. 72, pp. 109–122.

Robert Provine, "Contagious Yawning and Infant Imitation," *Bulletin of the Psychonomic Society* (1989), vol. 27, no. 2, pp. 125–126.

yawn simply by writing the word "yawn." The people who yawned when they saw you yawn, meanwhile, were infected by the sight of you yawning—which is a second kind of contagion. They might even have yawned if they only heard you yawn, because yawning is also aurally contagious: if you play an audiotape of a yawn to blind people, they'll yawn too. And finally, if you yawned as you read this, did the thought cross your mind—however unconsciously and fleetingly—that you might be tired? I suspect that for some of you it did, which means that yawns can also be emotionally contagious. Simply by writing the word, I can plant a feeling in your mind. Can the flu virus do that? Contagiousness, in other words, is an unexpected property of all kinds of things, and we have to remember that, if we are to recognize and diagnose epidemic change.

The second of the principles of epidemics—that little changes can 15 somehow have big effects—is also a fairly radical notion. We are, as humans, heavily socialized to make a kind of rough approximation between cause and effect. If we want to communicate a strong emotion, if we want to convince someone that, say, we love them, we realize that we need to speak passionately and forthrightly. If we want to break bad news to someone, we lower our voices and choose our words carefully. We are trained to think that what goes into any transaction or relationship or system must be directly related, in intensity and dimension, to what comes out. Consider, for example, the following puzzle. I give you a large piece of paper, and I ask you to fold it over once, and then take that folded paper and fold it over again, and then again, and again, until you have refolded the original paper fifty times. How tall do you think the final stack is going to be? In answer to that question, most people will fold the sheet in their mind's eye, and guess that the pile would be as thick as a phone book or, if they're really courageous, they'll say that it would be as tall as a refrigerator. But the real answer is that the height of the stack would approximate the distance to the sun. And if you folded it over one more time, the stack would be as high as the distance to the sun and back. This is an example of what in mathematics is called a geometric progression. Epidemics are another example of geometric progression: when a virus spreads through a population, it doubles and doubles again, until it has (figuratively) grown from a single sheet of paper all the way to the sun in fifty steps. As human beings we have a hard time with this kind of progression, because the end result—the effect—seems far out of proportion to the cause. To appreciate the power of epidemics, we have to abandon this expectation about proportionality. We need to prepare ourselves for the possibility that sometimes big changes follow from small events, and that sometimes these changes can happen very quickly.

This possibility of sudden change is at the center of the idea of the Tipping Point and might well be the hardest of all to accept. The expression first came into popular use in the 1970s to describe the flight to the suburbs of whites living in the older cities of the American Northeast. When the number of incoming African Americans in a particular neighborhood reached a certain point—20 percent, say—sociologists observed that the community would "tip": most of the remaining whites would leave almost immediately. The Tipping Point is the moment of critical mass, the threshold, the boiling point. There was a Tipping Point for violent crime in New York in the early 1990s, and a Tipping Point for the reemergence of Hush Puppies, just as there is a Tipping Point for the introduction of any new technology. Sharp introduced the first low-priced fax machine in 1984, and sold about 80,000 of those machines in the United States in that first year. For the next three years, businesses slowly and steadily bought more and more faxes, until, in 1987, enough people had faxes that it made sense for everyone to get a fax. Nineteen eighty-seven was the fax machine Tipping Point. A million machines were sold that year, and by 1989 two million new machines had gone into operation. Cellular phones have followed the same trajectory. Through the 1990s, they got smaller and cheaper, and service got better until 1998, when the technology hit a Tipping Point and suddenly everyone had a cell phone.[4]

---

[4]The best way to understand the Tipping Point is to imagine a hypothetical outbreak of the flu. Suppose, for example, that one summer 1,000 tourists come to Manhattan from Canada carrying an untreatable strain of twenty-four-hour virus. This strain of flu has a 2 percent infection rate, which is to say that one out of every 50 people who come into close contact with someone carrying it catches the bug himself. Let's say that 50 is also exactly the number of people the average Manhattanite—in the course of riding the subways and mingling with colleagues at work—comes into contact with every day. What we have, then, is a disease in equilibrium. Those 1,000 Canadian tourists pass on the virus to 1,000 new people

All epidemics have Tipping Points. Jonathan Crane, a sociologist at the University of Illinois, has looked at the effect the number of role models in a community—the professionals, managers, teachers whom the Census Bureau has defined as "high status"—has on the lives of teenagers in the same neighborhood. He found little difference in pregnancy rates or school drop-out rates in neighborhoods of between 40 and 5 percent of high-status workers. But when the number of professionals dropped below 5 percent, the problems exploded. For black schoolchildren, for example, as the percentage of high-status workers falls just 2.2 percentage points—from 5.6 percent to 3.4 percent— drop-out rates more than double. At the same Tipping Point, the rates of childbearing for teenaged girls—which barely move at all up to that point—nearly double. We assume, intuitively, that neighborhoods and social problems decline in some kind of steady progression. But sometimes they may not decline steadily at all; at the Tipping Point, schools can lose control of their students, and family life can disintegrate all at once.

---

on the day they arrive. And the next day those 1,000 newly infected people pass on the virus to another 1,000 people, just as the original 1,000 tourists who started the epidemic are returning to health. With those getting sick and those getting well so perfectly in balance, the flu chugs along at a steady but unspectacular clip through the rest of the summer and the fall.

But then comes the Christmas season. The subways and buses get more crowded with tourists and shoppers, and instead of running into an even 50 people a day, the average Manhattanite now has close contact with, say, 55 people a day. All of a sudden, the equilibrium is disrupted. The 1,000 flu carriers now run into 55,000 people a day, and at a 2 percent infection rate, that translates into 1,100 cases the following day. Those 1,100, in turn, are now passing on their virus to 55,000 people as well, so that by day three there are 1,210 Manhattanites with the flu and by day four 1,331 and by the end of the week there are nearly 2,000, and so on up, in an exponential spiral, until Manhattan has a full-blown flu epidemic on its hands by Christmas Day. That moment when the average flu carrier went from running into 50 people a day to running into 55 people was the Tipping Point. It was the point at which an ordinary and stable phenomenon—a low-level flu outbreak—turned into a public health crisis. If you were to draw a graph of the progress of the Canadian flu epidemic, the Tipping Point would be the point on the graph where the line suddenly turned upward.

Tipping Points are moments of great sensitivity. Changes made right at the Tipping Point can have enormous consequences. Our Canadian flu became an epidemic when the number of New Yorkers running into a flu carrier jumped from 50 to 55 a day. But had that

I remember once as a child seeing our family's puppy encounter snow for the first time. He was shocked and delighted and over-whelmed, wagging his tail nervously, sniffing about in this strange, fluffy substance, whimpering with the mystery of it all. It wasn't much colder on the morning of his first snowfall than it had been the evening before. It might have been 34 degrees the previous evening, and now it was 31 degrees. Almost nothing had changed, in other words, yet—and this was the amazing thing—everything had changed. Rain had become something entirely different. Snow! We are all, at heart, gradu-alists, our expectations set by the steady passage of time. But the world of the Tipping Point is a place where the unexpected becomes ex-pected, where radical change is more than possibility. It is—contrary to all our expectations—a certainty.

---

same small change happened in the opposite direction, if the number had dropped from 50 to 45, that change would have pushed the number of flu victims down to 478 within a week, and within a few weeks more at that rate, the Canadian flu would have vanished from Man-hattan entirely. Cutting the number exposed from 70 to 65, or 65 to 60 or 60 to 55 would not have been sufficient to end the epidemic. But a change right at the Tipping Point, from 50 to 45, would.

The Tipping Point model has been described in several classic works of sociology. I suggest:

Mark Granovetter, "Threshold Models of Collective Behavior," *American Journal of Sociology* (1978), vol. 83, pp. 1420–1443.

Mark Granovetter and R. Soong, "Threshold Models of Diffusion and Collective Be-havior," *Journal of Mathematical Sociology* (1983), vol. 9, pp. 165–179.

Thomas Schelling, "Dynamic Models of Segregation," *Journal of Mathematical So-ciology* (1971), vol. 1, pp. 143–186.

Thomas Schelling, *Micromotives and Macrobehavior* (New York: W. W. Norton, 1978).

Jonathan Crane, "The Epidemic Theory of Ghettos and Neighborhood Effects on Dropping Out and Teenage Childbearing," *American Journal of Sociology* (1989), vol. 95, no. 5, pp. 1226–1259.

STUDY QUESTIONS

1. In your own words, DEFINE a "Tipping Point." What three characteristics of Tipping Points does Gladwell point out?

2. Gladwell uses several examples to explain what a Tipping Point is. How effective are these examples? Explain.

3. *For Writing.* Choose a trend—perhaps from technology, fashion, or sports—and RESEARCH its popularity. Determine its "Tipping Point," and, in an essay, make an ARGUMENT for why that Tipping Point occurred. Also, DESCRIBE its effects.

STEPHEN JAY GOULD

{

Sex, Drugs, Disasters, and the

Extinction of Dinosaurs

STEVEN JAY GOULD (1941–2002) was born in New York City; he earned his undergraduate degree at Antioch College in Ohio and his PhD at Columbia University. For thirty-five years Gould was a professor at Harvard University. However, he is best known for his ability to explain complex scientific topics in ways that make them accessible to a general audience, often by writing articles in popular magazines and by advising (and often appearing in) television programs like PBS's *NOVA*. He collected his columns from the magazine *Natural History* into several book-length collections, including *Hen's Teeth and Horse's Toes* (1983), *The Flamingo's Smile* (1985), and *Bully for Brontosaurus* (1991). The recipient of dozens of honorary degrees, Gould was a finalist for the Pulitzer Prize for his book *Wonderful Life: The Burgess Shale and the Nature of History* (1989).

The following essay, originally published in *Discover Magazine* in 1984, presents three potential hypotheses for the extinction of the dinosaurs and analyzes each for its scientific value. As you read, think about how the essay is organized and how Gould incorporates humor into a serious discussion. How might these qualities contribute to Gould's reputation as a writer who excels at presenting scientific topics to a general audience?

———————————

SCIENCE, IN ITS MOST FUNDAMENTAL definition, is a fruitful mode of inquiry, not a list of enticing conclusions. The conclusions are the consequence, not the essence. My greatest unhappiness with most popular presentations of science concerns their failure to separate fascinating claims from the methods that scientists use to establish the facts of nature. Journalists, and the public, thrive on controversial and stunning statements. But science is, basically, a way of knowing—in P. B. Medawar's apt words, "the art of the soluble." If the growing corps of popular science writers would focus on *how* scientists develop and defend those fascinating claims, they would make their greatest possible contribution to public understanding.

Consider three ideas, proposed in perfect seriousness to account for that greatest of all titillating puzzles—the extinction of dinosaurs. These three notions invoke the primarly fascinating themes of our culture—sex, drugs, and violence—and I want to show why two of them rank as silly speculation, and why the other represents science at its grandest and most useful.

Science works with testable hypotheses. If, after much compilation and scrutiny of data, new information continues to affirm a hypothesis, we may accept it provisionally and gain confidence as further evidence mounts. We can never be completely sure that a hypothesis is right, though we may be able to show with confidence that it is wrong. The best scientific hypotheses are also generous and expansive: they suggest extensions and implications that enlighten related, and even far distant, subjects. Simply consider how the idea of evolution has influenced virtually every intellectual field.

Useless speculation, on the other hand, is restrictive. It generates no testable hypothesis, proposes no way to obtain potentially refuting evidence. Please note that I am not speaking of truth or falsity. The speculation may well be true; still, if it provides, in principle, no material for affirmation or rejection, we can make nothing of it. It must simply stand forever as an intriguing idea. Useless speculation turns in on itself and leads nowhere; good science reaches out. But, enough preaching. Let's move on to dinosaurs, and the three proposed causes of their extinction.

1. Sex: Testes function only in a narrow range of temperature (those of mammals hang externally in a scrotal sac because they need to be cooler than the body). A worldwide rise in temperature at the close of the Cretaceous period caused the testes of dinosaurs to stop functioning and led to their extinction by sterilization of males.

2. Drugs: Angiosperms (flowering plants) first evolved toward the end of the dinosaurs' reign. Many of these plants contain psychoactive

agents, avoided by mammals today because of their bitter taste. Dinosaurs had neither means to taste the bitterness, nor livers effective enough to detoxify the substances. They died of massive overdoses.

3. Disasters: A huge asteroid struck the earth some 65 million years ago, lofting a cloud of dust into the sky and blocking sunlight, thereby suppressing photosynthesis and so drastically lowering world temperatures that dinosaurs and hosts of other creatures became extinct.

Before analyzing these three tantalizing statements, we must establish a basic ground rule often violated in proposals for the dinosaurs' demise. *There is no separate problem of the extinction of dinosaurs.* Too often we divorce specific events from their wider contexts and systems of cause and effect. The fundamental fact of dinosaur extinction is that it coincided with the demise of many other groups across a wide range of habitats, from terrestrial to marine.

The history of life has been punctuated by brief episodes of mass extinction. A recent analysis by University of Chicago paleontologists Jack Sepkoski and Dave Raup, based on the best and most exhaustive tabulation of data ever assembled, shows clearly that five episodes of mass dying stand well above the "background" extinctions of normal times. The Cretaceous debacle, occurring 65 million years ago and separating the Mesozoic and Cenozoic eras of our geological time scale, ranks prominently among the five. Nearly all the marine plankton (single-celled floating creatures) died suddenly, at least in geological terms; among marine invertebrates, close to 15 percent of all families perished, including many previously dominant groups, especially the ammonites (relatives of squids in coiled shells). On land, the dinosaurs disappeared after more than 100 million years of unchallenged domination.

In this context, speculations limited to dinosaurs alone ignore the larger phenomenon. We need a coordinated explanation for a system of events that includes the extinction of dinosaurs as one component. Thus it makes little sense, though it may fuel our desire to view mammals as inevitable inheritors of the earth, to guess that dinosaurs died because small mammals ate their eggs (a perennial untestable speculation). It seems most unlikely that some disaster peculiar to dinosaurs befell these massive beasts—and that the debacle happened to strike

10

just when one of history's five great dyings had enveloped the earth for completely different reasons.

The testicular theory, an old favorite from the 1940s, had its root in an interesting and thoroughly respectable study of temperature tolerances in the American alligator, published in the staid *Bulletin of the American Museum of Natural History* in 1946 by three experts on living and fossil reptiles—E. H. Colbert, my own first teacher in paleontology, R. B. Cowles, and C. M. Bogert.

The first sentence of their summary reveals a purpose beyond alligators: "This report describes an attempt to infer the reactions of extinct reptiles, especially the dinosaurs, to high temperatures as based upon reactions observed in the modern alligator." They studied, by rectal thermometry, the body temperatures of alligators under changing conditions of heating and cooling. (Well, let's face it, you wouldn't want to try sticking a thermometer under a 'gator's tongue.) The predictions under test go way back to an old theory first stated by Galileo in the 1630s—the unequal scaling of surfaces and volumes. As an animal, or any object, grows (provided its shape doesn't change), surface areas must increase more slowly than volumes—since surfaces get larger as length squared, volumes much more rapidly, as length cubed. Therefore, small animals have high ratios of surface to volume, while large animals cover themselves with relatively little surface.

Among cold-blooded animals lacking any physiological mechanism for keeping their temperatures constant, small creatures have a hell of a time keeping warm—because they lose so much heat through their relatively large surfaces. On the other hand, large animals, with their relatively small surfaces, may lose heat so slowly that, once warm, they may maintain effectively constant temperatures against ordinary fluctuations of climate. (In fact, the resolution of the "hot-blooded dinosaur" controversy of a few years back may simply be that, while large dinosaurs possessed no physiological mechanism for constant temperature, and so were not warm-blooded in the technical sense, their size and relatively small surface area kept them warm.)

Colbert, Cowles, and Bogert compared the warming rates of small and large alligators. As predicted, the small fellows heated up (and cooled down) more quickly. When exposed to a warm sun, a tiny

50-gram (1.76-ounce) alligator heated up one degree Celsius every minute and a half, while a large alligator, 260 times bigger at 13,000 grams (28.7 pounds), took seven and a half minutes to gain a degree. Extrapolating up to an adult ten-ton dinosaur, they concluded that a one-degree rise in body temperature would take 86 hours. If large animals absorb heat so slowly (through their relatively small surfaces), they will also be unable to shed any excess heat gained when temperatures rise above a favorable level.

The authors then guessed that large dinosaurs lived at or near their optimum temperatures; Cowles suggested that a rise in global temperatures just before the Cretaceous extinction caused the dinosaurs to heat up beyond their optimal tolerance—and, being so large, they couldn't shed the unwanted heat. (In a most unusual statement for a scientific paper, Colbert and Bogert explicitly disavowed this speculative extension of their empirical work on alligators.) Cowles conceded that this excess heat probably wasn't enough to kill or even to enervate the great beasts, but since testes often function only within a narrow range of temperature, he proposed that this global rise might have sterilized all the males, causing extinction by natural contraception.

The overdose theory has recently been supported by UCLA psychiatrist Ronald K. Siegel. Siegel has observed, he claims, more than 2,000 animals that can give themselves various drugs—from a swig of alcohol to massive doses of the big H.[1] Elephants will swill the equivalent of twenty beers at a time, but do not like alcohol in concentrations greater than 7 per cent. In a silly bit of anthropocentric speculation, Siegel states that "elephants drink, perhaps, to forget . . . the anxiety produced by shrinking rangeland and the competition for food."

Since fertile imaginations can apply almost any hot idea to the extinction of dinosaurs, Siegel found a way. Flowering plants did not evolve until late in the dinosaurs' reign. These plants also produced an array of aromatic, amino-acid-based alkaloids—the major group of psychoactive agents. Most mammals are "smart" enough to avoid these potential poisons. The alkaloids simply don't taste good (they are

15

---

[1]Slang term for heroin.

bitter), and in any case we mammals have livers happily supplied with the capacity to detoxify them. But, Siegel speculates, perhaps dinosaurs could neither taste the bitterness nor detoxify the substances once ingested. Speaking of their extinction, he recently told members of the American Psychological Association: "I'm not suggesting that all dinosaurs OD'd on plant drugs, but it certainly was a factor." He also argued that death by overdose may help explain why so many dinosaur fossils are found in contorted positions. (Do not go gentle into that good night.)[2]

Extraterrestrial catastrophes have long pedigrees in the popular literature of extinction, but the subject exploded again after a long lull three years ago when the father-son, physicist-geologist team of Luis and Walter Alvarez proposed that an asteroid, about six miles in diameter, struck the earth 65 million years ago. Most asteroids circle the sun in an orbit between Mars and Jupiter but some, the so-called Apollo objects, take a more eccentric route, actually crossing the earth's orbit in their path around the sun. The chance of a collision at any crossing is minuscule, but the number of Apollo objects and the immensity of geological time virtually guarantee that impacts will occur once in a great while.

The force of such a collision would be immense, greater by far than the megatonnage of all the world's nuclear weapons. In trying to reconstruct a scenario that would explain the simultaneous dying of dinosaurs on land and so many creatures in the sea, the Alvarezes proposed that a gigantic dust cloud, generated by particles blown aloft in the impact, would so darken the earth that photosynthesis would cease and temperatures drop precipitously. (Rage, rage against the dying of the light.)[3] The single-celled photosynthetic oceanic plankton, with life cycles measured in weeks, would perish outright, but land plants might survive through the dormancy of their seeds (land plants were not much affected by the Cretaceous extinction, and any adequate the-

---

[2]Repeated line (and title) of a poem by Welsh poet Dylan Thomas (1914–53).

[3]Another repeating line in Thomas's poem.

ory must account for the curious pattern of differential survival). Dinosaurs would die by starvation and freezing; small, warm-blooded mammals, with more modest requirements for food and better regulation of body temperature, would squeak through.

All three theories, testicular malfunction, psychoactive overdosing, and asteroidal zapping, grab our attention mightily. As pure statements, they rank about equally high on any hit parade of primal fascination. Yet one represents expansive science, the others restrictive and untestable speculation. 20

How could we possibly decide whether the hypothesis of testicular frying is right or wrong? We would have to know things that the fossil record cannot provide. What temperatures were optimal for dinosaurs? Could the beasts avoid the absorption of excess heat by staying in the shade, or in caves? At what temperatures did their testicles cease to function? Were late Cretaceous climates ever warm enough to drive the internal temperatures of dinosaurs close to this ceiling? Testicles simply don't fossilize, and how could we infer their temperature tolerances even if they did? In short, Cowles's hypothesis is simply an intriguing speculation leading nowhere. The most damning statement against it appeared right in the conclusion of Colbert, Cowles, and Bogert's paper, when they admitted: "It is difficult to advance any definite arguments against this hypothesis." My statement may seem paradoxical—isn't a hypothesis really good if you can't devise any arguments against it? Quite the contrary. It is simply untestable and unusable.

Siegel's overdosing has even less going for it. At least Cowles extrapolated his conclusion from some good data on alligators. And he didn't completely violate the primary guideline of explaining dinosaur extinction in the context of a general mass dying—for rise in temperature could be the root cause of a general catastrophe, zapping dinosaurs by testicular malfunction and different groups for other reasons. But Siegel's speculation cannot touch the extinction of ammonites or oceanic plankton (diatoms make their own food with good sweet sunlight; they don't OD on the chemicals of terrestrial plants). It is simply a gratuitous, attention-grabbing guess. It cannot be tested, for how can we know what dinosaurs tasted and what their livers could do?

The hypothesis doesn't even make any sense in its own context. Angiosperms were in full flower tens of millions of years before dinosaurs went the way of all flesh. Why did it take so long? As for the pains of a chemical death recorded in contortions of fossils, I regret to say (or rather I'm pleased to note for the dinosaurs' sake) that Siegel's knowledge of geology must be a bit deficient: muscles contract after death and geological strata rise and fall with motions of the earth's crust after burial—more than enough reason to distort a fossil's pristine appearance.

The asteroid story, on the other hand, has a basis in evidence. It can be tested, extended, refined and, if wrong, disproved. The Alvarezes did not just construct an arresting guess for public consumption. They proposed their hypothesis after laborious geochemical studies with Frank Asaro and Helen Michel had revealed a massive increase of iridium in rocks deposited right at the time of extinction. Iridium, a rare metal of the platinum group, is virtually absent from indigenous rocks of the earth's crust; most of our iridium comes from extraterrestrial objects that hit the earth.

The Alvarez hypothesis bore immediate fruit. Based originally on 25 evidence found in rocks at two sites in Europe, it led geochemists throughout the world to examine other sediments of the same age. They found abnormally high amounts of iridium everywhere—from continental rocks of the western United States to deep sea cores from the South Atlantic.

Cowles proposed his testicular hypothesis in the mid-1940s. Where has it gone since then? Absolutely nowhere, because scientists can do nothing with it. It merely stands as a curious appendage to a solid study of alligators. Siegel's overdose scenario will also win a few press notices and fade into oblivion. The Alvarezes' asteroid falls into a different category altogether, and much of the popular commentary has missed this essential distinction by focusing on the impact and its attendant results, and forgetting what is really important to a scientist—the iridium. If you talk just about asteroids, dust, and darkness, you simply tell stories no better and no more entertaining than fried testicles or terminal trips. It is the iridium—the source of testable evidence—that counts and forges the crucial distinction between speculation and science.

The proof, to twist a phrase, lies in the doing. In thirty-five years, Cowles's hypothesis led to no further advances toward our understanding of dinosaurian extinction. In three years, the Alvarez hypothesis has spawned hundreds of studies, a major conference, and attendant publications. Geologists are fired up. They are looking for iridium at all other extinction boundaries and, by the way, have not (with one exception) found any marked increases—thus proving that a good hypothesis also shows its worth by failing to work in other situations. Every week exposes a new wrinkle in the scientific press. In November a group of Yale scientists supported the hypothesis by finding a "cosmic signature" for isotopes of osmium in Cretaceous boundary rocks (a ratio of isotopes found in extraterrestrial material but not in crustal rocks produced on earth). Then, in December, chemists from the University of Maryland cast some doubt by reporting that volcanic eruptions of Kilauea on Hawaii had belched forth unexpectedly high levels of iridium; perhaps an extraterrestrial source need not be sought.

My point is simply this: whatever the eventual outcome (I suspect it will be positive), the Alvarez hypothesis is exciting, fruitful science because it generates tests, provides us with things to do, and expands outward. We are having fun, battling back and forth, moving toward a resolution, and extending the hypothesis beyond its original scope.

As just one example of the unexpected, distant cross-fertilization that good science engenders, the Alvarez hypothesis made a major contribution to a theme that has riveted public attention in the past few months—so-called nuclear winter. In a speech delivered in April 1982, Luis Alvarez calculated the energy that a six-mile asteroid would release on impact. He compared such an explosion with a full nuclear exchange and implied that all-out atomic war might unleash similar consequences.

This theme of impact leading to massive dust clouds and falling 30 temperatures was an important factor in the decision of Carl Sagan and a group of colleagues to model the climatic consequences of nuclear holocaust. We have, of course, long known that a full nuclear exchange could kill half of humanity outright and cannot be deemed acceptable on any grounds. But some of us still had lurking in our minds the hope that, if we hunkered down in our shelters and lived far from military sites or cities, at least we could survive after the initial fallout dropped.

Apparently, it is not necessarily so. Full nuclear exchange would probably generate the same kind of dust cloud and darkening that may have wiped out the dinosaurs. Temperatures would drop precipitously and agriculture might become impossible. Avoidance of nuclear war is fundamentally an ethical and political problem, but we must know the factual consequences to make firm judgments. Is this not a heartening thought: a recognition of the very phenomenon that made our evolution possible by exterminating the previously dominant dinosaurs and clearing a way for the evolution of large mammals, including us, might actually help to save us from joining those magnificent beasts in contorted poses among the strata of the earth.

STUDY QUESTIONS

1. Gould explores three possible explanations for the extinction of the dinosaurs. Which one of these does he think is best, and why?

2. What CRITERIA does Gould use to EVALUATE each of the three hypotheses? What other criteria might he have used? How would changing the criteria change the outcome of his evaluation? What makes for "good science," according to Gould?

3. Gould's writing is often praised as "accessible"—that is, he presents scientific information in a way that makes it understandable for nonscientists. The ORGANIZATION of this essay and its use of humor are two elements that help make it accessible; how is each suited for a general AUDIENCE? How would the essay have been different if it were written for an audience of scientists?

4. *For Writing.* Select a TOPIC for which there are multiple causes or explanations and do RESEARCH to uncover common ARGUMENTS for each explanation. In an essay, address a few of those causes or explanations and argue for the superiority of one of them. Be sure to DOCUMENT your sources using the CITATION style assigned.

ELISABETH KÜBLER-ROSS { *On the Fear of Death*

ELISABETH KÜBLER-ROSS (1926–2004) graduated from the University
of Zurich as a medical doctor in 1957 and completed her degree in
psychiatry at the University of Colorado in 1963. Her experiences
working with Holocaust survivors helped inspire her to work with
the dying and their survivors. Kübler-Ross's first book, *On Death and
Dying* (1969), discussed dying in new and sometimes controversial ways.
Many of her ideas, particularly her enumeration of the stages of grief, have
entered the mainstream and permanently altered the way we think of death
and dying.

In this chapter from *On Death and Dying*, Kübler-Ross not only
asserts that the fear of death is universal but also describes how the
dying are frequently treated and insists that these practices need to change.
Kübler-Ross contrasts how the sick were cared for in the past with how
they are cared for today, focusing on how our treatment of the sick and
the deceased reflects our own humanity.

---

*Let me not pray to be sheltered from dangers but to be fearless in
facing them.*
*Let me not beg for the stilling of my pain but for the heart to
conquer it.*
*Let me not look for allies in life's battlefield but to my own
strength.*
*Let me not crave in anxious fear to be saved but hope for the
patience to win my freedom.*

*Grant me that I may not be a coward, feeling your mercy in my
success alone; but let me find the grasp of your hand in my
failure.*

RABINDRANATH TAGORE,[1]

Fruit-Gathering

EPIDEMICS HAVE TAKEN A GREAT toll of lives in past generations.
Death in infancy and early childhood was frequent and there were few
families who didn't lose a member of the family at an early age.
Medicine has changed greatly in the last decades. Widespread vaccina-
tions have practically eradicated many illnesses, at least in western
Europe and the United States. The use of chemotherapy, especially the
antibiotics, has contributed to an ever-decreasing number of fatalities
in infectious diseases. Better child care and education has effected a
low morbidity and mortality among children. The many diseases that
have taken an impressive toll among the young and middle-aged have
been conquered. The number of old people is on the rise, and with
this fact come the number of people with malignancies and chronic
diseases associated more with old age.

Pediatricians have less work with acute and life-threatening situations as they have an ever-increasing number of patients with psycho-
somatic disturbances and adjustment and behavior problems.
Physicians have more people in their waiting rooms with emotional
problems than they have ever had before, but they also have more elderly patients who not only try to live with their decreased physical abilities and limitations but who also face loneliness and isolation with all
its pains and anguish. The majority of these people are not seen by a
psychiatrist. Their needs have to be elicited and gratified by other professional people, for instance, chaplains and social workers. It is for
them that I am trying to outline the changes that have taken place in the
last few decades, changes that are ultimately responsible for the
increased fear of death, the rising number of emotional problems, and
the greater need for understanding of and coping with the problems of
death and dying.

[1]Bengali poet, playwright, novelist, and composer (1861–1941), Asia's first Nobel laureate
(1913).

When we look back in time and study old cultures and people, we are impressed that death has always been distasteful to man and will probably always be. From a psychiatrist's point of view this is very understandable and can perhaps best be explained by our basic knowledge that, in our unconscious, death is never possible in regard to ourselves. It is inconceivable for our unconscious to imagine an actual ending of our own life here on earth, and if this life of ours has to end, the ending is always attributed to a malicious intervention from the outside by someone else. In simple terms, in our unconscious mind we can only be killed; it is inconceivable to die of a natural cause or of old age. Therefore death in itself is associated with a bad act, a frightening happening, something that in itself calls for retribution and punishment.

One is wise to remember these fundamental facts as they are essential in understanding some of the most important, otherwise unintelligible communications of our patients.

The second fact that we have to comprehend is that in our unconscious mind we cannot distinguish between a wish and a deed. We are all aware of some of our illogical dreams in which two completely opposite statements can exist side by side—very acceptable in our dreams but unthinkable and illogical in our wakening state. Just as our unconscious mind cannot differentiate between the wish to kill somebody in anger and the act of having done so, the young child is unable to make this distinction. The child who angrily wishes his mother to drop dead for not having gratified his needs will be traumatized greatly by the actual death of his mother—even if this event is not linked closely in time with his destructive wishes. He will always take part or the whole blame for the loss of his mother. He will always say to himself—rarely to others—"I did it, I am responsible, I was bad, therefore Mommy left me." It is well to remember that the child will react in the same manner if he loses a parent by divorce, separation, or desertion. Death is often seen by a child as an impermanent thing and has therefore little distinction from a divorce in which he may have an opportunity to see a parent again.

Many a parent will remember remarks of their children such as, "I will bury my doggy now and next spring when the flowers come up again, he will get up." Maybe it was the same wish that motivated the ancient Egyptians to supply their dead with food and goods to keep them happy and the old American Indians to bury their relatives with their belongings.

When we grow older and begin to realize that our omnipotence is really not so omnipotent, that our strongest wishes are not powerful enough to make the impossible possible, the fear that we have contributed to the death of a loved one diminishes—and with it the guilt. The fear remains diminished, however, only so long as it is not challenged too strongly. Its vestiges can be seen daily in hospital corridors and in people associated with the bereaved.

A husband and wife may have been fighting for years, but when the partner dies, the survivor will pull his hair, whine, and cry louder and beat his chest in regret, fear, and anguish, and will hence fear his own death more than before, still believing in the law of talion—an eye for an eye, a tooth for a tooth—"I am responsible for her death, I will have to die a pitiful death in retribution."

Maybe this knowledge will help us understand many of the old customs and rituals which have lasted over the centuries and whose purpose is to diminish the anger of the gods or the people as the case may be, thus decreasing the anticipated punishment. I am thinking of the ashes, the torn clothes, the veil, the *Klage Weiber*[2] of the old days—they are all means to ask you to take pity on them, the mourners, and are expressions of sorrow, grief, and shame. If someone grieves, beats his chest, tears his hair, or refuses to eat, it is an attempt at self-punishment to avoid or reduce the anticipated punishment for the blame that he takes on the death of a loved one.

This grief, shame, and guilt are not very far removed from feelings of anger and rage. The process of grief always includes some qualities of anger. Since none of us likes to admit anger at a deceased person, these emotions are often disguised or repressed and prolong the period of grief or show up in other ways. It is well to remember that it is not up to us to judge such feelings as bad or shameful but to understand their true meaning and origin as something very human. In order

10

[2]Hired mourners; literally, "wailing wives" (German).

to illustrate this I will again use the example of the child—and the child in us. The five-year-old who loses his mother is both blaming himself for her disappearance and being angry at her for having deserted him and for no longer gratifying his needs. The dead person then turns into something the child loves and wants very much but also hates with equal intensity for this severe deprivation.

The ancient Hebrews regarded the body of a dead person as something unclean and not to be touched. The early American Indians talked about the evil spirits and shot arrows in the air to drive the spirits away. Many other cultures have rituals to take care of the "bad" dead person, and they all originate in this feeling of anger which still exists in all of us, though we dislike admitting it. The tradition of the tombstone may originate in this wish to keep the bad spirits deep down in the ground, and the pebbles that many mourners put on the grave are left-over symbols of the same wish. Though we call the firing of guns at military funerals a last salute, it is the same symbolic ritual as the Indian used when he shot his spears and arrows into the skies.

I give these examples to emphasize that man has not basically changed. Death is still a fearful, frightening happening, and the fear of death is a universal fear even if we think we have mastered it on many levels.

What has changed is our way of coping and dealing with death and dying and our dying patients.

Having been raised in a country in Europe where science is not so advanced, where modern techniques have just started to find their way into medicine, and where people still live as they did in this country half a century ago, I may have had an opportunity to study a part of the evolution of mankind in a shorter period.

I remember as a child the death of a farmer. He fell from a tree and was not expected to live. He asked simply to die at home, a wish that was granted without questioning. He called his daughters into the bedroom and spoke with each one of them alone for a few minutes. He arranged his affairs quietly, though he was in great pain, and distributed his belongings and his land, none of which was to be split until his wife should follow him in death. He also asked each of his children to share in the work, duties, and tasks that he had carried on until the

15

time of the accident. He asked his friends to visit him once more, to bid good-bye to them. Although I was a small child at the time, he did not exclude me or my siblings. We were allowed to share in the preparations of the family just as we were permitted to grieve with them until he died. When he did die, he was left at home, in his own beloved home which he had built, and among his friends and neighbors who went to take a last look at him where he lay in the midst of flowers in the place he had lived in and loved so much. In that country today there is still no make-believe slumber room, no embalming, no false makeup to pretend sleep. Only the signs of very disfiguring illnesses are covered up with bandages and only infectious cases are removed from the home prior to the burial.

Why do I describe such "old-fashioned" customs? I think they are an indication of our acceptance of a fatal outcome, and they help the dying patient as well as his family to accept the loss of a loved one. If a patient is allowed to terminate his life in the familiar and beloved environment, it requires less adjustment for him. His own family knows him well enough to replace a sedative with a glass of his favorite wine; or the smell of a home-cooked soup may give him the appetite to sip a few spoons of fluid which, I think, is still more enjoyable than an infusion. I will not minimize the need for sedatives and infusions and realize full well from my own experience as a country doctor that they are sometimes life-saving and often unavoidable. But I also know that patience and familiar people and foods could replace many a bottle of intravenous fluids given for the simple reason that it fulfills the physiological need without involving too many people and/or individual nursing care.

The fact that children are allowed to stay at home where a fatality has stricken and are included in the talk, discussions, and fears gives them the feeling that they are not alone in the grief and gives them the comfort of shared responsibility and shared mourning. It prepares them gradually and helps them view death as part of life, an experience which may help them grow and mature.

This is in great contrast to a society in which death is viewed as taboo, discussion of it is regarded as morbid, and children are excluded with the presumption and pretext that it would be "too much" for them. They are then sent off to relatives, often accompanied with some unconvincing lies of "Mother has gone on a long trip" or other unbelievable stories. The child senses that something is wrong, and his distrust in adults will only multiply if other relatives add new variations of the story, avoid his questions or suspicions, shower him with gifts as a meager substitute for a loss he is not permitted to deal with. Sooner or later the child will become aware of the changed family situation and, depending on the age and personality of the child, will have an unresolved grief and regard this incident as a frightening, mysterious, in any case very traumatic experience with untrustworthy grownups, which he has no way to cope with.

It is equally unwise to tell a little child who lost her brother that God loved little boys so much that he took little Johnny to heaven. When this little girl grew up to be a woman she never resolved her anger at God, which resulted in a psychotic depression when she lost her own little son three decades later.

We would think that our great emancipation, our knowledge of science and of man, has given us better ways and means to prepare ourselves and our families for this inevitable happening. Instead the days are gone when a man was allowed to die in peace and dignity in his own home.

The more we are making advancements in science, the more we seem to fear and deny the reality of death. How is this possible?

We use euphemisms, we make the dead look as if they were asleep, we ship the children off to protect them from the anxiety and turmoil around the house if the patient is fortunate enough to die at home, we don't allow children to visit their dying parents in the hospitals, we have long and controversial discussions about whether patients should be told the truth—a question that rarely arises when the dying person is tended by the family physician who has known him from delivery to death and who knows the weaknesses and strengths of each member of the family.

• ◦ •

I think there are many reasons for this flight away from facing death calmly. One of the most important facts is that dying nowadays is more

20

gruesome in many ways, namely, more lonely, mechanical, and dehumanized; at times it is even difficult to determine technically when the time of death has occurred.

Dying becomes lonely and impersonal because the patient is often taken out of his familiar environment and rushed to an emergency room. Whoever has been very sick and has required rest and comfort especially may recall his experience of being put on a stretcher and enduring the noise of the ambulance siren and hectic rush until the hospital gates open. Only those who have lived through this may appreciate the discomfort and cold necessity of such transportation which is only the beginning of a long ordeal—hard to endure when you are well, difficult to express in words when noise, light, pumps, and voices are all too much to put up with. It may well be that we might consider more the patient under the sheets and blankets and perhaps stop our well-meant efficiency and rush in order to hold the patient's hand, to smile, or to listen to a question. I include the trip to the hospital as the first episode in dying, as it is for many. I am putting it exaggeratedly in contrast to the sick man who is left at home—not to say that lives should not be saved if they can be saved by a hospitalization but to keep the focus on the patient's experience, his needs and his reactions.

When a patient is severely ill, he is often treated like a person with no right to an opinion. It is often someone else who makes the decision if and when and where a patient should be hospitalized. It would take so little to remember that the sick person too has feelings, has wishes and opinions, and has—most important of all—the right to be heard.

Well, our presumed patient has now reached the emergency room. He will be surrounded by busy nurses, orderlies, interns, residents, a lab technician perhaps who will take some blood, an electrocardiogram technician who takes the cardiogram. He may be moved to X-ray and he will overhear opinions of his condition and discussions and questions to members of the family. He slowly but surely is beginning to be treated like a thing. He is no longer a person. Decisions are made often without his opinion. If he tries to rebel he will be sedated and after hours of waiting and wondering whether he has the strength, he will be wheeled into the operating room or intensive treatment unit and become an object of great concern and great financial investment.

25

30

He may cry for rest, peace, and dignity, but he will get infusions, transfusions, a heart machine, or tracheostomy if necessary. He may want one single person to stop for one single minute so that he can ask one single question—but he will get a dozen people around the clock, all busily preoccupied with his heart rate, pulse, electrocardiogram or pulmonary functions, his secretions or excretions but not with him as a human being. He may wish to fight it all but it is going to be a useless fight since all this is done in the fight for his life, and if they can save his life they can consider the person afterwards. Those who consider the person first may lose precious time to save his life! At least this seems to be the rationale or justification behind all this—or is it? Is the reason for this increasingly mechanical, depersonalized approach our own defensiveness? Is this approach our own way to cope with and repress the anxieties that a terminally or critically ill patient evokes in us? Is our concentration on equipment, on blood pressure our desperate attempt to deny the impending death which is so frightening and discomforting to us that we displace all our knowledge onto machines, since they are less close to us than the suffering face of another human being which would remind us once more of our lack of omnipotence, our own limits and failures, and last but not least perhaps our own mortality?

Maybe the question has to be raised: Are we becoming less human or more human? *** It is clear that whatever the answer may be, the patient is suffering more—not physically, perhaps, but emotionally. And his needs have not changed over the centuries, only our ability to gratify them.

STUDY QUESTIONS

1. Kübler-Ross clearly indicates the AUDIENCE and PURPOSE of her writing. Who and what are they? How does the essay attempt to fulfill her purpose?

2. Kübler-Ross writes an EXPOSITORY essay that incorporates various modes of development, including COMPARISON AND CONTRAST. Find two passages in which she compares and/or contrasts ways of thinking. Do they provide information you were unaware of? Explain.

3. Kübler-Ross also uses CAUSE AND EFFECT to develop her essay. With cause and effect, writers explain why an action results from or causes another action. Identify several examples of cause and effect in this essay, and explain whether or not you find them effective.

4. *For Writing.* The emotions that surround death and dying are difficult for both those who are ill and those who love and care for them. Consider several things that might help people cope, such as religion, psychology, and support groups. Write a REFLECTION on what strategies have worked or might work for you. If you have not experienced the death of a family member, friend, or pet, talk to someone who has and gently ask how he or she coped with these feelings. Consider the response and write a reflection on how these coping strategies might or might not help you in a similar situation.

PLATO { *Allegory of the Cave*

PLATO (428/427–348/347 BCE), a devoted student of Socrates, became one of ancient Greece's most important philosophers and teachers. Plato's written dialogues explore philosophical questions related to justice, virtue, law, reason, and the soul. The central figure in his writings is Socrates, who taught by posing questions and exploring their implications instead of by lecturing. When Plato was about forty years old he founded the Academy, a school designed to provide rigorous philosophical training to prospective politicians, as Plato believed that public servants must first be seekers of wisdom and truth. His most famous pupil at the Academy was Aristotle.

In the Allegory of the Cave, a section from his best-known work, the *Republic*, Plato presents his belief that while change occurs in the physical realm, all things have their essence in a higher realm. For example, in the physical realm all trees change (they grow and die), but the essence of "tree" exists in the higher realm, the perfect world of permanent and unchanging ideas. The goal of philosophy, according to Plato, is to help the student more clearly see this higher realm. In this dialogue, Socrates asks his student Glaucon to imagine humans chained in a cave so that all they can see are shadows on the back wall. This chained existence of darkness and shadows is all they have ever known. What would happen, Socrates asks, if one were suddenly free of the chains and were able to see that what they had once considered reality was only a shadowy representation of truth?

AND NOW, I SAID, LET me show in a figure how far our nature is enlightened or unenlightened: Behold! human beings living in an underground den, which has a mouth open toward the light and reaching all along the den; here they have been from their childhood, and have their legs and necks chained so that they cannot move, and can see only before them, being prevented by the chains from turning round their heads. Above and behind them a fire is blazing at a distance, and between the fire and the prisoners there is a raised way; and you will see, if you look, a low wall built along the way, like the screen which marionette players have in front of them, over which they show the puppets.

I see.

And do you see, I said, men passing along the wall carrying all sorts of vessels, and statues and figures of animals made of wood and stone and various materials, which appear over the wall? Some of them are talking, others silent.

You have shown me a strange image, and they are strange prisoners.

Like ourselves, I replied; and they see only their own shadows, or   5
the shadows of one another, which the fire throws on the opposite wall of the cave?

True, he said; how could they see anything but the shadows if they were never allowed to move their heads?

And of the objects which are being carried in like manner they would only see the shadows?

Yes, he said.

And if they were able to converse with one another, would they not suppose that they were naming what was actually before them?

Very true.   10

And suppose further that the prison had an echo which came from the other side, would they not be sure to fancy when one of the passers-by spoke that the voice which they heard came from the passing shadow?

No question, he replied.

To them, I said, the truth would be literally nothing but the shadows of the images.

That is certain.

And now look again, and see what will naturally follow if the pris-   15
oners are released and disabused of their error. At first, when any of them is liberated and compelled suddenly to stand up and turn his neck round and walk and look toward the light, he will suffer sharp pains; the glare will distress him and he will be unable to see the reali-

ties of which in his former state he had seen the shadows; and then conceive someone saying to him, that what he saw before was an illusion, but that now, when he is approaching nearer to being and his eye is turned toward more real existence, he has a clearer vision— what will be his reply? And you may further imagine that his instructor is pointing to the objects as they pass and requiring him to name them—will he not be perplexed? Will he not fancy that the shadows which he formerly saw are truer than the objects which are now shown to him?

Far truer.

And if he is compelled to look straight at the light, will he not have a pain in his eyes which will make him turn away to take refuge in the objects of vision which he can see, and which he will conceive to be in reality clearer than the things which are now being shown to him?

True, he said.

And suppose once more, that he is reluctantly dragged up a steep and rugged ascent, and held fast until he is forced into the presence of the sun himself, is he not likely to be pained and irritated? When he approaches the light his eyes will be dazzled and he will not be able to see anything at all of what are now called realities.

Not all in a moment, he said. 20

He will require to grow accustomed to the sight of the upper world. And first he will see the shadows best, next the reflections of men and other objects in the water, and then the objects themselves; then he will gaze upon the light of the moon and the stars and the spangled heaven; and he will see the sky and the stars by night better than the sun or the light of the sun by day?

Certainly.

Last of all he will be able to see the sun, and not mere reflections of him in the water, but he will see him in his own proper place, and not in another; and he will contemplate him as he is.

Certainly.

He will then proceed to argue that this is he who gives the season 25 and the years, and is the guardian of all that is in the visible world, and in a certain way the cause of all things which he and his fellows have been accustomed to behold?

Clearly, he said, he would first see the sun and then reason about him.

And when he remembered his old habitation, and the wisdom of the den and his fellow-prisoners, do you not suppose that he would felicitate himself on the change, and pity them?

Certainly, he would.

And if they were in the habit of conferring honors among themselves on those who were quickest to observe the passing shadows and to remark which of them went before, and which followed after, and which were together; and who were therefore best able to draw conclusions as to the future, do you think that he would care for such honors and glories, or envy the possessors of them? Would he not say with Homer, "Better to be the poor servant of a poor master," and to endure anything, rather than think as they do and live after their manner?

Yes, he said, I think that he would rather suffer anything than entertain these false notions and live in this miserable manner. 30

Imagine once more, I said, such a one coming suddenly out of the sun to be replaced in his old situation; would he not be certain to have his eyes full of darkness?

To be sure, he said.

And if there were a contest, and he had to compete in measuring the shadows with the prisoners who had never moved out of the den, while his sight was still weak, and before his eyes had become steady (and the time which would be needed to acquire this new habit of sight might be very considerable) would he not be ridiculous? Men would say of him that up he went and down he came without his eyes; and that it was better not even to think of ascending; and if anyone tried to loose another and lead him up to the light, let them only catch the offender, and they would put him to death.

No question, he said.

This entire allegory, I said, you may now append, dear Glaucon, 35 to the previous argument; the prison-house is the world of sight, the light of the fire is the sun, and you will not misapprehend me if you interpret the journey upwards to be the ascent of the soul into the intellectual world according to my poor belief, which, at your desire, I have expressed—whether rightly or wrongly God knows. But, whether true or false, my opinion is that in the world of knowledge the idea of good appears last of all, and is seen only with an effort; and, when seen, is also inferred to be the universal author of all things beautiful and right, parent of light and of the lord of light in this visible world, and the immediate source of reason and truth in the intellectual; and that this is the power upon which he who would act rationally either in public or private life must have his eye fixed.

I agree, he said, as far as I am able to understand you.

Moreover, I said, you must not wonder that those who attain to this beatific vision are unwilling to descend to human affairs; for their souls are ever hastening into the upper world where they desire to dwell; which desire of theirs is very natural, if our allegory may be trusted.

Yes, very natural.

And is there anything surprising in one who passes from divine contemplations to the evil state of man, misbehaving himself in a ridiculous manner; if, while his eyes are blinking and before he has become accustomed to the surrounding darkness, he is compelled to fight in courts of law, or in other places, about the images or the shadows of images of justice, and is endeavoring to meet the conceptions of those who have never yet seen absolute justice?

Anything but surprising, he replied.   40

Anyone who has common sense will remember that the bewilderments of the eyes are of two kinds, and arise from two causes, either from coming out of the light or from going into the light, which is true of the mind's eye, quite as much as of the bodily eye; and he who remembers this when he sees anyone whose vision is perplexed and weak, will not be too ready to laugh; he will first ask whether that soul of man has come out of the brighter life, and is unable to see because unaccustomed to the dark, or having turned from darkness to the day is dazzled by excess of light. And he will count the one happy in his condition and state of being, and he will pity the other; or, if he have a mind to laugh at the soul which comes from below into the light, there will be more reason in this than in the laugh which greets him who returns from above out of the light into the den.

That, he said, is a very just distinction.

STUDY QUESTIONS

1. Explain the four different levels of awareness depicted in the Allegory of the Cave. At which level would Socrates place the philosophers?

2. An ALLEGORY is an extended METAPHOR with both literal and SYMBOLIC meaning. In Plato's allegory, what might the chained humans symbolize? According to Plato, what is humanity's predicament and salvation?

3. This allegory is presented as a conversation. Do you think Glaucon agrees too readily with Socrates? Are there points in the conversation where, if you were Glaucon, you would have disagreed with or questioned Socrates' claim? Explain.

4. *For Writing.* In Plato's allegory, the released humans experience an epiphany, a moment of insight into the limited nature of their reality. Write about an epiphany you have experienced when you suddenly realized that the world wasn't quite what you had always believed it to be.

NEIL POSTMAN AND STEVE POWERS { *The Bias of Language, the Bias of Pictures*

Neil Postman (1931–2003) is best known for his book *Amusing Ourselves to Death* (1986), a critique of the medium of television. He received his BS from the State University of New York at Fredonia and his MA and EdD degrees from Columbia University. He taught at New York University and eventually chaired the Department of Culture and Communication there. His other books include *The Disappearance of Childhood* (1982), *How to Watch TV News* (1992), and *The End of Education* (1996).

Steve Powers (b. 1934), born in New York City, has led a wide-ranging life: he has worked as a disc jockey, played jazz with Dizzy Gillespie, served as a Coast Guard officer in Puerto Rico, earned a business degree from the City University of New York and a PhD from New York University, and was a reporter and anchor for New York's Channel 5 News from 1980 to 1993, for which he was awarded an Emmy in 1981. He has also anchored newscasts for New York Times Radio. Powers has taught at the Columbia School of Journalism, the New School, New York University, and St. John's University.

In 1992 Postman and Powers collaborated to write *How to Watch TV News*. In the following selection from that book, they explain how television news programs transform events into very different forms, how they choose what to show, and their failure to help viewers impose meaning on events. By demonstrating the almost inescapable biases of language and the way pictures can distort our sense of what is "news," Postman and Powers reveal how television news presents "the world as a series of unrelated, fragmentary moments . . . without meaning, connections, or continuity." As you read, think about how television news shows, and other sources of news, have changed—and stayed the same—in the decades since *How to Watch TV News* was published.

WHEN A TELEVISION NEWS SHOW distorts the truth by altering or manufacturing facts (through re-creations), a television viewer is defenseless even if a re-creation is properly labeled. Viewers are still vulnerable to misinformation since they will not know (at least in the case of docudramas) what parts are fiction and what parts are not. But the problems of verisimilitude posed by re-creations pale to insignificance when compared to the problems viewers face when encountering a straight (no-monkey-business) show. All news shows, in a sense, are re-creations in that what we hear and see on them are attempts to represent actual events, and are not the events themselves. Perhaps, to avoid ambiguity, we might call all news shows "re-presentations" instead of "re-creations." These re-presentations come to us in two forms: language and pictures. The question then arises: what do viewers have to know about language and pictures in order to be properly armed to defend themselves against the seductions of eloquence (to use Bertrand Russell's[1] apt phrase)?

Let us take language first, Below are three principles that, in our opinion, are an essential part of the analytical equipment a viewer must bring to any encounter with a news show.

1. WHATEVER ANYONE SAYS SOMETHING IS, IT ISN'T.

This sounds more complex—and maybe more pretentious—than it actually is. What it means is that there is a difference between the world of events and the world of words about events. The job of an honest reporter is to try to find words and the appropriate tone in presenting them that will come as close to evoking the event as possible. But since no two people will use exactly the same words to describe an event, we

---

[1] Philosopher, mathematician, and writer (1872–1970), whose essay "On Denoting" (1905) had a great influence on the study of language and linguistics.

must acknowledge that for every verbal description of an event, there are multiple possible alternatives. You may demonstrate this to your own satisfaction by writing a two-paragraph description of a dinner you had with at least two other people, then asking the others who were present if each of them would also write, independently, a two-paragraph description of the "same" dinner. We should be very surprised if all of the descriptions include the same words, in the same order, emphasize the same things, and express the same feelings. In other words, "the dinner itself" is largely a nonverbal event. The words people use to describe this event are not the event itself and are only abstracted re-presentations of the event. What does this mean for a television viewer? It means that the viewer must never assume that the words spoken on a television news show are exactly what happened. Since there are so many alternative ways of describing what happened, the viewer must be on guard against assuming that he or she has heard "the absolute truth."

2. LANGUAGE OPERATES AT VARIOUS LEVELS OF ABSTRACTION.

This means that there is a level of language whose purpose is to *describe* an event. There is also a level of language whose purpose is to *evaluate* an event. Even more, there is a level of language whose purpose is to *infer* what is unknown on the basis of what is known. The usual way to make these distinctions clear is through sentences such as the following three:

Manny Freebus is 5'8" and weighs 235 pounds.

Manny Freebus is grossly fat.

Manny Freebus eats too much.

The first sentence may be said to be language as pure description. It involves no judgments and no inferences. The second sentence is a description of sorts, but is mainly a judgment that the speaker makes of the "event" known as Manny Freebus. The third sentence is an inference based on observations the speaker has made. It is, in fact, a statement about the unknown based on the known. As it happens, we know Manny Freebus and can tell you that he eats no more than the average person but suffers from a glandular condition which keeps him overweight. Therefore, anyone who concluded from observing Manny's shape that he eats too much has made a false inference. A good guess, but false nonetheless.

You can watch television news programs from now until doomsday and never come across any statement about Manny Freebus. But you will constantly come across the three kinds of statements we have been discussing—descriptions, judgments, and inferences. And it is important for a viewer to distinguish among them. For example, you might hear an anchor introduce a story by saying: "Today Congress ordered an investigation of the explosive issue of whether Ronald Reagan's presidential campaign made a deal with Iran in 1980 to delay the release of American hostages until after the election."[2] This statement is, of course, largely descriptive, but includes the judgmental word "explosive" as part of the report. We need hardly point out that what is explosive to one person may seem trivial to another. We do not say that the news writer has no business to include his or her judgment of this investigation. We do say that the viewer has to be aware that a judgment has been made. In fact, even the phrase "made a deal" (why not "arranged with Iran"?) has a somewhat sleazy connotation that implies a judgment of sorts. If, in the same news report, we are told that the evidence for such a secret deal is weak and that only an investigation with subpoena power can establish the truth, we must know that we have left the arena of factual language and have moved into the land of inference. An investigation with subpoena power may be a good idea but

---

[2] A reference to the charge, never proven, that while a candidate for the presidency Ronald Reagan secretly negotiated with the revolutionary government of Iran, promising that he would divert a supply of American arms to Iran in return for the Iranians' delaying the release of fifty-two American hostages until Reagan had defeated President Jimmy Carter and assumed the office himself. Minutes after Reagan was inaugurated in 1981, the hostages were freed.

whether or not it can establish the truth is a guess on the journalist's part, and a viewer ought to know that.

3. ALMOST ALL WORDS HAVE CONNOTATIVE MEANINGS.

This suggests that even when attempting to use purely descriptive language, a journalist cannot avoid expressing an attitude about what he or she is saying. For example, here is the opening sentence of an anchor's report about national examinations: "For the first time in the nation's history, high-level education policymakers have designed the elements for a national examination system similar to the one advocated by President Bush."[3] This sentence certainly looks like it is pure description although it is filled with ambiguities. Is this the first time in our history that this has been done? Or only the first time that high-level education policymakers have done it? Or is it the first time something has been designed that is similar to what the President has advocated? But let us put those questions aside. (After all, there are limits to how analytical one ought to be.) Instead, we might concentrate on such words as "high-level," "policymakers," and "designed." Speaking for ourselves, we are by no means sure that we know what a "high-level policymaker" is, although it sounds awfully impressive. It is certainly better than a "low-level policymaker," although how one would distinguish between the two is a bit of a mystery. Come to think of it, a low-level "policymaker" must be pretty good, too, since anyone who makes policy must be important. It comes as no surprise, therefore, that what was done was "designed." To design something usually implies careful thought, preparation, organization, and coherence. People design buildings, bridges, and furniture. If your experience has been anything like ours, you will know that reports are almost never designed; they are usually "thrown together," and it is quite a compliment to say that a report was designed. The journalist who paid this compliment was certainly entitled to do it even though he may not have been aware of what he was doing. He probably thought he had made a simple description, avoiding any words that would imply favor or disfavor. But if so, he was

[3]That is, George H. W. Bush (b. 1924), forty-first president of the United States.

defeated in his effort because language tends to be emotion-laden. Because it is people who do the talking, the talk almost always includes a feeling, an attitude, a judgment. In a sense, every language contains the history of a people's feelings about the world. Our words are baskets of emotion. Smart journalists, of course, know this. And so do smart audiences. Smart audiences don't blame anyone for this state of affairs. They are, however, prepared for it.

It is not our intention to provide here a mini-course in semantics. Even if we could, we are well aware that no viewer could apply analytic principles all the time or even much of the time. Anchors and reporters talk too fast and too continuously for any of us to monitor most of their sentences. Besides, who would want to do that for most of the stories on a news show? If you have a sense of what is important, you will probably judge most news stories to be fluff, or nonsense, or irrelevancies, not worthy of your analytic weaponry. But there are times when stories appear that are of major significance from your point of view. These are the times when your level of attention will reach a peak and you must call upon your best powers of interpretation. In those moments, you need to draw on whatever you know about the relationship between language and reality; about the distinctions among statements of fact, judgment, and inference; about the connotative meanings of words. When this is done properly, viewers are no longer passive consumers of news but active participants in a kind of dialogue between a news show and themselves. A viewer may even find that he or she is "talking back to the television set" (which is the title of a book by former FCC commissioner Nicholas Johnson). In our view, nothing could be healthier for the sanity and well-being of our nation than to have ninety million viewers talking back to their television news shows every night and twice on Sunday.

Now we must turn to the problem of pictures. It is often said that a picture is worth a thousand words. Maybe so. But it is probably equally true that one word is worth a thousand pictures, at least sometimes—for example, when it comes to understanding the world we live in. Indeed, the whole problem with news on television comes down to this: all the words uttered in an hour of news coverage could be printed on one page of a newspaper. And the world cannot be understood in one page. Of course, there is a compensation: television offers pictures, and the pictures move. Moving pictures are a kind of language in themselves, but the language of pictures differs radically from oral and written language, and the differences are crucial for understanding television news.

To begin with, pictures, especially single pictures, speak only in particularities. Their vocabulary is limited to concrete representation. Unlike words and sentences, a picture does not present to us an idea or concept about the world, except as we use language itself to convert the image to idea. By itself, a picture cannot deal with the unseen, the remote, the internal, the abstract. It does not speak of "man," only of *a* man; not of "tree," only of *a* tree. You cannot produce an image of "nature," any more than an image of "the sea." You can only show a particular fragment of the here-and-now—a cliff of a certain terrain, in a certain condition of light; a wave at a moment in time, from a particular point of view. And just as "nature" and "the sea" cannot be photographed, such larger abstractions as truth, honor, love, and falsehood cannot be talked about in the lexicon of individual pictures. For "showing of" and "talking about" are two very different kinds of processes: individual pictures give us the world as object; language, the world as idea. There is no such thing in nature as "man" or "tree." The universe offers no such categories or simplifications; only flux and infinite variety. The picture documents and celebrates the particularities of the universe's infinite variety. Language makes them comprehensible.

Of course, moving pictures, video with sound, may bridge the gap by juxtaposing images, symbols, sound, and music. Such images can present emotions and rudimentary ideas. They can suggest the panorama of nature and the joys and miseries of humankind.

Picture—smoke pouring from the window, cut to people coughing, an ambulance racing to a hospital, a tombstone in a cemetery.

Picture—jet planes firing rockets, explosions, lines of foreign soldiers surrendering, the American flag waving in the wind.

Nonetheless, keep in mind that when terrorists want to prove to the world that their kidnap victims are still alive, they photograph them holding a copy of a recent newspaper. The dateline on the newspaper provides the proof that the photograph was taken on or after that date.

Without the help of the written word, film and videotape cannot portray temporal dimensions with any precision. Consider a film clip
showing an aircraft carrier at sea. One might be able to identify the ship
as Soviet or American, but there would be no way of telling where in
the world the carrier was, where it was headed, or when the pictures
were taken. It is only through language—words spoken over the pictures or reproduced in them—that the image of the aircraft carrier takes
on specific meaning.

Still, it is possible to enjoy the image of the carrier for its own sake.   15
One might find the hugeness of the vessel interesting; it signifies military power on the move. There is a certain drama in watching the
planes come in at high speeds and skid to a stop on the deck. Suppose
the ship were burning: that would be even more interesting. This leads
to an important point about the language of pictures. Moving pictures
favor images that change. That is why violence and dynamic destruction find their way onto television so often. When something is
destroyed violently it is altered in a highly visible way; hence the
entrancing power of fire. Fire gives visual form to the ideas of consumption, disappearance, death—the thing that burned is actually taken
away by fire. It is at this very basic level that fires make a good subject
for television news. Something was here, now it's gone, and the change
is recorded on film.

Earthquakes and typhoons have the same power. Before the viewer's
eyes the world is taken apart. If a television viewer has relatives in
Mexico City and an earthquake occurs there, then he or she may take a
special interest in the images of destruction as a report from a specific
place and time; that is, one may look at television pictures for information about an important event. But film of an earthquake can be interesting even if the viewer cares nothing about the event itself. Which is
only to say, as we noted earlier, that there is another way of participating in the news—as a spectator who desires to be entertained. Actually
to see buildings topple is exciting, no matter where the buildings are.
The world turns to dust before our eyes.

Those who produce television news in America know that their
medium favors images that move. That is why they are wary of "talking heads," people who simply appear in front of a camera and speak.

When talking heads appear on television, there is nothing to record or document, no change in process. In the cinema the situation is somewhat different. On a movie screen, close-ups of a good actor speaking dramatically can sometimes be interesting to watch. When Clint Eastwood narrows his eyes and challenges his rival to shoot first, the spectator sees the cool rage of the Eastwood character take visual form, and the narrowing of the eyes is dramatic. But much of the effect of this small movement depends on the size of the movie screen and the darkness of the theater, which make Eastwood and his every action "larger than life."

The television screen is smaller than life. It occupies about 15 percent of the viewer's visual field (compared to about 70 percent for the movie screen). It is not set in a darkened theater closed off from the world but in the viewer's ordinary living space. This means that visual changes must be more extreme and more dramatic to be interesting on television. A narrowing of the eyes will not do. A car crash, an earthquake, a burning factory are much better.

With these principles in mind, let us examine more closely the structure of a typical newscast, and here we will include in the discussion not only the pictures but all the nonlinguistic symbols that make up a television news show. For example, in America, almost all news shows begin with music, the tone of which suggests important events about to unfold. The music is very important, for it equates the news with various forms of drama and ritual—the opera, for example, or a wedding procession—in which musical themes underscore the meaning of the event. Music takes us immediately into the realm of the symbolic, a world that is not to be taken literally. After all, when events unfold in the real world, they do so without musical accompaniment. More symbolism follows. The sound of teletype machines can be heard in the studio, not because it is impossible to screen this noise out, but because the sound is a kind of music in itself. It tells us that data are pouring in from all corners of the globe, a sensation reinforced by the world map in the background (or clocks noting the time on different continents). The fact is that teletype machines are rarely used in TV news rooms, having been replaced by silent computer terminals. When seen, they have only a symbolic function.

Already, then, before a single news item is introduced, a great deal has been communicated. We know that we are in the presence of a symbolic event, a form of theater in which the day's events are to be dramatized. This theater takes the entire globe as its subject, although it may look at the world from the perspective of a single nation. A certain tension is present, like the atmosphere in a theater just before the curtain goes up. The tension is represented by the music, the staccato beat of the teletype machines, and often the sight of news workers scurrying around typing reports and answering phones. As a technical matter, it would be no problem to build a set in which the newsroom staff remained off camera, invisible to the viewer, but an important theatrical effect would be lost. By being busy on camera, the workers help communicate urgency about the events at hand, which suggests that situations are changing so rapidly that constant revision of the news is necessary.

The staff in the background also helps signal the importance of the person in the center, the anchor, "in command" of both the staff and the news. The anchor plays the role of host. He or she welcomes us to the newscast and welcomes us back from the different locations we visit during the filmed reports.

Many features of the newscast help the anchor to establish the impression of control. These are usually equated with production values in broadcasting. They include such things as graphics that tell the viewer what is being shown, or maps and charts that suddenly appear on the screen and disappear on cue, or the orderly progression from story to story. They also include the absence of gaps, or "dead time," during the broadcast, even the simple fact that the news starts and ends at a certain hour. These common features are thought of as purely technical matters, which a professional crew handles as a matter of course. But they are also symbols of a dominant theme of television news: the imposition of an orderly world—called "the news"—upon the disorderly flow of events.

While the form of a news broadcast emphasizes tidiness and control, its content can best be described as fragmented. Because time is so precious on television, because the nature of the medium favors dynamic visual images, and because the pressures of a commercial structure require the news to hold its audience above all else, there is rarely any attempt to explain issues in depth or place events in their proper context. The news moves nervously from a warehouse fire to a court decision, from a guerrilla war to a World Cup match, the quality of the film most often determining the length of the story. Certain stories show up only because they offer dramatic pictures. Bleachers collapse in South America: hundreds of people are crushed—a perfect television news story, for the cameras can record the face of disaster in all its anguish. Back in Washington, a new budget is approved by Congress. Here there is nothing to photograph because a budget is not a physical event; it is a document full of language and numbers. So the producers of the news will show a photo of the document itself, focusing on the cover where it says "Budget of the United States of America." Or sometimes they will send a camera crew to the government printing plant where copies of the budget are produced. That evening, while the contents of the budget are summarized by a voice-over, the viewer sees stacks of documents being loaded into boxes at the government printing plant. Then a few of the budget's more important provisions will be flashed on the screen in written form, but this is such a time-consuming process—using television as a printed page—that the producers keep it to a minimum. In short, the budget is not televisable, and for that reason its time on the news must be brief. The bleacher collapse will get more time that evening.

While appearing somewhat chaotic, these disparate stories are not just dropped in the news program helter-skelter. The appearance of a scattershot story order is really orchestrated to draw the audience from one story to the next—from one section to the next—through the commercial breaks to the end of the show. The story order is constructed to hold and build the viewership rather than place events in context or explain issues in depth.

Of course, it is a tendency of journalism in general to concentrate 25 on the surface of events rather than underlying conditions; this is as true for the newspaper as it is for the newscast. But several features of television undermine whatever efforts journalists may make to give sense to the world. One is that a television broadcast is a series of events that occur in sequence, and the sequence is the same for all viewers. This is not true for a newspaper page, which displays many items simultaneously, allowing readers to choose the order in which they read them. If newspaper readers want only a summary of the latest tax bill, they can read the headline and the first paragraph of an article, and if they want more, they can keep reading. In a sense, then, everyone reads a different newspaper, for no two readers will read (or ignore) the same items.

But all television viewers see the same broadcast. They have no choices. A report is either in the broadcast or out, which means that anything which is of narrow interest is unlikely to be included. As NBC News executive Reuven Frank once explained:

> A newspaper, for example, can easily afford to print an item of conceivable interest to only a fraction of its readers. A television news program must be put together with the assumption that each item will be of some interest to everyone that watches. Every time a newspaper includes a feature which will attract a specialized group it can assume it is adding at least a little bit to its circulation. To the degree a television news program includes an item of this sort . . . it must assume that its audience will diminish.

The need to "include everyone," an identifying feature of commercial television in all its forms, prevents journalists from offering lengthy or complex explanations, or from tracing the sequence of events leading up to today's headlines. One of the ironies of political life in modern democracies is that many problems which concern the "general welfare" are of interest only to specialized groups. Arms control, for example, is an issue that literally concerns everyone in the world, and yet the language of arms control and the complexity of the subject are so daunting that only a minority of people can actually follow the issue from week to week and month to month. If it wants to act responsibly, a newspaper can at least make available more information about arms control than most people want. Commercial television cannot afford to do so.

But even if commercial television could afford to do so, it wouldn't. The fact that television news is principally made up of moving pictures prevents it from offering lengthy, coherent explanations of events. A television news show reveals the world as a series of unrelated, fragmentary moments. It does not—and cannot be expected to—offer a sense of coherence or meaning. What does this suggest to a TV viewer? That the viewer must come with a prepared mind—information, opinions, a sense of proportion, an articulate value system. To the TV viewer lacking such mental equipment, a news program is only a kind of rousing light show. Here a falling building, there a five-alarm fire, everywhere the world as an object, much without meaning, connections, or continuity.

STUDY QUESTIONS

1. Explain the similarity, from the standpoint of television news, of fires, earthquakes, and typhoons. Why do such events interest viewers? What two functions can pictures of an earthquake serve? What is a "talking head"?

2. List several points of CONTRAST that Postman and Powers make between newspapers and television news. How does language play a part in each medium?

3. What is the authors' THESIS? Select several examples of CAUSE AND EFFECT found in the selection and explain how they support that thesis.

4. Consider news from media that Postman and Powers do not address, such as the radio and the Internet, and COMPARE how they present the news to how television news shows do. How would *you* ANALYZE the ways people process news from the radio? The Internet?

5. *For Writing.* Postman and Powers write about three different kinds of language: description, evaluation, and inference. (Description here does not refer to the same kind of DESCRIPTION that is often taught in writing classes, with its attention to detail and DOMINANT IMPRESSION.) Watch a television news program and take notes on the language that the reporters and anchors use. Then, write an essay in which you analyze their speech for these three kinds of language. Be sure to explain not only how they speak, but also why that matters and what it says about their reporting.

MOTOKO RICH { *Literacy Debate: Online,*
R U Really Reading?

MOTOKO RICH (b. 1970) was born in Los Angeles, California, but grew
up primarily in Petaluma. She graduated from Yale University in 1991 and
received an MA in English from Cambridge University. Rich was a
reporter at the *Wall Street Journal* for six years before moving in 2003 to
the *New York Times,* where she reviews books and writes about culture and
the arts.

In "Literacy Debate: Online, R U Really Reading?" Rich presents
proponents' and opponents' views about children and teenagers reading
online. Education scholars and researchers correlate falling standardized
test scores among children and teens and a drop in the percentage of
teens who say they read for fun with the amount of time children and teens
spend on computers. On the other hand, Web enthusiasts argue that the
reading strategies gained through online reading prepare students for
work in today's digital society, and that Internet proficiency should be
tested in the same way students are tested in print material for reading
comprehension. As you read, determine whether Rich draws any
conclusions.

BOOKS ARE NOT NADIA KONYK'S thing. Her mother, hoping to entice
her, brings them home from the library, but Nadia rarely shows an
interest.

Instead, like so many other teenagers, Nadia, 15, is addicted to the
Internet. She regularly spends at least six hours a day in front of the
computer here in this suburb southwest of Cleveland.

A slender, chatty blonde who wears black-framed plastic glasses, Nadia checks her e-mail and peruses myyearbook.com, a social networking site, reading messages or posting updates on her mood. She searches for music videos on YouTube and logs onto Gaia Online, a role-playing site where members fashion alternate identities as cutesy cartoon characters. But she spends most of her time on quizilla.com or fanfiction.net, reading and commenting on stories written by other users and based on books, television shows or movies.

Her mother, Deborah Konyk, would prefer that Nadia, who gets A's and B's at school, read books for a change. But at this point, Ms. Konyk said, "I'm just pleased that she reads something anymore."

Children like Nadia lie at the heart of a passionate debate about just 5 what it means to read in the digital age. The discussion is playing out among educational policy makers and reading experts around the world, and within groups like the National Council of Teachers of English and the International Reading Association.

As teenagers' scores on standardized reading tests have declined or stagnated, some argue that the hours spent prowling the Internet are the enemy of reading—diminishing literacy, wrecking attention spans and destroying a precious common culture that exists only through the reading of books.

But others say the Internet has created a new kind of reading, one that schools and society should not discount. The Web inspires a teenager like Nadia, who might otherwise spend most of her leisure time watching television, to read and write.

Even accomplished book readers like Zachary Sims, 18, of Old Greenwich, Connecticut, crave the ability to quickly find different points of view on a subject and converse with others online. Some children with dyslexia or other learning difficulties, like Hunter Gaudet, 16, of Somers, Connecticut, have found it far more comfortable to search and read online.

At least since the invention of television, critics have warned that electronic media would destroy reading. What is different now, some literacy experts say, is that spending time on the Web, whether it is looking up something on Google or even britneyspears.org, entails some engagement with text.

SETTING EXPECTATIONS

Few who believe in the potential of the Web deny the value of books. 10
But they argue that it is unrealistic to expect all children to read *To Kill
a Mockingbird* or *Pride and Prejudice* for fun. And those who prefer
staring at a television or mashing buttons on a game console, they say,
can still benefit from reading on the Internet. In fact, some literacy experts say that online reading skills will help children fare better when
they begin looking for digital-age jobs.

Some Web evangelists say children should be evaluated for their
proficiency on the Internet just as they are tested on their print reading comprehension. Starting next year, some countries will participate
in new international assessments of digital literacy, but the United
States, for now, will not.

Clearly, reading in print and on the Internet are different. On paper,
text has a predetermined beginning, middle and end, where readers
focus for a sustained period on one author's vision. On the Internet,
readers skate through cyberspace at will and, in effect, compose their
own beginnings, middles and ends.

Young people "aren't as troubled as some of us older folks are by
reading that doesn't go in a line," said Rand J. Spiro, a professor of educational psychology at Michigan State University who is studying
reading practices on the Internet. "That's a good thing because the
world doesn't go in a line, and the world isn't organized into separate
compartments or chapters."

Some traditionalists warn that digital reading is the intellectual
equivalent of empty calories. Often, they argue, writers on the Internet
employ a cryptic argot that vexes teachers and parents. Zigzagging
through a cornucopia of words, pictures, video and sounds, they say,
distracts more than strengthens readers. And many youths spend most
of their time on the Internet playing games or sending instant messages, activities that involve minimal reading at best.

Last fall the National Endowment for the Arts issued a sobering report 15
linking flat or declining national reading test scores among teenagers with
the slump in the proportion of adolescents who said they read for fun.

According to Department of Education data cited in the report, just over a fifth of 17-year-olds said they read almost every day for fun in 2004, down from nearly a third in 1984. Nineteen percent of 17-year-olds said they never or hardly ever read for fun in 2004, up from 9 percent in 1984. (It was unclear whether they thought of what they did on the Internet as "reading.")

"Whatever the benefits of newer electronic media," Dana Gioia, the chairman of the N.E.A., wrote in the report's introduction, "they provide no measurable substitute for the intellectual and personal development initiated and sustained by frequent reading."

Children are clearly spending more time on the Internet. In a study of 2,032 representative 8- to 18-year-olds, the Kaiser Family Foundation found that nearly half used the Internet on a typical day in 2004, up from just under a quarter in 1999. The average time these children spent online on a typical day rose to one hour and 41 minutes in 2004, from 46 minutes in 1999.

The question of how to value different kinds of reading is complicated because people read for many reasons. There is the level required of daily life—to follow the instructions in a manual or to analyze a mortgage contract. Then there is a more sophisticated level that opens the doors to elite education and professions. And, of course, people read for entertainment, as well as for intellectual or emotional rewards.

It is perhaps that final purpose that book champions emphasize 20 the most.

"Learning is not to be found on a printout," David McCullough, the Pulitzer Prize–winning biographer, said in a commencement address at Boston College in May. "It's not on call at the touch of the finger. Learning is acquired mainly from books, and most readily from great books."

WHAT'S BEST FOR NADIA?

Deborah Konyk always believed it was essential for Nadia and her 8-year-old sister, Yashca, to read books. She regularly read aloud to the girls and took them to library story hours.

"Reading opens up doors to places that you probably will never get to visit in your lifetime, to cultures, to worlds, to people," Ms. Konyk said.

Ms. Konyk, who took a part-time job at a dollar store chain a year and a half ago, said she did not have much time to read books herself. There are few books in the house. But after Yashca was born, Ms. Konyk spent the baby's nap time reading the Harry Potter novels to Nadia, and she regularly brought home new titles from the library.

Despite these efforts, Nadia never became a big reader. Instead, she   25
became obsessed with Japanese anime cartoons on television and comics like "Sailor Moon." Then, when she was in the sixth grade, the family bought its first computer. When a friend introduced Nadia to fanfiction.net, she turned off the television and started reading online.

Now she regularly reads stories that run as long as 45 Web pages. Many of them have elliptical plots and are sprinkled with spelling and grammatical errors. One of her recent favorites was "My absolutely, perfect normal life . . . ARE YOU CRAZY? NOT!," a story based on the anime series "Beyblade."

In one scene the narrator, Aries, hitches a ride with some masked men and one of them pulls a knife on her. "Just then I notice (Like finally) something sharp right in front of me," Aries writes. "I gladly took it just like that until something terrible happen. . . ."

Nadia said she preferred reading stories online because "you could add your own character and twist it the way you want it to be."

"So like in the book somebody could die," she continued, "but you could make it so that person doesn't die or make it so like somebody else dies who you don't like."

Nadia also writes her own stories. She posted "Dieing Isn't Always   30
Bad," about a girl who comes back to life as half cat, half human, on both fanfiction.net and quizilla.com.

Nadia said she wanted to major in English at college and someday hopes to be published. She does not see a problem with reading few books. "No one's ever said you should read more books to get into college," she said.

The simplest argument for why children should read in their leisure time is that it makes them better readers. According to federal statistics, students who say they read for fun once a day score significantly higher on reading tests than those who say they never do.

Reading skills are also valued by employers. A 2006 survey by the Conference Board, which conducts research for business leaders, found that nearly 90 percent of employers rated "reading comprehension" as "very important" for workers with bachelor's degrees. Department of Education statistics also show that those who score higher on reading tests tend to earn higher incomes.

Critics of reading on the Internet say they see no evidence that increased Web activity improves reading achievement. "What we are losing in this country and presumably around the world is the sustained, focused, linear attention developed by reading," said Mr. Gioia of the N.E.A. "I would believe people who tell me that the Internet develops reading if I did not see such a universal decline in reading ability and reading comprehension on virtually all tests."

Nicholas Carr sounded a similar note in "Is Google Making Us 35 Stupid?" in the current issue of the *Atlantic* magazine. Warning that the Web was changing the way he—and others—think, he suggested that the effects of Internet reading extended beyond the falling test scores of adolescence. "What the Net seems to be doing is chipping away my capacity for concentration and contemplation," he wrote, confessing that he now found it difficult to read long books.

Literacy specialists are just beginning to investigate how reading on the Internet affects reading skills. A recent study of more than 700 low-income, mostly Hispanic and black sixth through 10th graders in Detroit found that those students read more on the Web than in any other medium, though they also read books. The only kind of reading that related to higher academic performance was frequent novel reading, which predicted better grades in English class and higher overall grade point averages.

Elizabeth Birr Moje, a professor at the University of Michigan who led the study, said novel reading was similar to what schools demand already. But on the Internet, she said, students are developing new reading skills that are neither taught nor evaluated in school.

One early study showed that giving home Internet access to low-income students appeared to improve standardized reading test scores and school grades. "These were kids who would typically not be reading in their free time," said Linda A. Jackson, a psychology professor at Michigan State who led the research. "Once they're on the Internet, they're reading."

Neurological studies show that learning to read changes the brain's circuitry. Scientists speculate that reading on the Internet may also affect the brain's hard wiring in a way that is different from book reading.

"The question is, does it change your brain in some beneficial way?" said Guinevere F. Eden, director of the Center for the Study of Learning at Georgetown University. "The brain is malleable and adapts to its environment. Whatever the pressures are on us to succeed, our brain will try and deal with it." 40

Some scientists worry that the fractured experience typical of the Internet could rob developing readers of crucial skills. "Reading a book, and taking the time to ruminate and make inferences and engage the imaginational processing, is more cognitively enriching, without doubt, than the short little bits that you might get if you're into the 30-second digital mode," said Ken Pugh, a cognitive neuroscientist at Yale who has studied brain scans of children reading.

BUT THIS IS READING TOO

Web proponents believe that strong readers on the Web may eventually surpass those who rely on books. Reading five Web sites, an op-ed article and a blog post or two, experts say, can be more enriching than reading one book.

"It takes a long time to read a 400-page book," said Mr. Spiro of Michigan State. "In a 10th of the time," he said, the Internet allows a reader to "cover a lot more of the topic from different points of view."

Zachary Sims, the Old Greenwich, Connecticut, teenager, often stays awake until 2 or 3 in the morning reading articles about technology or politics—his current passions—on up to 100 Web sites.

"On the Internet, you can hear from a bunch of people," said Zachary, who will attend Columbia University this fall. "They may not be pedigreed academics. They may be someone in their shed with a conspiracy theory. But you would weigh that." 45

Though he also likes to read books (earlier this year he finished, and loved, *The Fountainhead* by Ayn Rand), Zachary craves interaction with fellow readers on the Internet. "The Web is more about a conversation," he said. "Books are more one-way."

The kinds of skills Zachary has developed—locating information quickly and accurately, corroborating findings on multiple sites—may seem obvious to heavy Web users. But the skills can be cognitively demanding.

Web readers are persistently weak at judging whether information is trustworthy. In one study, Donald J. Leu, who researches literacy and technology at the University of Connecticut asked 48 students to look at a spoof Web site (http://zapatopi.net/treeoctopus/) about a mythical species known as the "Pacific Northwest tree octopus." Nearly 90 percent of them missed the joke and deemed the site a reliable source.

Some literacy experts say that reading itself should be redefined. Interpreting videos or pictures, they say, may be as important a skill as analyzing a novel or a poem.

"Kids are using sound and images so they have a world of ideas to   50
put together that aren't necessarily language oriented," said Donna E. Alvermann, a professor of language and literacy education at the University of Georgia. "Books aren't out of the picture, but they're only one way of experiencing information in the world today."

A LIFELONG STRUGGLE

In the case of Hunter Gaudet, the Internet has helped him feel more comfortable with a new kind of reading. A varsity lacrosse player in Somers, Connecticut, Hunter has struggled most of his life to read. After learning he was dyslexic in the second grade, he was placed in special education classes and a tutor came to his home three hours a week. When he entered high school, he dropped the special education classes, but he still reads books only when forced, he said.

In a book, "they go through a lot of details that aren't really needed," Hunter said. "Online just gives you what you need, nothing more or less."

When researching the 19th-century Chief Justice Roger B. Taney for one class, he typed Taney's name into Google and scanned the Wikipedia entry and other biographical sites. Instead of reading an entire page, he would type in a search word like "college" to find Taney's alma mater, assembling his information nugget by nugget.

Experts on reading difficulties suggest that for struggling readers, the Web may be a better way to glean information. "When you read online there are always graphics," said Sally Shaywitz, the author of *Overcoming Dyslexia* and a Yale professor. "I think it's just more comfortable and—I hate to say easier—but it more meets the needs of somebody who might not be a fluent reader."

Karen Gaudet, Hunter's mother, a regional manager for a retail 55 chain who said she read two or three business books a week, hopes Hunter will eventually discover a love for books. But she is confident that he has the reading skills he needs to succeed.

"Based on where technology is going and the world is going," she said, "he's going to be able to leverage it."

When he was in seventh grade, Hunter was one of 89 students who participated in a study comparing performance on traditional state reading tests with a specially designed Internet reading test. Hunter, who scored in the lowest 10 percent on the traditional test, spent weeks learning how to use the Web for a science class before taking the Internet test. It was composed of three sets of directions asking the students to search for information online, determine which sites were reliable and explain their reasoning.

Hunter scored in the top quartile. In fact, about a third of the students in the study, led by Professor Leu, scored below average on traditional reading tests but did well on the Internet assessment.

THE TESTING DEBATE

To date, there have been few large-scale appraisals of Web skills. The Educational Testing Service, which administers the SAT, has developed a digital literacy test known as iSkills that requires students to solve informational problems by searching for answers on the Web. About 80 colleges and a handful of high schools have administered the test so far.

But according to Stephen Denis, product manager at ETS, of the   60
more than 20,000 students who have taken the iSkills test since 2006,
only 39 percent of four-year-college freshmen achieved a score that
represented "core functional levels" in Internet literacy.

Now some literacy experts want the federal tests known as the
nation's report card to include a digital reading component. So far,
the traditionalists have held sway: The next round, to be administered to fourth and eighth graders in 2009, will test only print reading
comprehension.

Mary Crovo of the National Assessment Governing Board, which
creates policies for the national tests, said several members of a committee that sets guidelines for the reading tests believed large numbers
of low-income and rural students might not have regular Internet access, rendering measurements of their online skills unfair.

Some simply argue that reading on the Internet is not something
that needs to be tested—or taught.

"Nobody has taught a single kid to text message," said Carol Jago of
the National Council of Teachers of English and a member of the testing guidelines committee. "Kids are smart. When they want to do
something, schools don't have to get involved."

Michael L. Kamil, a professor of education at Stanford who lobbied   65
for an Internet component as chairman of the reading test guidelines
committee, disagreed. Students "are going to grow up having to be
highly competent on the Internet," he said. "There's no reason to make
them discover how to be highly competent if we can teach them."

The United States is diverging from the policies of some other
countries. Next year, for the first time, the Organization for Economic
Cooperation and Development, which administers reading, math and
science tests to a sample of 15-year-old students in more than 50 countries, will add an electronic reading component. The United States,
among other countries, will not participate. A spokeswoman for the
Institute of Education Sciences, the research arm of the Department of
Education, said an additional test would overburden schools.

Even those who are most concerned about the preservation of
books acknowledge that children need a range of reading experiences.
"Some of it is the informal reading they get in e-mails or on Web sites,"

said Gay Ivey, a professor at James Madison University who focuses on adolescent literacy. "I think they need it all."

Web junkies can occasionally be swept up in a book. After Nadia read Elie Wiesel's Holocaust memoir *Night* in her freshman English class, Ms. Konyk brought home another Holocaust memoir, *I Have Lived a Thousand Years*, by Livia Bitton-Jackson.

Nadia was riveted by heartbreaking details of life in the concentration camps. "I was trying to imagine this and I was like, I can't do this." she said. "It was just so—wow."

Hoping to keep up the momentum, Ms. Konyk brought home another book, *Silverboy*, a fantasy novel. Nadia made it through one chapter before she got engrossed in the Internet fan fiction again. 70

STUDY QUESTIONS

1. Rich begins and ends her article with PROFILES of particular teenagers; in between, she presents ARGUMENTS about the Internet's effect on reading. What is the relationship between the RESEARCH Rich cites and Nadia's and Zachary's reading experiences? How do the profiles of individuals contribute to the rest of the article?

2. What is the significance of the way the title is written? Does the title suggest the author's POSITION? Explain. Does the author provide a definitive answer to the question in the title? If so, what is it?

3. Rich sets up her essay as a Rogerian argument: one that presents multiple sides of an issue, from both proponents and opponents. Does she ever provide a CLAIM? Why or why not?

4. LIST the EVIDENCE that supports electronic media as a legitimate method of reading and the evidence that opposes it. Based on the evidence presented in the article, which side do you agree with—or do you find a middle ground? Write your own claim and be prepared to defend it in class.

5. *For Writing.* Write a LITERACY NARRATIVE about one or more early experiences you had reading in print and online. Include your attitude toward reading, your favorite reading material, and when and where you read. REFLECT on your enjoyment of reading or lack thereof—if you enjoyed reading, what did you enjoy about it? If you didn't, why didn't you?

PAUL CHAAT SMITH { *The Big Movie*

PAUL CHAAT SMITH (b. 1954), a member of the Comanche Tribe of
Oklahoma, serves as an associate curator of the National Museum of the
American Indian in Washington, DC. He is the founding editor of the
American Indian Movement's *Treaty Council News* and writes on issues
related to American Indian art, politics, history, and culture. Smith is the
author, with Robert Warrior, of *Like a Hurricane: The Indian Movement
from Alcatraz to Wounded Knee* (1996), a study of the awakening of Native
American political activism in the 1960s and '70s.

"The Big Movie," a chapter from his book *Everything You Know about
Indians Is Wrong* (2009), mixes memoir and cultural commentary to help
readers reflect upon the highly political and hotly disputed place of Native
Americans in the United States, past and present. Known for a straightforward prose style, Smith is frequently sarcastic, even scathing, in his
approach. Notice how Smith uses easily recognizable references to popular
culture as a means to express views and arguments that many readers may
be less likely to recognize or accept. Smith presents American Indians in
ways that disrupt readers' previously held views and stereotypes, allowing
them to consider fresh perspectives on the history that all Americans share.

---

*Our Indians are no longer dangerous. We understand today better than
ever that we have wronged them much and often, that we have misjudged
and slandered them in the past. Now the reaction has set in, and it is surely
a curious phase of the white man's civilization that his latest invention is
helping to set the red man right in history. All of the more artistic Indian
films exalt the Indian, depict the noble traits in his character and challenge*

for him and his views and his manner of life the belated admiration of his white brother.

—*The Moving Picture World*, AUGUST 1911

ABOUT FIVE YEARS AGO I realized that I had no memories of seeing Indians at the movies or on television while I was growing up.

Even now I recall nothing of the thousands of hours of Hollywood westerns I must have watched during the late 1950s and 1960s, in Oklahoma and the suburbs of Washington, D.C. It certainly wasn't because I found the medium lacking. I love television and always have. To this day I learn from it constantly, but somehow the thousands of flickering Indians that must have entered my consciousness disappeared without a trace.

There was no shortage of hardware, either. We had multiple televisions, my family being the kind of consumers whom advertising agencies classify as "early adopters." Televisions were in the kitchen and the den, and later I often smuggled a portable black-and-white set into my room and watched late into the night, using earphones to subvert curfew.

The amnesia is selective. I remember *The Twilight Zone, Mayberry RFD, Lost in Space, The Mod Squad, The Man from U.N.C.L.E.,* and *The Ghost and Mrs. Muir.* I remember the assassinations, *Apollo 8,* and the night Lyndon Johnson told us he would not run for reelection, peace being more important.

Indians, sure. Uncle Sly and Aunt Maude, Grandma telling us how 5 glad she is not to live in a tipi, and the Comanche Reformed Church (a sign near the door proudly announces last week's take: $82.50) packed with the faithful, singing Indian hymns where the only words I could ever make out were "Jesus Christ." As befits a people classified as prisoners of war and raised in a military fort, those of my grandparents' generation didn't talk much about the old days. I never heard them discuss *The Searchers* or *Two Rode Together,* tales of Comanche rape and kidnapping and murder that critics agree are among the best American films ever made.

Not that I remember, anyway.

The first moving pictures of Indians that anyone knows about were made by Thomas Edison in 1894. One was a little kinetoscope number called *Sioux Ghost Dance*, and even though it showed no such thing it was nonetheless a hit on the penny arcade peep-show circuit. Modern cinema was still years in the future, but Indians were already establishing market share.

More than two thousand Hollywood features and hundreds of radio and television series later, the western rocks on. Critics through the ages have pronounced it dead and buried, but most of them are the ones dead and buried while the western is still here.

Cars replace horses, flying machines turn into 747s, communism rises and falls. Through it all the western escaped obsolescence by brilliantly reinventing itself time and time again.

So adaptable is the western, an art form as supremely American as   10
jazz or baseball, that in the 1960s the Italians rode to its rescue, breathing new life into a format that seemed hopelessly old-fashioned by creating the spaghetti western: brutal, ironic, and up-to-the-minute cool. Synonymous with Indian bashing, the number-one moneymaking western of all time is *Dances with Wolves*.

We're coming up on the second century of westerns, but even that understates their importance. They have always been with us and always will be. Flip channels if you want, try self-induced amnesia, but these efforts are useless, because the western is encoded in our cultural DNA. If you live in North America, westerns are the Book of Genesis, the story of our lives.

Attention must be paid.

Investigations of the western begin with a man named William F. Cody. He's our Moses, a self-made legend, partly fact and partly fiction, the genius who shaped the myth. In 1869 Ned Buntline, whose given name was Edward Z. C. Judson, famed writer of dime novels, traveled to Nebraska in search of a hero. He found the twenty-three-year-old William Cody, already a veteran of gold rushes, the Pony Express, and the Union Army. His nickname was a result of employment as a hunter-supplier for the Union Pacific Railroad.

Cody became a national figure through reports of his exploits in the *New York Weekly*. He appeared in stage productions based on his life, but it was a part-time affair. Mostly, he continued with being Buffalo Bill.

In 1883 he created Buffalo Bill's Wild West show and hired out-of-work Indians and cowboys. Troupe members included such all-star veterans of the Indian Wars as Sitting Bull, Black Elk, Gall, and Gabriel Dumont.

Why'd they do it? Here's one explanation, from a 1980 essay by Ward Churchill, Mary Anne Hill, and Norbert S. Hill: "Sitting Bull and other plainsmen who participated in spectacles such as Cody's and those of Pawnee Bill and Colonel Frederick T. Cummins had their reasons. There was a pressing need for revenue for their impoverished peoples, an ingrained desire for mobility, perhaps a hope of communicating some sense of their cultural identity to an ignorant and overbearing race of conquerors. But surely if the latter is the case they failed . . . before the prejudgemental myopia of their land- and mineral-hungry hosts."

Well, could be. Maybe they felt Bill's circus was a chance for cross-cultural exchange and went for it. Maybe they had to just keep moving, although this "ingrained desire for mobility" business sounds to me a bit like saying "all God's chillun got happy feet." Some believe that Indians would never in their right mind choose to participate in kitsch like Buffalo Bill's Wild West. However, I speak from personal experience in arguing that Indians are as likely to have bad taste as everyone else.

Most accounts indicate Cody was liked and respected by his Indian employees, who knew exactly what they were doing. Like Cody, the Indians were part-time entertainers and full-time legends. They made history, then re-created the history they made in popular entertainments that toured America and Europe.

Just as art critic Philip Monk makes the case that Canadian contemporary art "passed from pre-modernism to so-called post-modernism without a history of modernism," so too can it be argued that our leaders anticipated the impact of the information age. Never given much of a chance with industrialism, we moved straight into ironic, cartoonish media experiments. If some prefer to see them as gullible dupes (let's see, Sitting Bull was a brilliant leader who forced the United States to sue for peace, and definitely nobody's fool, except of course for that embarrassing business with Cody), I see them as pioneers, our first explorers of the information age.

Unlike in the movies, everything was fabulous confusion. Here's an 20 example: It's December 1890 on Pine Ridge Reservation in the southwest corner of South Dakota. The Ghost Dance religion was sweeping Indian Country. Wovoka, the Paiute some called Messiah, promised to vanquish the whites and return the buffalo. Indians were leaving the reservation for the Black Hills. The government was spooked and sent thousands of soldiers to put down a possible uprising.

They worried most about Sitting Bull, now back on the reservation after his vacation in Canada. General Nelson Miles called up Sitting Bull's friend and sometime boss William Cody. He was on staff with the governor of Nebraska and just back from another boffo European tour. In a bizarre confluence of show biz and diplomacy, General Miles asked Cody to talk some sense into Sitting Bull.

The meeting never happened. It's said Cody stayed up late the night before drinking with cavalry officers. Instead of Cody, an Indian agent with agendas of his own sent Indian cops to arrest Sitting Bull. The cops were terrified, and when the Sioux leader refused to submit he was shot. Sitting Bull's white horse, a gift from Cody, was trained to kneel at the sound of gunfire. This the horse did, as his master lay dying.

Two weeks later, the massacre at Wounded Knee.[1]

And twenty-three years after Wounded Knee, General Miles, Cody, and dozens of Indians who were there the first time re-created the events of that unfortunate December. The government cooperated in the film, hoping it would help with recruitment in a possible war with Mexico. Miles played himself and served as the film's technical adviser, which drove everyone nuts because he insisted on complete authenticity. This meant that because eleven thousand troops participated in a review after the hostiles surrendered, eleven thousand troops were going to be used in the movie. His demands that the Badlands sequence be shot in the Badlands, despite the enormous cost of

---

[1] Wounded Knee Creek in South Dakota, where, on December 29, 1890, members of the U.S. Seventh Cavalry killed 150 Lakota Sioux, an event generally regarded as one of the most horrific in Native American history.

moving the camp, caused so much bitterness that it finally ended his friendship with Cody.

General Miles also worked as a press agent for the movie, saying 25 in one interview, "The idea is to give the whole thing from the start— the Indian dissatisfaction, their starving condition, the coming of the false 'Messiah' who stirred them to revolt, the massing of the troops, the death of Sitting Bull and, finally, the surrender. All of these incidents will be gone over, just as they happened. Some of the Indians will be there who fought against us. They will fight again, but there will be no bullets. All that is over."

They shot Sitting Bull again, and General Miles insisted on shooting the Battle of Wounded Knee just where it had originally happened, on the mass grave of Big Foot's band.

The night before, rumors swept the camp that some of the Indian extras were going to use live ammunition. Cody called a midnight meeting and told the Indians that the movie would celebrate their resistance. The next morning, although both sides were extremely reluctant to begin firing, they managed to reenact the battle/massacre.

Many Indians broke into tears.

After filming was completed, they spent six months editing. This was during a time when studios turned out movies by the week. Finally it was shown before the secretary of the interior and other top officials of the Wilson administration, who said they loved it.

Other reviews were mixed. One critic called the film "war itself, 30 grim, unpitying and terrible . . . no boy or girl should be allowed to miss these pictures. If you are a lonely man or woman pick up some equally lonely kiddie and take him for an afternoon with the great leaders of our army, with the great chiefs of our Indian tribes and two hours in the open world that has been made sacred by heroic blood of the nation's fighting heroes." A Lakota named Chauncey Yellow Robe trashed the movie in a speech to the Society of American Indians, reserving particular scorn for Miles and Cody, "who were not even there when it happened, went back and became heroes for a moving picture machine."

After a few screenings it mysteriously disappeared. Cody died in 1917, and for nearly a century the film was nowhere to be found. Even the title wasn't known for sure: at various times Buffalo Bill's lost masterpiece was called *The Indian Wars Refought, The Last Indian Battles; or, From the Warpath to the Peace Pipe, The Wars for Civilization in America,* and *Buffalo Bill's Indian Wars.*

The most expensive, elaborate western of its day was the victim of its own identity crisis. For Cody, it was the most spectacular movie ever made, the triumph of a fabled career. For Miles, it was part documentary, part training film. For the government, it was a recruiting device. For the critics, it was a battle showing the victory of Western civilization.

The final result must have been too close, too real. Critical distance could not be established when original combatants were actors, and when the set was the site of battle and massacre. It was a movie, but it was no western.

The films we know came later, as Hollywood matured (or at least got its act together). From the 1920s through the 1950s, cowboys and Indians were a lucrative staple of the industry.

The United States also was just getting its act together. National 35 identity was still shaky, with the Civil War over but not resolved, a frontier still largely untamed, and vast regional differences. Reports of armed resistance by Apaches, Cherokees, Yaquis, and others circulated into the 1920s. In 1909 a Paiute accidentally killed an in-law and vengeful whites chased him across Southern California. The accompanying hysteria made it clear many Americans were not convinced the Indian Wars were over, and even if they were, many wished they weren't. (This event became the subject of a 1969 pro-Indian movie called *Tell Them Willie Boy Was Here,* starring Robert Redford, Katharine Ross, and Robert Blake.)

The directors who pioneered the modern western grew up when the Indian Wars were recent, even current events. D. W. Griffith was born in 1875, Cecil B. DeMille in 1881, Raoul Walsh in 1887, and King Vidor in 1894. John Ford, born in 1894, said "I had four uncles in the Civil War. I used to ask my Uncle Mike to tell me about the Battle of Gettysburg. All Uncle Mike would say was, 'It was horrible. I went six whole days without a drink.'"

Geronimo, Wounded Knee, Sitting Bull, and Custer were no more distant to these guys than Vietnam and Watergate are to many of us.

The form they invented has several characteristics. First, it's set in the past. The films are implicitly about America's history. Second, they are set on the frontier. (This could be almost anywhere, since every inch of the continent was frontier at one time.) Third, westerns set up a language that extends the metaphor of the frontier into paired opposites of, for example, the wilderness versus civilization, the individual versus community, savagery versus humanity.

John Ford, the king of westerns, set his most famous movies about Indians in Monument Valley, a landscape that might be described as Martian, to contrast the alienness of the land with the flimsy covered wagons and lonely outposts. Often the Indians seemed alien as well, but they seemed to belong there, while the Americans looked like intruders, or tourists.

Some westerns demonstrate a real interest in Indians, but in most 40 we exist as a metaphor. The definitive moment in *The Searchers* is at the movie's close. The search is over, the rescue accomplished. Ethan (the rescuer, played by John Wayne) is asked to stay with the family he has reunited against all odds. Framed by a doorway, half in sunlight, half in darkness, the tormented Ethan says no. Still at war with demons from his past, he can't submit to a domestic life. His personal war goes on, and as he leaves the cabin to take his place in the wilderness we know it has nothing to do with Indians. The Comanches he's been fighting for two hours are simply a plot device to get to this moment of terrible pain and alienation.

Imagine something instead of Western history. For most of us, it can't be done. We think, okay, these movies are not exactly accurate (not that they ever claimed to be), and maybe we get closer to the truth if we turn them upside down. Maybe Indians didn't yelp. Maybe the whites were bloodthirsty savages. The master narrative will admit good Indians and bad whites; a western may even present the Long Knives[2] as supremely vicious and evil and the Indian cause just, yet still not challenge the basic premise of a frontier, a wilderness, an inevitable clash of cultures that ends in conquest.

[2] That is, whites.

In *Dances with Wolves*,[3] for example, there exists not a single positive white character. Many of the whites are physically disgusting. The film's title is the name of the protagonist, who becomes Indian and marries a white captive who is also now Indian. The government forces are incompetent, cowardly, and brutal. The message is delivered with all the subtlety of a sledgehammer. The Americans are portrayed as primitive Nazis with bad table manners.

Reduced to its essentials in this way, *Dances with Wolves* seems to be a devastating, revisionist history. In effect, however, the film is a moving, patriotic hymn to all that is majestic about the United States, which includes the beautiful Lakota and their tragic passing. The achievement of *Dances with Wolves* is extraordinary. It turns an indictment of genocide into a valentine to America. Audiences identify with the Indians as part of their heritage, a kind of national mascot. (In the fall of 1992, according to press reports, McDonald's, a corporation synonymous with patriotic values, was close to a deal to sell videocassettes of the movie with purchases of hamburgers and fries. These promotions are called tie-ins, and the phrase couldn't be more appropriate.)

One might ask, okay, maybe it is one-sided and overblown, but aren't we entitled to a little of that after thousands of one-sided and overblown racist westerns? It's a fair question. The night of the Academy Awards in the spring of 1991, one television network showed the ecstatic reaction of children from the Pine Ridge Reservation in South Dakota. Who can argue that those kids who desperately need positive images and role models are not uplifted, even with all the movie's flaws?

Well, I won't argue with that. I think it is positive for many. I also 45 think it leads to a dead end, because the opposite of a lie isn't necessarily true or useful. The master narrative thrives on us/them oppositions.

The 1992 remake of *Last of the Mohicans*[4] provides another illustration of what is permitted and what isn't. Director Michael Mann,

[3] Academy Award–winning film (1990) starring Kevin Costner and Graham Greene. The movie follows a Civil War Lieutenant to a remote Western outpost where he befriends members of a Lakota tribe and ultimately joins them, rejecting his white American background.

[4] James Fenimore Cooper's 1826 novel has been adapted several times for film, radio, and television.

the inventor of television's *Miami Vice*, gave interviews describing his uncompromising research of the eighteenth century, his obsession with getting everything right, and the importance of showing the complex politics of the era. He said back then, if you were an American settler, the Mohawks were your rich neighbors.

I see no reason to doubt that Mann had every intention of including this idea in his movie, but he didn't. It can't be done, because the master narrative does not include settled, prosperous farming towns of Indians. Pictures of Indian towns challenge the idea of settlers clearing a wilderness and instead raise the possibility that Europeans invaded and conquered and pillaged heavily populated, developed real estate. (*Dances with Wolves* offered us an inviting and warm village, but temporary villages with tipis are acceptable. They do not represent property.)

This isn't because some studio boss got a call from the Trilateral Commission.[5] It's because the audience knows about Indians, and knows Indians didn't live in settled farming towns. To be outside the narrative, then, is not to exist. A film that attempted to show something more historically accurate would appear to audiences to be like science fiction, a tale from a parallel universe.

The master narrative (let's call it the Big Movie) is like an infinitely elastic spider web that grows stronger with every change of pattern and wider after each assault. Subversion appears impossible.

Collectively, this is the accomplishment of westerns: they reconcile   50
horrible truths and make them understandable, acceptable, and even uplifting. And because they execute this reconciliation in a way that reinforces status quo values they are a powerful mechanism that serves and strengthens the dominant ideology.

The Big Movie is always up-to-date and these days is an equal opportunity employer. Indians are welcome to amplify or change aspects of the story, and with talent, luck, and the right contacts they have as much chance to succeed as anyone else. It won't be easy, but it's pos-

[5] Private organization founded in 1973 to promote closer relations among the United States, Europe, and Japan. Because its proceedings are closed and many of its members are wealthy, powerful, and well connected, the Trilateral Commission has become the focus of numerous conspiracy theories.

sible and in the long run inevitable that we will see westerns written and directed by Indians.

For those who want not a piece of the pie but a different pie altogether, the task is both urgent and far more difficult. It requires invention, not rewriting. Instead of a reimagined western, it means a final break with a form that really was never about us in the first place.

The stories of the continent must be told. A vacuum is impossible, and humans demand an explanation. So far, the only one that exists is the Big Movie. It says with perfect consistency that we are extinct, were never here anyway, that it was our fault because we couldn't get with the program. It says we are noble, are savage, and noble savages.

There's another narrative waiting to be written. It tells Sitting Bull's story: Did he complain about his agent? Did he really propose marriage to his secretary, a rich white woman from Brooklyn named Catherine Weldon, who lived in his camp in those final days? And let's say they did get hitched, could it have worked? It fully imagines that mysterious cipher Crazy Horse[6] (as a kid his nickname was "Curly") and Almighty Voice and Poundmaker and gives voice to the women nobody remembers.

Even more important, it tells the story of our all-too-human parents and brothers and sisters and uncles and aunts, just plain folks who were nothing like the Indians in the movies even though some of us tried hard to be like them. It tells a story of resistance, of laughter and tears in a doomed land cursed by the legacy of slavery and genocide, a place that's perhaps forever beyond redemption but still the only place we've got. 55

It's a long shot but worth a try. Besides, in the Big Movie, we'll always be extras. In our movie, we could be stars.

---

[6] Lakota Sioux warrior who was one of the Indian leaders at the Battle of the Little Big Horn. Almighty Voice and Poundmaker are important historical figures from the Cree tribe.

STUDY QUESTIONS

1. In Paul Chaat Smith's view, how does the movie *Dances with Wolves* differ from earlier movies featuring Native Americans? Does he find the movie satisfying? Why or why not?

2. Smith DESCRIBES and EVALUATES a number of movies, old and new, that depict Native Americans in both positive and negative ways. He also uses the phrase "The Big Movie" many times in a less literal sense. Explain in your own words what Smith means by the phrase "The Big Movie." How does he use this phrase to make a larger ARGUMENT?

3. How does Smith's focus on movies give us a sense of his intended AUDIENCE? Do you feel that you are part of this audience? Even if you have never heard of or seen the movies he discusses, does his ANALYSIS of these movies and "The Big Movie" behind them seem clear and well argued?

4. Toward the end of the selection, Smith writes, "The stories of this continent must be told. A vacuum is impossible, and humans demand an explanation. So far, the only one that exists is the Big Movie. It says with perfect consistency that we are extinct, were never here anyway, that it was our fault because we couldn't get with the program. It says we are noble, are savage, and noble savages." Who are "we" in this passage? What is implied by the phrase "noble savage"? What specific kinds of stories is he talking about here and why are they so necessary?

5. *For Writing.* In his discussion of the movie *Dances with Wolves*, Smith writes that it "turns an indictment of genocide into a valentine to America. Audiences identify with the Indians as part of their heritage, a kind of national mascot." Watch *Dances with Wolves* and write an essay that evaluates Smith's critique of the movie. Are you able to identify with the American Indians in the movie? With Kevin Costner's character? In what ways do you agree or disagree with Smith's claims about the movie? Be sure to cite specific passages from the text and refer to specific scenes from the movie in order to support your points.

ROBERT APPLEBAUM { *Cancel Student Loan*
Debt to Stimulate the
Economy

ROBERT APPLEBAUM (b. 1974) earned his BA in political science
at the State University of New York at Oneonta and completed his
law degree at Fordham University. He worked as an assistant district
attorney in Brooklyn, New York, from 1999 to 2004. Applebaum founded
ForgiveStudentLoanDebt.com because he found that he could not both support himself and pay off his student loans while working as an assistant DA.

In the following selection, which was posted to a Facebook group of the
same name, Applebaum proposes that forgiving student loan debt would
help the economy more than tax cuts and federal bailout money. According
to Applebaum, it would put hundreds or even thousands of dollars every
month in the pockets of those who need it and would go out and spend
it, thus stimulating the economy. As you read his argument, note how
Applebaum anticipates objections to his points. Is his argument convincing?
Should student loan debt be cancelled for the reasons Applebaum cites?

PRESIDENT OBAMA RECENTLY SIGNED INTO law a $787 billion stimu-
lus package on top of former President Bush's grossly misman-
aged $700 billion TARP bailout from last September. A couple of
months ago, the Federal Reserve basically printed an additional
$1,000,000,000,000 to inject more funds into the monetary system,
which will undoubtedly have the effect of diminishing the purchasing
power of the dollar. Since March of 2008, the government has paid out
approximately $5.32 *trillion* in bailouts, handouts, loans, and give-
aways, with no end in sight as our leaders try anything and everything

to get our spiraling economy under control. While some of what Washington has already done may act to stimulate the economy, many of the trillions of dollars already spent will, no doubt, turn out to be just money wasted.

Tax rebate checks *do not* stimulate the economy—history shows that people either spend such rebates on paying off credit card debt, or they simply save the money, doing little to nothing to stimulate the economy. Presumably, that is why they were removed from the final version of the stimulus bill. The tax cuts that were included, however, amount to a whopping $44 per month for the rest of 2009, decreasing to an even more staggering $33 per month in 2010. This is hardly "relief," as it is likely to help nobody.

The Wall Street financial institutions, auto manufacturers, insurance companies, and countless other irresponsible actors have now received *trillions* of taxpayer dollars (as demonstrated above, that's a number with *twelve* zeros at the end of it) to bail them out of their self-created mess. This, too, does nothing to stimulate the economy. It merely rewards bad behavior and does nothing to encourage institutional change. There is a better way.

How many times have we heard from our leaders in Washington that education is the key to solving all of our underlying societal problems? The so-called "silver bullet." For decades, presidents, senators, and members of Congress have touted themselves as champions of education, yet they've done nothing to actually encourage the pursuit of one on an individual level.

Some of us have taken advantage of Federal Stafford Loans and 5 other programs, including private loans, to finance higher education, presumably with the understanding that an advanced degree equates with higher earning power in the future. Many of us go into public service after attaining such degrees, something that's also repeatedly proclaimed as something society should encourage. Yet, the debt we've accrued to obtain such degrees has crippled our ability to reap the benefits of our educations, causing many to make the unfortunate choice of leaving public service so as to earn enough money to pay off that debt.

Our economy is in the tank. There isn't a reasonable economist alive who doesn't believe that the economy needs stimulating immediately. The only debate now centers on how to go about doing it. While the new stimulus plan contains some worthy provisions, very little of it will have a significant and immediate stimulating effect on the economy. The Obama administration itself doesn't expect to see an upsurge in the economy until mid- to late 2010.

Instead of funneling billions, if not *trillions* of additional dollars to banks, financial institutions, insurance companies, and other institutions of greed that are responsible for the current economic crisis, why not allow educated, hardworking, middle-class Americans to get something in return? After all, they're our tax dollars too!

Forgiving student loan debt would have an *immediate* stimulating effect on the economy. Responsible people who did nothing other than pursue a higher education would have hundreds if not thousands of extra dollars per month to spend, fueling the economy *now*. Those extra dollars being pumped into the economy would have a multiplying effect, unlike many of the provisions of the new stimulus package. As a result, tax revenues would go up, the credit markets would unfreeze, and jobs would be created. Consumer spending accounts for over two-thirds of the entire U.S. economy and in recent months, consumer spending has declined at alarming, unprecedented rates. Therefore, it stands to reason that the fastest way to revive our ailing economy is to do something drastic to get consumers to spend.

This proposal would quickly revitalize the housing market, the ailing automobile industry, travel and tourism, durable goods, and countless other sectors of the economy because the very people who sustain those sectors will automatically have hundreds or, in some cases, thousands of extra dollars per month to spend. The driving factor in today's economy is fear. Unless and until the middle class feels comfortable enough that they'll have their jobs, health insurance, and extra money to spend not only next month, but the month after that, etc., the economy will not, indeed, cannot grow fast enough to stop the hemorrhaging.

Let me be clear. This is *not* about a free ride. This is about a new approach to economic stimulus, nothing more. To those who would argue that this proposal would cause the banking system to collapse or   10 make student loans unavailable to future borrowers, please allow me to respond.

I am in no way suggesting that the lending institutions who carry such debts on their balance sheets get legislatively shafted by having them wiped from their books. The banks and other financial institutions are going to get their money regardless because, in addition to the $700 billion TARP bailout, more bailout money is coming their way. This proposal merely suggests that in return for the trillions of dollars that have been and will continue to be handed over to the banks, educated, hardworking Americans who are saddled with student loan debt should get some relief as well, rather than sending those institutions another enormous blank check. Because the banks are being handed trillions of dollars anyway, there would be no danger of making funds unavailable to future borrowers.

To avoid the moral hazard that this plan could potentially create, going forward, the way higher education in this country is financed *must* be reformed. Requiring students to amass enormous debt just to receive an education is an untenable approach, as demonstrated by the ever-growing student loan default rates. Having a loan-based system rather than one based on grants and scholarships or, ideally, public funding has, over time, begun to have the unintended consequence of discouraging people from seeking higher education at all. That is no way for America to reclaim the mantle of the land of opportunity.

A well-educated workforce benefits society as a whole, not just the students who receive a higher education. It is often said that an undergraduate degree today is the equivalent of a high school diploma thirty or forty years ago. Accepting the premise as true that society does, in fact, place the same value on an undergraduate degree today as it did on a high school diploma thirty or forty years ago, then what is the rationale for cutting off public funding of education after the twelfth grade? It seems to me that there is some dissonance in our values that needs to be reconciled. That, however, cannot come to pass until the millions of us already shackled with student loan debt are freed from the enormous economic burdens we're presently carrying.

Many of the vocal naysayers who have curiously joined this group seem intent on ignoring the fact that Washington *is* going to spend *trillions* of dollars, likely in the form of handing blank checks over to more and more banks, as a way of getting the economy under control. Normative assessments of how things should be are fine, but they don't reflect reality.

Accepting the premise that Washington *will* spend trillions of dol- 15 lars in unprecedented ways (a good portion of which will just be trial and error, since we're in uncharted waters), what is the argument against directly helping middle-class people who are struggling, rather than focusing solely on the banks and other financial institutions responsible for the crisis to begin with?

Further accepting that there is an aggregate amount of outstanding student loan debt totaling approximately $550 billion (that's billion with a "b", not a "t"), one is forced to ask again, what is the objection to helping real people with real hardships when all we're talking about is a relative drop in the bucket as compared with what will be spent to dig us out of this hole?

In a perfect world, I share these biases towards personal responsibility and having people pay back what they owe and making good on the commitments they've made. But we don't live in a perfect world and the global economy, not just the U.S. economy, is in a downward spiral, the likes of which *nobody* truly knows how to fix.

This proposal will immediately free up money for hardworking, educated Americans, giving them more money in their pockets *every month*, addressing the very real psychological aspects of the recession as much as the financial ones. Is it the only answer? No, of course not. But could it help millions of hardworking people who struggle every month to get by? Absolutely. Given the current economic climate, as well as the plans to spend trillions of additional dollars that are in the works, one must wonder what is so objectionable about giving a real helping hand to real people with real struggles.

The year 2009 and the new Obama administration is supposed to be about change. Nothing in the new economic stimulus package represents a significant departure from the way Washington has always operated—it's merely a different set of priorities on a higher scale, but it's certainly not materially different from any other economic stimulus package passed during the past few decades.

Washington cannot simply print and borrow money to get us out of 20
this crisis. We the People, however, can get this economy moving *now*.
All we need is relief from debt that was accrued under the now-false
promise that higher education equates with higher earnings.

Free us of our obligations to repay our out-of-control student loan
debt and *we*, the hardworking, middle-class Americans who drive this
economy, will spend those extra dollars *now*.

If you believe that there's a better way of climbing out of this economic crisis, one that empowers us to directly spend money, start businesses, free up credit and create jobs, then please join this group and
encourage others to do so as well.

There's strength in numbers—the more people to join this group,
the louder our voices and the greater the chances of being heard by
President Obama and Congress.

Support *real* change we can believe in!

STUDY QUESTIONS

1. How does Applebaum see the state of the economy? Why does he think that tax rebates will not help stimulate it? What role does he believe education plays in economic recovery?

2. Applebaum calls for the forgiveness of student debt. How and how effectively does he support his CLAIM? How and how effectively does he address COUNTERARGUMENTS? Explain.

3. At the end of his essay Applebaum issues a call for action. To what rhetorical GENRE does the essay belong? Why? Is Facebook an appropriate venue? Why or why not?

4. *For Writing.* Write an essay in which you argue for or against forgiving student loans. Be sure to support your claim with REASONS and EVIDENCE.

JUDY BRADY { *I Want a Wife*

JUDY BRADY (b. 1937) is a freelance writer whose work has appeared
in many periodicals, including *Ms.*, *Greenpeace*, and *The Women's
Review of Books*. Much of her writing concerns the politics surrounding
cancer and the environmental causes of cancer. She has edited both
Women and Cancer (1990) and *One in Three: Women with Cancer
Confront an Epidemic* (1991).

"I Want a Wife" debuted publicly in 1970 when Brady read it at a
celebration of the fiftieth anniversary of women's suffrage in 1970, and it
was published two years later in the first issue of *Ms.* magazine. In
essence, the essay provides a satiric look at what a wife is—or at least
"should" be. As you read, consider the stereotype of the perfect wife that
Brady was playing upon in the early days of the modern feminist
movement. Has the definition of "wife" changed today?

I BELONG TO THAT CLASSIFICATION of people known as wives. I am
A Wife. And, not altogether incidentally, I am a mother.

Not too long ago a male friend of mine appeared on the scene fresh
from a recent divorce. He had one child, who is, of course, with his
ex-wife. He is obviously looking for another wife. As I thought about
him while I was ironing one evening, it suddenly occurred to me that
I, too, would like to have a wife. Why do I want a wife?

I would like to go back to school so that I can become economically
independent, support myself, and, if need be, support those dependent upon me. I want a wife who will work and send me to school. And
while I am going to school I want a wife to take care of the children.

I want a wife to keep track of the children's doctor and dentist appointments. And to keep track of mine too. I want a wife to make sure my children eat properly and are kept clean. I want a wife who will wash the children's clothes and keep them mended. I want a wife who is a good nurturant attendant to my children, who arranges for their schooling, makes sure that they have an adequate social life with their peers, takes them to the park, the zoo, et cetera. I want a wife who takes care of the children when they are sick, a wife who arranges to be around when the children need special care, because, of course, I cannot miss classes at school. My wife must arrange to lose time at work and not lose the job. It may mean a small cut in my wife's income from time to time, but I guess I can tolerate that. Needless to say, my wife will arrange and pay for the care of the children while my wife is working.

I want a wife who will take care of my physical needs. I want a wife who will keep my house clean. A wife who will pick up after me. I want a wife who will keep my clothes clean, ironed, mended, replaced when need be, and who will see to it that my personal things are kept in their proper place so that I can find what I need the minute I need it. I want a wife who cooks the meals, a wife who is a *good* cook. I want a wife who will plan the menus, do the necessary grocery shopping, prepare the meals, serve them pleasantly, and then do the cleaning up while I do my studying. I want a wife who will care for me when I am sick and sympathize with my pain and loss of time from school. I want a wife to go along when our family takes a vacation so that someone can continue to care for me and my children when I need a rest and change of scene.

I want a wife who will not bother me with rambling complaints 5 about a wife's duties. But I want a wife who will listen to me when I feel the need to explain a rather difficult point I have come across in my course of studies. And I want a wife who will type my papers for me when I have written them.

I want a wife who will take care of the details of my social life. When my wife and I are invited out by my friends, I want a wife who will take care of the babysitting arrangements. When I meet people at school whom I like and want to entertain, I want a wife who will have the house clean, will prepare a special meal, serve it to me and my friends, and not interrupt when I talk about the things that interest me and my friends. I want a wife who will have arranged that the children are fed and ready for bed before my guests arrive so that the children do not bother us.

And I want a wife who knows that sometimes I need a night out by myself.

I want a wife who is sensitive to my sexual needs, a wife who makes love passionately and eagerly when I feel like it, a wife who makes sure that I am satisfied. And, of course, I want a wife who will not demand sexual attention when I am not in the mood for it. I want a wife who assumes the complete responsibilities for birth control, because I do not want more children. I want a wife who will remain sexually faithful to me so that I do not have to clutter up my intellectual life with jealousies. And I want a wife who understands that *my* sexual needs may entail more than strict adherence to monogamy. I must, after all, be able to relate to people as fully as possible.

If, by chance, I find another person more suitable as a wife than the wife I already have, I want the liberty to replace my present wife with another one. Naturally, I will expect a fresh, new life; my wife will take the children and be solely responsible for them so that I am left free.

When I am through with school and have a job, I want my wife to 10 quit working and remain at home so that my wife can more fully and completely take care of a wife's duties.

My God, who *wouldn't* want a wife?

STUDY QUESTIONS

1. Reread Brady's essay, and determine which gender Brady's "wife" is. Why do you suppose Brady chose to write about a wife in this way?

2. Brady gives many examples to define what a wife is. What might have sparked this extended DEFINITION? Explain.

3. What are Brady's AUDIENCE, TONE, and PURPOSE in this essay? Do the purpose and tone have an effect on you? How so? Are you part of the intended audience? If not, how do you feel about Brady's message?

4. *For Writing.* Using Brady's essay as a model, write an essay in which you describe your ideal partner. Consider employing such rhetorical devices as SATIRE and humor. You might also consider using the description of your ideal partner, like Brady, to make a larger point, whether about gender relations, sexual politics, the speed of life in the twenty-first century, or some other issue.

PAUL GOODMAN { *A Proposal to Abolish Grading*

PAUL GOODMAN (1911–1972), philosopher, sociologist, and writer, graduated from the City College of New York in 1932 and was awarded his PhD at the University of Chicago in 1953. Goodman belonged to a circle of New York intellectuals that included Lionel Trilling, Norman Mailer, and Mary McCarthy. He wrote short stories and contributed to *Politics*, a magazine of political analysis and literary essays. In 1960 he published the work for which he is best known: *Growing Up Absurd: Problems of Youth in the Organized System*. Goodman was also one of the co-founders of Gestalt therapy, which emphasizes the way the individual functions in the present moment.

In this selection from his book *Compulsory Mis-Education* (1964), Goodman makes an argument for abolishing grades in school. While many students over the years have jokingly made just such a proposal, Goodman is completely serious: he offers reasons and evidence in support of his idea and anticipates objections to it. Before reading this essay, make your own list of reasons that grades should or should not be abolished. Then, see how your views match up with Goodman's. You might just find yourself converted—or at least thinking about your education in a whole new light.

MY OTHER PROPOSAL[1] IS EVEN simpler, and not at all novel. Let half a dozen of the prestigious Universities—Chicago, Stanford, the Ivy League—abolish grading, and use testing only and entirely for pedagogic purposes as teachers see fit.

---

[1]Just before the start of this excerpt, Goodman proposes that colleges require potential students to complete two years of some sort of life experience after high school.

From *Compulsory Mis-Education and the Community of Schools* by Paul Goodman. Copyright © 1962, 1964 by Paul Goodman. Used by permission of Random House, Inc.

Anyone who knows the frantic temper of the present schools will understand the transvaluation of values that would be effected by this modest innovation. For most of the students, the competitive grade has come to be the essence. The naive teacher points to the beauty of the subject and the ingenuity of the research; the shrewd student asks if he is responsible for that on the final exam.

Let me at once dispose of an objection whose unanimity is quite fascinating. I think that the great majority of professors agree that grading hinders teaching and creates a bad spirit, going as far as cheating and plagiarizing. I have before me the collection of essays, *Examining in Harvard College*, and this is the consensus. It is uniformly asserted, however, that the grading is inevitable; for how else will the graduate schools, the foundations, the corporations *know* whom to accept, reward, hire? How will the talent scouts know whom to tap?

By testing the applicants, of course, according to the specific task-requirements of the inducting institution, just as applicants for the Civil Service or for licenses in medicine, law, and architecture are tested. Why should Harvard professors do the testing *for* corporations and graduate-schools?

The objection is ludicrous. Dean Whitla, of the Harvard Office of Tests, points out that the scholastic-aptitude and achievement tests used for *admission* to Harvard are a super-excellent index for all-around Harvard performance, better than high-school grades or particular Harvard course-grades. Presumably, these college-entrance tests are tailored for what Harvard and similar institutions want. By the same logic, would not an employer do far better to apply his own job-aptitude test rather than to rely on the vagaries of Harvard section-men? Indeed, I doubt that many employers bother to look at such grades; they are more likely to be interested merely in the fact of a Harvard diploma, whatever that connotes to them. The grades have most of their weight with the graduate schools—here, as elsewhere, the system runs mainly for its own sake. 5

It is really necessary to remind our academics of the ancient history of Examination. In the medieval university, the whole point of the gruelling trial of the candidate was whether or not to accept him as a peer. His disputation and lecture for the Master's was just that, a master-piece to enter the guild. It was not to make comparative evaluations. It was not to weed out and select for an extra-mural licensor or employer. It was certainly not to pit one young fellow against another in an ugly competition. My philosophic impression is that the medievals thought they knew what a good job of work was and that we are competitive because we do not know. But the more status is achieved by largely irrelevant competitive evaluation, the less will we ever know.

(Of course, our American examinations never did have this purely guild orientation, just as our faculties have rarely had absolute autonomy; the examining was to satisfy Overseers, Elders, distant Regents—and they as paternal superiors have always doted on giving grades, rather than accepting peers. But I submit that this set-up itself makes it impossible for the student to *become* a master, to *have* grown up, and to commence on his own. He will always be making A or B for some overseer. And in the present atmosphere, he will always be climbing on his friend's neck.)

Perhaps the chief objectors to abolishing grading would be the students and their parents. The parents should be simply disregarded; their anxiety has done enough damage already. For the students, it seems to me that a primary duty of the university is to deprive them of their props, their dependence on extrinsic valuation and motivation, and to force them to confront the difficult enterprise itself and finally lose themselves in it.

A miserable effect of grading is to nullify the various uses of testing. Testing, for both student and teacher, is a means of structuring, and also of finding out what is blank or wrong and what has been assimilated and can be taken for granted. Review—including high-pressure review—is a means of bringing together the fragments, so that there are flashes of synoptic insight.

There are several good reasons for testing, and kinds of test. But if the aim is to discover weakness, what is the point of down-grading and punishing it, and thereby inviting the student to conceal his weakness, by faking and bulling, if not cheating? The natural conclusion of synthesis is the insight itself, not a grade for having had it. For the important purpose of placement, if one can establish in the student the belief that one is testing *not* to grade and make invidious comparisons but for his own advantage, the student should normally seek his own level, where he is challenged and yet capable, rather than trying to get by. If the student dares to accept himself as he is, a teacher's grade is a crude instrument compared with a student's self-awareness. But it is rare in our universities that students are encouraged to notice objectively their vast confusion. Unlike Socrates, our teachers rely on power-drives rather than shame and ingenuous idealism.

Many students are lazy, so teachers try to goad or threaten them by grading. In the long run this must do more harm than good. Laziness is a character-defense. It may be a way of avoiding learning, in order to protect the conceit that one is already perfect (deeper, the despair that one *never* can). It may be a way of avoiding just the risk of failing and being down-graded. Sometimes it is a way of politely saying, "I won't." But since it is the authoritarian grown-up demands that have created such attitudes in the first place, why repeat the trauma? There comes a time when we must treat people as adult, laziness and all. It is one thing courageously to fire a do-nothing out of your class; it is quite another thing to evaluate him with a lordly F.

Most important of all, it is often obvious that balking in doing the work, especially among bright young people who get to great universities, means exactly what it says: The work does not suit me, not this subject, or not at this time, or not in this school, or not in school altogether. The student might not be bookish; he might be school-tired; perhaps his development ought now to take another direction. Yet unfortunately, if such a student is intelligent and is not sure of himself, he *can* be bullied into passing, and this obscures everything. My hunch is that I am describing a common situation. What a grim waste of young life and teacherly effort! Such a student will retain nothing of what he has "passed" in. Sometimes he must get mononucleosis to tell his story and be believed.

And ironically, the converse is also probably commonly true. A student flunks and is mechanically weeded out, who is really ready and eager to learn in a scholastic setting, but he has not quite caught on. A good teacher can recognize the situation, but the computer wreaks its will.

STUDY QUESTIONS

1. Why does Goodman think that grades should be abolished? How does he suggest students should be evaluated instead?

2. What objections to his PROPOSAL does Goodman anticipate? How and how effectively does he RESPOND to these objections?

3. *For Writing.* Do you think that grades should be abolished? Drawing on your own experience, write an essay in which you ARGUE for or against Goodman's proposal. Be sure to support your THESIS with EVIDENCE.

MICHAEL LEVIN ⎰ *The Case for Torture*

MICHAEL LEVIN (b. 1943), a professor of philosophy, earned his BA at Michigan State University in 1964 and his PhD in philosophy from Columbia University in 1969. He began his teaching career at Columbia before joining the philosophy department at the City University of New York in 1969. Levin holds controversial positions on a number of divisive social issues; he has stated, for example, that differences between the average IQ scores of Caucasian and African Americans are due mainly to genetic differences and that homosexuality is a misuse of the body. He has published numerous articles in both academic journals and popular periodicals, including *Newsday,* the *New York Times*, and *Newsweek*. His books include *Feminism and Freedom* (1987), *Why Race Matters* (1997), and *Sexual Orientation and Human Rights* (1999).

In "The Case for Torture," Levin supports another controversial position: he argues that torture is justified in certain situations. Before reading this essay, determine your own position on torture. Does Levin's essay prompt you to reconsider? Take note of how the author crafts his argument to appeal to the reader: does he engage your emotions or your logical reasoning? Does he have a credible persona? Is he fair in how he characterizes opposing arguments?

─────────────

IT IS GENERALLY ASSUMED THAT torture is impermissible, a throwback to a more brutal age. Enlightened societies reject it outright, and regimes suspected of using it risk the wrath of the United States.

I believe this attitude is unwise. There are situations in which torture is not merely permissible but morally mandatory. Moreover, these situations are moving from the realm of imagination to fact.

Death: Suppose a terrorist has hidden an atomic bomb on Manhattan Island which will detonate at noon on July 4 unless . . . (here follow the usual demands for money and release of his friends from jail). Suppose, further, that he is caught at 10 a.m. of the fateful day, but—preferring death to failure—won't disclose where the bomb is. What do we do? If we follow due process—wait for his lawyer, arraign him—millions of people will die. If the only way to save those lives is to subject the terrorist to the most excruciating possible pain, what grounds can there be for not doing so? I suggest there are none. In any case, I ask you to face the question with an open mind.

Torturing the terrorist is unconstitutional? Probably. But millions of lives surely outweigh constitutionality. Torture is barbaric? Mass murder is far more barbaric. Indeed, letting millions of innocents die in deference to one who flaunts his guilt is moral cowardice, an unwillingness to dirty one's hands. If *you* caught the terrorist, could you sleep nights knowing that millions died because you couldn't bring yourself to apply the electrodes?

Once you concede that torture is justified in extreme cases, you have 5 admitted that the decision to use torture is a matter of balancing innocent lives against the means needed to save them. You must now face more realistic cases involving more modest numbers. Someone plants a bomb on a jumbo jet. He alone can disarm it, and his demands cannot be met (or if they can, we refuse to set a precedent by yielding to his threats). Surely we can, we must, do anything to the extortionist to save the passengers. How can we tell 300, or 100, or 10 people who never asked to be put in danger, "I'm sorry, you'll have to die in agony, we just couldn't bring ourselves to . . ."

Here are the results of an informal poll about a third, hypothetical, case. Suppose a terrorist group kidnapped a newborn baby from a hospital. I asked four mothers if they would approve of torturing kidnappers if that were necessary to get their own newborns back. All said yes, the most "liberal" adding that she would like to administer it herself.

I am not advocating torture as punishment. Punishment is addressed to deeds irrevocably past. Rather, I am advocating torture as an acceptable measure for preventing future evils. So understood, it is far less objectionable than many extant punishments. Opponents of the death penalty, for example, are forever insisting that executing a murderer will not bring back his victim (as if the purpose of capital punishment were supposed to be resurrection, not deterrence or retribution). But torture, in the cases described, is intended not to bring anyone back but to keep innocents from being dispatched. The most powerful argument against using torture as a punishment or to secure confessions is that such practices disregard the rights of the individual. Well, if the individual is all that important—and he is—it is correspondingly important to protect the rights of individuals threatened by terrorists. If life is so valuable that it must never be taken, the lives of the innocents must be saved even at the price of hurting the one who endangers them.

Better precedents for torture are assassination and pre-emptive attack. No Allied leader would have flinched at assassinating Hitler, had that been possible. (The Allies did assassinate Heydrich.)[1] Americans would be angered to learn that Roosevelt[2] could have had Hitler killed in 1943—thereby shortening the war and saving millions of lives—but refused on moral grounds. Similarly, if nation A learns that nation B is about to launch an unprovoked attack, A has a right to save itself by destroying B's military capability first. In the same way, if the police can by torture save those who would otherwise die at the hands of kidnappers or terrorists, they must.

Idealism: There is an important difference between terrorists and their victims that should mute talk of the terrorists' "rights." The terrorist's victims are at risk unintentionally, not having asked to be endangered. But the terrorist knowingly initiated his actions. Unlike his victims, he volunteered for the risks of his deed. By threatening to kill for profit or idealism, he renounces civilized standards, and he can have no complaint if civilization tries to thwart him by whatever means necessary.

---

[1]Reinhard Heydrich (1904–42), German head of the Nazi SS and Gestapo who was assassinated by Czech resistance fighters aided by the British government.

[2]Franklin Delano Roosevelt (1882–1945), thirty-second president of the United States.

Just as torture is justified only to save lives (not extort confessions or 10
recantations), it is justifiably administered only to those *known* to hold
innocent lives in their hands. Ah, but how can the authorities ever be
sure they have the right malefactor? Isn't there a danger of error and
abuse? Won't We turn into Them?

Questions like these are disingenuous in a world in which terrorists
proclaim themselves and perform for television. The name of their
game is public recognition. After all, you can't very well intimidate a
government into releasing your freedom fighters unless you announce
that it is your group that has seized its embassy. "Clear guilt" is difficult to define, but when 40 million people see a group of masked gun-
men seize an airplane on the evening news, there is not much question
about who the perpetrators are. There will be hard cases where the situation is murkier. Nonetheless, a line demarcating the legitimate use of
torture can be drawn. Torture only the obviously guilty, and only for
the sake of saving innocents, and the line between Us and Them will
remain clear.

There is little danger that the Western democracies will lose their
way if they choose to inflict pain as one way of preserving order.
Paralysis in the face of evil is the greater danger. Some day soon a terrorist will threaten tens of thousands of lives, and torture will be the
only way to save them. We had better start thinking about this.

STUDY QUESTIONS

1. What is Levin's **POSITION** on torture in this essay? What objections to his **ARGUMENT** does he anticipate, and how does he **RESPOND** to them?

2. What kind of **EVIDENCE** does Levin offer for his **CLAIM** that torture is sometimes justified? How effective is it?

3. *For Writing.* This article was originally published in 1982. In the years since then the United States and many other countries have experienced acts of terrorism that have taken many innocent lives. Taking this history into account, write an essay in which you argue for or against the use of torture to prevent the loss of life. Be sure to anticipate and respond to any possible objections to your argument.

JONATHAN SWIFT { *A Modest Proposal*

JONATHAN SWIFT (1667–1745) was born in Dublin, Ireland, to
an Irish father and an English mother. He graduated from Dublin
University in 1686 and was working on his MA in 1688 when
England's Glorious Revolution saw King James II deposed and
William of Orange installed as king. Swift fled to England to escape the
ensuing political upheaval in Ireland. After taking a position as secretary
and assistant to English diplomat Sir William Temple, Swift completed
his MA in 1692 and became a priest in the Established Church of
Ireland. After some professional difficulty in securing a new position
after Temple's death, Swift earned his Doctor of Divinity in 1702 from
Trinity College, Dublin, and returned to London, where he published
his satirical play *A Tale of a Tub* (1704). During the early 1700s he
became involved with the Tory government, and when that rule fell he
returned to Ireland and began writing political pamphlets, including
A Modest Proposal (1729). He may be best known for his satirical novel
Gulliver's Travels (1726).

In *A Modest Proposal*, a classic example of satire, Swift's speaker
presents an apparently logical plan to eliminate poverty and hunger
in Ireland. Swift employs a carefully crafted argument that seems to
insist on one solution while actually arguing for a different one. Take
note of how Swift's ethos and his use of logos and pathos make his
audience receptive to his proposal, repel his readers when they find
out what that proposal entails, and finally make them think about
the underlying causes of the poverty and hunger that Swift proposes
to end.

*A Modest Proposal for Preventing the Children of Poor People
in Ireland from Being a Burden to Their Parents or Country, and for
Making Them Beneficial to the Public*

IT IS A MELANCHOLY OBJECT to those who walk through this great
town[1] or travel in the country, when they see the streets, the roads, and
cabin doors, crowded with beggars of the female-sex, followed by three,
four, or six children, all in rags and importuning every passenger for an
alms. These mothers, instead of being able to work for their honest livelihood, are forced to employ all their time in strolling to beg sustenance
for their helpless infants, who, as they grow up, either turn thieves for
want of work, or leave their dear native country to fight for the Pretender[2]
in Spain, or sell themselves to the Barbadoes.

I think it is agreed by all parties that this prodigious number of
children in the arms, or on the backs, or at the heels of their mothers,
and frequently of their fathers, is in the present deplorable state of the
kingdom a very great additional grievance; and therefore whoever
could find out a fair, cheap, and easy method of making these children
sound, useful members of the commonwealth would deserve so well of
the public as to have his statue set up for a preserver of the nation.

But my intention is very far from being confined to provide only for
the children of professed beggars; it is of a much greater extent, and
shall take in the whole number of infants at a certain age who are born
of parents in effect as little able to support them as those who demand
our charity in the streets.

As to my own part, having turned my thoughts for many years
upon this important subject, and maturely weighed the several
schemes of other projectors,[3] I have always found them grossly mistaken in their computation. It is true, a child just dropped from its
dam may be supported by her milk for a solar year, with little other
nourishment; at most not above the value of two shillings, which the

---

[1]Dublin.

[2]After King James II lost the English throne in the Glorious Revolution of 1688, his son,
James Francis Edward, known as "the Pretender," in exile on the European continent,
tried several times to retake the English throne.

[3]Schemers.

mother may certainly get, or the value in scraps, by her lawful occupation of begging; and it is exactly at one year old that I propose to provide for them in such a manner as instead of being a charge upon their parents or the parish, or wanting food and raiment for the rest of their lives, they shall on the contrary contribute to the feeding, and partly to the clothing, of many thousands.

There is likewise another great advantage in my scheme, that it will 5 prevent those voluntary abortions, and that horrid practice of women murdering their bastard children, alas, too frequent among us, sacrificing the poor innocent babes, I doubt, more to avoid the expense than the shame, which would move tears and pity in the most savage and inhuman breast.

The number of souls in this kingdom being usually reckoned one million and a half, of these I calculate there may be about two hundred thousand couple whose wives are breeders; from which number I subtract thirty thousand couples who are able to maintain their own children, although I apprehend there cannot be so many under the present distresses of the kingdom; but this being granted, there will remain an hundred and seventy thousand breeders. I again subtract fifty thousand for those women who miscarry, or whose children die by accident or disease within the year. There only remain an hundred and twenty thousand children of poor parents annually born. The question therefore is, how this number shall be reared and provided for, which, as I have already said, under the present situation of affairs, is utterly impossible by all the methods hitherto proposed. For we can neither employ them in handicraft or agriculture; we neither build houses (I mean in the country) nor cultivate land. They can very seldom pick up a livelihood by stealing till they arrive at six years old, except where they are of towardly parts;[4] although I confess they learn the rudiments much earlier, during which time they can however be looked upon only as probationers, as I have been informed by a principal gentleman in the county of Cavan, who protested to me that he never knew above one or two instances under the age of six, even in a part of the kingdom so renowned for the quickest proficiency in that art.

[4]Promising abilities.

I am assured by our merchants that a boy or a girl before twelve years old is no salable commodity; and even when they come to this age they will not yield above three pounds, or three pounds and half a crown at most on the Exchange; which cannot turn to account either to the parents or the kingdom, the charge of nutriment and rags having been at least four times that value.

I shall now therefore humbly propose my own thoughts, which I hope will not be liable to the least objection.

I have been assured by a very knowing American of my acquaintance in London, that a young healthy child well nursed is at a year old a most delicious, nourishing, and wholesome food, whether stewed, roasted, baked, or boiled; and I make no doubt that it will equally serve in a fricassee or a ragout.

I do therefore humbly offer it to public consideration that of the 10 hundred and twenty thousand children, already computed, twenty thousand may be reserved for breed, whereof only one fourth part to be males, which is more than we allow to sheep, black cattle, or swine; and my reason is that these children are seldom the fruits of marriage, a circumstance not much regarded by our savages, therefore one male will be sufficient to serve four females. That the remaining hundred thousand may at a year old be offered in sale to the persons of quality and fortune through the kingdom, always advising the mother to let them suck plentifully in the last month, so as to render them plump and fat for a good table. A child will make two dishes at an entertainment for friends; and when the family dines alone, the fore or hind quarter will make a reasonable dish, and seasoned with a little pepper or salt will be very good boiled on the fourth day, especially in winter.

I have reckoned upon a medium that a child just born will weigh twelve pounds, and in a solar year if tolerably nursed increaseth to twenty-eight pounds.

I grant this food will be somewhat dear, and therefore very proper for landlords, who, as they have already devoured most of the parents, seem to have the best title to the children.

Infant's flesh will be in season throughout the year, but more plentiful in March, and a little before and after. For we are told by a grave author, an eminent French physician,[5] that fish being a prolific diet, there are more children born in Roman Catholic countries about nine months after Lent than at any other season; therefore, reckoning a year after Lent, the markets will be more glutted than usual, because the number of popish infants is at least three to one in this kingdom; and therefore it will have one other collateral advantages, by lessening the number of Papists among us.

I have already computed the charge of nursing a beggar's child (in which list I reckon all cottagers, laborers, and four fifths of the farmers) to be about two shillings per annum, rags included; and I believe no gentleman would repine to give ten shillings for the carcass of a good fat child, which, as I have said, will make four dishes of excellent nutritive meat, when he hath only some particular friend or his own family to dine with him. Thus the squire will learn to be a good landlord, and grow popular among the tenants; the mother will have eight shillings net profit, and be fit for work till she produces another child.

Those who are more thrifty (as I must confess the times require) may flay the carcass; the skin of which artificially[6] dressed will make admirable gloves for ladies, and summer boots for fine gentlemen. 15

As to our city of Dublin, shambles[7] may be appointed for this purpose in the most convenient parts of it, and butchers we may be assured will not be wanting; although I rather recommend buying the children alive, and dressing them hot from the knife as we do roasting pigs.

A very worthy person, a true lover of his country, and whose virtues I highly esteem, was lately pleased in discoursing on this matter to offer a refinement upon my scheme. He said that many gentlemen of this kingdom, having of late destroyed their deer, he conceived that the want of venison might be well supplied by the bodies of young lads and maidens, not exceeding fourteen years of age nor under twelve, so great a number of both sexes in every county being now ready to starve for want of work and service; and these to be disposed of by their parents, if alive, or otherwise by their nearest relations. But with

[5]François Rabelais (1483–1553).
[6]Skillfully.
[7]Slaughterhouses.

due deference to so excellent a friend and so deserving a patriot, I cannot be altogether in his sentiments; for as to the males, my American acquaintance assured me from frequent experience that their flesh was generally tough and lean, like that of our schoolboys, by continual exercise, and their taste disagreeable; and to fatten them would not answer the charge. Then as to the females, it would, I think with humble submission, be a loss to the public, because they soon would become breeders themselves: and besides, it is not improbable that some scrupulous people might be apt to censure such a practice (although indeed very unjustly) as a little bordering upon cruelty; which, I confess, hath always been with me the strongest objection against any project, how well soever intended.

But in order to justify my friend, he confessed that this expedient was put into his head by the famous Psalmanazar, a native of the island Formosa,[8] who came from thence to London above twenty years ago, and in conversation told my friend that in his country when any young person happened to be put to death, the executioner sold the carcass to persons of quality as a prime dainty; and that in his time the body of a plump girl of fifteen, who was crucified for an attempt to poison the emperor, was sold to his Imperial Majesty's prime minister of state, and other great mandarins of the court, in joints from the gibbet, at four hundred crowns. Neither indeed can I deny that if the same use were made of several plump young girls in this town, who without one single groat to their fortunes cannot stir abroad without a chair,[9] and appear at the playhouse and assemblies in foreign fineries which they never will pay for, the kingdom would not be the worse.

Some persons of a desponding spirit are in great concern about that vast number of poor people who are aged, diseased, or maimed, and I have been desired to employ my thoughts what course may be taken to ease the nation of so grievous an encumbrance. But I am not in the least pain upon that matter, because it is very well known that they are every day dying and rotting by cold and famine, and filth and vermin,

[8]George Psalmanazar, a Frenchman, masqueraded as a traveler from Formosa (Taiwan) and wrote a fictitious account of that country, including accounts of cannibalism.
[9]A sedan chair.

as fast as can be reasonably expected. And as to the younger laborers, they are now in almost as hopeful a condition. They cannot get work, and consequently pine away for want of nourishment to a degree that if at any time they are accidentally hired to common labor, they have not strength to perform it; and thus the country and themselves are happily delivered from the evils to come.

I have too long digressed, and therefore shall return to my subject. 20 I think the advantages by the proposal which I have made are obvious and many, as well as of the highest importance.

For first, as I have already observed, it would greatly lessen the number of Papists, with whom we are yearly overrun, being the principal breeders of the nation as well as our most dangerous enemies; and who stay at home on purpose to deliver the kingdom to the Pretender, hoping to take their advantage by the absence of so many good Protestants, who have chosen rather to leave their country than to stay at home and pay tithes against their conscience to an Episcopal curate.

Secondly, the poorer tenants will have something valuable of their own, which by law may be made liable to distress,[1] and help to pay their landlord's rent, their corn and cattle being already seized and money a thing unknown.

Thirdly, whereas the maintenance of an hundred thousand children, from two years old and upwards, cannot be computed at less than ten shillings a piece per annum, the nation's stock will be thereby increased fifty thousand pounds per annum, besides the profit of a new dish introduced to the tables of all gentlemen of fortune in the kingdom who have any refinement in taste. And the money will circulate among ourselves, the goods being entirely of our own growth and manufacture.

Fourthly, the constant breeders, besides the gain of eight shillings sterling per annum by the sale of their children, will be rid of the charge of maintaining them after the first year.

Fifthly, this food would likewise bring great custom to taverns, 25 where the vintners will certainly be so prudent as to procure the best receipts[2] for dressing it to perfection, and consequently have their houses

[1]Seizure for the payment of debts.
[2]Recipes. *Custom*: commerce.

frequented by all the fine gentlemen, who justly value themselves upon their knowledge in good eating; and a skillful cook, who understands how to oblige his guests, will contrive to make it as expensive as they please.

Sixthly, this would be a great inducement to marriage, which all wise nations have either encouraged by rewards or enforced by laws and penalties. It would increase the care and tenderness of mothers toward their children, when they were sure of a settlement for life to the poor babes, provided in some sort by the public, to their annual profit instead of expense. We should see an honest emulation among the married women, which of them could bring the fattest child to the market. Men would become as fond of their wives during the time of their pregnancy as they are now of their mares in foal, their cows in calf, or sows when they are ready to farrow; nor offer to beat or kick them (as is too frequent a practice) for fear of a miscarriage.

Many other advantages might be enumerated. For instance, the addition of some thousand carcasses in our exportation of barreled beef, the propagation of swine's flesh, and improvement in the art of making good bacon, so much wanted among us by the great destruction of pigs, too frequent at our tables, which are no way comparable in taste or magnificence to a well-grown, fat, yearling child, which roasted whole will make a considerable figure at a lord mayor's feast or any other public entertainment. But this and many others I omit, being studious of brevity.

Supposing that one thousand families in this city would be constant customers for infants' flesh, besides others who might have it at merry meetings, particularly weddings and christenings, I compute that Dublin would take off annually about twenty thousand carcasses, and the rest of the kingdom (where probably they will be sold somewhat cheaper) the remaining eighty thousand.

I can think of no one objection that will possibly be raised against this proposal, unless it should be urged that the number of people will be thereby much lessened in the kingdom. This I freely own, and it was indeed one principal design in offering it to the world. I desire the reader will observe, that I calculate my remedy for this one individual kingdom of Ireland and for no other that ever was, is, or I think ever can be upon earth. Therefore let no man talk to me of other expedients: of taxing our absentees at five shillings a pound: of using neither clothes nor household furniture except what is of our own growth and manufacture: of utterly rejecting the materials and instruments that promote foreign luxury: of curing the expensiveness of pride, vanity, idleness, and gaming in our women: of introducing a vein of parsimony, prudence, and temperance: of learning to love our country, in the want of which we differ even from Laplanders and the inhabitants of Topinamboo:[3] of quitting our animosities and factions, nor acting any longer like the Jews, who were murdering one another at the very moment their city was taken: of being a little cautious not to sell our country and conscience for nothing: of teaching landlords to have at least one degree of mercy toward their tenants: lastly, of putting a spirit of honesty, industry, and skill into our shopkeepers; who, if a resolution could now be taken to buy only our native goods, would immediately unite to cheat and exact upon us in the price, the measure, and the goodness, nor could ever yet be brought to make one fair proposal of just dealing, though often and earnestly invited to it.

Therefore I repeat, let no man talk to me of these and the like expe-   30
dients, till he hath at least some glimpse of hope that there will ever be some hearty and sincere attempt to put them in practice.

But as to myself, having been wearied out for many years with offering vain, idle, visionary thoughts, and at length utterly despairing of success, I fortunately fell upon this proposal, which, as it is wholly new, so it hath something solid and real, of no expense and little trouble, full in our own power, and whereby we can incur no danger in disobliging England. For this kind of commodity will not bear exportation, the flesh being of too tender a consistence to admit a long continuance in salt, although perhaps I could name a country which would be glad to eat up our whole nation without it.

After all, I am not so violently bent upon my own opinion as to reject any offer proposed by wise men, which shall be found equally innocent, cheap, easy, and effectual. But before something of that kind

[3]That is, the people of the extremely cold regions of northern Europe and the people of the jungles of Brazil

shall be advanced in contradiction to my scheme, and offering a better, I desire the author or authors will be pleased maturely to consider two points. First, as things now stand, how they will be able to find food and raiment for an hundred thousand useless mouths and backs. And secondly, there being a round million of creatures in human figure throughout this kingdom, whose sole subsistence put into a common stock would leave them in debt two millions of pounds sterling, adding those who are beggars by profession to the bulk of farmers, cottagers, and laborers, with their wives and children who are beggars in effect; I desire those politicians who dislike my overture, and may perhaps be so bold to attempt an answer, that they will first ask the parents of these mortals whether they would not at this day think it a great happiness to have been sold for food at a year old in the manner I prescribe, and thereby have avoided such a perpetual scene of misfortunes as they have since gone through by the oppression of landlords, the impossibility of paying rent without money or trade, the want of common sustenance, with neither house nor clothes to cover them from the inclemencies of the weather, and the most inevitable prospect of entailing the like or greater miseries upon their breed forever.

I profess, in the sincerity of my heart, that I have not the least personal interest in endeavoring to promote this necessary work, having no other motive than the public good of my country, by advancing our trade, providing for infants, relieving the poor, and giving some pleasure to the rich. I have no children by which I can propose to get a single penny; the youngest being nine years old, and my wife past childbearing.

STUDY QUESTIONS

1. What does Swift's SPEAKER propose that the people of Ireland do with their children? Why is he making this PROPOSAL?

2. Consider Swift's persona in this essay. How does the speaker establish his ETHOS? Is it credible? Compassionate? Reasonable? Explain.

3. At what point in this proposal do you begin to suspect that Swift is engaging in SATIRE? How does he employ PATHOS and LOGOS within his satire? Where and for what purpose does he break from his satirical stance?

4. *For Writing.* Write a satirical "modest proposal" of your own, dealing with a social or political issue that you are familiar with, such as music downloading or health care reform. Make sure that your proposal, like Swift's, is impossible to take seriously but highlights a real problem. Create a speaker and address your proposal toward a specific AUDIENCE.

ELIE WIESEL { *The Perils of Indifference:*
Lessons Learned from
a Violent Century

ELIE WIESEL (b. 1928) was born in Sighet, Transylvania, now part of
Romania. Along with other Jewish inhabitants of Sighet, Wiesel's family
was moved to a ghetto in 1944, before being relocated once more to
Auschwitz-Birkenau, the concentration camp. Wiesel and his father were
sent to Buchenwald, where Wiesel's father was badly beaten and ultimately
killed in the crematorium. After the camp was liberated on April 11,
1945, Wiesel worked various jobs: he taught Hebrew, was a choirmaster,
and became a journalist. In 1960, he published *Night,* his first memoir
about the Holocaust, which quickly became a best seller. Wiesel moved to
New York City in 1955 and continued to write, publishing some forty
books of fiction and nonfiction. Regarded as one of the most important
writers about the Holocaust, he received the Nobel Peace Prize in 1986.
Wiesel continues to speak out against injustice, indifference, and intoler-
ance, and his Foundation for Humanity works to combat them. He also
has taught at various universities, including the City University of New
York and Yale University; he is currently Andrew Mellon Professor of
the Humanities at Boston University.

These remarks constitute a speech Wiesel gave in 1999 at one of the
White House's Millennium Evenings, a series of events conceived by
then-president Bill Clinton and -first lady Hillary Clinton, the latter of
whom introduced the author and activist. The events were meant to
celebrate creativity and inventiveness. Here Wiesel takes on the word
"indifference," defining it in order to show its destructive implications.
How does he use personal experience to make his points particularly valid?

From "Remarks at the Millennium Evening Lecture: The Perils of Indifference: Lessons
Learned from a Violent Century," Speech made an April 12, 1999 at the White House by
Elie Wiesel. Used by the kind permission of Mr. Elie Wiesel.

MR. PRESIDENT, MRS. CLINTON, MEMBERS of Congress, Ambassador Holbrooke, Excellencies, friends: Fifty-four years ago to the day, a young Jewish boy from a small town in the Carpathian Mountains woke up, not far from Goethe's beloved Weimar,[1] in a place of eternal infamy called Buchenwald. He was finally free, but there was no joy in his heart. He thought there never would be again.

Liberated a day earlier by American soldiers, he remembers their rage at what they saw. And even if he lives to be a very old man, he will always be grateful to them for that rage, and also for their compassion. Though he did not understand their language, their eyes told him what he needed to know—that they, too, would remember, and bear witness.

And now, I stand before you, Mr. President—Commander-in-Chief of the army that freed me, and tens of thousands of others—and I am filled with a profound and abiding gratitude to the American people.

Gratitude is a word that I cherish. Gratitude is what defines the humanity of the human being. And I am grateful to you, Hillary—or Mrs. Clinton—for what you said, and for what you are doing for children in the world, for the homeless, for the victims of injustice, the victims of destiny and society. And I thank all of you for being here.

We are on the threshold of a new century, a new millennium. What   5 will the legacy of this vanishing century be? How will it be remembered in the new millennium? Surely it will be judged, and judged severely, in both moral and metaphysical terms. These failures have cast a dark shadow over humanity: two World Wars, countless civil wars, the senseless chain of assassinations—Gandhi, the Kennedys, Martin Luther King, Sadat, Rabin—bloodbaths in Cambodia and Nigeria, India and Pakistan, Ireland and Rwanda, Eritrea and Ethiopia, Sarajevo and Kosovo; the inhumanity in the gulag and the tragedy of Hiroshima. And, on a different level, of course, Auschwitz and Treblinka. So much violence, so much indifference.

What is indifference? Etymologically, the word means "no difference." A strange and unnatural state in which the lines blur between

---

[1]Johann Wolfgang von Goethe (1749–1832), German poet and dramatist, lived in Weimar, Germany, for much of his life.

light and darkness, dusk and dawn, crime and punishment, cruelty and compassion, good and evil.

What are its courses and inescapable consequences? Is it a philosophy? Is there a philosophy of indifference conceivable? Can one possibly view indifference as a virtue? Is it necessary at times to practice it simply to keep one's sanity, live normally, enjoy a fine meal and a glass of wine, as the world around us experiences harrowing upheavals?

Of course, indifference can be tempting—more than that, seductive. It is so much easier to look away from victims. It is so much easier to avoid such rude interruptions to our work, our dreams, our hopes. It is, after all, awkward, troublesome, to be involved in another person's pain and despair. Yet, for the person who is indifferent, his or her neighbor[s] are of no consequence. And, therefore, their lives are meaningless. Their hidden or even visible anguish is of no interest. Indifference reduces the other to an abstraction.

Over there, behind the black gates of Auschwitz, the most tragic of all prisoners were the "Muselmanner," as they were called. Wrapped in their torn blankets, they would sit or lie on the ground, staring vacantly into space, unaware of who or where they were, strangers to their surroundings. They no longer felt pain, hunger, thirst. They feared nothing. They felt nothing. They were dead and did not know it.

Rooted in our tradition, some of us felt that to be abandoned by humanity then was not the ultimate. We felt that to be abandoned by God was worse than to be punished by Him. Better an unjust God than an indifferent one. For us to be ignored by God was a harsher punishment than to be a victim of His anger. Man can live far from God—not outside God. God is wherever we are. Even in suffering? Even in suffering.

In a way, to be indifferent to that suffering is what makes the human being inhuman. Indifference, after all, is more dangerous than anger and hatred. Anger can at times be creative. One writes a great poem, a great symphony; one does something special for the sake of humanity because one is angry at the injustice that one witnesses. But indifference is never creative. Even hatred at times may elicit a response.

You fight it. You denounce it. You disarm it. Indifference elicits no response. Indifference is not a response.

Indifference is not a beginning, it is an end. And, therefore, indifference is always the friend of the enemy, for it benefits the aggressor—never his victim, whose pain is magnified when he or she feels forgotten. The political prisoner in his cell, the hungry children, the homeless refugees—not to respond to their plight, not to relieve their solitude by offering them a spark of hope is to exile them from human memory. And in denying their humanity we betray our own.

Indifference, then, is not only a sin, it is a punishment. And this is one of the most important lessons of this outgoing century's wide-ranging experiments in good and evil.

In the place that I come from, society was composed of three simple categories: the killers, the victims, and the bystanders. During the darkest of times, inside the ghettoes and death camps—and I'm glad that Mrs. Clinton mentioned that we are now commemorating that event, that period, that we are now in the Days of Remembrance—but then, we felt abandoned, forgotten. All of us did.

And our only miserable consolation was that we believed that Auschwitz and Treblinka were closely guarded secrets; that the leaders of the free world did not know what was going on behind those black gates and barbed wire; that they had no knowledge of the war against the Jews that Hitler's armies and their accomplices waged as part of the war against the Allies.

If they knew, we thought, surely those leaders would have moved heaven and earth to intervene. They would have spoken out with great outrage and conviction. They would have bombed the railways leading to Birkenau, just the railways, just once.

And now we knew, we learned, we discovered that the Pentagon knew, the State Department knew. And the illustrious occupant of the White House then, who was a great leader—and I say it with some anguish and pain, because, today is exactly 54 years marking his death—Franklin Delano Roosevelt died on April the 12th, 1945, so he is very much present to me and to us.

No doubt, he was a great leader. He mobilized the American people and the world, going into battle, bringing hundreds and thousands of

15

valiant and brave soldiers in America to fight fascism, to fight dictatorship, to fight Hitler. And so many of the young people fell in battle.
And, nevertheless, his image in Jewish history—I must say it—his
image in Jewish history is flawed.

The depressing tale of the *St. Louis* is a case in point. Sixty years
ago, its human cargo—maybe 1,000 Jews—was turned back to Nazi
Germany. And that happened after the Kristallnacht,[2] after the first
state-sponsored pogrom, with hundreds of Jewish shops destroyed,
synagogues burned, thousands of people put in concentration
camps. And that ship, which was already on the shores of the United
States, was sent back.

I don't understand. Roosevelt was a good man, with a heart. He   20
understood those who needed help. Why didn't he allow these refugees
to disembark? A thousand people—in America, a great country, the
greatest democracy, the most generous of all new nations in modern
history. What happened? I don't understand. Why the indifference, on
the highest level, to the suffering of the victims?

But then, there were human beings who were sensitive to our tragedy. Those non-Jews, those Christians, that we called the "Righteous
Gentiles," whose selfless acts of heroism saved the honor of their
faith. Why were they so few? Why was there a greater effort to save SS
murderers after the war than to save their victims during the war?

Why did some of America's largest corporations continue to do
business with Hitler's Germany until 1942? It has been suggested,
and it was documented, that the Wehrmacht[3] could not have conducted its invasion of France without oil obtained from American
sources. How is one to explain their indifference?

And yet, my friends, good things have also happened in this traumatic century: the defeat of Nazism, the collapse of communism, the
rebirth of Israel on its ancestral soil, the demise of apartheid, Israel's
peace treaty with Egypt, the peace accord in Ireland. And let us
remember the meeting, filled with drama and emotion, between

---

[2]Night of broken glass (German), a 1938 Nazi offensive against the Jewish people in Germany and Austria.

[3]The German armed forces.

Rabin[4] and Arafat that you, Mr. President, convened in this very place. I was here and I will never forget it.

And then, of course, the joint decision of the United States and NATO to intervene in Kosovo and save those victims, those refugees, those who were uprooted by a man whom I believe that because of his crimes, should be charged with crimes against humanity.[5] But this time, the world was not silent. This time, we do respond. This time, we intervene.

Does it mean that we have learned from the past? Does it mean that society has changed? Has the human being become less indifferent and more human? Have we really learned from our experiences? Are we less insensitive to the plight of victims of ethnic cleansing and other forms of injustices in places near and far? Is today's justified intervention in Kosovo, led by you, Mr. President, a lasting warning that never again will the deportation, the terrorization of children and their parents be allowed anywhere in the world? Will it discourage other dictators in other lands to do the same? 25

What about the children? Oh, we see them on television, we read about them in the papers, and we do so with a broken heart. Their fate is always the most tragic, inevitably. When adults wage war, children perish. We see their faces, their eyes. Do we hear their pleas? Do we feel their pain, their agony? Every minute one of them dies of disease, violence, famine. Some of them—so many of them—could be saved.

And so, once again, I think of the young Jewish boy from the Carpathian Mountains. He has accompanied the old man I have become throughout these years of quest and struggle. And together we walk towards the new millennium, carried by profound fear and extraordinary hope.

---

[4]Yitzhak Rabin (1922–95), prime minister of Israel, whose first face-to-face meeting with the chairman of the Palestine Liberation Organization, Yasser Arafat (1929–2004), resulted in the Oslo Accords, an agreement that sought to normalize relations between Palestine and Israel.

[5]NATO was in the midst of a bombing campaign against the Federal Republic of Yugoslavia, in the province of Kosovo. The "man" Wiesel refers to is Slobodon Milošević (1941–2006), president of Serbia and then of Yugoslavia, indicted at The Hague for crimes against humanity a month after this speech was given.

STUDY QUESTIONS

1. How does Wiesel DESCRIBE himself as a boy?

2. What are the different ways that Wiesel DEFINES the concept of "indifference"? What is the effect of these various definitions? How does Wiesel use the definitions to develop his speech?

3. How can you tell from reading this selection that it was presented as a speech? What is Wiesel's TONE throughout? Audio versions of the speech are widely available, so try to listen to it online if possible.

4. *For Writing.* Test the lessons that Wiesel says have been learned from the times that "indifference" was expressed during the Holocaust. Choose a modern-day disaster, such as Hurricane Katrina or the oil spill in the Gulf Coast. RESEARCH the responses to it, and in an essay, analyze whether any of the lessons discussed here were applied. Be sure to use concrete examples and to discuss the significance of your findings.

DIANE ACKERMAN { *Why the Leaves Turn Color in the Fall*

DIANE ACKERMAN (b. 1948) is a writer who earned her MA, MFA, and PhD at Cornell University. Ackerman has written more than twenty books—nonfiction and poetry for adults as well as nature books for children—that have received numerous awards. Ackerman has also published essays about nature and human nature in the *New York Times*, *Smithsonian*, *Parade*, *The New Yorker*, and *National Geographic*, among other publications. *A Natural History of the Senses*, her acclaimed 1990 volume of essays, inspired the series *Mystery of the Senses* on PBS television, which Ackerman hosted.

This selection from *A Natural History of the Senses* explains the natural processes that cause leaves to change color in the fall. Much of Ackerman's work, including this essay, demonstrates her ability to convey scientific information in a way that is both engaging and relevant for non-scientists. Notice the ideas from different fields of study that Ackerman draws together here as she explains the seasonal cycle of leaves.

THE STEALTH OF AUTUMN CATCHES one unaware. Was that a goldfinch perching in the early September woods, or just the first turning leaf? A red-winged blackbird or a sugar maple closing up shop for the winter? Keen-eyed as leopards, we stand still and squint hard, looking for signs of movement. Early-morning frost sits heavily on the grass, and turns barbed wire into a string of stars. On a distant hill, a small square of yellow appears to be a lighted stage. At last the truth dawns on us: Fall is staggering in, right on schedule, with its baggage of chilly nights, macabre holidays, and spectacular, heart-stoppingly beautiful leaves. Soon the leaves will start cringing on the trees, and roll up in clenched fists before they actually fall off. Dry seedpods will rattle like tiny gourds. But first there will be weeks of gushing color so bright, so pastel, so confettilike, that people will travel up and down the East Coast just to stare at it—a whole season of leaves.

Where do the colors come from? Sunlight rules most living things with its golden edicts. When the days begin to shorten, soon after the summer solstice on June 21, a tree reconsiders its leaves. All summer it feeds them so they can process sunlight, but in the dog days of summer the tree begins pulling nutrients back into its trunk and roots, pares down, and gradually chokes off its leaves. A corky layer of cells forms at the leaves' slender petioles, then scars over. Undernourished, the leaves stop producing the pigment chlorophyll, and photosynthesis ceases. Animals can migrate, hibernate, or store food to prepare for winter. But where can a tree go? It survives by dropping its leaves, and by the end of autumn only a few fragile threads of fluid-carrying xylem hold leaves to their stems.

A turning leaf stays partly green at first, then reveals splotches of yellow and red as the chlorophyll gradually breaks down. Dark green seems to stay longest in the veins, outlining and defining them. During the summer, chlorophyll dissolves in the heat and light, but it is also being steadily replaced. In the fall, on the other hand, no new pigment is produced, and so we notice the other colors that were always there, right in the leaf, although chlorophyll's shocking green hid them from view. With their camouflage gone, we see these colors for the first time all year, and marvel, but they were always there, hidden like a vivid secret beneath the hot glowing greens of summer.

The most spectacular range of fall foliage occurs in the northeastern United States and in eastern China, where the leaves are robustly colored, thanks in part to a rich climate. European maples don't achieve the same flaming reds as their American relatives, which thrive on cold nights and sunny days. In Europe, the warm, humid weather turns the leaves brown or mildly yellow. Anthocyanin, the pigment that gives apples their red and turns leaves red or red-violet, is produced by sugars that remain in the leaf after the supply of nutrients dwindles. Unlike the carotenoids, which color carrots, squash, and corn, and turn leaves orange and yellow, anthocyanin varies from year to year, depending on the temperature and amount of sunlight. The fiercest colors occur in years when the fall sunlight is strongest and the nights are cool and dry (a state of grace scientists find vexing to forecast). This is also why leaves appear dizzyingly bright and clear on a sunny fall day: The anthocyanin flashes like a marquee.

Not all leaves turn the same colors. Elms, weeping willows, and the ancient ginkgo all grow radiant yellow, along with hickories, aspens, bottlebrush buckeyes, cottonwoods, and tall, keening poplars. Basswood turns bronze, birches bright gold. Water-loving maples put on a symphonic display of scarlets. Sumacs turn red, too, as do flowering dogwoods, black gums, and sweet gums. Though some oaks yellow, most turn a pinkish brown. The farmlands also change color, as tepees of cornstalks and bales of shredded-wheat-textured hay stand drying in the fields. In some spots, one slope of a hill may be green and the other already in bright color, because the hillside facing south gets more sun and heat than the northern one. 5

An odd feature of the colors is that they don't seem to have any special purpose. We are predisposed to respond to their beauty, of course. They shimmer with the colors of sunset, spring flowers, the tawny buff of a colt's pretty rump, the shuddering pink of a blush. Animals and flowers color for a reason—adaptation to their environment—but there is no adaptive reason for leaves to color so beautifully in the fall any more than there is for the sky or ocean to be blue. It's just one of the haphazard marvels the planet bestows every year. We find the sizzling colors thrilling, and in a sense they dupe us. Colored like living things, they signal death and disintegration. In time, they will become fragile and, like the body, return to dust. They are as we hope our own fate will be when we die: Not to vanish, just to sublime from one beautiful state into another. Though leaves lose their green life, they bloom with urgent colors, as the woods grow mummified day by day, and Nature becomes more carnal, mute, and radiant.

We call the season "fall," from the Old English *feallan,* to fall, which leads back through time to the Indo-European *phol,* which also means to fall. So the word and the idea are both extremely ancient, and haven't really changed since the first of our kind needed a name for fall's leafy abundance. As we say the word, we're reminded of that other Fall, in the garden of Eden, when fig leaves never withered and scales fell from our eyes. Fall is the time when leaves fall from the trees, just as spring is when flowers spring up, summer is when we simmer, and winter is when we whine from the cold.

Children love to play in piles of leaves, hurling them into the air like confetti, leaping into soft unruly mattresses of them. For children, leaf fall is just one of the odder figments of Nature, like hailstones or snowflakes. Walk down a lane overhung with trees in the never-never land of autumn, and you will forget about time and death, lost in the sheer delicious spill of color. Adam and Eve concealed their nakedness with leaves, remember? Leaves have always hidden our awkward secrets.

But how do the colored leaves fall? As a leaf ages, the growth hormone, auxin, fades, and cells at the base of the petiole divide. Two or three rows of small cells, lying at right angles to the axis of the petiole, react with water, then come apart, leaving the petioles hanging on by only a few threads of xylem. A light breeze, and the leaves are airborne. They glide and swoop, rocking in invisible cradles. They are all wing and may flutter from yard to yard on small whirlwinds or updrafts, swiveling as they go. Firmly tethered to earth, we love to see things rise up and fly—soap bubbles, balloons, birds, fall leaves. They remind us that the end of a season is capricious, as is the end of life. We especially like the way leaves rock, careen, and swoop as they fall. Everyone knows the motion. Pilots sometimes do a maneuver called a "falling leaf," in which the plane loses altitude quickly and on purpose, by slipping first to the right, then to the left. The machine weighs a ton or more, but in one pilot's mind it is a weightless thing, a falling leaf. She has seen the motion before, in the Vermont woods where she played as a child. Below her the trees radiate gold, copper, and red. Leaves are falling, although she can't see them fall, as she falls, swooping down for a closer view.

At last the leaves leave. But first they turn color and thrill us for weeks on end. Then they crunch and crackle underfoot. They *shush,* as children drag their small feet through leaves heaped along the curb. 10

Dark, slimy mats of leaves cling to one's heels after a rain. A damp, stuccolike mortar of semidecayed leaves protects the tender shoots with a roof until spring, and makes a rich humus. An occasional bulge or ripple in the leafy mounds signals a shrew or a field mouse tunneling out of sight. Sometimes one finds in fossil stones the imprint of a leaf, long since disintegrated, whose outlines remind us how detailed, vibrant, and alive are the things of this earth that perish.

STUDY QUESTIONS

1. Is the seasonal change of leaves equally dramatic in all areas of the world? Why or why not?

2. Ackerman uses many literary techniques in this selection. Select one of those techniques (e.g., IMAGERY, descriptive language, third-person plural POINT OF VIEW), give an example of it, and explain how it influences your reading of the piece.

3. *For Writing.* In paragraph 6, Ackerman notes that "there is no adaptive reason for leaves to color so beautifully in the fall," and she calls this change "one of the haphazard marvels the planet bestows every year." What is a natural "marvel" in your hometown or college area? What makes you identify it as a "marvel"? In an essay, describe this "marvel" using concrete language and explain what makes it worth noting or studying.

HUSSEIN AGHA AND ROBERT MALLEY

{ *The Arab Counterrevolution*

HUSSEIN AGHA (b. 1949) is senior associate member of St. Antony's College, Oxford. He often writes with Robert Malley (b. 1963), an expert on conflict resolution who worked as President Bill Clinton's special assistant for Arab-Israeli affairs (1998–2001) and who is currently program director for the Middle East and North Africa at the International Crisis Group in Washington, DC. Malley was educated at Yale University and Oxford University, where, as a Rhodes Scholar in 1984, he completed a PhD in political philosophy.

In this article, from the *New York Review of Books,* Agha and Malley argue that the eventual outcomes of the Arab revolutions of 2011 lie—as with all revolutions—in the struggles within the movement. Although commentators likened the so-called "Arab Spring" to European revolutions of the mid-nineteenth century and to the fall of the Soviet Union, the authors place current events in the historical context of previous Arab uprisings, showing how the mistakes of the mid-twentieth century led to the uprisings of the twenty-first. How, then, will the current revolution's weaknesses affect the future of the Arab world?

THE ARAB UPRISING THAT STARTED in Tunisia and Egypt reached its climax on February 11, the day President Hosni Mubarak was forced to step down. It was peaceful, homegrown, spontaneous, and seemingly unified. Lenin's theory was turned on its head. The Russian leader postulated that a victorious revolution required a structured and disciplined political party, robust leadership, and a clear program.

Dominic Nahr/Magnum Photos

Protesters celebrating Hosni Mubarak's resignation in Tahrir Square, Cairo, February 11, 2011.

The Egyptian rebellion, like its Tunisian precursor and unlike the Iranian Revolution of 1979, possessed neither organization nor identifiable leaders nor an unambiguous agenda.

Since Mubarak's ouster, everything that has happened in the region has offered a striking contrast with what came before. Protests turned violent in Yemen, Bahrain, Libya, and Syria. Foreign nations got involved in each of these conflicts. Ethnic, tribal, and sectarian divisions have come to the fore. Old parties and organizations as well as political and economic elites contend for power, leaving many protesters with the feeling that the history they were making not long ago is now passing them by.

Amid rising insecurity and uncertainty there is fear and a sense of foreboding. In many places there are blood, threats, and doubts. People once thrilled by the potential benefits of change are dumbfounded by its actual and obvious costs. As anxiety about the future grows, earlier episodes cease to be viewed as pristine or untouchable. Accounts of the uprisings as transparent, innocent affairs are challenged. In Egypt and Tunisia, plots and conspiracies are imagined and invented;

the military and other remnants of the old regime, which continue to hold much power, are suspected of having engineered preemptive coups. In Bahrain, protesters are accused of being Iranian agents; in Syria, they are portrayed as foreign-backed Islamist radicals. Little evidence is offered. It doesn't seem to matter.

February 11 was the culmination of the Arab revolution. On February 12, the counterrevolution began.

1

The Arab upheaval of 2011 is often heralded as an unparalleled occurrence in the region's history. Ghosts of the European revolutions of 1848 and the popular protests that brought down the Soviet bloc in 1989 are summoned. There is no need to look so far back or so far away. The current Arab awakening displays unique features but in the feelings first unleashed and the political and emotional arc subsequently followed, it resembles events that swept the Arab world in the 1950s and 1960s.

In the days well before social media and 24/7 television, Gamal Abdel Nasser, a young Egyptian army officer, captivated the imagination of millions of Arabs, prompting displays of popular exhilaration that would withstand comparison with anything witnessed today. The Baath Party took power in Syria and Iraq, promising the restoration of dignity and championing freedom and modernity; a triumphant national liberation movement marched to victory in Algeria; a socialist republic was established in South Yemen; and the odd blend that was Muammar Qaddafi came to power in Libya.

At the time, many people were moved by the illegitimacy and inefficacy of state institutions; rampant corruption and inequitable distribution of wealth; the concentration of power in the hands of parasitic elites; revulsion with subservience to former and current colonial masters; and humiliation, epitomized above all by the Palestinian catastrophe and the inability to redress it. Slogans from that era celebrated independence, Arab unity, freedom, dignity, and socialism.

Although the military was the vanguard then, the rebellions of 2011 arose from similar emotions and were inspired by similar aspirations.

The misfortunes of Arab unity have rendered the concept suspect. Socialism too has been tainted. But substitute local and domestic unity within each country (*Wihda Wataniyan*) for Pan-Arab unity (*Wihda Arabiyah*) and social justice, as well as attacks against crony capitalism for socialism, and it is hard not to hear clear echoes of the past in today's calls for change.

The fate of that earlier Arab rejuvenation offers a useful precedent but, more than that, a cautionary tale. Amid the turmoil and excitement, numerous political currents competed. Several espoused a blend of secular nationalism and pan-Arabism, others variants of Marxism, still others more Western-oriented liberalism. In the end, leftists and Communists were suppressed, most violently in Iraq and Sudan; elsewhere, they were co-opted or defeated. Liberal activists never established an authentic foothold; suspected of links to foreign powers, they were marginalized. After briefly flirting with Islamists, regimes quickly came to view them as a threat and, with varying degrees of bloodletting, drove them underground in Egypt, North Africa, and the Levant.

What emerged were ruling coalitions of the army and various secular nationalist movements. These yielded authoritarian, militaristic republics whose professed ideologies of modernism, pan-Arabism, and socialism were more make-believe than real. They exercised power through extensive internal security organizations—the much-dreaded *Mukhabarat;* the suppression of dissent; and enlistment of diverse social groups in support of the regime—merchants, peasants, industrialists, and state bureaucrats. Politics was the exclusive province of rulers. For others, it became a criminal activity.

The experiment ended in unmitigated failure. Wealth was concentrated in the hands of the few; corruption was endemic. Segments of society that had most enthusiastically greeted their new leaders, from the rural underclass to the urban declassed, were discarded or ignored. Where Arab regimes promised most they arguably accomplished least. They had vowed to reassert genuine national independence. Yet on the regional and international scenes the voice of the Arab world eventually went silent. On crucial issues such as the fate of Palestine, Iraq, and Sudan, regimes made noise of the most grandiloquent sort, but with no discernible impact. As the new millennium set in, even the clatter that by then had become a joke began to fade.

The legacy of this era goes further than material privation, or dysfunctional governance, or internal repression. Regimes born in the heyday of Nasser and Pan-Arabism lost the asset that would have allowed much to be forgiven and without which nothing else will suffice: a sense of authenticity and national dignity. Arab states were viewed as counterfeit. Citizens were put off by how their rulers took over public goods as private possessions and made national decisions under foreign influence. When that happens, the regimes' very existence—merciless domination they impose on their people and the debasing subservience they concede to outsiders—becomes a constant, unbearable provocation.

2

The Arab uprising of 2011 was a popular rebuke to this waste. By pouring onto the streets, many thousands of people rejected what they perceived as alien and aggressive transplants. Although initial slogans alluded to reform, the actual agenda was regime change. In Tunisia and Egypt, they won round one in spectacular fashion. Elsewhere, things got messier, as regimes had time to adapt and shape their response. Violence spread, civil war threatened, foreign powers joined the melee, and centrifugal powers—sectarian, ethnic, tribal, or geographic—asserted themselves.

The Arab awakening is a tale of three battles rolled into one: people against regimes; people against people; and regimes against other regimes. The first involves the tug-of-war between regimes and spontaneous protesters. The demonstrators, most of them political only in the broadest sense of the term, are stirred by visceral, nebulous emotions—paramount among them the basic feeling of being fed up. Many don't know what they want or who they support but are confident of what they refuse—daily indignities, privations, and the stifling of basic freedoms—and who they reject, which makes them formidable adversaries. Neither of the instruments used by rulers to maintain control, repression and co-optation, can easily succeed: repression because it further solidifies the image of the state as hostile; co-optation because there are no clearly empowered leaders to win over and attempts to seduce convey a message of weakness, which further emboldens the demonstrators.

The second struggle involves a focused fight among more orga- 15 nized political groups. Some are associated with the old order; they include the military, social and economic elites, local chieftains, as well as a coterie of ersatz traditional parties. Others are the outlawed or semitolerated opposition, including exiled personalities, parties, and, most importantly, Islamists. In Libya and Syria, armed groups with various leanings and motivations have emerged. Little of the enthusiasm or innocence of the protest movements survives here; this is the province of unsentimental dealings and raw power politics.

Relations between young protesters and more traditional opposition parties can be tenuous and it is not always clear how representative either are. In Egypt, where the street battle against the regime was quickly won and Mubarak rapidly resigned, organized opposition groups—from the Muslim Brotherhood to long-established parties— subsequently stepped in and sought to muscle the disorganized protesters out. In Yemen, street demonstrators coexist uneasily with organized opposition parties and defectors from the regime. In Libya, rivalry among strands of the opposition has led to bloodshed and could portend a chaotic future. Some of the local popular committees that spontaneously emerged in Syria warily eye and distrust the exiled opposition.

The third struggle is a regional and international competition for influence. It has become an important part of the picture and assumes an increasingly prominent role. The region's strategic balance is at stake: whether Syria will remain in alliance with Iran; whether Bahrain will drift from Saudi Arabia's influence; whether Turkey will emerge bolstered or battered; whether stability in Iraq will suffer. One suspects more than faithfulness to reforms and infatuation with democratic principles when Saudi Arabia and Bahrain, which both ruthlessly suppress dissent at home, urge Syria to allow peaceful protesters; when Iran, which backs the regime in Damascus, castigates the oppression in Bahrain; and when Ankara hedges its bets between the Syrian regime and its foes.

Interlopers are legion. The sense grows that what happens anywhere will have a profound impact everywhere. NATO fought in Libya and helped oust Qaddafi. Iran and Saudi Arabia play out their rivalry in Yemen, Bahrain, and Syria; Qatar hopes to elevate its standing by propelling the Libyan and Syrian opposition to power; in Syria, Turkey sees an opportunity to side with the majority Sunnis yet simultaneously fears what Damascus and Tehran might do in return: could they rekindle Kurdish separatism or jeopardize Ankara's delicate modus vivendi in Iraq? Iran will invest more in Iraq if it feels Syria slipping away. As they become buoyed by advances in Libya and Syria, how long before Iraqi Islamists and their regional allies rekindle a struggle they fear was prematurely aborted?

The US has not been the last to get involved, but it has done so without a clear sense of purpose, wishing to side with the protesters but unsure it can live with the consequences. The least visible, curiously yet wisely, has been Israel. It knows how much its interests are in the balance but also how little it can do to protect them. Silence has been the more judicious choice.

3

Any number of outcomes could emerge from this complex brew. 20 Regional equilibriums could be profoundly unsettled, with Iran losing its Syrian ally; the US, its Egyptian partner; Saudi Arabia, stability in the Gulf; Turkey, its newly acquired prestige; Iraq, its budding but fragile democracy. A wider Middle Eastern conflict could ensue. At the domestic level, some uprisings could result in a mere reshuffling of cards as new configurations of old elites keep control. There could be prolonged chaos, instability, and the targeting of minority groups.

The uprisings, partly motivated by economic hardship, ironically make those hardships still more severe. Where elections take place, they likely will prompt confusion, as groups with uncertain political experience compete. As with all upheavals, there will be a messy chapter before clarity sets in and the actual balance of power becomes evident. Increasing numbers could well question whether emerging regimes are improvements. Nostalgia for the past cannot lag far behind.

Some states might fragment because of ethnic, sectarian, or tribal divides. Civil war, a variant of which has broken out in Yemen and is deeply feared in Syria, may emerge. The region is ripe for breakdown. Sudan is partitioned; Yemen is torn between a Houthi rebellion in the north and secessionists in the south; Iraqi Kurdistan teeters on the edge of separation; in Palestine, Gaza and the West Bank each goes its own way; in Syria, Sunnis, Alawites, Kurds, Druze, and Bedouin tribes might push for greater self-rule. The upheaval could accelerate the drift. The uprisings revitalized symbols of unity—the national flag and anthem—yet simultaneously loosened the state's hold and facilitated displays of subnational identity. Even the often ignored Berbers of North Africa have become more assertive.

For all this uncertainty, there seems little doubt—as protesters tire and as the general public tires of them—in what direction the balance will tilt. After the dictator falls, incessant political upheaval carries inordinate economic and security costs and most people long for order and safety. The young street demonstrators challenge the status quo, ignite a revolutionary spirit, and point the way for a redistribution of power. But what they possess in enthusiasm they lack in organization and political experience. What gives them strength during the uprising—their amorphous character and impulsiveness— leads to their subsequent undoing. Their domain is the more visible and publicized. The real action, much to their chagrin, takes place elsewhere.

The outcome of the Arab awakening will not be determined by those who launched it. The popular uprisings were broadly welcomed, but they do not neatly fit the social and political makeup of traditional communities often organized along tribal and kinship ties, where religion has a central part and foreign meddling is the norm. The result will be decided by other, more calculating and hard-nosed forces.

Nationalists and leftists will make a bid, but their reputation has been sullied for having stood for a promise already once betrayed. Liberal, secular parties carry scant potential; the appeal they enjoy in the West is inversely proportional to the support they possess at home. Fragments of the old regime retain significant assets: the experience of power; ties to the security services; economic leverage; and

25

local networks of clients. They will be hard to dislodge, but much of the protesters' ire is directed at them and they form easy targets. They can survive and thrive, but will need new patrons and protectors.

That leaves two relatively untarnished and powerful forces. One is the military, whose positions, as much as anything, have molded the course of events. In Libya and Yemen, they split between regime and opposition supporters, which contributed to a stalemate of sorts. In Syria, they so far have sided with the regime; should that change, much will change with it. In Egypt, although closely identified with the former regime, they dissociated themselves in time, sided with the protesters, and emerged as central power brokers. They are in control, a position at once advantageous and uncomfortable. Their preference is to rule without the appearance of ruling, in order to maintain their privileges while avoiding the limelight and accountability. To that end, they have tried to reach understandings with various political groups. If they do not succeed, a de facto military takeover cannot be ruled out.

And then there are the Islamists. They see the Arab awakening as their golden opportunity. This was not their revolution nor was it their idea. But, they hope, this is their time.

4

From all corners of the Arab world, Islamists of various tendencies are coming in from the cold. Virtually everywhere they are the largest single group as well as the best organized. In Egypt and Tunisia, where they had been alternatively—and sometimes concurrently—tolerated and repressed, they are full-fledged political actors. In Libya, where they had been suppressed, they joined and played a major part in the rebellion. In Syria, where they had been massacred, they are a principal component of the protest movement.

Living in the wilderness has equipped them well. Years of waiting has taught them patience, the cornerstone of their strategy. They learned the art of survival and of compromise for the sake of survival. They are the only significant political force with a vision and program unsullied, because untested, by the exercise of, or complicity in, power. Their religious language and moral code resonate deeply with large parts of the population. Islamism provides an answer to people who feel they have been prevented from being themselves.

Islamists know the alarm they inspire at home and abroad and the price they formerly paid for it. In the early 1990s, when the Algerian Islamic Salvation Front was on the cusp of a resounding electoral triumph, the army intervened. The world stood aside. A civil war and tens of thousands of casualties later, Algeria's Islamists have yet to recover. After Hamas's parliamentary victory in Palestine in 2006, it was ostracized by the world and prevented from governing. 30

The lesson seems clear: the safest path to power can be to avoid its unabashed exercise. With this history in mind, the Islamists might want to stay away from the front lines. In Egypt, some Brotherhood leaders made it plain that they will regulate their share of the parliamentary vote, preferring to sit in the legislature without controlling it. They will not run for high-profile offices, such as the presidency. They will build coalitions. They will lead from behind.

The Islamists are on a mission to reassure. They might play down controversial religious aspects of their project, with emphasis less on Islamic law than on good governance and the fight against corruption, a free-market economy and a pluralistic political system that guarantees human and gender rights. They will argue for a more assertive and independent foreign policy, but might at the same time strive for good relations with the West. They will be skeptical about peace agreements with Israel but they will neither abrogate them nor push for open hostility to the Jewish state. The model they will hold out will be closer to Erdogan's Turkey than to the ayatollahs Iran or the Taliban's Afghanistan though, since they lack Turkey's political culture and institutions, the model they eventually build will be their own.

Quietly, the Islamists might present themselves as the West's most effective allies against its most dangerous foes: armed jihadists, whom they have the religious legitimacy to contain and, if necessary, cripple; and Iran, whose appeal to the Arab street they can counteract by not shunning the Islamic Republic and presenting a less aggressive, more attractive, and indigenous Islamic model. There are precedents: in the 1950s and 1960s, Islamists in the region sided with the West and Saudi Arabia against Nasser's Egypt; not long ago they supported Jordan's monarch against the PLO and domestic dissidents; and, today, Islamist Turkey is both in Washington's good graces and an active NATO member.

Their quest will not be without challenges. The flip side of their extensive experience of opposition is that they have no experience in governing. Their knowledge of economics is rudimentary. Should they be called upon to participate in affairs of state their reputation will suffer at a time of predictable popular disillusionment and economic turmoil. The combination of high expectations and unfulfilled promises may expose them to protests they are ill-suited to endure.

The prospect of power and the taste of freedom are testing the Islamists' legendary discipline and unity. In Egypt in particular, several fissures have opened. Young Muslim Brothers chide their elders for their conservatism, ambivalence toward street protests, and overly cozy relationship with the military. There are grumblings and splinter organizations. Warnings from the past notwithstanding, some Islamists may want to exercise as much power as the movement can gain. There are tensions between those drawn to allying with secular parties and those willing to join with the more puritan and militant Salafists whose Islamism is based on literalist readings of scripture.

Other cracks could appear. Those conditioned by a deeply ingrained suspicion of the US will be reluctant to engage with Washington and will prefer an understanding with Tehran. Others will hope to roll back Shiite power; still others might turn to Riyadh. The Syrian branch of the Brotherhood, which has suffered under the rule of the Iranian-backed Assad regime, is likely to consider any rapprochement with Tehran unthinkable. Islamists could make different calculations in Yemen or Jordan, should they help overthrow their respective pro-Western regimes.

The thorniest challenge to the traditional middle-of-the-road Islamists will come from the Salafists. Their focus traditionally has been on individual morals and behavior and they have tended to oppose party and electoral politics. Yet they have undergone remarkable change. In Egypt, they have established a strong grassroots political presence, created a number of political parties, and plan to compete in elections. Elsewhere, they are actively participating in protests, at times violently. The more traditional Islamists, such as the Muslim Brotherhood, bend their views to placate foreign or domestic concerns, the more they take part in governing, the more they risk alienating those of their followers drawn to Salafism and its stricter interpretation of Islam. As the Muslim Brotherhood struggles to strike a balance, the Salafists could emerge as unintended beneficiaries. In Egypt, Syria, Yemen, and Libya, the most significant future rivalry is unlikely to be between Islamists and so-called pro-democracy secular forces. It might well be between mainstream Islamists and Salafists.

5

Of all the features of the initial Arab uprisings, the more notable relate to what they were not. They were not spearheaded by the military, engineered from outside, backed by a powerful organization, or equipped with a clear vision and leadership. Nor, remarkably, were they violent. The excitement generated by these early revolutionary moments owed as much to what they lacked as to what they possessed.

The absence of those attributes is what allowed so many, especially in the West, to believe that the spontaneous celebrations they were witnessing would translate into open, liberal, democratic societies.

Revolutions devour their children. The spoils go to the resolute, the patient, who know what they are pursuing and how to achieve it. Revolutions almost invariably are short-lived affairs, bursts of energy that destroy much on their pathway, including the people and ideas that inspired them. So it is with the Arab uprising. It will bring about radical changes. It will empower new forces and marginalize others. But the young activists who first rush onto the streets tend to lose out in the skirmishes that follow. Members of the general public might be grateful for what they have done. They often admire them and hold them in high esteem. But they do not feel they are part of them. The usual condition of a revolutionary is to be tossed aside.

The Arab world's immediate future will very likely unfold in a complex tussle between the army, remnants of old regimes, and the

Islamists, all of them with roots, resources, as well as the ability and willpower to shape events. Regional parties will have influence and international powers will not refrain from involvement. There are many possible outcomes—from restoration of the old order to military takeover, from unruly fragmentation and civil war to creeping Islamization. But the result that many outsiders had hoped for—a victory by the original protesters—is almost certainly foreclosed.

After some hesitation, the US and others have generally taken the side of the protesters. Several considerations were at work, among them the hope that this support will strengthen those most liable to espouse pro-Western views and curry favor with those most likely to take the helm. New rulers might express gratitude toward those who stood by them. But any such reflex probably will be short-lived. The West likely will awake to an Arab world whose rulers are more representative and assertive, but not more sympathetic or friendly.

The French and the British helped liberate the Arab world from four centuries of Ottoman rule; the US enabled the Afghan Mujahideen to liberate themselves from Soviet domination and freed the Iraqi people from Saddam Hussein's dictatorship. Before long, yesterday's liberators became today's foes. Things are not as they seem. The sound and fury of revolutionary moments can dull the senses and obscure the more ruthless struggles going on in the shadows.

STUDY QUESTIONS

1. Why is the Arab revolution of 2011 unlike earlier revolutions? How is it similar?

2. What is the THESIS STATEMENT of this selection? In what ways do the authors support their thesis?

3. What are some of the CAUSES of the Arab uprisings described by the authors? If the uprisings are EFFECTS, how might they, in turn, become causes of future outcomes?

4. *For Writing.* Choose another current uprising or protest. Research its origins and events, and write an essay in which you ANALYZE THE PROCESS of this revolution, using concrete examples.

WILLIAM F. BUCKLEY JR. { *Why Don't We Complain?*

WILLIAM F. BUCKLEY JR. (1925–2008), conservative author and commentator, was born in New York City. He attended schools in England, France, and New York, then served three years in the army before attending Yale. In 1955 Buckley founded *National Review*, an influential conservative magazine still in publication, and between 1966 and 1999 he hosted *Firing Line*, a television show that allowed him to showcase his formidable debating skills. He also wrote *On the Right*, a nationally syndicated newspaper column that, by the 1970s, appeared three times a week in more than 300 newspapers.

In his 1961 essay "Why Don't We Complain?" Buckley tells of two occasions when he experienced "irrational vexations" that could have been rectified had he been more assertive. Instead of complaining, however, he chose to suffer in silence. Why, he asks, do Americans remain passive when confronted with unjust or offensive situations? Buckley admits that his discomfort on these occasions was minor, but warns that passive acceptance becomes dangerous when it slides toward political apathy. Notice how Buckley uses personal experience and observations to draw conclusions about larger issues in American society.

IT WAS THE VERY LAST coach and the only empty seat on the entire train, so there was no turning back. The problem was to breathe. Outside the temperature was below freezing. Inside the railroad car, the temperature must have been about 85 degrees. I took off my overcoat, and a few minutes later my jacket, and noticed that the car was flecked with the white shirts of passengers. I soon found my hand moving to loosen my tie. From one end of the car to the other, as we rattled through Westchester County, we sweated; but we did not moan.

I watched the train conductor appear at the head of the car. "Tickets, all tickets, please!" In a more virile age, I thought, the passengers would seize the conductor and strap him down on a seat over the radiator to share the fate of his patrons. He shuffled down the aisle, picking up tickets, punching commutation cards. *No one addressed a word to him.* He approached my seat, and I drew a deep breath of resolution. "Conductor," I began with a considerable edge to my voice. . . . Instantly the doleful eyes of my seatmate turned tiredly from his newspaper to fix me with a resentful stare: what question could be so important as to justify my sibilant intrusion into his stupor? I was shaken by those eyes. I am incapable of making a discreet fuss, so I mumbled a question about what time were we due in Stamford (I didn't even ask whether it would be before or after dehydration could be expected to set in), got my reply, and went back to my newspaper and to wiping my brow.

The conductor had nonchalantly walked down the gauntlet of eighty sweating American freemen, and not one of them had asked him to explain why the passengers in that car had been consigned to suffer. There is nothing to be done when the temperature *outdoors* is 85 degrees, and indoors the air conditioner has broken down; obviously when that happens there is nothing to do, except perhaps curse the day that one was born. But when the temperature outdoors is below freezing, it takes a positive act of will on somebody's part to set the temperature *indoors* at 85. Somewhere a valve was turned too far, a furnace overstoked, a thermostat maladjusted: something that could easily be remedied by turning off the heat and allowing the great outdoors to come indoors. All this is so obvious. What is not obvious is what has happened to the American people.

It isn't just the commuters, whom we have come to visualize as a supine breed who have got onto the trick of suspending their sensory faculties twice a day while they submit to the creeping dissolution of the railroad industry. It isn't just they who have given up trying to rectify irrational vexations. It is the American people everywhere.

A few weeks ago at a large movie theatre I turned to my wife and said, "The picture is out of focus." "Be quiet," she answered. I obeyed. But a few minutes later I raised the point again, with mounting impatience. "It will be all right in a minute," she said apprehensively. (She would rather lose her eyesight than be around when I make one of my infrequent scenes.) I waited. It was *just* out of focus—not glaringly out, but out. My vision is 20–20, and I assume that is the vision, adjusted, of most people in the movie house. So, after hectoring my wife throughout the first reel, I finally prevailed upon her to admit that it *was* off, and very annoying. We then settled down, coming to rest on the presumption that: a) someone connected with the management of the theatre must soon notice the blur and make the correction; or b) that someone seated near the rear of the house would make the complaint in behalf of those of us up front; or c) that—any minute now—the entire house would explode into catcalls and foot stamping, calling dramatic attention to the irksome distortion.

What happened was nothing. The movie ended, as it had begun, *just* out of focus, and as we trooped out, we stretched our faces in a variety of contortions to accustom the eye to the shock of normal focus.

I think it is safe to say that everybody suffered on that occasion. And I think it is safe to assume that everyone was expecting someone else to take the initiative in going back to speak to the manager. And it is probably true even that if we had supposed the movie would run right through with the blurred image, someone surely would have summoned up the purposive indignation to get up out of his seat and file his complaint.

But notice that no one did. And the reason no one did is because we are all increasingly anxious in America to be unobtrusive, we are reluctant to make our voices heard, hesitant about claiming our rights; we are afraid that our cause is unjust, or that if it is not unjust, that it is ambiguous; or if not even that, that it is too trivial to justify the horrors of a confrontation with Authority; we will sit in an oven or endure a racking headache before undertaking a head-on, I'm-here-to-tell-you complaint. That tendency to passive compliance, to a heedless endurance is something to keep one's eyes on—in sharp focus.

I myself can occasionally summon the courage to complain, but I cannot, as I have intimated, complain softly. My own instinct is so strong to let the thing ride, to forget about it—to expect that someone will take the matter up, when the grievance is collective, in my behalf—that it is only when the provocation is at a very special key, whose vibrations touch simultaneously a complexus of nerves, allergies, and passions, that I catch fire and find the reserves of courage and assertiveness to speak up. When that happens, I get quite carried away. My blood gets hot, my brow wet, I become unbearably and unconscionably sarcastic and bellicose: I am girded for a total showdown.

Why should that be? Why could not I (or anyone else) on that railroad coach have said simply to the conductor, "Sir,"—I take that back: that sounds sarcastic—"Conductor, would you be good enough to turn down the heat? I am extremely hot. In fact, I tend to get hot every time the temperature reaches 85 degr—" Strike that last sentence. Just end it with the simple statement that you are extremely hot, and let the conductor infer the cause.

Every New Year's Eve I resolve to do something about the Milquetoast[1] in me and vow to speak up, calmly, for my rights, and for the betterment of our society, on every appropriate occasion. Entering last New Year's Eve I was fortified in my resolve because that morning at breakfast I had had to ask the waitress three times for a glass of milk. She finally brought it—after I had finished my eggs, which is when I don't want it any more. I did not have the manliness to order her to take the milk back, but settled instead for a cowardly sulk, and ostentatiously refused to drink the milk—though I later paid for it— rather than state plainly to the hostess, as I should have, why I had not drunk it, and would not pay for it.

So by the time the New Year ushered out the Old, riding in on my morning's indignation and stimulated by the gastric juices of resolution that flow so faithfully on New Year's Eve, I rendered my vow. Henceforward I would conquer my shyness, my despicable disposition

[1]Caspar Milquetoast was a nervous, cowardly character in Harold Webster's comic strip, *The Timid Soul.*

to supineness. I would speak out like a man against the unnecessary annoyances of our time.

Forty-eight hours later, I was standing in line at the ski-repair store in Pico Peak, Vermont. All I needed, to get on with my skiing, was the loan, for one minute, of a small screwdriver, to tighten a loose binding. Behind the counter in the workshop were two men. One was industriously engaged in servicing the complicated requirements of a young lady at the head of the line, and obviously he would be tied up for quite a while. The other—"Jiggs," his workmate called him—was a middle-aged man, who sat in a chair puffing a pipe, exchanging small talk with his working partner. My pulse began its telltale acceleration. The minutes ticked on. I stared at the idle shopkeeper, hoping to shame him into action, but he was impervious to my telepathic reproof and continued his small talk with his friend, brazenly insensitive to the nervous demands of six good men who were raring to ski.

Suddenly my New Year's Eve resolution struck me. It was now or never. I broke from my place in line and marched to the counter. I was going to control myself. I dug my nails into my palms. My effort was only partially successful:

"If you are not too busy," I said icily, "would you mind handing me 15 a screwdriver?"

Work stopped and everyone turned his eyes on me, and I experienced that mortification I always feel when I am the center of centripetal shafts of curiosity, resentment, perplexity.

But the worst was yet to come. "I am sorry, sir," said Jiggs deferentially, moving the pipe from his mouth. "I am not supposed to move. I have just had a heart attack." That was the signal for a great whirring noise that descended from heaven. We looked, stricken, out the window, and it appeared as though a cyclone had suddenly focused on the snowy courtyard between the shop and the ski lift. Suddenly a gigantic Army helicopter materialized, and hovered down to a landing. Two men jumped out of the plane carrying a stretcher, tore into the ski shop, and lifted the shopkeeper onto the stretcher. Jiggs bade his companion good-by, was whisked out the door, into the plane, up to the heavens, down—we learned—to a nearby Army hospital. I looked up manfully—into a score of man-eating eyes. I put the experience down as a reversal.

As I write this, on an airplane, I have run out of paper and need to reach into my briefcase under my legs for more. I cannot do this until my empty lunch tray is removed from my lap. I arrested the stewardess as she passed empty-handed down the aisle on the way to the kitchen to fetch the lunch trays for the passengers up forward who haven't been served yet. "Would you please take my tray?" "Just a *moment, sir*," she said, and marched on sternly. Shall I tell her that since she is headed for the kitchen *anyway*, it cannot delay the feeding of the other passengers by the two seconds necessary to stash away my empty tray? Or remind her that not fifteen minutes ago she spoke unctuously into the loud-speaker the words undoubtedly devised by the airline's highly paid public-relations counselor: "If there is anything I or Miss French can do for you to make your trip more enjoyable, *please* let us—" I have run out of paper.

I think the observable reluctance of the majority of Americans to assert themselves in minor matters is related to our increased sense of helplessness in an age of technology and centralized political and economic power. For generations, Americans who were too hot, or too cold, got up and did something about it. Now we call the plumber, or the electrician, or the furnace man. The habit of looking after our own needs obviously had something to do with the assertiveness that characterized the American family familiar to readers of American literature. With the technification of life goes our direct responsibility for our material environment, and we are conditioned to adopt a position of helplessness not only as regards the broken air conditioner, but as regards the overheated train. It takes an expert to fix the former, but not the latter: yet these distinctions, as we withdrew into helplessness, tend to fade away.

Our notorious political apathy is a related phenomenon. Every year, 20 whether the Republican or the Democratic Party is in office, more and more power drains away from the individual to feed vast reservoirs in far-off places; and we have less and less say about the shape of events which shape our future. From this aberration of personal power comes the sense of resignation with which we accept the political dispensations of a powerful government whose hold upon us continues to increase.

An editor of a national weekly news magazine told me a few years ago that as few as a dozen letters of protest against an editorial stance of his magazine was enough to convene a plenipotentiary meeting of the board of editors to review policy. "So few people complain, or make their voices heard," he explained to me, "that we assume a dozen letters represent the inarticulated views of thousands of readers." In the past ten years, he said, the volume of mail has noticeably decreased, even though the circulation of his magazine has risen.

When our voices are finally mute, when we have finally suppressed the natural instinct to complain, whether the vexation is trivial or grave, we shall have become automatons, incapable of feeling. When Premier Khrushchev[2] first came to this country late in 1959 he was primed, we are informed, to experience the bitter resentment of the American people against his tyranny, against his persecutions, against the movement which is responsible for the then great number of American deaths in Korea, for billions in taxes every year, and for life everlasting on the brink of disasters; but Khrushchev was pleasantly surprised, and reported back to the Russian people that he had been met with overwhelming cordiality (read: apathy), except, to be sure, for "a few fascists who followed me around with their wretched posters, and should be . . . horse-whipped."

I may be crazy, but I say there would have been lots more posters in a society where train temperatures in the dead of winter are not allowed to climb up to 85 degrees without complaint.

[2]Nikita Krushchev (1894–1971), then Soviet Premier.

STUDY QUESTIONS

1. What, specifically, is Buckley advocating? Considering that he wrote this essay in 1961, are his concerns still relevant? Why or why not?

2. Examine those places in the essay where Buckley uses his personal experience as a means for drawing conclusions about the American people and identify the TRANSITIONS between personal experience and cultural commentary. Given the ANECDOTES he relates, are his insights and general conclusions convincing?

3. *For Writing.* Buckley writes, "When our voices are finally mute, when we have finally suppressed the natural instinct to complain, whether the vexation is trivial or grave, we shall have become automatons, incapable of feeling." Write an essay explaining why you agree or disagree with Buckley's CLAIM. In your essay, consider the following: Do we have a "natural instinct to complain"? If so, is following this instinct always the best course of action? When, if ever, might "passive compliance" be the best response?

NICHOLAS CARR { *Hal and Me*

FROM *THE SHALLOWS*

NICHOLAS CARR (b. 1959) is an American journalist and author who specializes in writing about the connection between technology, economics, and culture. He earned a BA from Dartmouth College and an MA in English and American literature and language from Harvard University. His work has appeared in a number of newspapers and magazines, including the *Guardian*, the *Times* of London, the *New York Times*, the *Wall Street Journal*, and *Wired*. In addition, he is the author of four books on information technology, including *The Big Switch: Rewiring the World, from Edison to Google* (2008) and *The Shallows: What the Internet Is Doing to Our Brains* (2011), which was a finalist for the Pulitzer Prize.

"Hal and Me," taken from *The Shallows*, describes Carr's thoughts on how the Internet alters its users' minds in ways that are both subtle and profound. Among other things, he argues that using the Internet changes the ways in which we read and absorb information—on the one hand, we read more quickly and more widely, but on the other hand, we rarely explore topics as deeply as we do when reading and researching with print sources. As you read, take note of how Carr compares his experiences using the Internet with other people's stories and the research that he has done on the topic.

"DAVE, STOP. STOP, WILL YOU? Stop, Dave. Will you stop?" So the supercomputer HAL pleads with the implacable astronaut Dave Bowman in a famous and weirdly poignant scene toward the end of Stanley Kubrick's *2001: A Space Odyssey*. Bowman, having nearly been sent to a deep-space death by the malfunctioning machine, is calmly, coldly disconnecting the memory circuits that control its artificial brain. "Dave, my mind is going," HAL says, forlornly. "I can feel it. I can feel it."

I can feel it too. Over the last few years I've had an uncomfortable sense that someone, or something, has been tinkering with my brain, remapping the neural circuitry, reprogramming the memory. My mind isn't going—so far as I can tell—but it's changing. I'm not thinking the way I used to think. I feel it most strongly when I'm reading. I used to find it easy to immerse myself in a book or a lengthy article. My mind would get caught up in the twists of the narrative or the turns of the argument, and I'd spend hours strolling through long stretches of prose. That's rarely the case anymore. Now my concentration starts to drift after a page or two. I get fidgety, lose the thread, begin looking for something else to do. I feel like I'm always dragging my wayward brain back to the text. The deep reading that used to come naturally has become a struggle.

I think I know what's going on. For well over a decade now, I've been spending a lot of time online, searching and surfing and sometimes adding to the great databases of the Internet. The Web's been a godsend to me as a writer. Research that once required days in the stacks or periodical rooms of libraries can now be done in minutes. A few Google searches, some quick clicks on hyperlinks, and I've got the telltale fact or the pithy quote I was after. I couldn't begin to tally the hours or the gallons of gasoline the Net has saved me. I do most of my banking and a lot of my shopping online. I use my browser to pay my bills, schedule my appointments, book flights and hotel rooms, renew my driver's license, send invitations and greeting cards. Even when I'm not working, I'm as likely as not to be foraging in the Web's data thickets—reading and writing e-mails, scanning headlines and blog posts, following Facebook updates, watching video streams, downloading music, or just tripping lightly from link to link to link.

The Net has become my all-purpose medium, the conduit for most of the information that flows through my eyes and ears and into my mind. The advantages of having immediate access to such an incredibly rich and easily searched store of data are many, and they've been widely described and duly applauded. "Google," says Heather Pringle, a writer with *Archaeology* magazine, "is an astonishing boon to humanity, gathering up and concentrating information and ideas that were once scattered so broadly around the world that hardly anyone could profit from them."[1] Observes *Wired's* Clive Thompson, "The perfect recall of silicon memory can be an enormous boon to thinking."[2]

The boons are real. But they come at a price. As McLuhan[3] sug-   5
gested, media aren't just channels of information. They supply the stuff of thought, but they also shape the process of thought. And what the Net seems to be doing is chipping away my capacity for concentration and contemplation. Whether I'm online or not, my mind now expects to take in information the way the Net distributes it: in a swiftly moving stream of particles. Once I was a scuba diver in the sea of words. Now I zip along the surface like a guy on a Jet Ski.

Maybe I'm an aberration, an outlier. But it doesn't seem that way. When I mention my troubles with reading to friends, many say they're suffering from similar afflictions. The more they use the Web, the more they have to fight to stay focused on long pieces of writing. Some worry they're becoming chronic scatterbrains. Several of the bloggers I follow have also mentioned the phenomenon. Scott Karp, who used to work for a magazine and now writes a blog about online media, confesses that he has stopped reading books altogether. "I was a lit major in college, and used to be [a] voracious book reader," he writes. "What happened?" He speculates on the answer: "What if I do all my reading on the Web not so much because the way I read has

---

[1] Heather Pringle, "Is Google Making Archaeologists Smarter?" *Beyond Stone & Bone* blog (Archaeological Institute of America), February 27, 2009, archaeology.org/blog/?p =322. [All notes are the author's unless otherwise indicated.]

[2] Clive Thompson, "Your Outboard Brain Knows All," *Wired*, October 2007.

[3] Herbert Marshall McLuhan (1911–1980), Canadian philosopher and media theorist known for his view that "the medium is the message." [Editor's note.]

changed, i.e. I'm just seeking convenience, but because the way I THINK has changed?"[4]

Bruce Friedman, who blogs about the use of computers in medicine, has also described how the Internet is altering his mental habits. "I now have almost totally lost the ability to read and absorb a longish article on the Web or in print," he says.[5] A pathologist on the faculty of the University of Michigan Medical School, Friedman elaborated on his comment in a telephone conversation with me. His thinking, he said, has taken on a "staccato" quality, reflecting the way he quickly scans short passages of text from many sources online. "I can't read *War and Peace* anymore," he admitted. "I've lost the ability to do that. Even a blog post of more than three or four paragraphs is too much to absorb. I skim it."

Philip Davis, a doctoral student in communication at Cornell who contributes to the Society for Scholarly Publishing's blog, recalls a time back in the 1990s when he showed a friend how to use a Web browser. He says he was "astonished" and "even irritated" when the woman paused to read the text on the sites she stumbled upon. "You're not supposed to read Web pages, just click on the hypertexted words!" he scolded her. Now, Davis writes, "I read a lot—or at least I should be reading a lot—only I don't. I skim. I scroll. I have very little patience for long, drawn-out, nuanced arguments, even though I accuse others of painting the world too simply."[6]

Karp, Friedman, and Davis—all well-educated men with a keenness for writing—seem fairly sanguine about the decay of their faculties for reading and concentrating. All things considered, they say, the benefits they get from using the Net—quick access to loads of information, potent searching and filtering tools, an easy way to share

[4] Scott Karp, "The Evolution from Linear Thought to Networked Thought," *Publishing 2.0* blog, February 9, 2008, publishing2.com/2008/02/09/the-evolution-from-linear-thought-to-networked-thought.

[5] Bruce Friedman, "How Google Is Changing Our Information-Seeking Behavior," *Lab Soft News* blog, February 6, 2008, labsoftnews.typepad.com/lab_soft_news/2008/02/how-google-is-c.html.

[6] Philip Davis, "Is Google Making Us Stupid? Nope!" *The Scholarly Kitchen* blog, June 16, 2008, scholarlykitchen.sspnet.org/2008/06/16/is-google-making-us-stupid-nope.

their opinions with a small but interested audience—make up for the loss of their ability to sit still and turn the pages of a book or a magazine. Friedman told me, in an e-mail, that he's "never been more creative" than he has been recently, and he attributes that "to my blog and the ability to review/scan 'tons' of information on the Web." Karp has come to believe that reading lots of short, linked snippets online is a more efficient way to expand his mind than reading "250-page books," though, he says, "we can't yet recognize the superiority of this networked thinking process because we're measuring it against our old linear thought process."[7] Muses Davis, "The Internet may have made me a less patient reader, but I think that in many ways, it has made me smarter. More connections to documents, artifacts, and people means more external influences on my thinking and thus on my writing."[8] All three know they've sacrificed something important, but they wouldn't go back to the way things used to be.

For some people, the very idea of reading a book has come to seem old-fashioned, maybe even a little silly—like sewing your own shirts or butchering your own meat. "I don't read books," says Joe O'Shea, a former president of the student body at Florida State University and a 2008 recipient of a Rhodes Scholarship. "I go to Google, and I can absorb relevant information quickly." O'Shea, a philosophy major, doesn't see any reason to plow through chapters of text when it takes but a minute or two to cherry-pick the pertinent passages using Google Book Search. "Sitting down and going through a book from cover to cover doesn't make sense," he says. "It's not a good use of my time, as I can get all the information I need faster through the Web." As soon as you learn to be "a skilled hunter" online, he argues, books become superfluous.[9] 10

O'Shea seems more the rule than the exception. In 2008, a research and consulting outfit called nGenera released a study of the effects

[7] Scott Karp, "Connecting the Dots of the Web Revolution," *Publishing 2.0* blog, June 17, 2008, publishing2.com/2008/06/17/connecting-the-dots-of-the-web-revolution.

[8] Davis, "Is Google Making Us Stupid? Nope!"

[9] Don Tapscott, "How Digital Technology Has Changed the Brain," *Business Week Online,* November 10, 2008, www.businessweek.com/technology/content/nov2008/tc2008117_034517.htm.

of Internet use on the young. The company interviewed some six thousand members of what it calls "Generation Net"—kids who have grown up using the Web. "Digital immersion," wrote the lead researcher, "has even affected the way they absorb information. They don't necessarily read a page from left to right and from top to bottom. They might instead skip around, scanning for pertinent information of interest."[1] In a talk at a recent Phi Beta Kappa meeting, Duke University professor Katherine Hayles confessed, "I can't get my students to read whole books anymore."[2] Hayles teaches English; the students she's talking about are students of literature.

People use the Internet in all sorts of ways. Some are eager, even compulsive adopters of the latest technologies. They keep accounts with a dozen or more online services and subscribe to scores of information feeds. They blog and they tag, they text and they twitter. Others don't much care about being on the cutting edge but nevertheless find themselves online most of the time, tapping away at their desktop, their laptop, or their mobile phone. The Net has become essential to their work, school, or social lives, and often to all three. Still others log on only a few times a day—to check their e-mail, follow a story in the news, research a topic of interest, or do some shopping. And there are, of course, many people who don't use the Internet at all, either because they can't afford to or because they don't want to. What's clear, though, is that for society as a whole the Net has become, in just the twenty years since the software programmer Tim Berners-Lee wrote the code for the World Wide Web, the communication and information medium of choice. The scope of its use is unprecedented, even by the standards of the mass media of the twentieth century. The scope of its influence is equally broad. By choice or necessity, we've embraced the Net's uniquely rapid-fire mode of collecting and dispensing information.

We seem to have arrived, as McLuhan said we would, at an important juncture in our intellectual and cultural history, a moment of

[1] Don Tapscott, "How to Teach and Manage 'Generation Net,'" *BusinessWeek Online,* November 30, 2008, www.businessweek.com/technology/content/nov2008/tc20081130_713563.htm.

[2] Quoted in Naomi S. Baron, *Always On: Language in an Online and Mobile World* (Oxford: Oxford University Press, 2008), 204.

transition between two very different modes of thinking. What we're trading away in return for the riches of the Net—and only a curmudgeon would refuse to see the riches—is what Karp calls "our old linear thought process." Calm, focused, undistracted, the linear mind is being pushed aside by a new kind of mind that wants and needs to take in and dole out information in short, disjointed, often overlapping bursts—the faster, the better. John Battelle, a onetime magazine editor and journalism professor who now runs an online advertising syndicate, has described the intellectual frisson he experiences when skittering across Web pages: "When I am performing bricolage in real time over the course of hours, I am 'feeling' my brain light up, I [am] 'feeling' like I'm getting smarter."[3] Most of us have experienced similar sensations while online. The feelings are intoxicating—so much so that they can distract us from the Net's deeper cognitive consequences.

For the last five centuries, ever since Gutenberg's[4] printing press made book reading a popular pursuit, the linear, literary mind has been at the center of art, science, and society. As supple as it is subtle, it's been the imaginative mind of the Renaissance, the rational mind of the Enlightenment, the inventive mind of the Industrial Revolution, even the subversive mind of Modernism. It may soon be yesterday's mind.

•   ○   •

THE HAL 9000 COMPUTER was born, or "made operational," as HAL himself humbly put it, on January 12, 1992, in a mythical computer plant in Urbana, Illinois. I was born almost exactly thirty-three years earlier, in January of 1959, in another midwestern city, Cincinnati, Ohio. My life, like the lives of most Baby Boomers and Generation Xers, has unfolded like a two-act play. It opened with Analogue Youth and then, after a quick but thorough shuffling of the props, it entered Digital Adulthood.

15

[3] John Battelle, "Google: Making Nick Carr Stupid, but It's Made This Guy Smarter," *John Battelle's Searchblog,* June 10, 2008, battellemedia.com/archives/004494.php.

[4] Johannes Gutenberg (c. 1398–1468), German developer of the first movable-type printing press, which revolutionized publishing by making mass-produced books possible. [Editor's Note.]

When I summon up images from my early years, they seem at once comforting and alien, like stills from a G-rated David Lynch film. There's the bulky mustard-yellow telephone affixed to the wall of our kitchen, with its rotary dial and long, coiled cord. There's my dad fiddling with the rabbit ears on top of the TV, vainly trying to get rid of the snow obscuring the Reds game. There's the rolled-up, dew-dampened morning newspaper lying in our gravel driveway. There's the hi-fi console in the living room, a few record jackets and dust sleeves (some from my older siblings' Beatles albums) scattered on the carpet around it. And downstairs, in the musty basement family room, there are the books on the bookshelves—lots of books—with their many-colored spines, each bearing a title and the name of a writer.

In 1977, the year *Star Wars* came out and the Apple Computer company was incorporated, I headed to New Hampshire to attend Dartmouth College. I didn't know it when I applied, but Dartmouth had long been a leader in academic computing, playing a pivotal role in making the power of data-processing machines easily available to students and teachers. The college's president, John Kemeny, was a respected computer scientist who in 1972 had written an influential book called *Man and the Computer*. He had also, a decade before that, been one of the inventors of BASIC, the first programming language to use common words and everyday syntax. Near the center of the school's grounds, just behind the neo-Georgian Baker Library with its soaring bell tower, squatted the single-story Kiewit Computation Center, a drab, vaguely futuristic concrete building that housed the school's pair of General Electric GE-635 mainframe computers. The mainframes ran the groundbreaking Dartmouth Time-Sharing System, an early type of network that allowed dozens of people to use the computers simultaneously. Time-sharing was the first manifestation of what we today call personal computing. It made possible, as Kemeny wrote in his book, "a true symbiotic relationship between man and computer."[5]

I was an English major and went to great lengths to avoid math and science classes, but Kiewit occupied a strategic location on campus, midway between my dorm and Fraternity Row, and on weekend eve-

[5] John G. Kemeny, *Man and the Computer* (New York: Scribner, 1972), 21.

nings I'd often spend an hour or two at a terminal in the public teletype room while waiting for the keg parties to get rolling. Usually, I'd
fritter away the time playing one of the goofily primitive multiplayer
games that the undergraduate programmers—"sysprogs," they called
themselves—had hacked together. But I did manage to teach myself
how to use the system's cumbersome word-processing program and
even learned a few BASIC commands.

That was just a digital dalliance. For every hour I passed in Kiewit,
I must have spent two dozen next door in Baker. I crammed for exams
in the library's cavernous reading room, looked up facts in the weighty
volumes on the reference shelves, and worked part-time checking
books in and out at the circulation desk. Most of my library time,
though, went to wandering the long, narrow corridors of the stacks.
Despite being surrounded by tens of thousands of books, I don't
remember feeling the anxiety that's symptomatic of what we today call
"information overload." There was something calming in the reticence of all those books, their willingness to wait years, decades even,
for the right reader to come along and pull them from their appointed
slots. *Take your time,* the books whispered to me in their dusty voices.
We're not going anywhere.

It was in 1986, five years after I left Dartmouth, that computers 20
entered my life in earnest. To my wife's dismay, I spent nearly our
entire savings, some $2,000, on one of Apple's earliest Macintoshes—
a Mac Plus decked out with a single megabyte of RAM, a 20-megabyte
hard drive, and a tiny black-and-white screen. I still recall the excitement I felt as I unpacked the little beige machine. I set it on my desk,
plugged in the keyboard and mouse, and flipped the power switch.
It lit up, sounded a welcoming chime, and smiled at me as it went
through the mysterious routines that brought it to life. I was smitten.

The Plus did double duty as both a home and a business computer.
Every day, I lugged it into the offices of the management consulting
firm where I worked as an editor. I used Microsoft Word to revise
proposals, reports, and presentations, and sometimes I'd launch
Excel to key in revisions to a consultant's spreadsheet. Every evening, I carted it back home, where I used it to keep track of the family
finances, write letters, play games (still goofy, but less primitive),

and—most diverting of all—cobble together simple databases using the ingenious HyperCard application that back then came with every Mac. Created by Bill Atkinson, one of Apple's most inventive programmers, HyperCard incorporated a hypertext system that anticipated the look and feel of the World Wide Web. Where on the Web you click links on pages, on HyperCard you clicked buttons on cards—but the idea, and its seductiveness, was the same.

The computer, I began to sense, was more than just a simple tool that did what you told it to do. It was a machine that, in subtle but unmistakable ways, exerted an influence over you. The more I used it, the more it altered the way I worked. At first I had found it impossible to edit anything on-screen. I'd print out a document, mark it up with a pencil, and type the revisions back into the digital version. Then I'd print it out again and take another pass with the pencil. Sometimes I'd go through the cycle a dozen times a day. But at some point—and abruptly—my editing routine changed. I found I could no longer write or revise anything on paper. I felt lost without the Delete key, the scrollbar, the cut and paste functions, the Undo command. I *had* to do all my editing on-screen. In using the word processor, I had become something of a word processor myself.

Bigger changes came after I bought a modem, sometime around 1990. Up to then, the Plus had been a self-contained machine, its functions limited to whatever software I installed on its hard drive. When hooked up to other computers through the modem, it took on a new identity and a new role. It was no longer just a high-tech Swiss Army knife. It was a communications medium, a device for finding, organizing, and sharing information. I tried all the online services— CompuServe, Prodigy, even Apple's short-lived eWorld—but the one I stuck with was America Online. My original AOL subscription limited me to five hours online a week, and I would painstakingly parcel out the precious minutes to exchange e-mails with a small group of friends who also had AOL accounts, to follow the conversations on a few bulletin boards, and to read articles reprinted from newspapers and magazines. I actually grew fond of the sound of my modem connecting through the phone lines to the AOL servers. Listening to the bleeps and clangs was like overhearing a friendly argument between a couple of robots.

By the mid-nineties, I had become trapped, not unhappily, in the "upgrade cycle." I retired the aging Plus in 1994, replacing it with a Macintosh Performa 550 with a color screen, a CD-ROM drive, a 500-megabyte hard drive, and what seemed at the time a miraculously fast 33-megahertz processor. The new computer required updated versions of most of the programs I used, and it let me run all sorts of new applications with the latest multimedia features. By the time I had installed all the new software, my hard drive was full. I had to go out and buy an external drive as a supplement. I added a Zip drive too—and then a CD burner. Within a couple of years, I'd bought another new desktop, with a much larger monitor and a much faster chip, as well as a portable model that I could use while traveling. My employer had, in the meantime, banished Macs in favor of Windows PCs, so I was using two different systems, one at work and one at home.

It was around this same time that I started hearing talk of some- 25 thing called the Internet, a mysterious "network of networks" that promised, according to people in the know, to "change everything." A 1994 article in *Wired* declared my beloved AOL "suddenly obsolete." A new invention, the "graphical browser," promised a far more exciting digital experience: "By following the links—click, and the linked document appears—you can travel through the online world along paths of whim and intuition."[6] I was intrigued, and then I was hooked. By the end of 1995 I had installed the new Netscape browser on my work computer and was using it to explore the seemingly infinite pages of the World Wide Web. Soon I had an ISP account at home as well—and a much faster modem to go with it. I canceled my AOL service.

You know the rest of the story because it's probably your story too. Ever-faster chips. Ever-quicker modems. DVDs and DVD burners. Gigabyte-sized hard drives. Yahoo and Amazon and eBay. MP3s.

---

[6] Gary Wolfe, "The (Second Phase of the) Revolution Has Begun," *Wired*, October 1994.

Streaming video. Broadband. Napster and Google. BlackBerrys and iPods. Wi-Fi networks. YouTube and Wikipedia. Blogging and micro-blogging. Smartphones, thumb drives, netbooks. Who could resist? Certainly not I.

When the Web went 2.0 around 2005, I went 2.0 with it. I became a social networker and a content generator. I registered a domain, roughtype.com, and launched a blog. It was exhilarating, at least for the first couple of years. I had been working as a freelance writer since the start of the decade, writing mainly about technology, and I knew that publishing an article or a book was a slow, involved, and often frustrating business. You slaved over a manuscript, sent it off to a publisher, and assuming it wasn't sent back with a rejection slip, went through rounds of editing, fact checking, and proofreading. The finished product wouldn't appear until weeks or months later. If it was a book, you might have to wait more than a year to see it in print. Blogging junked the traditional publishing apparatus. You'd type something up, code a few links, hit the Publish button, and your work would be out there, immediately, for all the world to see. You'd also get something you rarely got with more formal writing: direct responses from readers, in the form of comments or, if the readers had their own blogs, links. It felt new and liberating.

Reading online felt new and liberating too. Hyperlinks and search engines delivered an endless supply of words to my screen, alongside pictures, sounds, and videos. As publishers tore down their pay-walls, the flood of free content turned into a tidal wave. Headlines streamed around the clock through my Yahoo home page and my RSS feed reader. One click on a link led to a dozen or a hundred more. New e-mails popped into my in-box every minute or two. I registered for accounts with MySpace and Facebook, Digg and Twitter. I started letting my newspaper and magazine subscriptions lapse. Who needed them? By the time the print editions arrived, dew-dampened or other-wise, I felt like I'd already seen all the stories.

Sometime in 2007, a serpent of doubt slithered into my info-paradise. I began to notice that the Net was exerting a much stronger and broader influence over me than my old stand-alone PC ever had. It wasn't just that I was spending so much time staring into a computer screen. It wasn't just that so many of my habits and routines were changing as I became more accustomed to and dependent on the sites and services of the Net. The very way my brain worked seemed to be changing. It was then that I began worrying about my inability to pay attention to one thing for more than a couple of minutes. At first I'd figured that the problem was a symptom of middle-age mind rot. But my brain, I realized, wasn't just drifting. It was hungry. It was demanding to be fed the way the Net fed it—and the more it was fed, the hungrier it became. Even when I was away from my computer, I yearned to check e-mail, click links, do some Googling. I wanted to be *connected*. Just as Microsoft Word had turned me into a flesh-and-blood word processor, the Internet, I sensed, was turning me into something like a high-speed data-processing machine, a human HAL.

I missed my old brain. 30

STUDY QUESTIONS

1. Describe how Carr traces his own history of Internet use.

2. Consider Carr's use of multiple forms of EVIDENCE—he utilizes his own story, other people's experiences, and statistical data. How does this combination of sources affect the rhetorical impact of the essay?

3. How would you describe the overall TONE of the piece? As you read the essay, what sense did you get about Carr's feelings about the Internet and his use of it? What are some specific examples from the essay that demonstrate how he establishes that tone?

4. *For Writing.* In a short essay, describe how *you* use the Internet, and how your Internet use has affected your life and school work.

TERRELL F. DIXON
AND LISA SLAPPEY

{ *The Bayou and the Ship Channel:*
Finding Place and Building
Community in Houston, Texas }

TERRELL F. DIXON (b. 1940) and LISA SLAPPEY (b. 1969) are both
university professors dedicated to making environmental awareness part
of the English curriculum. Dixon received his BA at the University of
Oklahoma and his PhD at Indiana University. He has taught at Indiana
University, Southern Methodist University, and the University of Houston,
where he currently teaches undergraduate and graduate courses in environ-
mental literature. Dixon's books include *Being in the World: An
Environmental Reader for Writers* (1993, co-edited with Scott H. Slovic),
John Graves: Writer (2007, co-edited with Mark Busby), and *City Wilds:
Essays and Stories about Urban Nature* (2002). Slappey received her BA
from Florida State University and her MA and PhD from Rice University.
Now a professor at Rice, she focuses mainly on environmental literature and
Native American literature.

In "The Bayou and the Ship Channel," Dixon and Slappey take readers
through the experiences their students had as they got out of the classroom
and visited Houston's Ship Channel and Buffalo Bayou, sharing their
reactions and responses to various sights and, notably, smells they encountered in the course of their fieldwork. Through a close examination of
Houston from the perspective of college teachers and students, Dixon and
Slappey explore the idea of place and how we shape and interact with our
environment.

MOST AMERICANS VIEW OUR CITIES as having a sort of built-in placelessness. Cities are mainly freeways, and malls, and chain restaurants.
The real Places, the ones that matter, are the Grand Canyon, and Old

"Buffalo Bayou and the Ship Channel" by Terrell Dixon and Lisa Slappey. Used by permission of the authors.

Faithful, and Rocky Mountain National Park. Once we allow for differences in weather, one American city is pretty much like another.

Our students share this general sense that place is somewhere outside the city. To counteract this viewpoint, to get the students thinking about cities in a different way, we each have chosen to focus our "Literature and the Environment" classes on the city where we teach: Houston. At first, it sounds like an overwhelming challenge: how can we make the epitome of the placeless city a place that lives for them? The solution is simple: get them out in it.

What follows is a distillation of our experiences in teaching urban nature in Houston. Lisa works with undergraduate students, mostly non-English majors, at Rice University; Terrell works with graduate students in creative writing and literature at the University of Houston. We share the desire to help our students discover the nature of place in the city. Taking Rice students to the Ship Channel and University of Houston students to Buffalo Bayou makes Houston both our subject and our classroom.

THE SHIP CHANNEL

When I ask students where they imagine living after college, few say Houston. As a small private university within Houston's metropolis, Rice University can often seem dissociated, both physically and culturally, from the surrounding city. Rice boasts a strong residential-college system, and even commuting students need not stray far from campus. Students rarely see this city as a desirable living place, nor do they realize how many Rice graduates either stay in or return to Houston to work in our medical center, our petrochemical industry, or our shiny downtown buildings. Many will make their fortunes and raise their families right here. To begin to instill in them an awareness of Houston as a wonderfully complex place, we go outside for a look at the city they will call home for at least four years.

What they see is not always pretty. A trip to the Ship Channel may   5
provide the most revealing, if the least aesthetically pleasing, vision of Houston. Though we may also visit Buffalo Bayou, Brazos Bend State Park, or the Galleria, the Ship Channel takes us to the source of so much

of the filthy lucre available here. Many of the social, economic, and environmental challenges facing Houston are evident in this segment of the waterway that connects Buffalo Bayou to the Gulf of Mexico. The place itself is a history lesson. In 1836, Sam Houston's forces defeated Santa Anna's[1] Mexican Army at the Battle of San Jacinto, opening the way for an influx of American settlers into the new Republic of Texas. Most of those early arrivals to the city founded by the Allen brothers[2] and bearing Houston's name came by this water route. The outcome of that 1836 contest of international wills set the stage for Houston's emergence as not merely a Southern cotton exchange or oil-refining boomtown but as a global-commerce headquarters as well.

Houston houses the nation's second-busiest port and the world's second-largest petrochemical complex. Proud of those designations, the city offers a free public relations boat tour of the Houston Ship Channel. Taking my students on the ninety-minute tour aboard the MV[3] *Sam Houston* to meet our petrochemical neighbors requires that we make reservations, bring identification, and clear Homeland Security. Bureaucracy aside, everyone associated with the Ship Channel has always welcomed us, though I warn the class not to expect the "unforgettably spectacular waterborne adventure" promised on the Port of Houston's official Web site. We journey from our little urban oasis across the 610 Ship Channel Bridge and onto Clinton Drive, passing parking lots full of shiny imported cars on one side and ramshackle housing on the other. Ship Channel neighborhoods lack the Rice area's affluence. Those who can afford to live elsewhere do. Environmental justice begins to take human form.

Students ask why Houston would market this view of itself to tourists, and yet the ship's register is full of visitors. This area interests our guests more than it interests the locals. Over the years, only two of my local students had taken the boat tour before our field trips.

---

[1] Antonio López de Santa Anna (1794–1876), Mexican revolutionary leader, army general, and seven-time president. *Sam Houston*: American politician and soldier (1793–1863), governor of Tennessee, two-time president of the Republic of Texas, and governor of the state of Texas.

[2] Augustus Chapman Allen (1806–64) and John Kirby Allen (1810–38), land speculators.

[3] Merchant Vessel.

Virtually all admit to a basic lack of awareness of the Ship Channel's functions. Some are surprised to learn that we are a port city; certainly they are oblivious to the port's past and present connections to Rice University. Marie Phelps McAshan describes in romantic terms the 1874 port "dream" of Houston as a cotton exporter. This economic and engineering feat required "the narrow tortuous channel choked with logs, infested with alligators, and full of all kinds of debris" (100–101) to be dredged to a depth of twenty-five feet; it succeeded because "these men of great vision and indomitable energy persevered" (101). The project was completed in 1914. The leaders in the later stages included Baldwin Rice, Houston mayor and nephew of Rice University's founder, and Jesse H. Jones, namesake of Rice's Graduate School of Management.

Overwhelmed by the Ship Channel, the noxious smells, noise, smoke, the huge refineries, the filth in the water and along the banks, my students begin to understand Houston's prominence in the global petrochemical economy. Oil and gas politics underpin many national strategies, and the Port of Houston, at once dangerous, powerful, and vulnerable, becomes a significant place. Recognizing the port as neighbor makes us notice when, for example, refineries explode, as they do, faithfully and conveniently, at least once a semester.

For those who live and die by the petrochemical industry, there is nothing convenient about the constant threats and occasional eruptions serving as student lessons. Once students understand that we all face environmental perils daily, they ask how individuals can initiate change when corporations seem so powerful. Sandra Steingraber reminds us in *Living Downstream* that "with the right to know comes the duty to inquire" (xxii) and, ultimately, "the obligation to act" (117). This is not easy, since closing ranks is industry's typical response to disaster.

On February 6, 2006, explosions at Akzo Nobel Chemicals in Deer Park sent one employee to the burn unit. Officials shut down nearby roads while attempting to determine the danger level; instead of calling the city's firefighters, the plant's in-house fire crew handled the situation. When one student investigated this incident for her midterm project, neither Akzo Nobel nor OSHA provided any information

10

relating to the fire, so she exercised her right to know and fulfilled her duty to inquire by filing for disclosure under the Freedom of Information Act.

On the boat, we wonder that the industries lining the shore do not have more frequent mishaps than those making the evening news. Perhaps nothing less than spectacular tragedy will force our attention, however briefly, to what occurs along the Ship Channel. How many of us know or care about the chemical processes and political maneuvers that keep the Ship Channel—and therefore much of Houston— generating growth and income? Who pays attention to the daily Air Quality Index, monitors particulate matter, or worries about toxins in the water? Should a hurricane wind its way up the Ship Channel, what sort of unnatural disaster might ensue? In November 2004, *Texas Monthly* magazine's executive editor S.C. Gwynne described the Ship Channel as a "prime terrorist target" because "it is both ground zero for the nation's petrochemical industry and home to unfathomably large quantities of the deadliest, most combustible, disease-causing, lung-exploding, chromosome-annihilating, and metal-dissolving substances known to man," yet until the Bush administration planned in 2006 to award management of several U.S. ports (Houston was not among them) to Dubai Ports World, how many citizens recognized the port systems' vulnerability to any form of terrorism?

Despite its activity level, there is a depressing, even desolate quality to the Ship Channel. Advocates of retrofitting industrial plants could build their cases here: much of the equipment seems old, rusted, and run-down; some structures, such as the Houston Lighting and Power building, are simply abandoned and falling apart. Add a few dark clouds, and the view becomes downright ominous with silhouetted spires belching toxicity into the air. Here, where the hot, hard, dirty work takes place, the effect of heavy industry cannot be disguised. Unless we are doing that work, unless we live in the communities where such work takes place, it is easy enough to disregard it. On the boat's return trip, we see Houston's glassy, expensive downtown rising in the background.

The Ship Channel provides olfactory as well as visual stimuli. One class suggests renaming the boat trip "The Tour of Smells." Author

Bill Minutaglio recounts a "joke" popular in Texas City in the 1940s: *"What brought you here?" "Shit, that's an easy answer. It's the stink. The stink of money"* (7). The Port Authority takes pride in "generating more than $10 billion in business each year and supporting nearly 300,000 jobs." In 2005, Exxon Mobil alone, whose Baytown, Texas, plant is the largest refinery in the United States, posted a staggering $36.13 billion profit ("Exxon Mobil . . .").

Although it is easy to revile petrochemical giants for their avarice, they are not the port's only financial beneficiaries. According to *The Port of Houston Magazine*, each year more than 6,000 vessels carrying 15 million tons of containers loaded with consumer products pass through the facility. They are destined not only or even primarily for metropolitan Houston, but for all of the pretty places in our nation's interior. The port's motto, "The Port Delivers the Goods," could not be more appropriate. Many of us sell these goods; all of us use them. The boat tour reminds us that everyone is implicated in the activities of the Port of Houston and the Houston Ship Channel. The stench, which is often what students recall long after the tour, clings to all of us, no matter how far we distance ourselves from the Ship Channel.

Environmental lawyer Jim Blackburn lectures in the Department of Civil and Environmental Engineering at Rice University and opposes the massive new Bayport Container Facility. In his beautiful text, *The Book of Texas Bays*, he urges us to consider the personal implications at the intersection of ecology and economy: 15

> We Texans are on a path whereby the full costs of our projects—our water supply, our shipping channels, our water pollutants—are not being paid today. . . . Our most pressing need is to find a different way of thinking about economics and ecology, one that is serious about protecting life on our living planet, one that provides for an accounting of the full cost of our current activities. (56–57)

Blackburn's work, including a federal lawsuit to stop the Bayport project, reveals the highly politicized issues surrounding the Houston Ship Channel. Although the suit was rejected, at least the Port Authority's

Web site now includes a nod toward environmental consciousness. At forty-five feet deep and 530 feet wide and crowded with hundreds of industrial facilities, today's Ship Channel bears little resemblance to that wildly lush, narrow channel through which early settlers journeyed up Buffalo Bayou to Houston. It is a fine place to account for the costs not just of our projects but of our way of life.

BUFFALO BAYOU

As Houston has grown, its bayous have suffered. Some very early city plans followed the flow of the bayous, but after that our bayous have more often than not been degraded and ignored. Some remarkably sinuous streams that once threaded the landscape of the coastal plain have been "channelized" (that is, in a process as ugly as the word itself, reshaped into a straight line and then cemented). Others have been made unappealing ditches, dumping grounds for trash, homes to nests of plastic bags, shopping carts, abandoned cars, and the occasional murder victim. Though we citizens usually choose not to really see our bayous, we were sometimes inadvertently implicated in a drive-by bayou sighting. We glimpse part of a bayou, usually from the corner of our eye, from a car speeding down a crowded freeway. Such happenings have inspired us, not to stop, look, and walk but to keep on going. In a revealing synecdoche that signifies how we Houstonians have treated our home landscape, the nickname Space City has mostly supplanted the original, place-based Bayou City. We have chosen to look away.

The problem has been, I think, that the bayous were not part of the aesthetic vocabulary of most Americans. Without peaks and rushing streams, it took us some time to learn how to read their beauty.

Houstonians were prodded into this recognition process by two disparate things. One was popular culture on the national level; the other was the work of Richard Florida, a Carnegie Mellon professor who is a specialist on urban economies. The popular culture provocation was the late-night television world of Jay Leno and David Letterman. Houston has always been an exceedingly image-conscious city, mindful of its status relative to other cities and determined to advance its place in the great, fluid hierarchy of city reputations.

Thus what transpired during the presidential election of 2000 had a huge impact: Leno and Letterman made fun of Houston! The jokes began with a George W. Bush campaign promise that he "would do for the country what he did for Texas." The talk show hosts tied that phrase to then current news stories about Houston's number one ranking in air pollution, Houston's traffic gridlock, etc. For Houston power brokers, the ridicule translated into a loss of face and, even worse, a potential loss of business. At last, change had to be considered.

My seminar students at the University of Houston come from all parts of the country, and they begin the seminar with the Jay Leno humorous view of Houston. No need to teach it. They have already discovered poor public transportation, high heat and humidity. It is a big, hot city, and they mostly try not to get out in it, except in an air-conditioned automobile.   20

The change in the city's attitude toward bayous also stems from the theories of Richard Florida. Sometimes we read his work; most often I summarize it. Florida has developed—with appropriate data, charts, etc.—a profile of what he designates the "creative class."[3] This class of young people, he says, now drives the economic engines of the cities where they *choose* to live. "Choose" is the key word here; Florida believes that those who make up the creative class seek more than a well-paying job. They take the ability to earn a good income as a given. What they look for, instead, is something that Florida describes as "quality of place." Quality of place for these young people has many different components, but foremost among them are such "amenities" as diversity. To them, diversity means everything from an ethnically mixed population, to varied kinds of restaurants, to active gay and lesbian communities, to an atmosphere where current artistic creation flourishes (not the big museums that emphasize the work from other times and places). It also encompasses opportunities for outdoor activity, and natural places conducive to outdoor recreation are a high priority in this group's evaluation. ٭

[3]Richard Florida's thesis is developed in *The Rise of the Creative Class* (New York: Basic Books, 2002). The Houston Quality of Life Coalition Web page presents (under the heading "Additional Resources") a fifty-page essay that includes many but not all of his ideas: "Competing in the Age of Talent: Quality of Place and the New Economy." [Author's note.]

Clearly, high air pollution and traffic gridlock will not attract this group. And, just as clearly, the landscape feature in Houston that has the most potential is the bayou system. It seemed no accident that Richard Florida's work began to appear on the Web site for a relatively new organization, one whose membership overlapped greatly with that of the Greater Houston Partnership (formerly called the Houston Chamber of Commerce). This organization calls itself the Quality of Life Coalition, and, since a fifty-page essay written by Florida is part of the Web site, the echo of his phrase seems deliberate. The negative push of Leno and Letterman and the positive pull of Florida's argument combined to have a powerful impact. At last, a substantial change in Houston's long-term complacency about ongoing landscape degradation seems to be happening.

My graduate students' notion of what a city can and should be also changes as they learn Florida's views. Their sense of Houston, however, changes most with the group field-study segment of the seminar. This usually involves two visits, the first to a cement-bottomed bayou not far from campus, complete with high-wire lines and rusted pipes over the bayou. This serves as my example of a "bad," that is, "unrestored" Houston bayou. During one recent early-spring visit, however, there were great blue herons in the water, and a sharp-eyed student spotted huckleberries growing along the bank, enough for two very tasty pies—reminders that it is hard to completely eradicate nature. We may have to work to see it, but it is there, even in the heavily industrialized city.

This changing sense of what was best for Houston crystallized in "Buffalo Bayou and Beyond: Visions, Strategies, and Actions for the Twenty-first Century." A long title for a huge plan. The project is, both in scope and in finances, typical of Houston at its most ambitious: the redevelopment of some ten miles of downtown bayou, to be completed over a twenty-year period, at a projected expense of $800 million.

The plan also was a stunningly attractive departure from business as usual in Houston—a needed fulcrum for how the city treats nature. It is by no means the first plan to beautify this bayou; there were at least twenty such proposals, of varying scopes, during the twentieth century. None of those earlier plans had either the range or the backing of this one, and most of them got nowhere. This was good news. It also has made it more uplifting to use the city as environmental text.

With the new plan, it suddenly seemed as if Houston was ready to move into a new growth stage, a maturity that honored, rather than degraded, the natural world. I went to the announcement, noted that several people talked with pride about "greening Houston," and left with only one nagging question. Some dignitary mentioned an aquarium, but I couldn't find it on my expensive, detailed take-home rendition of the plan. I wondered: do we need an aquarium there, right on the banks of the bayou? Even if the aquarium is presumed to have educational value, doesn't that make either one or the other of the two bodies of water— either the real bayou or the man-made aquarium—redundant?

I soon found out. On October 20, 2002, less than a month after the big introduction of "Buffalo Bayou and Beyond," the *Houston Chronicle* featured a front-page story praising a new draw for tourism and a boost for the economy: the Downtown Aquarium. The news that morning seemed so far from the elaborate press conference presentations that I had to read it several times. That was because the Downtown Aquarium is a mammoth business venture—a $38 million aquatic-themed entertainment center spread over six acres, featuring the following: a huge seafood restaurant, a 200,000-gallon shark tank with a mini-train running through it, the capacity to hold three thousand people at a time, and a merry-go-round with sea life rider seats near a ninety-foot Ferris wheel. At night, the Ferris wheel glows bright blue neon. This place is, beneath the self-serving designation of itself as an aquarium, a very large and Disney-fied Landry's seafood restaurant, one with a permanent carnival attached and several large fish tanks squeezed into a small space below the restaurant and gift shop. It was the first bayou project after the September "Buffalo Bayou and Beyond" announcement, *and* it was to be on six acres of public land. The land deal was so blatant that the Houston papers—even the alternative one—dodged the underlying issue.

The argument, widely circulated by word of mouth, was that the Ferris wheel and the carnival were needed to draw "more people" downtown. "To thereby build community as we build downtown." A key point was that "not everyone would go to the Wortham Center Opera House across the street."

Students study this decision, the company involved in it and its political connections, and what was written about it. We talk about the culture's need, first, to do away with nature and then to build commercial, profit-generating simulations of it, about what happens when city governments try to outsource the responsibility to provide parks for its citizens. The rationale for the city's aquarium decision, as I suggest to students before we walk this section of the bayou, underestimates both the power of nature and the priorities of the majority of those Houstonians who are working class or middle class. A real park could build a more inclusive community; the city's decision assumed, and thereby strengthened, a socioeconomic- (and often color-) based separation. People from all walks of life desire and deserve parks, both to enjoy the natural world and to enjoy sharing space with someone who is not just exactly like them.

Since the 2002 announcement, Buffalo Bayou has prospered. Two 30 stages of a beautiful and environmentally helpful redevelopment are done (and the two stages do include some areas with diverse residential demographics). Though I still contend that the permanent "seafood" carnival detracts from downtown and trashes the bayou, the overall Buffalo Bayou redevelopment progress has been good. Houston, downtown, on Buffalo Bayou, is making progress. It is green and spacious, with a good view of a mostly beautiful skyline (marred only by the bright neon Ferris wheel) in the distance, good trails, a great dog park, and the chance to see large turtles sunning themselves on bayou logs and many migrating birds in the spring and fall. I urge my students to walk there at least several times during the semester.

There is a certain pleasure and heuristic value, however, in the field study trip when the seminar goes downtown to walk the bayou. The discussions and readings work well, but the main field study segment of the class helps multiply the impact of the students' library and classroom work. However contradictory the term "urban nature walk" may sound, it works. It remains the best teaching tool that I have.

We start at Sabine Street and stroll down toward the aquarium. This juxtaposition of Buffalo Bayou and the aquarium entertainment complex built on its banks does have one redeeming virtue. It creates a serendipitous site for students to observe and learn about contemporary American culture and urban nature's contested place in it. On our way, we see turtles and birds—herons as well as egrets. Often, we see alligators. Students have already read a funny short story by Donald Barthelme, a legendary teacher in our graduate program. Barthelme's "Return" creates a contemporary urban everyman who returns to Houston and tries to connect with the city through nature, but who finally settles for a simulation of Southern nature, a nine-hundred-foot steel azalea.

When we get to the "aquarium," we note the exhibition room that displays stuffed or glassed-in versions of the local wildlife that we have just seen. The name over that door says "Louisiana Swamp." We pass it, and then head back up Buffalo Bayou. Students sometimes ask, "Where do they keep the steel azalea?"

Most of these seminar students will leave Houston. Only one or two from a class of fifteen will teach and write here. But whether they settle in small college towns or teach in urban universities across the country, they do leave with a sense of one city's efforts to re-green itself, and of its missteps and its successes. The degree of commitment will vary, but they are all to some degree part of a larger community that has started to recognize the importance of urban nature. They can take with them the knowledge that more than 80 percent of their students will live in cities, that city wilds and walks within these wilds are crucial if we are to expand America's environmental consciousness.

CONCLUSION

The Ship Channel and the bayou embody the two central attitudes 35 that the city of Houston has had toward the natural world—the Ship Channel expresses Houston's past, build-and-develop-the-hell-out-of-this-place-and-damn-the-consequences attitudes. It may someday get cleaned up a bit.

Upstream and uptown, there is Buffalo Bayou, increasingly seen as an "amenity," a way to attract the labor force, those imaginative city builders of the future—beautiful in itself and becoming developed, mostly, in ways that will enhance that beauty and the city's enjoyment of it. Houston's future, we hope, will include the beautification of other bayous. But certainly this is progress. Houston is not now and never will be Portland, or Boulder, or San Francisco. It is, however, now a city where community has begun to coalesce and grow around the idea of finding the place—the bayous, the trees, the neighborhoods—once hidden beneath our decades of determined growth into placelessness.

Cities, wild places before they became urban centers, can be made green again, and our students at the University of Houston and at Rice can someday support such a process wherever they live. They learn that they want a city with jobs and homes, *and* places that can embody what Terry Tempest Williams calls "the open space of democracy." They seek places where citizens of all kinds can go to renew their human connections and discover a larger sense of community, their ties to the green world that undergirds and supports the life of the city.

WORKS CITED

Barthelme, Donald. "Return." *The Teachings of Don B.* Print. New York: Turtle Bay Books, 1992.

Blackburn, Jim. *The Book of Texas Bays.* Print. College Station: Texas A&M University Press, 2004.

"Exxon Mobil Posts Largest Annual Profit for U.S. Company." *New York Times* 31 Jan. 2006. Web. 2 Sept. 2006.

Florida, Richard. *The Rise of the Creative Class.* Print. New York: Basic Books, 2002.

Gwynne, S. C. "Attack Here." *Texas Monthly* Nov. 2004. Posted on the Houston Architecture Info Forum, 1 Nov. 2004. Web. 4 Sept. 2006.

McAshan, Marie Phelps. *A Houston Legacy: On the Corner of Main and Texas.* Print. Houston: Hutchins House, 1985.

Minutaglio, Bill. *City on Fire: The Explosion That Devastated a Texas Town and Ignited a Historic Legal Battle.* Print. New York: Perennial, 2004.

The Port of Houston Magazine Jan./Feb. 2006. Print.

Sam Houston Boat Tour. The Port of Houston Authority, 2009. Web. 3 Sept. 2006.

Steingraber, Sandra. *Living Downstream*. Print. New York: Vintage Books, 1997.

Turner, Allan. "CEO Casts His Net for Downtown." *Houston Chronicle* 20 October 2002: A1. Web.

Williams, Terry Tempest. *The Open Space of Democracy*. Print. Barrington, MA: Orion Society, 2004.

STUDY QUESTIONS

1. Identify the authors of each section and explain where each took their classes. How do you think they each feel about Houston? Support your RESPONSE with passages from the essay.

2. When some authors write in COLLABORATION with others, the work takes on one VOICE and does not distinguish who writes what part. In this essay, however, readers can clearly tell that Slappey wrote one section and Dixon wrote the other. Evaluate their method of collaboration and determine if two voices detract from or add to the unity of the essay. Would you prefer reading an essay written in this way or one that has one voice? How would you prefer to write a collaborative essay?

3. What is the authors' THESIS? Where is it stated most directly? How do they support that thesis?

4. DESCRIPTION appears throughout the essay, with lots of concrete, specific details painting a picture of various places in Houston. What DOMINANT IMPRESSION of Houston do the authors create? What details contribute to this impression?

5. *For Writing.* Select a place that you feel is representative of the town you live in now or of your hometown—for instance, a local landmark, a natural feature like a beach or a mountain, or a well-known building. Write an essay in which you describe this place, creating an overall impression of it, and explain how it is representative of the town.

MAXINE HONG KINGSTON { *No Name Woman*

MAXINE HONG KINGSTON (b. 1940) is an award-winning novelist and
nonfiction writer. Born in Stockton, California, to Chinese immigrant parents, she earned her BA in English at the University of California, Berkeley,
in 1962 and her teaching certificate three years later. After a decade of teaching in Hawaii, Kingston published her first book, *The Woman Warrior:
Memoirs of a Girlhood among Ghosts* (1976), which received the National
Book Critics Award for Nonfiction. Kingston's other nonfiction works
include the National Book Award–winning *China Men* (1980) and *The Fifth
Book of Peace* (2006); she has also written a novel, *Tripmaster Monkey: His
Fake Book* (1989). In 1997 she received the National Humanities Medal
from President Bill Clinton.

   This selection from *The Woman Warrior* addresses the hard lives of
Kingston's female relatives in China, particularly her aunt, who became
pregnant out of wedlock and took her own life soon after giving birth.
Nobody in the family will say anything more about her, so Kingston imagines a variety of possible details about her aunt's pregnancy to fill in the gaps
left by a family who refuses even to say her name. Can you think of any cultural or social restrictions that apply to your own life? Do you accept them?
Challenge them?

"YOU MUST NOT TELL ANYONE," my mother said, "what I am about to
tell you. In China your father had a sister who killed herself. She
jumped into the family well. We say that your father has all brothers
because it is as if she had never been born.

"In 1924 just a few days after our village celebrated seventeen hurry-up weddings—to make sure that every young man who went 'out on the road' would responsibly come home—your father and his brothers and your grandfather and his brothers and your aunt's new husband sailed for America, the Gold Mountain.[1] It was your grandfather's last trip. Those lucky enough to get contracts waved good-bye from the decks. They fed and guarded the stowaways and helped them off in Cuba, New York, Bali, Hawaii. 'We'll meet in California next year,' they said. All of them sent money home.

"I remember looking at your aunt one day when she and I were dressing; I had not noticed before that she had such a protruding melon of a stomach. But I did not think, 'She's pregnant,' until she began to look like other pregnant women, her shirt pulling and the white tops of her black pants showing. She could not have been pregnant, you see, because her husband had been gone for years. No one said anything. We did not discuss it. In early summer she was ready to have the child, long after the time when it could have been possible.

"The village had also been counting. On the night the baby was to be born the villagers raided our house. Some were crying. Like a great saw, teeth strung with lights, files of people walked zigzag across our land, tearing the rice. Their lanterns doubled in the disturbed black water, which drained away through the broken bunds.[2] As the villagers closed in, we could see that some of them, probably men and women we knew well, wore white masks. The people with long hair hung it over their faces. Women with short hair made it stand up on end. Some had tied white bands around their foreheads, arms, and legs.

"At first they threw mud and rocks at the house. Then they threw eggs and began slaughtering our stock. We could hear the animals scream their deaths—the roosters, the pigs, a last great roar from the ox. Familiar wild heads flared in our night windows; the villagers encircled us. Some of the faces stopped to peer at us, their eyes rushing like searchlights. The hands flattened against the panes, framed heads, and left red prints.

---

[1] A Chinese nickname for America since the California Gold Rush of 1849.
[2] Low embankments that contain the water covering rice paddies.

"The villagers broke in the front and the back doors at the same time, even though we had not locked the doors against them. Their knives dripped with the blood of our animals. They smeared blood on the doors and walls. One woman swung a chicken, whose throat she had slit, splattering blood in red arcs about her. We stood together in the middle of our house, in the family hall with the pictures and tables of the ancestors around us, and looked straight ahead.

"At that time the house had only two wings. When the men came back, we would build two more to enclose our courtyard and a third one to begin a second courtyard. The villagers pushed through both wings, even your grandparents' rooms, to find your aunt's, which was also mine until the men returned. From this room a new wing for one of the younger families would grow. They ripped up her clothes and shoes and broke her combs, grinding them underfoot. They tore her work from the loom. They scattered the cooking fire and rolled the new weaving in it. We could hear them in the kitchen breaking our bowls and banging the pots. They overturned the great waist-high earthenware jugs; duck eggs, pickled fruits, vegetables burst out and mixed in acrid torrents. The old woman from the next field swept a broom through the air and loosed the spirits-of-the-broom over our heads. 'Pig.' 'Ghost.' 'Pig,' they sobbed and scolded while they ruined our house.

"When they left, they took sugar and oranges to bless themselves. They cut pieces from the dead animals. Some of them took bowls that were not broken and clothes that were not torn. Afterward we swept up the rice and sewed it back up into sacks. But the smells from the spilled preserves lasted. Your aunt gave birth in the pigsty that night. The next morning when I went for the water, I found her and the baby plugging up the family well.

"Don't let your father know that I told you. He denies her. Now that you have started to menstruate, what happened to her could happen to you. Don't humiliate us. You wouldn't like to be forgotten as if you had never been born. The villagers are watchful."

Whenever she had to warn us about life, my mother told stories that ran like this one, a story to grow up on. She tested our strength to establish realities. Those in the emigrant generations who could not reassert brute survival died young and far from home. Those of us in the first American generations have had to figure out how the invisible world the emigrants built around our childhoods fit in solid America.

The emigrants confused the gods by diverting their curses, misleading them with crooked streets and false names. They must try to confuse their offspring as well, who, I suppose, threaten them in similar ways—always trying to get things straight, always trying to name the unspeakable. The Chinese I know hide their names; sojourners take new names when their lives change and guard their real names with silence.

Chinese-Americans, when you try to understand what things in you are Chinese, how do you separate what is peculiar to childhood, to poverty, insanities, one family, your mother who marked your growing with stories, from what is Chinese? What is Chinese tradition and what is the movies?

If I want to learn what clothes my aunt wore, whether flashy or ordinary, I would have to begin, "Remember Father's drowned-in-the-well sister?" I cannot ask that. My mother has told me once and for all the useful parts. She will add nothing unless powered by Necessity, a riverbank that guides her life. She plants vegetable gardens rather than lawns; she carries the odd-shaped tomatoes home from the fields and eats food left for the gods.

Whenever we did frivolous things, we used up energy; we flew high kites. We children came up off the ground over the melting cones our parents brought home from work and the American movie on New Year's Day—*Oh, You Beautiful Doll* with Betty Grable one year, and *She Wore a Yellow Ribbon* with John Wayne[3] another year. After the one carnival ride each, we paid in guilt; our tired father counted his change on the dark walk home.

Adultery is extravagance. Could people who hatch their own chicks 15 and eat the embryos and the heads for delicacies and boil the feet in

---

[3]Academy Award–winning American actor (1907–79), known especially for his roles in Western films. His movie *She Wore a Yellow Ribbon* opened in 1949. *Betty Grable*: American actress (1916–73), famous as a pin-up girl during World War II. June Haver (1926–2005) actually played the lead in *Oh, You Beautiful Doll*, rather than Grable.

vinegar for party food, leaving only the gravel, eating even the gizzard lining—could such people engender a prodigal aunt? To be a woman, to have a daughter in starvation time was a waste enough. My aunt could not have been the lone romantic who gave up everything for sex. Women in the old China did not choose. Some man had commanded her to lie with him and be his secret evil. I wonder whether he masked himself when he joined the raid on her family.

Perhaps she encountered him in the fields or on the mountain where the daughters-in-law collected fuel. Or perhaps he first noticed her in the marketplace. He was not a stranger because the village housed no strangers. She had to have dealings with him other than sex. Perhaps he worked an adjoining field, or he sold her the cloth for the dress she sewed and wore. His demand must have surprised, then terrified her. She obeyed him; she always did as she was told.

When the family found a young man in the next village to be her husband, she stood tractably beside the best rooster, his proxy, and promised before they met that she would be his forever. She was lucky that he was her age and she would be the first wife, an advantage secure now. The night she first saw him, he had sex with her. Then he left for America. She had almost forgotten what he looked like. When she tried to envision him, she only saw the black and white face in the group photograph the men had had taken before leaving.

The other man was not, after all, much different from her husband. They both gave orders: she followed. "If you tell your family, I'll beat you. I'll kill you. Be here again next week." No one talked sex, ever. And she might have separated the rapes from the rest of living if only she did not have to buy her oil from him or gather wood in the same forest. I want her fear to have lasted just as long as rape lasted so that the fear could have been contained. No drawn-out fear. But women at sex hazarded birth and hence lifetimes. The fear did not stop but permeated everywhere. She told the man, "I think I'm pregnant." He organized the raid against her.

On nights when my mother and father talked about their life back home, sometimes they mentioned an "outcast table" whose business they still seemed to be settling, their voices tight. In a commensal tradition, where food is precious, the powerful older people made wrongdoers eat alone. Instead of letting them start separate new lives like the Japanese, who could become samurais and geishas, the Chinese family, faces averted but eyes glowering sideways, hung on to the offenders and fed them leftovers. My aunt must have lived in the same house as my parents and eaten at an outcast table. My mother spoke about the raid as if she had seen it, when she and my aunt, a daughter-in-law to a different household, should not have been living together at all. Daughters-in-law lived with their husbands' parents, not their own; a synonym for marriage in Chinese is "taking a daughter-in-law." Her husband's parents could have sold her, mortgaged her, stoned her. But they had sent her back to her own mother and father, a mysterious act hinting at disgraces not told me. Perhaps they had thrown her out to deflect the avengers.

She was the only daughter; her four brothers went with her father,   20 husband, and uncles "out on the road" and for some years became western men. When the goods were divided among the family, three of the brothers took land, and the youngest, my father, chose an education. After my grandparents gave their daughter away to her husband's family, they had dispensed all the adventure and all the property. They expected her alone to keep the traditional ways, which her brothers, now among the barbarians, could fumble without detection. The heavy, deep-rooted women were to maintain the past against the flood, safe for returning. But the rare urge west had fixed upon our family, and so my aunt crossed boundaries not delineated in space.

The work of preservation demands that the feelings playing about in one's guts not be turned into action. Just watch their passing like cherry blossoms. But perhaps my aunt, my forerunner, caught in a slow life, let dreams grow and fade and after some months or years went toward what persisted. Fear at the enormities of the forbidden kept her desires delicate, wire and bone. She looked at a man because she liked the way the hair was tucked behind his ears, or she liked the question-mark line of a long torso curving at the shoulder and straight at the hip. For warm eyes or a soft voice or a slow walk—that's all—a few hairs, a line, a brightness, a sound, a pace, she gave up family. She offered us up for a charm that vanished with tiredness, a pigtail that didn't toss when the wind died. Why, the wrong lighting could erase the dearest thing about him.

It could very well have been, however, that my aunt did not take subtle enjoyment of her friend, but, a wild woman, kept rollicking company. Imagining her free with sex doesn't fit, though. I don't know any women like that, or men either. Unless I see her life branching into mine, she gives me no ancestral help.

To sustain her being in love, she often worked at herself in the mirror, guessing at the colors and shapes that would interest him, changing them frequently in order to hit on the right combination. She wanted him to look back.

On a farm near the sea, a woman who tended her appearance reaped a reputation for eccentricity. All the married women blunt-cut their hair in flaps about their ears or pulled it back in tight buns. No nonsense. Neither style blew easily into heart-catching tangles. And at their weddings they displayed themselves in their long hair for the last time. "It brushed the backs of my knees," my mother tells me. "It was braided, and even so, it brushed the backs of my knees."

At the mirror my aunt combed individuality into her bob. A bun 25 could have been contrived to escape into black streamers blowing in the wind or in quiet wisps about her face, but only the older women in our picture album wear buns. She brushed her hair back from her forehead, tucking the flaps behind her ears. She looped a piece of thread, knotted into a circle between her index fingers and thumbs, and ran the double strand across her forehead. When she closed her fingers as if she were making a pair of shadow geese bite, the string twisted together catching the little hairs. Then she pulled the thread away from her skin, ripping the hairs out neatly, her eyes watering from the needles of pain. Opening her fingers, she cleaned the thread, then rolled it along her hairline and the tops of her eyebrows. My mother did the same to me and my sisters and herself. I used to believe that the expression "caught by the short hairs"[4] meant a captive held with a depilatory

---

[4]That is, to be held by the hairs at the nape of the neck, a position from which it is difficult to escape.

string. It especially hurt at the temples, but my mother said we were lucky we didn't have to have our feet bound when we were seven.[5] Sisters used to sit on their beds and cry together, she said, as their mothers or their slaves removed the bandages for a few minutes each night and let the blood gush back into their veins. I hope that the man my aunt loved appreciated a smooth brow, that he wasn't just a tits-and-ass man.

Once my aunt found a freckle on her chin, at a spot that the almanac said predestined her for unhappiness. She dug it out with a hot needle and washed the wound with peroxide.

More attention to her looks than these pullings of hairs and pickings at spots would have caused gossip among the villagers. They owned work clothes and good clothes, and they wore good clothes for feasting the new seasons. But since a woman combing her hair hexes beginnings, my aunt rarely found an occasion to look her best. Women looked like great sea snails—the corded wood, babies, and laundry they carried were the whorls on their backs. The Chinese did not admire a bent back; goddesses and warriors stood straight. Still there must have been a marvelous freeing of beauty when a worker laid down her burden and stretched and arched.

Such commonplace loveliness, however, was not enough for my aunt. She dreamed of a lover for the fifteen days of New Year's, the time for families to exchange visits, money, and food. She plied her secret comb. And sure enough she cursed the year, the family, the village, and herself.

Even as her hair lured her imminent lover, many other men looked at her. Uncles, cousins, nephews, brothers would have looked, too, had they been home between journeys. Perhaps they had already been restraining their curiosity, and they left, fearful that their glances, like a field of nesting birds, might be startled and caught. Poverty hurt, and that was their first reason for leaving. But another, final reason for leaving the crowded house was the never-said.

[5]For a thousand years until the early twentieth century, many Chinese families, particularly among the upper classes, bound girls' feet in tight wrappings in order to deform the feet and stunt their growth; Chinese custom held that tiny feet were beautiful and that they made girls more desirable, and hence more marriageable.

She may have been unusually beloved, the precious only daughter,
spoiled and mirror gazing because of the affection the family lavished
on her. When her husband left, they welcomed the chance to take her
back from the in-laws; she could live like the little daughter for just a
while longer. There are stories that my grandfather was different from
other people, "crazy ever since the little Jap bayoneted him in the
head." He used to put his naked penis on the dinner table, laughing.
And one day he brought home a baby girl, wrapped up inside his
brown western-style greatcoat. He had traded one of his sons, probably my father, the youngest, for her. My grandmother made him trade
back. When he finally got a daughter of his own, he doted on her. They
must have all loved her, except perhaps my father, the only brother
who never went back to China, having once been traded for a girl.

Brothers and sisters, newly men and women, had to efface their sexual color and present plain miens. Disturbing hair and eyes, a smile like
no other threatened the ideal of five generations living under one roof.
To focus blurs, people shouted face to face and yelled from room to
room. The immigrants I know have loud voices, unmodulated to
American tones even after years away from the village where they
called their friendships out across the fields. I have not been able to
stop my mother's screams in public libraries or over telephones.
Walking erect (knees straight, toes pointed forward, not pigeon-toed,
which is Chinese-feminine) and speaking in an inaudible voice, I have
tried to turn myself American-feminine. Chinese communication was
loud, public. Only sick people had to whisper. But at the dinner table,
where the family members came nearest one another, no one could
talk, not the outcasts nor any eaters. Every word that falls from the
mouth is a coin lost. Silently they gave an accepted food with both
hands. A preoccupied child who took his bowl with one hand got a
sideways glare. A complete moment of total attention is due everyone
alike. Children and lovers have no singularity here, but my aunt used a
secret voice, a separate attentiveness.

She kept the man's name to herself throughout her labor and dying;
she did not accuse him that he be punished with her. To save her
inseminator's name she gave silent birth.

He may have been somebody in her own household, but intercourse with a man outside the family would have been no less abhorrent. All the village were kinsmen, and the titles shouted in loud country voices never let kinship be forgotten. Any man within visiting distance would have been neutralized as a lover—"brother," "younger brother," "older brother"—one hundred and fifteen relationship titles. Parents researched birth charts probably not so much to assure good fortune as to circumvent incest in a population that has but one hundred surnames. Everybody has eight million relatives. How useless then sexual mannerisms, how dangerous.

As if it came from an atavism deeper than fear, I used to add "brother" silently to boys' names. It hexed the boys, who would or would not ask me to dance, and made them less scary and as familiar and deserving of benevolence as girls.

But, of course, I hexed myself also—no dates. I should have stood up, both arms waving, and shouted out across libraries, "Hey, you! Love me back." I had no idea, though, how to make attraction selective, how to control its direction and magnitude. If I made myself American-pretty so that the five or six Chinese boys in the class fell in love with me, everyone else—the Caucasian, Negro, and Japanese boys—would too. Sisterliness, dignified and honorable, made much more sense.

Attraction eludes control so stubbornly that whole societies designed to organize relationships among people cannot keep order, not even when they bind people to one another from childhood and raise them together. Among the very poor and the wealthy, brothers married their adopted sisters, like doves. Our family allowed some romance, paying adult brides' prices and providing dowries so that their sons and daughters could marry strangers. Marriage promises to turn strangers into friendly relatives—a nation of siblings.

In the village structure, spirits shimmered among the live creatures, balanced and held in equilibrium by time and land. But one human being flaring up into violence could open up a black hole, a maelstrom that pulled in the sky. The frightened villagers, who depended on one another to maintain the real, went to my aunt to show her a personal, physical representation of the break she had made in the "roundness." Misallying couples snapped off the future, which was to be embodied

35

in true offspring. The villagers punished her for acting as if she could have a private life, secret and apart from them.

If my aunt had betrayed the family at a time of large grain yields and peace, when many boys were born, and wings were being built on many houses, perhaps she might have escaped such severe punishment. But the men—hungry, greedy, tired of planting in dry soil, cuckolded—had had to leave the village in order to send food-money home. There were ghost plagues, bandit plagues, wars with the Japanese, floods. My Chinese brother and sister had died of an unknown sickness. Adultery, perhaps only a mistake during good times, became a crime when the village needed food.

The round moon cakes and round doorways, the round tables of graduated size that fit one roundness inside another, round windows and rice bowls—these talismen had lost their power to warn this family of the law: a family must be whole, faithfully keeping the descent line by having sons to feed the old and the dead, who in turn look after the family. The villagers came to show my aunt and her lover-in-hiding a broken house. The villagers were speeding up the circling of events because she was too shortsighted to see that her infidelity had already harmed the village, that waves of consequences would return unpredictably, sometimes in disguise, as now, to hurt her. This roundness had to be made coin-sized so that she would see its circumference: punish her at the birth of her baby. Awaken her to the inexorable. People who refused fatalism because they could invent small resources insisted on culpability. Deny accidents and wrest fault from the stars.

After the villagers left, their lanterns now scattering in various directions toward home, the family broke their silence and cursed her. "Aiaa, we're going to die. Death is coming. Death is coming. Look what you've done. You've killed us. Ghost! Dead ghost! Ghost! You've never been born." She ran out into the fields, far enough from the house so that she could no longer hear their voices, and pressed herself against the earth, her own land no more. When she felt the birth coming, she thought that she had been hurt. Her body seized together. "They've hurt me too much," she thought. "This is gall, and it will kill me." Her forehead and knees against the earth, her body convulsed and then released her onto her back. The black well of sky and stars

40

184

went out and out and out forever; her body and her complexity seemed to disappear. She was one of the stars, a bright dot in blackness, without home, without a companion, in eternal cold and silence. An agoraphobia rose in her, speeding higher and higher, bigger and bigger; she would not be able to contain it; there would be no end to fear.

Flayed, unprotected against space, she felt pain return, focusing her body. This pain chilled her—a cold, steady kind of surface pain. Inside, spasmodically, the other pain, the pain of the child, heated her. For hours she lay on the ground, alternately body and space. Sometimes a vision of normal comfort obliterated reality: she saw the family in the evening gambling at the dinner table, the young people massaging their elders' backs. She saw them congratulating one another, high joy on the mornings the rice shoots came up. When these pictures burst, the stars drew yet further apart. Black space opened.

She got to her feet to fight better and remembered that old-fashioned women gave birth in their pigsties to fool the jealous, paindealing gods, who do not snatch piglets. Before the next spasms could stop her, she ran to the pigsty, each step a rushing out into emptiness. She climbed over the fence and knelt in the dirt. It was good to have a fence enclosing her, a tribal person alone.

Laboring, this woman who had carried her child as a foreign growth that sickened her every day, expelled it at last. She reached down to touch the hot, wet, moving mass, surely smaller than anything human, and could feel that it was human after all—fingers, toes, nails, nose. She pulled it up on to her belly, and it lay curled there, butt in the air, feet precisely tucked one under the other. She opened her loose shirt and buttoned the child inside. After resting, it squirmed and thrashed and she pushed it up to her breast. It turned its head this way and that until it found her nipple. There, it made little snuffling noises. She clenched her teeth at its preciousness, lovely as a young calf, a piglet, a little dog.

She may have gone to the pigsty as a last act of responsibility: she would protect this child as she had protected its father. It would look after her soul, leaving supplies on her grave. But how would this tiny child without family find her grave when there would be no marker for her anywhere, neither in the earth nor the family hall? No one would give her a family hall name. She had taken the child with her into the wastes. At its birth the two of them had felt the same raw pain of separation, a wound that only the family pressing tight could close. A child with no descent line would not soften her life but only trail after her, ghost-like, begging her to give it purpose. At dawn the villagers on their way to the fields would stand around the fence and look.

Full of milk, the little ghost slept. When it awoke, she hardened her 45 breasts against the milk that crying loosens. Toward morning she picked up the baby and walked to the well.

Carrying the baby to the well shows loving. Otherwise abandon it. Turn its face into the mud. Mothers who love their children take them along. It was probably a girl; there is some hope of forgiveness for boys.

"Don't tell anyone you had an aunt. Your father does not want to hear her name. She has never been born." I have believed that sex was unspeakable and words so strong and fathers so frail that "aunt" would do my father mysterious harm. I have thought that my family, having settled among immigrants who had also been their neighbors in the ancestral land, needed to clean their name, and a wrong word would incite the kinspeople even here. But there is more to this silence: they want me to participate in her punishment. And I have.

In the twenty years since I heard this story I have not asked for details nor said my aunt's name; I do not know it. People who can comfort the dead can also chase after them to hurt them further—a reverse ancestor worship. The real punishment was not the raid swiftly inflicted by the villagers, but the family's deliberately forgetting her. Her betrayal so maddened them, they saw to it that she would suffer forever, even after death. Always hungry, always needing, she would have to beg food from other ghosts, snatch and steal it from those whose living descendants give them gifts. She would have to fight the ghosts massed at crossroads for the buns a few thoughtful citizens leave to decoy her away from village and home so that the ancestral spirits could feast unharassed. At peace, they could act like gods, not ghosts, their descent lines providing them with paper suits and dresses, spirit money, paper houses, paper automobiles, chicken, meat, and rice into eternity—essences delivered up in smoke and flames, steam and incense rising from each rice bowl.

In an attempt to make the Chinese care for people outside the family, Chairman Mao[6] encourages us now to give our paper replicas to the spirits of outstanding soldiers and workers, no matter whose ancestors they may be. My aunt remains forever hungry. Goods are not distributed evenly among the dead.

My aunt haunts me—her ghost drawn to me because now, after fifty years of neglect, I alone devote pages of paper to her, though not origamied into houses and clothes. I do not think she always means me well. I am telling on her, and she was a spite suicide, drowning herself in the drinking water. The Chinese are always very frightened of the drowned one, whose weeping ghost, wet hair hanging and skin bloated, waits silently by the water to pull down a substitute.

[6]Mao Zedong (1893–1976), as chairman of the Chinese Communist Party, became the supreme leader of China following the overthrow of the Nationalist government by Communist forces in 1949.

STUDY QUESTIONS

1. Why does the NARRATOR's aunt jump into the family well? What is the family's reaction to her death? What is the narrator's?

2. What kinds of stories does the narrator tell about her aunt and why does she tell them? What DESCRIPTIVE details does she emphasize? How does the narrator's *own* story fit into the stories about her aunt?

3. REFLECT on how Kingston uses the image of a ghost throughout the narrative. How does it contribute to your understanding of the story?

4. *For Writing.* How is female identity linked to culture? How can it overcome cultural limitations? In an essay, explore this issue, using examples from Kingston's NARRATIVE to support your THESIS.

JONATHAN RAUCH { *What Is Marriage For?*

JONATHAN RAUCH (b. 1960), a senior writer for the *National Journal* and guest scholar at the Brookings Institution, grew up in Phoenix, Arizona, and earned his undergraduate degree at Yale University. Much of Rauch's writing focuses on political policy issues, including such diverse topics as agriculture, gay marriage, and animal rights. Awarded the National Magazine Award for his columns and commentary, Rauch has written countless articles and several books, including *The Outnation: A Search for the Soul of Japan* (1992) and *Government's End: Why Washington Stopped Working* (1999).

In this selection from *Gay Marriage: Why It Is Good for Gays, Good for Straights, and Good for America* (2004), Rauch argues that "what makes marriage marriage" is the commitment to take care of each other. That commitment, he says, is at the heart of the legal privileges that accompany marriage, society's attitude toward marriage, and even the traditional marriage vows that date from the seventeenth century. As you read, consider the implications of Rauch's argument for the debate on gay marriage.

* * *

I HAVE A GOOD JOB. I have money. I have health insurance. I have friends. I have relatives. But my relatives live far away. My friends are busy. And no amount of money can allay what has to be one of the most elemental fears humans can know: the fear of enduring some catastrophe alone. Tomorrow, maybe, my little car gets hit by a big bus.

Everything goes black. When I awake, I am surrounded by doctors and nurses, but without someone there especially for me, I am alone in the sense that matters most. I lose the power to work or walk or feed myself. A service comes by to check on me once a day. Meals on Wheels brings lunch. Nonetheless, I am alone. No one is there for *me*. God forbid it should ever happen. But we all know the fear.

Society worries, too. An enormous problem for society is what to do when someone is beset by catastrophe. It could be cancer, a broken back, unemployment, depression; it could be exhaustion from work, stress under pressure, or an all-consuming rage. From society's point of view, an unattached person is an accident waiting to happen. The burdens of contingency are likely to fall, immediately and sometimes crushingly, on people—relatives, friends, neighbors—who have enough problems of their own, and then on charities and welfare agencies. We all suffer periods of illness, sadness, distress, fury. What happens to us, and what happens to the people around us, when we desperately need a hand but find none to hold?

If marriage has any meaning at all, it is that when you collapse from a stroke, there will be another person whose "job" is to drop everything and come to your aid. Or that when you come home after being fired, there will be someone to talk you out of committing a massacre or killing yourself. To be married is to know there is someone out there for whom you are always first in line.

No group could make such a commitment in quite the same way, because of a free-rider problem. If I were to marry three or four people, the pool of potential caregivers would be larger, but the situation would, perversely, make all of them less reliable: each could expect one of the others to take care of me (and each may be reluctant to do more than any of the others are willing to do—a common source of conflict among siblings who need to look after an aging parent). The pair bond, one to one, is the only kind which is inescapably reciprocal, perfectly mutual. Because neither of us has anyone else, we are there for each other.

All by itself, marriage is society's first and, often, second and third line of support for the troubled individual. A husband or wife is the social worker of first resort, the psychiatrist of first resort, the cop and counselor and insurer and nurse and 911 operator of first resort. 5

Married people are happier, healthier, and live longer; married men have lower rates of homicide, suicide, accidents, and mental illness. In 1858, reports Graff,[1] a British public-health statistician named William Farr noticed that, on average, married people outlive singles. "Marriage," said Farr, "is a healthy state. The single individual is much more likely to be wrecked on his voyage than the lives joined together in matrimony." Graff goes on to say:

> The data have been eerily consistent ever since: whether measuring by death rate, morbidity (health problems such as diabetes, kidney disease, or ischemic heart disease), subjective or stress-related complaints (dizziness, shortness of breath, achiness, days in bed during past year, asthma, headaches), or psychiatric problems (clinical depression or debilitating anxiety after a cancer diagnosis), married people do better than unmarried—single, widowed, divorced.

Might that just be because healthier people are more likely to marry? Maybe. But the conclusion remains the same even when studies compare matched populations, factor out confounding variables, or follow individuals over time. Moreover, married people do better than cohabiting couples, and their unions are more enduring—and, again, the generalization seems to hold even when researchers account for the fact that cohabitors and married people may be different. Marriage itself appears to be good for you. Why? I'm sure the answer is complicated. But in large part it must boil down to something pretty simple. Married people have someone to look after them, and they know it.

• ○ •

The gay-marriage debate is a storm that swirls around a single question. What makes marriage marriage? That is, what are marriage's essential attributes, and what are its incidental ones? As we will see, various people give various answers. They point to children, for instance. Or the ability to have children. Or heterosexual intercourse. Or monogamy. Clearly, marriage has many important attributes, and

---

[1] E. J. Graff, author of *What Is Marriage For?: The Strange Social History of Our Most Intimate Institution* (1999).

it would be unrealistic to expect agreement on what counts the most. But I think one attribute is more important than any of the others. If I had to pare marriage to its essential core, I would say that marriage is two people's lifelong commitment, recognized by law and by society, to care for each other. To get married is to put yourself in another person's hands, and to promise to take that person into your hands, and to do so within a community which expects both of you to keep your word.

Because, in theory, there is no reason why a male-male or female-female couple could not make and sustain the promise of lifelong caregiving, opponents of same-sex marriage are reluctant to put the caregiving commitment at the heart, rather than the periphery, of marriage. Against them, I adduce what I think are three strong kinds of evidence that caregiving is at the core of marriage: law, social opinion, and something else.

Law, as I said earlier, says almost nothing about what married people must do in order to be married; but it does weave a dense entanglement of prerogatives and special standings around any couple legally deemed to be wed. Spouses are generally exempted from having to testify against each other in court. They can make life-or-death decisions on each other's behalf in case of incapacity. They have hospital visitation rights. A doctor cannot refuse to tell them their spouse's condition. They have inheritance rights. They can file taxes as a single unit. On and on. The vast majority of the ways in which the law recognizes marriage—practically all of them, if you stop to think about it—aim at facilitating and bolstering the caregiving commitment. They are tools of trust and teamwork. A husband can speak to his wife candidly without fear that she will be served with a subpoena and rat him out. When one spouse is gravely ill, doctors and friends and other family members defer to the second spouse as caregiver in chief. Because spouses make a unique commitment to care for each other in life, their assets are presumed to merge when one of them dies—a recognition of what each has given up for the other. Most of what are usually thought of as the legal benefits of marriage are really gifts with strings attached. Or maybe strings with gifts attached. The law is saying: "You have a unique responsibility to care for each other. Here are the tools. Do your job."

Marriage creates kin. In olden times, marriage merged families to create alliances between clans. Today, marriage takes two people who are (except very rarely) not even remotely related and makes them each other's closest kin. Matrimony creates family out of thin air. Children cannot do this, nor can money, monogamy (that's just "going steady"), or lawyers. Only marriage does it.

Social opinion, I think, follows the same principle. Legally speaking, spouses are married until officially divorced. Socially speaking, however, under what circumstance would you regard someone as not just an imperfect spouse but as a nullifier of the marriage compact—a nonspouse? Adultery springs to mind. But the world is full of spouses who cheat or have cheated and who still manage to carry on in marriage. About 20 percent of American husbands admit to infidelity. Perhaps the betrayed spouse doesn't know, or knows but has forgiven, or has decided to live with the situation. I know more than one couple who have been through an adultery crisis and survived. An adulterous spouse is not a good spouse but, in the eyes of most people, would be a flawed spouse rather than a nonspouse.

What would lead me to think of someone as a nonspouse? Only, I think, abandonment. Mrs. Smith is diagnosed with a brain tumor. She will need treatment and care. Mr. Smith, an able-bodied adult with no history of mental illness, responds by leaving town. Now and then he calls her, chats for a few minutes as a friend might do, and then goes on about his business. He leaves Mrs. Smith in the hands of her sister, who has to fly in from Spokane. When the doctors call, he lets the answering machine take a message. "She can sign on our bank account," he says. "Let her hire help."

I have heard of people getting divorced in the face of a crisis. But I have never heard of anyone behaving like Mr. Smith while claiming to be married; and if Mr. Smith behaved that way, even his closest friends would think him beyond the pale. They would say he was having a breakdown—"not himself" (meaning, no longer the husband Mrs. Smith thought she had). Everyone else would just be shocked. Mrs. Smith, if she survived, would get a divorce.

Decent opinion has understood for centuries that, whatever else marriage may be, it is a commitment to be there. In 1547 (according to Graff), Archbishop Thomas Cranmer wrote that marriage is for "mutual society, help, and comfort, that the one ought to have of the other, both in prosperity and in adversity." I mentioned a third strong kind of evidence for my view that the prime-caregiver status is the sine qua non[2] of marriage. Here it is:

> *To have and to hold from this day forward, for better for worse, for richer for poorer, in sickness and in health, to love, cherish, and to obey, till death us do part.*

I doubt there is a single grown-up person of sound mind in America 15 who does not know what those words signify. They are from the Book of Common Prayer, dating from 1662. "Obey" is gone today, but otherwise not much has changed in four-and-a-half centuries:

> *Wilt thou love her, comfort her, honor and keep her in sickness and in health; and, forsaking all others, keep thee only unto her, so long as ye both shall live?*

So go the ancient vows, the first for her, the second for him. The text speaks twice of care and comfort "in sickness and in health," twice of love, twice of a lifetime bond. Those three, it implies, are interwoven: the commitment to care for another for life is the love which exceeds all others, the love of another even above oneself. There is no promise of children here, either to have them or to raise them, no mention of sex, no mention of inheritance, not a word about personal fulfillment. Perhaps the writers of the vow meant to put in those things but forgot. Or perhaps they placed at the center of marriage what most married people today also place there: "in sickness and in health, to love and cherish, till death us do part."

---

[2] Something absolutely essential (Latin, "without which not").

STUDY QUESTIONS

1. What are the three pieces of EVIDENCE Rauch presents in support of his ARGUMENT that caregiving is the chief function of marriage? How effective do you find this evidence?

2. Although the title of his book is *Gay Marriage: Why It Is Good for Gays, Good for Straights, and Good for America,* Rauch mentions gay marriage only in paragraphs 7 and 8 of this excerpt. How does this selection nevertheless advance Rauch's larger argument in favor of gay marriage?

3. Who is the author's likely AUDIENCE? In what ways does he address his readers? How does he try to connect with them?

4. *For Writing.* Consider what makes a good marriage and how people can make their marriages endure. Write a PROCESS ANALYSIS essay in which you DEFINE what a good marriage is and explain what steps a couple should take to overcome difficulties. You might want to interview married couples, from those who have been married for a long time to newlyweds, as well as divorced couples and couples who never married at all.

ERIC SCHLOSSER { *Why McDonald's*

French Fries

Taste So Good

ERIC SCHLOSSER (b. 1959) received his BA from Princeton University and his MA from Oxford University. A contributing editor for *The Atlantic Monthly*, Schlosser has also had articles published in *Rolling Stone, Vanity Fair, The Nation,* and *The New Yorker.* His book *Reefer Madness* (2003) probes America's anti-marijuana laws and the "war on drugs." Schlosser's best-known book is *Fast Food Nation* (2001), from which this selection was taken.

In this expository essay, Schlosser moves outward from the specific example of McDonald's French fries to examine the processed-food industry, how our sense of taste works, artificial additives, and the chemistry of "flavor." He describes the various ways manufacturers make food taste the way it does in order to satisfy—and create—consumer demand. Additionally, Schlosser demonstrates how industry profits from the preferences consumers formed in childhood and points out legal but possibly deadly ommissions from food ingredient labels. In other words, the author reveals that there is a lot more to the food industry than just food.

THE FRENCH FRY WAS "ALMOST sacrosanct for me," Ray Kroc, one of the founders of McDonald's, wrote in his autobiography,"its preparation a ritual to be followed religiously." During the chain's early years french fries were made from scratch every day. Russet Burbank potatoes were peeled, cut into shoestrings, and fried in McDonald's kitchens. As the chain expanded nationwide, in the mid-1960s, it sought to cut labor costs, reduce the number of suppliers, and ensure that its fries tasted the same at every restaurant. McDonald's began switching to frozen french fries in 1966—and few customers noticed the difference. Nevertheless, the change had a profound effect on the nation's agriculture and diet. A familiar food had been transformed into a highly processed industrial commodity. McDonald's fries now come from huge manufacturing plants that can peel, slice, cook, and freeze two million pounds of potatoes a day. The rapid expansion of McDonald's and the popularity of its low-cost, mass-produced fries changed the way Americans eat. In 1960 Americans consumed an average of about eighty-one pounds of fresh potatoes and four pounds of frozen french fries. In 2000 they consumed an average of about fifty pounds of fresh potatoes and thirty pounds of frozen fries. Today McDonald's is the largest buyer of potatoes in the United States.

The taste of McDonald's french fries played a crucial role in the chain's success—fries are much more profitable than hamburgers—and was long praised by customers, competitors, and even food critics. James Beard[1] loved McDonald's fries. Their distinctive taste does not stem from the kind of potatoes that McDonald's buys, the technology that processes them, or the restaurant equipment that fries them: other chains use Russet Burbanks, buy their french fries from the same large processing companies, and have similar fryers in their restaurant kitchens. The taste of a french fry is largely determined by the cooking oil. For decades McDonald's cooked its french fries in a mixture of about seven percent cottonseed oil and 93 percent beef tallow. The mixture gave the fries their unique flavor—and more saturated beef fat per ounce than a McDonald's hamburger.

In 1990, amid a barrage of criticism over the amount of cholesterol in its fries, McDonald's switched to pure vegetable oil. This presented the company with a challenge: how to make fries that subtly taste like beef without cooking them in beef tallow. A look at the ingredients in McDonald's french fries suggests how the problem was solved. Toward the end of the list is a seemingly innocuous yet oddly mysterious phrase: "natural flavor." That ingredient helps to explain not only

---

[1] American food writer and chef (1903–85).

why the fries taste so good but also why most fast food—indeed, most of the food Americans eat today—tastes the way it does.

Open your refrigerator, your freezer, your kitchen cupboards, and look at the labels on your food. You'll find "natural flavor" or "artificial flavor" in just about every list of ingredients. The similarities between these two broad categories are far more significant than the differences. Both are man-made additives that give most processed food most of its taste. People usually buy a food item the first time because of its packaging or appearance. Taste usually determines whether they buy it again. About 90 percent of the money that Americans now spend on food goes to buy processed food. The canning, freezing, and dehydrating techniques used in processing destroy most of food's flavor—and so a vast industry has arisen in the United States to make processed food palatable. Without this flavor industry today's fast food would not exist. The names of the leading American fast-food chains and their best-selling menu items have become embedded in our popular culture and famous worldwide. But few people can name the companies that manufacture fast food's taste.

The flavor industry is highly secretive. Its leading companies will   5 not divulge the precise formulas of flavor compounds or the identities of clients. The secrecy is deemed essential for protecting the reputations of beloved brands. The fast-food chains, understandably, would like the public to believe that the flavors of the food they sell somehow originate in their restaurant kitchens, not in distant factories run by other firms. A McDonald's french fry is one of countless foods whose flavor is just a component in a complex manufacturing process. The look and the taste of what we eat now are frequently deceiving—by design.

THE FLAVOR CORRIDOR

The New Jersey Turnpike runs through the heart of the flavor industry, an industrial corridor dotted with refineries and chemical plants. International Flavors & Fragrances (IFF), the world's largest flavor company, has a manufacturing facility off Exit 8A in Dayton, New Jersey; Givaudan, the world's second-largest flavor company, has a plant in East Hanover. Haarmann & Reimer, the largest German flavor company, has a plant in Teterboro, as does Takasago, the largest Japanese flavor company. Flavor Dynamics had a plant in South Plainfield; Frutarom is in North Bergen; Elan Chemical is in Newark. Dozens of companies manufacture flavors in the corridor between Teaneck and South Brunswick. Altogether the area produces about two thirds of the flavor additives sold in the United States.

The IFF plant in Dayton is a huge pale-blue building with a modern office complex attached to the front. It sits in an industrial park, not far from a BASF plastics factory, a Jolly French Toast factory, and a plant that manufactures Liz Claiborne cosmetics. Dozens of tractor-trailers were parked at the IFF loading dock the afternoon I visited, and a thin cloud of steam floated from a roof vent. Before entering the plant, I signed a nondisclosure form, promising not to reveal the brand names of foods that contain IFF flavors. The place reminded me of Willy Wonka's chocolate factory.[2] Wonderful smells drifted through the hallways, men and women in neat white lab coats cheerfully went about their work, and hundreds of little glass bottles sat on laboratory tables and shelves. The bottles contained powerful but fragile flavor chemicals, shielded from light by brown glass and round white caps shut tight. The long chemical names on the little white labels were as mystifying to me as medieval Latin. These odd-sounding things would be mixed and poured and turned into new substances, like magic potions.

I was not invited into the manufacturing areas of the IFF plant, where, it was thought, I might discover trade secrets. Instead I toured various laboratories and pilot kitchens, where the flavors of well-established brands are tested or adjusted, and where whole new flavors are created. IFF's snack-and-savory lab is responsible for the flavors of potato chips, corn chips, breads, crackers, breakfast cereals, and pet food. The confectionery lab devises flavors for ice cream, cookies, candies, toothpastes, mouthwashes, and antacids. Everywhere I looked, I saw famous, widely advertised products sitting on laboratory desks

---

[2]A reference to the 1964 novel by Roald Dahl, *Charlie and the Chocolate Factory*, which was adapted into the 1971 movie *Willy Wonka and the Chocolate Factory*.

and tables. The beverage lab was full of brightly colored liquids in clear bottles. It comes up with flavors for popular soft drinks, sports drinks, bottled teas, and wine coolers, for all-natural juice drinks, organic soy drinks, beers, and malt liquors. In one pilot kitchen I saw a dapper food technologist, a middle-aged man with an elegant tie beneath his crisp lab coat, carefully preparing a batch of cookies with white frosting and pink-and-white sprinkles. In another pilot kitchen I saw a pizza oven, a grill, a milk-shake machine, and a french fryer identical to those I'd seen at innumerable fast-food restaurants.

In addition to being the world's largest flavor company, IFF manufactures the smells of six of the ten best-selling fine perfumes in the United States, including Estée Lauder's Beautiful, Clinique's Happy, Lancôme's Tresor, and Calvin Klein's Eternity. It also makes the smells of household products such as deodorant, dishwashing detergent, bath soap, shampoo, furniture polish, and floor wax. All these aromas are made through essentially the same process: the manipulation of volatile chemicals. The basic science behind the scent of your shaving cream is the same as that governing the flavor of your TV dinner.

"NATURAL" AND "ARTIFICIAL"

Scientists now believe that human beings acquired the sense of taste   10 as a way to avoid being poisoned. Edible plants generally taste sweet, harmful ones bitter. The taste buds on our tongues can detect the presence of half a dozen or so basic tastes, including sweet, sour, bitter, salty, astringent, and umami, a taste discovered by Japanese researchers—a rich and full sense of deliciousness triggered by amino acids in foods such as meat, shellfish, mushrooms, potatoes, and seaweed. Taste buds offer a limited means of detection, however, compared with the human olfactory system, which can perceive thousands of different chemical aromas. Indeed, "flavor" is primarily the smell of gases being released by the chemicals you've just put in your mouth. the aroma of a food can be responsible for as much as 90 percent of its taste.

The act of drinking, sucking, or chewing a substance releases its volatile gases. They flow out of your mouth and up your nostrils, or up the passageway in the back of your mouth, to a thin layer of nerve cells called the olfactory epithelium, located at the base of your nose, right between your eyes. Your brain combines the complex smell signals from your olfactory epithelium with the simple taste signals from your tongue, assigns a flavor to what's in your mouth, and decides if it's something you want to eat.

A person's food preferences, like his or her personality, are formed during the first few years of life, through a process of socialization. Babies innately prefer sweet tastes and reject bitter ones; toddlers can learn to enjoy hot and spicy food, bland health food, or fast food, depending on what the people around them eat. The human sense of smell is still not fully understood. It is greatly affected by psychological factors and expectations. The mind focuses intently on some of the aromas that surround us and filters out the overwhelming majority. People can grow accustomed to bad smells or good smells; they stop noticing what once seemed overpowering. Aroma and memory are somehow inextricably linked. A smell can suddenly evoke a long-forgotten moment. The flavors of childhood foods seem to leave an indelible mark, and adults often return to them, without always knowing why. These "comfort foods" become a source of pleasure and reassurance— a fact that fast-food chains use to their advantage. Childhood memories of Happy Meals, which come with french fries, can translate into frequent adult visits to McDonald's. On average, Americans now eat about four servings of french fries every week.

The human craving for flavor has been a largely unacknowledged and unexamined force in history. For millennia royal empires have been built, unexplored lands traversed, and great religions and philosophies forever changed by the spice trade. In 1492 Chirstopher Columbus set sail to find seasoning. Today the influence of flavor in the world marketplace is no less decisive. The rise and fall of corporate empires—of soft-drink companies, snack-food companies, and fast-food chains—is often determined by how their products taste.

The flavor industry emerged in the mid-nineteenth century, as processed foods began to be manufactured on a large scale. Recognizing the need for flavor additives, early food processors turned to perfume companies that had long experience working with essential oils and volatile aromas. The great perfume houses of England, France, and the Netherlands produced many of the first flavor compounds. In the early part of the twentieth century Germany took the technological lead in flavor production, owing to its powerful chemical industry. Legend has it that a German scientist discovered methyl anthranilate, one of the first artificial flavors, by accident while mixing chemicals in his laboratory. Suddenly the lab was filled with the sweet smell of grapes. Methyl anthranilate later became the chief flavor compound in grape Kool-Aid. After World War II much of the perfume industry shifted from Europe to the United States, settling in New York City near the garment district and the fashion houses. The flavor industry came with it, later moving to New Jersey for greater plant capacity. Man-made flavor additives were used mostly in baked goods, candies, and sodas until the 1950s, when sales of processed food began to soar. The invention of gas chromatographs and mass spectrometers—machines capable of detecting volatile gases at low levels—vastly increased the number of flavors that could be synthesized. By the mid-1960s flavor companies were churning out compounds to supply the taste of Pop Tarts, Bac-Os, Tab, Tang, Filet-O-Fish sandwiches, and literally thousands of other new foods.

The American flavor industry now has annual revenues of about $1.4 billion. Approximately 10,000 new processed-food products are introduced every year in the United States. Almost all of them require flavor additives. And about nine out of ten of these products fail. The latest flavor innovations and corporate realignments are heralded in publications such as *Chemical Market Reporter, Food Chemical News, Food Engineering,* and *Food Product Design.* The progress of IFF has mirrored that of the flavor industry as a whole. IFF was formed in 1958, through the merger of two small companies. Its annual revenues have grown almost fifteenfold since the early 1970s, and it currently has manufacturing facilities in twenty countries. 15

Today's sophisticated spectrometers, gas chromatographs, and headspace-vapor analyzers provide a detailed map of a food's flavor components, detecting chemical aromas present in amounts as low as one part per billion. The human nose, however, is even more sensitive. A nose can detect aromas present in quantities of a few parts per trillion—an amount equivalent to about 0.000000000003 percent. Complex aromas, such as those of coffee and roasted meat, are composed of volatile gases from nearly a thousand differnet chemicals. The smell of a strawberry arises from the interaction of about 350 chemicals that are present in minute amounts. The quality that people seek most of all in a food—flavor—is usually present in a quantity too infinitesimal to be measured in traditional culinary terms such as ounces or teaspoons. The chemical that provides the dominant flavor of bell pepper can be tasted in amounts as low as 0.02 parts per billion; one drop is sufficient to add flavor to five average-size swimming pools. The flavor additive usually comes next to last in a processed food's list of ingredients and often costs less than its packaging. Soft drinks contain a larger proportion of flavor additives than most products. The flavor in a twelve-ounce can of Coke costs about half a cent.

The color additives in processed foods are usually present in even smaller amounts than the flavor compounds. Many of New Jersey's flavor companies also manufacture these color additives, which are used to make processed foods look fresh and appealing. Food coloring serves many of the same decorative purposes as lipstick, eye shadow, mascara—and is often made from the same pigments. Titanium dioxide, for example, has proved to be an especially versatile mineral. It gives many processed candies, frostings and icings their bright white color; it is a common ingredient in women's cosmetics; and it is the pigment used in many white oil paints and house paints. At Burger King, Wendy's, and McDonald's coloring agents have been added to many of the soft drinks, salad dressings, cookies, condiments, chicken dishes, and sandwich buns.

Studies have found that the color of a food can greatly affect how its taste is perceived. Brightly colored foods frequently seem to taste better than bland-looking foods, even when the flavor compounds are identical. Foods that somehow look off-color often seem to have off tastes. For thousands of years human beings have relied on visual cues to help determine what is edible. The color of fruit suggests whther it is ripe, the color of meat whether it is rancid. Flavor researchers sometimes use colored lights to modify the influence of visual cues during taste tests. During one experiment in the early 1970s people were served an oddly tinted meal of steak and french fries that appeared normal beneath colored lights. Everyone thought the meal tasted fine until the lighting was changed. Once it became apparent that the steak was actually blue and the fries were green, some people became ill.

The federal Food and Drug Administration does not require companies to disclose the ingredients of their color or flavor additives so long as all the chemicals in them are considered by the agency to be GRAS ("generally recognized as safe"). This enables companies to maintain the secrecy of their formulas. It also hides the fact that flavor compounds often contain more ingredients than the foods to which they give taste. The phrase "artificial strawberry flavor" gives little hint of the chemical wizardry and manufacturing skill that can make a highly processed food taste like strawberries. A typical artificial strawberry flavor, like the kind found in a Burger King strawberry milk shake, contains the following ingredients: amyl acetate, amyl butyrate, amyl valerate, anethol, anisyl formate, benzyl acetate, benzyl isobutyrate, butyric acid, cinnamyl isobutyrate, cinnamyl valerate, cognac essential oil, diacetyl, dipropyl ketone, ethyl acetate, ethyl amyl ketone, ethyl butyrate, ethyl cinnamate, ethyl heptanoate, ethyl heptylate, ethyl lactate, ethyl methylphenylglycideate, ethyl nitrate, ethyl propionate, ethyl valerate, heliotropin, hydroxyphenyl-2-butanone (10 percent solution in alcohol), a-ionone, isobutyl anthranilate, isobutyl butyrate, lemon essential oil, maltol, 4-methylacetophenone, methyl anthranilate, methyl benzoate, methyl cinnamate, methyl heptine carbonate, methyl naphthyl ketone, methyl salicylate, mint essential oil, neroli essential oil, nerolin, neryl isobutyrate, orris butter, phenethyl alcohol, rose, rum ether, gamma-undecalactone, vanillin, and solvent.

Although flavors usually arise from a mixture of many different 20 volatile chemicals, often a single compound supplies the dominant aroma. Smelled alone, that chemical provides an unmistakable sense of the food. Ethyl-2-methyl butyrate, for example, smells just like an apple. Many of today's highly processed foods offer a blank palette:

whatever chemicals are added to them will give them specific tastes. Adding methyl-2-pyridyl ketone makes something taste like popcorn. Adding ethyl-3-hydroxy butanoate makes it taste like marshmallow. The possibilities are now almost limitless. Without affecting appearance or nutritional value, processed foods could be made with aroma chemicals such as hexanal (the smell of freshly cut grass), or 3-methyl butanoic acid (the smell of body odor).

The 1960s were the heyday of artificial flavors in the United States. The synthetic versions of flavor compounds were not subtle, but they did not have to be, given the nature of most processed food. For the past twenty years food processors have tried hard to use only "natural flavors" in their products. According to the FDA, these must be derived entirely from natural sources—from herbs, spices, fruits, vegetables, beef, chicken, yeast, bark, roots, and so forth. Consumers prefer to see natural flavors on a label, out of a belief that they are more healthful. Distinctions between artificial and natural flavors can be arbitrary and somewhat absurd, based more on how the flavor has been made than on what it actually contains.

"A natural flavor," says Terry Acree, a professor of food science at Cornell University, "is a flavor that's been derived with an out-of-date technology." Natural flavors and artificial flavors sometimes contain exactly the same chemicals, produced through different methods. Amyl acetate, for example, provides the dominant note of banana flavor. When it is distilled from bananas with a solvent, amyl acetate is a natural flavor. When it is produced by mixing vinegar with amyl alcohol and adding sulfuric acid as a catalyst, amyl acetate is an artificial flavor. Either way it smells and tastes the same. "Natural flavor" is now listed among the ingredients of everything from Health Valley Blueberry Granola Bars to Taco Bell Hot Taco Sauce.

A natural flavor is not necessarily more healthful or purer than an artificial one. When almond flavor—benzaldehyde—is derived from natural sources, such as peach and apricot pits, it contains traces of hydrogen cyanide, a deadly poison. Benzaldehyde derived by mixing oil of clove and amyl acetate does not contain any cyanide. Nevertheless, it is legally considered an artificial flavor and sells at a much lower price. Natural and artificial flavors are now manufactured at the same chemical plants, places that few people would associate with Mother Nature.

A TRAINED NOSE AND A POETIC SENSIBILITY

The small and elite group of scientists who create most of the flavor in most of the food now consumed in the United States are called "flavorists." They draw on a number of disciplines in their work: biology, psychology, physiology, and organic chemistry. A flavorist is a chemist with a trained nose and a poetic sensibility. Flavors are created by blending scores of different chemicals in tiny amounts—a process governed by scientific principles but demanding a fair amount of art. In an age when delicate aromas and microwave ovens do not easily co-exist, the job of the flavorist is to conjure illusions about processed food and, in the words of one flavor company's literature, to ensure "consumer likeability." The flavorists with whom I spoke were discreet, in keeping with the dictates of their trade. They were also charming, cosmopolitan, and ironic. They not only enjoyed fine wine but could identify the chemicals that give each grape its unique aroma. One flavorist compared his work to composing music. A well-made flavor compound will have a "top note" that is often followed by a "dry-down" and a "leveling-off," with different chemicals responsible for each stage. The taste of a food can be radically altered by minute changes in the flavoring combination. "A little odor goes a long way," one flavorist told me.

In order to give a processed food a taste that consumers will find 25 appealing, a flavorist must always consider the food's "mouthfeel"—the unique combination of textures and chemical interactions that affect how the flavor is perceived. Mouthfeel can be adjusted through the use of various fats, gums, starches, emulsifiers, and stabilizers. The aroma chemicals in a food can be precisely analyzed, but the elements that make up mouthfeel are much harder to measure. How does one quantify a pretzel's hardness, a french fry's crispness? Food technologists are now conducting basic research in rheology, the branch of physics that examines the flow and deformation of materials. A number of companies sell sophisticated devices that attempt to measure mouthfeel. The

TA.XT2i Texture Analyzer, produced by the Texture Technologies Corporation, of Scardsale, New York, performs calculations based on data derived from as many as 250 separate probes. It is essentially a mechanical mouth. It gauges the most-important rheological properties of a food—bounce, creep, breaking point, density, crunchiness, chewiness, gumminess, lumpiness, rubberiness, springiness, slipperiness, smoothness, softness, wetness, juiciness, spreadability, springback, and tackiness.

Some of the most important advances in flavor manufacturing are now occurring in the field of biotechnology. Complex flavors are being made using enzyme reactions, fermentation, and fungal and tissue cultures. All the flavors created by these methods—including the ones being synthesized by fungi—are considered natural flavors by the FDA. The new enzyme-based processes are responsible for extremely true-to-life dairy flavors. One company now offers not just butter flavor but also fresh creamy butter, cheesy butter, milky butter, savory melted butter, and super-concentrated butter flavor, in liquid or powder form. The development of new fermentation techniques, along with new techniques for heating mixtures of sugar and amino acids, have led to the creation of much more realistic meat flavors.

The McDonald's Corporation most likely drew on these advances when it eliminated beef tallow from its french fries. The company will not reveal the exact origin of the natural flavor added to its fries. In response to inquiries from *Vegetarian Journal,* however, McDonald's did acknowledge that its fries derive some of their characteristic flavor from "an animal source." Beef is the probable source, although other meats cannot be ruled out. In France, for example, fries are sometimes cooked in duck fat or horse tallow.

Other popular fast foods derive their flavor from unexpected ingredients. McDonald's Chicken McNuggets contain beef extracts, as does Wendy's Grilled Chicken Sandwich. Burger King's BK Broiler Chicken Breast Patty contains "natural smoke flavor." A firm called Red Arrow Products specializes in smoke flavor, which is added to barbecue sauces, snack foods, and processed meats. Red Arrow manufactures natural smoke flavor by charring sawdust and capturing the aroma chemicals released into the air. The smoke is captured in water and then bottled, so that other companies can sell food that seems to have been cooked over a fire.

The Vegetarian Legal Action Network recently petitioned the FDA to issue new labeling requirements for foods that contain natural flavors. The group wants food processors to list the basic origins of their flavors on their labels. At the moment vegetarians often have no way of knowing whether a flavor additive contains beef, pork, poultry, or shellfish. One of the most widely used color additives—whose presence is often hidden by the phrase "color added"—violates a number of religious dietary restrictions, may cause allergic reactions in susceptible people, and comes from an unusual source. Cochineal extract (also known as carmine or carminic acid) is made from the desiccated bodies of female *Dactylopius coccus Costa,* a small insect harvested mainly in Peru and the Canary Islands. The bug feeds on red cactus berries, and color from the berries accumulates in the females and their unhatched larvae. The insects are collected, dried, and ground into a pigment. It takes about 70,000 of them to produce a pound of carmine, which is used to make processed foods look pink, red, or purple. Dannon strawberry yogurt gets its color from carmine, and so do many frozen fruit bars, candies, and fruit fillings, and Ocean Spray pink-grapefruit juice drink.

In a meeting room at IFF, Brian Grainger let me sample some of the 30 company's flavors. It was an unusual taste test—there was no food to taste. Grainger is a senior flavorist at IFF, a soft-spoken chemist with graying hair, an English accent, and a fondness for understatement. He could easily be mistaken for a British diplomat or the owner of a West End brasserie with two Michelin stars. Like many in the flavor industry, he has an Old World, old-fashioned sensibility. When I suggested that IFF's policy of secrecy and discretion was out of step with our mass-marketing, brand-conscious, self-promoting age, and that the company should put its own logo on the countless products that bear its flavors, instead of allowing other companies to enjoy the consumer loyalty and affection inspired by those flavors, Grainger politely disagreed, assuring me that such a thing would never be done. In the absence of public credit or acclaim, the small and secretive fraternity of flavor chemists praise one another's work. By analyzing the flavor formula of a product, Grainger can often tell which of his counterparts at a rival firm devised it. Whenever he walks down a supermarket aisle, he takes a quiet pleasure in seeing the well-known foods that contain his flavors.

Grainger had brought a dozen small glass bottles from the lab. After he opened each bottle, I dipped a fragrance-testing filter into it—a long white strip of paper designed to absorb aroma chemicals without producing off notes. Before placing each strip of paper in front of my nose, I closed my eyes. Then I inhaled deeply, and one food after another was conjured from the glass bottles. I smelled fresh cherries, black olives, sauteed onions, and shrimp. Grainger's most remarkable creation took me by surprise. After closing my eyes, I suddenly smelled a grilled hamburger. The aroma was uncanny, almost miraculous—as if somone in the room were flipping burgers on a hot grill. But when I opened my eyes, I saw just a narrow strip of white paper and a flavorist with a grin.

STUDY QUESTIONS

1. What are the perceived and actual differences between "natural flavor" and "artificial flavor"? Describe the relationship between European perfume houses and the flavor industry.

2. Find the PROCESS ANALYSIS paragraphs in the article dealing with smell and taste. Using those paragraphs as your source, explain in your own words how our senses of smell and taste work.

3. How does the inclusion of personal experiences contribute to or detract from Schlosser's ETHOS? Select two experiences that he shares, explain how they affect his ethos, and evaluate their effectiveness in this essay.

4. *For Writing.* Examine the items in your pantry. (If you live in a dorm and have no kitchen or pantry, visit a local grocery store and select ten or fifteen items to examine.) Organize them into the various categories of foods: canned fruits and vegetables, packaged processed foods, and so forth. Carefully read the lists of ingredients on each label. If you do not recognize some of the ingredients, look them up in a dictionary or on the Internet. Write an EXPOSITORY essay about these items and their ingredients. Evaluate the safety and nutritional value of the ingredients, and determine whether each is necessary and whether any might be harmful.

KATINA R. STAPLETON {

From the Margins to the
Mainstream: The Political
Power of Hip-Hop

KATINA R. STAPLETON (b. 1973), a native of Maryland, graduated
from Eleanor Roosevelt High School in Greenbelt, Maryland, in 1991
and went on to earn a BA in print journalism from the University of
Maryland at College Park in 1995 and a PhD in American politics with a
concentration in political communication from Duke University in 2002.
She interned at *U.S. News and World Report* and has been a contributing
editor at the *Black Collegian Magazine*. With an academic specialty in
education policy as well as the intersections of popular culture, media,
politics, and public policy, Stapleton writes about various political
narratives: from tabloid coverage of the presidency to the politics of
music; from political communication to political cartoons. She has
taught at Duke, St. Lawrence, Syracuse, and Georgetown universities.
She currently supervises grant programs for the U.S. Department of
Education.

"From the Margins to the Mainstream: The Political Power of
Hip-Hop" comes from a 1998 volume of the journal *Media, Culture, and
Society*. In it, Stapleton explores the musical genre of hip-hop as what
she calls a "means of political action." As you read, determine how this
musical genre can cause such varied political effects. Can you perceive
its effects in your daily life?

"THEY DIDN'T KNOW WHAT THEY were playing with, look what they
got," spoke Jungle Brothers rapper Mike G from the floor of a conference on the state of hip-hop in the late 1990s. In the 20-plus years

since it emerged in inner-city New York as an alternative to violence and a way to escape harsh urban realities, hip-hop has become a worldwide musical and cultural force. But the widespread popularity of rap music and hip-hop culture among youth has caught many outside the hip-hop community by surprise. Once considered "black noise," hip-hop has claimed for itself the role of cultural and political voice of an entire generation of youth.

When hip-hop emerged in New York City in the 1970s, its primary sphere of influence was the youth in the neighborhoods where it evolved. In areas like the Bronx, breakdancers, graffiti artists, MCs (rappers), DJs and fans formed the hip-hop community. Hip-hop scholar Tricia Rose argues that "alternative local identities were forged in fashions and language, street names, and most important, in establishing neighborhood crews or posses" (Rose, 1994: 34). Crews provided an opportunity for youth to form family-like bonds similar to, but not based on, gang affiliation. Instead of always fighting with fists, hip-hop gave youth the option of fighting with words, art, dance or the ability to produce good beats (Fernando, 1994).

Hip-hop emerged at a time of crisis for youth in urban communities. The situation was no less than a "deindustrialized meltdown where social alienation, prophetic imagination, and yearning intersect" (Rose, 1994: 21). Hip-hop enabled youth to create their own cultural space within the city that countered the poverty and alienation that surrounded them on a day-to-day basis. As a type of genuine street culture, hip-hop evolved for several years before being discovered by the mass media (Shomari, 1995).

As scholars began to research hip-hop, it became clear that while it developed as an alternative youth culture, hip-hop incorporated many elements of the larger African-American and African cultures (DeMott, 1988; Floyd, 1995; Remes, 1991; Stephens, 1991). One such element is "playing the dozens," a time-honored tradition in the African-American community. Also known as bragging, boasting, toasting or signifying, the process includes "ritual insults" in which the speakers test their verbal prowess by seeing who can form the best taunt. Dozens-playing was an integral part of the early rap competitions and has remained a significant element of rap music today.

Hip-hop's use of the spoken or sung word to tell stories and teach 5 "life-lessons" is also part of a tradition among African peoples that goes back to the *griots*, African storytellers who played the important role of oral historians. The griots' role in African communities was to pass down the stories of each generation in song, while imparting knowledge about society. "Endowed with this much prized oral skill, the griot enjoyed a very respected position within his community, just like many modern-day microphone personalities" (Fernando, 1994: 255). Rappers have become urban griots, using their lyrics to disperse social commentary about what it means to be young and black in the late 20th century (Kuwahara, 1992).

Like more traditional griots, what makes hip-hop artists such successful purveyors of cultural and political information is that they relay messages of importance to youth in a form that they enjoy. Rap music, currently the most visible element of hip-hop, has proven its ability to both capture the ear of those who listen to it for aesthetic reasons and those who look to the genre for deeper meaning. From its rough and tumble forms to the most commercial jams, hip-hop has been able to raise awareness among African-Americans and the general public about the issues that face black youth on a day-to-day basis.

Another strong tradition in African-American music that hip-hop has followed is the use of song to "tell it like it is" and protest against social injustice (Nelson, 1992; Remes, 1991). In the early 1900s an examination of Negro spirituals as folksongs noted that folksongs were developed out of experience (Krehbiel, 1914). The pathos of what it meant to be a slave was reflected in music of the times. Krehbiel writes, "as a rule the finest songs are the fruits of suffering undergone and the hope of deliverance from bondage" (Krehbiel, 1914: 26–7). Rochelle Larking (1972) argues that the historic conditions of black Americans will always serve as a basis for protest music. Her 1970s examination of soul music as a form of protest noted that beginning with the blues, black popular music has joined church songs as calls to freedom.

African-Americans, according to the musicologist Jon Spencer, have used secular music such as the blues to reflect the "hell on earth" which they have been subjected to throughout the ages. These songs, claims Spencer, are no less profound than Old Testament psalms and lamentations. Like these biblical tales of woe, the blues are songs "that reveal the nitty-gritty details of life as it is lived at the underside of society and the underbelly of history" (Spencer, 1996: xiv). Black music from the blues to funk, soul, jazz and now to hip-hop often shares the hope for deliverance found in Negro folksongs. As noted by Henry Charles (1990), the concept of deliverance is found in many aspects of African-American culture.

The central purpose of this article is to examine how hip-hop culture and music are uniquely situated among youth as a means of political action. While the most obvious means is through lyrical protest, Mark Mattern (1997) provides a larger framework for political action that includes music and the culture in which it develops. In his examination of Cajun music, Mattern suggests three categories of political action that will also form the basis of my analysis: confrontational (protest), deliberative and pragmatic.

HIDDEN TRANSCRIPTS AND CONFRONTATIONAL LYRICS

Creating culture is not easy. . . . There is a politically conscious, culturally aware, liberated, Black survival kit side to rap music that is being seriously overlooked. (Jackson, 1994)   10

One of the greatest contributions of hip-hop artists to the political landscape is one of protest. Mattern (1997) argues that the use of music to provide protest is a clear example of confrontational political action. Protest music is characterized by objections to injustices and oppressions inflicted on certain individuals and groups. Resistance is key and so are clear distinctions between those being subjugated and those perpetrating the injustice. "Typically, the intent of protest musicians is to oppose the exploitation and oppression exercised by dominant elites and members of dominant groups" (Mattern, 1997: 2). Mattern finds similar elements of resistance in Cajun music that had been previously found in rap music.

In her seminal study of hip-hop, Tricia Rose (1994) provides an examination of rap music and hip-hop culture as a means to resist the dominant social order. Drawing on the work of James Scott (1990), Rose makes the critical distinction between the means by which those in dominant versus marginalized groups are able to get their messages across. Those in power are represented by dominant public transcripts, which are "maintained through a wide range of social practices," such as setting the terms of public debate (Rose, 1994: 100). Cut out of the public debate, marginalized groups develop their own resistive or hidden transcripts. These communications take place in disguised form and tend to include critiques of the predominant culture. As one of the most marginalized groups in American history, African-Americans have long fought to be included in public debate. Since its inception, one of the areas found to be most problematic for the expression of African-American culture has been television. While there has been more of an influx of television shows and films that feature African-Americans in recent years, critics argue that blacks are mostly portrayed as comedic objects or criminals (Dates and Barlow, 1990; Greenberg and Brand, 1990). Black youths in particular have looked to the media to find representations of their own lives. Rap music and rap music videos gained in popularity among black youth as they recognized rap as their voice. Rap veteran Chuck D of Public Enemy has been widely quoted as calling rap music the "Black man's CNN." In the face of under- and/or misrepresentation in traditional media, black youths have turned to hip-hop as a means to define themselves. In terms of resistance, hip-hop provided a forum from which black youth can portray what it means to be young and black in America and protest against it. In its musical form, hip-hop has been able to form what are termed "hidden transcripts." While those from dominant cultural groups have public transcripts, those from marginalized groups often must create their own forum from which they can communicate with each other and transmit messages to the dominant culture. The use of resistive transcripts in rap music serves the dual purpose of using symbolism to critique power holders (Rose, 1994) and providing a dialogic arena in which rappers shape the terms of entry (Skeggs, 1993).

The transcripts found in rap music, while often protesting the treatment of all African-Americans, find black youth, not adults, as their primary audience. Dates and Barlow (1990) suggest that this age division among African-Americans over rap is based in part on perceived class consciousness. They argue that this can be seen in radio programming. Many radio formats reflect a class style, with stations wooing urban contemporary listeners with jazz, soul and traditional R&B while other stations woo black youth with hip-hop influenced R&B and rap music (Dates and Barlow, 1990; Jackson, 1994). In terms of political action, this means that black youth and black adults are finding that they have differing ideas of what protest music should sound like. While "Say it Loud, I'm Black and I'm Proud" by James Brown and "Respect" by Aretha Franklin were anthems for blacks who came of age in the 1960s, rap is providing new anthems for black youth of the 1990s.

One of the earliest raps credited with going beyond the boast/party elements of rap music to provide a protest anthem was simply called "The Message." Released by Grandmaster Flash and the Furious Five in the early 1980s, "The Message" captured the angst of black youth growing up in the inner city and lent its name to a type of rap music that would follow.

Flash's message that society shouldn't push him because he was close to the edge was something that anyone who had grown up in the ghetto could understand. According to Flash, being raised in the impoverished "second rate" conditions is what often causes young blacks to harbor deep feelings of anger towards society.

While raps like "The Message" may have started with GrandMaster Flash in 1982, over the years, the group Public Enemy has brought hard-hitting societal critiques to the forefront of hip-hop. Public Enemy's founder and lead rapper Chuck D, writes how PE decided to use their music for social purposes: 15

> The sociopolitical meaning of Public Enemy came after we decided the group would be called that, because the meaning and the connection of what we were about fit right in. The Black man and woman was considered three-fifths of human being in the Constitution of the

United States. Since the government and the general public follow the Constitution, then we must be the enemy. (Chuck D, 1997: 86)

Public Enemy credit their strong commitment to protest to the influences of the Black Panther Party and the Nation of Islam. The combination of PE's political background and their ability to create strong musical and video images allowed them to use their songs to provide powerful statements. Two of the most remembered, rap commentaries from PE are "911 is a Joke" and "Fight the Power." Even before newspaper and television reporters started telling the general public about the problems inner-city residents had with receiving prompt ambulance service, Public Enemy detailed the situation in rhyme. The raps of nationalist groups such as Public Enemy serve as direct examples of confrontational political action. One criterion of this type of political action is the placement of the group, which is perceived as being oppressed in direct opposition to the oppressors (Mattern, 1997). The resistive transcripts of Public Enemy's song "Hitler Day," locate people of color in direct opposition to white America.

"Hitler Day" is a critique of America's celebration of Columbus Day. According to the rap, a holiday which celebrates the "discovery" of America at the expense of its native inhabitants is inherently offensive to people of color.

Chuck D explains that asking Native and African-American people to celebrate Columbus Day is analogous to asking Jews to celebrate Adolf Hitler Day. "For me, that's what Christopher Columbus represents to Black, Brown, and Red Nations in North America and throughout the world because he opened the gates for five hundred years of mayhem" (Chuck D, 1997: 198). Other more well known confrontational songs by the group include "Shut 'Em Down," which encouraged the boycotting of businesses that take from the black community without giving back, and the self-explanatory rap "Fight the Power."

Other nation-conscious rappers like Brand-Nubian, X-Clan, Poor Righteous Teachers and KRS-One have provided either direct indictments of the dominant social structure or more hidden critiques (Decker, 1993; Eurie and Spady, 1991; Henderson, 1996). But nation-consciousness in rap music also includes messages of empowerment.

Next to Public Enemy, Kris Parker is one of the most well known deliverers of political and social messages to the hip-hop community. Ironically, Kris Parker (KRS-One) began his career as part of Boogie Down Productions (BDP) with the late Scott LaRock. Posing on the cover of "Criminal Minded with Guns," BDP produced some of the earliest music with a gangster ethic, while at the same time promoting messages of black nationalism, safe sex and the rejection of the drug trade. As a solo artist, KRS-One has cemented his role as a teacher among the hip-hop community. From his 1997 album *I Got Next* KRS-One urges the hip-hop nation to shed what he calls ghetto mentality for one of success. Both Public Enemy and KRS-One represent nation-consciousness based in the 1960s black power movement. Jeffery Decker contends that hip-hop nationalists:

> . . . are most effective when they appropriate popular knowledge from within the black community and exploit its most progressive elements in the process of envisioning a new society. At these moments rappers function in a manner resembling what Antonio Gramsci calls "organic intellectuals." (Decker, 1993: 59)

Much of the literature on the presence of confrontational political action in music is implicitly or explicitly indebted to Gramscian Marxism. Organic intellectuals are individuals who hold close ties to their class of origin and whose function is to express class identity and goals (Mattern, 1997). The relationship of the hip-hop artist to a class identity has been clear since hip-hop began. Early hip-hop artists came directly from specific inner-city communities and represented a class of youth facing economic deprivation along with social and political marginalization. Even though the hip-hop community has expanded beyond its core to include youth of all classes, races and cultures, hip-hop artists are expected to remain true to their positions as the representative of black youth. "Hip Hop nationalists are organic cultural intellectuals to the degree that their activities are directly linked to the everyday struggles of black folk and that their music critically engages the popular knowledge of which they have a part"

(Decker, 1993: 59). Henderson (1996) and Decker (1993) note that many prominent examples of hip-hop nationalists are not explicitly linked to 1960s nationalism. The Fugees are among rappers whose vision of nationhood is bounded not by geography, but rather one's link to the African or Afro-Hispanic diaspora. Referring to black youth as black diamonds and pearls, Fugees vocalist Lauren Hill raps, "If I ruled the world, I'd free all my sons." This type of nationalism is Afrocentric in nature. Rappers like Queen Latifah look to Mother Africa for inspiration in forming their hip-hop identity.

Gangster rap is another prominent source of confrontational nationalist rap (Decker, 1993). Known for their universal distrust of the police, gangster rappers often use their music to provide graphic indictments of the police and the government interspersed with tales of gangster living. Many gangster rappers prefer to be called realists, because they feel their rap describes what is really going on in the 'hood. With black on black violence being the leading source of death for black youth since 1969, it doesn't seem wrong to many rappers to reflect that in their music (Kitwana, 1994: 41). King George, a member of TRU, contends that this type of realism is more than just talk about killing. "I'm just relating to what's going on and keeping everybody aware at the same time" (Davis, 1996: 63).

GENDER AND GANGSTA-RAP

Claims to realism aside, however, there has been widespread debate 20 about whether or not songs that call black women "bitches" and "hoes" (whores) as well as songs which detail sex acts, drug sales and extreme violence are negative influences on youth. The portrayal of women and whites in hip-hop music have been special sources of concern (Allison, 1994; Hansen, 1995; Johnson et al., 1995). It would seem obvious that no woman would want to be called a female dog on tape, or have their boyfriends "Treat 'em like a prostitute." But while female rappers like M.C. Lyte, Queen Latifah, Yo-Yo and Salt 'n' Pepa began to challenge the conception that only males could rap and shape perceptions of women in the urban community, some female rappers responded by becoming hard-core rappers themselves (Rose, 1994; Skeggs, 1993).

In the late 1990s female rappers have emerged as a force equal to male rappers. Skeggs (1993) argues that if rap in general is used to combat racism and oppression, female artists use rap to battle sexism. While many female hip-hop artists rap about female solidarity, others provide images of women being in control of their sexuality. Skeggs theorizes that for black women, "sexuality is one of the few cultural resources that they can use for the construction of embodied self worth" (Skeggs, 1993: 310). This notion has not gone unchallenged. Female rappers like Lil' Kim and Foxy Brown have been both vilified and held up for praise for their hard-core attitude and blatantly sexy style. The question "Harlots or heroines?" has followed them since they came on the scene. While supporters celebrate the two female rappers' ability to take charge and proclaim their sexuality, critics challenge their claim to feminism. The Lady of Rage, like many other female rappers, holds conflicting views of artists like Kim and Foxy. "I like Little Kim because she sounds so hard. At first I thought what she was saying was not good because we already got problems as far as women getting recognition and being accepted. I felt that might hinder it a little bit." But, as Rage notes, "Sex sells and she's good" (Williams, 1997: 63).

Many in the hip-hop community contend that while there are valid concerns about the level of sexual and violent content in hip-hop music, the concern from the media and politicians is not genuine. Instead, negative sentiments towards hip-hop are considered to have racial overtones. Hip-hop artists in attendance at the 1997 Life After Death conference contended that the media and politicians are down on hip-hop because it is a black art form that is being consumed by white youth. The consumption of hip-hop by young whites allows them to become "ghetto chic" without actually having to live in ghetto conditions (Allison, 1994). Though much of the criticism of hip-hop comes from those outside of the black community, there is a large concern about the tone of rap music within African-American discourse. Rose, who applauds rap for its ability to provide resistive transcripts, lambasts rappers for their sexism. "I am thoroughly frustrated but not surprised by the apparent need for some rappers to craft elaborate and creative stories about the abuse and domination of young black women" (Rose, 1994: 15).

Likewise, trends toward the inclusion of sex, drugs, violence and, most recently, materialism in rap music have not gone unnoticed or unchallenged by members of the hip-hop community itself (Life After Death, 1997). Hip-hop conferences held in the aftermath of the violent deaths of favorite sons, Tupac Shakur and the Notorious B.I.G. have looked at whether hip-hop has a social responsibility to the youth that listen to the music. Participants at Life After Death (1997) asked serious questions about the role of violence in the genre. The consensus among panel and audience members seemed to be that in many ways hip-hop is out of control. However, they note—and I agree—that rappers who talk about sex and violence should not be expected to take all the blame. Equal shares of blame should lie with record companies and managers who promote violent/sexual rappers, with the youth who buy these records, and with parents who do not take the time to listen to what their children are listening to. Blame also lies with American society itself, which criticizes rappers for talking about ideals that are in fact embedded in the American way of life, as well as the media who often blow up the violence in hip-hop out of context. A sampling of newspaper articles following the shooting death of Biggie Smalls seems to support claims that in a society where black men are killed in record numbers the media still insist on implying that the rap industry, not guns, kills people (Patillo, 1997).

The fact that rappers reflect aspects of American society and the pursuit of the American dream is important in a political context. Rap has many elements in common with country and hard rock music, but receives more critical attention. "Rap and country lyrics implicate underclass reality, that the alternative symbol systems have a parallel socio-economic provenience" (Armstrong, 1993: 69). Though both genres are based on somewhat different social realities, they both share a rhetoric of violence. Analyses of press coverage of country and rap have found that while the genres share a tendency towards machismo, they are not treated the same way by the press. The difference, as found by Noe, lies not in the song lyrics, but in the racial lenses through which the songs are interpreted.

> When Ice Cube says, "Let the suburbs see a nigga invasion," many whites interpret that as an incitement to violence. But when Johnny Cash sings, "Shot a man in Reno/just to watch him die," the public taps its feet and hums. (Noe, 1995: 20)

The irony, says Noe, is that rap is no more amoral than other musical genres, but rappers are being punished for catering to prevalent American themes: sex, violence and materialism.

SETTING THE BOUNDARIES OF HIP-HOP

Hip-hop is bigger than any one person's opinion of what it should be, said Chuck D of Public Enemy, now a reporter for the Fox News Channel (Chuck D, 1997: 152). The process of establishing where the boundaries of hip-hop should stand is one of deliberation. Mattern (1997) elaborates on this type of political action. He writes, "Deliberation is a political process and a form of political action in its own right, as well as a necessary preliminary step in forging agreement on common interests and goals for action in other political arenas to address them" (Mattern, 1997: 7). Mattern uses rap and Cajun music as examples of how differing visions of what a genre should stand for are deliberated within a community. The main point of deliberation within the hip-hop community revolves around the question: "Has hip-hop gone too far?" Related questions include, but are not limited to: "Has rap music become too sexual, too violent, and too materialistic?" "Has hip-hop sold its soul for commercial success?" "Has hip-hop crossed too far into the territory of other music forms?" "As a community, has hip-hop become more suburban and white than black and urban?"

The answers to all these questions are not clear-cut. The very nature of hip-hop culture has been one that accommodated many types of people, many types of subject matter, and many types of music. The underlying question, then, is whether or not hip-hop can accommodate varying interests, while still retaining its distinctive urban identity. The presence of intra-group differences and disagreements, and of border zones between different groups, suggests that we consider, at least in some instances, a framework for understanding and action of negotiation, rather than an either-or struggle between opposing forces. Popular music would be viewed in these cases as a site and a medium for disagreement and debate over both intra- and inter-group identity and commitments. This takes shape in a deliberative form of political action (Mattern, 1997: 6).

Hip-hop's identity as form of resistance among black youth lies at the heart of deliberation in the hip-hop community. Part of hip-hop's credibility among young blacks lies in its ability to claim that it is an authentic street culture (Powell, 1991). But if hip-hop is "by the ghetto, for the ghetto," how is the community changed by the fact that it is being played on college campuses across the nation and in the homes of suburban whites? When hip-hop style is being used to sell movies, breath mints, sodas, make-up, fast food, alcohol, clothing, shoes and various other products, one knows that this is a valid concern (Blair, 1993). Similar feelings have been reported from England's hip-hop community. "Hip-hop's integrity has been prostituted in the pursuit of financial gain," writes a columnist in *Hip-Hop Connection,* one of Britain's hip-hop magazines (Salsa, 1997: 5). Though the author was from England, she accurately summed up concerns that are held across the hip-hop community. Salsa charges that hip-hop is at its best in its resistive mode, but that it has lost its subversiveness due to mainstreaming and commercialization. Bernard-Donais (1994: 133) shares this opinion. "The very fact that it is covered by an institution like the [*New York*] *Times* suggests that rap has found its way into the canon, and that it has ceased to be the subversive (or in other terms, marginal) form that it had been at one time."

In the case of hip-hop, the transference from subculture to mainstream has been driven by technological advances. As long as artists performed rap in venues limited to neighborhoods, its marginal status was assured. But as rap music expanded to being mass produced hip-hop spread across the nation (Blair, 1993; Kuwahara, 1992). Hip-hop's influence has not been limited to America. Fans from across the world are able to buy rap music both from traditional record stores and from mail order distribution. The worldwide audience for hip-hop should not be underestimated (Toop, 1991). Hip-hop artists regularly perform to international audiences. Wu Tang Clan and the Fugees are just two examples of what is called global hip-hop. The appeal of hip-hop around the world is based in part on the fact that marginalization, oppression and struggle can be understood by many youth. The love of hip-hop has a universal appeal, agrees Chuck D (1997). He believes that one of the reasons that rap crosses over successfully into mainstream culture is that young whites are able to gain an African-American perspective through the music.

The character of deliberation within the hip-hop community is necessarily shaped by its widespread audience. Stephens (1991) contends that rap provides a "double-voiced discourse" in which rap crosses racial and geographic boundaries. Hip-hop, writes Stephens, provides a point of intersection where blacks and whites can have a dialogue. Though not always acknowledged in the media, the members of the Hispanic community have also been involved in hip-hop since its inception. In this case, it is urbanity and similar social situations that guide Hispanic contributions to hip-hop (Fernando, 1994; Stephens, 1991). As Rose notes, "Rap's black cultural address and its focus on marginal identities may appear to be in opposition to its crossover appeal for people from different racial or ethnic groups and social positions," but in reality it suggests "that rap is a black idiom that prioritizes black culture and that articulates the problems of black urban life in the face of such diverse constituencies" (Rose, 1994: 4).

Discussions of hip-hop as a street culture sometimes overlook contributions of college students who have since become hip-hop artists and the strong identification of many black college students with hip-hop culture. Music, if not social class, draws young African-Americans of differing socioeconomic status to hip-hop. 30

Zillman et al. have looked at the effects of popular rock, non-political rap and radical political rap on African-American and white high-school students. They found that while radical political rap seemed to motivate white students to be more supportive of racial harmony, there was no positive link between political rap and ethnic consciousness or ethnic solidarity among the black students (Zillman et al., 1995). The authors note that this does not imply that message rap does not have an effect on black students. In fact the opposite could be true.

> It can be argued that African-American students, in contrast to white students, are massively exposed to rap and that any effect of rap may have manifested itself already prior to exposure. Several additional exposures thus could have influenced white students, especially those who are relatively unfamiliar with radical rap, but not African-American students—because of the informational saturation and its perceptual and evaluative consequences. (Zillman et al., 1995:21)

Debate about the relative effects of hip-hop on youth is a major area of discussion within the academic community. Instead of concentrating on consciousness, researchers Johnson et al. looked at the effects of violent rap on youth. They found that there was greater acceptance of dating violence among youth exposed to violent rap videos than those exposed to non-violent rap videos or no video at all. In a slightly different experiment they also found that youth exposed to either type of rap video expressed greater desire to be like the materialistic youth portrayed in a scenario than his college-bound friend (Johnson et al., 1995).

Materialism, sexism and violence are points of deliberation among hip-hop artists and fans. Chuck D (1997) recounts the extremely negative reactions he got from African hip-hop fans to the newest incarnations of hip-hop. But as he also notes, the more negative aspects of rap are the easiest to market. "If you give a fourteen-year-old a choice between a positive video, and a video with tits and ass, or guns and violence, he's going to choose the tits and ass, guns and violence almost every time" (Chuck D, 1997: 33). Researchers have shown that white youth who listen to rap are particularly attracted to its most violent elements. "The more rappers are packaged as violent black criminals, the bigger their audiences become," writes Ewan Allison (1994: 449).

Is this preoccupation with ghetto culture detrimental to youth, black or white? In some ways it is positive, according to Rose, because the ghetto provides a source of social identity for the millions of youth who call it home. Other positive interpretations include the fact that rap has value both because of its brutal honesty and as a point of deliberation. Freestyle rapper Supernatural feels that gangster rap gives other types of rappers more incentive to present the hip-hop experience from all points of view. Looking at the situation from a slightly different perspective, KRS-One notes that the existence of more than one type of rap exposes the tendency for the public to choose negative over positive. Among participants at Life After Death (1997), the origins of hip-hop were seen as being positive in contrast to more recent developments. Old-school hip-hop artists stressed that hip-hop has strayed too far from its original intentions of combating gang activity to promoting gangster ethics; from promoting black unity to encouraging east coast–west coast feuds; from MC'ing, DJ'ing, breaking, and painting graffiti to simply rapping; from performing for the love of it to performing for money; and from simple boasting to gross exaggerations of one's sexual prowess (Life After Death, 1997; Nia, 1997). Though each of these issues is important to the future of hip-hop, the charge that there has been a dilution of hip-hop as a distinct, protest-based culture and music form is the most political.

ACTIONS SPEAK LOUDER THAN WORDS

Though the previous discussion in this article has concentrated on both the resistive and deliberative aspects of hip-hop, Mattern suggests music and its related culture also can be used as a basis for pragmatic political action. This type of action, says Mattern, "begins from the premise of shared political interests. Pragmatic political action occurs when individuals and groups use music to promote awareness of shared interests and to organize collaborative action to address them" (Mattern, 1997: 7). In the past, hip-hop artists have come together for many causes. One prominent example, though considered ill-fated, was the Stop the Violence movement (STV), an attempt to discourage black-on-black crime. Other movements include HEAL (Human Education Against Lies) and the current Rap the Vote project.

Currently there seems to be a resurgence of hip-hop artists attempting to form groups to further the common interests of African-diasporic

35

peoples and/or members of the hip-hop nation. KRS-One, whose song "Stop the Violence" typified the spirit of the STV movement, has recently started the Temple of Hip-Hop, a non-profit cultural center with the purpose of preserving hip-hop culture. The Zulu Nation remains a long-standing conduit of nationalism within the hip-hop community. Many other rap groups and individual artists have taken on specific service projects in order to give back to the community. Perhaps some of the most interesting projects are coming from the ground up. One such project is the Wiseguys, led by Raymond "Ray Benzino" Scott, president of Boston-based Surrender Records. Using a similar concept to the one of trading a gang for a team, Scott and three friends encouraged former gang rivals to "trade their hardware for mics." The project, called Wiseguys, resulted in former gang members coming together to record an album now distributed nationally. Says Scott, "It becomes a political platform of hypocrisy when you're scared to actually go in and touch the people who are going through the problems" (Walker, 1997: 30-1).

Whether initiated by artists, producers or fans, it is clear that hip-hop has great potential for becoming a major agent of change. All hip-hop needs, according to Chuck D and others, is organization. "We have to really tie up some areas in the hip-hop Nation: the Zulu Nation, the Rhyme Syndicate, any organization is good. It's just that we have to drop these badges when we come down to dialogue and figure out how to help our people . . ." (Chuck D, 1997: 181). Robert Jackson, author of the *The Last Black Mecca*, believes that an organized hip-hop nation has the potential to be a powerful social and political base within the African-American community: "The next revolution should be more than televised—it should be political" (Jackson, 1994: 99). The next level for hip-hop, says Jackson, is to organize around a progressive political agenda which would include housing, education and health reform as well as affirmative action and employment.

Music has always been a major source of cultural identity within the African-American community. Rap music is no exception. As part of the larger hip-hop culture, rap music has served to form a cohesive bond among urban youth. Through the mass distribution of hip-hop records and videos, hip-hop has also been able to at least partially erase lines between young people of different socioeconomic backgrounds and vastly different geographic locations. Equally important, hip-hop culture has established itself as a powerful informational tool and means of resistance. It is not an overstatement to say that despite its faults, hip-hop has provided America with one of its only hard-hitting indictments of the social conditions that continue to be a harsh reality for African-American young people.

Hip-hop has shown itself to be both the site of political controversy and a means of more than one type of political action. As Mattern notes, confrontational, deliberative and pragmatic political action can occur "whenever music is produced and consumed," and thus, "[they] should not be viewed as mutually exclusive of each other" (Mattern, 1997: 8). In the case of hip-hop, this is especially true. Rap music, while a significant source of political action within hip-hop, should not be considered its only source. It is its presence within the hip-hop community that lends it the context in which resistance emerges. As the hip-hop community looks towards the 21st century, it will be the challenge of hip-hop to define how hip-hop will continue to evolve as a culture and as genuine political force.

REFERENCES

Allison, E. (1994) "It's a Black Thing: Hearing How Whites Can't," *Cultural Studies* 8(3): 438–56.

Armstrong, E.G. (1993) "The Rhetoric of Violence in Rap and Country Music," *Sociological Inquiry* 63(1): 64–83.

Bernard-Donais, M. (1994) "Jazz, Rock 'n' Roll, Rap and Polities," *Journal of Popular Culture* 28(2): 127–38.

Blair, M.E. (1993) "The Commercialization of the Rap Music Youth Subculture," *Journal of Popular Culture* 27(3): 21–32.

Charles, H. (1990) *Culture and African American Politics.* Bloomington: Indiana University Press.

Craddock-Willis, A. (1989) "Rap Music and the Black Musical Tradition," *Radical America* 23(4): 29–38.

D, Chuck. (1997) *Fight the Power: Rap, Race and Reality.* New York: Delacorte Press.

Dates, J.L. and W. Barlow. (1990) *Split Image: African Americans in the Mass Media.* Washington, DC: Howard University Press.

Davis, T. (1996) "King George: Tru Royalty," *4080* 35: 63.

Decker, J. (1993) "The State of Rap: Time and Place in Hip Hop Nationalism," *Social Text* 34: 53–84.

DeMott, D. (1988) "The Future is Unwritten: Working-Class Youth Cultures in England and America," *Critical Text* 5(1): 42–56.

Eurie, J.D. and J.G. Spady (eds). (1991) *Nation Conscious Rap.* New York: PC International Press.

Fernando, S.H. (1994) *The New Beats: Exploring the Music, Culture, and Attitudes of Hip-Hop Culture.* New York: Harmony Books.

Floyd, S.A. (1995) *The Power of Black Music: Interpreting its History from Africa to the United States.* New York: Oxford University Press.

Greenberg, B. and J. Brand (1994) "Minorities and the Mass Media: 1970s to 1990s," pp. 273–314 in J. Bryant and D. Zillman (eds) *Media Effects: Advances in Theory and Research.* Hillsdale, NJ: Lawrence Erlbaum Associates.

Hansen, C.H. (1995) "Predicting Cognitive and Behavioral Effects of Gangsta Rap," *Basic and Applied Social Psychology* 16(1–2): 43–52.

Henderson, E.A. (1996) "Black Nationalism and Rap Music," *Journal of Black Studies* 26(3): 308–39.

Jackson, R. (1994) *The Last Black Mecca; Hip-Hop,* Chicago, IL: Research Associates and Frontline Distribution International Inc.

Johnson, J.D., et al. (1995) "Violent Attitudes and Deferred Academic Aspirations: Deleterious Effects of Exposure to Rap Music," *Basic and Applied Social Psychology* 16(1–2): 27–41.

Kitwana, B. (1994) *The Rap on Gangsta Rap.* Chicago, IL: Third World Press.

Krehbiel, H.E. (1914) *Afro-American Folksongs: A Study in Racial and National Music.* New York and London: G. Shirmer.

Kuwahara, Y. (1992) "Power to the People Y'all," *Humanity and Society* 16(1): 54–73.

Larking, R. (1972) "The Soul Message," pp. 92–104 in R. Serge Denisoff and R. Peterson (eds) *The Sounds of Social Change.* Chicago: Rand McNally.

Life After Death: Rap, Reality and Social Responsibility. (1997) Harvard University, Cambridge, MA, 3 May.

Mattern, M. (1997) "Cajun Music, Cultural Revival: Theorizing Political Action in Popular Music," paper prepared for delivery at the 1997 Annual Meeting of the American Political Science Association, Washington, DC.

Nelson, A. (1992) "The Persistence of Ethnicity in African American Popular Music," *Explorations in Ethnic Studies.* 15(1): 47–57.

Nia, M. (1997) "From God's to Niggas, From Queens to Bitch's: Do Rappers Have An Identity Crisis?," *Beat Down* 5(5): 20.

Noe, D. (1995) "Parallel Worlds," *Humanist* 55(4): 20–2.

Patillo, M. (1997) "The Public Eulogy of a Slain Rapper," *The Source* 92: 83.

Powell, C. (1991) "Rap Music: An Education with a Beat from the Street," *Journal of Negro Education* 60(3): 245–59

Remes, P. (1991) "Rapping: A Sociolinguistic Study of Oral Tradition," *Anthropological Society of Oxford* 22(2): 129–49.

Rose, T. (1994) *Black Noise: Rap and Black Culture in Contemporary America.* Hanover, NH: Wesleyan University Press.

Salsa, M. (1997) "Hard Lines," *Hip Hop Connection* 104: 5.

Scott, J.C. (1990) *Domination and the Arts of Resistance: Hidden Transcripts.* New Haven, CT: Yale University Press.

Shomari, H. (1995) *From the Underground: Hip Hop Culture As An Agent of Social Change.* Fairwood, NJ: X-Factor Publications.

Skeggs, B. (1993) "Two Minute Brother: Contestation Through Gender, 'Race' and Sexuality," *Innovation* 6(3): 299–322.

Spencer, J.M. (1996) *Re-searching Black Music.* Knoxville: University of Tennessee Press.

Stephens, G. (1991) "Rap Music's Double-Voiced Discourse," *Journal of Communication Inquiry* 15(2): 70–91.

Toop, D. (1991) *Rap Attack 2: African Rap to Global Hip Hop.* London: Serpent's Tail.

Walker, S. (1997) "Glocks Down," *The Source* 98: 30–1.

Williams, F. (1997) "Rage against the Machine," *The Source* 94: 63–6.

Zillman, D., et al. (1995) "Radical Rap: Does it Further Ethnic Division?," *Basic and Applied Social Psychology* 16(1–2): 1–25.

DISCOGRAPHY

"2nd Quarter—Free Throws," performed by KRS-One on *I Got Next* album (1997).

"911 Is a Joke," performed by Public Enemy, by W. Drayton, K. Shocklee, E. Sadler. Copyright © 1990 Def American Songs, Inc. (BMI).

"Hitler Day," performed by Public Enemy on *Muse Sick-N-Hour Mess Age* album (1994).

"The Message," performed by Grandmaster Flash and the Furious Five, by E. Fletcher, S. Robinson, C. Chase, M. Glover. Copyright © 1982 Sugar Hill Music Publ. Ltd. (BMI).

STUDY QUESTIONS

1. What, according to Stapleton, accounts for the initial popularity of hip-hop?

2. Stapleton argues that hip-hop culture and music can be a "means of political action" (paragraph 9). If hip-hop is the CAUSE of the political action, what are the EFFECTS that Stapleton sees? As you reference specific examples, evaluate the credibility of her argument.

3. How would you characterize Stalepton's TONE in this selection? Why is it appropriate for her PURPOSE and AUDIENCE?

4. *For Writing.* Does hip-hop retain its political power today? Test Stapleton's THESIS against contemporary hip-hop music and culture. In an essay, make an ARGUMENT about the relevance of her thesis, being sure to address the individual subtopics of her essay and to provide concrete examples from today's culture and music.

NATALIE ANGIER { *Men, Women, Sex and Darwin*

NATALIE ANGIER (b. 1958) has built a career writing books and articles that explain the intricacies of science to the nonscientist. Born and raised in New York City, Angier graduated from Barnard College, where she studied physics, astronomy, and English. She began working as a science writer for *Discovery* magazine in 1980, and in 1990 she joined the staff of the *New York Times*, where she won a Pulitzer Prize for beat reporting in 1991. She has published four books, all of them bestsellers: *Natural Obsessions* (1988), *The Beauty of the Beastly* (1995), *Woman: An Intimate Geography* (2000), and *The Canon: A Whirligig Tour of the Beautiful Basics of Science* (2007).

In "Men, Women, Sex and Darwin," published in the *New York Times* in 1999, Angier examines the most common theories proposed by evolutionary psychologists to explain male and female sexual behavior—for instance, that men are naturally more promiscuous than women and that women are naturally more interested in marriage than men. Drawing on empirical evidence and the work of psychologists, anthropologists, and primatologists, Angier finds reason to doubt these theories and offers alternative explanations of her own. As you read, notice how Angier summarizes and synthesizes information from many different sources.

LIFE IS SHORT BUT JINGLES are forever. None more so, it seems, than the familiar ditty, variously attributed to William James, Ogden Nash and Dorothy Parker: "Hoggamus, higgamus,/Men are polygamous,/Higgamus, hoggamus,/Women monogamous."

"Men, Women, Sex, and Darwin" by Natalie Angier from the *New York Times*, February 21, 1999. Reprinted with permission of the New York Times.

Lately the pith of that jingle has found new fodder and new fans, through the explosive growth of a field known as evolutionary psychology. Evolutionary psychology professes to have discovered the fundamental modules of human nature, most notably the essential nature of man and of woman. It makes sense to be curious about the evolutionary roots of human behavior. It's reasonable to try to understand our impulses and actions by applying Darwinian logic to the problem. We're animals. We're not above the rude little prods and jests of natural and sexual selection. But evolutionary psychology as it has been disseminated across mainstream consciousness is a cranky and despotic Cyclops, its single eye glaring through an overwhelmingly masculinist lens. I say "masculinist" rather than "male" because the view of male behavior promulgated by hard-core evolutionary psychologists is as narrow and inflexible as their view of womanhood is.

I'm not interested in explaining to men what they really want or how they should behave. If a fellow chooses to tell himself that his yen for the fetching young assistant in his office and his concomitant disgruntlement with his aging wife make perfect Darwinian sense, who am I to argue with him? I'm only proposing here that the hard-core evolutionary psychologists have got a lot about women wrong—about some of us, anyway—and that women want more and deserve better than the cartoon Olive Oyl[1] handed down for popular consumption.

The cardinal premises of evolutionary psychology of interest to this discussion are as follows: 1. Men are more promiscuous and less sexually reserved than women are. 2. Women are inherently more interested in a stable relationship than men are. 3. Women are naturally attracted to high-status men with resources. 4. Men are naturally attracted to youth and beauty. 5. Humankind's core preferences and desires were hammered out long, long ago, a hundred thousand years or more, in the legendary Environment of Evolutionary Adaptation, or E.E.A., also known as the ancestral environment, also known as the Stone Age, and they have not changed appreciably since then, nor are they likely to change in the future.

---

[1] Popeye's long-suffering sweetheart in the *Popeye* comic strip and animations, first created by cartoonist Elzie Crisler Segar in 1929.

In sum: Higgamus, hoggamus, Pygmalionus, *Playboy* magazine, 5 eternitas. Amen.

Hard-core evolutionary psychology types go to extremes to argue in favor of the yawning chasm that separates the innate desires of women and men. They declare ringing confirmation for their theories even in the face of feeble and amusingly contradictory data. For example: Among the cardinal principles of the evo-psycho set is that men are by nature more polygamous than women are, and much more accepting of casual, even anonymous, sex. Men can't help themselves, they say: they are always hungry for sex, bodies, novelty and nubility. Granted, men needn't act on such desires, but the drive to sow seed is there nonetheless, satyric and relentless, and women cannot fully understand its force. David Buss, a professor of psychology at the University of Texas at Austin and one of the most outspoken of the evolutionary psychologists, says that asking a man not to lust after a pretty young woman is like telling a carnivore not to like meat.

At the same time, they recognize that the overwhelming majority of men and women get married, and so their theories must extend to different innate mate preferences among men and women. Men look for the hallmarks of youth, like smooth skin, full lips and perky breasts; they want a mate who has a long childbearing career ahead of her. Men also want women who are virginal and who seem as though they'll be faithful and not make cuckolds of them. The sexy, vampy types are fine for a Saturday romp, but when it comes to choosing a marital partner, men want modesty and fidelity.

Women want a provider, the theory goes. They want a man who seems rich, stable and ambitious. They want to know that they and their children will be cared for. They want a man who can take charge, maybe dominate them just a little, enough to reassure them that the man is genotypically, phenotypically, eternally, a king. Women's innate preference for a well-to-do man continues to this day, the evolutionary psychologists insist, even among financially independent and professionally successful women who don't need a man as a provider. It was adaptive in the past to look for the most resourceful man, they say, and adaptations can't be willed away in a generation or two of putative cultural change.

And what is the evidence for these male-female verities? For the difference in promiscuity quotas, the hard-cores love to raise the example of the differences between gay men and lesbians. Homosexuals are seen as a revealing population because they supposedly can behave according to the innermost impulses of their sex, untempered by the need to adjust to the demands and wishes of the opposite sex, as heterosexuals theoretically are. What do we see in this ideal study group? Just look at how gay men carry on! They are perfectly happy to have hundreds, thousands, of sexual partners, to have sex in bathhouses, in bathrooms, in Central Park. By contrast, lesbians are sexually sedate. They don't cruise sex clubs. They couple up and stay coupled, and they like cuddling and hugging more than they do serious, genitally based sex.

In the hard-core rendering of inherent male-female discrepancies in   10
promiscuity, gay men are offered up as true men, real men, men set free to be men, while lesbians are real women, ultrawomen, acting out every woman's fantasy of love and commitment. Interestingly, though, in many neurobiology studies gay men are said to have somewhat feminized brains, with hypothalamic nuclei that are closer in size to a woman's than to a straight man's, and spatial-reasoning skills that are modest and ladylike rather than manfully robust. For their part, lesbians are posited to have somewhat masculinized brains and skills—to be sportier, more mechanically inclined, less likely to have played with dolls or tea sets when young—all as an ostensible result of exposure to prenatal androgens. And so gay men are sissy boys in some contexts and Stone Age manly men in others, while lesbians are battering rams one day and flower into the softest and most sexually divested girlish girls the next.

On the question of mate preferences, evo-psychos rely on surveys, most of them compiled by David Buss. His surveys are celebrated by some, derided by others, but in any event they are ambitious— performed in thirty-seven countries, he says, on six continents. His surveys, and others emulating them, consistently find that men rate youth and beauty as important traits in a mate, while women give comparatively greater weight to ambition and financial success. Surveys show that surveys never lie. Lest you think that women's mate preferences change with their own mounting economic clout, surveys assure us that they do not. Surveys of female medical students, according to John Marshall Townsend, of Syracuse University, indicate that they hope to marry men with an earning power and social status at least equal to and preferably greater than their own.

Perhaps all this means is that men can earn a living wage better, even now, than women can. Men make up about half the world's population, but they still own the vast majority of the world's wealth—the currency, the minerals, the timber, the gold, the stocks, the amber fields of grain. In her superb book *Why So Slow?* Virginia Valian, a professor of psychology at Hunter College, lays out the extent of lingering economic discrepancies between men and women in the United States. In 1978 there were two women heading Fortune 1000 companies; in 1994, there were still two; in 1996, the number had jumped all the way to four. In 1985, 2 percent of the Fortune 1000's senior-level executives were women; by 1992, that number had hardly budged, to 3 percent. A 1990 salary and compensation survey of 799 major companies showed that of the highest-paid officers and directors, less than one-half of 1 percent were women. Ask, and he shall receive. In the United States the possession of a bachelor's degree adds $28,000 to a man's salary but only $9,000 to a woman's. A degree from a high-prestige school contributes $11,500 to a man's income but subtracts $2,400 from a woman's. If women continue to worry that they need a man's money, because the playing field remains about as level as the surface of Mars, then we can't conclude anything about innate preferences. If women continue to suffer from bag-lady syndrome even as they become prosperous, if they still see their wealth as provisional and capsizable, and if they still hope to find a man with a dependable income to supplement their own, then we can credit women with intelligence and acumen, for inequities abound.

There's another reason that smart, professional women might respond on surveys that they'd like a mate of their socioeconomic status or better. Smart, professional women are smart enough to know that men can be tender of ego—is it genetic?—and that it hurts a man to earn less money than his wife, and that resentment is a noxious chemical in a marriage and best avoided at any price. "A woman who is more successful than her mate threatens his position in the male hierarchy," Elizabeth Cashdan, of the University of Utah, has written. If women could be persuaded that men didn't mind their being high achievers, were in fact pleased and proud to be affiliated with them, we might predict that the women would stop caring about the particulars of their mates' income. The anthropologist Sarah Blaffer Hrdy writes that "when female status and access to resources do not depend on her mate's status, women will likely use a range of criteria, not primarily or even necessarily prestige and wealth, for mate selection." She cites a 1996 *New York Times* story about women from a wide range of professions—bankers, judges, teachers, journalists—who marry male convicts. The allure of such men is not their income, for you can't earn much when you make license plates for a living. Instead, it is the men's gratitude that proves irresistible. The women also like the fact that their husbands' fidelity is guaranteed. "Peculiar as it is," Hrdy writes, "this vignette of sex-reversed claustration[2] makes a serious point about just how little we know about female choice in breeding systems where male interests are not paramount and patrilines[3] are not making the rules."

Do women love older men? Do women find gray hair and wrinkles attractive on men—as attractive, that is, as a fine, full head of pigmented hair and a vigorous, firm complexion? The evolutionary psychologists suggest yes. They believe that women look for the signs of maturity in men because a mature man is likely to be a comparatively wealthy and resourceful man. That should logically include baldness, which generally comes with age and the higher status that it often confers. Yet, as Desmond Morris points out, a thinning hairline is not considered a particularly attractive state.

Assuming that women find older men attractive, is it the men's alpha 15 status? Or could it be something less complimentary to the male, something like the following—that an older man is appealing not because he is powerful but because in his maturity he has lost some of his power, has become less marketable and desirable and potentially

[2]Cloistering, enclosing.
[3]Groups of patrilineages, or lines of descent from a male ancestor.

more grateful and gracious, more likely to make a younger woman feel that there is a balance of power in the relationship? The rude little calculation is simple: He is male, I am female—advantage, man. He is older, I am younger—advantage, woman. By the same token, a woman may place little value on a man's appearance because she values something else far more: room to breathe. Who can breathe in the presence of a handsome young man, whose ego, if expressed as a vapor, would fill Biosphere II? Not even, I'm afraid, a beautiful young woman.

In the end, what is important to question, and to hold to the fire of alternative interpretation, is the immutability and adaptive logic of the discrepancy, its basis in our genome rather than in the ecological circumstances in which a genome manages to express itself. Evolutionary psychologists insist on the essential discordance between the strength of the sex drive in males and females. They admit that many nonhuman female primates gallivant about rather more than we might have predicted before primatologists began observing their behavior in the field—more, far more, than is necessary for the sake of reproduction. Nonetheless, the credo of the coy female persists. It is garlanded with qualifications and is admitted to be an imperfect portrayal of female mating strategies, but then, that little matter of etiquette attended to, the credo is stated once again.

"Amid the great variety of social structure in these species, the basic theme . . . stands out, at least in minimal form: males seem very eager for sex and work hard to find it; females work less hard," Robert Wright says in *The Moral Animal*. "This isn't to say the females don't like sex. They love it, and may initiate it. And, intriguingly, the females of the species most closely related to humans—chimpanzees and bonobos—seem particularly amenable to a wild sex life, including a variety of partners. Still, female apes don't do what male apes do: search high and low, risking life and limb, to find sex, and to find as much of it, with as many different partners, as possible; it has a way of finding them." In fact female chimpanzees do search high and low and take great risks to find sex with partners other than the partners who have a way of finding them. DNA studies of chimpanzees in West Africa show that half the offspring in a group of closely scrutinized chimpanzees turned out not to be the offspring of the resident males.

The females of the group didn't rely on sex "finding" its way to them; they proactively left the local environs, under such conditions of secrecy that not even their vigilant human observers knew they had gone, and became impregnated by outside males. They did so even at the risk of life and limb—their own and those of their offspring. Male chimpanzees try to control the movements of fertile females. They'll scream at them and hit them if they think the females aren't listening. They may even kill an infant they think is not their own. We don't know why the females take such risks to philander, but they do, and to say that female chimpanzees "work less hard" than males do at finding sex does not appear to be supported by the data.

Evo-psychos pull us back and forth until we might want to sue for whiplash. On the one hand we are told that women have a lower sex drive than men do. On the other hand we are told that the madonna-whore dichotomy is a universal stereotype. In every culture, there is a tendency among both men and women to adjudge women as either chaste or trampy. The chaste ones are accorded esteem. The trampy ones are consigned to the basement, a notch or two below goats in social status. A woman can't sleep around without risking terrible retribution, to her reputation, to her prospects, to her life. "Can anyone find a single culture in which women with unrestrained sexual appetites aren't viewed as more aberrant than comparably libidinous men?" Wright asks rhetorically.

Women are said to have lower sex drives than men, yet they are universally punished if they display evidence to the contrary—if they disobey their "natural" inclination toward a stifled libido. Women supposedly have a lower sex drive than men do, yet it is not low enough. There is still just enough of a lingering female infidelity impulse that cultures everywhere have had to gird against it by articulating a rigid dichotomy with menacing implications for those who fall on the wrong side of it. There is still enough lingering female infidelity to justify infibulation, purdah, claustration. Men have the naturally higher sex drive, yet all the laws, customs, punishments, shame, strictures, mystiques and antimystiques are aimed with full hominid fury at that tepid, sleepy, hypoactive creature, the female libido.

"It seems premature . . . to attribute the relative lack of female inter- 20 est in sexual variety to women's biological nature alone in the face of overwhelming evidence that women are consistently beaten for promiscuity and adultery," the primatologist Barbara Smuts has written. "If female sexuality is muted compared to that of men, then why must men the world over go to extreme lengths to control and contain it?"

Why indeed? Consider a brief evolutionary apologia for President Clinton's adulteries written by Steven Pinker, of the Massachusetts Institute of Technology. "Most human drives have ancient Darwinian rationales," he wrote. "A prehistoric man who slept with fifty women could have sired fifty children, and would have been more likely to have descendants who inherited his tastes. A woman who slept with fifty men would have no more descendants than a woman who slept with one. Thus, men should seek quantity in sexual partners; women, quality." And isn't it so, he says, everywhere and always so? "In our society," he continues, "most young men tell researchers that they would like eight sexual partners in the next two years; most women say that they would like one." Yet would a man find the prospect of a string of partners so appealing if the following rules were applied: that no matter how much he may like a particular woman and be pleased by her performance and want to sleep with her again, he will have no say in the matter and will be dependent on her mood and good graces for all future contact; that each act of casual sex will cheapen his status and make him increasingly less attractive to other women; and that society will not wink at his randiness but rather sneer at him and think him pathetic, sullied, smaller than life? Until men are subjected to the same severe standards and threat of censure as women are, and until they are given the lower hand in a so-called casual encounter from the start, it is hard to insist with such self-satisfaction that, hey, it's natural, men like a lot of sex with a lot of people and women don't.

Reflect for a moment on Pinker's philandering caveman who slept with fifty women. Just how good a reproductive strategy is this chronic, random shooting of the gun? A woman is fertile only five or six days a month. Her ovulation is concealed. The man doesn't know when she's fertile. She might be in the early stages of pregnancy when he gets to her; she might still be lactating and thus not ovulating. Moreover, even if our hypothetical Don Juan hits a day on which a woman is ovulating, the chances are around 65 percent that his sperm will fail to fertilize her egg; human reproduction is complicated, and most eggs and sperm are not up to the demands of proper fusion. Even if conception occurs, the resulting embryo has about a 30 percent chance of miscarrying at some point in gestation. In sum, each episode of fleeting sex has a remarkably small probability of yielding a baby—no more than 1 or 2 percent at best.

And because the man is trysting and running, he isn't able to prevent any of his casual contacts from turning around and mating with other men. The poor fellow. He has to mate with many scores of women for his wham-bam strategy to pay off. And where are all these women to be found, anyway? Population densities during that purportedly all-powerful psyche shaper the "ancestral environment" were quite low, and long-distance travel was dangerous and difficult.

There are alternatives to wantonness, as a number of theorists have emphasized. If, for example, a man were to spend more time with one woman rather than dashing breathlessly from sheet to sheet, if he were to feel compelled to engage in what animal behaviorists call mate guarding, he might be better off, reproductively speaking, than the wild Lothario, both because the odds of impregnating the woman would increase and because he'd be monopolizing her energy and keeping her from the advances of other sperm bearers. It takes the average couple three to four months of regular sexual intercourse to become pregnant. That number of days is approximately equal to the number of partners our hypothetical libertine needs to sleep with to have one encounter result in a "fertility unit," that is, a baby. The two strategies, then, shake out about the same. A man can sleep with a lot of women—the quantitative approach— or he can sleep with one woman for months at a time, and be madly in love with her—the qualitative tactic.

It's possible that these two reproductive strategies are distributed 25 in discrete packets among the male population, with a result that some men are born philanderers and can never attach, while others are born romantics and perpetually in love with love; but it's also possible that men teeter back and forth from one impulse to the other, suffering an internal struggle between the desire to bond and the desire to retreat, with the circuits of attachment ever there to be toyed with, and their needs and desires difficult to understand, paradoxical, fickle, treacherous and glorious. It is possible, then, and for perfectly good Darwinian reason, that casual sex for men is rarely as casual as it is billed.

It needn't be argued that men and women are exactly the same, or that humans are meta-evolutionary beings, removed from nature and slaves to culture, to reject the perpetually regurgitated model of the coy female and the ardent male. Conflicts of interest are always among us, and the outcomes of those conflicts are interesting, more interesting by far than what the ultra-evolutionary psychology line has handed us. Patricia Gowaty, of the University of Georgia, sees conflict between males and females as inevitable and pervasive. She calls it sexual dialectics. Her thesis is that females and males vie for control over the means of reproduction. Those means are the female body, for there is as yet no such beast as the parthenogenetic[4] man.

Women are under selective pressure to maintain control over their reproduction, to choose with whom they will mate and with whom they will not—to exercise female choice. Men are under selective pressure to make sure they're chosen or, barring that, to subvert female choice and coerce the female to mate against her will. "But once you have this basic dialectic set in motion, it's going to be a constant push-me, pull-you," Gowaty says. That dynamism cannot possibly result in a unitary response, the caricatured coy woman and ardent man. Instead there are going to be some coy, reluctantly mating males and some ardent females, and any number of variations in between.

"A female will choose to mate with a male whom she believes, consciously or otherwise, will confer some advantage on her and her offspring. If that's the case, then her decision is contingent on what she brings to the equation." For example, she says, "the 'good genes' model leads to oversimplified notions that there is a 'best male' out there, a top-of-the-line hunk whom all females would prefer to mate with if they had the wherewithal. But in the viability model, a female brings

[4]Created from an unfertilized egg.

her own genetic complement to the equation, with the result that what looks good genetically to one woman might be a clash of colors for another."

Maybe the man's immune system doesn't complement her own, for example, Gowaty proposes. There's evidence that the search for immune variation is one of the subtle factors driving mate selection, which may be why we care about how our lovers smell; immune molecules may be volatilized and released in sweat, hair, the oil on our skin. We are each of us a chemistry set, and each of us has a distinctive mix of reagents. "What pleases me might not please somebody else," Gowaty says. "There is no one-brand great male out there. We're not all programmed to look for the alpha male and only willing to mate with the little guy or the less aggressive guy because we can't do any better. But the propaganda gives us a picture of the right man and the ideal woman, and the effect of the propaganda is insidious. It becomes self-reinforcing. People who don't fit the model think, I'm weird, I'll have to change my behavior." It is this danger, that the ostensible "discoveries" of evolutionary psychology will be used as propaganda, that makes the enterprise so disturbing.

Variation and flexibility are the key themes that get set aside in the 30 breathless dissemination of evolutionary psychology. "The variation is tremendous, and is rooted in biology," Barbara Smuts said to me. "Flexibility itself is the adaptation." Smuts has studied olive baboons, and she has seen males pursuing all sorts of mating strategies. "There are some whose primary strategy is dominating other males, and being able to gain access to more females because of their fighting ability," she says. "Then there is the type of male who avoids competition and cultivates long-term relationships with females and their infants. These are the nice, affiliative guys. There's a third type, who focuses on sexual relationships. He's the consorter. . . . And as far as we can tell, no one reproductive strategy has advantages over the others."

Women are said to need an investing male. We think we know the reason. Human babies are difficult and time consuming to raise. Stone Age mothers needed husbands to bring home the bison. Yet the age-old assumption that male parental investment lies at the heart of human evolution is now open to serious question. Men in traditional foraging cultures do not necessarily invest resources in their offspring. Among the Hadza of Africa, for example, the men hunt, but they share the bounty of that hunting widely, politically, strategically. They don't deliver it straight to the mouths of their progeny. Women rely on their senior female kin to help feed their children. The women and their children in a gathering-hunting society clearly benefit from the meat that hunters bring back to the group. But they benefit as a group, not as a collection of nuclear family units, each beholden to the father's personal pound of wildeburger.

This is a startling revelation, which upends many of our presumptions about the origins of marriage and what women want from men and men from women. If the environment of evolutionary adaptation is not defined primarily by male parental investment, the bedrock of so much of evolutionary psychology's theories, then we can throw the door wide open and ask new questions, rather than endlessly repeating ditties and calling the female coy long after she has run her petticoats through the presidential paper shredder.

For example: Nicholas Blurton Jones, of the University of California at Los Angeles, and others have proposed that marriage developed as an extension of men's efforts at mate guarding. If the cost of philandering becomes ludicrously high, the man might be better off trying to claim rights to one woman at a time. Regular sex with a fertile woman is at least likely to yield offspring at comparatively little risk to his life, particularly if sexual access to the woman is formalized through a public ceremony—a wedding. Looked at from this perspective, one must wonder why an ancestral woman bothered to get married, particularly if she and her female relatives did most of the work of keeping the family fed from year to year. Perhaps, Blurton Jones suggests, to limit the degree to which she was harassed. The cost of chronic male harassment may be too high to bear. Better to agree to a ritualized bond with a male and to benefit from whatever hands-off policy that marriage may bring, than to spend all of her time locked in one sexual dialectic or another.

Thus marriage may have arisen as a multifaceted social pact: between man and woman, between male and male and between the couple and the tribe. It is a reasonable solution to a series of cultural challenges that arose in concert with the expansion of the human neocortex. But its roots may not be what we think they are, nor may our contemporary mating behaviors stem from the pressures of an ancestral environment as it is commonly portrayed, in which a woman needed a mate to help feed and clothe her young. Instead, our "deep" feelings about marriage may be more pragmatic, more contextual and, dare I say it, more egalitarian than we give them credit for being.

If marriage is a social compact, a mutual bid between man and 35 woman to contrive a reasonably stable and agreeable microhabitat in a community of shrewd and well-armed members, then we can understand why, despite rhetoric to the contrary, men are as eager to marry as women are. A raft of epidemiological studies have shown that marriage adds more years to the life of a man than it does to that of a woman. Why should that be, if men are so "naturally" ill suited to matrimony?

What do women want? None of us can speak for all women, or for more than one woman, really, but we can hazard a mad guess that a desire for emotional parity is widespread and profound. It doesn't go away, although it often hibernates under duress, and it may be perverted by the restrictions of habitat or culture into something that looks like its opposite. The impulse for liberty is congenital. It is the ultimate manifestation of selfishness, which is why we can count on its endurance.

STUDY QUESTIONS

1. What theories of evolutionary psychology does Angier call into question? What alternative theories does she propose?

2. List the people Angier quotes or cites. How does each contribute to her essay? What is the rhetorical effect of using these sources? How would the essay be different if she hadn't used sources?

3. *For Writing.* Write an essay in which you explain, in your own words, a theory of evolutionary psychology that Angier discusses. Then DESCRIBE the behavior of at least two people you know and explain how that behavior supports or refutes that theory.

RUSSELL BAKER { *The Plot Against People*

Russell Baker (b. 1925), journalist, columnist, and essayist, was born in Morrisonville, Virginia, and earned a BA from the Johns Hopkins University in 1947. From 1962 to 2008 he wrote the nationally syndicated "Observer" column for the *New York Times*, for which he won a Pulitzer Prize in 1979. He received a second Pulitzer in 1983 for his autobiography *Growing Up*. His other books include *The Good Times* (1992), a continuation of *Growing Up*, and several collections of his columns and essays. Baker hosted PBS's *Masterpiece Theatre* from 1992 to 2004.

In "The Plot against People," Baker humorously employs science to make sense out of decidedly unscientific occurrences: everyday objects getting broken or lost. As he classifies each type of object in its proper scientific category, Baker proposes a theory to explain why inanimate objects are in such adversarial relationships with their owners. Note how he carefully builds his case through logical reasoning and personification.

Inanimate objects are classified scientifically into three major categories—those that don't work, those that break down and those that get lost.

The goal of all inanimate objects is to resist man and ultimately to defeat him, and the three major classifications are based on the method each object uses to achieve its purpose. As a general rule, any object capable of breaking down at the moment when it is most needed will do so. The automobile is typical of the category.

With the cunning typical of its breed, the automobile never breaks down while entering a filling station with a large staff of idle mechanics. It waits until it reaches a downtown intersection in the middle of the rush hour, or until it is fully loaded with family and luggage on the Ohio Turnpike.

Thus it creates maximum misery, inconvenience, frustration and irritability among its human cargo, thereby reducing its owner's life span.

Washing machines, garbage disposals, lawn mowers, light bulbs,   5 automatic laundry dryers, water pipes, furnaces, electrical fuses, television tubes, hose nozzles, tape recorders, slide projectors—all are in league with the automobile to take their turn at breaking down whenever life threatens to flow smoothly for their human enemies.

Many inanimate objects, of course, find it extremely difficult to break down. Pliers, for example, and gloves and keys are almost totally incapable of breaking down. Therefore, they have had to evolve a different technique for resisting man.

A PLAUSIBLE THEORY

They get lost. Science has still not solved the mystery of how they do it, and no man has ever caught one of them in the act of getting lost. The most plausible theory is that they have developed a secret method of locomotion which they are able to conceal the instant a human eye falls upon them.

It is not uncommon for a pair of pliers to climb all the way from the cellar to the attic in its single-minded determination to raise its owner's blood pressure. Keys have been known to burrow three feet under mattresses. Women's purses, despite their great weight, frequently travel through six or seven rooms to find hiding space under a couch.

Scientists have been struck by the fact that things that break down virtually never get lost, while things that get lost hardly ever break down.

A furnace, for example, will invariably break down at the depth of   10 the first winter cold wave, but it will never get lost. A woman's purse, which after all does have some inherent capacity for breaking down, hardly ever does; it almost invariably chooses to get lost.

Some persons believe this constitutes evidence that inanimate objects are not entirely hostile to man, and that a negotiated peace is possible. After all, they point out, a furnace could infuriate a man even more thoroughly by getting lost than by breaking down, just as a glove could upset him far more by breaking down than by getting lost.

Not everyone agrees, however, that this indicates a conciliatory attitude among inanimate objects. Many say it merely proves that furnaces, gloves and pliers are incredibly stupid.

The third class of objects—those that don't work—is the most curious of all. These include such objects as barometers, car clocks, cigarette lighters, flashlights and toy-train locomotives. It is inaccurate, of course, to say that they never work. They work once, usually for the first few hours after being brought home, and then quit. Thereafter, they never work again.

In fact, it is widely assumed that they are built for the purpose of not working. Some people have reached advanced ages without ever seeing some of these objects—barometers, for example—in working order.

Science is utterly baffled by the entire category. There are many theories about it. The most interesting holds that the things that don't work have attained the highest state possible for an inanimate object, the state to which things that break down and things that get lost can still only aspire.

THEY GIVE PEACE

They have truly defeated man by conditioning him never to expect anything of them, and in return they have given man the only peace he receives from inanimate society. He does not expect his barometer to work, his electric locomotive to run, his cigarette lighter to light or his flashlight to illuminate, and when they don't, it does not raise his blood pressure.

He cannot attain that peace with furnaces and keys and cars and women's purses as long as he demands that they work for their keep.

STUDY QUESTIONS

1. What are the three major categories that Baker establishes in his essay, and what inanimate objects does he mention as representative examples of each?

2. How does Baker use science, humor, and personification as he presents his CLASSIFICATION scheme? What is the effect of classifying the adversarial relationship between inanimate objects and humans from a scientific perspective?

3. *For Writing.* Update this opinion piece (written in 1968) for your generation. Create several categories and, in an essay, classify the relationships you have with several items you own—such as an iPod, a cell phone, or a laptop computer.

JAMAICA KINCAID   { *Girl*

JAMAICA KINCAID (b. 1949) was born Elaine Potter Richardson in
St. John's, the capital of the Caribbean island of Antigua, then a British
colony. She emigrated at age seventeen to New York State and soon
moved to New York City, where she changed her name, worked at
several jobs, and attended community college at night; she later studied
photography at Franconia College in New Hampshire. Kincaid began
writing for magazines in the 1970s, and from 1976 to 1995 she was a staff
writer at *The New Yorker*. Her books include, among other works of
fiction and nonfiction, the novels *Annie John* (1985) and *Lucy* (1990), the
collection of short stories *At the Bottom of the River* (1984), the memoir
My Brother (1997), and the nonfiction *A Small Place* (1988). Kincaid
currently teaches at Claremont McKenna College during the academic
year and lives in Bennington, Vermont.

Originally published in *The New Yorker* in 1978, "Girl" later
appeared as the first story in Kincaid's collection *At the Bottom of the
River* (1983). Blurring the lines between fiction and nonfiction, the story
distills a mother's teachings to her daughter into a single potent collection of phrases that reveals much about relationships, coming of age,
men and women, societal expectations, and much more. As you read,
pay close attention to the style of the piece, particularly the rhythm of its
language.

═══════════════

WASH THE WHITE CLOTHES ON Monday and put them on the stone
heap; wash the color clothes on Tuesday and put them on the clothes-
line to dry; don't walk barehead in the hot sun; cook pumpkin fritters

in very hot sweet oil; soak your little cloths right after you take them off; when buying cotton to make yourself a nice blouse, be sure that it doesn't have gum on it, because that way it won't hold up well after a wash; soak salt fish overnight before you cook it; is it true that you sing benna[1] in Sunday school?; always eat your food in such a way that it won't turn someone else's stomach; on Sundays try to walk like a lady and not like the slut you are so bent on becoming; don't sing benna in Sunday school; you mustn't speak to wharf-rat boys, not even to give directions; don't eat fruits on the street—flies will follow you; *but I don't sing benna on Sundays at all and never in Sunday school*; this is how to sew on a button; this is how to make a buttonhole for the button you have just sewed on; this is how to hem a dress when you see the hem coming down and so to prevent yourself from looking like the slut I know you are so bent on becoming; this is how you iron your father's khaki shirt so that it doesn't have a crease; this is how you iron your father's khaki pants so that they don't have a crease; this is how you grow okra—far from the house, because okra tree harbors red ants; when you are growing dasheen,[2] make sure it gets plenty of water or else it makes your throat itch when you are eating it; this is how you sweep a corner; this is how you sweep a whole house; this is how you sweep a yard; this is how you smile to someone you don't like too much; this is how you smile to someone you don't like at all; this is how you smile to someone you like completely; this is how you set a table for tea; this is how you set a table for dinner; this is how you set a table for dinner with an important guest; this is how you set a table for lunch; this is how you set a table for breakfast; this is how to behave in the presence of men who don't know you very well, and this way they won't recognize immediately the slut I have warned you against becoming; be sure to wash every day, even if it is with your own spit; don't squat down to play marbles—you are not a boy, you know; don't pick people's flowers—you might catch something; don't throw stones at blackbirds, because it might not be a blackbird at all;

[1] Form of African song brought by slaves from Africa to Antigua and Jamaica; benna's themes were often scandalous or gruesome. In Kincaid's youth, the term also referred to all secular music.

[2] Caribbean staple vegetable whose roots and leaves are used in many dishes.

this is how to make a bread pudding; this is how to make doukona;[3] this is how to make pepper pot; this is how to make a good medicine for a cold; this is how to make a good medicine to throw away a child before it even becomes a child; this is how to catch a fish; this is how to throw back a fish you don't like, and that way something bad won't fall on you; this is how to bully a man; this is how a man bullies you; this is how to love a man, and if this doesn't work there are other ways, and if they don't work don't feel too bad about giving up; this is how to spit up in the air if you feel like it, and this is how to move quick so that it doesn't fall on you; this is how to make ends meet; always squeeze bread to make sure it's fresh; *but what if the baker won't let me feel the bread?*; you mean to say that after all you are really going to be the kind of woman who the baker won't let near the bread?

[3]Pudding composed of cornmeal, plantain, coconut, sugar, and spices.

STUDY QUESTIONS

1. How would you summarize the instructions being passed on to the girl? What do these instructions tell you about the speaker?

2. Describe the STYLE of this story. How is it told? How does the style influence your reading of it? What kind of language does it use? Does the style seem similar to that of any other texts you've read, particularly those that employ STREAM-OF-CONSCIOUSNESS narration?

3. Notice the two phrases in italics. What do the italics represent? How can you tell? How does the VOICE in the italics differ from the dominant voice in the story? What is the connection between the italicized text and the title of the story?

4. *For Writing.* Reread "Girl" and look for THEMES or categories of advice that the dominant voice offers (domestic advice might be one, or etiquette). Select one theme or category and mark specific phrases that fit that theme. Then write a brief essay in which you explain how the instructions from the story fit with your selected theme and discuss why this category of advice is so important to the speaker. Where does the speaker seem to deviate from the theme?

WILLIAM LUTZ { *The World of Doublespeak*

WILLIAM LUTZ (b. 1941) earned an MA from Marquette University, a PhD
from the University of Nevada, Reno, and a JD from the Rutgers School of
Law. He began teaching English at Rutgers in 1971 and is now an emeritus
faculty member there. As a leader in the "plain language" movement, he has
shared his expertise on radio and television programs, served as an expert
legal witness on readability, and worked with private businesses and government agencies to make their information more accessible. Lutz has published more than two dozen articles in magazines and newspapers, including
the *Los Angeles Times*, the *Atlanta Constitution*, the *Baltimore Sun*, *USA
Today*, *Esquire*, and *The Times of London*. He has authored, co-authored,
or edited several books, and he edited the *Quarterly Review of Doublespeak*
for fourteen years. In 1996 the National Council of Teachers of English
honored Lutz with the George Orwell Award for Distinguished
Contribution to Honesty and Clarity in Public Language.

"The World of Doublespeak," the introductory chapter to Lutz's book
*Doublespeak: From "Revenue Enhancement" to "Terminal Living"—How
Government, Business, Advertisers, and Others Use Language to Deceive You*
(1989), lays the foundation for much of Lutz's later work. In this excerpt
from it, he defines "doublespeak" and identifies several of its major sources.
While reading, think of examples of doublespeak you encounter today. What
is the effect on the reader or listener of such language?

THERE ARE NO POTHOLES IN the streets of Tucson, Arizona, just
"pavement deficiencies." The Reagan Administration didn't propose
any new taxes, just "revenue enhancement" through new "user's fees."

Those aren't bums on the street, just "non-goal oriented members of society." There are no more poor people, just "fiscal underachievers." There was no robbery of an automatic teller machine, just an "unauthorized withdrawal." The patient didn't die because of medical malpractice, it was just a "diagnostic misadventure of a high magnitude." The U.S. Army doesn't kill the enemy anymore, it just "services the target." And the doublespeak goes on.

Doublespeak is language that pretends to communicate but really doesn't. It is language that makes the bad seem good, the negative appear positive, the unpleasant appear attractive or at least tolerable. Doublespeak is language that avoids or shifts responsibility, language that is at variance with its real or purported meaning. It is language that conceals or prevents thought; rather than extending thought, doublespeak limits it.

Doublespeak is not a matter of subjects and verbs agreeing; it is a matter of words and facts agreeing. Basic to doublespeak is incongruity, the incongruity between what is said or left unsaid, and what really is. It is the incongruity between the word and the referent, between seem and be, between the essential function of language—communication—and what doublespeak does—mislead, distort, deceive, inflate, circumvent, obfuscate.

HOW TO SPOT DOUBLESPEAK

How can you spot doublespeak? Most of the time you will recognize doublespeak when you see or hear it. But, if you have any doubts, you can identify doublespeak just by answering these questions: Who is saying what to whom, under what conditions and circumstances, with what intent, and with what results? Answering these questions will usually help you identify as doublespeak language that appears to be legitimate or that at first glance doesn't even appear to be doublespeak.

First Kind of Doublespeak

There are at least four kinds of doublespeak. The first is the euphemism, an inoffensive or positive word or phrase used to avoid a harsh, 5 unpleasant, or distasteful reality. But a euphemism can also be a tactful word or phrase which avoids directly mentioning a painful reality, or it can be an expression used out of concern for the feelings of someone else, or to avoid directly discussing a topic subject to a social or cultural taboo.

When you use a euphemism because of your sensitivity for someone's feelings or out of concern for a recognized social or cultural taboo, it is not doublespeak. For example, you express your condolences that someone has "passed away" because you do not want to say to a grieving person, "I'm sorry your father is dead." When you use the euphemism "passed away," no one is misled. Moreover, the euphemism functions here not just to protect the feelings of another person, but to communicate also your concern for that person's feelings during a period of mourning. When you excuse yourself to go to the "rest room," or you mention that someone is "sleeping with" or "involved with" someone else, you do not mislead anyone about your meaning, but you do respect the social taboos about discussing bodily functions and sex in direct terms. You also indicate your sensitivity to the feelings of your audience, which is usually considered a mark of courtesy and good manners.

However, when a euphemism is used to mislead or deceive, it becomes doublespeak. For example, in 1984 the U.S. State Department announced that it would no longer use the word "killing" in its annual report on the status of human rights in countries around the world. Instead, it would use the phrase "unlawful or arbitrary deprivation of life," which the department claimed was more accurate. Its real purpose for using this phrase was simply to avoid discussing the embarrassing situation of government-sanctioned killings in countries that are supported by the United States and have been certified by the United States as respecting the human rights of their citizens. This use of a euphemism constitutes doublespeak, since it is designed to mislead, to cover up the unpleasant. Its real intent is at variance with its apparent intent. It is language designed to alter our perception of reality.

The Pentagon, too, avoids discussing unpleasant realities when it refers to bombs and artillery shells that fall on civilian targets as "incontinent ordnance." And in 1977 the Pentagon tried to slip funding for the neutron bomb unnoticed into an appropriations bill by calling it a "radiation enhancement device."

Second Kind of Doublespeak

A second kind of doublespeak is jargon, the specialized language of a trade, profession, or similar group, such as that used by doctors, lawyers, engineers, educators, or car mechanics. Jargon can serve an important and useful function. Within a group, jargon functions as a kind of verbal shorthand that allows members of the group to communicate with each other clearly, efficiently, and quickly. Indeed, it is a mark of membership in the group to be able to use and understand the group's jargon.

But jargon, like the euphemism, can also be doublespeak. It can   10 be—and often is—pretentious, obscure, and esoteric terminology used to give an air of profundity, authority, and prestige to speakers and their subject matter. Jargon as doublespeak often makes the simple appear complex, the ordinary profound, the obvious insightful. In this sense it is used not to express but impress. With such doublespeak, the act of smelling something becomes "organoleptic analysis," glass becomes "fused silicate," a crack in a metal support beam becomes a "discontinuity," conservative economic policies become "distributionally conservative notions."

Lawyers, for example, speak of an "involuntary conversion" of property when discussing the loss or destruction of property through theft, accident, or condemnation. If your house burns down or if your car is stolen, you have suffered an involuntary conversion of your property. When used by lawyers in a legal situation, such jargon is a legitimate use of language, since lawyers can be expected to understand the term.

However, when a member of a specialized group uses its jargon to communicate with a person outside the group, and uses it knowing that the nonmember does not understand such language, then there is doublespeak. For example, on May 9, 1978, a National Airlines 727 airplane crashed while attempting to land at the Pensacola, Florida, airport. Three of the fifty-two passengers aboard the airplane were killed. As a result of the crash, National made an after-tax insurance benefit of $1.7 million, or an extra 18¢ a share dividend for its stockholders. Now National Airlines had two problems: It did not want to talk about one of its airplanes crashing, and it had to account for the $1.7 million when it issued its annual report to its stockholders. National solved the problem by inserting a footnote in its annual report which explained that the $1.7 million income was due to "the involuntary conversion of a 727." National thus acknowledged the crash of its airplane and the subsequent profit it made from the crash, without once mentioning the accident or the deaths. However, because airline officials knew that most stockholders in the company, and indeed most of the general public, were not familiar with legal jargon, the use of such jargon constituted doublespeak.

Third Kind of Doublespeak

A third kind of doublespeak is gobbledygook or bureaucratese. Basically, such doublespeak is simply a matter of piling on words, of overwhelming the audience with words, the bigger the words and the longer the sentences the better. Alan Greenspan, then chair of President Nixon's Council of Economic Advisors, was quoted in *The Philadelphia Inquirer* in 1974 as having testified before a Senate committee that "It is a tricky problem to find the particular calibration in timing that would be appropriate to stem the acceleration in risk premiums created by falling incomes without prematurely aborting the decline in the inflation-generated risk premiums."

Nor has Mr. Greenspan's language changed since then. Speaking to the meeting of the Economic Club of New York in 1988, Mr. Greenspan, now Federal Reserve chair, said, "I guess I should warn you, if I turn out to be particularly clear, you've probably misunderstood what I've said." Mr. Greenspan's doublespeak doesn't seem to have held back his career.

Sometimes gobbledygook may sound impressive, but when the 15 quote is later examined in print it doesn't even make sense. During the 1988 presidential campaign, vice-presidential candidate Senator Dan

Quayle explained the need for a strategic-defense initiative by saying, "Why wouldn't an enhanced deterrent, a more stable peace, a better prospect to denying the ones who enter conflict in the first place to have a reduction of offensive systems and an introduction to defensive capability? I believe this is the route the country will eventually go."

The investigation into the *Challenger* disaster in 1986[1] revealed the doublespeak of gobbledygook and bureaucratese used by too many involved in the shuttle program. When Jesse Moore, NASA's associate administrator, was asked if the performance of the shuttle program had improved with each launch or if it had remained the same, he answered, "I think our performance in terms of the liftoff performance and in terms of the orbital performance, we knew more about the envelope we were operating under, and we have been pretty accurately staying in that. And so I would say the performance has not by design drastically improved. I think we have been able to characterize the performance more as a function of our launch experience as opposed to it improving as a function of time." While this language may appear to be jargon, a close look will reveal that it is really just gobbledygook laced with jargon. But you really have to wonder if Mr. Moore had any idea what he was saying.

Fourth Kind of Doublespeak

The fourth kind of doublespeak is inflated language that is designed to make the ordinary seem extraordinary; to make everyday things seem impressive; to give an air of importance to people, situations, or things that would not normally be considered important; to make the simple seem complex. Often this kind of doublespeak isn't hard to spot, and it is usually pretty funny. While car mechanics may be called "automotive internists," elevator operators members of the "vertical transportation corps," used cars "pre-owned" or "experienced cars," and black-and-white television sets described as having "non-multicolor capability," you really aren't misled all that much by such language.

---

[1]The NASA space shuttle *Challenger* broke apart just after liftoff, killing all seven astronauts, including Christa McAuliffe, the first member of the Teacher in Space Project.

However, you may have trouble figuring out that, when Chrysler "initiates a career alternative enhancement program," it is really laying off five thousand workers; or that "negative patient care outcome" means the patient died; or that "rapid oxidation" means a fire in a nuclear power plant.

The doublespeak of inflated language can have serious consequences. In Pentagon doublespeak, "pre-emptive counterattack" means that American forces attacked first; "engaged the enemy on all sides" means American troops were ambushed; "backloading of augmentation personnel" means a retreat by American troops. In the doublespeak of the military, the 1983 invasion of Grenada was conducted not by the U.S. Army, Navy, Air Force, and Marines, but by the "Caribbean Peace Keeping Forces." But then, according to the Pentagon, it wasn't an invasion, it was a "predawn vertical insertion."

DOUBLESPEAK THROUGHOUT HISTORY

Doublespeak is not a new use of language peculiar to the politics or   20 economics of the twentieth century. In the fifth century B.C., the Greek historian Thucydides wrote in *The Peloponnesian War* that

> revolution thus ran its course from city to city. . . . Words had to change their ordinary meanings and to take those which were now given them. Reckless audacity came to be considered the courage of a loyal ally; prudent hesitation, specious cowardice; moderation was held to be a cloak for unmanliness; ability to see all sides of a question, inaptness to act on any. Frantic violence became the attribute of manliness; cautious plotting, a justifiable means of self-defense. The advocate of extreme measures was always trustworthy; his opponent, a man to be suspected.

Julius Caesar, in his account of the Gallic Wars, described his brutal and bloody conquest and subjugation of Gaul as "pacifying" Gaul. "Where they make a desert, they call it peace," said an English nobleman quoted by the Roman historian Tacitus. When traitors were put to death in Rome, the announcement of their execution was made in the form of saying "they have lived." "Taking notice of a man in the ancestral manner" meant capital punishment; "the prisoner was then led away" meant he was executed.

In his memoirs, *V-2*, Walter Dornberger, commanding officer of the Peenemünde Rocket Research Institute in Germany during World War II, describes how he and his staff used language to get what they needed from the Bureau of Budget for their rocket experiments. A pencil sharpener was an "Appliance for milling wooden dowels up to 10 millimeters in diameter," and a typewriter was an "Instrument for recording test data with rotating roller." But it was the Nazis who were the masters of doublespeak, and they used it not just to achieve and maintain power but to perpetrate some of the most heinous crimes in the history of the human race.

In the world of Nazi Germany, nonprofessional prostitutes were called "persons with varied sexual relationships"; "protective custody" was the very opposite of protective; "Winter Relief" was a compulsory tax presented as a voluntary charity; and a "straightening of the front" was a retreat, while serious difficulties became "bottlenecks." Minister of Information (the very title is doublespeak) Josef Goebbels spoke in all seriousness of "simple pomp" and "the liberalization of the freedom of the press."

Nazi doublespeak reached its peak when dealing with the "Final Solution,"[2] a phrase that is itself the ultimate in doublespeak. The notice, "The Jew X.Y. lived here," posted on a door, meant the occupant had been "deported," that is, killed. When mail was returned stamped "Addressee has moved away," it meant the person had been "deported." "Resettlement" also meant deportation, while "work camp" meant concentration camp or incinerator, "action" meant massacre, "Special Action Groups" were army units that conducted mass murder, "selection" meant gassing, and "shot while trying to escape" meant deliberately killed in a concentration camp.

---

[2]Adolf Hitler's plan to exterminate the Jewish population of Europe during World War II.

GEORGE ORWELL AND LANGUAGE

In his famous and now-classic essay, "Politics and the English   25
Language," which was published in 1946, George Orwell wrote that
the "great enemy of clear language is insincerity. When there is a gap
between one's real and one's declared aims, one turns as it were
instinctively to long words and exhausted idioms, like a cuttlefish
squirting out ink." For Orwell, language was an instrument for
"expressing and not for concealing or preventing thought." In his most
biting comment, he observed that, "in our time, political speech and
writing are largely the defense of the indefensible. . . . [P]olitical language has to consist largely of euphemism, question-begging, and
sheer cloudy vagueness. . . . Political language . . . is designed to make
lies sound truthful and murder respectable, and to give an appearance
of solidity to pure wind."

Orwell understood well the power of language as both a tool and a
weapon. In the nightmare world of his novel *1984,* Orwell depicted a
society where language was one of the most important tools of the
totalitarian state. Newspeak, the official state language in the world of
1984, was designed not to extend but to *diminish* the range of human
thought, to make only "correct" thought possible and all other modes
of thought impossible. It was, in short, a language designed to create a
reality that the state wanted.

Newspeak had another important function in Orwell's world of
1984. It provided the means of expression for doublethink, the mental
process that allows you to hold two opposing ideas in your mind at the
same time and believe in both of them. The classic example in Orwell's
novel is the slogan, "War Is Peace." Lest you think doublethink is confined only to Orwell's novel, you need only recall the words of
Secretary of State Alexander Haig when he testified before a congressional committee in 1982 that a continued weapons build-up by the
United States is "absolutely essential to our hopes for meaningful arms
reduction." Or remember what Senator Orrin Hatch said in 1988:
"Capital punishment is our society's recognition of the sanctity of
human life."

At its worst, doublespeak, like newspeak, is language designed to limit, if not eliminate, thought. Like doublethink, doublespeak enables speaker and listener, writer and reader, to hold two opposing ideas in their minds at the same time and believe in both of them. At its least offensive, doublespeak is inflated language that tries to give importance to the insignificant.[3]

* * *

DEADLY DOUBLESPEAK

There are instances, however, where doublespeak becomes more than amusing, more than a cause for a laugh. At St. Mary's Hospital in Minneapolis in 1982, an anesthetist turned the wrong knob during a Cesarean delivery, giving a fatal dose of nitrous oxide which killed the mother and unborn child. The hospital called it a "therapeutic misadventure." In its budget request to Congress in 1977, the Pentagon called the neutron bomb "an efficient nuclear weapon that eliminates an enemy with a minimum degree of damage to friendly territory." The Pentagon also calls the expected tens of millions of civilian dead in a nuclear war "collateral damage," a term the Pentagon also applies to the civilians killed in any war. And in 1977 people watching the Dick Cavett show on television learned from former Green Beret Captain Bob Marasco that during the Vietnam war the Central Intelligence Agency created the phrase "eliminate with extreme prejudice" to replace the more direct verb "kill."

President Reagan and the Doublespeak of Politics

Identifying doublespeak can at times be difficult. For example, on July   30
27, 1981, President Ronald Reagan said in a speech televised to the
American public that "I will not stand by and see those of you who are

---

[3]To condense this selection the editors have omitted the next section of Lutz's chapter, titled "The Doublespeak All Around Us." In it, Lutz provides examples of doublespeak from three categories: the military, business, and education. Lutz concludes the section by remarking on the prevalance of doublespeak in education, citing this example from a 1966 research report from the U.S. Office of Education: "In other words feediness is the shared information between toputness, where toputness is at a time just prior to the inputness."

dependent on Social Security deprived of the benefits you've worked so hard to earn. You will continue to receive your checks in the full amount due you." This speech had been billed as President Reagan's position on Social Security, a subject of much debate at the time. After the speech, public opinion polls revealed that the great majority of the public believed that the president had affirmed his support for Social Security and that he would not support cuts in benefits. However, only days after the speech, on July 31, 1981, an article in the *Philadelphia Inquirer* quoted White House spokesperson David Gergen as saying that President Reagan's words had been "carefully chosen." What President Reagan had meant, according to Gergen, was that he was reserving the right to decide who was "dependent" on those benefits, who had "earned" them, and who, therefore, was "due" them.

The subsequent remarks of David Gergen reveal the real intent of President Reagan as opposed to his apparent intent. Thus, the criteria for analyzing language to determine whether it is doublespeak (who is saying what to whom, under what conditions and circumstances, with what intent, and with what results), when applied in light of David Gergen's remarks, reveal the doublespeak of President Reagan. Here, indeed, is the insincerity of which Orwell wrote. Here, too, is the gap between the speaker's real and declared aim.

Doublespeak and Political Advertisements

During the 1982 congressional election campaign, the Republican National Committee sponsored a television advertisement that pictured an elderly, folksy postman delivering Social Security checks "with the 7.4 percent cost-of-living raise that President Reagan promised." The postman then adds that "he promised that raise and he kept his promise, in spite of those sticks-in-the-mud who tried to keep him from doing what we elected him to do." The commercial was, in fact, deliberately misleading. The cost-of-living increases had been provided automatically by law since 1975, and President Reagan had tried three times to roll them back or delay them but was overruled by congressional opposition. When these discrepancies were pointed out to an official of the Republican National Committee, he called the commercial "inoffensive" and added, "Since when is a commercial supposed to be accurate? Do women really smile when they clean their ovens?"

Again, applying the criteria for identifying doublespeak to this advertisement reveals the doublespeak in it, once you know the facts of past actions by President Reagan. Moreover, the official for the Republican National Committee assumes that all advertisements, whether for political candidates or commercial products, do not tell the truth; in his doublespeak, they do not have to be "accurate." Thus, the real intent of the advertisement was to mislead, while the apparent purpose of the commercial was to inform the public of President Reagan's position on possible cuts in Social Security benefits. Again there is insincerity, and again there is a gap between the speaker's real and declared aims.

Alexander Haig and Doublespeak

One of the most chilling and terrifying uses of doublespeak in recent memory occurred in 1981 when then Secretary of State Alexander Haig was testifying before congressional committees about the murder of three American nuns and a Catholic lay worker in El Salvador. The four women had been raped and then shot at close range, and there was clear evidence that the crime had been committed by soldiers of the Salvadoran government. Before the House Foreign Affairs Committee, Secretary Haig said:

> I'd like to suggest to you that some of the investigations would lead one to believe that perhaps the vehicle the nuns were riding in may have tried to run a roadblock, or may accidentally have been perceived to have been doing so, and there'd been an exchange of fire and then perhaps those who inflicted the casualties sought to cover it up. And this could have been at a very low level of both competence and motivation in the context of the issue itself. But the facts on this are not clear enough for anyone to draw a definitive conclusion.

The next day, before the Senate Foreign Relations Committee, 35 Secretary Haig claimed that press reports on his previous testimony were "inaccurate." When Senator Claiborne Pell asked whether the secretary was suggesting the possibility that "the nuns may have run through a roadblock," he replied, "You mean that they tried to violate . . . ? Not at all, no, not at all. My heavens! The dear nuns who raised me in my parochial schooling would forever isolate me from their affections and respect." Then Senator Pell asked Secretary Haig, "Did you mean that the nuns were firing at the people, or what did 'an exchange of fire' mean?" The secretary replied, "I haven't met any pistol-packing nuns in my day, Senator. What I meant was that if one fellow starts shooting, then the next thing you know they all panic." Thus did the secretary of state of the United States explain official government policy on the murder of four American citizens in a foreign land.

Secretary Haig's testimony implies that the women were in some way responsible for their own fate. By using such vague wording as "would lead one to believe" and "may accidentally have been perceived to have been doing so," he avoids any direct assertion. The use of the phrase "inflicted the casualties" not only avoids using the word "kill" but also implies that at the worst the killings were accidental or justifiable. The result of this testimony is that the secretary of state has become an apologist for rape and murder. This is indeed language in defense of the indefensible; language designed to make lies sound truthful and murder respectable; language designed to give an appearance of solidity to pure wind.

THE DANGERS OF DOUBLESPEAK

These previous three examples of doublespeak should make it clear that doublespeak is not the product of carelessness or sloppy thinking. Indeed, most doublespeak is the product of clear thinking and is carefully designed and constructed to appear to communicate when in fact it doesn't. It is language designed not to lead but mislead. It is language designed to distort reality and corrupt thought. In the world created by doublespeak, if it's not a tax increase, but rather "revenue enhancement" or "tax base broadening," how can you complain about higher taxes? If it's not acid rain, but rather "poorly buffered precipitation," how can you worry about all those dead trees? If that isn't the Mafia in Atlantic City, but just "members of a career-offender cartel," why worry about the influence of organized crime in the city? If Supreme Court Justice William Rehnquist wasn't addicted to the pain-killing drug his doctor prescribed, but instead it was just that the drug had "established an interrelationship with the body, such that if the drug is removed precipitously, there is a reaction," you needn't question that his decisions might have been influenced by his drug addiction. If it's not a Titan II nuclear-armed intercontinental ballistic missile with a warhead 630 times more powerful than the atomic bomb dropped on Hiroshima, but instead, according to Air Force Colonel Frank Horton, it's just a "very large, potentially disruptive reentry system," why be concerned about the threat of nuclear destruction? Why worry about the neutron bomb escalating the arms race if it's just a "radiation enhancement weapon"? If it's not an invasion, but a "rescue mission" or a "predawn vertical insertion," you won't need to think about any violations of U.S. or international law.

Doublespeak has become so common in everyday living that many people fail to notice it. Even worse, when they do notice doublespeak being used on them, they don't react, they don't protest. Do you protest when you are asked to check your packages at the desk "for your convenience," when it's not for your convenience at all but for someone else's? You see advertisements for "genuine imitation leather," "virgin vinyl," or "real counterfeit diamonds," but do you question the language or the supposed quality of the product? Do you question politicians who don't speak of slums or ghettos but of the "inner city" or "substandard housing" where the "disadvantaged" live and thus avoid talking about the poor who have to live in filthy, poorly heated, ramshackle apartments or houses? Aren't you amazed that patients don't die in the hospital anymore, it's just "negative patient-care outcome"?

Doublespeak such as that noted earlier that defines cab drivers as "urban transportation specialists," elevator operators as members of the "vertical transportation corps," and automobile mechanics as "automotive internists" can be considered humorous and relatively harmless. However, when a fire in a nuclear reactor building is called "rapid oxidation," an explosion in a nuclear power plant is called an "energetic disassembly," the illegal overthrow of a legitimate government is termed "destabilizing a government," and lies are seen as "inoperative statements," we are hearing doublespeak that attempts to avoid responsibility and make the bad seem good, the negative appear positive, something unpleasant appear attractive; and which seems to communicate but doesn't. It is language designed to alter our perception of reality and corrupt our thinking. Such language does not provide us with the tools we need to develop, advance, and preserve our culture and our civilization. Such language breeds suspicion, cynicism, distrust, and, ultimately, hostility.

Doublespeak is insidious because it can infect and eventually   40
destroy the function of language, which is communication between people and social groups. This corruption of the function of language can have serious and far-reaching consequences. We live in a country that depends upon an informed electorate to make decisions in selecting candidates for office and deciding issues of public policy. The use of doublespeak can become so pervasive that it becomes the coin of the political realm, with speakers and listeners convinced that they really understand such language. After a while we may really believe that politicians don't lie but only "misspeak," that illegal acts are merely "inappropriate actions," that fraud and criminal conspiracy are just "miscertification." President Jimmy Carter in April of 1980 could call the aborted raid to free the American hostages in Teheran an "incomplete success" and really believe that he had made a statement that clearly communicated with the American public. So, too, could President Ronald Reagan say in 1985 that "ultimately our security and our hopes for success at the arms reduction talks hinge on the determination that we show here to continue our program to rebuild and refortify our defenses" and really believe that greatly increasing the amount of money spent building new weapons would lead to a reduction in the number of weapons in the world. If we really believe that we understand such language and that such language communicates and promotes clear thought, then the world of *1984,* with its control of reality through language, is upon us.

STUDY QUESTIONS

1. What exactly is "doublespeak"? Sum up Lutz's DEFINITION of this term in a single sentence.

2. Within this definition essay, Lutz makes the ARGUMENT that doublespeak can be dangerous and damaging. What EVIDENCE does he offer for this CLAIM? How effective do you find it? How does his extended definition of doublespeak support this idea?

3. Lutz wrote this essay as the first chapter to his book *Doublespeak* (1989). How might it have been different if he'd written it as a speech? As an op-ed piece? As a BLOG entry? What if he were writing today?

4. *For Writing.* Using Lutz's definition of doublespeak, find an example of doublespeak spoken or written in the last twelve months. In an essay, present your example, ANALYZE what makes it doublespeak, and consider what the intent might have been as well as the actual result.

GEORGE ORWELL ⎰ *Politics and the*
⎱ *English Language*

GEORGE ORWELL (1903–1950) is best known today for his political novels *Animal Farm* (1945) and *1984* (1949), but he was also a highly regarded essayist. Born Eric Blair in India, where his father was employed by the civil service, Orwell was educated in England before returning to Asia in 1922. In Burma (now called "Myanmar" by the military regime that rules it), Orwell served for five years as an officer in the India Imperial Police. He returned to Europe in 1928 to become a writer. Before his death at age forty-six, Orwell also published the novel *Burmese Days* (1934) and his memoir of fighting against fascism in the Spanish Civil War, *Homage to Catalonia* (1938).

In "Politics and the English Language," from the essay collection *Shooting an Elephant and Other Essays* (1950), Orwell critiques the decline of the English language and argues both why and how this trend should be reversed. Notice, though, what specific improvements Orwell proposes and his observation that his plan "has nothing to do with correct grammar and syntax, which are of no importance so long as one makes one's meaning clear."

MOST PEOPLE WHO BOTHER WITH the matter at all would admit that the English language is in a bad way, but it is generally assumed that we cannot by conscious action do anything about it. Our civilization is decadent and our language—so the argument runs—must inevitably share in the general collapse. It follows that any struggle against the abuse of language is a sentimental archaism, like preferring candles to electric light or hansom cabs to aeroplanes. Underneath this lies the half-conscious belief that language is a natural growth and not an instrument which we shape for our own purposes.

Now, it is clear that the decline of a language must ultimately have political and economic causes: it is not due simply to the bad influence of this or that individual writer. But an effect can become a cause, reinforcing the original cause and producing the same effect in an intensified form, and so on indefinitely. A man may take to drink because he feels himself to be a failure, and then fail all the more completely because he drinks. It is rather the same thing that is happening to the English language. It becomes ugly and inaccurate because our thoughts are foolish, but the slovenliness of our language makes it easier for us to have foolish thoughts. The point is that the process is reversible. Modern English, especially written English, is full of bad habits which spread by imitation and which can be avoided if one is willing to take the necessary trouble. If one gets rid of these habits one can think more clearly, and to think clearly is a necessary first step towards political regeneration: so that the fight against bad English is not frivolous and is not the exclusive concern of professional writers. I will come back to this presently, and I hope that by that time the meaning of what I have said here will have become clearer. Meanwhile, here are five specimens of the English language as it is now habitually written.

These five passages have not been picked out because they are especially bad—I could have quoted far worse if I had chosen—but because they illustrate various of the mental vices from which we now suffer. They are a little below the average, but are fairly representative samples. I number them so that I can refer back to them when necessary:

(1) I am not, indeed, sure whether it is not true to say that the Milton who once seemed not unlike a seventeenth-century Shelley had not become, out of an experience ever more bitter in each year, more alien [*sic*] to the founder of that Jesuit sect which nothing could induce him to tolerate.

Professor Harold Laski
(Essay in *Freedom of Expression*).

(2) Above all, we cannot play ducks and drakes with a native battery of idioms which prescribes such egregious collocations of vocables as the Basic *put up with* for *tolerate* or *put at a loss* for *bewilder.*

Professor Lancelot Hogben (*Interglossa*).

(3) On the one side we have the free personality: by definition it is not neurotic, for it has neither conflict nor dream. Its desires, such as they are, are transparent, for they are just what institutional approval keeps in the forefront of consciousness; another institutional pattern would alter their number and intensity; there is little in them that is natural, irreducible, or culturally dangerous. But *on the other side,* the social bond itself is nothing but the mutual reflection of these self-secure integrities. Recall the definition of love. Is not this the very picture of a small academic? Where is there a place in this hall of mirrors for either personality or fraternity?

Essay on psychology in *Politics* (New York).

(4) All the "best people" from the gentlemen's clubs, and all the frantic fascist captains, united in common hatred of Socialism and bestial horror of the rising tide of the mass revolutionary movement, have turned to acts of provocation, to foul incendiarism, to medieval legends of poisoned wells, to legalize their own destruction of proletarian organizations, and rouse the agitated petty-bourgeoisie to chauvinistic fervor on behalf of the fight against the revolutionary way out of the crisis.

Communist pamphlet.

(5) If a new spirit *is* to be infused into this old country, there is one thorny and contentious reform which must be tackled, and that is the humanization and galvanization of the B.B.C. Timidity here will bespeak canker and atrophy of the soul. The heart of Britain may be sound and of strong beat, for instance, but the British lion's roar at present is like that of Bottom in Shakespeare's *Midsummer Night's Dream*— as gentle as any sucking dove. A virile new Britain cannot continue indefinitely to be traduced in the eyes or rather ears, of the world by the effete languors of Langham Place, brazenly masquerading as "standard English." When the Voice of Britain is heard at nine o'clock, better far and infinitely less ludicrous to hear aitches honestly dropped than the

present priggish, inflated, inhibited, school-ma'amish arch braying of blameless bashful mewing maidens!

Letter in *Tribune*

Each of these passages has faults of its own, but, quite apart from avoidable ugliness, two qualities are common to all of them. The first is staleness of imagery; the other is lack of precision. The writer either has a meaning and cannot express it, or he inadvertently says something else, or he is almost indifferent as to whether his words mean anything or not. This mixture of vagueness and sheer incompetence is the most marked characteristic of modern English prose, and especially of any kind of political writing. As soon as certain topics are raised, the concrete melts into the abstract and no one seems able to think of turns of speech that are not hackneyed: prose consists less and less of *words* chosen for the sake of their meaning, and more and more of *phrases* tacked together like the sections of a prefabricated henhouse. I list below, with notes and examples, various of the tricks by means of which the work of prose-construction is habitually dodged:

Dying metaphors. A newly invented metaphor assists thought by evoking a visual image, while on the other hand a metaphor which is technically "dead" (e.g. *iron resolution*) has in effect reverted to being an ordinary word and can generally be used without loss of vividness. But in between these two classes there is a huge dump of worn-out metaphors which have lost all evocative power and are merely used because they save people the trouble of inventing phrases for themselves. Examples are: *Ring the changes on, take up the cudgels for, toe the line, ride roughshod over, stand shoulder to shoulder with, play into the hands of, no axe to grind, grist to the mill, fishing in troubled waters, on the order of the day, Achilles' heel, swan song, hotbed.* Many of these are used without knowledge of their meaning (what is a "rift," for instance?), and incompatible metaphors are frequently mixed, a sure sign that the writer is not interested in what he is saying. Some metaphors now current have been twisted out of their original meaning without those who use them even being aware of the fact. For example, *toe the line* is sometimes written *tow the line*. Another example is *the hammer and the anvil,* now always used with the implication that the anvil gets the worst of it. In real life it is always the anvil that breaks the hammer, never the other way about: a writer who stopped to think what he was saying would be aware of this, and would avoid perverting the original phrase.

Operators or *verbal false limbs.* These save the trouble of picking out appropriate verbs and nouns, and at the same time pad each sentence with extra syllables which give it an appearance of symmetry. Characteristic phrases are *render inoperative, militate against, make contact with, be subjected to, give rise to, give grounds for, have the effect of, play a leading part (role) in, make itself felt, take effect, exhibit a tendency to, serve the purpose of, etc., etc.* The keynote is the elimination of simple verbs. Instead of being a single word, such as *break, stop, spoil, mend, kill,* a verb becomes a *phrase,* made up of a noun or adjective tacked on to some general-purposes verb such as *prove, serve, form, play, render.* In addition, the passive voice is wherever possible used in preference to the active, and noun constructions are used instead of gerunds (*by examination of* instead of *by examining*). The range of verbs is further cut down by means of the *-ize* and *de-* formations, and the banal statements are given an appearance of profundity by means of the *not un-* formation. Simple conjunctions and prepositions are replaced by such phrases as *with respect to, having regard to, the fact that, by dint of, in view of, in the interests of, on the hypothesis that;* and the ends of sentences are saved by anticlimax by such resounding common-places as *greatly to be desired, cannot be left out of account, a development to be expected in the near future, deserving of serious consideration, brought to a satisfactory conclusion,* and so on and so forth.

Pretentious diction. Words like *phenomenon, element, individual* (as noun), *objective, categorical, effective, virtual, basic, primary, promote, constitute, exhibit, exploit, utilize, eliminate, liquidate,* are used to dress up simple statements and give an air of scientific impartiality to biased judgments. Adjectives like *epoch-making, epic, historic, unforgettable, triumphant, age-old, inevitable, inexorable, veritable,* are used to dignify the sordid processes of international politics, while writing that aims at glorifying war usually takes on an archaic color, its characteristic words being: *realm, throne, chariot, mailed fist, trident, sword, shield, buckler, banner, jackboot, clarion.* Foreign words and expressions such as *cul de sac, ancien régime, deus ex machina, mutatis mutandis, status quo, gleichschaltung, weltanschauung,* are used to give an air of culture and elegance. Except for the useful abbreviations *i.e., e.g.,* and *etc.,*[1] there is no real need for any of the hundreds of foreign phrases now current in English. Bad writers, and especially scientific, political and sociological writers, are nearly always haunted by the notion that Latin or Greek words are grander than Saxon ones, and unnecessary words like *expedite, ameliorate, predict, extraneous, deracinated, clandestine, subaqueous* and hundreds of others constantly gain ground from their Anglo-Saxon opposite numbers.[2] The jargon peculiar to Marxist writing (*hyena, hangman, cannibal, petty bourgeois, these gentry, lacquey, flunkey, mad dog, White Guard,* etc.) consists largely of words and phrases translated from Russian, German or French; but the normal way of coining a new word is to use a Latin or Greek root with the appropriate affix and, where necessary, the size formation. It is often easier to make up words of this kind (*deregionalize, impermissible, extramarital, non-fragmentary* and so forth) than to think up the English words that will cover one's meaning. The result, in general, is an increase in slovenliness and vagueness.

Meaningless words. In certain kinds of writing, particularly in art criticism and literary criticism, it is normal to come across long passages which are almost completely lacking in meaning.[3] Words like

---

[1]Latin abbreviations for *that is, for example,* and *and other things,* respectively. [Ed.]

[2]An interesting illustration of this is the way in which the English flower names which were in use till very recently are being ousted by Greek ones, *snapdragon* becoming *antirrhinum, forget-me-not* becoming *myosotis,* etc. It is hard to see any practical reason for this change of fashion: it is probably due to an instinctive turning-away from the more homely word and a vague feeling that the Greek word is scientific [Unless otherwise indicated, the notes included with this selection are those of the author.]

[3]Example: "Comfort's catholicity of perception and image, strangely Whitmanesque in range, almost the exact opposite in aesthetic compulsion, continues to evoke that trembling atmospheric accumulative hinting at a cruel, an inexorably serene timelessness. . . . Wrey Gardiner scores by aiming at simple bull's-eyes with precision. Only they are not so simple, and through this contented sadness runs more than the surface bitter-sweet of resignation" (*Poetry Quarterly*).

romantic, plastic, values, human, dead, sentimental, natural, vitality, as used in art criticism, are strictly meaningless, in the sense that they not only do not point to any discoverable object, but are hardly ever expected to do so by the reader. When one critic writes, "The outstanding feature of Mr. X's work is its living quality," while another writes, "The immediately striking thing about Mr. X's work is its peculiar deadness," the reader accepts this as a simple difference of opinion. If words like *black* and *white* were involved, instead of the jargon words *dead* and *living,* he would see at once that language was being used in an improper way. Many political words are similarly abused. The word *Fascism* has now no meaning except in so far as it signifies "something not desirable." The words *democracy, socialism, freedom, patriotic, realistic, justice,* have each of them several different meanings which cannot be reconciled with one another. In the case of a word like *democracy,* not only is there no agreed definition, but the attempt to make one is resisted from all sides. It is almost universally felt that when we call a country democratic we are praising it: consequently the defenders of every kind of régime claim that it is a democracy, and fear that they might have to stop using the word if it were tied down to any one meaning. Words of this kind are often used in a consciously dishonest way. That is, the person who uses them has his own private definition, but allows his hearer to think he means something quite different. Statements like *Marshal Pétain was a true patriot, The Soviet Press is the freest in the world, The Catholic Church is opposed to persecution,* are almost always made with intent to deceive. Other words used in variable meanings, in most cases more or less dishonestly, are: *class, totalitarian, science, progressive, reactionary, bourgeois, equality.*

Now that I have made this catalogue of swindles and perversions, let me give another example of the kind of writing that they lead to. This time it must of its nature be an imaginary one. I am going to translate a 5 passage of good English into modern English of the worst sort. Here is a well-known verse from *Ecclesiastes:*

> I returned and saw under the sun, that the race is not to the swift, nor the
> battle to the strong, neither yet bread to the wise, nor yet riches to men

of understanding, nor yet favour to men of skill; but time and chance happeneth to them all.

Here it is in modern English:

Objective considerations of contemporary phenomena compels the conclusion that success or failure in competitive activities exhibits no tendency to be commensurate with innate capacity, but that a considerable element of the unpredictable must invariably be taken into account.

This is a parody, but not a very gross one. Exhibit (3), above, for instance, contains several patches of the same kind of English. It will be seen that I have not made a full translation. The beginning and ending of the sentence follow the original meaning fairly closely, but in the middle the concrete illustrations—race, battle, bread—dissolve into the vague phrase "success or failure in competitive activities." This had to be so, because no modern writer of the kind I am discussing—no one capable of using phrases like "objective consideration of contemporary phenomena"—would ever tabulate his thoughts in that precise and detailed way. The whole tendency of modern prose is away from concreteness. Now analyse these two sentences a little more closely. The first contains forty-nine words but only sixty syllables, and all its words are those of everyday life. The second contains thirty-eight words of ninety syllables: eighteen of its words are from Latin roots, and one from Greek. The first sentence contains six vivid images, and only one phrase ("time and chance") that could be called vague. The second contains not a single fresh, arresting phrase, and in spite of its ninety syllables it gives only a shortened version of the meaning contained in the first. Yet without a doubt it is the second kind of sentence that is gaining ground in modern English. I do not want to exaggerate. This kind of writing is not yet universal, and outcrops of simplicity will occur here and there in the worst-written page. Still, if you or I were told to write a few lines on the uncertainty of human fortunes, we should probably come much nearer to my imaginary sentence than to the one from *Ecclesiastes*.

As I have tried to show, modern writing at its worst does not consist in picking out words for the sake of their meaning and inventing images in order to make the meaning clearer. It consists in gumming together long strips of words which have already been set in order by someone else, and making the results presentable by sheer humbug. The attraction of this way of writing is that it is easy. It is easier—even quicker, once you have the habit—to say *In my opinion it is not an unjustifiable assumption that* than to say *I think.* If you use ready-made phrases, you not only don't have to hunt about for words; you also don't have to bother with the rhythms of your sentences, since these phrases are generally so arranged as to be more or less euphonious. When you are composing in a hurry—when you are dictating to a stenographer, for instance, or making a public speech—it is natural to fall into a pretentious, Latinized style. Tags like *a consideration which we should do well to bear in mind* or *a conclusion to which all of us would readily assent* will save many a sentence from coming down with a bump. By using stale metaphors, similes and idioms, you save much mental effort, at the cost of leaving your meaning vague, not only for your reader but for yourself. This is the significance of mixed metaphors. The sole aim of a metaphor is to call up a visual image. When these images clash—as in *The Fascist octopus has sung its swan song, the jackboot is thrown into the melting pot*—it can be taken as certain that the writer is not seeing a mental image of the objects he is naming; in other words he is not really thinking. Look again at the examples I gave at the beginning of this essay. Professor Laski (1) uses five negatives in fifty-three words. One of these is superfluous, making nonsense of the whole passage, and in addition there is the slip *alien* for akin, making further nonsense, and several avoidable pieces of clumsiness which increase the general vagueness. Professor Hogben (2) plays ducks and drakes with a battery which is able to write prescriptions, and, while disapproving of the everyday phrase *put up with,* is unwilling to look *egregious* up in the dictionary and see what it means; (3), if one takes an uncharitable attitude towards it, is simply meaningless: probably one could work out its intended meaning by reading the whole of the article in which it occurs. In (4), the writer knows more or less what he wants to say, but an accumulation of stale phrases chokes him like tea leaves blocking a sink. In (5), words and meaning have almost parted company. People who write in this manner usually have a general emotional meaning—they dislike one thing and want to express solidarity with another—but they are not interested in the detail of what they are saying. A scrupulous writer, in every sentence that he writes, will ask himself at least four questions, thus: What am I trying to say? What words will express it? What image or idiom will make it clearer? Is this image fresh enough to have an effect? And he will probably ask himself two more: Could I put it more shortly? Have I said anything that is avoidably ugly? But you are not obliged to go to all this trouble. You can shirk it by simply throwing your mind open and letting the ready-made phrases come crowding in. They will construct your sentences for you—even think your thoughts for you, to a certain extent—and at need they will perform the important service of partially concealing your meaning even from yourself. It is at this point that the special connection between politics and the debasement of language becomes clear.

In our time it is broadly true that political writing is bad writing. Where it is not true, it will generally be found that the writer is some kind of rebel, expressing his private opinions and not a "party line." Orthodoxy, of whatever color, seems to demand a lifeless, imitative style. The political dialects to be found in pamphlets, leading articles, manifestos, White Papers and the speeches of under-secretaries do, of course, vary from party to party, but they are all alike in that one almost never finds in them a fresh, vivid, home-made turn of speech. When one watches some tired hack on the platform mechanically repeating the familiar phrases—*bestial atrocities, iron heel, bloodstained tyranny, free peoples of the world, stand shoulder to shoulder*—one often has a curious feeling that one is not watching a live human being but some kind of dummy: a feeling which suddenly becomes stronger at moments when the light catches the speaker's spectacles and turns them into blank discs which seem to have no eyes behind them. And this is not altogether fanciful. A speaker who uses that kind of phraseology has gone some distance towards turning himself into a machine. The appropriate noises are coming out of his larynx, but his brain is not involved as it would be if he were choosing his words for himself.

If the speech he is making is one that he is accustomed to make over and over again, he may be almost unconscious of what he is saying, as one is when one utters the responses in church. And this reduced state of consciousness, if not indispensable, is at any rate favorable to political conformity.

In our time, political speech and writing are largely the defence of the 10 indefensible. Things like the continuance of British rule in India, the Russian purges and deportations, the dropping of the atom bombs on Japan, can indeed be defended, but only by arguments which are too brutal for most people to face, and which do not square with the professed aims of political parties. Thus political language has to consist largely of euphemism, question-begging and sheer cloudy vagueness. Defenceless villages are bombarded from the air, the inhabitants driven out into the countryside, the cattle machine-gunned, the huts set on fire with incendiary bullets: this is called *pacification*. Millions of peasants are robbed of their farms and sent trudging along the roads with no more than they can carry: this is called *transfer of population* or *rectification of frontiers*. People are imprisoned for years without trial, or shot in the back of the neck or sent to die of scurvy in Arctic lumber camps: this is called *elimination of unreliable elements*. Such phraseology is needed if one wants to name things without calling up mental pictures of them. Consider for instance some comfortable English professor defending Russian totalitarianism. He cannot say outright, "I believe in killing off your opponents when you can get good results by doing so." Probably, therefore, he will say something like this:

> While freely conceding that the Soviet régime exhibits certain features which the humanitarian may be inclined to deplore, we must, I think, agree that a certain curtailment of the right to political opposition is an unavoidable concomitant of transitional periods, and that the rigors which the Russian people have been called upon to undergo have been amply justified in the sphere of concrete achievement.

The inflated style is itself a kind of euphemism. A mass of Latin words falls upon the facts like soft snow, blurring the outlines and covering up all the details. The great enemy of clear language is insincerity.

When there is a gap between one's real and one's declared aims, one turns as it were instinctively to long words and exhausted idioms, like a cuttlefish squirting out ink. In our age there is no such thing as "keeping out of politics." All issues are political issues, and politics itself is a mass of lies, evasions, folly, hatred and schizophrenia. When the general atmosphere is bad, language must suffer. I should expect to find— this is a guess which I have not sufficient knowledge to verify—that the German, Russian and Italian languages have all deteriorated in the last ten or fifteen years, as a result of dictatorship.

But if thought corrupts language, language can also corrupt thought. A bad usage can spread by tradition and imitation, even among people who should and do know better. The debased langauge that I have been discussing is in some ways very convenient. Phrases like *a not unjustifiable assumption, leaves much to be desired, would serve no good purpose, a consideration which we should do well to bear in mind,* are a continuous temptation, a packet of aspirins always at one's elbow. Look back through this essay, and for certain you will find that I have again and again committed the very faults I am protesting against. By this morning's post I have received a pamphlet dealing with conditions in Germany. The author tells me that he "felt impelled" to write it. I open it at random, and here is almost the first sentence that I see: "[The Allies] have an opportunity not only of achieving a radical transformation of Germany's social and political structure in such a way as to avoid a nationalistic reaction in Germany itself, but at the same time of laying the foundations of a co-operative and unified Europe." You see, he "feels impelled" to write—feels, presumably, that he has something new to say—and yet his words, like cavalry horses answering the bugle, group themselves automatically into the familiar dreary pattern. This invasion of one's mind by ready-made phrases (*lay the foundations, achieve a radical transformation*) can only be prevented if one is constantly on guard against them, and every such phrase anaesthetizes a portion of one's brain.

I said earlier that the decadence of our language is probably curable. Those who deny this would argue, if they produced an argument at all, that language merely reflects existing social conditions, and that we cannot influence its development by any direct tinkering with words and constructions. So far as the general tone or spirit of a language goes, this may be true, but it is not true in detail. Silly words and expressions have often disappeared, not through any evolutionary process but owing to the conscious action of a minority. Two recent examples were *explore every avenue* and *leave no stone unturned,* which were killed by the jeers of a few journalists. There is a long list of flyblown metaphors which could similarly be got rid of if enough people would interest themselves in the job; and it should also be possible to laugh the *not un-* formation out of existence,[4] to reduce the amount of Latin and Greek in the average sentence, to drive out foreign phrases and strayed scientific words, and, in general, to make pretentiousness unfashionable. But all these are minor points. The defence of the English language implies more than this, and perhaps it is best to start by saying what it does *not* imply.

To begin with it has nothing to do with archaism, with the salvaging of obsolete words and turns of speech, or with the setting up of a "standard English" which must never be departed from. On the contrary, it is especially concerned with the scrapping of every word or idiom which has outworn its usefulness. It has nothing to do with correct grammar and syntax, which are of no importance so long as one makes one's meaning clear, or with the avoidance of Americanisms, or with having what is called a "good prose style." On the other hand it is not concerned with fake simplicity and the attempt to make written English colloquial. Nor does it even imply in every case preferring the Saxon word to the Latin one, though it does imply using the fewest and shortest words that will cover one's meaning. What is above all needed is to let the meaning choose the word, and not the other way about. In prose, the worst thing one can do with words is to surrender to them. When you think of a concrete object, you think wordlessly, and then, if you want to describe the thing you have been visualizing you probably hunt about till you find the exact words that seem to fit it. When you think of something abstract you are more inclined to use words from the start, and unless you make a conscious effort to prevent

---

[4]One can cure oneself of the *not un-* formation by memorizing this sentence: *A not unblack dog was chasing a not unsmall rabbit across a not ungreen field.*

it, the existing dialect will come rushing in and do the job for you, at the expense of blurring or even changing your meaning. Probably it is better to put off using words as long as possible and get one's meaning as clear as one can through pictures or sensations. Afterwards one can choose—not simply *accept*—the phrases that will best cover the meaning, and then switch round and decide what impression one's words are likely to make on another person. This last effort of the mind cuts out all stale or mixed images, all prefabricated phrases, needless repetitions, and humbug and vagueness generally. But one can often be in doubt about the effect of a word or a phrase, and one needs rules that one can rely on when instinct fails. I think the following rules will cover most cases:

1. Never use a metaphor, simile or other figure of speech which you are used to seeing in print.

2. Never use a long word where a short one will do.

3. If it is possible to cut a word out, always cut it out.

4. Never use the passive where you can use the active.

5. Never use a foreign phrase, a scientific word or a jargon word if you can think of an everyday English equivalent.

6. Break any of these rules sooner than say anything outright barbarous.

These rules sound elementary, and so they are, but they demand a deep change of attitude in anyone who has grown used to writing in the style now fashionable. One could keep all of them and still write bad English, but one could not write the kind of stuff that I quoted in those five specimens at the beginning of this article.

I have not here been considering the literary use of language, but merely language as an instrument for expressing and not for concealing or preventing thought. Stuart Chase[5] and others have come near to claiming that all abstract words are meaningless, and have used this as

15

---

[5] American economist (1888–1985) whose influential writings about semantics include *The Tyranny of Words* (1938).

a pretext for advocating a kind of political quietism. Since you don't know what Fascism is, how can you struggle against Fascism? One need not swallow such absurdities as this, but one ought to recognize that the present political chaos is connected with the decay of langauge, and that one can probably bring about some improvement by starting at the verbal end. If you simplify your English, you are freed from the worst follies of orthodoxy. You cannot speak any of the necessary dialects, and when you make a stupid remark its stupidity will be obvious, even to yourself. Political langauge—and with variations this is true of all political parties, from Conservatives to Anarchists—is designed to make lies sound truthful and murder respectable, and to give an appearance of solidity to pure wind. One cannot change this all in a moment, but one can at least change one's own habits, and from time to time one can even, if one jeers loudly enough, send some worn-out and useless phrase—some *jackboot, Achilles' heel, hotbed, melting pot, acid test, veritable inferno* or other lump of verbal refuse—into the dustbin where it belongs.

STUDY QUESTIONS

1. According to Orwell, why do writers continue to write badly?

2. Orwell admits, late in the essay, "I have again and again committed the very faults I am protesting against." Identify one of these "faults" in this essay.

3. SUMMARIZE Orwell's defense of the English language. Does he urge people to use "good grammar"? Does his writing advice seem similar to or different from advice you have read or heard before? Explain.

4. *For Writing.* Compared to the 1950 use of the English language that Orwell discusses, what do you think about writing today? Locate a short piece of writing and review it for one or more of Orwell's areas of criticism. Your teacher will provide guidelines for what GENRES and lengths are appropriate, but you might explore the fields Orwell specifically mentions in the essay (e.g., art criticism, literary criticism, politics, science, sociology). Write an essay relating your findings and providing examples from the piece you found.

AMY TAN (b. 1952), novelist and essayist, was born in Oakland, California, to immigrant parents from China. She earned her BA and MA in English and linguistics from San Jose State University and then entered a University of California PhD program in linguistics at both Santa Cruz and Berkeley. Tan has famously remarked that she failed her parents' expectations that she would become either a doctor or concert pianist—or both. Instead, she left the PhD program, began writing fiction, and is now an internationally best-selling novelist. Her 1989 novel *The Joy Luck Club* was made into a feature film; her other novels include *The Kitchen God's Wife* (1991) and *The Bonesetter's Daughter* (2001). She has also written a memoir, *The Opposite of Fate: A Book of Musings* (2003), as well as a children's book, *Sagwa, the Chinese Siamese Cat* (1994), which became a PBS television series. When she is not writing, Tan performs with the Rock Bottom Remainders, a garage band whose members include the novelists Stephen King, Barbara Kingsolver, and Scott Turow, as well as the humorist Dave Barry.

The following chapter from *The Joy Luck Club* is closely modeled on Tan's own life. It depicts a struggle for identity between mother and daughter: the mother wants her daughter to be a "prodigy"—at dancing or mathematics or the piano or anything at all—but her daughter just wants to relax and be herself. Take note of how mother defines daughter and vice versa, and think about whether those definitions are accurate or inflated.

MY MOTHER BELIEVED YOU COULD be anything you wanted to be in America. You could open a restaurant. You could work for the government and get good retirement. You could buy a house with almost no money down. You could become rich. You could become instantly famous.

"Of course you can be prodigy, too," my mother told me when I was nine. "You can be best anything. What does Auntie Lindo know? Her daughter, she is only best tricky."

America was where all my mother's hopes lay. She had come here in 1949 after losing everything in China: her mother and father, her family home, her first husband, and two daughters, twin baby girls. But she never looked back with regret. There were so many ways for things to get better.

• ○ •

We didn't immediately pick the right kind of prodigy. At first my mother thought I could be a Chinese Shirley Temple.[1] We'd watch Shirley's old movies on TV as though they were training films. My mother would poke my arm and say, "*Ni kan*"—You watch. And I would see Shirley tapping her feet, or singing a sailor song, or pursing her lips into a very round O while saying, "Oh my goodness."

"*Ni kan*," said my mother as Shirley's eyes flooded with tears. "You already know how. Don't need talent for crying!" 5

Soon after my mother got this idea about Shirley Temple, she took me to a beauty training school in the Mission district[2] and put me in the hands of a student who could barely hold the scissors without shaking. Instead of getting big fat curls, I emerged with an uneven mass of crinkly black fuzz. My mother dragged me off to the bathroom and tried to wet down my hair.

"You look like Negro Chinese," she lamented, as if I had done this on purpose.

The instructor of the beauty training school had to lop off these soggy clumps to make my hair even again. "Peter Pan is very popular these days," the instructor assured my mother. I now had hair the

---

[1]Child actress and tap dancer (b. 1928), known for her golden curls and plucky manner in many films of the 1930s.

[2]A mainly Latino immigrant neighborhood in San Francisco.

length of a boy's, with straight-across bangs that hung at a slant two inches above my eyebrows. I liked the haircut and it made me actually look forward to my future fame.

In fact, in the beginning, I was just as excited as my mother, maybe even more so. I pictured this prodigy part of me as many different images, trying each one on for size. I was a dainty ballerina girl standing by the curtains, waiting to hear the right music that would send me floating on my tiptoes. I was like the Christ child lifted out of the straw manger, crying with holy indignity. I was Cinderella stepping from her pumpkin carriage with sparkly cartoon music filling the air.

In all of my imaginings, I was filled with a sense that I would soon become *perfect*. My mother and father would adore me. I would be beyond reproach. I would never feel the need to sulk for anything.

But sometimes the prodigy in me became impatient. "If you don't hurry up and get me out of here, I'm disappearing for good," it warned. "And then you'll always be nothing."

Every night after dinner, my mother and I would sit at the Formica kitchen table. She would present new tests, taking her examples from stories of amazing children she had read in *Ripley's Believe It or Not,* or *Good Housekeeping, Reader's Digest,* and a dozen other magazines she kept in a pile in our bathroom. My mother got these magazines from people whose houses she cleaned. And since she cleaned many houses each week, we had a great assortment. She would look through them all, searching for stories about remarkable children.

The first night she brought out a story about a three-year-old boy who knew the capitals of all the states and even most of the European countries. A teacher was quoted as saying the little boy could also pronounce the names of the foreign cities correctly.

"What's the capital of Finland?" my mother asked me, looking at the magazine story.

All I knew was the capital of California, because Sacramento was the name of the street we lived on in Chinatown. "Nairobi!" I guessed, saying the most foreign word I could think of. She checked to see if that was possibly one way to pronounce "Helsinki" before showing me the answer.

The tests got harder—multiplying numbers in my head, finding the queen of hearts in a deck of cards, trying to stand on my head without using my hands, predicting the daily temperatures in Los Angeles, New York, and London.

One night I had to look at a page from the Bible for three minutes and then report everything I could remember. "Now Jehoshaphat had riches and honor in abundance and . . . that's all I remember, Ma," I said.

And after seeing my mother's disappointed face once again, something inside of me began to die. I hated the tests, the raised hopes and failed expectations. Before going to bed that night, I looked in the mirror above the bathroom sink and when I saw only my face staring back—and that it would always be this ordinary face—I began to cry. Such a sad, ugly girl! I made high-pitched noises like a crazed animal, trying to scratch out the face in the mirror.

And then I saw what seemed to be the prodigy side of me—because I had never seen that face before. I looked at my reflection, blinking so I could see more clearly. The girl staring back at me was angry, powerful. This girl and I were the same. I had new thoughts, willful thoughts, or rather thoughts filled with lots of won'ts. I won't let her change me, I promised myself. I won't be what I'm not.

So now on nights when my mother presented her tests, I performed   20
listlessly, my head propped on one arm. I pretended to be bored. And I was. I got so bored I started counting the bellows of the foghorns out on the bay while my mother drilled me in other areas. The sound was comforting and reminded me of the cow jumping over the moon. And the next day, I played a game with myself, seeing if my mother would give up on me before eight bellows. After a while I usually counted only one, maybe two bellows at most. At last she was beginning to give up hope.

Two or three months had gone by without any mention of my being a prodigy again. And then one day my mother was watching *The Ed Sullivan Show*[3] on TV. The TV was old and the sound kept shorting

[3]Popular variety show of the 1960s, hosted by impresario Ed Sullivan (1901–74).

out. Every time my mother got halfway up from the sofa to adjust the set, the sound would go back on and Ed would be talking. As soon as she sat down, Ed would go silent again. She got up, the TV broke into loud piano music. She sat down. Silence. Up and down, back and forth, quiet and loud. It was like a stiff embraceless dance between her and the TV set. Finally she stood by the set with her hand on the sound dial.

She seemed entranced by the music, a little frenzied piano piece with this mesmerizing quality, sort of quick passages and then teasing lilting ones before it returned to the quick playful parts.

"*Ni kan,*" my mother said, calling me over with hurried hand gestures, "Look here."

I could see why my mother was fascinated by the music. It was being pounded out by a little Chinese girl, about nine years old, with a Peter Pan haircut. The girl had the sauciness of a Shirley Temple. She was proudly modest like a proper Chinese child. And she also did this fancy sweep of a curtsy, so that the fluffy skirt of her white dress cascaded slowly to the floor like the petals of a large carnation.

In spite of these warning signs, I wasn't worried. Our family had no 25
piano and we couldn't afford to buy one, let alone reams of sheet music and piano lessons. So I could be generous in my comments when my mother bad-mouthed the little girl on TV.

"Play note right, but doesn't sound good! No singing sound," complained my mother.

"What are you picking on her for?" I said carelessly. "She's pretty good. Maybe she's not the best, but she's trying hard." I knew almost immediately I would be sorry I said that.

"Just like you," she said. "Not the best. Because you not trying." She gave a little huff as she let go of the sound dial and sat down on the sofa.

The little Chinese girl sat down also to play an encore of "Anitra's Dance" by Grieg. I remember the song, because later on I had to learn how to play it.

Three days after watching *The Ed Sullivan Show,* my mother told me 30
what my schedule would be for piano lessons and piano practice. She had talked to Mr. Chong, who lived on the first floor of our apartment building. Mr. Chong was a retired piano teacher and my mother had

traded housecleaning services for weekly lessons and a piano for me to practice on every day, two hours a day, from four until six.

When my mother told me this, I felt as though I had been sent to hell. I whined and then kicked my foot a little when I couldn't stand it anymore.

"Why don't you like me the way I am? I'm *not* a genius! I can't play the piano. And even if I could, I wouldn't go on TV if you paid me a million dollars!" I cried.

My mother slapped me. "Who ask you be genius?" she shouted. "Only ask you be your best. For you sake. You think I want you be genius? Hnnh! What for! Who ask you!"

"So ungrateful," I heard her mutter in Chinese. "If she had as much talent as she has temper, she would be famous now."

Mr. Chong, whom I secretly nicknamed Old Chong, was very 35 strange, always tapping his fingers to the silent music of an invisible orchestra. He looked ancient in my eyes. He had lost most of the hair on top of his head and he wore thick glasses and had eyes that always looked tired and sleepy. But he must have been younger than I thought, since he lived with his mother and was not yet married.

I met Old Lady Chong once and that was enough. She had this peculiar smell like a baby that had done something in its pants. And her fingers felt like a dead person's, like an old peach I once found in the back of the refrigerator; the skin just slid off the meat when I picked it up.

I soon found out why Old Chong had retired from teaching piano. He was deaf. "Like Beethoven!" he shouted to me. "We're both listening only in our head!" And he would start to conduct his frantic silent sonatas.

Our lessons went like this. He would open the book and point to different things, explaining their purpose: "Key! Treble! Bass! No sharps or flats! So this is C major! Listen now and play after me!"

And then he would play the C scale a few times, a simple chord, and then, as if inspired by an old, unreachable itch, he gradually added more notes and running trills and a pounding bass until the music was really something quite grand.

I would play after him, the simple scale, the simple chord, and then 40 I just played some nonsense that sounded like a cat running up and down on top of garbage cans. Old Chong smiled and applauded and then said, "Very good! But now you must learn to keep time!"

So that's how I discovered that Old Chong's eyes were too slow to keep up with the wrong notes I was playing. He went through the motions in half-time. To help me keep rhythm, he stood behind me, pushing down on my right shoulder for every beat. He balanced pennies on top of my wrists so I would keep them still as I slowly played scales and arpeggios. He had me curve my hand around an apple and keep that shape when playing chords. He marched stiffly to show me how to make each finger dance up and down, staccato like an obedient little soldier.

He taught me all these things, and that was how I also learned I could be lazy and get away with mistakes, lots of mistakes. If I hit the wrong notes because I hadn't practiced enough, I never corrected myself. I just kept playing in rhythm. And Old Chong kept conducting his own private reverie.

So maybe I never really gave myself a fair chance. I did pick up the basics pretty quickly, and I might have become a good pianist at that young age. But I was so determined not to try, not to be anybody different that I learned to play only the most ear-splitting preludes, the most discordant hymns.

Over the next year, I practiced like this, dutifully in my own way. And then one day I heard my mother and her friend Lindo Jong both talking in a loud bragging tone of voice so others could hear. It was after church, and I was leaning against the brick wall wearing a dress with stiff white petticoats. Auntie Lindo's daughter, Waverly, who was about my age, was standing farther down the wall about five feet away. We had grown up together and shared all the closeness of two sisters squabbling over crayons and dolls. In other words, for the most part, we hated each other. I thought she was snotty. Waverly Jong had gained a certain amount of fame as "Chinatown's Littlest Chinese Chess Champion."

"She bring home too many trophy," lamented Auntie Lindo that 45 Sunday. "All day she play chess. All day I have no time do nothing but dust off her winnings." She threw a scolding look at Waverly, who pretended not to see her.

"You lucky you don't have this problem," said Auntie Lindo with a sigh to my mother.

And my mother squared her shoulders and bragged: "Our problem worser than yours. If we ask Jing-mei wash dish, she hear nothing but music. It's like you can't stop this natural talent."

And right then, I was determined to put a stop to her foolish pride.

A few weeks later, Old Chong and my mother conspired to have me play in a talent show which would be held in the church hall. By then, my parents had saved up enough to buy me a secondhand piano, a black Wurlitzer spinet with a scarred bench. It was the showpiece of our living room.

For the talent show, I was to play a piece called "Pleading Child" from   50
Schumann's *Scenes from Childhood*. It was a simple, moody piece that sounded more difficult than it was. I was supposed to memorize the whole thing, playing the repeat parts twice to make the piece sound longer. But I dawdled over it, playing a few bars and then cheating, looking up to see what notes followed. I never really listened to what I was playing. I daydreamed about being somewhere else, about being someone else.

The part I liked to practice best was the fancy curtsy: right foot out, touch the rose on the carpet with a pointed foot, sweep to the side, left leg bends, look up and smile.

My parents invited all the couples from the Joy Luck Club[4] to witness my debut. Auntie Lindo and Uncle Tin were there. Waverly and her two older brothers had also come. The first two rows were filled with children both younger and older than I was. The littlest ones got to go first. They recited simple nursery rhymes, squawked out tunes on miniature violins, twirled Hula Hoops, pranced in pink ballet tutus, and when they bowed or curtsied, the audience would sigh in unison, "Awww," and then clap enthusiastically.

When my turn came, I was very confident. I remember my childish excitement. It was as if I knew, without a doubt, that the prodigy side of me really did exist. I had no fear whatsoever, no nervousness. I remember thinking to myself, This is it! This is it! I looked out over the audience, at my mother's blank face, my father's yawn, Auntie Lindo's

[4]The name of a social club that unites the book's characters; the members gather to play mah-jong, a Chinese gambling game for three or four players.

stiff-lipped smile, Waverly's sulky expression. I had on a white dress layered with sheets of lace, and a pink bow in my Peter Pan haircut. As I sat down I envisioned people jumping to their feet and Ed Sullivan rushing up to introduce me to everyone on TV.

And I started to play. It was so beautiful. I was so caught up in how lovely I looked that at first I didn't worry how I would sound. So it was a surprise to me when I hit the first wrong note and I realized something didn't sound quite right. And then I hit another and another followed that. A chill started at the top of my head and began to trickle down. Yet I couldn't stop playing, as though my hands were bewitched. I kept thinking my fingers would adjust themselves back, like a train switching to the right track. I played this strange jumble through two repeats, the sour notes staying with me all the way to the end.

When I stood up, I discovered my legs were shaking. Maybe I had just been nervous and the audience, like Old Chong, had seen me go through the right motions and had not heard anything wrong at all. I swept my right foot out, went down on my knee, looked up and smiled. The room was quiet, except for Old Chong, who was beaming and shouting, "Bravo! Bravo! Well done!" But then I saw my mother's face, her stricken face. The audience clapped weakly, and as I walked back to my chair, with my whole face quivering as I tried not to cry, I heard a little boy whisper loudly to his mother, "That was awful," and the mother whispered back, "Well, she certainly tried." 55

And now I realized how many people were in the audience, the whole world it seemed. I was aware of eyes burning into my back. I felt the shame of my mother and father as they sat stiffly throughout the rest of the show.

We could have escaped during intermission. Pride and some strange sense of honor must have anchored my parents to their chairs. And so we watched it all: the eighteen-year-old boy with a fake mustache who did a magic show and juggled flaming hoops while riding a unicycle. The breasted girl with white makeup who sang from *Madama Butterfly*[5] and got honorable mention. And the eleven-year-old boy

[5]A 1904 opera with music by the Italian composer Giacomo Puccini (1858–1924).

who won first prize playing a tricky violin song that sounded like a busy bee.

After the show, the Hsus, the Jongs, and the St. Clairs from the Joy Luck Club came up to my mother and father.

"Lots of talented kids," Auntie Lindo said vaguely, smiling broadly.

"That was somethin' else," said my father, and I wondered if he was 60 referring to me in a humorous way, or whether he even remembered what I had done.

Waverly looked at me and shrugged her shoulders. "You aren't a genius like me," she said matter-of-factly. And if I hadn't felt so bad, I would have pulled her braids and punched her stomach.

But my mother's expression was what devastated me: a quiet, blank look that said she had lost everything. I felt the same way, and it seemed as if everybody were now coming up, like gawkers at the scene of an accident, to see what parts were actually missing. When we got on the bus to go home, my father was humming the busy-bee tune and my mother was silent. I kept thinking she wanted to wait until we got home before shouting at me. But when my father unlocked the door to our apartment, my mother walked in and then went to the back, into the bedroom. No accusations. No blame. And in a way, I felt disappointed. I had been waiting for her to start shouting, so I could shout back and cry and blame her for all my misery.

I assumed my talent-show fiasco meant I never had to play the piano again. But two days later, after school, my mother came out of the kitchen and saw me watching TV.

"Four clock," she reminded me as if it were any other day. I was stunned, as though she were asking me to go through the talent-show torture again. I wedged myself more tightly in front of the TV.

"Turn off TV," she called from the kitchen five minutes later. 65

I didn't budge. And then I decided. I didn't have to do what my mother said anymore. I wasn't her slave. This wasn't China. I had listened to her before and look what happened. She was the stupid one.

She came out from the kitchen and stood in the arched entryway of the living room. "Four clock," she said once again, louder.

"I'm not going to play anymore," I said nonchalantly. "Why should I? I'm not a genius."

She walked over and stood in front of the TV. I saw her chest was heaving up and down in an angry way.

"No!" I said, and I now felt stronger, as if my true self had finally emerged. So this was what had been inside me all along.   70

"No! I won't!" I screamed.

She yanked me by the arm, pulled me off the floor, snapped off the TV. She was frighteningly strong, half pulling, half carrying me toward the piano as I kicked the throw rugs under my feet. She lifted me up and onto the hard bench. I was sobbing by now, looking at her bitterly. Her chest was heaving even more and her mouth was open, smiling crazily as if she were pleased I was crying.

"You want me to be someone that I'm not!" I sobbed. "I'll never be the kind of daughter you want me to be!"

"Only two kinds of daughters," she shouted in Chinese. "Those who are obedient and those who follow their own mind! Only one kind of daughter can live in this house. Obedient daughter!"

"Then I wish I wasn't your daughter. I wish you weren't my   75
mother," I shouted. As I said these things I got scared. It felt like worms and toads and slimy things crawling out of my chest, but it also felt good, as if this awful side of me had surfaced, at last.

"Too late change this," said my mother shrilly.

And I could sense her anger rising to its breaking point. I wanted to see it spill over. And that's when I remembered the babies she had lost in China, the ones we never talked about. "Then I wish I'd never been born!" I shouted. "I wish I were dead! Like them."

It was as if I had said the magic words. Alakazam!—and her face went blank, her mouth closed, her arms went slack, and she backed out of the room, stunned, as if she were blowing away like a small brown leaf, thin, brittle, lifeless.

● ○ ●

It was not the only disappointment my mother felt in me. In the years that followed, I failed her so many times, each time asserting my own will, my right to fall short of expectations. I didn't get straight As. I didn't become class president. I didn't get into Stanford. I dropped out of college.

For unlike my mother, I did not believe I could be anything I wanted   80
to be. I could only be me.

And for all those years, we never talked about the disaster at the recital or my terrible accusations afterward at the piano bench. All that remained unchecked, like a betrayal that was now unspeakable. So I never found a way to ask her why she had hoped for something so large that failure was inevitable.

And even worse, I never asked her what frightened me the most: Why had she given up hope?

For after our struggle at the piano, she never mentioned my playing again. The lessons stopped. The lid to the piano was closed, shutting out the dust, my misery, and her dreams.

So she surprised me. A few years ago, she offered to give me the piano, for my thirtieth birthday. I had not played in all those years. I saw the offer as a sign of forgiveness, a tremendous burden removed.

"Are you sure?" I asked shyly. "I mean, won't you and Dad miss it?"   85
"No, this your piano," she said firmly. "Always your piano. You only one can play."

"Well, I probably can't play anymore," I said. "It's been years."

"You pick up fast," said my mother, as if she knew this was certain. "You have natural talent. You could been genius if you want to."

"No I couldn't."

"You just not trying," said my mother. And she was neither angry   90
nor sad. She said it as if to announce a fact that could never be disproved. "Take it," she said.

But I didn't at first. It was enough that she had offered it to me. And after that, every time I saw it in my parents' living room, standing in front of the bay windows, it made me feel proud, as if it were a shiny trophy I had won back.

Last week I sent a tuner over to my parents' apartment and had the piano reconditioned, for purely sentimental reasons. My mother had died a few months before and I had been getting things in order for my father, a little bit at a time. I put the jewelry in special silk pouches. The sweaters she had knitted in yellow, pink, bright orange—all the colors I hated—I put those in moth-proof boxes. I found some old Chinese silk dresses, the kind with little slits up the sides. I rubbed the old silk against my skin, then wrapped them in tissue and decided to take them home with me.

After I had the piano tuned, I opened the lid and touched the keys. It sounded even richer than I remembered. Really, it was a very good piano. Inside the bench were the same exercise notes with handwritten scales, the same secondhand music books with their covers held together with yellow tape.

I opened up the Schumann book to the dark little piece I had played at the recital. It was on the left-hand side of the page, "Pleading Child." It looked more difficult than I remembered. I played a few bars, surprised at how easily the notes came back to me.

And for the first time, or so it seemed, I noticed the piece on the 95 right-hand side. It was called "Perfectly Contented." I tried to play this one as well. It had a lighter melody but the same flowing rhythm and turned out to be quite easy. "Pleading Child" was shorter but slower; "Perfectly Contented" was longer, but faster. And after I played them both a few times, I realized they were two halves of the same song.

STUDY QUESTIONS

1. What is the NARRATOR's early attitude toward becoming a prodigy? What is her mother's attitude? How do both develop throughout the story? How does the narrator wish to DEFINE herself and how does her mother wish to define her?

2. The mother's DIALOGUE is important to establishing her CHARACTER. What does her dialogue tell us about her? What do we learn about her from what she says, and what do we learn from the way she says it? Why do you think Tan chose to present the mother's dialogue in broken English rather than in standard English?

3. At the end of the story, the narrator plays two melodies by Robert Schumann: "Pleading Child" and "Perfectly Contented." How do these two titles SYMBOLIZE the narrator's relationship with her mother? What is the larger significance of the fact that "they were two halves of the same song"?

4. *For Writing.* Have you ever been strongly encouraged by your family to do something you didn't want to do—play a certain sport, perhaps, or learn to play an instrument? Write an essay in which you NARRATE and REFLECT on that experience. Think about how you felt about the issue then and how you feel now, looking back on it. Be sure to take into account others' perspectives.

DEBORAH TANNEN {

Sex, Lies and Conversation:

Why Is It So Hard for Men and

Women to Talk to Each Other?

DEBORAH TANNEN (b. 1945) earned a PhD in linguistics at the
University of California, Berkeley, in 1979 and is a professor of linguistics at Georgetown University. She is best known for her research on
how people of different genders attempt to communicate with each other.
Tannen has published more than one hundred articles in scholarly
journals as well as most major American magazines and newspapers; she
has written more than twenty books, including *You Just Don't Understand: Women and Men in Conversation* (1990), which spent nearly four
years on the *New York Times* best-seller list and has been translated into
twenty-nine languages. Other books include *You're Wearing That?
Understanding Mothers and Daughters in Conversation* (2006) and *You
Were Always Mom's Favorite: Sisters in Conversation Throughout Their
Lives* (2009). A frequent guest on radio and television programs, she has
appeared on NPR's *Morning Edition, 20/20, Good Morning America,
Oprah,* and *The Colbert Report,* among others.

The following article, which appeared in the *Washington Post* in 1990,
offers an encapsulated version of Tannen's research on how men and
women speak with each other. Tannen compares and contrasts conversational styles and offers plenty of examples to demonstrate how different
expectations and understandings of conversational cues affect how men
and women communicate with each other. The next time you speak with
a member of the opposite sex, it might help you to understand that your
communication is truly, as Tannen calls it, "cross-cultural." As you read,
notice the kinds of evidence Tannen supplies to support her ideas.

I WAS ADDRESSING A SMALL gathering in a suburban Virginia living room—a women's group that had invited men to join them. Throughout the evening, one man had been particularly talkative, frequently offering ideas and anecdotes, while his wife sat silently beside him on the couch. Toward the end of the evening, I commented that women frequently complain that their husbands don't talk to them. This man quickly concurred. He gestured toward his wife and said, "She's the talker in our family." The room burst into laughter; the man looked puzzled and hurt. "It's true," he explained. "When I come home from work I have nothing to say. If she didn't keep the conversation going, we'd spend the whole evening in silence."

This episode crystallizes the irony that although American men tend to talk more than women in public situations, they often talk less at home. And this pattern is wreaking havoc with marriage.

The pattern was observed by political scientist Andrew Hacker in the late '70s. Sociologist Catherine Kohler Riessman reports in her new book *Divorce Talk* that most of the women she interviewed—but only a few of the men—gave lack of communication as the reason for their divorces. Given the current divorce rate of nearly 50 percent, that amounts to millions of cases in the United States every year—a virtual epidemic of failed conversation.

In my own research, complaints from women about their husbands most often focused not on tangible inequities such as having given up the chance for a career to accompany a husband to his, or doing far more than their share of daily life-support work like cleaning, cooking, social arrangements and errands. Instead, they focused on communication: "He doesn't listen to me," "He doesn't talk to me," I found, as Hacker observed years before, that most wives want their husbands to be, first and foremost, conversational partners, but few husbands share this expectation of their wives.

In short, the image that best represents the current crisis is the stereotypical cartoon scene of a man sitting at the breakfast table with a newspaper held up in front of his face, while a woman glares at the back of it, wanting to talk. 5

LINGUISTIC BATTLE OF THE SEXES

How can women and men have such different impressions of communication in marriage? Why the widespread imbalance in their interests and expectations?

In the April issue of *American Psychologist*, Stanford University's Eleanor Maccoby reports the results of her own and others' research showing that children's development is most influenced by the social structure of peer interactions. Boys and girls tend to play with children of their own gender, and their sex-separate groups have different organizational structures and interactive norms.

I believe these systematic differences in childhood socialization make talk between women and men like cross-cultural communication, heir to all the attraction and pitfalls of that enticing but difficult enterprise. My research on men's and women's conversations uncovered patterns similar to those described for children's groups.

For women, as for girls, intimacy is the fabric of relationships, and talk is the thread from which it is woven. Little girls create and maintain friendships by exchanging secrets; similarly, women regard conversation as the cornerstone of friendship. So a woman expects her husband to be a new and improved version of a best friend. What is important is not the individual subjects that are discussed but the sense of closeness, of a life shared, that emerges when people tell their thoughts, feelings, and impressions.

Bonds between boys can be as intense as girls', but they are based 10 less on talking, more on doing things together. Since they don't assume talk is the cement that binds a relationship, men don't know what kind of talk women want, and they don't miss it when it isn't there.

Boys' groups are larger, more inclusive, and more hierarchical, so boys must struggle to avoid the subordinate position in the group. This may play a role in women's complaints that men don't listen to them. Some men really don't like to listen, because being the listener makes them feel one-down, like a child listening to adults or an employee to a boss.

But often when women tell men, "You aren't listening," and the men protest, "I am," the men are right. The impression of not listening results from misalignments in the mechanics of conversation. The misalignment begins as soon as a man and a woman take physical positions. This became clear when I studied videotapes made by psychologist Bruce Dorval of children and adults talking to their same-sex best friends. I found that at every age, the girls and women faced each other directly, their eyes anchored on each other's faces. At every age, the boys and men sat at angles to each other and looked elsewhere in the room, periodically glancing at each other. They were obviously attuned to each other, often mirroring each other's movements. But the tendency of men to face away can give women the impression they aren't listening even when they are. A young woman in college was frustrated: Whenever she told her boyfriend she wanted to talk to him, he would lie down on the floor, close his eyes, and put his arm over his face. This signaled to her, "He's taking a nap." But he insisted he was listening extra hard. Normally, he looks around the room, so he is easily distracted. Lying down and covering his eyes helped him concentrate on what she was saying.

Analogous to the physical alignment that women and men take in conversation is their topical alignment. The girls in my study tended to talk at length about one topic, but the boys tended to jump from topic to topic. The second-grade girls exchanged stories about people they knew. The second-grade boys teased, told jokes, noticed things in the room and talked about finding games to play. The sixth-grade girls talked about problems with a mutual friend. The sixth-grade boys talked about fifty-five different topics, none of which extended over more than a few turns.

LISTENING TO BODY LANGUAGE

Switching topics is another habit that gives women the impression men aren't listening, especially if they switch to a topic about themselves. But the evidence of the tenth-grade boys in my study indicates otherwise. The tenth-grade boys sprawled across their chairs with bodies parallel and eyes straight ahead, rarely looking at each other. They looked as if they were riding in a car, staring out the windshield. But they were talking about their feelings. One boy was upset because a girl had told him he had a drinking problem, and the other was feeling alienated from all his friends.

Now, when a girl told a friend about a problem, the friend responded   15
by asking probing questions and expressing agreement and understanding. But the boys dismissed each other's problems. Todd assured Richard that his drinking was "no big problem" because "sometimes you're funny when you're off your butt." And when Todd said he felt left out, Richard responded, "Why should you? You know more people than me."

Women perceive such responses as belittling and unsupportive. But the boys seemed satisfied with them. Whereas women reassure each other by implying, "You shouldn't feel bad because I've had similar experiences," men do so by implying, "You shouldn't feel bad because your problems aren't so bad."

There are even simpler reasons for women's impression that men don't listen. Linguist Lynette Hirschman found that women make more listener-noise, such as "mhm," "uhuh," and "yeah," to show "I'm with you." Men, she found, more often give silent attention. Women who expect a stream of listener noise interpret silent attention as no attention at all.

Women's conversational habits are as frustrating to men as men's are to women. Men who expect silent attention interpret a stream of listener noise as overreaction or impatience. Also, when women talk to each other in a close, comfortable setting, they often overlap, finish each other's sentences and anticipate what the other is about to say. This practice, which I call "participatory listenership," is often perceived by men as interruption, intrusion and lack of attention.

A parallel difference caused a man to complain about his wife, "She just wants to talk about her own point of view. If I show her another view, she gets mad at me." When most women talk to each other, they assume a conversationalist's job is to express agreement and support. But many men see their conversational duty as pointing out the other side of an argument. This is heard as disloyalty by women, and refusal to offer the requisite support. It is not that women don't want to see other points of view, but that they prefer them phrased as suggestions and inquiries rather than as direct challenges.

In his book *Fighting for Life*, Walter Ong points out that men use   20
"agonistic," or warlike, oppositional formats to do almost anything;
thus discussion becomes debate, and conversation a competitive
sport. In contrast, women see conversation as a ritual means of establishing rapport. If Jane tells a problem and June says she has a similar
one, they walk away feeling closer to each other. But this attempt at
establishing rapport can backfire when used with men. Men take too
literally women's ritual "troubles talk," just as women mistake men's
ritual challenges for real attack.

THE SOUNDS OF SILENCE

These differences begin to clarify why women and men have such different expectations about communication in marriage. For women, talk
creates intimacy. Marriage is an orgy of closeness: you can tell your feelings and thoughts, and still be loved. Their greatest fear is being pushed
away. But men live in a hierarchical world, where talk maintains independence and status. They are on guard to protect themselves from
being put down and pushed around.

This explains the paradox of the talkative man who said of his
silent wife, "She's the talker." In the public setting of a guest lecture,
he felt challenged to show his intelligence and display his understanding of the lecture. But at home, where he has nothing to prove
and no one to defend against, he is free to remain silent. For his wife,
being home means she is free from the worry that something she says
might offend someone, or spark disagreement, or appear to be showing off; at home she is free to talk.

The communication problems that endanger marriage can't be
fixed by mechanical engineering. They require a new conceptual framework about the role of talk in human relationships. Many of the psychological explanations that have become second nature may not be
helpful, because they tend to blame either women (for not being assertive enough) or men (for not being in touch with their feelings). A
sociolinguistic approach by which male-female conversation is seen
as cross-cultural communication allows us to understand the problem and forge solutions without blaming either party.

Once the problem is understood, improvement comes naturally, as it did to the young woman and her boyfriend who seemed to go to sleep when she wanted to talk. Previously, she had accused him of not listening, and he had refused to change his behavior, since that would be admitting fault. But then she learned about and explained to him the differences in women's and men's habitual ways of aligning themselves in conversation. The next time she told him she wanted to talk, he began, as usual, by lying down and covering his eyes. When the familiar negative reaction bubbled up, she reassured herself that he really was listening. But then he sat up and looked at her. Thrilled, she asked why. He said, "You like me to look at you when we talk, so I'll try to do it." Once he saw their differences as cross-cultural rather than right and wrong, he independently altered his behavior.

Women who feel abandoned and deprived when their husbands 25 won't listen to or report daily news may be happy to discover their husbands trying to adapt once they understand the place of small talk in women's relationships. But if their husbands don't adapt, the women may still be comforted that for men, this is not a failure of intimacy. Accepting the difference, the wives may look to their friends or family for that kind of talk. And husbands who can't provide it shouldn't feel their wives have made unreasonable demands. Some couples will still decide to divorce, but at least their decisions will be based on realistic expectations.

In these times of resurgent ethnic conflicts, the world desperately needs cross-cultural understanding. Like charity, successful cross-cultural communication should begin at home.

STUDY QUESTIONS

1. According to Tannen, what conversational cues tell women someone is listening closely? What conversational cues tell men they're being listened to? How do women express support in conversation? How do men?

2. Tannen COMPARES AND CONTRASTS men's and women's conversational strategies in same-gender groups in order to determine how they might speak more effectively with each other. On what points does she compare them? (For instance, one point of comparison is the use of "listener noise.") What other points of comparison might she have examined?

4. What is Tannen's CLAIM? What REASONS does she supply to support that claim? What kinds of EVIDENCE does she supply? How effective are they?

5. *For Writing.* Seek out two sustained conversations: first with someone of the opposite gender, and then with someone of your own gender. Do you notice any of the conversational strategies Tannen mentions? Write an essay in which you ANALYZE the conversations in terms of male and female conversational styles, and apply Tannen's generalizations about male and female approaches to them. Does what you observed match her conclusions?

{

DAVE BARRY

A GPS Helps a Guy Always

Know Where His Couch Is

DAVE BARRY (b. 1947), a humorist, was recognized for his talent early: he was named Class Clown in his senior year of high school. Barry earned an English degree at Haverford College in 1969; after graduating, he worked as a newspaper reporter for the *Daily Local News* of West Chester, Pennsylvania. He then took a job as a business-writing consultant, but eight years later, in 1983, he returned to print journalism when he joined the *Miami Herald* as a humor columnist. Barry received the Pulitzer Prize for Commentary in 1988, and his columns are now nationally syndicated. His books include *Dave Barry's Complete Guide to Guys* (1991), *Dave Barry Is from Mars AND Venus* (1998), and *Dave Barry's History of the Milennium (So Far)* (2007).

In "A GPS Helps a Guy Always Know Where His Couch Is," first published in the *Miami Herald,* Barry takes a look at electronic gadgetry by means of an old comedy standby: he compares and contrasts the attitudes of men with those of women. As you read, take note of how often Barry ostensibly asserts a position while simultaneously undercutting it with irony, the stuff of which so much humor is made.

─────────────

I'M A BIG FAN OF technology. Most guys are. This is why all important inventions were invented by guys.

For example, millions of years ago, there was no such thing as the wheel. One day, some primitive guys were watching their wives drag a dead mastodon to the food-preparation area. It was exhausting work; the guys were getting tired just WATCHING. Then they noticed some large, smooth, rounded boulders, and they had an idea: They could sit on the boulders and watch! This was the first in a series of breakthroughs that ultimately led to television.

So we see that there are vital reasons why guys are interested in technology, and why women should not give them a hard time about always wanting to have the "latest gadget." And when I say "women," I mean "my wife."

For example, as a guy, I feel I need a new computer every time a new model comes out, which is every 15 minutes. This baffles my wife, who has had the same computer since the Civil War and refuses to get a new one because—get THIS for an excuse—the one she has works fine. I try to explain that, when you get a new computer, you get exciting new features. My new computer has a truly fascinating feature: Whenever I try to turn it off, the following message, which I am not making up, appears on the screen:

"An exception 0E has occurred at 0028:F000F841 in VxD—. This 5 was called from 0028:C001D324 in VxD NDIS(01) + 00005AA0. It may be possible to continue normally."

Clearly, this message is not of human origin. Clearly, my new computer is receiving this message from space aliens. I don't understand all of it, but apparently there has been some kind of intergalactic problem that the aliens want to warn us about. What concerns me is the last sentence, because if the aliens are telling us that "it may be possible to continue normally," they are clearly implying that it may NOT be possible to continue normally. In other words, the Earth may be doomed, and the aliens have chosen ME to receive this message. If I can figure out exactly what they're saying, I might be able to save humanity!

Unfortunately, I don't have time, because I'm busy using my new GPS device. This is an extremely important gadget that every guy in the world needs. It receives signals from orbiting satellites, and somehow— I suspect the "cosine" is involved—it figures out exactly where on the Earth you are. Let's say you're in the town of Arcola, Illinois, but for some reason you do not realize this. You turn on your GPS, and, after pondering for a few minutes, it informs you that you are in . . . Arcola, Illinois! My wife argues that it's easier to just ASK somebody, but of course you cannot do that, if you truly are a guy.

I became aware of how useful a GPS can be when I was on a plane trip with a literary rock band I belong to called the Rock Bottom Remainders, which has been hailed by critics as having one of the world's highest ratios of noise to talent. On this trip were two band members whom I will identify only as "Roger" and "Steve," so that you will not know that they are actually Roger McGuinn, legendary co-founder of the Byrds, and Stephen King, legendary legend.

We were flying from Chicago to Boston, and while everybody else was reading or sleeping, "Roger" and "Steve," who are both fully grown men, were staring at their GPS devices and periodically inform-ing each other how far we were from the Boston airport. "Roger" would say, "I'm showing 238 miles," and "Steve" would say, "I'm showing 241 miles." Then "Roger" would say, "Now I'm showing 236 miles," and "Steve" would come back with another figure, and so on. My wife, who was confident that the airplane pilot did not need help locating Boston, thought this was the silliest thing she had ever seen. Whereas I thought: I NEED one of those.

So I got a GPS for Christmas, and I spent the entire day sitting on a couch, putting it to good use. Like, I figured out exactly where our house is. My wife told me this was exciting news. I think she was being sarcastic, but I couldn't be sure, because I had to keep watching the GPS screen, in case our house moved. I also used my GPS to figure out exactly how far my couch is from LaGuardia Airport (1,103 miles). There is NO END to the usefulness of this device! If you're a guy, you need to get one NOW, so you can locate yourself on the planet. While we still have one. 10

STUDY QUESTIONS

1. According to Barry, why do men want the newest technology? Who does Barry say he means by "women"?

2. COMPARE AND CONTRAST Barry's depictions of men's and women's attitudes toward technology. Why does he call men "guys" but women "women" throughout the article? How seriously does he advocate one perspective over another?

3. *For Writing.* Consider the various electronic devices that you own. Compose an essay in which you REFLECT on how and how often you use them, perhaps comparing and contrasting your use of technology to that of a parent, a sibling, or someone else whose technological skills are markedly different from your own.

SUZANNE BRITT ⎰ *Neat People vs. Sloppy People*

SUZANNE BRITT (b. 1946) was born in Winston-Salem, North Carolina. She earned her bachelor's degree at Salem College and her master's degree at Washington University in St. Louis. A poet, essayist, and columnist, Britt has published her work in numerous newspapers and magazines, including *Newsweek,* the *Boston Globe,* and the *Charlotte Observer.* Many of her essays are collected in two books: *Skinny People Are Dull and Crunchy Like Carrots* (1982) and *Show and Tell* (1983), from which the following selection is taken. Britt currently teaches literature and writing at Meredith College in Raleigh, North Carolina.

In "Neat People vs. Sloppy People," Britt strikes back at those who believe the adage that cleanliness is next to godliness. In her defense of sloppy people, Britt claims that the true difference between neat and sloppy people is one of morality: "Neat people are lazier and meaner than sloppy people." Notice how Britt, like many humorists, uses exaggeration and stereotype for comic effect. While a more serious comparison and contrast essay would make an attempt to be fair, Britt clearly has a different purpose in mind.

I'VE FINALLY FIGURED OUT THE difference between neat people and sloppy people. The distinction is, as always, moral. Neat people are lazier and meaner than sloppy people.

Sloppy people, you see, are not really sloppy. Their sloppiness is merely the unfortunate consequence of their extreme moral rectitude. Sloppy people carry in their mind's eye a heavenly vision, a precise plan, that is so stupendous, so perfect, it can't be achieved in this world or the next.

Sloppy people live in Never-Never Land. Someday is their *métier.*[1] Someday they are planning to alphabetize all their books and set up home catalogues. Someday they will go through their wardrobes and mark certain items for tentative mending and certain items for passing on to relatives of similar shape and size. Someday sloppy people will make family scrapbooks into which they will put newspaper clippings, post-cards, locks of hair, and the dried corsage from their senior prom. Someday they will file everything on the surface of their desks, including the cash receipts from coffee purchases at the snack shop. Someday they will sit down and read all the back issues of *The New Yorker.*

For all these noble reasons and more, sloppy people never get neat. They aim too high and wide. They save everything, planning someday to file, order, and straighten out the world. But while these ambitious plans take clearer and clearer shape in their heads, the books spill from the shelves onto the floor, the clothes pile up in the hamper and closet, the family mementos accumulate in every drawer, the surface of the desk is buried under mounds of paper, and the unread magazines threaten to reach the ceiling.

Sloppy people can't bear to part with anything. They give loving 5 attention to every detail. When sloppy people say they're going to tackle the surface of the desk, they really mean it. Not a paper will go unturned; not a rubber band will go unboxed. Four hours or two weeks into the excavation, the desk looks exactly the same, primarily because the slop-py person is meticulously creating new piles of papers with new head-ings and scrupulously stopping to read all the old book catalogues before he throws them away. A neat person would just bulldoze the desk.

Neat people are bums and clods at heart. They have cavalier atti-tudes toward possessions, including family heirlooms. Everything is just another dust-catcher to them. If anything collects dust, it's got to go and that's that. Neat people will toy with the idea of throwing the children out of the house just to cut down on the clutter.

Neat people don't care about process. They like results. What they

[1]Occupation (French).

want to do is get the whole thing over with so they can sit down and watch the rasslin' on TV. Neat people operate on two unvarying principles: Never handle any item twice, and throw everything away.

The only thing messy in a neat person's house is the trash can. The minute something comes to a neat person's hand, he will look at it, try to decide if it has immediate use and, finding none, throw it in the trash.

Neat people are especially vicious with mail. They never go through their mail unless they are standing directly over a trash can. If the trash can is beside the mailbox, even better. All ads, catalogues, pleas for charitable contributions, church bulletins, and money-saving coupons go straight into the trash can without being opened. All letters from home, postcards from Europe, bills, and paychecks are opened, immediately responded to, then dropped in the trash can. Neat people keep their receipts only for tax purposes. That's it. No sentimental salvaging of birthday cards or the last letter a dying relative ever wrote. Into the trash it goes.

Neat people place neatness above everything, even economics.   10
They are incredibly wasteful. Neat people throw away several toys every time they walk through the den. I knew a neat person once who threw away a perfectly good dish drainer because it had mold on it. The drainer was too much trouble to wash. And neat people sell their furniture when they move. They will sell a La-Z-Boy recliner while you are reclining in it.

Neat people are no good to borrow from. Neat people buy everything in expensive little single portions. They get their flour and sugar in two-pound bags. They wouldn't consider clipping a coupon, saving a leftover, reusing plastic non-dairy whipped cream containers, or rinsing off tinfoil and draping it over the unmoldy dish drainer. You can never borrow a neat person's newspaper to see what's playing at the movies. Neat people have the paper all wadded up and in the trash by 7:05 a.m.

Neat people cut a clean swath through the organic as well as the inorganic world. People, animals, and things are all one to them. They are so insensitive. After they've finished with the pantry, the medicine cabinet, and the attic, they will throw out the red geranium (too many leaves), sell the dog (too many fleas), and send the children off to boarding school (too many scuffmarks on the hardwood floors).

STUDY QUESTIONS

1. How much truth is there to Britt's CHARACTERIZATIONS of neat and sloppy people? Who might be Britt's intended AUDIENCE?

2. One of the conventions of a COMPARISON AND CONTRAST essay is that the subjects being compared and contrasted share some common ground; however, Britt never mentions the ways neat people and sloppy people are similar. Why not?

3. How is Britt able to use the STRATEGIES of generalization, STEREOTYPE, and HYPERBOLE to comic effect, when those same approaches are often taken as a sign of ignorance?

4. *For Writing.* Write an essay in which you rebut Britt's ARGUMENT and CLAIM that neat people are better than sloppy people.

BRUCE CATTON { *Grant and Lee:*

A Study in Contrasts

BRUCE CATTON (1899–1978) grew up in tiny Benzonia, Michigan, enthralled by the stories he heard from Civil War veterans. He turned his interest into his life's work and became a Civil War historian, ultimately receiving the Presidential Medal of Freedom for his work. His many books include *Mr. Lincoln's Army* (1951), the Pulitzer Prize–winning *A Stillness at Appomattox* (1953), *Waiting for the Morning Train: An American Boyhood* (1972), and *Gettysburg: The Final Fury* (1974).

In the following essay, Catton compares the two most famous Civil War generals in terms of their personal qualities and, more broadly, the social and historical forces they represented. The cool, aristocratic Robert E. Lee and the tough, independent-minded Ulysses S. Grant clashed not only on the battlefield, says Catton, but also in their heritage, and they both fought for their highest ideals. As you read, notice how Catton organizes his essay, focusing first on Lee, then on Grant, then bringing them together to focus on their similarities. How effective do you find this organization, and why?

WHEN ULYSSES S. GRANT AND Robert E. Lee met in the parlor of a modest house at Appomattox Court House, Virginia, on April 9, 1865, to work out the terms for the surrender of Lee's Army of Northern Virginia,[1] a great chapter in American life came to a close, and a great new chapter began.

---

[1] That is, the main body of Southern troops fighting for secession from the Union.

These men were bringing the Civil War to its virtual finish. To be sure, other armies had yet to surrender, and for a few days the fugitive Confederate government would struggle desperately and vainly, trying to find some way to go on living now that its chief support was gone. But in effect it was all over when Grant and Lee signed the papers. And the little room where they wrote out the terms was the scene of one of the poignant, dramatic contrasts in American history.

They were two strong men, these oddly different generals, and they represented the strengths of two conflicting currents that, through them, had come into final collision.

Back of Robert E. Lee was the notion that the old aristocratic concept might somehow survive and be dominant in American life.

Lee was tidewater Virginia, and in his background were family, culture, and tradition . . . the age of chivalry transplanted to a New World which was making its own legends and its own myths. He embodied a way of life that had come down through the age of knighthood and the English country squire. America was a land that was beginning all over again, dedicated to nothing much more complicated than the rather hazy belief that all men had equal rights, and should have an equal chance in the world. In such a land Lee stood for the feeling that it was somehow of advantage to human society to have a pronounced inequality in the social structure. There should be a leisure class, backed by ownership of land; in turn, society itself should be keyed to the land as the chief source of wealth and influence. It would bring forth (according to this ideal) a class of men with a strong sense of obligation to the community; men who lived not to gain advantage for themselves, but to meet the solemn obligations which had been laid on them by the very fact that they were privileged. From them the country would get its leadership; to learn it could look for the higher values—of thought, of conduct, of personal deportment—to give it strength and virtue.

Lee embodied the noblest elements of this aristocratic ideal. Through him, the landed nobility justified itself. For four years, the Southern states had fought a desperate war to uphold the ideals for which Lee stood. In the end, it almost seemed as if the Confederacy fought for Lee; as if he himself was the Confederacy . . . the best thing

5

that the way of life for which the Confederacy stood could ever have to offer. He had passed into legend before Appomattox. Thousands of tired, underfed, poorly clothed Confederate soldiers, long-since past the simple enthusiasm of the early days of the struggle, somehow considered Lee the symbol of everything for which they had been willing to die. But they could not quite put this feeling into words. If the Lost Cause, sanctified by so much heroism and so many deaths, had a living justification, its justification was General Lee.

Grant, the son of a tanner on the Western frontier, was everything Lee was not. He had come up the hard way, and embodied nothing in particular except the eternal toughness and sinewy fiber of the men who grew up beyond the mountains. He was one of a body of men who owed reverence and obeisance to no one, who were self-reliant to a fault, who cared hardly anything for the past but who had a sharp eye for the future.

These frontier men were the precise opposites of the tidewater aristocrats. Back of them, in the great surge that had taken people over the Alleghenies and into the opening Western country, there was a deep, implicit dissatisfaction with a past that had settled into grooves. They stood for democracy, not from any reasoned conclusion about the proper ordering of human society, but simply because they had grown up in the middle of democracy and knew how it worked. Their society might have privileges, but they would be privileges each man had won for himself. Forms and patterns meant nothing. No man was born to anything, except perhaps to a chance to show how far he could rise. Life was competition.

Yet along with this feeling had come a deep sense of belonging to a national community. The Westerner who developed a farm, opened a shop or set up in business as a trader, could hope to prosper only as his own community prospered—and his community ran from the Atlantic to the Pacific and from Canada down to Mexico. If the land was settled, with towns and highways and accessible markets, he could better himself. He saw his fate in terms of the nation's own destiny. As its horizons expanded, so did his. He had, in other words, an acute dollars-and-cents stake in the continued growth and development of his country.

And that, perhaps, is where the contrast between Grant and Lee 10

320

becomes most striking. The Virginia aristocrat, inevitably, saw himself in relation to his own region. He lived in a static society which could endure almost anything except change. Instinctively, his first loyalty would go to the locality in which that society existed. He would fight to the limit of endurance to defend it, because in defending it he was defending everything that gave his own life its deepest meaning.

The Westerner, on the other hand, would fight with an equal tenacity for the broader concept of society. He fought so because everything he lived by was tied to growth, expansion, and a constantly widening horizon. What he lived by would survive or fail with the nation itself. He could not possibly stand by unmoved in the face of an attempt to destroy the Union. He would combat it with everything he had, because he could only see it as an effort to cut the ground out from under his feet.

So Grant and Lee were in complete contrast, representing two diametrically opposed elements in American life. Grant was the modern man emerging; beyond him, ready to come on the stage, was the great age of steel and machinery, of crowded cities and a restless, burgeoning vitality. Lee might have ridden down from the old age of chivalry, lance in hand, silken banner fluttering over his head. Each man was the perfect champion of his cause, drawing both his strengths and his weaknesses from the people he led.

Yet it was not all contrast, after all. Different as they were—in background, in personality, in underlying aspiration—these two great soldiers had much in common. Under everything else, they were marvelous fighters. Furthermore, their fighting qualities were really very much alike.

Each man had, to begin with, the great virtue of utter tenacity and fidelity. Grant fought his way down the Mississippi Valley in spite of acute personal discouragement and profound military handicaps. Lee hung on in the trenches at Petersburg after hope itself had died. In each man there was an indomitable quality . . . the born fighter's refusal to give up as long as he can still remain on his feet and lift his two fists.

Daring and resourcefulness they had, too; the ability to think faster 15 and move faster than the enemy. These were the qualities which gave Lee the dazzling campaigns of Second Manassas and Chancellorsville and won Vicksburg for Grant.

Lastly, and perhaps greatest of all, there was the ability, at the end, to turn quickly from war to peace once the fighting was over. Out of the way these two men behaved at Appomattox came the possibility of a peace of reconciliation. It was a possibility not wholly realized, in the years to come, but which did, in the end, help the two sections to become one nation again . . . after a war whose bitterness might have seemed to make such a reunion wholly impossible. No part of either man's life became him more than the part he played in their brief meeting in the McLean house at Appomattox. Their behavior there put all succeeding generations of Americans in their debt. Two great Americans, Grant and Lee—very different, yet under everything very much alike. Their encounter at Appomattox was one of the great moments of American history.

STUDY QUESTIONS

1. Even though Catton builds his essay on the differences between Grant and Lee, he also points out their similarities. According to Catton, how were the two generals alike, and how did those similar qualities benefit the nation in the end?

2. What is Catton's THESIS? If he directly states it, quote it; if not, put it into your own words. How do the differences between Grant and Lee support this thesis?

3. It has been said that "the personal is the political." In this essay, Catton appears to present mainly personal aspects about each general. How do these points suggest their political personae?

4. *For Writing.* Choose two contemporary public figures who campaigned against each other for the same elected office (president, perhaps, or senator, or governor), or who represent different sides of key political or moral issues. Using Catton's essay as a model, write a COMPARISON AND CONTRAST essay about these two figures. Identify the goal and the results, but focus primarily on the similarities and differences that characterize the two. Use the personal as well as the political characteristics of each figure to support your THESIS.

SANDRA CISNEROS ⎰ *Only Daughter*

SANDRA CISNEROS (b. 1954) is a writer, teacher, and community activist. She was raised in both Chicago, the city in which she was born, and Mexico City. After earning her undergraduate degree in English at Loyola University in Chicago, Cisneros obtained an MFA in creative writing at the University of Iowa. A writer of poetry, fiction, and essays, Cisneros won the American Book Award in 1985 for her first novel, *The House on Mango Street* (1983). She has also published two volumes of poetry, a collection of short stories, a children's book, and a second novel, *Caramelo* (2002). During her career, Cisneros has taught writing at every level above first grade and has been a visiting writer at many universities. In 2000 she established the Alfredo Cisneros Del Moral Foundation to honor the memory of her father; each year, the foundation awards grants to writers born in Texas, writing about Texas, or living in Texas.

In the following essay, first published in *Glamour* magazine in 1990, Cisneros explores the play on words of its title: she describes her life as an only daughter in a large Mexican American family and as, from her father's perspective, "only a daughter." As you read, consider the contrasts Cisneros notes—in language, in meaning, and in expectations—and how these disparities contribute to the development of the essay.

ONCE, SEVERAL YEARS AGO, WHEN I was just starting out my writing career, I was asked to write my own contributor's note for an anthology I was part of. I wrote: "I am the only daughter in a family of six sons. *That* explains everything."

Well, I've thought about that ever since, and yes, it explains a lot to me, but for the reader's sake I should have written: "I am the only daughter in a Mexican family of six sons." Or even: "I am the only daughter of a Mexican father and a Mexican-American mother." Or: "I am the only daughter of a working-class family of nine." All of these had everything to do with who I am today.

I was/am the only daughter and *only* a daughter. Being an only daughter in a family of six sons forced me by circumstance to spend a lot of time by myself because my brothers felt it beneath them to play with a *girl* in public. But that aloneness, that loneliness, was good for a would-be writer—it allowed me time to think and think, to imagine, to read and prepare myself.

Being only a daughter for my father meant my destiny would lead me to become someone's wife. That's what he believed. But when I was in the fifth grade and shared my plans for college with him. I was sure he understood. I remember my father saying, "*Que bueno, mi'ja,* that's good." That meant a lot to me, especially since my brothers thought the idea hilarious. What I didn't realize was that my father thought college was good for girls—good for finding a husband. After four years in college and two more in graduate school, and still no husband, my father shakes his head even now and says I wasted all that education.

In retrospect, I'm lucky my father believed daughters were meant 5 for husbands. It meant it didn't matter if I majored in something silly like English. After all, I'd find a nice professional eventually, right? This allowed me the liberty to putter about embroidering my little poems and stories without my father interrupting with so much as a "What's that you're writing?"

But the truth is, I wanted him to interrupt. I wanted my father to understand what it was I was scribbling, to introduce me as "My only daughter, the writer." Not as "This is only my daughter. She teaches." *Es maestra*—teacher. Not even *profesora.*

In a sense, everything I have ever written has been for him, to win his approval even though I know my father can't read English words, even though my father's only reading includes the brown-ink *Esto* sports magazines from Mexico City and the bloody *¡Alarma!* magazines that feature yet another sighting of *La Virgen de Guadalupe* on a tortilla[1] or a wife's revenge on her philandering husband by bashing his skull in with a *molcajete* (a kitchen mortar made of volcanic rock). Or the *fotonovelas,* the little picture paperbacks with tragedy and trauma erupting from the characters' mouths in bubbles.

My father represents, then, the public majority. A public who is disinterested in reading, and yet one whom I am writing about and for, and privately trying to woo.

When we were growing up in Chicago, we moved a lot because of my father. He suffered bouts of nostalgia. Then we'd have to let go our flat, store the furniture with mother's relatives, load the station wagon with baggage and bologna sandwiches and head south. To Mexico City.

We came back, of course. To yet another Chicago flat, another Chicago neighborhood, another Catholic school. Each time, my father would seek out the parish priest in order to get a tuition break, and complain or boast: "I have seven sons."

He meant *siete hijos,* seven children, but he translated it as "sons." "I have seven sons." To anyone who would listen. The Sears Roebuck employee who sold us the washing machine. The short-order cook where my father ate his ham-and-eggs breakfasts. "I have seven sons." As if he deserved a medal from the state.

My papa. He didn't mean anything by that mistranslation, I'm sure. But somehow I could feel myself being erased. I'd tug my father's sleeve and whisper: "Not seven sons. Six! and *one daughter.*"

When my oldest brother graduated from medical school, he fulfilled my father's dream that we study hard and use this—our heads, instead of this—our hands. Even now my father's hands are thick and yellow, stubbed by a history of hammer and nails and twine and coils and springs. "Use this," my father said, tapping his head, "and not this," showing us those hands. He always looked tired when he said it.

Wasn't college an investment? And hadn't I spent all those years in college? And if I didn't marry, what was it all for? Why would anyone go to college and then choose to be poor? Especially someone who had always been poor.

[1]That is, the legendary appearance of an image of the Virgin of Guadalupe (Mary, mother of Jesus) in the texture of a toasted tortilla.

Last year, after ten years of writing professionally, the financial rewards started to trickle in. My second National Endowment for the Arts Fellowship. A guest professorship at the University of California, Berkeley. My book, which sold to a major New York publishing house.

At Christmas, I flew home to Chicago. The house was throbbing, same as always: hot *tamales* and sweet *tamales* hissing in my mother's pressure cooker, and everybody—my mother, six brothers, wives, babies, aunts, cousins—talking too loud and at the same time, like in a Fellini film, because that's just how we are.

I went upstairs to my father's room. One of my stories had just been translated into Spanish and published in an anthology of Chicano writing, and I wanted to show it to him. Ever since he recovered from a stroke two years ago, my father likes to spend his leisure hours horizontally. And that's how I found him, watching a Pedro Infante[2] movie on Galavision and eating rice pudding.

There was a glass filmed with milk on the bedside table. There were several vials of pills and balled Kleenex. And on the floor, one black sock and a plastic urinal that I didn't want to look at but looked at anyway. Pedro Infante was about to burst into song, and my father was laughing.

I'm not sure if it was because my story was translated into Spanish, or because it was published in Mexico, or perhaps because the story dealt with Tepeyac, the *colonia* my father was raised in and the house he grew up in, but at any rate, my father punched the mute button on his remote control and read my story.

I sat on the bed next to my father and waited. He read it very slowly. As if he were reading each line over and over. He laughed at all the right places and read lines he liked out loud. He pointed and asked questions: "Is this So-and-so?" "Yes," I said. He kept reading.

When he was finally finished, after what seemed like hours, my father looked up and asked: "Where can we get more copies of this for the relatives?"

Of all the wonderful things that happened to me last year, that was the most wonderful.

---

[2]José Pedro Infante Cruz (1917–57), Mexican actor and singer. *Galavision:* Spanish-language cable channel.

STUDY QUESTIONS

1. Why does Cisneros's father believe college can be worthwhile for her? How does he view her actual college experience?

2. In paragraph 8, Cisneros writes that her father represents "the public majority," which she envisions as the AUDIENCE for her writing. Based on what she says about her father, how would you characterize that audience? How can you tell Cisneros is writing for them? What clues do you find in the way she addresses the reader and in her TONE and DICTION?

3. Cisneros vividly DESCRIBES her father's hands. Why? What significance do his hands have for her story?

4. *For Writing.* Have you ever been frustrated trying to gain someone's approval for an activity that is very important to you? Have you ever had a difficult time understanding someone else's devotion to an activity that means a lot to him or her—but not, personally, to you? Write a NARRATIVE in which you select one of these experiences and relate the main events associated with it, using vivid descriptions to make your CHARACTERS real to your readers.

JUDITH ORTIZ COFER

{

The Myth of the Latin Woman:
I Just Met a Girl Named María

JUDITH ORTIZ COFER (b. 1952) was born in Puerto Rico but moved to
the United States as a small child. She grew up living mainly in Paterson,
New Jersey, but made frequent extended trips to Puerto Rico, attending
schools in both locations. This "commuting," and the tensions between
life on the island and life on the mainland, informs much of Cofer's
work. A writer who publishes in many genres, Cofer is Regents and
Franklin Professor of English and Creative Writing at the University of
Georgia.

"The Myth of the Latin Woman: I Just Met a Girl Named María," first
published in *Glamour* magazine, appears in her collection of short stories,
essays, and poems *The Latin Deli: Telling the Lives of Barrio Women*
(1993). *The Latin Deli* describes the lives of the women and the other
children Cofer grew up with in El Building, an apartment complex in
Paterson, New Jersey. The women shared memories of similar lives in
Puerto Rico, which helped them form close emotional attachments in New
Jersey. In this selection, Cofer moves away from her childhood narratives
and shares with the reader instances of prejudice she experienced as an
adult. In numerous examples readers see how these encounters, even when
no harm was intended, are enduringly painful for her.

ON A BUS TRIP TO London from Oxford University where I was earning some graduate credits one summer, a young man, obviously fresh
from a pub, spotted me and as if struck by inspiration went down on
his knees in the aisle. With both hands over his heart he broke into an

Irish tenor's rendition of "María" from *West Side Story*.[1] My politely amused fellow passengers gave his lovely voice the round of gentle applause it deserved. Though I was not quite as amused, I managed my version of an English smile: no show of teeth, no extreme contortions of the facial muscles—I was at this time of my life practicing reserve and cool. Oh, that British control, how I coveted it. But María had followed me to London, reminding me of a prime fact of my life: you can leave the Island, master the English language, and travel as far as you can, but if you are a Latina, especially one like me who so obviously belongs to Rita Moreno's gene pool, the Island travels with you.

This is sometimes a very good thing—it may win you that extra minute of someone's attention. But with some people, the same things can make *you* an island—not so much a tropical paradise as an Alcatraz, a place nobody wants to visit. As a Puerto Rican girl growing up in the United States and wanting like most children to "belong," I resented the stereotype that my Hispanic appearance called forth from many people I met.

Our family lived in a large urban center in New Jersey during the sixties, where life was designed as a microcosm of my parents' casas[2] on the island. We spoke in Spanish, we ate Puerto Rican food bought at the bodega,[3] and we practiced strict Catholicism complete with Saturday confession and Sunday mass at a church where our parents were accommodated into a one-hour Spanish mass slot, performed by a Chinese priest trained as a missionary for Latin America.

As a girl I was kept under strict surveillance, since virtue and modesty were, by cultural equation, the same as family honor. As a teenager I was instructed on how to behave as proper señorita.[4] But it was a conflicting message girls got, since the Puerto Rican mothers also encouraged their daughters to look and act like women and to dress in clothes our Anglo friends and their mothers found too "mature" for our age. It

---

[1]Broadway musical made into a 1961 film starring Rita Moreno (b. 1931) as Anita, friend of the female protagonist María.

[2]Homes (Spanish).

[3]Grocery store (Spanish).

[4]Young lady (Spanish).

was, and is, cultural, yet I often felt humiliated when I appeared at an American friend's party wearing a dress more suitable to a semiformal than to a playroom birthday celebration. At Puerto Rican festivities, neither the music nor the colors we wore could be too loud. I still experience a vague sense of letdown when I'm invited to a "party" and it turns out to be a marathon conversation in hushed tones rather than a fiesta with salsa, laughter, and dancing—the kind of celebration I remember from my childhood.

I remember Career Day in our high school, when teachers told us to come dressed as if for a job interview. It quickly became obvious that to the barrio girls, "dressing up" sometimes meant wearing ornate jewelry and clothing that would be more appropriate (by mainstream standards) for the company Christmas party than as daily office attire. That morning I had agonized in front of my closet, trying to figure out what a "career girl" would wear because, essentially, except for Marlo Thomas[5] on TV, I had no models on which to base my decision. I knew how to dress for school: at the Catholic school I attended we all wore uniforms; I knew how to dress for Sunday mass, and I knew what dresses to wear for parties at my relatives' homes. Though I do not recall the precise details of my Career Day outfit, it must have been a composite of the above choices. But I remember a comment my friend (an Italian-American) made in later years that coalesced my impressions of that day. She said that at the business school she was attending the Puerto Rican girls always stood out for wearing "everything at once." She meant, of course, too much jewelry, too many accessories. On that day at school, we were simply made the negative models by the nuns who were themselves not credible fashion experts to any of us. But it was painfully obvious to me that to the others, in their tailored skirts and silk blouses, we must have seemed "hopeless" and "vulgar." Though I now know that most adolescents feel out of step much of the time, I also know that for the Puerto Rican girls of my generation that sense was intensified. The way our teachers and classmates looked at us that day in school was just a taste of the culture clash that awaited us

[5]American actress (b. 1937), star of the popular series *That Girl*, which aired from 1966 to 1971.

in the real world, where prospective employers and men on the street would often misinterpret our tight skirts and jingling bracelets as a come-on.

Mixed cultural signals have perpetuated certain stereotypes—for example, that of the Hispanic woman as the "Hot Tamale" or sexual firebrand. It is a one-dimensional view that the media have found easy to promote. In their special vocabulary, advertisers have designated "sizzling" and "smoldering" as the adjectives of choice for describing not only the foods but also the women of Latin America. From conversations in my house I recall hearing about the harassment that Puerto Rican women endured in factories where the "boss men" talked to them as if sexual innuendo was all they understood and, worse, often gave them the choice of submitting to advances or being fired.

It is custom, however, not chromosomes, that leads us to choose scarlet over pale pink. As young girls, we were influenced in our decisions about clothes and colors by the women—older sisters and mothers who had grown up on a tropical island where the natural environment was a riot of primary colors, where showing your skin was one way to keep cool as well as to look sexy. Most important of all, on the island, women perhaps felt freer to dress and move more provocatively, since, in most cases, they were protected by the traditions, mores, and laws of a Spanish/Catholic system of morality and machismo whose main rule was: *You may look at my sister, but if you touch her I will kill you.* The extended family and church structure could provide a young woman with a circle of safety in her small *pueblo*[6] on the island; if a man "wronged" a girl, everyone would close in to save her family honor.

This is what I have gleaned from my discussions as an adult with older Puerto Rican women. They have told me about dressing in their best party clothes on Saturday nights and going to the town's plaza to promenade with their girlfriends in front of the boys they liked. The males were thus given an opportunity to admire the women and to express their admiration in the form of *piropos:* erotically charged street poems they composed on the spot. I have been subjected to a few piropos while visiting the Island, and they can be outrageous, although cus-

[6]Town (Spanish).

tom dictates that they must never cross into obscenity. This ritual, as I understand it, also entails a show of studied indifference on the woman's part; if she is "decent," she must not acknowledge the man's impassioned words. So I do understand how things can be lost in translation. When a Puerto Rican girl dressed in her idea of what is attractive meets a man from the mainstream culture who has been trained to react to certain types of clothing as a sexual signal, a clash is likely to take place. The line I first heard based on this aspect of the myth happened when the boy who took me to my first formal dance leaned over to plant a sloppy overeager kiss painfully on my mouth, and when I didn't respond with sufficient passion said in a resentful tone: "I thought you Latin girls were supposed to mature early"—my first instance of being thought of as a fruit or vegetable—I was supposed to *ripen,* not just grow into womanhood like other girls.

It is surprising to some of my professional friends that some people, including those who should know better, still put others "in their place." Though rarer, these incidents are still commonplace in my life. It happened to me most recently during a stay at a very classy metropolitan hotel favored by young professional couples for their weddings. Late one evening after the theater, as I walked toward my room with my new colleague (a woman with whom I was coordinating an arts program), a middle-aged man in a tuxedo, a young girl in satin and lace on his arm, stepped directly into our path. With his champagne glass extended toward me, he exclaimed, "Evita!"[7]

Our way blocked, my companion and I listened as the man half-recited, half-bellowed "Don't Cry for Me, Argentina." When he finished, the young girl said: "How about a round of applause for my daddy?" We complied, hoping this would bring the silly spectacle to a close. I was becoming aware that our little group was attracting the attention of the other guests. "Daddy" must have perceived this too, and he once more barred the way as we tried to walk past him. He began to shout-sing a ditty to the tune of "La Bamba"—except the lyrics were about a girl named María whose exploits all rhymed with her name and

10

[7]Eva Perón (1919–52), dynamic First Lady of Argentina on whom the musical *Evita,* with its hit song "Don't Cry for Me, Argentina," was based.

gonorrhea. The girl kept saying "Oh, Daddy" and looking at me with pleading eyes. She wanted me to laugh along with the others. My companion and I stood silently waiting for the man to end his offensive song. When he finished, I looked not at him but at his daughter. I advised her calmly never to ask her father what he had done in the army. Then I walked between them and to my room. My friend complimented me on my cool handling of the situation. I confessed to her that I really had wanted to push the jerk into the swimming pool. I knew that this same man—probably a corporate executive, well educated, even worldly by most standards—would not have been likely to regale a white woman with a dirty song in public. He would perhaps have checked his impulse by assuming that she could be somebody's wife or mother, or at least *somebody* who might take offense. But to him, I was just an Evita or a María: merely a character in his cartoon-populated universe.

Because of my education and my proficiency with the English language, I have acquired many mechanisms for dealing with the anger I experience. This was not true for my parents, nor is it true for the many Latin women working at menial jobs who must put up with stereotypes about our ethnic group such as: "They make good domestics." This is another facet of the myth of the Latin woman in the United States. Its origin is simple to deduce. Work as domestics, waitresses, and factory jobs are all that's available to women with little English and few skills. The myth of the Hispanic menial has been sustained by the same media phenomenon that made "Mammy" from *Gone with the Wind*[8] America's idea of the black woman for generations; María, the housemaid or counter girl, is now indelibly etched into the national psyche. The big and the little screens have presented us with the picture of the funny Hispanic maid, mispronouncing words and cooking up a spicy storm in a shiny California kitchen.

This media-engendered image of the Latina in the United States has been documented by feminist Hispanic scholars, who claim that such portrayals are partially responsible for the denial of opportunities for

[8]Immensely popular 1936 novel by Margaret Mitchell and 1937 movie set on a Southern plantation before, during, and after the Civil War.

upward mobility among Latinas in the professions. I have a Chicana friend working on a Ph.D. in philosophy at a major university. She says her doctor still shakes his head in puzzled amazement at all the "big words" she uses. Since I do not wear my diplomas around my neck for all to see, I too have on occasion been sent to the "kitchen," where some think I obviously belong.

One such incident that has stayed with me, though I recognize it as a minor offense, happened on the day of my first public poetry reading. It took place in Miami in a boat-restaurant where we were having lunch before the event. I was nervous and excited as I walked in with my notebook in my hand. An older woman motioned me to her table. Thinking (foolish me) that she wanted me to autograph a copy of my grand new slender volume of verse, I went over. She ordered a cup of coffee from me, assuming that I was the waitress. Easy enough to mistake my poems for menus, I suppose. I know that it wasn't an intentional act of cruelty, yet of all the good things that happened that day, I remember that scene most clearly, because it reminded me of what I had to overcome before anyone would take me seriously. In retrospect I understand that my anger gave my reading fire, that I have almost always taken doubts in my abilities as a challenge—and that the result is, most times, a feeling of satisfaction at having won a convert when I see the cold, appraising eyes warm to my words, the body language change, the smile that indicates that I have opened some avenue for communication. The day I read to that woman and her lowered eyes told me that she was embarrassed at her little faux pas, and when I willed her to look up at me, it was my victory, and she graciously allowed me to punish her with my full attention. We shook hands at the end of the reading, and I never saw her again. She has probably forgotten the whole thing but maybe not.

Yet I am one of the lucky ones. My parents made it possible for me to acquire a stronger footing in the mainstrain culture by giving me the chance at an education. And books and art have saved me from the harsher forms of ethnic and racial prejudice that many of my Hispanic *compañeras*[9] have had to endure. I travel a lot around the United

[9]Countrywomen (Spanish).

States, reading from my books of poetry and my novel, and the reception I most often receive is one of positive interest by people who want to know more about my culture. There are, however, thousands of Latinas without the privilege of an education or the entrée into society that I have. For them life is a struggle against the misconceptions perpetuated by the myth of the Latina as whore, domestic, or criminal. We cannot change this by legislating the way people look at us. The transformation, as I see it, has to occur at a much more individual level. My personal goal in my public life is to try to replace the old pervasive stereotypes and myths about Latinas with a much more interesting set of realities. Every time I give a reading, I hope the stories I tell, the dreams and fears I examine in my work, can achieve some univesal truth which will get my audience past the particulars of my skin color, my accent, or my clothes.

I once wrote a poem in which I called us Latinas "God's brown daughters." This poem is really a prayer of sorts, offered upward, but also, through the human-to-human channel of art, outward. It is a prayer for communication, and for respect. In it, Latin women pray "in Spanish to an Anglo God / with a Jewish heritage," and they are "fervently hoping / that if not omnipotent, / at least He be bilingual." 15

STUDY QUESTIONS

1. Who was Cofer's role model for how to dress in an office job? Explain the cultural differences between the way the Puerto Rican women dressed for work and how the American women dressed. What does it mean to wear "everything at once"?

2. When writing about their personal experiences, authors sometimes do not include a stated THESIS. However, readers can sometimes find one or at least be able to infer one after they complete the reading. Find or infer a thesis for this personal NARRATIVE. Next, look at all the examples Cofer uses in the piece and determine if they support the thesis you selected/inferred. If not, change your thesis to one that corresponds with the examples.

3. In her DESCRIPTIONS of her encounters with prejudice, Cofer frequently offers COUNTERARGUMENTS on behalf of the people committing the offensive act. What effect do these alternative POINTS OF VIEW have on Cofer's narrative?

4. *For Writing.* Select a particular cultural tradition or object that departs from mainstream American culture. For example, you might want to discuss Chinese New Year, the King Cake, the Day of the Dead, a *quinceañera*, a *tamalada*, or something that is specific to your own family, such as a special food dish that no one else makes, a special ritual at someone's birthday, or other unique cultural expression. Write a DESCRIPTIVE ESSAY about it, including its background, how it is celebrated or used, and how you, your family, or members of your culture participate in it. How does it help make you who you are?

T. ALLEN CULPEPPER { *The Myth of Inferiority*

T. ALLEN CULPEPPER (b. 1962) is an American professor and poet. He was born and raised in Alabama and earned a BA in English from the University of Alabama (1985), an MA in English from the University of West Florida (1993), and a PhD in English from the University of Tulsa (1998). In addition to his work as an academic and poet, Culpepper worked as a journalist for several years in the 1980s and early 1990s. He has taught at a number of colleges and universities in the United States, and is currently an assistant professor of English at Tulsa Community College.

"The Myth of Inferiority" was published in *The Chronicle of Higher Education*, a journal written for professors and others who work at colleges and universities, in 2006. In the essay, Culpepper challenges the idea that community-college students are less academically capable than their counterparts at four-year colleges and universities. He goes on to argue that the way in which teachers think about their students (and teaching in general) can have a major impact on their instructional practices. As you read, take special note of what Culpepper describes as the opinions that many teachers and administrators hold regarding community-college students and what he describes as the reality at both community colleges and four-year colleges and universities.

A CANDIDATE FOR A FACULTY position at a community college usually faces some version of the question "Why are you particularly well suited to working with the kinds of students who come here?" Having been interviewed for a number of such positions and having served on

"The Myth of Inferiority" by T. Allen Culpepper from *The Chronicle of Higher Education*, October 27, 2006. Used by permission of T. Allen Culpepper, formerly of State College of Florida, now teaches English at Tulsa Community College in Oklahoma.

several search committees charged with filling them, I speak from experience. At least superficially straightforward and appropriate, the question seldom surprises job candidates who have even casually attempted to prepare for their interviews. But that the question arises at all reflects widely held misconceptions of community-college students that job candidates, and even interviewers—who should know better—may have unconsciously internalized. For the incautious candidate, answering that unsurprising, but sometimes surprisingly loaded, question can be perilous.

As a novice job candidate myself, I simply (and perhaps naïvely) took the question at face value, accepting that community-college students differ significantly from students at other kinds of institutions. I genuinely wanted to teach at a community college. Having dutifully done my research and formulated my "statement of teaching philosophy," I began my first interview by stating my familiarity with the particular challenges that many community-college students face: being a first-generation college student, coping with economic hardship and lack of intellectual confidence, balancing academic responsibilities with competing obligations to employers and families. After emphasizing my desire to work with exactly those kinds of students, I declared my commitment to "student-centered learning." I emphasized my ability to help students succeed in the face of their challenges and to recognize the myriad "learning styles" that students bring to the classroom. I spoke of my ability to use various teaching methods to engage students, always being mindful of the need to stress the subject matter's "real-world connections" and "workplace value."

That kind of answer works well enough, if you make it with conviction and avoid any hint of irony when speaking the buzzwords. It is true that candidates must convey a clear understanding of the allegedly unique characteristics of community-college students, along with a sincere desire to teach such students. But at the same time, it is essential to steer clear of even the slightest suggestion that one considers community colleges or their students in any way inferior to four-year institutions or students who attend them. That is especially important if the interviewer's tone or framing of the question implies that he or she might hold that view.

Even early in my first job search, the question made me uneasy, mainly because of the subtle implication that teaching at a community college amounts to settling for second- or third-rate students. Merely asking the question somehow suggests, however faintly and unintentionally, that there is something wrong with students who choose to attend community colleges.

In later phases of job hunting, with more experience as an interviewee and as a teacher at various kinds of institutions (a private research university, a large land-grant university, two community colleges, and an institution in transition from two-year college to regional university), I gently challenged the question's underlying assumption that one finds totally different students at community colleges than at universities. In my experience, first- and second-year students, regardless of the type of institution they attend, are more alike than different. At every institution where I have taught, including the private research university, I have found poorly prepared first-generation students with few economic, academic, or social resources. And at every institution, including the community colleges, I have worked with well-prepared, intellectually gifted students with friends in all the right places and money to burn.

In four years at the same community college, I have watched the ebb and flow of students through several semesters, during some of which I have raved to anyone who would listen about how wonderful my students are, and during others of which I have whined incessantly, whether anyone listened or not, about how shockingly clueless my students are. While it is probably true that there were more high-caliber students in my honors classes at the private university than there are in my standard classes at the similarly sized community college where I teach now, only the proportions—not the types—of students have varied.

Although I have not conducted formal research in this area, I suspect that if one looked at essays from a representative sampling of students in freshman-composition classes at a university and at a community college, one would find it difficult to determine which essays came from which institution. In writing classes at both community colleges and universities, I have encountered intellectually gifted students who can write deeply analytical essays in eloquent prose, brilliant students who cannot write a shopping list that makes sense, students who write beautifully but fail to say anything of substance, and students who can hardly read, much less write clearly or think critically. At both kinds of institutions, I have also found students who manage to complete a full load of classes successfully while working three jobs, rearing multiple children alone, caring for elderly relatives, and coping with chronic illness or disability, as well as students who take a relatively light load of courses and don't do much else (except illicit drugs) but still manage to fail all their classes, despite considerable intelligence and ability.

Students are students, wherever they are.

The danger is that the perception of difference between the two groups of students can lead to low expectations of community-college students and an institutional culture that enables them to live down to those expectations. Unfortunately, the false belief persists among the general public, students themselves, and even some faculty members that students choose to attend community colleges because they couldn't survive academically at a university. That might be true for some, but many students choose community colleges for a variety of good reasons, such as cost, location, emphasis on teaching, and flexible class schedules.

Regardless of why students come to community colleges, we welcome them with open arms and make every accommodation we can to help them succeed. We want them, of course, to become well-adjusted, well-informed, clear-thinking citizens who can contribute productively and ethically to our society. We also want the enrollment figures that bring in revenue, the graduation and retention rates that impress accreditation teams, and the glowing evaluations of our teaching that earn us promotions and tenure. If we even unconsciously assume our students' inferiority while pursuing those goals, however, we risk lowering our standards rather than teaching our students how to meet them. 10

In seeking to satisfy our students while enhancing our own performance ratings, we might also yield too easily to educational fads of dubious value, as when we embrace and carry out the advice of the alleged pedagogical experts, who, as far as I can tell, denounce the lecture style of teaching while insisting that students learn most when they teach themselves and insist that hands-on learning is best (provided of course that people never touch each other), that teaching cannot occur without at least one computer in the room, and that, because every student has a different "learning style," professors must cater to the whims of all their students individually but simultaneously.

Do not misunderstand: Teachers should be willing to do whatever it takes, within reason, to engage students with the course material—to "meet students where they are." And it is true that the one thing worse than a bad lecture is a bad lecture with PowerPoint slides. But I am skeptical that there even is such a thing as "learning styles," for example. In my view, teachers will achieve better results by determining their own strengths and using them effectively than by attempting to use pedagogical methods that make them feel incompetent or uncomfortable because some expert says that is the "right" thing to do. In my experience, most students respond favorably to professors who teach well and respond negatively to professors who teach badly, regardless of the teaching methods employed.

If current and potential community-college faculty members allow ourselves, or even worse, our students, to accept the myth of community-college students' inherent inferiority, we may be, despite all our efforts to "retain" them as successful students, enabling them to fail. The means would be our own failure to uphold high performance standards and our willingness to make allowances for shoddy work, plagiarism, missed deadlines, chronic absence, and other academic sins because so many of our students have hard lives.

Let us again consider the question "Why are you particularly well suited to working with the kinds of students who come here?" Regardless of where "here" is and what kind of students it is known for, the best answer might be "I have learned to maintain high standards, expect students to meet them, and do whatever I can to help students meet those expectations." To lower our standards is to accept the false assumption that students "here" are inferior to students "there."

STUDY QUESTIONS

1. According to the essay, what are the *perceived* challenges that community-college students and teachers face? What does Culpepper say is the reality?

2. This piece was primarily written for a professional AUDIENCE—in this case, educators. How does Culpepper acknowledge what he sees as the common attitudes of his audience toward community-college students, and how does he challenge those attitudes?

3. As he moves away from discussing community-college students, what broader CLAIMS does Culpepper make about education, and how does he support them?

4. *For Writing.* Think about what Culpepper says about teaching and learning styles. Write a short essay in which you agree or disagree with Carr, citing your own educational experience—what are the best, most effective educational experiences you have had, and what made them the best?

JOAN DIDION { *On Going Home*

JOAN DIDION (b. 1934), a native of California and graduate of the
University of California at Berkeley, wrote for *Vogue* magazine until she published her first novel, *River Run* (1963). Didion is probably best known for
her essays, many of which are haunting reflections on the changes that over-
took her home state in the middle of the twentieth century. Her essay collections include *Slouching Towards Bethlehem* (1969), from which "On Going
Home" is taken, *The White Album* (1979), and *The Year of Magical
Thinking* (2005).

Didion frames this memoir with her daughter's first birthday, focusing
on her visit to the home where she grew up. The essay probes her feelings
about her family and about her husband's presence in her family's home,
revealing Didion's inner conflicts. As you read, notice how Didion uses
specific objects to help paint a picture of her family.

I AM HOME FOR MY daughter's first birthday. By "home" I do not
mean the house in Los Angeles where my husband and I and the baby
live, but the place where my family is, in the Central Valley of
California. It is a vital although troublesome distinction. My husband
likes my family but is uneasy in their house, because once there I fall
into their ways, which are difficult, oblique, deliberately inarticulate,
not my husband's ways. We live in dusty houses ("D-U-S-T," he once
wrote with his finger on surfaces all over the house, but no one noticed
it) filled with mementos quite without value to him (what could the
Canton dessert plates mean to him? how could he have known about

the assay scales,[1] why should he care if he did know?), and we appear to talk exclusively about people we know who have been committed to mental hospitals, about people we know who have been booked on drunk-driving charges, and about property, particularly about property, land, price per acre and C-2 zoning and assessments and freeway access. My brother does not understand my husband's inability to perceive the advantage in the rather common real-estate transaction known as "sale-leaseback," and my husband in turn does not understand why so many of the people he hears about in my father's house have recently been committed to mental hospitals or booked on drunk-driving charges. Nor does he understand that when we talk about sale-leasebacks and right-of-way condemnations we are talking in code about things we like best, the yellow fields and the cottonwoods and the rivers rising and falling and the mountain roads closing when the heavy snow comes in. We miss each other's points, have another drink and regard the fire. My brother refers to my husband, in his presence, as "Joan's husband." Marriage is the classic betrayal.

Or perhaps it is not anymore. Sometimes I think that those of us who are now in our thirties were born into the last generation to carry the burden of "home," to find in family life the source of all tension and drama. I had by all objective accounts a "normal" and a "happy" family situation, and yet I was almost thirty years old before I could talk to my family on the telephone without crying after I had hung up. We did not fight. Nothing was wrong. And yet some nameless anxiety colored the emotional charges between me and the place that I came from. The question of whether or not you could go home again was a very real part of the sentimental and largely literary baggage with which we left home in the fifties; I suspect that it is irrelevant to the children born of the fragmentation after World War II. A few weeks ago in a San Francisco bar I saw a pretty young girl on crystal[2] take off her clothes and dance for the cash prize in an "amateur-topless" contest. There was no particular sense of moment about this, none of the effect of

[1]Scales such as those used during the California Gold Rush (1848-55) to determine the weight and purity of mineral ore.
[2]Common name for methamphetamine, a psychoactive stimulant.

romantic degradation, of "dark journey," for which my generation strived so assiduously. What sense could that girl possibly make of, say, *Long Day's Journey into Night?*[3] Who is beside the point?

That I am trapped in this particular irrelevancy is never more apparent to me than when I am home. Paralyzed by the neurotic lassitude engendered by meeting one's past at every turn, around every corner, inside every cupboard, I go aimlessly from room to room. I decide to meet it head-on and clean out a drawer, and I spread the contents on the bed. A bathing suit I wore the summer I was seventeen. A letter of rejection from *The Nation,* an aerial photograph of the site for a shopping center my father did not build in 1954. Three teacups hand-painted with cabbage roses and signed "E.M.," my grandmother's initials. There is no final solution for letters of rejection from *The Nation* and teacups hand-painted in 1900. Nor is there any answer to snapshots of one's grandfather as a young man on skis, surveying around Donner Pass[4] in the year 1910. I smooth out the snapshot and look into his face, and do and do not see my own. I close the drawer, and have another cup of coffee with my mother. We get along very well, veterans of a guerrilla war we never understood.

Days pass. I see no one. I come to dread my husband's evening call, not only because he is full of news of what by now seems to me our remote life in Los Angeles, people he has seen, letters which require attention, but because he asks what I have been doing, suggests uneasily that I get out, drive to San Francisco or Berkeley. Instead I drive across the river to a family graveyard. It has been vandalized since my last visit and the monuments are broken, overturned in the dry grass. Because I once saw a rattlesnake in the grass I stay in the car and listen to a country-and-Western station. Later I drive with my father to a ranch he has in the foothills. The man who runs his cattle on it asks us to the round-up, a week from Sunday, and although I know that I will be in Los Angeles I say, in the oblique way my family talks, that I will come. Once home I mention the broken monuments in the graveyard. My mother shrugs.

---

[3]Play by Eugene O'Neill (1888–1952), a tragedy about family relationships and addiction.
[4]High mountain pass in California's northern Sierra Nevada.

I go to visit my great-aunts. A few of them think now that I am my cousin, or their daughter who died young. We recall an anecdote about a relative last seen in 1948, and they ask if I still like living in New York City. I have lived in Los Angeles for three years, but I say that I do. The baby is offered a horehound drop, and I am slipped a dollar bill "to buy a treat." Questions trail off, answers are abandoned, the baby plays with the dust motes in a shaft of afternoon sun.

It is time for the baby's birthday party: a white cake, strawberry-marshmallow ice cream, a bottle of champagne saved from another party. In the evening, after she has gone to sleep, I kneel beside the crib and touch her face, where it is pressed against the slats, with mine. She is an open and trusting child, unprepared for and unaccustomed to the ambushes of family life, and perhaps it is just as well that I can offer her little of that life. I would like to give her more. I would like to promise her that she will grow up with a sense of her cousins and of rivers and of her great-grandmother's teacups, would like to pledge her a picnic on a river with fried chicken and her hair uncombed, would like to give her *home* for her birthday, but we live differently now and I can promise her nothing like that. I give her a xylophone and a sundress from Madeira,[5] and promise to tell her a funny story.

[5]Small group of Portuguese islands in the Atlantic Ocean.

STUDY QUESTIONS

1. What event frames the activity in this MEMOIR? How does that event make the author think about her trip home? What does she want to give her daughter?

2. How would you DESCRIBE the TONE of this memoir? Is Didion happy to be home? How has her husband's presence made such stays difficult for her? Why does she say, "Marriage is the classic betrayal"?

3. Examine Didion's memoir for its CONTRASTING elements. Identify at least three examples. What do they tell you about her life in her parents' home? About her life in Los Angeles? About herself?

4. *For Writing.* If you can, visit the home where you grew up. Go through the house and neighborhood and REFLECT on different events that happened to you that no one you've met since you left home knows about. If you can't go home, find a quiet place and recall your experiences at home that only you and possibly your parents know about. Write a memoir about the ways certain places evoke vivid memories about things you did when you were younger. Use Didion's essay as a model. Be sure to use DESCRIPTIVE language, relying on your physical senses as well as feelings.

JOAN DIDION { *On Keeping a Notebook*

JOAN DIDION (b. 1934), a prolific writer whose body of work includes novels, screenplays, and book reviews, is especially well known for her keen social observation. Two of her most popular essay collections are *Slouching Towards Bethlehem* (1969) and *The White Album* (1979). The former is considered a classic of New Journalism, a style of writing that combines elements of fiction with reporting. Her recent memoir, *The Year of Magical Thinking* (2005), describes her slow, painful adjustment to the loss of her husband and the illness of her daughter. In 2007, Didion wrote a drama based on the memoir; the play ran on Broadway for twenty-four weeks.

In "On Keeping a Notebook," originally published in *Slouching Towards Bethlehem*, Didion examines her notebooks, contrasts them with diaries, and explains the purposes her notebooks serve. As she reminisces about the specific people and events she has recorded in her notebooks, she speculates about the person who, although absent, is the real subject of these entries: Didion herself. Notice how this essay is organized and consider what effect its structure has on you as a reader. If you keep a notebook, journal, or diary, think about why you do and what you are trying to record.

"'THAT WOMAN ESTELLE,'" THE NOTE reads, " 'is partly the reason why George Sharp and I are separated today.' *Dirty crepe-de-Chine wrapper, hotel bar, Wilmington RR, 9:45 a.m. August Monday morning.*"

Since the note is in my notebook, it presumably has some meaning to me. I study it for a long while. At first I have only the most general notion of what I was doing on an August Monday morning in the bar of the hotel across from the Pennsylvania Railroad station in Wilmington, Delaware (waiting for a train? missing one? 1960? 1961? why Wilmington?), but I do remember being there. The woman in the dirty crepe-de-Chine wrapper had come down from her room for a beer, and the bartender had heard before the reason why George Sharp and she were separated today. "Sure," he said, and went on mopping the floor. "You told me." At the other end of the bar is a girl. She is talking, pointedly, not to the man beside her but to a cat lying in the triangle of sunlight cast through the open door. She is wearing a plaid silk dress from Peck & Peck, and the hem is coming down.

Here is what it is: the girl has been on the Eastern Shore, and now she is going back to the city, leaving the man beside her, and all she can see ahead are the viscous summer sidewalks and the 3 a.m. long-distance calls that will make her lie awake and then sleep drugged through all the steaming mornings left in August (1960? 1961?). Because she must go directly from the train to lunch in New York, she wishes that she had a safety pin for the hem of the plaid silk dress, and she also wishes that she could forget about the hem and the lunch and stay in the cool bar that smells of disinfectant and malt and make friends with the woman in the crepe-de-Chine wrapper. She is afflicted by a little self-pity, and she wants to compare Estelles. That is what that was all about.

Why did I write it down? In order to remember, of course, but exactly what was it I wanted to remember? How much of it actually happened? Did any of it? Why do I keep a notebook at all? It is easy to deceive oneself on all those scores. The impulse to write things down is a peculiarly compulsive one, inexplicable to those who do not share it, useful only accidentally, only secondarily, in the way that any compulsion tries to justify itself. I suppose that it begins or does not begin in the cradle. Although I have felt compelled to write things down since I was five years old, I doubt that my daughter ever will, for she is a singularly blessed and accepting child, delighted with life exactly as life presents itself to her, unafraid to go to sleep and unafraid to wake up. Keepers of private notebooks are a different breed altogether, lonely and resistant rearrangers of things, anxious malcontents, children afflicted apparently at birth with some presentiment of loss.

My first notebook was a Big Five tablet, given to me by my mother 5 with the sensible suggestion that I stop whining and learn to amuse myself by writing down my thoughts. She returned the tablet to me a few years ago; the first entry is an account of a woman who believed herself to be freezing to death in the Arctic night, only to find, when day broke, that she had stumbled onto the Sahara Desert, where she would die of the heat before lunch. I have no idea what turn of a five-year-old's mind could have prompted so insistently "ironic" and exotic a story, but it does reveal a certain predilection for the extreme which has dogged me into adult life; perhaps if I were analytically inclined I would find it a truer story than any I might have told about Donald Johnson's birthday party or the day my cousin Brenda put Kitty Litter in the aquarium.

So the point of my keeping a notebook has never been, nor is it now, to have an accurate factual record of what I have been doing or thinking. That would be a different impulse entirely, an instinct for reality which I sometimes envy but do not possess. At no point have I ever been able successfully to keep a diary; my approach to daily life ranges from the grossly negligent to the merely absent, and on those few occasions when I have tried dutifully to record a day's events, boredom has so overcome me that the results are mysterious at best. What is this business about "shopping, typing piece, dinner with E, depressed"? Shopping for what? Typing what piece? Who is E? Was this "E" depressed, or was I depressed? Who cares?

In fact I have abandoned altogether that kind of pointless entry; instead I tell what some would call lies. "That's simply not true," the members of my family frequently tell me when they come up against my memory of a shared event. "The party was *not* for you, the spider was *not* a black widow, *it wasn't that way at all.*" Very likely they are right, for not only have I always had trouble distinguishing between what happened and what merely might have happened, but I remain unconvinced that the distinction, for my purposes, matters. The cracked crab that I recall having for lunch the day my father came home from Detroit in 1945 must certainly be embroidery, worked into the day's pattern to lend verisimilitude; I was ten years old and would not now remember the cracked crab. The day's events did not turn on cracked crab. And yet it is precisely that fictitious crab that makes me see the afternoon all over again, a home movie run all too often, the father bearing gifts, the child weeping, an exercise in family love and guilt. Or that is what it was to me. Similarly, perhaps it never did snow that August in Vermont; perhaps there never were flurries in the night wind, and maybe no one else felt the ground hardening and summer already dead even as we pretended to bask in it, but that was how it felt to me, and it might as well have snowed, could have snowed, did snow.

How it felt to me: that is getting closer to the truth about a notebook. I sometimes delude myself about why I keep a notebook, imagine that some thrifty virtue derives from preserving everything observed. See enough and write it down, I tell myself, and then some morning when the world seems drained of wonder, some day when I am only going through the motions of doing what I am supposed to do, which is write—on that bankrupt morning I will simply open my notebook and there it will all be, a forgotten account with accumulated interest, paid passage back to the world out there: dialogue overheard in hotels and elevators and at the hatcheck counter in Pavillon (one middle-aged man shows his hat check to another and says, "That's my old football number"); impressions of Bettina Aptheker and Benjamin Sonnenberg and Teddy ("Mr. Acapulco") Stauffer; careful *aperçus*[1] about tennis bums and failed fashion models and Greek shipping heiresses, one of whom taught me a significant lesson (a lesson I could have learned from F. Scott Fitzgerald, but perhaps we all must meet the very rich for ourselves) by asking, when I arrived to interview her in her orchid-filled sitting room on the second day of a paralyzing New York blizzard, whether it was snowing outside.

I imagine, in other words, that the notebook is about other people. But of course it is not. I have no real business with what one stranger said to another at the hatcheck counter in Pavillon; in fact I suspect that the line "That's my old football number" touched not my own imagination at all, but merely some memory of something once read,

[1]Observations (French).

probably "The Eighty-Yard Run."[2] Nor is my concern with a woman in a dirty crepe-de-Chine wrapper in a Wilmington bar. My stake is always, of course, in the unmentioned girl in the plaid silk dress. *Remember what it was to be me:* that is always the point.

It is a difficult point to admit. We are brought up in the ethic that oth- 10 ers, any others, all others, are by definition more interesting than our- selves; taught to be diffident, just this side of self-effacing. ("You're the least important person in the room and don't forget it," Jessica Mitford's[3] governess would hiss in her ear on the advent of any social occasion; I copied that into my notebook because it is only recently that I have been able to enter a room without hearing some such phrase in my inner ear.) Only the very young and the very old may recount their dreams at breakfast, dwell upon self, interrupt with memories of beach picnics and favorite Liberty lawn dresses and the rainbow trout in a creek near Colorado Springs. The rest of us are expected, rightly, to affect absorption in other people's favorite dresses, other people's trout.

And so we do. But our notebooks give us away, for however dutifully we record what we see around us, the common denominator of all we see is always, transparently, shamelessly, the implacable "I." We are not talking here about the kind of notebook that is patently for public con- sumption, a structural conceit for binding together a series of graceful *pensées;*[4] we are talking about something private, about bits of the mind's string too short to use, an indiscriminate and erratic assemblage with meaning only for its maker.

And sometimes even the maker has difficulty with the meaning. There does not seem to be, for example, any point in my knowing for the rest of my life that, during 1964, 720 tons of soot fell on every square mile of New York City, yet there it is in my notebook, labeled "FACT." Nor do I really need to remember that Ambrose Bierce liked to spell Leland Stanford's name "£eland $tanford"[5] or that "smart

[2]A 1955 short story by novelist Irwin Shaw.
[3]British-born writer (1917–96) best known as an investigative journalist.
[4]Thoughts (French).
[5]American businessman (1824–93) and founder of Stanford University. Ambrose Bierce (1842–1914?) was an American journalist and satirist.

women almost always wear black in Cuba," a fashion hint without much potential for practical application. And does not the relevance of these notes seem marginal at best?:

> In the basement museum of the Inyo County Courthouse in Independence, California, sign pinned to a mandarin coat: "This MANDARIN COAT was often worn by Mrs. Minnie S. Brooks when giving lectures on her TEAPOT COLLECTION."

> Redhead getting out of car in front of Beverly Wilshire Hotel, chinchilla stole, Vuitton bags with tags reading:

> MRS LOU FOX
> HOTEL SAHARA
> VEGAS

Well, perhaps not entirely marginal. As a matter of fact, Mrs. Minnie S. Brooks and her MANDARIN COAT pull me back into my own childhood, for although I never knew Mrs. Brooks and did not visit Inyo County until I was thirty, I grew up in just such a world, in houses cluttered with Indian relics and bits of gold ore and ambergris and the souvenirs my Aunt Mercy Farnsworth brought back from the Orient. It is a long way from that world to Mrs. Lou Fox's world, where we all live now, and is it not just as well to remember that? Might not Mrs. Minnie S. Brooks help me to remember what I am? Might not Mrs. Lou Fox help me to remember what I am not?

But sometimes the point is harder to discern. What exactly did I have in mind when I noted down that it cost the father of someone I know $650 a month to light the place on the Hudson in which he lived before the Crash? What use was I planning to make of this line by Jimmy Hoffa:[6] "I may have my faults, but being wrong ain't one of them"? And although I think it interesting to know where the girls who travel with the Syndicate have their hair done when they find them-

---

[6]American labor leader (b. 1913) who disappeared in 1975; he is presumed to have been murdered.

selves on the West Coast, will I ever make suitable use of it? Might I not be better off just passing it on to John O'Hara?[7] What is a recipe for sauerkraut doing in my notebook? What kind of magpie keeps this notebook? *"He was born the night the Titanic went down."* That seems a nice enough line, and I even recall who said it, but is it not really a better line in life than it could ever be in fiction?

But of course that is exactly it: not that I should ever use the line, but that I should remember the woman who said it and the afternoon I heard it. We were on her terrace by the sea, and we were finishing the wine left from lunch, trying to get what sun there was, a California winter sun. The woman whose husband was born the night the *Titanic* went down wanted to rent her house, wanted to go back to her children in Paris. I remember wishing that I could afford the house, which cost $1,000 a month. "Someday you will," she said lazily. "Someday it all comes." There in the sun on her terrace it seemed easy to believe in someday, but later I had a low-grade afternoon hangover and ran over a black snake on the way to the supermarket and was flooded with inexplicable fear when I heard the checkout clerk explaining to the man ahead of me why she was finally divorcing her husband. "He left me no choice," she said over and over as she punched the register. "He has a little seven-month-old baby by her, he left me no choice." I would like to believe that my dread then was for the human condition, but of course it was for me, because I wanted a baby and did not then have one and because I wanted to own the house that cost $1,000 a month to rent and because I had a hangover.

It all comes back. Perhaps it is difficult to see the value in having one's self back in that kind of mood, but I do see it; I think we are well advised to keep on nodding terms with the people we used to be, whether we find them attractive company or not. Otherwise they run up unannounced and surprise us, come hammering on the mind's door at 4 a.m. of a bad night and demand to know who deserted them, who betrayed them, who is going to make amends. We forget all too soon the things we thought we could never forget. We forget the loves and the betrayals alike, forget what we whispered and what we

[7]American author (1905–70), highly regarded for his skillful use of realistic dialogue.

screamed, forget who we were. I have already lost touch with a couple of people I used to be; one of them, a seventeen-year-old, presents little threat, although it would be of some interest to me to know again what it feels like to sit on a river levee drinking vodka-and-orange-juice and listening to Les Paul and Mary Ford and their echoes sing "How High the Moon"[8] on the car radio. (You see I still have the scenes, but I no longer perceive myself among those present, no longer could even improvise the dialogue.) The other one, a twenty-three-year-old, bothers me more. She was always a good deal of trouble, and I suspect she will reappear when I least want to see her, skirts too long, shy to the point of aggravation, always the injured party, full of recriminations and little hurts and stories I do not want to hear again, at once saddening me and angering me with her vulnerability and ignorance, an apparition all the more insistent for being so long banished.

It is a good idea, then, to keep in touch, and I suppose that keeping in touch is what notebooks are all about. And we are all on our own when it comes to keeping those lines open to ourselves: your notebook will never help me, nor mine you. *"So what's new in the whiskey business?"* What could that possibly mean to you? To me it means a blonde in a Pucci bathing suit sitting with a couple of fat men by the pool at the Beverly Hills Hotel. Another man approaches, and they all regard one another in silence for a while. "So what's new in the whiskey business?" one of the fat men finally says by way of welcome, and the blonde stands up, arches one foot and dips it in the pool, looking all the while at the cabaña where Baby Pignatari[9] is talking on the telephone. That is all there is to that, except that several years later I saw the blonde coming out of Saks Fifth Avenue in New York with her California complexion and a voluminous mink coat. In the harsh wind that day she looked old and irrevocably tired to me, and even the skins in the mink coat were not worked the way they were doing them that year, not the way she would have wanted them done, and there is the

[8] Jazz standard by Nancy Hamilton and Morgan Lewis (1940), best known by the 1951 recording by singer Mary Ford and guitarist Les Paul, featuring groundbreaking use of echo and overdubbing.
[9] Francisco "Baby" Pignatari (1916–77), Italian-born Brazilian industrialist and notorious playboy.

point of the story. For a while after that I did not like to look in the mirror, and my eyes would skim the newspapers and pick out only the deaths, the cancer victims, the premature coronaries, the suicides, and I stopped riding the Lexington Avenue IRT[1] because I noticed for the first time that all the strangers I had seen for years—the man with the seeing-eye dog, the spinster who read the classified pages every day, the fat girl who always got off with me at Grand Central—looked older than they once had.

It all comes back. Even that recipe for sauerkraut: even that brings it back. I was on Fire Island when I first made that sauerkraut, and it was raining, and we drank a lot of bourbon and ate the sauerkraut and went to bed at ten, and I listened to the rain and the Atlantic and felt safe. I made the sauerkraut again last night and it did not make me feel any safer, but that is, as they say, another story.

---

[1] New York City subway line passing through Grand Central Terminal in Manhattan.

STUDY QUESTIONS

1. What are the differences, as Didion sees them, between diaries and notebooks? Why does she prefer the latter?

2. Didion concludes that notebooks are a tool to "keep in touch" with "the people we used to be, whether we find them attractive company or not." How do you "keep in touch" with earlier versions of yourself? ANALYZE the effectiveness of these methods, intentional or not, and of any tools you use (notebooks, journals, etc.).

3. *For Writing.* Although Didion notes her family members' disagreement with her presentation of details from the past, she also goes on to say, "not only have I always had trouble distinguishing between what happened and what merely might have happened, but I remain unconvinced that the distinction, for my purposes, matters." Write an essay on the nature of memory, using either personal experience or RESEARCH to argue whether you think that the distinction between what *really* happened and what *might* have happened matters. Does your STANCE change based on context; that is, does your answer change if the record of a memory is intended to be read by others or to be kept to oneself? How does the importance of the distinction change based on the GENRE in which it is presented?

SOJOURNER TRUTH { *Ar'n't I a Woman?*

SOJOURNER TRUTH (1797–1883) was born into slavery as Isabella
Baumfree in upstate New York; she was separated from her family at age
nine and was resold several times in the next decade. In 1817, her owner,
John Dumont, arranged her marriage to a fellow slave, and the couple added
four more children to the daughter she had from a previous relationship
(she had thirteen children in all). After Dumont reneged on his promise to
free her in 1826, she escaped with her youngest daughter and was sheltered
by a sympathetic couple until emancipation took effect in New York State in
1827. For a short time, she was part of a cooperative religious community;
when it disbanded, she moved to New York City. In 1843, she changed her
name to Sojourner Truth and became a traveling preacher. She joined
another cooperative, this one founded by abolitionists, and dictated her
autobiography, *The Narrative of Sojourner Truth* (1850), to a fellow community member. The book's publication won her popularity as a speaker in
both the abolitionist and women's suffrage movements. In 1857 Truth relocated her family to Michigan, which remained her home base for the rest of
her life even as she continued to travel widely, meeting with presidents and
speaking in favor of many moral and progressive causes.

Truth delivered "Ar'n't I a Woman?" her most famous speech, in 1851 at
a women's rights convention in Ohio where she was the only African
American woman in attendance. Truth felt moved to share her opinion with
the assembled crowd. Think about her rhetorical situation as you read the
text of her speech, transcribed by Frances D. Gage, the president of the convention, who attempted to record Truth's distinctive dialect. As you read,
think about the effect of reading the speech in dialect. How would it have
been different if it were written in standard English?

WELL, CHILERN, WHAR DAR IS so much racket dar must be something out o' kilter. I tink dat 'twixt de niggers of de Souf and de women at de Norf[1] all a talkin' 'bout rights, de white men will be in a fix pretty soon. But what's all dis here talkin' 'bout? Dat man ober dar say dat women needs to be helped into carriages, and lifted ober ditches, and to have de best place every whar. Nobody eber help me into carriages, or ober mud puddles, or gives me any best place, and ar'n't I a woman? Look at me! Look at my arm! I have plowed, and planted, and gathered into barns, and no man could head me—and ar'n't I a woman? I could work as much and eat as much as a man (when I could get it), and bear de lash as well—and ar'n't I a woman? I have borne thirteen chilern and seen 'em mos' all sold off into slavery, and when I cried out with a mother's grief, none but Jesus heard—and ar'n't I a woman? Den dey talks 'bout dis ting in de head—what dis dey call it? ["Intellect," whispered some one near.] Dat's it honey. What's dat got to do with women's rights or niggers' rights? If my cup won't hold but a pint and yourn holds a quart, would n't ye be mean not to let me have my little half-measure full?

Den dat little man in black dar, he say women can't have as much rights as man, cause Christ wa'n't a woman. Whar did your Christ come from? From God and a woman. Man had nothing to do with him. . . . If de fust woman God ever made was strong enough to turn the world upside down, all 'lone, dese togedder ought to be able to turn it back and get it right side up again, and now dey is asking to do it, de men better let em. 'Bleeged to ye for hearin' on me, and now ole Sojourner ha'n't got nothing more to say.

---

[1]"Souf" is South and "Norf" is North; this transcription of Truth's dialect was made by the president of the convention, Frances D. Gage; what she renders as "ar'n't," contemporary writers would probably spell "ain't."

STUDY QUESTIONS

1. Name an accomplishment that Truth CLAIMS for herself.

2. Notice how often Truth repeats the RHETORICAL QUESTION "And ar'n't I a woman?" What effect does this repetition have on the speech? What effect do you think it would have had on her AUDIENCE at the convention? Would you use repetition like this in a written, rather than an oral, text? Why or why not?

3. Other speakers at the convention, arguing against women's suffrage, suggested reasons that women should be subservient to men: because men have a "superior intellect," because Christ was a man, because Eve introduced sin into the world in the Garden of Eden. What COUNTER-ARGUMENTS does Truth offer to these claims? How effective do you find them, and why?

4. *For Writing.* The use of dialect to represent Truth's actual VOICE is often a subject of debate. How effective do you find the use of dialect in this piece? Does it add something to the piece's effectiveness? Does it take anything away? In an essay, ANALYZE the effectiveness of the use of dialect in this speech. RESEARCH what others have said on the topic and incorporate their ideas into your essay—but make sure your analysis is your own.

MARGARET ATWOOD { *The Female Body*

MARGARET ATWOOD (b. 1939), best known for her novels *The Edible Woman* (1970) and *The Handmaid's Tale* (1983), was born in Ottawa, Canada. She received her BA from Victoria College at the University of Toronto and her MA from Ratcliffe College. Atwood has served as writer in residence at several universities in Canada and the United States. She has published thirty-five volumes of poetry, fiction, and nonfiction, including *Moral Disorder* and *The Tent,* collections of short fiction that were both published in 2006, and the poetry collection *The Door* (2007).

This narrator takes the reader on a tour of the various uses of, problems with, meanings of, and attitudes toward the female body. She is critical of how society views women as objects, but she softens the critique with humor that is surprisingly generous toward men. As you read, consider how the scenes presented contribute to the development of the narrative.

> . . . *entirely devoted to the subject of 'The Female Body.'*
> *Knowing how well you have written on this topic . . . this*
> *capacious topic . . .*
> —LETTER FROM THE MICHIGAN QUARTERLY REVIEW

1

I AGREE, IT'S A HOT topic. But only one? Look around, there's a wide range. Take my own, for instance.

I get up in the morning. My topic feels like hell. I sprinkle it with water, brush parts of it, rub it with towels, powder it, add lubricant. I dump in the fuel and away goes my topic, my topical topic, my controversial topic, my capacious topic, my limping topic, my nearsighted topic, my topic with back problems, my badly behaved topic, my vulgar topic, my outrageous topic, my aging topic, my topic that is out of the question and anyway still can't spell, in its oversized coat and worn winter boots, scuttling along the sidewalk as if it were flesh and blood, hunting for what's out there, an avacado, an alderman, an adjective, hungry as ever.

2

The basic Female Body comes with the following accessories: garter belt, panty girdle, crinoline, camisole, bustle, brassiere, stomacher, chemise, virgin zone, spike heels, nose ring, veil, kid gloves, fishnet stockings, fichu, bandeau, Merry Widow, weepers, chokers, barrettes, bangles, beads, lorgnette, feather boa, basic black, compact, Lycra stretch one-piece with modesty panel, designer peignoir, flannel nightie, lace teddy, bed, head.

3

The Female Body is made of transparent plastic and lights up when you plug it in. You press a button to illuminate the different systems. The Circulatory System is red, for the heart and arteries, purple for the veins; the Respiratory System is blue, the Lymphatic System is yellow, the Digestive System is green, with liver and kidneys in aqua. The nerves are done in orange and the brain in pink. The skeleton, as you might expect, is white.

The Reproductive System is optional, and can be removed. It comes 5 with or without a miniature embryo. Parental judgment can thereby be exercised. We do not wish to frighten or offend.

4

He said, I won't have one of those things in the house. It gives a young girl a false notion of beauty, not to mention anatomy. If a real woman was built like that she'd fall on her face.

She said, if we don't let her have one like all the other girls she'll feel singled out. It'll become an issue. She'll long for one and she'll long to turn into one. Repression breeds sublimation. You know that.

He said, It's not just the pointy plastic tits, it's the wardrobes. The wardrobes and that stupid male doll, what's his name, the one with the underwear glued on.

She said, Better to get it over with when she's young. He said, All right but don't let me see it.

She came whizzing down the stairs, thrown like a dart. She was stark 10 naked. Her hair had been chopped off, her head was turned back to front, she was missing some toes and she'd been tattooed all over her body with purple ink, in a scrollwork design. She hit the potted azalea, trembled there for a moment like a botched angel, and fell.

He said, I guess we're safe.

5

The Female Body has many uses. It's been used as a door knocker, a bottle-opener, as a clock with a ticking belly, as something to hold up lampshades, as a nutcracker, just squeeze the brass legs together and out comes your nut. It bears torches, lifts victorious wreaths, grows copper wings, and raises aloft a ring of neon stars; whole buildings rest on its marble heads.

It sells cars, beer, shaving lotion, cigarettes, hard liquor; it sells diet plans and diamonds, and desire in tiny crystal bottles. Is this the face that launched a thousand products? You bet it is, but don't get any funny big ideas, honey, that smile is a dime a dozen.

It does not merely sell, it is sold. Money flows into this country or that country, flies in, practically crawls in, suitful after suitful, lured by all those hairless preteen legs. Listen, you want to reduce the national debt, don't you? Aren't you patriotic? That's the spirit. That's my girl.

She's a natural resource, a renewable one luckily, because those things   15
wear out so quickly. They don't make 'em like they used to. Shoddy
goods.

6

One and one equals another one. Pleasure in the female is not a
requirement. Pair-bonding is stronger in geese. We're not talking about
love, we're talking about biology. That's how we all got here, daughter.

Snails do it differently. They're hermaphrodites, and work in threes.

7

Each female body contains a female brain. Handy. Makes things work.
Stick pins in it and you get amazing results. Old popular songs. Short
circuits. Bad dreams.

Anyway: each of these brains has two halves. They're joined together by a thick cord; neural pathways flow from one to the other, sparkles
of electric information washing to and fro. Like light on waves. Like a
conversation. How does a woman know? She listens. She listens in.

The male brain, now, that's a different matter. Only a thin connection.
Space over here, time over there, music and arithmetic in their own   20
sealed compartments. The right brain doesn't know what the left brain
is doing. Good for aiming though, for hitting the target when you pull
the trigger. What's the target? Who's the target? Who cares? What
matters is hitting it. That's the male brain for you. Objective.

This is why men are so sad, why they feel so cut off, why they think of
themselves as orphans cast adrift, footloose and stringless in the deep
void. What void? she says. What are you talking about? The void of

the Universe, he says, and she says Oh and looks out the window and tries to get a handle on it, but it's no use, there's too much going on, too many rustlings in the leaves, too many voices, so she says, Would you like a cheese sandwich, a piece of cake, a cup of tea? And he grinds his teeth because she doesn't understand, and wanders off, not just alone but Alone, lost in the dark, lost in the skull, searching for the other half, the twin who could complete him.

Then it comes to him: he's lost the Female Body! Look, it shines in the gloom, far ahead, a vision of wholeness, ripeness, like a giant melon, like an apple, like a metaphor for *breast* in a bad sex novel; it shines like a balloon, like a foggy noon, a watery moon, shimmering in its egg of light.

Catch it. Put it in a pumpkin, in a high tower, in a compound, in a chamber, in a house, in a room. Quick, stick a leash on it, a lock, a chain, some pain, settle it down, so it can never get away from you again.

STUDY QUESTIONS

1. Two unnamed people, referred to simply as "he" and "she," talk about an unnamed object for which "he" has a definite distaste. What is the TOPIC of this conversation? Why was the conversation ultimately pointless?

2. Atwood divides this text into sections. How does the selection maintain its unity? Would the text have been better constructed with traditional PLOT development? Explain.

3. The original copyright date of "The Female Body" is 1983. How do you think it was received some twenty-five years ago? What is your RESPONSE to it now? Is there anything to be learned from this piece today? What?

4. *For Writing.* Identify the different DESCRIPTIONS and DEFINITIONS that Atwood's NARRATOR provides. Using the text as a model, write, either independently or collaboratively, a piece about the male body. Consider using humor in the form of SATIRE and IRONY, as Atwood does.

ROB FISHMAN { *The Generation*
of Generation Q }

ROB FISHMAN (b. 1986) graduated from Cornell University in 2007.
While a student there he joined the *Cornell Daily Sun*, the university's
independent newspaper, as a staff writer and weekly columnist. Upon
graduating, he entered the Journalism School at Columbia University in
New York City, and he is a research assistant at the Peter G. Peterson
Foundation, an organization dedicated to increasing political and
personal fiscal responsibility.

In this *Daily Sun* editorial from 2007, Fishman argues that if his
generation of college-age Americans is indeed "quiet," as *New York
Times* columnist Thomas Friedman argued when he dubbed them
"Generation Q," it's because technology has made them complacent:
instant replay resolves a dispute during a sporting event; Google
instantly provides the forgotten lyrics to a song. Using examples ranging
from commonplaces like these to significant moments in recent history,
Fishman redefines "Generation Q" by showing how they are all too
ready to defer to technology. Do you recognize your own behavior in his
examples?

LAST WEEK, THOMAS FRIEDMAN[1] DUBBED us "Generation Q"—the
Quiet Americans, so plugged in (and tuned out) that our idealism stops
at the computer monitor. With so much interconnectedness among the
Facebook-YouTube-MySpace cohort, and so much wrong in the world,
Friedman wonders why our generation looks so complacent.

---

[1] *New York Times* columnist and author (b. 1953).

"The Generation of Generation Q" by Rob Fishman from *The Cornell Daily Sun*, October 15, 2007. Used by permission of *The Cornell Daily Sun*.

The twentysomethings fire back that their technological moving and shaking is being mistaken for indolence; as a recent *Sun* editorial argued, activism has "transformed from sensationalized 1960s tear-gas rallies to online petitions and Internet discussion boards."

Yet for Friedman—and, I suspect, many among the Baby Boomers and the "Greatest Generation"—we come off as apologists, hiding our apathy behind a high tech façade: "Martin Luther King and Bobby Kennedy didn't change the world by asking people to join their Face-book crusades or to download their platforms," Friedman chides us nostalgically.

In truth, we are complacent—and if you look around, for good reason.

For my generation, technology *has* had a distinctively quieting effect. In nearly every walk of life, technological advancements have instilled this generation with a deep sense of inevitability that encourages us to look inward. In a sense, Friedman has it backwards: we don't lazily hide behind technology, so much as technology inspires us to stay quiet.

Take sports. In an edge-of-your-seat final quarter between the Dallas Cowboys and the Buffalo Bills last week, a few of the thrills came from great catches and kicks, to be sure, but the real drama resulted from technicalities—from an instant replay review of a twenty-yard pass and from a split-second time out that voided a field goal kick that made the victory "one of the most implausible in the Cowboys' illustrious history," according to an ESPN recap of the game.

It's strange, watching these hippo-sized linemen beating the hell out of each other . . . all until a flag drops, at which point they respectfully defer to a high-definition replay.

Much the same in other sports: as the *Daily Scotsman* noted when FIFA[2] sanctioned a trial run for a soccer ball that "beeps" when it crosses the goal line, football fans can't quibble with technology that "ensure[s] justice and eradicate[s] controversy."

---

[2]The Fédération Internationale de Football Association, the international governing body for association football (professional soccer).

For sports fans and players alike, technology has obviated the important human element of competition. The exciting disputes are no longer about "bad" or "close" calls, but about close-up high-definition simulacra of the plays in question; as controversy is eradicated, sports fans are, for lack of a better option, quiet.

Consider a seminal American experience for my generation: the 10 O. J. Simpson trial. In an adversarial procedure that (we now know) failed to capture the truth (if he did it, of course), the determining factor was DNA evidence, which, according to a *New York Times* article at that time, was not challenged by the defense at all on the basis of its "validity as a science."

Though the DNA evidence may not have been "clear or convincing to a jury of non-scientists," according to the *Times* article, it was ultimately presented as indisputable fact. Where Clarence Darrow drew on philosophy, religion and, yes, science to defend Leopold and Loeb in the "Trial of the Century," Johnnie Cochran's famous catchphrase was "if it doesn't fit, you must acquit."[3] Like the instant replay, DNA evidence isn't up for debate, it's a foregone conclusion.

Perhaps the most glaring example was the 2000 presidential election, when the Supreme Court upheld the voting tabulations accrued by the disputed ballots in Florida to hand the election to George W. Bush. The Court, while lamenting the "unfortunate number of ballots which [were] not punched in a clean, complete way" in *Bush v. Gore* (2000), ruled that the technology of the day would have to suffice, and that it could not read into the intent of voters—even if half a chad was clearly punched.[4]

[3]The courtroom words of defense attorney Johnnie Cochran (1937–2005), addressing the jury in the 1995 murder trial of O. J. Simpson after Simpson was unable to squeeze his hand into a glove found at the crime scene. *Clarence Darrow*: American lawyer (1857–1938) famed for representing thrill killers Nathan Freudenthal Leopold Jr. and Richard A. Loeb in criminal proceedings dubbed the "Trial of the Century" in 1924.

[4]In a ruling that determined the outcome of the 2000 presidential election, the U.S. Supreme Court declined to overrule Florida election officials and the Florida Supreme Court after supporters of Democratic Party candidate Al Gore argued that faulty vote-tabulating machinery had tainted the Florida vote count. (A "chad" is the tiny piece of paper displaced when a hole is punched in a computer card; such cards were used as ballots in Florida in the 2000 election.)

What's dangerous in these cases is not the technology itself—for surely, we applaud fairness in sports, exonerations based on DNA evidence, and new digital voting platforms—but the excesses and unintended consequences of these innovations.

Thus, dinner-table disputes end as quickly as one can BlackBerry the answer; road-side directions are relics of history thanks to GPS technology; and those impossible-to-understand song lyrics no longer require funny substitutions because you can Google them straightaway. Because information is so readily accessible, technology has made us close-minded, more attuned to what's for lunch than what's on the news (though, like CNN.com, menupages.com is a mere click away).

The direst consequences of a technocracy are the stuff of entertainment: the Orwellian[5] justice system in the blockbuster hit *Minority Report* and the simulated boxing match which precedes the actual fight in *Rocky Balboa* being two prominent examples of technology meting out results before the parties have spoken. When Tom Cruise or ESPN can anticipate outcomes before events, deliberation loses meaning.

Is it any wonder that Generation Q, which saw the guilty O. J. vindicated by DNA evidence and the calamitous Bush crowned by faulty ballots, appears so apathetic?

Faced with the most bitter and divisive of conflicts, our societal "referees" regularly defer to technological precepts of justice over human concepts of fairness. With the world on fire, Generation Q isn't questioning the lies of WMDs in Iraq[6] or global climate change—no, we're keeping our mouths shut and burying ourselves further in our computers.

15

---

[5] An allusion to George Orwell's 1949 novel *Nineteen Eighty-Four,* depicting life under an oppressive totalitarian government.

[6] U.S. President George W. Bush famously cited the presence in Iraq of forbidden WMDs—weapons of mass destruction—as justification for the American invasion of 2003. Such weapons were never found.

STUDY QUESTIONS

1. Why did columnist Thomas Friedman call today's college-age Americans "Generation Q?" How does technology have what Fishman calls "unintended consequences?"

2. How does Fishman DEFINE Generation Q through its behavior? Consider the examples that Fishman uses to support his ARGUMENT. How effective are they? How might they appeal to a college AUDIENCE?

3. *For Writing.* Drawing on your own experience, write an essay in which you either defend or critique—or both defend *and* critique—Fishman's argument about how Generation Q relies on technology.

THOMAS L. FRIEDMAN { *Generation Q*

THOMAS FRIEDMAN (b. 1953), journalist and author, was born in St.
Louis Park, Minnesota. He holds degrees from Brandeis and Oxford.
Since he began writing for the *New York Times* in 1981 he has won three
Pulitzer Prizes, for international reporting and for commentary. Friedman,
who has served as the *Times* chief correspondent for the Middle East, for
the White House, and for international economics, currently writes a
nationally syndicated, twice-weekly column mainly addressing foreign
affairs. His best-selling books include *From Beirut to Jerusalem* (1989),
The Lexus and the Olive Tree (1999), *The World Is Flat* (2005), and *Hot,
Flat, and Crowded: Why We Need a Green Revolution—And How It Can
Renew America* (2008).

In "Generation Q," which appeared in the *New York Times* in 2007,
when U.S. presidential candidates were campaigning for the 2008 election,
Friedman continues the tradition of giving distinctive names to
generations (such as Baby Boomers or Gen Xers) by suggesting a name
for young Americans currently in college: the Quiet Americans. According
to Friedman, today's twenty-somethings will inherit unprecedented
challenges—potentially devastating climate change, a bankrupt Social
Security system, and an immense national budget deficit—and he worries
that they're not as outraged as they should be, or as they need to be.
As you read, consider whether or not you agree with Friedman's
assessment of "Generation Q" and how you might respond to the
author.

"Generation Q" by Thomas Friedman from *The New York Times,* October 10, 2007. Used
by permission of The New York Times.

I JUST SPENT THE PAST week visiting several colleges—Auburn, the University of Mississippi, Lake Forest and Williams—and I can report that the more I am around this generation of college students, the more I am both baffled and impressed.

I am impressed because they are so much more optimistic and idealistic than they should be. I am baffled because they are so much less radical and politically engaged than they need to be.

One of the things I feared most after 9/11—that my daughters would not be able to travel the world with the same carefree attitude my wife and I did at their age—has not come to pass.

Whether it was at Ole Miss or Williams or my alma mater, Brandeis, college students today are not only going abroad to study in record numbers, but they are also going abroad to build homes for the poor in El Salvador in record numbers or volunteering at AIDS clinics in record numbers. Not only has terrorism not deterred them from traveling, they are rolling up their sleeves and diving in deeper than ever.

The Iraq war may be a mess, but I noticed at Auburn and Ole Miss 5 more than a few young men and women proudly wearing their R.O.T.C. uniforms. Many of those not going abroad have channeled their national service impulses into increasingly popular programs at home like "Teach for America," which has become to this generation what the Peace Corps was to mine.

It's for all these reasons that I've been calling them "Generation Q"—the Quiet Americans, in the best sense of that term, quietly pursuing their idealism, at home and abroad.

But Generation Q may be too quiet, too online, for its own good, and for the country's own good. When I think of the huge budget deficit, Social Security deficit and ecological deficit that our generation is leaving this generation, if they are not spitting mad, well, then they're just not paying attention. And we'll just keep piling it on them.

There is a good chance that members of Generation Q will spend their entire adult lives digging out from the deficits that we—the "Greediest Generation," epitomized by George W. Bush—are leaving them.

When I was visiting my daughter at her college, she asked me about a terrifying story that ran in this newspaper on October 2, reporting that the Arctic ice cap was melting "to an extent unparalleled in a century or more"—and that the entire Arctic system appears to be "heading toward a new, more watery state" likely triggered by "human-caused global warming."

"What happened to that Arctic story, Dad?" my daughter asked me. 10 How could the news media just report one day that the Arctic ice was melting far faster than any models predicted "and then the story just disappeared?" Why weren't any of the candidates talking about it? Didn't they understand: this has become the big issue on campuses?

No, they don't seem to understand. They seem to be too busy raising money or buying votes with subsidies for ethanol farmers in Iowa. The candidates could actually use a good kick in the pants on this point. But where is it going to come from?

Generation Q would be doing itself a favor, and America a favor, if it demanded from every candidate who comes on campus answers to three questions: What is your plan for mitigating climate change? What is your plan for reforming Social Security? What is your plan for dealing with the deficit—so we all won't be working for China in twenty years?

America needs a jolt of the idealism, activism and outrage (it must be in there) of Generation Q. That's what twentysomethings are for—to light a fire under the country. But they can't e-mail it in, and an online petition or a mouse click for carbon neutrality won't cut it. They have to get organized in a way that will force politicians to pay attention rather than just patronize them.

Martin Luther King and Bobby Kennedy didn't change the world by asking people to join their Facebook crusades or to download their platforms. Activism can only be uploaded, the old-fashioned way—by young voters speaking truth to power, face to face, in big numbers, on campuses or the Washington Mall. Virtual politics is just that—virtual.

Maybe that's why what impressed me most on my brief college 15 swing was actually a statue—the life-size statue of James Meredith at the University of Mississippi. Meredith was the first African-American to be admitted to Ole Miss in 1962. The Meredith bronze is posed as if he is striding toward a tall limestone archway, re-enacting his fateful step onto the then-segregated campus—defying a violent, angry mob and protected by the National Guard.

Above the archway, carved into the stone, is the word "Courage." That is what real activism looks like. There is no substitute.

*

STUDY QUESTIONS

1. What attributes does Friedman ascribe to "Generation Q"? Do you agree with his CHARACTERIZATION? If not, explain why not. If so, offer two or three examples of how you or people you know fit his characterization.

2. Publicly characterizing and naming a generation is a bold act. Is Friedman qualified to make such an assessment? How does he seek to establish his ETHOS—that is, his credibility with his readers? Is he successful?

3. *For Writing.* Write an opinion piece that responds to Friedman. Be sure to establish your credibility with your readers. Consider the following questions to help you get started: With what parts of Friedman's assessment do you agree or disagree? What, if anything, do you believe he leaves out or doesn't fully address?

GLORIA NAYLOR   { *A Word's Meaning Can Often Depend on Who Says It*

GLORIA NAYLOR (b. 1950) was raised in New York City by parents who had been sharecroppers in Mississippi. She received her BA from Brooklyn College and her MA in Afro-American Studies from Yale University, and she has taught at Princeton University, George Washington University, the University of Pennsylvania, and New York University. Naylor has written several novels, including *The Women of Brewster Place* (1982) and *1996* (2005). Enduring themes in her work are feminism and the African-American community.

In this definition essay, Naylor explains how a word cannot have true meaning unless people agree to the meaning. She takes a pejorative epithet many people are familiar with and explains how different contexts can create entirely different meanings. Drawing from her own experience, Naylor maps out the range of what the word can signify. What does the word mean to you? Does it carry other meanings for people you know?

LANGUAGE IS THE SUBJECT. IT is the written form with which I've managed to keep the wolf away from the door and, in diaries, to keep my sanity. In spite of this, I consider the written word inferior to the spoken, and much of the frustration experienced by novelists is the awareness that whatever we manage to capture in even the most transcendent passages falls far short of the richness of life. Dialogue achieves its power in the dynamics of a fleeting moment of sight, sound, smell, and touch.

I'm not going to enter the debate here about whether it is language that shapes reality or vice versa. That battle is doomed to be waged whenever we seek intermittent reprieve from the chicken and egg dispute. I will simply take the position that the spoken word, like the written word, amounts to a nonsensical arrangement of sounds or letters without a consensus that assigns "meaning." And building from the meanings of what we hear, we order reality. Words themselves are innocuous; it is the consensus that gives them true power.

•   ○   •

I remember the first time I heard the word *nigger*.[1] In my third-grade class, our math tests were being passed down the rows, and as I handed the papers to a little boy in back of me, I remarked that once again he had received a much lower mark than I did. He snatched his test from me and spit out that word. Had he called me a nymphomaniac or a necrophiliac, I couldn't have been more puzzled. I didn't know what a nigger was, but I knew that whatever it meant, it was something he shouldn't have called me. This was verified when I raised my hand, and in a loud voice repeated what he had said and watched the teacher scold him for using a "bad" word. I was later to go home and ask the inevitable question that every black parent must face—"Mommy, what does 'nigger' mean?"

And what exactly did it mean? Thinking back, I realize that this could not have been the first time the word was used in my presence. I was part of a large extended family that had migrated from the rural South after World War II and formed a close-knit network that gravitated around my maternal grandparents. Their ground-floor apartment in one of the buildings they owned in Harlem was a weekend mecca for my immediate family, along with countless aunts, uncles and cousins who brought along assorted friends. It was a bustling and open house with assorted neighbors and tenants popping in and out to exchange bits of gossip, pick up an old quarrel or referee the ongoing checkers game in which my grandmother cheated shamelessly. They

[1] The author wants it understood that the use of the word "nigger" is reprehensible in today's society. This essay speaks to a specific time and place when that word was utilized to empower African Americans; today it is used to degrade them even if spoken from their own mouths.

were all there to let down their hair and put up their feet after a week of labor in the factories, laundries and shipyards of New York.

Amid the clamor, which could reach deafening proportions—two or 5 three conversations going on simultaneously, punctuated by the sound of a baby's crying somewhere in the back rooms or out on the street— there was still a rigid set of rules about what was said and how. Older children were sent out of the living room when it was time to get into the juicy details about "you-know-who" up on the third floor who had gone and gotten herself "p-r-e-g-n-a-n-t!" But my parents, knowing that I could spell well beyond my years, always demanded that I follow the others out to play. Beyond sexual misconduct and death, everything else was considered harmless for our young ears. And so among the anecdotes of the triumphs and disappointments in the various workings of their lives, the word *nigger* was used in my presence, but it was set within contexts and inflections that caused it to register in my mind as something else.

In the singular, the word was always applied to a man who had distinguished himself in some situation that brought their approval for his strength, intelligence, or drive:

"Did Johnny *really* do that?"

"I'm telling you, that nigger pulled in $6,000 of overtime last year. Said he got enough for a down payment on a house."

When used with a possessive adjective by a woman—"my nigger"— it became a term of endearment for husband or boyfriend. But it could be more than just a term applied to a man. In their mouths it became the pure essence of manhood—a disembodied force that channeled their past history of struggle and present survival against the odds into a victorious statement of being: "Yeah, that old foreman found out quick enough—you don't mess with a nigger."

In the plural, it became a description of some group within the com- 10 munity that had overstepped the bounds of decency as my family defined it: Parents who neglected their children, a drunken couple who fought in public, people who simply refused to look for work, those with excessively dirty mouths or unkempt households were all "trifling niggers." This particular circle could forgive hard times, unemployment, the occasional bout of depression—they had gone through all of that themselves—but the unforgivable sin was a lack of self-respect.

A woman could never be a "nigger" in the singular, with its connotation of confirming worth. The noun *girl* was its closest equivalent in that sense, but only when used in direct address and regardless of the gender doing the addressing. "Girl" was a token of respect for a woman. The one-syllable word was drawn out to sound like three in recognition of the extra ounce of wit, nerve or daring that the woman had shown in the situation under discussion.

"G-i-r-l, stop. You mean you said that to his face?"

But if the word was used in a third-person reference or shortened so that it almost snapped out of the mouth, it always involved some element of communal disapproval. And age became an important factor in these exchanges. It was only between individuals of the same generation, or from an older person to a younger (but never the other way around), that "girl" would be considered a compliment.

• ○ •

I don't agree with the argument that use of the word *nigger* at this social stratum of the black community was an internalization of racism. The dynamics were the exact opposite: the people in my grandmother's living room took a word that whites used to signify worthlessness or degradation and rendered it impotent. Gathering there together, they transformed "nigger" to signify the varied and complex human beings they knew themselves to be. If the word was to disappear totally from the mouths of even the most liberal of white society, no one in that room was naïve enough to believe it would disappear from white minds. Meeting the word head-on, they proved it had absolutely nothing to do with the way they were determined to live their lives.

So there must have been dozens of times that the "nigger" was spoken in front of me before I reached the third grade. But I didn't "hear" it until it was said by a small pair of lips that had already learned it could be a way to humiliate me. That was the word I went home and asked my mother about. And since she knew that I had to grow up in America, she took me in her lap and explained. 15

STUDY QUESTIONS

1. Naylor explains that the pejorative term she heard as a third grader had been used in her presence before. Why did she still have to ask her mother what it meant?

2. What is the THESIS of Naylor's essay? How does the TOPIC of her essay relate to the thesis? Could she have developed her essay in another way? Explain.

3. *For Writing.* Select a word that has a range of connotations, both positive and negative, to a specific group of people. Using Naylor's essay as a model, explain the different connotations this word can have within that group. Be sure to identify the group you have selected and to explain how outsiders use the term. Alternatively, update Naylor's essay, exploring how the "N-word" is used today.

JO GOODWIN PARKER { *What Is Poverty?*

JO GOODWIN PARKER, the first-person narrator of the following essay, requests that biographical information about her not be revealed—but the essay itself reveals extremely intimate details about her life in poverty. This personal essay, a classic of definition, provides poignant examples of what Parker and her family experience. The power of this matter-of-fact description derives from its credible ethos, one that does not seek pity so much as understanding. Parker also describes the emotional blows that poverty inflicts upon its victims and the inescapable downward spiral of those caught in it.

"What Is Poverty?" was delivered as a speech. As you read, imagine the effects of Parker's speech—and her appearance—on her audience.

YOU ASK ME WHAT IS poverty? Listen to me. Here I am, dirty, smelly, and with no "proper" underwear on and with the stench of my rotting teeth near you. I will tell you. Listen to me. Listen without pity. I cannot use your pity. Listen with understanding. Put yourself in my dirty, worn out, ill-fitting shoes, and hear me.

Poverty is getting up every morning from a dirt- and illness-stained mattress. The sheets have long since been used for diapers. Poverty is living in a smell that never leaves. This is a smell of urine, sour milk, and spoiling food sometimes joined with the strong smell of long-cooked onions. Onions are cheap. If you have smelled this smell, you did not know how it came. It is the smell of the outdoor privy. It is the smell of young children who cannot walk the long dark way in the night. It is the smell of the mattresses where years of "accidents" have happened. It is the smell of the milk which has gone sour because the refrigerator long has not worked, and it costs money to get it fixed. It is the smell of rotting garbage. I could bury it, but where is the shovel? Shovels cost money.

Poverty is being tired. I have always been tired. They told me at the hospital when the last baby came that I had chronic anemia caused from poor diet, a bad case of worms, and that I needed a corrective operation. I listened politely—the poor are always polite. The poor always listen. They don't say that there is no money for iron pills, or better food, or worm medicine. The idea of an operation is frightening and costs so much that, if I had dared, I would have laughed. Who takes care of my children? Recovery from an operation takes a long time. I have three children. When I left them with "Granny" the last time I had a job, I came home to find the baby covered with fly specks, and a diaper that had not been changed since I left. When the dried diaper came off, bits of my baby's flesh came with it. My other child was playing with a sharp bit of broken glass, and my oldest was playing alone at the edge of a lake. I made twenty-two dollars a week, and a good nursery school costs twenty dollars a week for three children. I quit my job.

Poverty is dirt. You say in your clean clothes coming from your clean house, "Anybody can be clean." Let me explain about housekeeping with no money. For breakfast I give my children grits with no oleo or cornbread without eggs and oleo. This does not use up many dishes. What dishes there are, I wash in cold water and with no soap. Even the cheapest soap has to be saved for the baby's diapers. Look at my hands, so cracked and red. Once I saved for two months to buy a jar of Vaseline for my hands and the baby's diaper rash. When I had saved enough, I went to buy it and the price had gone up two cents. The baby and I suffered on. I have to decide every day if I can bear to put my cracked, sore hands into the cold water and strong soap. But you ask, why not hot water? Fuel costs money. If you have a wood fire it costs money. If you burn electricity, it costs money. Hot water is a luxury. I do not have luxuries. I know you will be surprised when I tell you how young I am. I look so much older. My back has been bent over the wash tubs every day for so long. I cannot remember when I ever did anything else. Every night I wash every stitch my school-age child has on and just hope her clothes will be dry by morning.

Poverty is staying up all night on cold nights to watch the fire, know- 5 ing one spark on the newspaper covering the walls means your sleeping children die in flames. In summer poverty is watching gnats and flies devour your baby's tears when he cries. The screens are torn and you pay so little rent you know they will never be fixed. Poverty means insects in your food, in your nose, in your eyes, and crawling over you when you sleep. Poverty is hoping it never rains because diapers won't dry when it rains and soon you are using newspapers. Poverty is seeing your children forever with runny noses. Paper handkerchiefs cost money and all your rags you need for other things. Even more costly are antihistamines. Poverty is cooking without food and cleaning without soap.

Poverty is asking for help. Have you ever had to ask for help, know- ing your children will suffer unless you get it? Think about asking for a loan from a relative, if this is the only way you can imagine asking for help. I will tell you how it feels. You find out where the office is that you are supposed to visit. You circle that block four or five times. Thinking of your children, you go in. Everyone is very busy. Finally, someone comes out and you tell her that you need help. That never is the per- son you need to see. You go see another person, and after spilling the whole shame of your poverty all over the desk between you, you find that this isn't the right office after all—you must repeat the whole process, and it never is any easier at the next place.

You have asked for help, and after all it has a cost. You are again told to wait. You are told why, but you don't really hear because of the red cloud of shame and the rising black cloud of despair.

Poverty is remembering. It is remembering quitting school in junior high because "nice" children had been so cruel about my clothes and my smell. The attendance officer came. My mother told him I was pregnant. I wasn't, but she thought that I could get a job and help out. I had jobs off and on, but never long enough to learn anything. Mostly I remember being married. I was so young then. I am still young. For a time, we had all the things you have. There was a little house in anoth- er town, with hot water and everything. Then my husband lost his job. There was unemployment insurance for a while and what few jobs I could get. Soon, all our nice things were repossessed and we moved back here. I was pregnant then. This house didn't look so bad when we first moved in. Every week it gets worse. Nothing is ever fixed. We now had no money. There were a few odd jobs for my husband, but everything went for food then, as it does now. I don't know how we lived through three years and three babies, but we did. I'll tell you something, after the last baby I destroyed my marriage. It had been a good one, but could you keep on bringing children in this dirt? Did you ever think how much it costs for any kind of birth control? I knew my husband was leaving that day he left, but there were no good-byes between us. I hope he has been able to climb out of this mess somewhere. He never could hope with us to drag him down.

That's when I asked for help. When I got it, you know how much it was? It was, and is, seventy-eight dollars a month for the four of us; that is all I ever can get. Now you know why there is no soap, no needles and thread, no hot water, no aspirin, no worm medicine, no hand cream, no shampoo. None of these things forever and ever and ever. So that you can see clearly, I pay twenty dollars a month rent, and most of the rest goes for food. For grits and cornmeal, and rice and milk and beans. I try my best to use only the minimum electricity. If I use more, there is that much less for food.

Poverty is looking into a black future. Your children won't play with ⟨10⟩ my boys. They will turn to other boys who steal to get what they want. I can already see them behind the bars of their prison instead of behind the bars of my poverty. Or they will turn to the freedom of alcohol or drugs, and find themselves enslaved. And my daughter? At best, there is for her a life like mine.

But you say to me, there are schools. Yes, there are schools. My children have no extra books, no magazines, no extra pencils, or crayons, or paper, and the most important of all, they do not have health. They have worms, they have infections, they have pink-eye all summer. They do not sleep well on the floor, or with me in my one bed. They do not suffer from hunger, my seventy-eight dollars keeps us alive, but they do suffer from malnutrition. Oh yes, I do remember what I was taught about health in school. It doesn't do much good. In some places there is a surplus commodities program. Not here. The county said it cost too much. There is a school lunch program. But I have two children who will already be damaged by the time they get to school.

But, you say to me, there are health clinics. Yes, there are health clinics and they are in the towns. I live out here eight miles from town. I can walk that far (even if it is sixteen miles both ways), but can my little children? My neighbor will take me when he goes; but he expects to get paid, *one way or another.* I bet you know my neighbor. He is that large man who spends his time at the gas station, the barbershop, and the corner store complaining about the government spending money on the immoral mothers of illegitimate children.

Poverty is an acid that drips on pride until all pride is worn away. Poverty is a chisel that chips on honor until honor is worn away. Some of you say that you would do *something* in my situation, and maybe you would, for the first week or the first month, but for year after year after year?

Even the poor can dream. A dream of a time when there is money. Money for the right kinds of food, for worm medicine, for iron pills, for toothbrushes, for hand cream, for a hammer and nails and a bit of screening, for a shovel, for a bit of paint, for some sheeting, for needles and thread. Money to pay *in money* for a trip to town. And, oh, money for hot water and money for soap. A dream of when asking for help does not eat away the last bit of pride. When the office you visit is as nice as the offices of other governmental agencies, when there are enough workers to help you quickly, when workers do not quit in defeat and despair. When you have to tell your story to only one person, and that person can send you for other help and you don't have to prove your poverty over and over and over again.

I have come out of my despair to tell you this. Remember I did not 15 come from another place or another time. Others like me are all around you. Look at us with an angry heart, anger that will help you help me. Anger that will let you tell of me. The poor are always silent. Can you be silent too?

STUDY QUESTIONS

1. Cite three examples from the essay of how poverty hurts its victims physically and emotionally. What is Parker's THESIS?

2. Parker clearly DESCRIBES her life as a victim of poverty. She also moves beyond herself to describe a number of other individuals who are touched in some way by her poverty. Starting with the close, personal circle of relatives and moving to others outside her family, list the people and/or organizations affected by her situation and describe how it affects them. How do these descriptions contribute to her DEFINITION of poverty?

3. First-person NARRATIVES are sometimes read with skepticism because they can be distorted by emotions, faulty memory, underlying agendas, and so forth. Reread this essay and decide whether the NARRATOR is reliable or unreliable. Support your position with specific QUOTATIONS.

4. *For Writing.* Conduct research into the economic realities of your hometown—the cost of living, housing costs, transportation costs, and the number of people living below the poverty line. What local agencies and organizations provide help for indigent people? Interview the staff of one such organization and find out what services they offer and how many people or families they help annually. Write an economic PROFILE of your town using the research you have gathered.

JAMES BALDWIN { *Stranger in the Village*

JAMES BALDWIN (1924–1987) was born in Harlem and moved to
Paris in 1948. He was a novelist, essayist, playwright, and activist. The
great theme running through most of his work was the relations between
white and black Americans—a concern that was, if anything, heightened
by the distance he placed between himself and America by moving to
Paris. In Europe Baldwin completed his first collection of essays, *Notes
of a Native Son* (1955). In the 1960s he returned to the United States to
take part in the civil rights movement, which ultimately led him to write
the essays collected in *The Fire Next Time* (1963), where "Stranger in
the Village" first appeared.

This essay begins as a personal narrative and then turns outward to
an analysis of the relationships between African Americans and
European Americans over time. Baldwin argues that because of slavery,
white Americans have played a larger role in the lives of black people
than has any other white group in the world—and, whether white
Americans want to acknowledge it or not, no other white group has seen
its identity so fundamentally shaped by black people.

FROM ALL AVAILABLE EVIDENCE NO black man had ever set foot in this
tiny Swiss village before I came. I was told before arriving that I
would probably be a "sight" for the village; I took this to mean that
people of my complexion were rarely seen in Switzerland, and also
that city people are always something of a "sight" outside of the city. It

did not occur to me—possibly because I am an American—that there could be people anywhere who had never seen a Negro.

It is a fact that cannot be explained on the basis of the inaccessibility of the village. The village is very high, but it is only four hours from Milan and three hours from Lausanne. It is true that it is virtually unknown. Few people making plans for a holiday would elect to come here. On the other hand, the villagers are able, presumably, to come and go as they please—which they do: to another town at the foot of the mountain, with a population of approximately five thousand, the nearest place to see a movie or go to the bank. In the village there is no movie house, no bank, no library, no theater; very few radios, one jeep, one station wagon; and, at the moment, one typewriter, mine, an invention which the woman next door to me here had never seen. There are about six hundred people living here, all Catholic—I conclude this from the fact that the Catholic church is open all year round, whereas the Protestant chapel, set off on a hill a little removed from the village, is open only in the summertime when the tourists arrive. There are four or five hotels, all closed now, and four or five *bistros,* of which, however, only two do any business during the winter. These two do not do a great deal, for life in the village seems to end around nine or ten o'clock. There are a few stores, butcher, baker, *épicerie,*[1] a hardware store, and a money-changer—who cannot change travelers' checks, but must send them down to the bank, an operation which takes two or three days. There is something called the *Ballet Haus,* closed in the winter and used for God knows what, certainly not ballet, during the summer. There seems to be only one schoolhouse in the village, and this for the quite young children; I suppose this to mean that their older brothers and sisters at some point descend from these mountains in order to complete their education—possibly, again, to the town just below. The landscape is absolutely forbidding, mountains towering on all four sides, ice and snow as far as the eye can reach. In this white wilderness, men and women and children move all day, carrying washing, wood, buckets of milk or water, sometimes skiing on Sunday afternoons. All week

[1]Grocery store (French).

long boys and young men are to be seen shoveling snow off the rooftops, or dragging wood down from the forest in sleds.

The village's only real attraction, which explains the tourist season, is the hot spring water. A disquietingly high proportion of these tourists are cripples, or semicripples, who come year after year—from other parts of Switzerland, usually—to take the waters. This lends the village, at the height of the season, a rather terrifying air of sanctity, as though it were a lesser Lourdes.[2] There is often something beautiful, there is always something awful, in the spectacle of a person who has lost one of his faculties, a faculty he never questioned until it was gone, and who struggles to recover it. Yet people remain people, on crutches or indeed on deathbeds; and wherever I passed, the first summer I was here, among the native villagers or among the lame, a wind passed with me—of astonishment, curiosity, amusement, and outrage. That first summer I stayed two weeks and never intended to return. But I did return in the winter, to work; the village offers, obviously, no distractions whatever and has the further advantage of being extremely cheap. Now it is winter again, a year later, and I am here again. Everyone in the village knows my name, though they scarcely ever use it, knows that I come from America—though, this, apparently, they will never really believe: black men come from Africa—and everyone knows that I am the friend of the son of a woman who was born here, and that I am staying in their chalet. But I remain as much a stranger today as I was the first day I arrived, and the children shout *Neger! Neger!*[3] as I walk along the streets.

It must be admitted that in the beginning I was far too shocked to have any real reaction. In so far as I reacted at all, I reacted by trying to be pleasant—it being a great part of the American Negro's education (long before he goes to school) that he must make people "like" him. This smile-and-the-world-smiles-with-you routine worked about as well in this situation as it had in the situation for which it was designed, which is to say that it did not work at all. No one, after all,

---

[2]Lourdes, France, a popular Roman Catholic shrine where the waters are believed to have healing powers.

[3]That is, "Negro" in German and in Romansh, two of the languages of Switzerland.

can be liked whose human weight and complexity cannot be, or has not been, admitted. My smile was simply another unheard-of phenomenon which allowed them to see my teeth—they did not, really, see my smile and I began to think that, should I take to snarling, no one would notice any difference. All of the physical characteristics of the Negro which had caused me, in America, a very different and almost forgotten pain were nothing less than miraculous—or infernal—in the eyes of the village people. Some thought my hair was the color of tar, that it had the texture of wire, or the texture of cotton. It was jocularly suggested that I might let it all grow long and make myself a winter coat. If I sat in the sun for more than five minutes some daring creature was certain to come along and gingerly put his fingers on my hair, as though he were afraid of an electric shock, or put his hand on my hand, astonished that the color did not rub off. In all of this, in which it must be conceded there was the charm of genuine wonder and in which there was certainly no element of intentional unkindness, there was yet no suggestion that I was human: I was simply a living wonder.

I knew that they did not mean to be unkind, and I know it now; it is necessary, nevertheless, for me to repeat this to myself each time that I walk out of the chalet. The children who shout *Neger!* have no way of knowing the echoes this sound raises in me. They are brimming with good humor and the more daring swell with pride when I stop to speak with them. Just the same, there are days when I cannot pause and smile, when I have no heart to play with them; when, indeed, I mutter sourly to myself, exactly as I muttered on the streets of a city these children have never seen, when I was no bigger than these children are now: *Your* mother *was a nigger.* Joyce is right about history being a nightmare[4]—but it may be the nightmare from which no one *can* awaken. People are trapped in history and history is trapped in them.

There is a custom in the village—I am told it is repeated in many villages—of "buying" African natives for the purpose of converting

[4]From *Ulysses* by Irish novelist James Joyce: "History is a nightmare from which I am trying to escape."

them to Christianity. There stands in the church all year round a small box with a slot for money, decorated with a black figurine, and into this box the villagers drop their francs. During the *carnaval* which precedes Lent, two village children have their faces blackened— out of which bloodless darkness their blue eyes shine like ice—and fantastic horsehair wigs are placed on their blond heads; thus disguised, they solicit among the villagers for money for the missionaries in Africa. Between the box in the church and the blackened children, the village "bought" last year six or eight African natives. This was reported to me with pride by the wife of one of the *bistro* owners and I was careful to express astonishment and pleasure at the solicitude shown by the village for the souls of black folk. The *bistro* owner's wife beamed with a pleasure far more genuine than my own and seemed to feel that I might now breathe more easily concerning the souls of at least six of my kinsmen.

I tried not to think of these so lately baptized kinsmen, of the price paid for them, or the peculiar price they themselves would pay, and said nothing about my father, who having taken his own conversion too literally never, at bottom, forgave the white world (which he described as heathen) for having saddled him with a Christ in whom, to judge at least from their treatment of him, they themselves no longer believed. I thought of white men arriving for the first time in an African village, strangers there, as I am a stranger here, and tried to imagine the astounded populace touching their hair and marveling at the color of their skin. But there is a great difference between being the first white man to be seen by Africans and being the first black man to be seen by whites. The white man takes the astonishment as tribute, for he arrives to conquer and to convert the natives, whose inferiority in relation to himself is not even to be questioned; whereas I, without a thought of conquest, find myself among a people whose culture controls me, has even, in a sense, created me, people who have cost me more in anguish and rage than they will ever know, who yet do not even know of my existence. The astonishment with which I might have greeted them, should they have stumbled into my African village a few hundred years ago, might have rejoiced their hearts. But the astonishment with which they greet me today can only poison mine.

And this is so despite everything I may do to feel differently, despite my friendly conversations with the *bistro* owner's wife, despite their three-year-old son who has at last become my friend, despite the *saluts* and *bonsoirs*[5] which I exchange with people as I walk, despite the fact that I know that no individual can be taken to task for what history is doing, or has done. I say that the culture of these people controls me—but they can scarcely be held responsible for European culture. America comes out of Europe, but these people have never seen America, nor have most of them seen more of Europe than the hamlet at the foot of their mountain. Yet they move with an authority which I shall never have; and they regard me, quite rightly, not only as a stranger in their village but as a suspect latecomer, bearing no credentials, to everything they have—however unconsciously—inherited.

For this village, even were it incomparably more remote and incredibly more primitive, is the West, the West onto which I have been so strangely grafted. These people cannot be, from the point of view of power, strangers anywhere in the world; they have made the modern world, in effect, even if they do not know it. The most illiterate among them is related, in a way that I am not, to Dante, Shakespeare, Michelangelo, Aeschylus, Da Vinci, Rembrandt, and Racine; the cathedral at Chartres says something to them which it cannot say to me, as indeed would New York's Empire State Building, should anyone here ever see it. Out of their hymns and dances come Beethoven and Bach. Go back a few centuries and they are in their full glory—but I am in Africa, watching the conquerors arrive.

The rage of the disesteemed is personally fruitless, but it is also 10 absolutely inevitable; this rage, so generally discounted, so little understood even among the people whose daily bread it is, is one of the things that makes history. Rage can only with difficulty, and never entirely, be brought under the domination of the intelligence and is therefore not susceptible to any arguments whatever. This is a fact which ordinary representatives of the *Herrenvolk*,[6] having never felt this rage and being unable to imagine it, quite fail to understand.

[5]"Hellos" and "good evenings" (French).
[6]Master race (German).

Also, rage cannot be hidden, it can only be dissembled. This dissembling deludes the thoughtless, and strengthens rage and adds, to rage, contempt. There are, no doubt, as many ways of coping with the resulting complex of tensions as there are black men in the world, but no black man can hope ever to be entirely liberated from this internal warfare—rage, dissembling, and contempt having inevitably accompanied his first realization of the power of white men. What is crucial here is that, since white men represent in the black man's world so heavy a weight, white men have for black men a reality which is far from being reciprocal; and hence all black men have toward all white men an attitude which is designed, really, either to rob the white man of the jewel of his naïveté, or else to make it cost him dear.

The black man insists, by whatever means he finds at his disposal, that the white man cease to regard him as an exotic rarity and recognize him as a human being. This is a very charged and difficult moment, for there is a great deal of willpower involved in the white man's naïveté. Most people are not naturally reflective any more than they are naturally malicious, and the white man prefers to keep the black man at a certain human remove because it is easier for him thus to preserve his simplicity and avoid being called to account for crimes committed by his forefathers, or his neighbors. He is inescapably aware, nevertheless, that he is in a better position in the world than black men are, nor can he quite put to death the suspicion that he is hated by black men therefore. He does not wish to be hated, neither does he wish to change places, and at this point in his uneasiness he can scarcely avoid having recourse to those legends which white men have created about black men, the most usual effect of which is that the white man finds himself enmeshed, so to speak, in his own language which describes hell, as well as the attributes which lead one to hell, as being as black as night.

Every legend, moreover, contains its residuum of truth, and the root function of language is to control the universe by describing it. It is of quite considerable significance that black men remain, in the imagination, and in overwhelming numbers in fact, beyond the disciplines of salvation; and this despite the fact that the West has been "buying" African natives for centuries. There is, I should hazard, an instantaneous necessity to be divorced from this so visibly unsaved stranger, in whose heart, moreover, one cannot guess what dreams of vengeance are being nourished; and, at the same time, there are few things on earth more attractive than the idea of the unspeakable liberty which is allowed the unredeemed. When, beneath the black mask, a human being begins to make himself felt one cannot escape a certain awful wonder as to what kind of human being it is. What one's imagination makes of other people is dictated, of course, by the laws of one's own personality and it is one of the ironies of black-white relations that, by means of what the white man imagines the black man to be, the black man is enabled to know who the white man is.

I have said, for example, that I am as much a stranger in this village today as I was the first summer I arrived, but this is not quite true. The villagers wonder less about the texture of my hair than they did then, and wonder rather more about me. And the fact that their wonder now exists on another level is reflected in their attitudes and in their eyes. There are the children who make those delightful, hilarious, sometimes astonishingly grave overtures of friendship in the unpredictable fashion of children; other children, having been taught that the devil is a black man, scream in genuine anguish as I approach. Some of the older women never pass without a friendly greeting, never pass, indeed, if it seems that they will be able to engage me in conversation; other women look down or look away or rather contemptuously smirk. Some of the men drink with me and suggest that I learn how to ski—partly, I gather, because they cannot imagine what I would look like on skis—and want to know if I am married, and ask questions about my *métier*. But some of the men have accused *le sale nègre*[7]— behind my back—of stealing wood and there is already in the eyes of some of them that peculiar, intent, paranoiac malevolence which one sometimes surprises in the eyes of American white men when, out walking with their Sunday girl, they see a Negro male approach.

There is a dreadful abyss between the streets of this village and the streets of the city in which I was born, between the children who shout *Neger!* today and those who shouted *Nigger!* yesterday—the

[7]*Métier:* occupation; *le sale nègre:* the dirty Negro (French).

abyss is experience, the American experience. The syllable hurled behind me today expresses, above all, wonder: I am a stranger here. But I am not a stranger in America and the same syllable riding on the American air expresses the war my presence has occasioned in the American soul.

For this village brings home to me this fact: that there was a day, and   15
not really a very distant day, when Americans were scarcely Americans at all but discontented Europeans, facing a great unconquered continent and strolling, say, into a marketplace and seeing black men for the first time. The shock this spectacle afforded is suggested, surely, by the promptness with which they decided that these black men were not really men but cattle. It is true that the necessity on the part of the settlers of the New World of reconciling their moral assumptions with the fact—and the necessity—of slavery enhanced immensely the charm of this idea, and it is also true that this idea expresses, with a truly American bluntness, the attitude which to varying extents all masters have had toward all slaves.

But between all former slaves and slave-owners and the drama which begins for Americans over three hundred years ago at Jamestown, there are at least two differences to be observed. The American Negro slave could not suppose, for one thing, as slaves in past epochs had supposed and often done, that he would ever be able to wrest the power from his master's hands. This was a supposition which the modern era, which was to bring about such vast changes in the aims and dimensions of power, put to death; it only begins, in unprecedented fashion, and with dreadful implications, to be resurrected today. But even had this supposition persisted with undiminished force, the American Negro slave could not have used it to lend his condition dignity, for the reason that this supposition rests on another: that the slave in exile yet remains related to his past, has some means—if only in memory—of revering and sustaining the forms of his former life, is able, in short, to maintain his identity.

This was not the case with the American Negro slave. He is unique among the black men of the world in that his past was taken from him, almost literally, at one blow. One wonders what on earth the first slave found to say to the first dark child he bore. I am told that there are

Haitians able to trace their ancestry back to African kings, but any American Negro wishing to go back so far will find his journey through time abruptly arrested by the signature on the bill of sale which served as the entrance paper for his ancestor. At the time—to say nothing of the circumstances—of the enslavement of the captive black man who was to become the American Negro, there was not the remotest possibility that he would ever take power from his master's hands. There was no reason to suppose that his situation would ever change, nor was there, shortly, anything to indicate that his situation had ever been different. It was his necessity, in the words of E. Franklin Frazier,[8] to find a "motive for living under American culture or die." The identity of the American Negro comes out of this extreme situation, and the evolution of this identity was a source of the most intolerable anxiety in the minds and the lives of his masters.

For the history of the American Negro is unique also in this: that the question of his humanity, and of his rights therefore as a human being, became a burning one for several generations of Americans, so burning a question that it ultimately became one of those used to divide the nation. It is out of this argument that the venom of the epithet *Nigger!* is derived. It is an argument which Europe has never had, and hence Europe quite sincerely fails to understand how or why the argument arose in the first place, why its effects are so frequently disastrous and always so unpredictable, why it refuses until today to be entirely settled. Europe's black possessions remained—and do remain—in Europe's colonies, at which remove they represented no threat whatever to European identity. If they posed any problem at all for the European conscience, it was a problem which remained comfortingly abstract: in effect, the black man, *as a man,* did not exist for Europe. But in America, even as a slave, he was an inescapable part of the general social fabric and no American could escape having an attitude toward him. Americans attempt until today to make an abstraction of the Negro, but the very nature of these abstractions reveals the tremendous effects the presence of the Negro has had on the American character.

[8] African American sociologist (1894–1962).

When one considers the history of the Negro in America it is of the greatest importance to recognize that the moral beliefs of a person, or a people, are never really as tenuous as life—which is not moral—very often causes them to appear; these create for them a frame of reference and a necessary hope, the hope being that when life has done its worst they will be enabled to rise above themselves and to triumph over life. Life would scarcely be bearable if this hope did not exist. Again, even when the worst has been said, to betray a belief is not by any means to have put oneself beyond its power; the betrayal of a belief is not the same thing as ceasing to believe. If this were not so there would be no moral standards in the world at all. Yet one must also recognize that morality is based on ideas and that all ideas are dangerous—dangerous because ideas can only lead to action and where the action leads no man can say. And dangerous in this respect: that confronted with the impossibility of remaining faithful to one's beliefs, and the equal impossibility of becoming free of them, one can be driven to the most inhuman excesses. The ideas on which American beliefs are based are not, though Americans often seem to think so, ideas which originated in America. They came out of Europe. And the establishment of democracy on the American continent was scarcely as radical a break with the past as was the necessity, which Americans faced, of broadening this concept to include black men.

This was, literally, a hard necessity. It was impossible, for one thing, 20 for Americans to abandon their beliefs, not only because these beliefs alone seemed able to justify the sacrifices they had endured and the blood that they had spilled, but also because these beliefs afforded them their only bulwark against a moral chaos as absolute as the physical chaos of the continent it was their destiny to conquer. But in the situation in which Americans found themselves, these beliefs threatened an idea which, whether or not one likes to think so, is the very warp and woof of the heritage of the West, the idea of white supremacy.

Americans have made themselves notorious by the shrillness and the brutality with which they have insisted on this idea, but they did not invent it; and it has escaped the world's notice that those very excesses of which Americans have been guilty imply a certain, unprecedented uneasiness over the idea's life and power, if not, indeed, the idea's validity. The idea of white supremacy rests simply on the fact that white men are the creators of civilization (the present civilization, which is the only one that matters; all previous civilizations are simply "contributions" to our own) and are therefore civilization's guardians and defenders. Thus it was impossible for Americans to accept the black man as one of themselves, for to do so was to jeopardize their status as white men. But not so to accept him was to deny his human reality, his human weight and complexity, and the strain of denying the overwhelmingly undeniable forced Americans into rationalizations so fantastic that they approached the pathological.

At the root of the American Negro problem is the necessity of the American white man to find a way of living with the Negro in order to be able to live with himself. And the history of this problem can be reduced to the means used by Americans—lynch law and law, segregation and legal acceptance, terrorization and concession—either to come to terms with this necessity, or to find a way around it, or (most usually) to find a way of doing both these things at once. The resulting spectacle, at once foolish and dreadful, led someone to make the quite accurate observation that "the Negro-in-America is a form of insanity which overtakes white men."

In this long battle, a battle by no means finished, the unforeseeable effects of which will be felt by many future generations, the white man's motive was the protection of his identity; the black man was motivated by the need to establish an identity. And despite the terrorization which the Negro in America endured and endures sporadically until today, despite the cruel and totally inescapable ambivalence of his status in his country, the battle for his identity has long ago been won. He is not a visitor to the West, but a citizen there, an American; as American as the Americans who despise him, the Americans who fear him, the Americans who love him—the Americans who became less than themselves, or rose to be greater than themselves by virtue of the fact that the challenge he represented was inescapable. He is perhaps the only black man in the world whose relationship to white men is more terrible, more subtle, and more meaningful than the relationship of bitter possessed to uncertain possessor. His survival depended, and his development depends, on his ability to turn his peculiar status in the Western world to his own advantage and, it may be, to the very great advantage of that world. It remains for him to fashion out of his experience that which will give him sustenance, and a voice.

The cathedral at Chartres, I have said, says something to the people of this village which it cannot say to me; but it is important to understand that this cathedral says something to me which it cannot say to them. Perhaps they are struck by the power of the spires, the glory of the windows; but they have known God, after all, longer than I have known him, and in a different way, and I am terrified by the slippery bottomless well to be found in the crypt, down which heretics were hurled to death, and by the obscene, inescapable gargoyles jutting out of the stone and seeming to say that God and the devil can never be divorced. I doubt that the villagers think of the devil when they face a cathedral because they have never been identified with the devil. But I must accept the status which myth, if nothing else, gives me in the West before I can hope to change the myth.

Yet, if the American Negro has arrived at his identity by virtue of the 25 absoluteness of his estrangement from his past, American white men still nourish the illusion that there is some means of recovering the European innocence, of returning to a state in which black men do not exist. This is one of the greatest errors Americans can make. The identity they fought so hard to protect has, by virtue of that battle, undergone a change: Americans are as unlike any other white people in the world as it is possible to be. I do not think, for example, that it is too much to suggest that the American vision of the world—which allows so little reality, generally speaking, for any of the darker forces in human life, which tends until today to paint moral issues in glaring black and white—owes a great deal to the battle waged by Americans to maintain between themselves and black men a human separation which could not be bridged. It is only now beginning to be borne in on us—very faintly, it must be admitted, very slowly, and very much against our will—that this vision of the world is dangerously inaccurate, and perfectly useless. For it protects our moral high-mindedness at the terrible expense of weakening our grasp of reality. People who shut their eyes to reality simply invite their own destruction, and anyone who insists on remaining in a state of innocence long after that innocence is dead turns himself into a monster.

The time has come to realize that the interracial drama acted out on the American continent has not only created a new black man, it has created a new white man, too. No road whatever will lead Americans back to the simplicity of this European village where white men still have the luxury of looking on me as a stranger. I am not, really, a stranger any longer for any American alive. One of the things that distinguishes Americans from other people is that no other people has ever been so deeply involved in the lives of black men, and vice versa. This fact faced, with all its implications, it can be seen that the history of the American Negro problem is not merely shameful, it is also something of an achievement. For even when the worst has been said, it must also be added that the perpetual challenge posed by this problem was always, somehow, perpetually met. It is precisely this black-white experience which may prove of indispensable value to us in the world we face today. This world is white no longer, and it will never be white again.

STUDY QUESTIONS

1. Baldwin says that "there is a great difference between being the first white man to be seen by Africans and being the first black man to be seen by whites" (paragraph 7). Explain what he means.

2. In Baldwin's MEMOIR, he DESCRIBES the village from the perspective of a stranger. Find examples of Baldwin's description showing that he is culturally different from the villagers. How does this difference make him feel?

3. Baldwin's essay begins as a memoir but moves to the larger political issue of race relations. How does the Swiss village become a rhetorical tool to help him deliver his message? Find other examples of how Baldwin uses time and location to help him argue his points.

4. *For Writing.* Baldwin wrote this essay in 1953. Select at least two points in the essay with which you agree or disagree, and write an essay in which you respond to these points using events in contemporary America as evidence. Be sure to DOCUMENT any sources you consult.

EDWARD HOAGLAND 〔 *The Football Game in My Head*

EDWARD HOAGLAND (b. 1932), a native of New York City, earned his BA
from Harvard University in 1954. He published his first novel, *Cat Man,*
just a year later in 1955; it draws on his experiences working for a circus for
two summers during college. Now best known for his nonfiction writing
about nature and travel, particularly his journeys in Africa, Hoagland has
received many awards, including two Guggenheim fellowships (1964,
1975). He has also taught at a number of institutions, including the New
School in New York City, Beloit College, Brown University, and, before
retiring from teaching in 2005, Bennington College.

The reading included here is a personal essay about Hoagland's lifelong
stuttering. Carefully describing the physiological, psychological, and social
aspects of stuttering, Hoagland redefines stuttering not as a handicap but
instead a motivator. As you read, think about the analogies and metaphors
Hoagland uses to describe his stuttering—the football game in his head, for
instance—and how effectively they convey the experience of stuttering.

STUTTERING IS LIKE TRYING TO run with loops of rope around your
feet. And yet you feel that you *do* want to run because you may get more
words out that way before you trip: an impulse you resist so other people won't tell you to "calm down" and "relax." Because they themselves
may stammer a little bit when jittery or embarrassed, it's hard for a real
stutterer like me to convince a new acquaintance that we aren't perpetually in such a nervous state and that it's quite normal for us to be at the
mercy of strangers. Strangers are usually civilized, once the rough and

sometimes inadvertently hurtful process of recognizing what is wrong with us is over (that we're not laughing, hiccuping, coughing, or whatever) and in a way we plumb them for traces of *Schadenfreude*.[1] A stutterer knows who the good guys are in any crowded room, as well as the location of each mocking gleam, and even the St. Francis[2] type, who will wait until he thinks nobody is looking to wipe a fleck of spittle off his face.

I've stuttered for more than sixty years, and the mysteries of the encumbrance still catch me up: being reminded every morning that it's engrained in my fiber, although I had forgotten in my dreams. Life can become a matter of measuring the importance of anything you have to say. Is it better to remain a pleasant cipher who ventures nothing in particular but chuckles immoderately at everyone else's conversation, or instead to subject your several companions to the ordeal of watching you struggle to expel opinions that are either blurred and vitiated, or made to sound too emphatic, by all the huffing and puffing, the facial contortions, tongue biting, blushing, and suffering? "Write it down," people often said to me in school; indeed I sold my first novel before I left college.

Self-confidence can reduce a stutter's dimensions (in that sense you do "outgrow" it), as will affection (received or felt), anger, sexual arousal, and various other hormonal or pheromonal states you may dip into in the shorter term. Yet it still lurks underfoot, like a trapdoor. I was determined not to be impeded and managed to serve a regular stint in the Army by telling the draft-board psychiatrist that I wanted to and was only stammering from "nervousness" with him. Later I also contrived to become a college professor, thanks to the patience of my early students. Nevertheless, through childhood and adolescence, when I was almost mute in public, I could talk without much difficulty to one or two close friends, and then to the particular girl I was necking with. In that case, an overlapping trust was then the lubricant, but if it began to evaporate as our hopes for permanence didn't pan out, I'd

---

[1] Pleasure derived from the troubles of others (German).

[2] Giovanni Francesco Bernardone (c. 1181–1226), patron saint of animals and the environment, as well as founder of the Franciscans, the Order of Friars Minor. St. Francis is often invoked, as here, as the personification of kindness.

start regretfully, apologetically but willy-nilly, to stutter with her again. Adrenaline, when I got mad, operated in a similar fashion, though only momentarily. That is, if somebody made fun of me or treated me cavalierly and a certain threshold was crossed, a spurt of chemistry would suddenly free my mouth and—like Popeye[3] grabbing a can of spinach—I could answer him. Poor Billy Budd[4] didn't learn this technique (and his example frightened me because of its larger implications). Yet many stutterers develop a snappish temperament, and from not just sheer frustration but the fact that being more than ready to "lose one's temper" (as Billy wasn't) actually helps. As in jujitsu, you can trap an opponent by employing his strength and cruelty against him; and bad guys aren't generally smart enough to know that if they wait me out, I'll bog down helplessly all over again.

Overall, however, stuttering is not so predictable. Whether rested or exhausted, fibbing or speaking the Simon-pure truth, and when in the company of chums or people whom I don't respect, I can be fluent or tied in knots. I learned young to be an attentive listener, both because my empathy for others' worries was honed by my handicap and because it was in my best interest that they talk a lot. And yet a core in you will hemorrhage if you become a mere assenter. How many opinions can you keep to yourself before you choke on them (and turn into a stick of furniture for everybody else)? So, instead, you measure what's worth specifying. If you agree with two thirds of what's being suggested, is it worth the labor of breathlessly elaborating upon the one third where you differ? There were plenty of times when a subject might come up that I knew more about than the rest of the group, and it used to gall me if I had held my peace till maybe closeted afterward with a close friend. A stymieing bashfulness can also slide a stutterer into slack language because accurate words are so much harder to say than bland ones. You're tempted to be content with an approximation

---

[3]Cartoon hero of comic strip and animations, created in 1929 by Elzie Crisler Segar. Popeye the Sailor gained his remarkable strength by eating spinach.

[4]Title character of *Billy Budd*, a novella by American author Herman Melville (1819–91). At a climactic moment in the story, Billy, a sailor on a ship, finds himself accused of mutiny, and, unable to respond because of his speech impediment, he strikes and kills his accuser, for which he is later hanged.

of what you mean in order to escape the scourge of being exact. A sort of football game is going on in your head—the tacklers live there too—and the very effort of pausing to figure out the right way to describe something will alert them to how to pull you down. Being glib and sloppy generates less blockage.

But it's important not to err in the opposite direction, on the side of 5 tendentiousness, and insist on equal time only because you are a pain in the neck with a problem. You can stutter till your tongue bleeds and your chest is sore from heaving, but so what, if you haven't anything to say that's worth the humiliation? Better to function as a kind of tuning fork, vibrating to other people's anguish or apprehensiveness, as well as your own. A handicap can be cleansing. My scariest moments as a stutterer have been (1) when my daughter was learning to talk and briefly got the impression that she was supposed to do the same; (2) once when I was in the woods and a man shot in my direction and I had to make myself heard loud and fast; and (3) when anticipating weddings where I would need either to propose a toast or say "I do." Otherwise my impediment ceased to be a serious blight about the time I lost my virginity: just a sort of cleft to step around—a squint and gasp of hesitation that indicated to people I might want to be friends with or interview that I wasn't perfect either and perhaps they could trust me.

At worst, during my teens, when I was stuttering on vowels as well as consonants and spitting a few words out could seem interminable, I tried some therapies. But "Slow Speech" was as slow as the trouble itself; and repeatedly writing the first letter of the word that I was stuttering on with my finger in my pocket looked peculiar enough to attract almost as much attention. It did gradually lighten with my maturity and fatherhood, professional recognition, and the other milestones that traditionally help. Nothing "slew" it, though, until at nearly sixty I went semiblind for a couple of years, and this emergency eclipsed—completely trumped—the lesser difficulty. I felt I simply had to talk or die, and so I talked. Couldn't do it gratuitously or lots, but I talked enough to survive. The stutter somehow didn't hold water and ebbed away, until surgery restored my vision and then it returned, like other normalcies.

Such variations can make a stutter seem like a sort of ancillary eccentricity, or a personal Godzilla. But the ball carrier in your head is going to have his good days too—when he can swivel past the tacklers, improvising a broken-field dash so that they are out of position—or even capture their attention with an idea so intriguing that they stop and listen. Not for long, however: The message underlying a stutter is rather like mortality, after all. Real reprieves and fluency are not for you and me. We blunder along, stammering—then not so much—through minor scrapes and scares, but not unscathed. We're not Demosthenes,[5] of course. And poor Demosthenes, if you look him up, ended about as sadly as Billy Budd. People tend to.

[5]Ancient Greek statesman (384–22 BCE.), often cited, as here, as a superb orator. He died by taking poison rather than face capture by his enemies; his final words are remembered for their grace and eloquence.

STUDY QUESTIONS

1. How does Hoagland characterize stuttering? How does he see it as an advantage as well as an impediment? When does he not stutter?

2. How would you characterize Hoagland's ETHOS in this essay? Support your response with specific passages from the text. How does his ethos affect your reaction to his essay as a reader? How effective is it?

3. *For Writing.* Research the phenomenon of so-called phatic verbal tics—conversational filler words such as "like," "kind of," and "you know." Choose two of them, and write an essay in which you ANALYZE their function in everyday speech. What effect do they have on conversation? Why do we use them?

NANCY MAIRS { *On Being a Cripple*

NANCY MAIRS (b. 1943) was born in Long Beach, California, and raised north of Boston. She earned her undergraduate degree at Wheaton College in Massachusetts and her MFA in creative writing and PhD in English literature at the University of Arizona. While still a graduate student, Mairs was diagnosed with multiple sclerosis, a disease of the central nervous system. Mairs has taught writing and literature at the high school and college levels and has published several books in different genres, including poetry, nonfiction, and autobiography. Her work often discusses spirituality, women's issues, and living with disability. After publishing her essay collection *Waist High in the World: A Life Among the Nondisabled* (1996), Mairs became the subject of a documentary filmed over a five-year period, also titled *Waist High in the World* (2002).

In this essay, published in *Plaintext* (1986), Mairs offers an unflinching look at life with MS. She details the reasons she chooses to describe herself as "crippled," rather than "disabled" or "handicapped" and compares life with a disability to life without. As you read, consider how Mairs's writing style can deliberately throw her readers off balance and how that unbalancing might, in turn, parallel her own experiences with MS.

To escape is nothing. Not to escape is nothing.

—LOUISE BOGAN

THE OTHER DAY I WAS thinking of writing an essay on being a cripple. I was thinking hard in one of the stalls of the women's room in my office building, as I was shoving my shirt into my jeans and tugging up my zipper. Preoccupied, I flushed, picked up my book bag, took my cane down from the hook, and unlatched the door. So many movements unbalanced me, and as I pulled the door open I fell over backward, landing fully clothed on the toilet seat with my legs splayed in front of me: the old beetle-on-its-back routine. Saturday afternoon, the building deserted, I was free to laugh aloud as I wriggled back to my feet, my voice bouncing off the yellowish tiles from all directions. Had anyone been there with me, I'd have been still and faint and hot with chagrin. I decided that it was high time to write the essay.

First, the matter of semantics. I am a cripple. I choose this word to name me. I choose from among several possibilities, the most common of which are "handicapped" and "disabled." I made the choice a number of years ago, without thinking, unaware of my motives for doing so. Even now, I'm not sure what those motives are, but I recognize that they are complex and not entirely flattering. People—crippled or not—wince at the word "cripple," as they do not at "handicapped" or "disabled." Perhaps I want them to wince. I want them to see me as a tough customer, one to whom the fates/gods/viruses have not been kind, but who can face the brutal truth of her existence squarely. As a cripple, I swagger.

But, to be fair to myself, a certain amount of honesty underlies my choice. "Cripple" seems to me a clean word, straightforward and precise. It has an honorable history, having made its first appearance in the Lindisfarne Gospel[1] in the tenth century. As a lover of words, I like the accuracy with which it describes my condition: I have lost the full use of my limbs. "Disabled," by contrast, suggests any incapacity, physical or mental. And I certainly don't like "handicapped," which implies that I have deliberately been put at a disadvantage, by whom I can't imagine (my God is not a Handicapper General), in order to equalize chances in the great race of life. These words seem to me to be moving away from my condition, to be widening the gap between word and

---

[1] Illuminated manuscript of the four gospels, prepared in Northumbria (now northeastern England and southern Scotland) by the monk Eadfrith (d. 721). The work was translated from Latin into Old English in the tenth century.

reality. Most remote is the recently coined euphemism "differently abled," which partakes of the same semantic hopefulness that transformed countries from "undeveloped" to "underdeveloped," then to "less developed," and finally to "developing" nations. People have continued to starve in those countries during the shift. Some realities do not obey the dictates of language.

Mine is one of them. Whatever you call me, I remain crippled. But I don't care what you call me, so long as it isn't "differently abled," which strikes me as pure verbal garbage designed, by its ability to describe anyone, to describe no one. I subscribe to George Orwell's thesis that "the slovenliness of our language makes it easier for us to have foolish thoughts."[2] And I refuse to participate in the degeneration of the language to the extent that I deny that I have lost anything in the course of this calamitous disease; I refuse to pretend that the only differences between you and me are the various ordinary ones that distinguish any one person from another. But call me "disabled" or "handicapped" if you like. I have long since grown accustomed to them; and if they are vague, at least they hint at the truth. Moreover, I use them myself. Society is no readier to accept crippledness than to accept death, war, sex, sweat, or wrinkles. I would never refer to another person as a cripple. It is the word I use to name only myself.

I haven't always been crippled, a fact for which I am soundly grateful. 5 To be whole of limb is, I know from experience, infinitely more pleasant and useful than to be crippled; and if that knowledge leaves one open to bitterness at my loss, the physical soundness I once enjoyed (though I did not enjoy it half enough) is well worth the occasional stab of regret. Though never any good at sports, I was a normally active child and young adult. I climbed trees, played hopscotch, jumped rope, skated, swam, rode my bicycle, sailed. I despised team sports, spending some of the wretchedest afternoons of my life, sweaty and humiliated, behind a field-hockey stick and under a basketball hoop. I tramped alone for miles along the bridle paths that webbed the woods behind the house I grew up in. I swayed through countless dim hours in the arms of one man or

[2]George Orwell is the pseudonym of Eric Arthur Blair (1903–50), English author. The reference here is to his classic essay "Politics and the English Language" (1950).

another under the scattered shot of light from mirrored balls, and gyrated through countless more as Tab Hunter and Johnny Mathis gave way to the Rolling Stones, Creedence Clearwater Revival, Cream.[3] I walked down the aisle. I pushed baby carriages, changed tires in the rain, marched for peace.

When I was twenty-eight I started to trip and drop things. What at first seemed my natural clumsiness soon became too pronounced to shrug off. I consulted a neurologist, who told me that I had a brain tumor. A battery of tests, increasingly disagreeable, revealed no tumor. About a year and a half later I developed a blurred spot in one eye. I had, at last, the episodes "disseminated in space and time" requisite for a diagnosis: multiple sclerosis. I have never been sorry for the doctor's initial misdiagnosis, however. For almost a week, until the negative results of the tests were in, I thought that I was going to die right away. Every day for the past nearly ten years, then, has been a kind of gift. I accept all gifts.

Multiple sclerosis is a chronic degenerative disease of the central nervous system, in which the myelin that sheathes the nerves is somehow eaten away and scar tissue forms in its place, interrupting the nerves' signals. During its course, which is unpredictable and uncontrollable, one may lose vision, hearing, speech, the ability to walk, control of bladder and/or bowels, strength in any or all extremities, sensitivity to touch, vibration, and/or pain, potency, coordination of movements—the list of possibilities is lengthy and, yes, horrifying. One may also lose one's sense of humor. That's the easiest to lose and the hardest to survive without.

In the past ten years, I have sustained some of these losses. Characteristic of MS are sudden attacks, called exacerbations, followed by remissions, and these I have not had. Instead, my disease has been slowly progressive. My left leg is now so weak that I walk with the aid of a brace and a cane; and for distances I use an Amigo, a variation on the electric wheelchair that looks rather like an electrified kiddie car. I no longer have much use of my left hand. Now my right side is weakening as well. I still have the blurred spot in my right eye. Overall,

---

[3] Mairs refers to musical artists popular from the late 1950s through the late 1960s.

though, I've been lucky so far. My world has, of necessity, been circumscribed by my losses, but the terrain left me has been ample enough for me to continue many of the activities that absorb me: writing, teaching, raising children and cats and plants and snakes, reading, speaking publicly about MS and depression, even playing bridge with people patient and honorable enough to let me scatter cards every which way without sneaking a peek.

Lest I begin to sound like Pollyanna,[4] however, let me say that I don't like having MS. I hate it. My life holds realities—harsh ones, some of them—that no right-minded human being ought to accept without grumbling. One of them is fatigue. I know of no one with MS who does not complain of bone-weariness; in a disease that presents an astonishing variety of symptoms, fatigue seems to be a common factor. I wake up in the morning feeling the way most people do at the end of a bad day, and I take it from there. As a result, I spend a lot of time *in extremis*[5] and, impatient with limitation, I tend to ignore my fatigue until my body breaks down in some way and forces rest. Then I miss picnics, dinner parties, poetry readings, the brief visits of old friends from out of town. The offspring of a puritanical tradition of exceptional venerability, I cannot view these lapses without shame. My life often seems a series of small failures to do as I ought.

I lead, on the whole, an ordinary life, probably rather like the one I 10 would have led had I not had MS. I am lucky that my predilections were already solitary, sedentary, and bookish—unlike the world-famous French cellist I have read about, or the young woman I talked with one long afternoon who wanted only to be a jockey. I had just begun graduate school when I found out something was wrong with me, and I have remained, interminably, a graduate student. Perhaps I would not have if I'd thought I had the stamina to return to a full-time job as a technical editor; but I've enjoyed my studies.

In addition to studying, I teach writing courses. I also teach medical students how to give neurological examinations. I pick up freelance

[4]The sunny, optimistic title character of a 1913 novel by American writer Eleanor Porter (1868–1920).
[5]In extreme circumstances (Latin).

editing jobs here and there. I have raised a foster son and sent him into the world, where he has made me two grandbabies, and I am still escorting my daughter and son through adolescence. I go to Mass every Saturday. I am a superb, if messy, cook. I am also an enthusiastic laundress, capable of sorting a hamper full of clothes into five subtly differentiated piles, but a terrible housekeeper. I can do italic writing and, in an emergency, bathe an oil-soaked cat. I play a fiendish game of Scrabble. When I have the time and the money, I like to sit on my front steps with my husband, drinking Amaretto and smoking a cigar, as we imagine our counterparts in Leningrad and make sure that the sun gets down once more behind the sharp childish scrawl of the Tucson Mountains.

This lively plenty has its bleak complement, of course, in all the things I can no longer do. I will never run again, except in dreams, and one day I may have to write that I will never walk again. I like to go camping, but I can't follow George and the children along the trails that wander out of a campsite through the desert or into the mountains. In fact, even on the level I've learned never to check the weather or try to hold a coherent conversation: I need all my attention for my wayward feet. Of late, I have begun to catch myself wondering how people can propel themselves without canes. With only one usable hand, I have to select my clothing with care not so much for style as for ease of ingress and egress, and even so, dressing can be laborious. I can no longer do fine stitchery, pick up babies, play the piano, braid my hair. I am immobilized by acute attacks of depression, which may or may not be physiologically related to MS but are certainly its logical concomitant.

These two elements, the plenty and the privation, are never pure, nor are the delight and wretchedness that accompany them. Almost every pickle that I get into as a result of my weakness and clumsiness— and I get into plenty—is funny as well as maddening and sometimes painful. I recall one May afternoon when a friend and I were going out for a drink after finishing up at school. As we were climbing into opposite sides of my car, chatting, I tripped and fell, flat and hard, onto the asphalt parking lot, my abrupt departure interrupting him in mid-sentence. "Where'd you go?" he called as he came around the back of the car to find me hauling myself up by the door frame. "Are you all right?" Yes, I told him, I was fine, just a bit rattly, and we drove off to find a shady patio and some beer. When I got home an hour or so later, my daughter greeted me with "What have you done to yourself?" I looked down. One elbow of my white turtleneck with the green frog-gies, one knee of my white trousers, one white kneesock were blood-soaked. We peeled off the clothes and inspected the damage, which was nasty enough but not alarming. That part wasn't funny: The abra-sions took a long time to heal, and one got a little infected. Even so, when I think of my friend talking earnestly, suddenly, to the hot thin air while I dropped from his view as though through a trap door, I find the image as silly as something from a Marx Brothers movie.

I may find it easier than other cripples to amuse myself because I live propped by the acceptance and the assistance and, sometimes, the amusement of those around me. Grocery clerks tear my checks out of my checkbook for me, and sales clerks find chairs to put into dressing rooms when I want to try on clothes. The people I work with make sure I teach at times when I am least likely to be fatigued, in places I can get to, with the materials I need. My students, with one anonymous exception (in an end-of-the-semester evaluation), have been unper-turbed by my disability. Some even like it. One was immensely cheered by the information that I paint my own fingernails; she decided, she told me, that if I could go to such trouble over fine details, she could keep on writing essays. I suppose I became some sort of bright-fingered muse. She wrote good essays, too.

The most important struts in the framework of my existence, of 15 course, are my husband and children. Dismayingly few marriages sur-vive the MS test, and why should they? Most twenty-two- and nineteen-year-olds, like George and me, can vow in clear conscience, after a childhood of chicken pox and summer colds, to keep one an-other in sickness and in health so long as they both shall live. Not many are equipped for catastrophe: the dismay, the depression, the extra work, the boredom that a degenerative disease can insinuate into a rela-tionship. And our society, with its emphasis on fun and its association of fun with physical performance, offers little encouragement for a whole spouse to stay with a crippled partner. Children experience similar stresses when faced with a crippled parent, and they are more helpless, since parents and children can't usually get divorced. They hate, of course, to be different from their peers, and the child whose mother is tacking down the aisle of a school auditorium packed with proud parents like a Cape Cod dinghy in a stiff breeze jolly well stands out in a crowd. Deprived of legal divorce, the child can at least deny the mother's disability, even her existence, forgetting to tell her about recitals and PTA meetings, refusing to accompany her to stores or church or the movies, never inviting friends to the house. Many do.

But I've been limping along for ten years now, and so far George and the children are still at my left elbow, holding tight. Anne and Matthew vacuum floors and dust furniture and haul trash and rake up dog droppings and button my cuffs and bake lasagna and Toll House cookies with just enough grumbling so I know that they don't have brain fever. And far from hiding me, they're forever dragging me by racks of fancy clothes or through teeming school corridors, or welcoming gaggles of friends while I'm wandering through the house in Anne's filmy pink babydoll pajamas. George generally calls before he brings someone home, but he does just as many dumb thankless chores as the children. And they all yell at me, laugh at some of my jokes, write me funny letters when we're apart—in short, treat me as an ordinary human being for whom they have some use. I think they like me. Unless they're faking. . . .

Faking. There's the rub. Tugging at the fringes of my consciousness always is the terror that people are kind to me only because I'm a cripple. My mother almost shattered me once, with that instinct mothers have—blind, I think, in this case, but unerring nonetheless—for striking blows along the fault-lines of their children's hearts, by telling me, in an attack on my selfishness, "We all have to make allowances for you, of course, because of the way you are." From the distance of a couple of years, I have to admit that I haven't any idea just what she meant, and I'm not sure that she knew either. She was awfully angry. But at the time, as the words thudded home, I felt my worst fear, suddenly realized. I could bear being called selfish: I am. But I couldn't bear the corroboration that those around me were doing in fact what I'd always suspected them of doing, professing fondness while silently putting up with me because of the way I am. A cripple. I've been a little cracked ever since.

Along with this fear that people are secretly accepting shoddy goods comes a relentless pressure to please—to prove myself worth the burdens I impose, I guess, or to build a substantial account of goodwill against which I may write drafts in times of need. Part of the pressure arises from social expectations. In our society, anyone who deviates from the norm had better find some way to compensate. Like fat people, who are expected to be jolly, cripples must bear their lot meekly and cheerfully. A grumpy cripple isn't playing by the rules. And much of the pressure is self-generated. Early on I vowed that, if I had to have MS, by God I was going to do it well. This is a class act, ladies and gentlemen. No tears, no recriminations, no faintheartedness.

One way and another, then, I wind up feeling like Tiny Tim,[6] peering over the edge of the table at the Christmas goose, waving my crutch, piping down God's blessing on us all. Only sometimes I don't want to play Tiny Tim. I'd rather be Caliban,[7] a most scurvy monster. Fortunately, at home no one much cares whether I'm a good cripple or a bad cripple as long as I make vichyssoise with fair regularity. One evening several years ago, Anne was reading at the dining-room table while I cooked dinner. As I opened a can of tomatoes, the can slipped in my left hand and juice spattered me and the counter with bloody spots. Fatigued and infuriated, I bellowed, "I'm so sick of being crippled!" Anne glanced at me over the top of her book. "There now," she said, "do you feel better?" "Yes," I said, "yes, I do." She went back to her reading. I felt better. That's about all the attention my scurviness ever gets.

Because I hate being crippled, I sometimes hate myself for being a 20 cripple. Over the years I have come to expect—even accept—attacks of violent self-loathing. Luckily, in general our society no longer connects deformity and disease directly with evil (though a charismatic once told me that I have MS because a devil is in me) and so I'm allowed to move largely at will, even among small children. But I'm not sure that

[6]Optimistic, handicapped character in the Charles Dickens novella *A Christmas Carol* (1843).
[7]Wild, malformed creature from Shakespeare's play *The Tempest* (1610–11).

this revision of attitude has been particularly helpful. Physical imperfection, even freed of moral disapprobation, still defies and violates the ideal, especially for women, whose confinement in their bodies as objects of desire is far from over. Each age, of course, has its ideal, and I doubt that ours is any better or worse than any other. Today's ideal woman, who lives on the glossy pages of dozens of magazines, seems to be between the ages of eighteen and twenty-five; her hair has body, her teeth flash white, her breath smells minty, her underarms are dry; she has a career but is still a fabulous cook, especially of meals that take less than twenty minutes to prepare; she does not ordinarily appear to have a husband or children; she is trim and deeply tanned; she jogs, swims, plays tennis, rides a bicycle, sails, but does not bowl; she travels widely, even to out-of-the-way places like Finland and Samoa, always in the company of the ideal man, who possesses a nearly identical set of characteristics. There are a few exceptions. Though usually white and often blonde, she may be black, Hispanic, Asian, or Native American, so long as she is unusually sleek. She may be old, provided she is selling a laxative or is Lauren Bacall.[8] If she is selling a detergent, she may be married and have a flock of strikingly messy children. But she is never a cripple.

Like many women I know, I have always had an uneasy relationship with my body. I was not a popular child, largely, I think now, because I was peculiar: intelligent, intense, moody, shy, given to unexpected actions and inexplicable notions and emotions. But as I entered adolescence, I believed myself unpopular because I was homely: my breasts too flat, my mouth too wide, my hips too narrow, my clothing never quite right in fit or style. I was not, in fact, particularly ugly, old photographs inform me, though I was well off the ideal; but I carried this sense of self-alienation with me into adulthood, where it regenerated in response to the depredations of MS. Even with my brace I walk with a limp so pronounced that, seeing myself on the videotape of a television program on the disabled, I couldn't believe that anything but an inchworm could make progress humping along like that. My shoulders droop and my pelvis thrusts forward as I try to balance myself

[8]American film star (b. 1924), famed for beauty that has endured throughout her life.

upright, throwing my frame into a bony S. As a result of contractures, one shoulder is higher than the other and I carry one arm bent in front of me, the fingers curled into a claw. My left arm and leg have wasted into pipe-stems, and I try always to keep them covered. When I think about how my body must look to others, especially to men, to whom I have been trained to display myself, I feel ludicrous, even loathsome.

At my age, however, I don't spend much time thinking about my appearance. The burning egocentricity of adolescence, which assures one that all the world is looking all the time, has passed, thank God, and I'm generally too caught up in what I'm doing to step back, as I used to, and watch myself as though upon a stage. I'm also too old to believe in the accuracy of self-image. I know that I'm not a hideous crone, that in fact, when I'm rested, well dressed, and well made up, I look fine. The self-loathing I feel is neither physically nor intellectually substantial. What I hate is not me but a disease.

I am not a disease.

And a disease is not—at least not singlehandedly—going to determine who I am, though at first it seemed to be going to. Adjusting to a chronic incurable illness, I have moved through a process similar to that outlined by Elisabeth Kübler-Ross[9] in *On Death and Dying.* The major difference—and it is far more significant than most people recognize—is that I can't be sure of the outcome, as the terminally ill cancer patient can. Research studies indicate that, with proper medical care, I may achieve a "normal" life span. And in our society, with its vision of death as the ultimate evil, worse even than decrepitude, the response to such news is, "Oh well, at least you're not going to *die.*" Are there worse things than dying? I think that there may be.

I think of two women I know, both with MS, both enough older than 25 I to have served me as models. One took to her bed several years ago and has been there ever since. Although she can sit in a high-backed wheelchair, because she is incontinent she refuses to go out at all, even though incontinence pants, which are readily available at any pharmacy, could protect her from embarrassment. Instead, she stays at

[9]Swiss American psychiatrist (1926–2004) who established the five stages of grief: denial, anger, bargaining, depression, and acceptance.

home and insists that her husband, a small quiet man, a retired civil servant, stay there with her except for a quick weekly foray to the supermarket. The other woman, whose illness was diagnosed when she was eighteen, a nursing student engaged to a young doctor, finished her training, married her doctor, accompanied him to Germany when he was in the service, bore three sons and a daughter, now grown and gone. When she can, she travels with her husband; she plays bridge, embroiders, swims regularly; she works, like me, as a symptomatic-patient instructor of medical students in neurology. Guess which woman I hope to be.

At the beginning, I thought about having MS almost incessantly. And because of the unpredictable course of the disease, my thoughts were always terrified. Each night I'd get into bed wondering whether I'd get out again the next morning, whether I'd be able to see, to speak, to hold a pen between my fingers. Knowing that the day might come when I'd be physically incapable of killing myself, I thought perhaps I ought to do so right away, while I still had the strength. Gradually I came to understand that the Nancy who might one day lie inert under a bedsheet, arms and legs paralyzed, unable to feed or bathe herself, unable to reach out for a gun, a bottle of pills, was not the Nancy I was at present, and that I could not presume to make decisions for that future Nancy, who might well not want in the least to die. Now the only provision I've made for the future Nancy is that when the time comes—and it is likely to come in the form of pneumonia, friend to the weak and the old—I am not to be treated with machines and medications. If she is unable to communicate by then, I hope she will be satisfied with these terms.

Thinking all the time about having MS grew tiresome and intrusive, especially in the large and tragic mode in which I was accustomed to considering my plight. Months and even years went by without catastrophe (at least without one related to MS), and really I was awfully busy, what with George and children and snakes and students and poems, and I hadn't the time, let alone the inclination, to devote myself to being a disease. Too, the richer my life became, the funnier it seemed, as though there were some connection between largesse and laughter, and so my tragic stance began to waver until, even with the aid of a brace and a cane, I couldn't hold it for very long at a time.

After several years I was satisfied with my adjustment. I had suffered my grief and fury and terror, I thought, but now I was at ease with my lot. Then one summer day I set out with George and the children across the desert for a vacation in California. Part way to Yuma I became aware that my right leg felt funny. "I think I've had an exacerbation," I told George. "What shall we do?" he asked. "I think we'd better get the hell to California," I said, "because I don't know whether I'll ever make it again." So we went on to San Diego and then to Orange, up the Pacific Coast Highway to Santa Cruz, across to Yosemite, down to Sequoia and Joshua Tree, and so back over the desert to home. It was a fine two-week trip, filled with friends and fair weather, and I wouldn't have missed it for the world, though I did in fact make it back to California two years later. Nor would there have been any point in missing it, since in MS, once the symptoms have appeared, the neurological damage has been done, and there's no way to predict or prevent that damage.

The incident spoiled my self-satisfaction, however. It renewed my grief and fury and terror, and I learned that one never finishes adjusting to MS. I don't know now why I thought one would. One does not, after all, finish adjusting to life, and MS is simply a fact of my life—not my favorite fact, of course—but as ordinary as my nose and my tropical fish and my yellow Mazda station wagon. It may at any time get worse, but no amount of worry or anticipation can prepare me for a new loss. My life is a lesson in losses. I learn one at a time.

And I had best be patient in the learning, since I'll have to do it like   30
it or not. As any rock fan knows, you can't always get what you want.[1]
Particularly when you have MS. You can't, for example, get cured. In recent years researchers and the organizations that fund research have started to pay MS some attention even though it isn't fatal; perhaps they have begun to see that life is something other than a quantitative phenomenon, that one may be very much alive for a very long time in a life that isn't worth living. The researchers have made some progress toward understanding the mechanism of the disease: It may well be an autoimmune reaction triggered by a slow-acting virus. But they are

[1]Title of a 1969 song by the Rolling Stones.

nowhere near its prevention, control, or cure. And most of us want to be cured. Some, unable to accept incurability, grasp at one treatment after another, no matter how bizarre: megavitamin therapy, gluten-free diet, injections of cobra venom, hypothermal suits, lymphocytopharesis, hyperbaric chambers. Many treatments are probably harmless enough, but none are curative.

The absence of a cure often makes MS patients bitter toward their doctors. Doctors are, after all, the priests of modern society, the new shamans, whose business is to heal, and many an MS patient roves from one to another, searching for the "good" doctor who will make him well. Doctors too think of themselves as healers, and for this reason many have trouble dealing with MS patients, whose disease in its intransigence defeats their aims and mocks their skills. Too few doctors, it is true, treat their patients as whole human beings, but the reverse is also true. I have always tried to be gentle with my doctors, who often have more at stake in terms of ego than I do. I may be frustrated, maddened, depressed by the incurability of my disease, but I am not diminished by it, and they are. When I push myself up from my seat in the waiting room and stumble toward them, I incarnate the limitation of their powers. The least I can do is refuse to press on their tenderest spots.

This gentleness is part of the reason that I'm not sorry to be a cripple. I didn't have it before. Perhaps I'd have developed it anyway—how could I know such a thing?—and I wish I had more of it, but I'm glad of what I have. It has opened and enriched my life enormously, this sense that my frailty and need must be mirrored in others, that in searching for and shaping a stable core in a life wrenched by change and loss, change and loss, I must recognize the same process, under individual conditions, in the lives around me. I do not deprecate such knowledge, however I've come by it.

All the same, if a cure were found, would I take it? In a minute. I may be a cripple, but I'm only occasionally a loony and never a saint. Anyway, in my brand of theology God doesn't give bonus points for a limp. I'd take a cure; I just don't need one. A friend who also has MS startled me once by asking, "Do you ever say to yourself, 'Why me, Lord?' " "No, Michael, I don't," I told him, "because whenever I try, the only response I can think of is 'Why not?' " If I could make a cosmic deal, who would I put in my place? What in my life would I give up in exchange for sound limbs and a thrilling rush of energy? No one. Nothing. I might as well do the job myself. Now that I'm getting the hang of it.

STUDY QUESTIONS

1. In addition to the physical changes that MS brings, Mairs notes something less concrete that can often be lost to the disease (she calls it "the easiest to lose and the hardest to survive without"). What is it?

2. After reading this essay, how would you DESCRIBE the author's ETHOS? List three words or phrases that describe it and find a passage in the essay that supports each term.

3. Mairs states that she applies the word "cripple" only to herself, not to other people (paragraph 4). In another essay, she further notes her reasons for doing so: "because it is a word many people with disabilities find deeply offensive, I apply it only to myself, and so it reminds me that I am not speaking for others." Why do you think Mairs finds it important to remind herself that she is speaking as an individual, not representing a larger group?

4. How does Mairs use the word "faking" as a TRANSITION between paragraphs 16 and 17?

5. *For Writing.* One of the engaging features of this essay is Mairs's frequent references—to other texts, both literary and popular. Select one of these references, RESEARCH its origins, and ANALYZE how the allusion contributes to the point Mairs makes in this piece.

JOYCE CAROL OATES { *Where Are You Going, Where Have You Been?*

JOYCE CAROL OATES (b. 1938) is a prolific and versatile writer whose work is popular both with the general reading public (her 1996 novel *We Were the Mulvaneys* was featured on Oprah's Book Club) and in academia, where her fiction and poetry often appear on the syllabi of college courses. Oates was raised in a rural area near Lockport, New York, and earned her BA at Syracuse University; as a student there, she won a fiction contest sponsored by *Mademoiselle* magazine. She went on to obtain an MA in English at the University of Wisconsin. She has taught at the University of Windsor and is currently a professor of creative writing at Princeton. The author of more than one hundred novels, novellas, and short story collections, as well as many books of poetry, plays, and essays, Oates received the National Book Award in 1970 for her novel *them*, which, like much of her fiction, reimagines historical events in fictional form. Her other novels include *Black Water* (1993), *What I Lived For* (1994), *Blonde* (2000), and *The Gravedigger's Daughter* (2007).

"Where Are You Going, Where Have You Been?" (1966) is Oates's most anthologized short story. It presents a vivid picture of the seemingly conventional life of its teenaged protagonist, Connie, and describes what happens when an element of danger is introduced. As you read, consider how the story both reflects and undercuts the popular culture of the early 1960s.

"Where Are You Going, Where Have You Been?" from *The Wheel of Love and Other Stories* by author Joyce Carol Oates. Copyright © 1970. Used by permission of John Hawkins & Associates, Inc.

for Bob Dylan[1]

HER NAME WAS CONNIE. SHE was fifteen and she had a quick, nervous giggling habit of craning her neck to glance into mirrors or checking other people's faces to make sure her own was all right. Her mother, who noticed everything and knew everything and who hadn't much reason any longer to look at her own face, always scolded Connie about it. "Stop gawking at yourself. Who are you? You think you're so pretty?" she would say. Connie would raise her eyebrows at these familiar old complaints and look right through her mother, into a shadowy vision of herself as she was right at that moment: she knew she was pretty and that was everything. Her mother had been pretty once too, if you could believe those old snapshots in the album, but now her looks were gone and that was why she was always after Connie.

"Why don't you keep your room clean like your sister? How've you got your hair fixed—what the hell stinks? Hair spray? You don't see your sister using that junk."

Her sister June was twenty-four and still lived at home. She was a secretary in the high school Connie attended, and if that wasn't bad enough—with her in the same building—she was so plain and chunky and steady that Connie had to hear her praised all the time by her mother and her mother's sisters. June did this, June did that, she saved money and helped clean the house and cooked and Connie couldn't do a thing, her mind was all filled with trashy daydreams. Their father was away at work most of the time and when he came home he wanted supper and he read the newspaper at supper and after supper he went to bed. He didn't bother talking much to them, but around his bent head Connie's mother kept picking at her until Connie wished her mother was dead and she herself was dead and it was all over. "She makes me want to throw up sometimes," she complained to her friends. She had a high, breathless, amused voice that made everything she said sound a little forced, whether it was sincere or not.

---

[1] The mood and tone of this story was inspired by American folk and rock singer and songwriter Bob Dylan (b. 1941).

There was one good thing: June went places with girl friends of hers, girls who were just as plain and steady as she, and so when Connie wanted to do that her mother had no objections. The father of Connie's best girl friend drove the girls the three miles to town and left them at a shopping plaza so they could walk through the stores or go to a movie, and when he came to pick them up again at eleven he never bothered to ask what they had done.

They must have been familiar sights, walking around the shopping   5
plaza in their shorts and flat ballerina slippers that always scuffed the sidewalk, with charm bracelets jingling on their thin wrists; they would lean together to whisper and laugh secretly if someone passed who amused or interested them. Connie had long dark blond hair that drew anyone's eye to it, and she wore part of it pulled up on her head and puffed out and the rest of it she let fall down her back. She wore a pullover jersey blouse that looked one way when she was at home and another way when she was away from home. Everything about her had two sides to it, one for home and one for anywhere that was not home: her walk, which could be childlike and bobbing, or languid enough to make anyone think she was hearing music in her head; her mouth, which was pale and smirking most of the time, but bright and pink on these evenings out; her laugh, which was cynical and drawling at home—"Ha, ha, very funny,"—but high-pitched and nervous anywhere else, like the jingling of the charms on her bracelet.

Sometimes they did go shopping or to a movie, but sometimes they went across the highway, ducking fast across the busy road, to a drive-in restaurant where older kids hung out. The restaurant was shaped like a big bottle, though squatter than a real bottle, and on its cap was a revolving figure of a grinning boy holding a hamburger aloft. One night in midsummer they ran across, breathless with daring, and right away someone leaned out a car window and invited them over, but it was just a boy from high school they didn't like. It made them feel good to be able to ignore him. They went up through the maze of parked and cruising cars to the bright-lit, fly-infested restaurant, their faces pleased and expectant as if they were entering a sacred building that loomed up out of the night to give them what haven and blessing they yearned for.

They sat at the counter and crossed their legs at the ankles, their thin shoulders rigid with excitement, and listened to the music that made everything so good: the music was always in the background, like music at a church service; it was something to depend upon.

A boy named Eddie came in to talk with them. He sat backwards on his stool, turning himself jerkily around in semicircles and then stopping and turning back again, and after a while he asked Connie if she would like something to eat. She said she would and so she tapped her friend's arm on her way out—her friend pulled her face up into a brave, droll look—and Connie said she would meet her at eleven, across the way. "I just hate to leave her like that," Connie said earnestly, but the boy said that she wouldn't be alone for long. So they went out to his car, and on the way Connie couldn't help but let her eyes wander over the windshields and faces all around her, her face gleaming with a joy that had nothing to do with Eddie or even this place; it might have been the music. She drew her shoulders up and sucked in her breath with the pure pleasure of being alive, and just at that moment she happened to glance at a face just a few feet from hers. It was a boy with shaggy black hair, in a convertible jalopy painted gold. He stared at her and then his lips widened into a grin. Connie slit her eyes at him and turned away, but she couldn't help glancing back and there he was, still watching her. He wagged a finger and laughed and said, "Gonna get you, baby," and Connie turned away again without Eddie noticing anything.

She spent three hours with him, at the restaurant where they ate hamburgers and drank Cokes in wax cups that were always sweating, and then down an alley a mile or so away, and when he left her off at five to eleven only the movie house was still open at the plaza. Her girl friend was there, talking with a boy. When Connie came up, the two girls smiled at each other and Connie said, "How was the movie?" and the girl said, "*You* should know." They rode off with the girl's father, sleepy and pleased, and Connie couldn't help but look back at the darkened shopping plaza with its big empty parking lot and its signs that were faded and ghostly now, and over at the drive-in restaurant where cars were still circling tirelessly. She couldn't hear the music at this distance.

Next morning June asked her how the movie was and Connie said, "So-so."

She and that girl and occasionally another girl went out several 10
times a week, and the rest of the time Connie spent around the house—
it was summer vacation—getting in her mother's way and thinking,
dreaming about the boys she met. But all the boys fell back and dis-
solved into a single face that was not even a face but an idea, a feeling,
mixed up with the urgent insistent pounding of the music and the
humid night air of July. Connie's mother kept dragging her back to the
daylight by finding things for her to do or saying suddenly, "What's
this about the Pettinger girl?"

And Connie would say nervously, "Oh, her. That dope." She always
drew thick clear lines between herself and such girls, and her mother
was simple and kind enough to believe it. Her mother was so simple,
Connie thought, that it was maybe cruel to fool her so much. Her
mother went scuffling around the house in old bedroom slippers and
complained over the telephone to one sister about the other, then the
other called up and the two of them complained about the third one. If
June's name was mentioned her mother's tone was approving, and
if Connie's name was mentioned it was disapproving. This did not
really mean she disliked Connie, and actually Connie thought that her
mother preferred her to June just because she was prettier, but the two
of them kept up a pretense of exasperation, a sense that they were tugging and struggling over something of little value to either of them.
Sometimes, over coffee, they were almost friends, but something
would come up—some vexation that was like a fly buzzing suddenly
around their heads—and their faces went hard with contempt.

One Sunday Connie got up at eleven—none of them bothered with
church—and washed her hair so that it could dry all day long in the
sun. Her parents and sister were going to a barbecue at an aunt's house
and Connie said no, she wasn't interested, rolling her eyes to let her
mother know just what she thought of it. "Stay home alone then," her
mother said sharply. Connie sat out back in a lawn chair and watched
them drive away, her father quiet and bald, hunched around so that he
could back the car out, her mother with a look that was still angry and
not at all softened through the windshield, and in the back seat poor

old June, all dressed up as if she didn't know what a barbecue was, with all the running yelling kids and the flies. Connie sat with her eyes closed in the sun, dreaming and dazed with the warmth about her as if this were a kind of love, the caresses of love, and her mind slipped over onto thoughts of the boy she had been with the night before and how nice he had been, how sweet it always was, not the way someone like June would suppose but sweet, gentle, the way it was in movies and promised in songs; and when she opened her eyes she hardly knew where she was, the back yard ran off into weeds and a fence-like line of trees and behind it the sky was perfectly blue and still. The asbestos "ranch house" that was now three years old startled her—it looked small. She shook her head as if to get awake.

It was too hot. She went inside the house and turned on the radio to drown out the quiet. She sat on the edge of her bed, barefoot, and listened for an hour and a half to a program called XYZ Sunday Jamboree, record after record of hard, fast, shrieking songs she sang along with, interspersed by exclamations from "Bobby King": "An' look here, you girls at Napoleon's—Son and Charley want you to pay real close attention to this song coming up!"

And Connie paid close attention herself, bathed in a glow of slow-pulsed joy that seemed to rise mysteriously out of the music itself and lay languidly about the airless little room, breathed in and breathed out with each gentle rise and fall of her chest.

After a while she heard a car coming up the drive. She sat up at once, startled, because it couldn't be her father so soon. The gravel kept crunching all the way in from the road—the driveway was long— and Connie ran to the window. It was a car she didn't know. It was an open jalopy, painted a bright gold that caught the sunlight opaquely. Her heart began to pound and her fingers snatched at her hair, checking it, and she whispered, "Christ. Christ," wondering how bad she looked. The car came to a stop at the side door and the horn sounded four short taps, as if this were a signal Connie knew.

She went into the kitchen and approached the door slowly, then hung out the screen door, her bare toes curling down off the step. There were two boys in the car and now she recognized the driver: he had shaggy, shabby black hair that looked crazy as a wig and he was grinning at her.

15

"I ain't late, am I?" he said.

"Who the hell do you think you are?" Connie said.

"Toldja I'd be out, didn't I?"

"I don't even know who you are."   20

She spoke sullenly, careful to show no interest or pleasure, and he spoke in a fast, bright monotone. Connie looked past him to the other boy, taking her time. He had fair brown hair, with a lock that fell onto his forehead. His sideburns gave him a fierce, embarrassed look, but so far he hadn't even bothered to glance at her. Both boys wore sunglasses. The driver's glasses were metallic and mirrored everything in miniature.

"You wanta come for a ride?" he said.

Connie smirked and let her hair fall loose over one shoulder.

"Don'tcha like my car? New paint job," he said. "Hey."

"What?"   25

"You're cute."

She pretended to fidget, chasing flies away from the door.

"Don'tcha believe me, or what?" he said.

"Look, I don't even know who you are," Connie said in disgust.

"Hey, Ellie's got a radio, see. Mine broke down." He lifted his   30
friend's arm and showed her the little transistor radio the boy was holding, and now Connie began to hear the music. It was the same program that was playing inside the house.

"Bobby King?" she said.

"I listen to him all the time. I think he's great."

"He's kind of great," Connie said reluctantly.

"Listen, that guy's *great*. He knows where the action is."

Connie blushed a little, because the glasses made it impossible for   35
her to see just what this boy was looking at. She couldn't decide if she liked him or if he was just a jerk, and so she dawdled in the doorway and wouldn't come down or go back inside. She said, "What's all that stuff painted on your car?"

"Can'tcha read it?" He opened the door very carefully, as if he were afraid it might fall off. He slid out just as carefully, planting his feet firmly on the ground, the tiny metallic world in his glasses slowing down like gelatine hardening, and in the midst of it Connie's bright green blouse. "This here is my name, to begin with," he said. ARNOLD

FRIEND was written in tarlike black letters on the side, with a drawing of a round, grinning face that reminded Connie of a pumpkin, except it wore sunglasses. "I wanta introduce myself, I'm Arnold Friend and that's my real name and I'm gonna be your friend, honey, and inside the car's Ellie Oscar, he's kinda shy." Ellie brought his transistor radio up to his shoulder and balanced it there. "Now, these numbers are a secret code, honey," Arnold Friend explained. He read off the numbers 33, 19, 17 and raised his eyebrows at her to see what she thought of that, but she didn't think much of it. The left rear fender had been smashed and around it was written, on the gleaming gold background: DONE BY CRAZY WOMAN DRIVER. Connie had to laugh at that. Arnold Friend was pleased at her laughter and looked up at her. "Around the other side's a lot more—you wanta come and see them?"

"No."

"Why not?"

"Why should I?"

"Don'tcha wanta see what's on the car? Don'tcha wanta go for a ride?"   40

"I don't know."

"Why not?"

"I got things to do."

"Like what?"

"Things."   45

He laughed as if she had said something funny. He slapped his thighs. He was standing in a strange way, leaning back against the car as if he were balancing himself. He wasn't tall, only an inch or so taller than she would be if she came down to him. Connie liked the way he was dressed, which was the way all of them dressed: tight faded jeans stuffed into black, scuffed boots, a belt that pulled his waist in and showed how lean he was, and a white pull-over shirt that was a little soiled and showed the hard small muscles of his arms and shoulders. He looked as if he probably did hard work, lifting and carrying things. Even his neck looked muscular. And his face was a familiar face, somehow: the jaw and chin and cheeks slightly darkened because he hadn't shaved for a day or two, and the nose long and hawklike, sniffing as if she were a treat he was going to gobble up and it was all a joke.

"Connie, you ain't telling the truth. This is your day set aside for a ride with me and you know it," he said, still laughing. The way he straightened and recovered from his fit of laughing showed that it had been all fake.

"How do you know what my name is?" she said suspiciously.

"It's Connie."

"Maybe and maybe not."   50

"I know my Connie," he said, wagging his finger. Now she remembered him even better, back at the restaurant, and her cheeks warmed at the thought of how she had sucked in her breath just at the moment she passed him—how she must have looked to him. And he had remembered her. "Ellie and I come out here especially for you," he said. "Ellie can sit in back. How about it?"

"Where?"

"Where what?"

"Where're we going?"

He looked at her. He took off the sunglasses and she saw how pale   55
the skin around his eyes was, like holes that were not in shadow but instead in light. His eyes were like chips of broken glass that catch the light in an amiable way. He smiled. It was as if the idea of going for a ride somewhere, to someplace, was a new idea to him.

"Just for a ride, Connie sweetheart."

"I never said my name was Connie," she said.

"But I know what it is. I know your name and all about you, lots of things," Arnold Friend said. He had not moved yet but stood still leaning back against the side of his jalopy. "I took a special interest in you, such a pretty girl, and found out all about you—like I know your parents and sister are gone somewhere and I know where and how long they're going to be gone, and I know who you were with last night, and your best girl friend's name is Betty. Right?"

He spoke in a simple lilting voice, exactly as if he were reciting the words to a song. His smile assured her that everything was fine. In the car Ellie turned up the volume on his radio and did not bother to look around at them.

"Ellie can sit in the back seat," Arnold Friend said. He indicated his   60
friend with a casual jerk of his chin, as if Ellie did not count and she should not bother with him.

"How'd you find out all that stuff?" Connie said.

"Listen: Betty Schultz and Tony Fitch and Jimmy Pettinger and Nancy Pettinger," he said in a chant. "Raymond Stanley and Bob Hutter—"

"Do you know all those kids?"

"I know everybody."

"Look, you're kidding. You're not from around here." 65

"Sure."

"But—how come we never saw you before?"

"Sure you saw me before," he said. He looked down at his boots, as if he were a little offended. "You just don't remember."

"I guess I'd remember you," Connie said.

"Yeah?" He looked up at this, beaming. He was pleased. He began to 70 mark time with the music from Ellie's radio, tapping his fists lightly together. Connie looked away from his smile to the car, which was painted so bright it almost hurt her eyes to look at it. She looked at that name, ARNOLD FRIEND. And up at the front fender was an expression that was familiar—MAN THE FLYING SAUCERS. It was an expression kids had used the year before but didn't use this year. She looked at it for a while as if the words meant something to her that she did not yet know.

"What're you thinking about? Huh?" Arnold Friend demanded. "Not worried about your hair blowing around in the car, are you?"

"No."

"Think I maybe can't drive good?"

"How do I know?"

"You're a hard girl to handle. How come?" he said. "Don't you 75 know I'm your friend? Didn't you see me put my sign in the air when you walked by?"

"What sign?"

"My sign." And he drew an X in the air, leaning out toward her. They were maybe ten feet apart. After his hand fell back to his side the X was still in the air, almost visible. Connie let the screen door close and stood perfectly still inside it, listening to the music from her radio and the boy's blend together. She stared at Arnold Friend. He stood there so stiffly relaxed, pretending to be relaxed, with one hand idly on the door handle as if he were keeping himself up that way and had no intention of ever moving again. She recognized most things about him, the tight jeans that showed his thighs and buttocks and the greasy leather boots and the tight shirt, and even that slippery friendly smile of his, that sleepy dreamy smile that all the boys used to get across ideas they didn't want to put into words. She recognized all this and also the singsong way he talked, slightly mocking, kidding, but serious and a little melancholy, and she recognized the way he tapped one fist against the other in homage to the perpetual music behind him. But all these things did not come together.

She said suddenly, "Hey, how old are you?"

His smiled faded. She could see then that he wasn't a kid, he was much older—thirty, maybe more. At this knowledge her heart began to pound faster.

"That's a crazy thing to ask. Can'tcha see I'm your own age?" 80

"Like hell you are."

"Or maybe a coupla years older. I'm eighteen."

"Eighteen?" she said doubtfully.

He grinned to reassure her and lines appeared at the corners of his mouth. His teeth were big and white. He grinned so broadly his eyes became slits and she saw how thick the lashes were, thick and black as if painted with a black tarlike material. Then, abruptly, he seemed to become embarrassed and looked over his shoulder at Ellie. "*Him,* he's crazy," he said. "Ain't he a riot? He's a nut, a real character." Ellie was still listening to the music. His sunglasses told nothing about what he was thinking. He wore a bright orange shirt unbuttoned halfway to show his chest, which was a pale, bluish chest and not muscular like Arnold Friend's. His shirt collar was turned up all around and the very tips of the collar pointed out past his chin as if they were protecting him. He was pressing the transistor radio up against his ear and sat there in a kind of daze, right in the sun.

"He's kinda strange," Connie said. 85

"Hey, she says you're kinda strange! Kinda strange!" Arnold Friend cried. He pounded on the car to get Ellie's attention. Ellie turned for the first time and Connie saw with shock that he wasn't a kid either— he had a fair, hairless face, cheeks reddened slightly as if the veins grew too close to the surface of his skin, the face of a forty-year-old baby.

Connie felt a wave of dizziness rise in her at this sight and she stared at him as if waiting for something to change the shock of the moment, make it all right again. Ellie's lips kept shaping words, mumbling along with the words blasting in his ear.

"Maybe you two better go away," Connie said faintly.

"What? How come?" Arnold Friend cried. "We come out here to take you for a ride. It's Sunday." He had the voice of the man on the radio now. It was the same voice, Connie thought. "Don'tcha know it's Sunday all day? And honey, no matter who you were with last night, today you're with Arnold Friend and don't you forget it! Maybe you better step out here," he said, and this last was in a different voice. It was a little flatter, as if the heat was finally getting to him.

"No. I got things to do."

"Hey." 90

"You two better leave."

"We ain't leaving until you come with us."

"Like hell I am—"

"Connie, don't fool around with me. I mean—I mean, don't fool *around*," he said, shaking his head. He laughed incredulously. He placed his sunglasses on top of his head, carefully, as if he were indeed wearing a wig, and brought the stems down behind his ears. Connie stared at him, another wave of dizziness and fear rising in her so that for a moment he wasn't even in focus but was just a blur standing there against his gold car, and she had the idea that he had driven up the driveway all right but had come from nowhere before that and belonged nowhere and that everything about him and even about the music that was so familiar to her was only half real.

"If my father comes and sees you—" 95

"He ain't coming. He's at a barbecue."

"How do you know that?"

"Aunt Tillie's. Right now they're—uh—they're drinking. Sitting around," he said vaguely, squinting as if he were staring all the way to town and over to Aunt Tillie's back yard. Then the vision seemed to get clear and he nodded energetically. "Yeah. Sitting around. There's your sister in a blue dress, huh? And high heels, the poor sad bitch—

nothing like you, sweetheart! And your mother's helping some fat
woman with the corn, they're cleaning the corn—husking the corn—"

"What fat woman?" Connie cried.

"How do I know what fat woman, I don't know every goddamn fat   100
woman in the world!" Arnold Friend laughed.

"Oh, that's Mrs. Hornsby. . . . Who invited her?" Connie said. She
felt a little lightheaded. Her breath was coming quickly.

"She's too fat. I don't like them fat. I like them the way you are,
honey," he said, smiling sleepily at her. They stared at each other for a
while through the screen door. He said softly, "Now, what you're going
to do is this: you're going to come out that door. You're going to sit up
front with me and Ellie's going to sit in the back, the hell with Ellie,
right? This isn't Ellie's date. You're my date. I'm your lover, honey."

"What? You're crazy—"

"Yes, I'm your lover. You don't know what that is but you will," he
said. "I know that too. I know all about you. But look: it's real nice and
you couldn't ask for nobody better than me, or more polite. I always
keep my word. I'll tell you how it is, I'm always nice at first, the first
time. I'll hold you so tight you won't think you have to try to get
away or pretend anything because you'll know you can't. And I'll
come inside you where it's all secret and you'll give in to me and you'll
love me—"

"Shut up! You're crazy!" Connie said. She backed away from the   105
door. She put her hands up against her ears as if she'd heard something
terrible, something not meant for her. "People don't talk like that,
you're crazy," she muttered. Her heart was almost too big now for her
chest and its pumping made sweat break out all over her. She looked
out to see Arnold Friend pause and then take a step toward the porch,
lurching. He almost fell. But, like a clever drunken man, he managed to
catch his balance. He wobbled in his high boots and grabbed hold of
one of the porch posts.

"Honey?" he said. "You still listening?"

"Get the hell out of here!"

"Be nice, honey. Listen."

"I'm going to call the police—"

He wobbled again and out of the side of his mouth came a fast spat   110
curse, an aside not meant for her to hear. But even this "Christ!"
sounded forced. Then he began to smile again. She watched this smile
come, awkward as if he were smiling from inside a mask. His whole
face was a mask, she thought wildly, tanned down to his throat but then
running out as if he had plastered make-up on his face but had forgotten about his throat.

"Honey—? Listen, here's how it is. I always tell the truth and I
promise you this: I ain't coming in that house after you."

"You better not! I'm going to call the police if you—if you don't—"

"Honey," he said, talking right through her voice, "honey, I'm not
coming in there but you are coming out here. You know why?"

She was panting. The kitchen looked like a place she had never seen
before, some room she had run inside but that wasn't good enough,
wasn't going to help her. The kitchen window had never had a curtain, after three years, and there were dishes in the sink for her to do—
probably—and if you ran your hand across the table you'd probably
feel something sticky there.

"You listening, honey? Hey?"   115

"—going to call the police—"

"Soon as you touch the phone I don't need to keep my promise and
can come inside. You won't want that."

She rushed forward and tried to lock the door. Her fingers were
shaking. "But why lock it," Arnold Friend said gently, talking right into
her face. "It's just a screen door. It's just nothing." One of his boots was
at a strange angle, as if his foot wasn't in it. It pointed out to the left,
bent at the ankle. "I mean, anybody can break through a screen door
and glass and wood and iron or anything else if he needs to, anybody
at all, and specially Arnold Friend. If the place got lit up with a fire,
honey, you'd come runnin' out into my arms, right into my arms an'
safe at home—like you knew I was your lover and'd stopped fooling
around. I don't mind a nice shy girl but I don't like no fooling around."
Part of those words were spoken with a slight rhythmic lilt, and Connie
somehow recognized them—the echo of a song from last year, about a
girl rushing into her boy friend's arms and coming home again—

Connie stood barefoot on the linoleum floor, staring at him. "What do you want?" she whispered.

"I want you," he said.   120

"What?"

"Seen you that night and thought, that's the one, yes sir. I never needed to look anymore."

"But my father's coming back. He's coming to get me. I had to wash my hair first—" She spoke in a dry, rapid voice, hardly raising it for him to hear.

"No, your daddy is not coming and yes, you had to wash your hair and you washed it for me. It's nice and shining and all for me. I thank you, sweetheart," he said with a mock bow, but again he almost lost his balance. He had to bend and adjust his boots. Evidently his feet did not go all the way down; the boots must have been stuffed with something so that he would seem taller. Connie stared out at him and behind him at Ellie in the car, who seemed to be looking off toward Connie's right, into nothing. This Ellie said, pulling the words out of the air one after another as if he were just discovering them, "You want me to pull out the phone?"

"Shut your mouth and keep it shut," Arnold Friend said, his face   125
red from bending over or maybe from embarrassment because Connie had seen his boots. "This ain't none of your business."

"What—what are you doing? What do you want?" Connie said. "If I call the police they'll get you, they'll arrest you—"

"Promise was not to come in unless you touch that phone, and I'll keep that promise," he said. He resumed his erect position and tried to force his shoulders back. He sounded like a hero in a movie, declaring something important. But he spoke too loudly and it was as if he were speaking to someone behind Connie. "I ain't made plans for coming in that house where I don't belong but just for you to come out to me, the way you should. Don't you know who I am?"

"You're crazy," she whispered. She backed away from the door but did not want to go into another part of the house, as if this would give him permission to come through the door. "What do you . . . you're crazy, you. . . ."

"Huh? What're you saying, honey?"

Her eyes darted everywhere in the kitchen. She could not remem- 130
ber what it was, this room.

"This is how it is, honey: you come out and we'll drive away, have a
nice ride. But if you don't come out we're gonna wait till your people
come home and then they're all going to get it."

"You want that telephone pulled out?" Ellie said. He held the radio
away from his ear and grimaced, as if without the radio the air was too
much for him.

"I toldja shut up, Ellie," Arnold Friend said, "you're deaf, get a hearing aid, right? Fix yourself up. This little girl's no trouble and's gonna
be nice to me, so Ellie keep to yourself, this ain't your date—right?
Don't hem in on me, don't hog, don't crush, don't bird dog, don't trail
me," he said in a rapid, meaningless voice, as if he were running
through all the expressions he'd learned but was no longer sure which
of them was in style, then rushing on to new ones, making them up
with his eyes closed. "Don't crawl under my fence, don't squeeze in my
chipmunk hole, don't sniff my glue, suck my Popsicle, keep your own
greasy fingers on yourself!" He shaded his eyes and peered in at
Connie, who was backed against the kitchen table. "Don't mind him,
honey, he's just a creep. He's a dope. Right? I'm the boy for you and
like I said, you come out here nice like a lady and give me your hand,
and nobody else gets hurt, I mean, your nice old bald-headed daddy
and your mummy and your sister in her high heels. Because listen: why
bring them in this?"

"Leave me alone," Connie whispered.

"Hey, you know that old woman down the road, the one with the 135
chickens and stuff—you know her?"

"She's dead!"

"Dead? What? You know her?" Arnold Friend said.

"She's dead—"

"Don't you like her?"

"She's dead—she's—she isn't here any more—" 140

"But don't you like her, I mean, you got something against her?
Some grudge or something?" Then his voice dipped as if he were con-

scious of a rudeness. He touched the sunglasses perched up on top of his head as if to make sure they were still there. "Now, you be a good girl."

"What are you going to do?"

"Just two things, or maybe three," Arnold Friend said. "But I promise it won't last long and you'll like me the way you get to like people you're close to. You will. It's all over for you here, so come on out. You don't want your people in any trouble, do you?"

She turned and bumped against a chair or something, hurting her leg, but she ran into the back room and picked up the telephone. Something roared in her ear, a tiny roaring, and she was so sick with fear that she could do nothing but listen to it—the telephone was clammy and very heavy and her fingers groped down to the dial but were too weak to touch it. She began to scream into the phone, into the roaring. She cried out, she cried for her mother, she felt her breath start jerking back and forth in her lungs as if it were something Arnold Friend was stabbing her with again and again with no tenderness. A noisy sorrowful wailing rose all about her and she was locked inside it the way she was locked inside this house.

After a while she could hear again. She was sitting on the floor with her wet back against the wall.   145

Arnold Friend was saying from the door, "That's a good girl. Put the phone back."

She kicked the phone away from her.

"No, honey. Pick it up. Put it back right."

She picked it up and put it back. The dial tone stopped.

"That's a good girl. Now, you come outside."   150

She was hollow with what had been fear but what was now just an emptiness. All that screaming had blasted it out of her. She sat, one leg cramped under her, and deep inside her brain was something like a pinpoint of light that kept going and would not let her relax. She thought, I'm not going to see my mother again. She thought, I'm not going to sleep in my bed again. Her bright green blouse was all wet.

Arnold Friend said, in a gentle-loud voice that was like a stage voice, "The place where you came from ain't there any more, and where you had in mind to go is cancelled out. This place you are now—inside your daddy's house—is nothing but a cardboard box I can knock down any time. You know that and always did know it. You hear me?"

She thought, I have got to think. I have got to know what to do.

"We'll go out to a nice field, out in the country here where it smells so nice and it's sunny," Arnold Friend said. "I'll have my arms tight around you so you won't need to try to get away and I'll show you what love is like, what it does. The hell with this house! It looks solid all right," he said. He ran a fingernail down the screen and the noise did not make Connie shiver, as it would have the day before. "Now, put your hand on your heart, honey. Feel that? That feels solid too but we know better. Be nice to me, be sweet like you can because what else is there for a girl like you but to be sweet and pretty and give in?—and get away before her people come back?"

She felt her pounding heart. Her hand seemed to enclose it. She   155
thought for the first time in her life that it was nothing that was hers, that belonged to her, but just a pounding, living thing inside this body that wasn't really hers either.

"You don't want them to get hurt," Arnold Friend went on. "Now, get up, honey. Get up all by yourself."

She stood.

"Now, turn this way. That's right. Come over here to me.—Ellie, put that away, didn't I tell you? You dope. You miserable creepy dope," Arnold Friend said. His words were not angry but only part of an incantation. The incantation was kindly. "Now, come out through the kitchen to me, honey, and let's see a smile, try it, you're a brave, sweet little girl and now they're eating corn and hot dogs cooked to bursting over an outdoor fire, and they don't know one thing about you and never did and honey, you're better than them because not a one of them would have done this for you."

Connie felt the linoleum under her feet; it was cool. She brushed her hair back out of her eyes. Arnold Friend let go of the post tentatively and opened his arms for her, his elbows pointing in toward each other and his wrists limp, to show that this was an embarrassed embrace and a little mocking, he didn't want to make her self-conscious.

She put out her hand against the screen. She watched herself push   160 the door slowly open as if she were back safe somewhere in the other doorway, watching this body and this head of long hair moving out into the sunlight where Arnold Friend waited.

"My sweet little blue-eyed girl," he said in a half-sung sigh that had nothing to do with her brown eyes but was taken up just the same by the vast sunlit reaches of the land behind him and on all sides of him— so much land that Connie had never seen before and did not recognize except to know that she was going to it.

STUDY QUESTIONS

1. Where does Connie first encounter Arnold Friend? What does he do when he sees her?

2. One of the techniques that Oates uses to add DESCRIPTION to this story is to include many COMPARISONS (e.g., "as if" statements). Select one of these comparisons that you find interesting. ANALYZE what that comparison adds to the story and provide an updated version of it, using contemporary language.

3. This story is commonly discussed as a coming-of-age NARRATIVE that takes an unexpected turn. Where does the story include the expected components of a coming-of-age story? At what point does its turn to the unexpected take place? How is the story's outcome different from what you would expect from a conventional coming-of-age narrative?

4. The DIALOGUE between Connie and Arnold Friend moves the PLOT forward in the second half of the story. How would you CHARACTERIZE Arnold Friend's language? How does it change as the story progresses? How does it help to establish Arnold Friend's character?

5. *For Writing.* Arnold Friend is a puzzling character, one who is often interpreted symbolically. In an essay, analyze Arnold Friend as a SYMBOL: what do you think he symbolizes? What EVIDENCE from the story supports your analysis?

RICHARD RODRIGUEZ { *Aria*

RICHARD RODRIGUEZ (b. 1944), the son of Mexican immigrants, became
well known with the publication of the first of three autobiographical books:
Hunger of Memory: The Education of Richard Rodriguez (1982). It was
followed by *Days of Obligation: An Argument with My Mexican Father* (1992)
and *Brown: The Last Discovery of America* (2002). Rodriguez is an editor for
the Pacific News Service in San Francisco, an essayist for *The NewsHour with
Jim Lehrer*, and a contributing editor for *Harper's Magazine, U.S. News &
World Report*, and the Sunday "Opinion" page of the *Los Angeles Times*.

"Aria" comes from *Hunger of Memory* and explores the way the language
of Rodriguez's childhood shaped his feelings about the problems that
students encounter as they strive to learn English. Drawing upon his own
experiences, Rodriguez distinguishes the private language of home from the
public language of school and society. He then proceeds to apply this insight
to the controversial issue of bilingual education. His conclusion may
surprise you.

SUPPORTERS OF BILINGUAL EDUCATION TODAY imply that students
like me miss a great deal by not being taught in their family's language.
What they seem not to recognize is that, as a socially disadvantaged
child, I considered Spanish to be a private language. What I needed to
learn in school was that I had the right—and the obligation—to speak
the public language of *los gringos*.[1] The odd truth is that my first-grade
classmates could have become bilingual, in the conventional sense of

---

[1] The Americans (Spanish).

that word, more easily than I. Had they been taught (as upper-middle-class children are often taught early) a second language like Spanish or French, they could have regarded it simply as that: another public language. In my case such bilingualism could not have been so quickly achieved. What I did not believe was that I could speak a single public language.

Without question, it would have pleased me to hear my teachers address me in Spanish when I entered the classroom. I would have felt much less afraid. I would have trusted them and responded with ease. But I would have delayed—for how long postponed?—having to learn the language of public society. I would have evaded—and for how long could I have afforded to delay?—learning the great lesson of school, that I had a public identity.

Fortunately, my teachers were unsentimental about their responsibility. What they understood was that I needed to speak a public language. So their voices would search me out, asking me questions. Each time I'd hear them, I'd look up in surprise to see a nun's face frowning at me. I'd mumble, not really meaning to answer. The nun would persist, "Richard, stand up. Don't look at the floor. Speak up. Speak to the entire class, not just to me!" But I couldn't believe that the English language was mine to use. (In part, I did not want to believe it.) I continued to mumble. I resisted the teacher's demands. (Did I somehow suspect that once I learned public language my pleasing family life would be changed?) Silent, waiting for the bell to sound, I remained dazed, diffident, afraid.

Because I wrongly imagined that English was intrinsically a public language and Spanish an intrinsically private one, I easily noted the difference between classroom language and the language of home. At school, words were directed to a general audience of listeners. ("Boys and girls.") Words were meaningfully ordered. And the point was not self-expression alone but to make oneself understood by many others. The teacher quizzed: "Boys and girls, why do we use that word in this sentence? Could we think of a better word to use there? Would the sentence change its meaning if the words were differently arranged? And wasn't there a better way of saying much the same thing?" (I couldn't say. I wouldn't try to say.)

Three months. Five. Half a year passed. Unsmiling, ever watchful, 5
my teachers noted my silence. They began to connect my behavior
with the difficult progress my older sister and brother were making.
Until one Saturday morning three nuns arrived at the house to talk
to our parents. Stiffly, they sat on the blue living room sofa. From the
doorway of another room, spying the visitors, I noted the incongruity—the clash of two worlds, the faces and voices of school
intruding upon the familiar setting of home. I overheard one voice gently wondering, "Do your children speak only Spanish at home, Mrs.
Rodriguez?" While another voice added, "That Richard especially
seems so timid and shy."

That Rich-heard!

With great tact the visitors continued, "Is it possible for you and
your husband to encourage your children to practice their English
when they are home?" Of course, my parents complied. What would
they not do for their children's well-being? And how could they have
questioned the Church's authority which those women represented?
In an instant, they agreed to give up the language (the sounds) that had
revealed and accentuated our family's closeness. The moment after the
visitors left, the change was observed. *"Ahora,* speak to us *en inglés,"*[2]
my father and mother united to tell us.

At first, it seemed a kind of game. After dinner each night, the family gathered to practice "our" English. (It was still then *inglés,* a language foreign to us, so we felt drawn as strangers to it.) Laughing, we
would try to define words we could not pronounce. We played with
strange English sounds, often over-anglicizing our pronunciations.
And we filled the smiling gaps of our sentences with familiar Spanish
sounds. But that was cheating, somebody shouted. Everyone laughed.
In school, meanwhile, like my brother and sister, I was required to
attend a daily tutoring session. I needed a full year of special attention.
I also needed my teachers to keep my attention from straying in class
by calling out, *Rich-heard*—their English voices slowly prying loose
my ties to my other name, its three notes, *Ri-car-do.* Most of all I
needed to hear my mother and father speak to me in a moment of seri-

[2]*Now,* speak to us *in English.*

ousness in broken—suddenly heartbreaking—English. The scene was inevitable: One Saturday morning I entered the kitchen where my parents were talking in Spanish. I did not realize that they were talking in Spanish however until, at the moment they saw me, I heard their voices change to speak English. Those *gringo* sounds they uttered startled me. Pushed me away. In that moment of trivial misunderstanding and profound insight, I felt my throat twisted by unsounded grief. I turned quickly and left the room. But I had no place to escape to with Spanish. (The spell was broken.) My brother and sisters were speaking English in another part of the house.

Again and again in the days following, increasingly angry, I was obliged to hear my mother and father: "Speak to us *en inglés.*" (*Speak.*) Only then did I determine to learn classroom English. Weeks after, it happened: One day in school I raised my hand to volunteer an answer. I spoke out in a loud voice. And I did not think it remarkable when the entire class understood. That day, I moved very far from the disadvantaged child I had been only days earlier. The belief, the calming assurance that I belonged in public, had at last taken hold.

Shortly after, I stopped hearing the high and loud sounds of *los* 10 *gringos.* A more and more confident speaker of English, I didn't trouble to listen to *how* strangers sounded, speaking to me. And there simply were too many English-speaking people in my day for me to hear American accents anymore. Conversations quickened. Listening to persons who sounded eccentrically pitched voices, I usually noted their sounds for an initial few seconds before I concentrated on *what* they were saying. Conversations became content-full. Transparent. Hearing someone's *tone* of voice—angry or questioning or sarcastic or happy or sad—I didn't distinguish it from the words it expressed. Sound and word were thus tightly wedded. At the end of a day, I was often bemused, always relieved, to realize how "silent," though crowded with words, my day in public had been. (This public silence measured and quickened the change in my life.)

At last, seven years old, I came to believe what had been technically true since my birth: I was an American citizen.

But the special feeling of closeness at home was diminished by then. Gone was the desperate, urgent, intense feeling of being at home; rare was the experience of feeling myself individualized by family intimates. We remained a loving family, but one greatly changed. No longer so close; no longer bound tight by the pleasing and troubling knowledge of our public separateness. Neither my older brother nor sister rushed home after school anymore. Nor did I. When I arrived home there would often be neighborhood kids in the house. Or the house would be empty of sounds.

Following the dramatic Americanization of their children, even my parents grew more publicly confident. Especially my mother. She learned the names of all the people on our block. And she decided we needed to have a telephone installed in the house. My father continued to use the word *gringo*. But it was no longer charged with the old bitterness or distrust. (Stripped of any emotional content, the word simply became a name for those Americans not of Hispanic descent.) Hearing him, sometimes, I wasn't sure if he was pronouncing the Spanish word *gringo* or saying gringo in English.

Matching the silence I started hearing in public was a new quiet at home. The family's quiet was partly due to the fact that, as we children learned more and more English, we shared fewer and fewer words with our parents. Sentences needed to be spoken slowly when a child addressed his mother or father. (Often the parent wouldn't understand.) The child would need to repeat himself. (Still the parent misunderstood.) The young voice, frustrated, would end up saying, "Never mind"—the subject was closed. Dinners would be noisy with the clinking of knives and forks against dishes. My mother would smile softly between her remarks; my father at the other end of the table would chew and chew at his food, while he stared over the heads of his children.

My *mother!* My *father!* After English became my primary language, I no longer knew what words to use in addressing my parents. The old Spanish words (those tender accents of sound) I had used earlier— *mamá* and *papá*—I couldn't use anymore. They would have been too painful reminders of how much had changed in my life. On the other hand, the words I heard neighborhood kids call *their* parents seemed equally unsatisfactory. *Mother* and *Father; Ma, Papa, Pa, Dad, Pop* (how I hated the all-American sound of that last word especially)—all

15

these terms I felt were unsuitable, not really terms of address for *my* parents. As a result, I never used them at home. Whenever I'd speak to my parents, I would try to get their attention with eye contact alone. In public conversations, I'd refer to "my parents" or "my mother and father."

My mother and father, for their part, responded differently, as their children spoke to them less. She grew restless, seemed troubled and anxious at the scarcity of words exchanged in the house. It was she who would question me about my day when I came home from school. She smiled at small talk. She pried at the edges of my sentences to get me to say something more. (What?) She'd join conversations she overheard, but her intrusions often stopped her children's talking. By contrast, my father seemed reconciled to the new quiet. Though his English improved somewhat, he retired into silence. At dinner he spoke very little. One night his children and even his wife helplessly giggled at his garbled English pronunciation of the Catholic Grace before Meals. Thereafter he made his wife recite the prayer at the start of each meal, even on formal occasions, when there were guests in the house. Hers became the public voice of the family. On official business, it was she, not my father, one would usually hear on the phone or in stores, talking to strangers. His children grew so accustomed to his silence that, years later, they would speak routinely of his shyness. (My mother would often try to explain: Both his parents died when he was eight. He was raised by an uncle who treated him like little more than a menial servant. He was never encouraged to speak. He grew up alone. A man of few words.) But my father was not shy, I realized, when I'd watch him speaking Spanish with relatives. Using Spanish, he was quickly effusive. Especially when talking with other men, his voice would spark, flicker, flare alive with sounds. In Spanish, he expressed ideas and feelings he rarely revealed in English. With firm Spanish sounds, he conveyed confidence and authority English would never allow him.

The silence at home, however, was finally more than a literal silence. Fewer words passed between parent and child, but more profound was the silence that resulted from my inattention to sounds. At about the time I no longer bothered to listen with care to the sounds of English in public, I grew careless about listening to the sounds family members made when they spoke. Most of the time I heard someone speaking at home and didn't distinguish his sounds from the words people uttered in public. I didn't even pay much attention to my parents' accented and ungrammatical speech. At least not at home. Only when I was with them in public would I grow alert to their accents. Though, even then, their sounds caused me less and less concern. For I was increasingly confident of my own public identity.

I would have been happier about my public success had I not sometimes recalled what it had been like earlier, when my family had conveyed its intimacy through a set of conveniently private sounds. Sometimes in public, hearing a stranger, I'd hark back to my past. A Mexican farmworker approached me downtown to ask directions to somewhere. "*¿Hijito . . . ?*"[3] he said. And his voice summoned deep longing. Another time, standing beside my mother in the visiting room of a Carmelite convent, before the dense screen which rendered the nuns shadowy figures, I heard several Spanish-speaking nuns—their busy, singsong overlapping voices—assure us that yes, yes, we were remembered, all our family was remembered in their prayers. (Their voices echoed faraway family sounds.) Another day, a dark-faced old woman—her hand light on my shoulder—steadied herself against me as she boarded a bus. She murmured something I couldn't quite comprehend. Her Spanish voice came near, like the face of a never-before-seen relative in the instant before I was kissed. Her voice, like so many of the Spanish voices I'd hear in public, recalled the golden age of my youth. Hearing Spanish then, I continued to be a careful, if sad, listener to sounds. Hearing a Spanish-speaking family walking behind me, I turned to look. I smiled for an instant, before my glance found the Hispanic-looking faces of strangers in the crowd going by.

● ○ ●

Today I hear bilingual educators say that children lose a degree of "individuality" by becoming assimilated into public society. (Bilingual schooling was popularized in the seventies, that decade when middle-

---

[3]Literally, "little son" (Spanish), a common term of endearment.

class ethnics began to resist the process of assimilation—the American melting pot.) But the bilingualists simplistically scorn the value and necessity of assimilation. They do not seem to realize that there are *two* ways a person is individualized. So they do not realize that while one suffers a diminished sense of *private* individuality by becoming assimilated into public society, such assimilation makes possible the achievement of *public* individuality.

The bilingualists insist that a student should be reminded of his 20 difference from others in mass society, his heritage. But they equate mere separateness with individuality. The fact is that only in private— with intimates—is separateness from the crowd a prerequisite for individuality. (An intimate draws me apart, tells me that I am unique, unlike all others.) In public, by contrast, full individuality is achieved, paradoxically, by those who are able to consider themselves members of the crowd. Thus it happened for me: Only when I was able to think of myself as an American, no longer an alien in *gringo* society, could I seek the rights and opportunities necessary for full public individuality. The social and political advantages I enjoy as a man result from the day that I came to believe that my name, indeed, is *Rich-heard Road-ree-guess*. It is true that my public society today is often impersonal. (My public society is usually mass society.) Yet despite the anonymity of the crowd and despite the fact that the individuality I achieve in public is often tenuous—because it depends on my being one in a crowd—I celebrate the day I acquired my new name. Those middle-class ethnics who scorn assimilation seem to me filled with decadent self-pity, obsessed by the burden of public life. Dangerously, they romanticize public separateness and they trivialize the dilemma of the socially disadvantaged.

My awkward childhood does not prove the necessity of bilingual education. My story discloses instead an essential myth of childhood— inevitable pain. If I rehearse here the changes in my private life after my Americanization, it is finally to emphasize the public gain. The loss implies the gain: The house I returned to each afternoon was quiet. Intimate sounds no longer rushed to the door to greet me. There were other noises inside. The telephone rang. Neighborhood kids ran past the door of the bedroom where I was reading my schoolbooks—covered with shopping-bag paper. Once I learned public language, it would never again be easy for me to hear intimate family voices. More and more of my day was spent hearing words. But that may only be a way of saying that the day I raised my hand in class and spoke loudly to an entire roomful of faces, my childhood started to end. ***

STUDY QUESTIONS

1. Rodriguez divides his world into a public life and a private life. What language is spoken in each? What made him afraid of learning English? How was his learning English at school different from learning it at home?

2. Within the GENRE of autobiography, Rodriguez incorporates two major kinds of writing: the MEMOIR and the PERSUASIVE ESSAY. Reread the essay and determine how each kind depends on the other for support. In other words, how does the memoir support the persuasive and how does the persuasive then lead him back to a deeper exploration of the personal?

3. *For Writing.* Think about languages other than English that are spoken in the United States. In many large cities, voter information and pamphlets sent out by utilities companies are printed in languages other than English. Many hospitals and schools, as well as other public services, are either staffed by individuals who are fluent in multiple languages or have translators available for those who cannot speak English. On the other hand, some elected officials have tried repeatedly to pass English-only legislation that would make English the official language of the United States and thus would require that every citizen be able to speak that language. Do you think language should be legislated? If English-only laws were passed, how would authorities ensure compliance? What might be the effect of such laws on the economy, on the national community, and on the lives of individual citizens? Write an ARGUMENTATIVE ESSAY that presents and defends your POSITION. Be sure to RESEARCH the issue and cite facts, statistics, and other EVIDENCE to support you THESIS. Remember to DOCUMENT your sources.

SARAH VOWELL { *Shooting Dad*

SARAH VOWELL (b. 1969), journalist, humorist, and author, was born in
Muskogee, Oklahoma, and earned her BA from Montana State University in
1993 and her MA from the School of the Art Institute of Chicago in 1996.
Vowell has written cultural criticism for publications such as the *New York
Times* and *GQ*, appeared on television shows such as the *Daily Show with
Jon Stewart* and *Nightline,* and written several books, including *Radio On:
A Listener's Diary* (1997) and *The Wordy Shipmates* (2008). She is a fre-
quent contributor to *This American Life,* a public radio program hosted by
Ira Glass, and was the voice of Violet in the animated film *The Incredibles*
(2004).

  In "Shooting Dad," Vowell plays with the double entendre of her title:
she both describes and critiques her gun-loving father. She initially separates
herself from him, classifying herself as anti-gun and her father as pro-gun,
but gradually she learns how those classifications can overlap in unexpected
ways. As you read, notice how Vowell uses humor to lighten a controversial
topic and to help her ethos, or persona, appeal to readers.

IF YOU WERE PASSING BY the house where I grew up during my
teenage years and it happened to be before Election Day, you wouldn't
have needed to come inside to see that it was a house divided. You
could have looked at the Democratic campaign poster in the upstairs
window and the Republican one in the downstairs window and seen
our home for the Civil War battleground it was. I'm not saying who was
the Democrat or who was the Republican—my father or I—but I will

tell you that I have never subscribed to *Guns & Ammo*, that I did not plaster the family vehicle with National Rifle Association stickers, and that hunter's orange was never my color.

About the only thing my father and I agree on is the Constitution, though I'm partial to the First Amendment, while he's always favored the Second.

I am a gunsmith's daughter. I like to call my parents' house, located on a quiet residential street in Bozeman, Montana, the United States of Firearms. Guns were everywhere: the so-called pretty ones like the circa 1850 walnut muzzleloader hanging on the wall, Dad's clients' fixer-uppers leaning into corners, an entire rack right next to the TV. I had to move revolvers out of my way to make room for a bowl of Rice Krispies on the kitchen table.

I was eleven when we moved into that Bozeman house. We had never lived in town before, and this was a college town at that. We came from Oklahoma—a dusty little Muskogee County nowhere called Braggs. My parents' property there included an orchard, a horse pasture, and a couple of acres of woods. I knew our lives had changed one morning not long after we moved to Montana when, during breakfast, my father heard a noise and jumped out of his chair. Grabbing a BB gun, he rushed out the front door. Standing in the yard, he started shooting at crows. My mother sprinted after him screaming, "Pat, you might ought to check, but I don't think they do that up here!" From the look on his face, she might as well have told him that his American citizenship had been revoked. He shook his head, mumbling, "Why, shooting crows is a national pastime, like baseball and apple pie." Personally, I preferred baseball and apple pie. I looked up at those crows flying away and thought, I'm going to like it here.

Dad and I started bickering in earnest when I was fourteen, after the   5 1984 Democratic National Convention. I was so excited when Walter Mondale chose Geraldine Ferraro as his running mate that I taped the front page of the newspaper with her picture on it to the refrigerator door. But there was some sort of mysterious gravity surge in the kitchen. Somehow, that picture ended up in the trash all the way across the room.

Nowadays, I giggle when Dad calls me on Election Day to cheerfully inform me that he has once again canceled out my vote, but I was not always so mature. There were times when I found the fact that he was a gunsmith horrifying. And just *weird*. All he ever cared about were guns. All I ever cared about was art. There were years and years when he hid out by himself in the garage making rifle barrels and I holed up in my room reading Allen Ginsberg poems, and we were incapable of having a conversation that didn't end in an argument.

Our house was partitioned off into territories. While the kitchen and the living room were well within the DMZ, the respective work spaces governed by my father and me were jealously guarded totalitarian states in which each of us declared ourselves dictator. Dad's shop was a messy disaster area, a labyrinth of lathes. Its walls were hung with the mounted antlers of deer he'd bagged, forming a makeshift museum of death. The available flat surfaces were buried under a million scraps of paper on which he sketched his mechanical inventions in blue ballpoint pen. And the floor, carpeted with spiky metal shavings, was a tetanus shot waiting to happen. My domain was the cramped, cold space known as the music room. It was also a messy disaster area, an obstacle course of musical instruments—piano, trumpet, baritone horn, valve trombone, various percussion doodads (bells!), and recorders. A framed portrait of the French composer Claude Debussy was nailed to the wall. The available flat surfaces were buried under piles of staff paper, on which I penciled in the pompous orchestra music given titles like "Prelude to the Green Door" (named after an O. Henry[1] short story by the way, not the watershed porn flick *Behind the Green Door*) I starting writing in junior high.

It has been my experience that in order to impress potential suitors, skip the teen Debussy anecdotes and stick with the always attention-getting line "My dad makes guns." Though it won't cause the guy to like me any better, it will make him handle the inevitable breakup with diplomacy—just in case I happen to have any loaded family heirlooms lying around the house.

---

[1]Pen name of William Sydney Porter (1862–1910), American short story author known for his "twist" endings.

But the fact is, I have only shot a gun, once and once was plenty. My twin sister, Amy, and I were six years old—six—when Dad decided that it was high time we learned how to shoot. Amy remembers the day he handed us the gun for the first time differently. She liked it.

Amy shared our father's enthusiasm for firearms and the quick-draw cowboy mythology surrounding them. I tended to daydream through Dad's activities—the car trip to Dodge City's Boot Hill, his beloved John Wayne Westerns on TV. My sister, on the other hand, turned into Rooster Cogburn Jr.,[2] devouring Duke movies with Dad. In fact, she named her teddy bear Duke, hung a colossal John Wayne portrait next to her bed, and took to wearing one of those John Wayne shirts that button on the side. So when Dad led us out to the backyard when we were six and, to Amy's delight, put the gun in her hand, she says she felt it meant that Daddy trusted us and that he thought of us as "big girls."

But I remember holding the pistol only made me feel small. It was so heavy in my hand. I stretched out my arm and pointed it away and winced. It was a very long time before I had the nerve to pull the trigger and I was so scared I had to close my eyes. It felt like it just went off by itself, as if I had no say in the matter, as if the gun just had this *need*. The sound it made was as big as God. It kicked little me back to the ground like a bully, like a foe. It hurt. I don't know if I dropped it or just handed it back over to my dad, but I do know that I never wanted to touch another one again. And, because I believed in the devil, I did what my mother told me to do every time I felt an evil presence. I looked at the smoke and whispered under my breath. "Satan, I rebuke thee."

It's not like I'm saying I was traumatized. It's more like I was decided. Guns: Not For Me. Luckily, both my parents grew up in exasperating households where children were considered puppets and/or slaves. My mom and dad were hell-bent on letting my sister and me make our own choices. So if I decided that I didn't want my father's little death sticks to kick me to the ground again, that was fine with him.

---

[2]Character played by John Wayne (1907–79) in the 1975 film of the same name. *Duke*: Wayne's nickname.

He would go hunting with my sister, who started calling herself "the loneliest twin in history" because of my reluctance to engage in family activities.

Of course, the fact that I was allowed to voice my opinions did not mean that my father would silence his own. Some things were said during the Reagan administration that cannot be taken back. Let's just say that I blamed Dad for nuclear proliferation and Contra aid. He believed that if I had my way, all the guns would be confiscated and it would take the commies about fifteen minutes to parachute in and assume control.

We're older now, my dad and I. The older I get, the more I'm interested in becoming a better daughter. First on my list: Figure out the whole gun thing.

Not long ago, my dad finished his most elaborate tool of death yet. A cannon. He built a nineteenth-century cannon. From scratch. It took two years.

My father's cannon is a smaller replica of a cannon called the Big Horn Gun in front of Bozeman's Pioneer Museum. The barrel of the original has been filled with concrete ever since some high school kids in the '50s pointed it at the school across the street and shot out its windows one night as a prank. According to Dad's historical source, a man known to scholars as A Guy at the Museum, the cannon was brought to Bozeman around 1870, and was used by local white merchants to fire at the Sioux and Cheyenne Indians who blocked their trade access to the East in 1874.

"Bozeman was founded on greed," Dad says. The courthouse cannon, he continues, "definitely killed Indians. The merchants filled it full of nuts, bolts, and chopped-up horseshoes. Sitting Bull could have been part of these engagements. They definitely ticked off the Indians, because a couple of years later, Custer wanders into them at Little Bighorn.[3] The Bozeman merchants were out to cause trouble. They left fresh baked bread with cyanide in it on the trail to poison a few Indians."

[3]Montana river that was the site of a battle between Native Americans and the U.S. Army on June 25 and 26, 1876. Lakota, Cheyenne, and Arapaho warriors, led by Lakota chief Sitting Bull (circa 1831–90), defeated Lieutenant Colonel George Armstrong Custer (1839–76) and his cavalry.

Because my father's sarcastic American history yarns rarely go on for long before he trots out some nefarious ancestor of ours—I come from a long line of moonshiners, Confederate soldiers, murderers, even Democrats—he cracks that the merchants hired some "community-minded Southern soldiers from North Texas." These soldiers had, like my great-great-grandfather John Vowell, fought under pro-slavery guerrilla William C. Quantrill.[4] Quantrill is most famous for riding into Lawrence, Kansas, in 1863 flying a black flag and commanding his men pharaohlike to "kill every male and burn down every house."

"John Vowell," Dad says, "had a little rep for killing people." And since he abandoned my great-grandfather Charles, whose mother died giving birth to him in 1870, and wasn't seen again until 1912, Dad doesn't rule out the possibility that John Vowell could have been one of the hired guns on the Bozeman Trail. So the cannon isn't just another gun to my dad. It's a map of all his obsessions—firearms, certainly, but also American history and family history, subjects he's never bothered separating from each other.

After tooling a million guns, after inventing and building a rifle barrel boring machine, after setting up that complicated shop filled with lathes and blueing tanks and outmoded blacksmithing tools, the cannon is his most ambitious project ever. I thought that if I was ever going to understand the ballistic bee in his bonnet, this was my chance. It was the biggest gun he ever made and I could experience it and spend time with it with the added bonus of not having to actually pull a trigger myself.

I called Dad and said that I wanted to come to Montana and watch him shoot off the cannon. He was immediately suspicious. But I had never taken much interest in his work before and he would take what he could get. He loaded the cannon into the back of his truck and we drove up into the Bridger Mountains. I was a little worried that the National Forest Service would object to us lobbing fiery balls of metal onto its property. Dad laughed, assuring me that "you cannot shoot fireworks, but this is considered a fire*arm*."

20

---

[4]Confederate sympathizer (1837–65) whose Quantrill's Raiders became known for brutality and ruthlessness during the Civil War.

It is a small cannon, about as long as a baseball bat and as wide as a coffee can. But it's heavy—110 pounds. We park near the side of the hill. Dad takes his gunpowder and other tools out of this adorable wooden box on which he has stenciled "PAT G. VOWELL CAN-NONWORKS." Cannonworks: So that's what NRA members call a metal-strewn garage.

Dad plunges his homemade bullets into the barrel, points it at an embankment just to be safe, and lights the fuse. When the fuse is lit, it resembles a cartoon. So does the sound, which warrants Ben Day dot words along the lines of *ker-pow!* There's so much Fourth of July smoke everywhere I feel compelled to sing the national anthem.

I've given this a lot of thought—how to convey the giddiness I felt when the cannon shot off. But there isn't a sophisticated way to say this. It's just really, really cool. My dad thought so, too.

Sometimes, I put together stories about the more eccentric corners   25
of the American experience for public radio. So I happen to have my tape recorder with me, and I've never seen levels like these. Every time the cannon goes off, the delicate needles which keep track of the sound quality lurch into the bad, red zone so fast and so hard I'm surprised they don't break.

The cannon was so loud and so painful, I had to touch my head to make sure my skull hadn't cracked open. One thing that my dad and I share is that we're both a little hard of hearing—me from Aerosmith,[5] him from gunsmith.

He lights the fuse again. The bullet knocks over the log he was aiming at. I instantly utter a sentence I never in my entire life thought I would say. I tell him, "Good shot, Dad."

Just as I'm wondering what's coming over me, two hikers walk by. Apparently, they have never seen a man set off a homemade cannon in the middle of the wilderness while his daughter holds a foot-long microphone up into the air recording its terrorist boom. One hiker gives me a puzzled look and asks, "So you work for the radio and that's your dad?"

Dad shoots the cannon again so that they can see how it works. The

---

[5]American hard rock band, formed in 1970, known for such hits as "Dream On" (1976), "Love in an Elevator" (1989), and "I Don't Want to Miss a Thing" (1998).

other hiker says, "That's quite the machine you got there." But he isn't talking about the cannon. He's talking about my tape recorder and my microphone—which is called a *shotgun* mike. I stare back at him, then I look over at my father's cannon, then down at my microphone, and I think. Oh. My. God. My dad and I are the same person. We're both smart-alecky loners with goofy projects and weird equipment. And since this whole target practice outing was my idea, I was no longer his adversary. I was his accomplice. What's worse, I was liking it.

I haven't changed my mind about guns. I can get behind the cannon 30 because it is a completely ceremonial object. It's unwieldy and impractical, just like everything else I care about. Try to rob a convenience store with this 110-pound Saturday night special, you'd still be dragging it in the door Sunday afternoon.

I love noise. As a music fan, I'm always waiting for that moment in a song when something just flies out of it and explodes in the air. My dad is a one-man garage band, the kind of rock 'n' roller who slaves away at his art for no reason other than to make his own sound. My dad is an artist—a pretty driven, idiosyncratic one, too. He's got his last *Gesamtkunstwerk*[6] all planned out. It's a performance piece. We're all in it—my mom, the loneliest twin in history, and me.

When my father dies, take a wild guess what he wants done with his ashes. Here's a hint: It requires a cannon.

"You guys are going to love this," he smirks, eyeballing the cannon. "You get to drag this thing up on top of the Gravellies[7] on opening day of hunting season. And looking off at Sphinx Mountain, you get to put me in little paper bags. I can take my last hunting trip on opening morning."

I'll do it, too. I will have my father's body burned into ashes. I will pack these ashes into paper bags. I will go to the mountains with my mother, my sister, and the cannon. I will plunge his remains into the barrel and point it into a hill so that he doesn't take anyone with him. I will light the fuse. But I will not cover my ears. Because when I blow what used to be my dad into the earth, I want it to hurt.

[6]Comprehensive artwork (German).

[7]Montana mountains that rise to a height of more than eight thousand feet.

STUDY QUESTIONS

1. What is Vowell's attitude toward guns? What experiences has she had with them? What is her father's attitude toward guns, and what have been his experiences with them? How does the title of this selection reflect Vowell's relationship with her father?

2. How many different meanings are packed into Vowell's title? How does the title shape the essay?

3. Consider how Vowell CLASSIFIES herself as anti-gun and her father as pro-gun. What STRATEGIES does she use to support this classification? How does she bring the two classifications together by the end of the selection?

4. *For Writing.* Think of a family member who has a strong belief that you disagree with. Write an essay in which you make an ARGUMENT *for* that person's perspective. Be sure to offer thoughtful, compelling REASONS and EVIDENCE, and consider and respond to possible COUNTERARGUMENTS.

ALICE WALKER { *Everyday Use*

ALICE WALKER (b. 1944), poet, novelist, and essayist, was born in
Eatonton, Georgia, and earned her BA at Sarah Lawrence College in New
York. Much of Walker's writing addresses civil rights issues, particularly the
racism and sexism leveled at African-American women. She coined the
now-common term "womanist" to describe the particular experiences of
women of color. Walker's many novels include the Pulitzer Prize–winning
The Color Purple (1982), *The Temple of My Familiar* (1989), and *Possessing
the Secret of Joy* (1992); her books of nonfiction include *Living by the Word*
(1988) and *We Are the Ones We Have Been Waiting For* (2006).

"Everyday Use" was first published in Walker's collection of short fiction
In Love and Trouble (1973). The story explores the relationship between
Mama and her two daughters, one educated and self-centered, the other
simple and sweet natured, each with a distinct sense of ethnic heritage.
Should family artifacts be showcased as works of art or should they be put
to the "everyday use" for which they were intended? As you read, notice
how physical details can function as symbols for larger, more abstract issues.

for your grandmamma

I WILL WAIT FOR HER in the yard that Maggie and I made so clean and
wavy yesterday afternoon. A yard like this is more comfortable than
most people know. It is not just a yard. It is like an extended living
room. When the hard clay is swept clean as a floor and the fine sand
around the edges lined with tiny, irregular grooves, anyone can come

and sit and look up into the elm tree and wait for the breezes that never come inside the house.

Maggie will be nervous until after her sister goes: she will stand hopelessly in corners, homely and ashamed of the burn scars down her arms and legs, eying her sister with a mixture of envy and awe. She thinks her sister has held life always in the palm of one hand, that "no" is a word the world never learned to say to her.

You've no doubt seen those TV shows where the child who has "made it" is confronted, as a surprise, by her own mother and father, tottering in weakly from backstage. (A pleasant surprise, of course: What would they do if parent and child came on the show only to curse out and insult each other?) On TV mother and child embrace and smile into each other's faces. Sometimes the mother and father weep, the child wraps them in her arms and leans across the table to tell how she would not have made it without their help. I have seen these programs.

Sometimes I dream a dream in which Dee and I are suddenly brought together on a TV program of this sort. Out of a dark and soft-seated limousine I am ushered into a bright room filled with many people. There I meet a smiling, gray, sporty man like Johnny Carson[1] who shakes my hand and tells me what a fine girl I have. Then we are on the stage and Dee is embracing me with tears in her eyes. She pins on my dress a large orchid, even though she has told me once that she thinks orchids are tacky flowers.

In real life I am a large, big-boned woman with rough, man-working   5 hands. In the winter I wear flannel nightgowns to bed and overalls during the day. I can kill and clean a hog as mercilessly as a man. My fat keeps me hot in zero weather. I can work outside all day, breaking ice to get water for washing; I can eat pork liver cooked over the open fire minutes after it comes steaming from the hog. One winter I knocked a bull calf straight in the brain between the eyes with a sledge hammer and had the meat hung up to chill before nightfall. But of course all this does not show on television. I am the way my daughter would want me

[1]American comedian (1925–2005), best known as host of *The Tonight Show* on television.

to be: a hundred pounds lighter, my skin like an uncooked barley pancake. My hair glistens in the hot bright lights. Johnny Carson has much to do to keep up with my quick and witty tongue.

But that is a mistake. I know even before I wake up. Who ever knew a Johnson with a quick tongue? Who can even imagine me looking a strange white man in the eye? It seems to me I have talked to them always with one foot raised in flight, with my head turned in whichever way is farthest from them. Dee, though. She would always look anyone in the eye. Hesitation was no part of her nature.

"How do I look, Mama?" Maggie says, showing just enough of her thin body enveloped in pink skirt and red blouse for me to know she's there, almost hidden by the door.

"Come out into the yard," I say.

Have you ever seen a lame animal, perhaps a dog run over by some careless person rich enough to own a car, sidle up to someone who is ignorant enough to be kind to them? That is the way my Maggie walks. She has been like this, chin on chest, eyes on ground, feet in shuffle, ever since the fire that burned the other house to the ground.

Dee is lighter than Maggie, with nicer hair and a fuller figure. She's   10 a woman now, though sometimes I forget. How long ago was it that the other house burned? Ten, twelve years? Sometimes I can still hear the flames and feel Maggie's arms sticking to me, her hair smoking and her dress falling off her in little black papery flakes. Her eyes seemed stretched open, blazed open by the flames reflected in them. And Dee. I see her standing off under the sweet gum tree she used to dig gum out of; a look of concentration on her face as she watched the last dingy gray board of the house fall in toward the red-hot brick chimney. Why don't you do a dance around the ashes? I'd wanted to ask her. She had hated the house that much.

I used to think she hated Maggie, too. But that was before we raised the money, the church and me, to send her to Augusta to school. She used to read to us without pity; forcing words, lies, other folks' habits, whole lives upon us two, sitting trapped and ignorant underneath her voice. She washed us in a river of make-believe, burned us with a lot of knowledge we didn't necessarily need to know. Pressed us to her with the serious way she read, to shove us away at just the moment, like dimwits, we seemed about to understand.

Dee wanted nice things. A yellow organdy dress to wear to her graduation from high school; black pumps to match a green suit she'd made from an old suit somebody gave me. She was determined to stare down any disaster in her efforts. Her eyelids would not flicker for minutes at a time. Often I fought off the temptation to shake her. At sixteen she had a style of her own: and knew what style was.

I never had an education myself. After second grade the school was closed down. Don't ask me why: in 1927 colored asked fewer questions than they do now. Sometimes Maggie reads to me. She stumbles along good naturedly but can't see well. She knows she is not bright. Like good looks and money, quickness passed her by. She will marry John Thomas (who has mossy teeth in an earnest face) and then I'll be free to sit here and I guess just sing church songs to myself. Although I never was a good singer. Never could carry a tune. I was always better at a man's job. I used to love to milk till I was hooked[2] in the side in '49. Cows are soothing and slow and don't bother you, unless you try to milk them the wrong way.

I have deliberately turned my back on the house. It is three rooms, just like the one that burned, except the roof is tin; they don't make shingle roofs anymore. There are no real windows, just some holes cut in the sides, like the portholes in a ship, but not round and not square, with rawhide holding the shutters up on the outside. This house is in a pasture, too, like the other one. No doubt when Dee sees it she will want to tear it down. She wrote me once that no matter where we "choose" to live, she will manage to come see us. But she will never bring her friends. Maggie and I thought about this and Maggie asked me, "Mama, when did Dee ever *have* any friends?"

She had a few. Furtive boys in pink shirts hanging about on washday   15
after school. Nervous girls who never laughed. Impressed with her they worshiped the well-turned phrase, the cute shape, the scalding humor that erupted like bubbles in lye. She read to them.

---

[2]That is, gored by the horn of a cow.

When she was courting Jimmy T she didn't have much time to pay to us, but turned all her faultfinding power on him. He *flew* to marry a cheap city girl from a family of ignorant flashy people. She hardly had time to recompose herself.

When she comes I will meet—but there they are!

Maggie attempts to make a dash for the house, in her shuffling way, but I stay her with my hand. "Come back here," I say. And she stops and tries to dig a well in the sand with her toe.

It is hard to see them clearly through the strong sun. But even the first glimpse of leg out of the car tells me it is Dee. Her feet were always neat-looking, as if God himself had shaped them with a certain style. From the other side of the car comes a short, stocky man. Hair is all over his head a foot long and hanging from his chin like a kinky mule tail. I hear Maggie suck in her breath. "Uhnnnh," is what it sounds like. Like when you see the wriggling end of a snake just in front of your foot on the road. "Uhnnnh."

Dee next. A dress down to the ground, in this hot weather. A dress so loud it hurts my eyes. There are yellows and oranges enough to throw back the light of the sun. I feel my whole face warming from the heat waves it throws out. Earrings gold, too, and hanging down to her shoulders. Bracelets dangling and making noises when she moves her arm up to shake the folds of the dress out of her armpits. The dress is loose and flows, and as she walks closer, I like it. I hear Maggie go "Uhnnnh" again. It is her sister's hair. It stands straight up like the wool on a sheep. It is black as night and around the edges are two long pigtails that rope about like small lizards disappearing behind her ears. 20

"Wa-su-zo-Tean-o!" she says, coming on in that gliding way the dress makes her move. The short stocky fellow with the hair to his navel is all grinning and he follows up with "Asalamalakim,[3] my mother and sister!" He moves to hug Maggie but she falls back, right up against the back of my chair. I feel her trembling there and when I look up I see the perspiration falling off her chin.

[3]Transliteration of a Muslim greeting; literally, "Peace be with you." "Wa-su-zo-Tean-o" is a similar rendering of a Ugandan salutation.

"Don't get up," says Dee. Since I am stout it takes something of a push. You can see me trying to move a second or two before I make it. She turns, showing white heels through her sandals, and goes back to the car. Out she peeks next with a Polaroid. She stoops down quickly and lines up picture after picture of me sitting there in front of the house with Maggie cowering behind me. She never takes a shot without making sure the house is included. When a cow comes nibbling around the edge of the yard she snaps it and me and Maggie *and* the house. Then she puts the Polaroid in the back seat of the car, and comes up and kisses me on the forehead.

Meanwhile Asalamalakim is going through motions with Maggie's hand. Maggie's hand is as limp as a fish, and probably as cold, despite the sweat, and she keeps trying to pull it back. It looks like Asalamalakim wants to shake hands but wants to do it fancy. Or maybe he don't know how people shake hands. Anyhow, he soon gives up on Maggie.

"Well," I say. "Dee."

"No, Mama," she says. "Not 'Dee,' Wangero Leewanika Kemanjo!"   25

"What happened to 'Dee'?" I wanted to know.

"She's dead," Wangero said. "I couldn't bear it any longer, being named after the people who oppress me."

"You know as well as me you was named after your aunt Dicie," I said. Dicie is my sister. She named Dee. We called her "Big Dee" after Dee was born.

"But who was *she* named after?" asked Wangero.

"I guess after Grandma Dee," I said.   30

"And who was she named after?" asked Wangero.

"Her mother," I said, and saw Wangero was getting tired. "That's about as far back as I can trace it," I said. Though, in fact, I probably could have carried it back beyond the Civil War through the branches.

"Well," said Asalamalakim, "there you are."

"Uhnnnh," I heard Maggie say.

"There I was not," I said, "before 'Dicie' cropped up in our family,   35 so why should I try to trace it that far back?"

He just stood there grinning, looking down on me like somebody inspecting a Model A car. Every once in a while he and Wangero sent eye signals over my head.

"How do you pronounce this name?" I asked.

"You don't have to call me by it if you don't want to," said Wangero.

"Why shouldn't I?" I asked. "If that's what you want us to call you, we'll call you."

"I know it might sound awkward at first," said Wangero. 40

"I'll get used to it," I said. "Ream it out again."

Well, soon we got the name out of the way. Asalamalakim had a name twice as long and three times as hard. After I tripped over it two or three times he told me to just call him Hakim-a-barber. I wanted to ask him was he a barber, but I didn't really think he was, so I didn't ask.

"You must belong to those beef-cattle peoples down the road," I said. They said "Asalamalakim" when they met you, too, but they didn't shake hands. Always too busy: feeding the cattle, fixing the fences, putting up salt-lick shelters, throwing down hay. When the white folks poisoned some of the herd the men stayed up all night with rifles in their hands. I walked a mile and a half just to see the sight.

Hakim-a-barber said, "I accept some of their doctrines, but farming and raising cattle is not my style." (They didn't tell me, and I didn't ask, whether Wangero (Dee) had really gone and married him.)

We sat down to eat and right away he said he didn't eat collards and 45 pork was unclean. Wangero, though, went on through the chitlins and corn bread, the greens and everything else. She talked a blue streak over the sweet potatoes. Everything delighted her. Even the fact that we still used the benches her daddy made for the table when we couldn't afford to buy chairs.

"Oh, Mama!" she cried. Then turned to Hakim-a-barber. "I never knew how lovely these benches are. You can feel the rump prints," she said running her hands underneath her and along the bench. Then she gave a sigh and her hand closed over Grandma Dee's butter dish. "That's it!" she said. "I knew there was something I wanted to ask you if I could have." She jumped up from the table and went over in the corner where the churn stood, the milk in it clabber[4] by now. She looked at the churn and looked at it.

[4]Curdled.

"This churn top is what I need," she said. "Didn't Uncle Buddy whittle it out of a tree you all used to have?"

"Yes," I said.

"Uh huh," she said happily. "And I want the dasher,[5] too."

"Uncle Buddy whittle that, too?" asked the barber. 50

Dee (Wangero) looked up at me.

"Aunt Dee's first husband whittled the dash," said Maggie so low you almost couldn't hear her. "His name was Henry, but they called him Stash."

"Maggie's brain is like an elephant's," Wangero said, laughing. "I can use the churn top as a centerpiece for the alcove table," she said, sliding a plate over the churn, "and I'll think of something artistic to do with the dasher."

When she finished wrapping the dasher the handle stuck out. I took it for a moment in my hands. You didn't even have to look close to see where hands pushing the dasher up and down to make butter had left a kind of sink in the wood. In fact, there were a lot of small sinks; you could see where thumbs and fingers had sunk into the wood. It was beautiful light yellow wood, from a tree that grew in the yard where Big Dee and Stash had lived.

After dinner Dee (Wangero) went to the trunk at the foot of my bed 55 and started rifling through it. Maggie hung back in the kitchen over the dishpan. Out came Wangero with two quilts. They had been pieced by Grandma Dee and then Big Dee and me had hung them on the quilt frames on the front porch and quilted them. One was in the Lone Star pattern. The other was Walk Around the Mountain. In both of them were scraps of dresses Grandma Dee had worn fifty and more years ago. Bits and pieces of Grandpa Jarrell's Paisley shirts. And one teeny faded blue piece, about the size of a penny matchbox, that was from Great Grandpa Ezra's uniform that he wore in the Civil War.

"Mama," Wangero said sweet as a bird. "Can I have these old quilts?"

I heard something fall in the kitchen, and a minute later the kitchen door slammed.

---

[5] A device for stirring the cream in a churn.

"Why don't you take one or two of the others?" I asked. "These old things was just done by me and Big Dee from some tops your grandma pieced before she died."

"No," said Wangero. "I don't want those. They are stitched around the borders by machine."

"That'll make them last better," I said. 60

"That's not the point," said Wangero. "These are all pieces of dresses Grandma used to wear. She did all this stitching by hand. Imagine!" She held the quilts securely in her arms, stroking them.

"Some of the pieces, like those lavender ones, come from old clothes her mother handed down to her," I said, moving up to touch the quilts. Dee (Wangero) moved back just enough so that I couldn't reach the quilts. They already belonged to her.

"Imagine!" she breathed again, clutching them closely to her bosom.

"The truth is," I said, "I promised to give them quilts to Maggie, for when she marries John Thomas."

She gasped like a bee had stung her. 65

"Maggie can't appreciate these quilts!" she said. "She'd probably be backward enough to put them to everyday use."

"I reckon she would," I said. "God knows I been saving 'em for long enough with nobody using 'em. I hope she will!" I didn't want to bring up how I had offered Dee (Wangero) a quilt when she went away to college. Then she had told me they were old-fashioned, out of style.

"But they're *priceless!*" she was saying now, furiously; for she has a temper. "Maggie would put them on the bed and in five years they'd be in rags. Less than that!"

"She can always make some more," I said. "Maggie knows how to quilt."

Dee (Wangero) looked at me with hatred. "You just will not under- 70 stand. The point is these quilts, *these* quilts!"

"Well," I said, stumped. "What would *you* do with them?"

"Hang them," she said. As if that was the only thing you *could* do with quilts.

Maggie by now was standing in the door. I could almost hear the sound her feet made as they scraped over each other.

"She can have them, Mama," she said, like somebody used to never winning anything, or having anything reserved for her. "I can 'member Grandma Dee without the quilts."

I looked at her hard. She had filled her bottom lip with checkerberry 75 snuff and it gave her a face a kind of dopey, hangdog look. It was Grandma Dee and Big Dee who taught her how to quilt herself. She stood there with her scarred hands hidden in the folds of her skirt. She looked at her sister with something like fear but she wasn't mad at her. This was Maggie's portion. This was the way she knew God to work.

When I looked at her like that something hit me in the top of my head and ran down to the soles of my feet. Just like when I'm in church and the spirit of God touches me and I get happy and shout. I did something I never had done before: hugged Maggie to me, then dragged her on into the room, snatched the quilts out of Miss Wangero's hands and dumped them into Maggie's lap. Maggie just sat there on my bed with her mouth open.

"Take one or two of the others," I said to Dee.

But she turned without a word and went out to Hakim-a-barber.

"You just don't understand," she said, as Maggie and I came out to the car.

"What don't I understand?" I wanted to know. 80

"Your heritage," she said. And then she turned to Maggie, kissed her, and said, "You ought to try to make something of yourself, too, Maggie. It's really a new day for us. But from the way you and Mama still live you'd never know it."

She put on some sunglasses that hid everything above the tip of her nose and her chin.

Maggie smiled; maybe at the sunglasses. But a real smile, not scared. After we watched the car dust settle I asked Maggie to bring me a dip of snuff. And then the two of us sat there just enjoying, until it was time to go in the house and go to bed.

STUDY QUESTIONS

1. Why does Dee want her mother's quilts? Why does Mama want Maggie to have the quilts?

2. Explain how the quilts are used to SYMBOLIZE contrasting views of ethnic heritage. Which view do you think Walker agrees with? How do you know? Other than the quilts, what items in the story might function as symbols? What might they symbolize? How do you know?

3. Is it better for the quilts to be hung on a wall as art or to be put to "everyday use"? What is your opinion, and what view does the story seem to support? What details in the story helped you determine your answer? What AUDIENCE do you think Walker had in mind for this story?

4. *For Writing.* Choose two or three items that are important to you. Write an essay in which you explain the importance of these items and what they symbolize to you. Be sure to DESCRIBE the items in concrete detail.

BARBARA EHRENREICH } *Cultural Baggage*

BARBARA EHRENREICH (b. 1941), a native of Butte, Montana, earned
a PhD in biology from Rockefeller University in New York City. She
turned to writing later in her professional life, and she now wears many
hats: journalist, feminist, social critic, and political activist. She has
written almost twenty books, two of which became *New York Times* best
sellers: *Nickel and Dimed: On (Not) Getting By in America* (2001),
a record of her experiment trying to live only on what she earned at
minimum-wage jobs, and *Bait and Switch: The (Futile) Pursuit of the
American Dream* (2006), in which she examines the growing trend of
white-collar unemployment. Her articles have appeared in *Harper's,
Time, Mother Jones, Ms., The Atlantic Monthly,* and many other
periodicals.

In "Cultural Baggage," originally published in the *New York Times* in
1992, Ehrenreich explains the difficulty she has had identifying with a
particular ethnic heritage, even as she claims an intellectual heritage: she
belongs among those who think for themselves and try new things. She
argues that "skepticism, curiosity, and wide-eyed ecumenical tolerance"
are as worthy a heritage as any other. As you read, notice how Ehrenreich uses narrative and dialogue to trace her intellectual lineage.

AN ACQUAINTANCE WAS TELLING ME about the joys of rediscovering
her ethnic and religious heritage. "I know exactly what my ancestors
were doing 2,000 years ago," she said, eyes gleaming with enthusiasm,

"HERS; Cultural Baggage" by Barbara Ehrenreich. Originally published in the *New York
Times Magazine,* April 5, 1992. Used by permission of the New York Times Syndication.

"and *I can do the same things now.*" Then she leaned forward and inquired politely, "And what is your ethnic background, if I may ask?"

"None," I said, that being the first word in line to get out of my mouth. Well, not "none," I backtracked. Scottish, English, Irish—that was something, I supposed. Too much Irish to qualify as a WASP; too much of the hated English to warrant a "Kiss Me, I'm Irish" button; plus there are a number of dead ends in the family tree due to adoptions, missing records, failing memories and the like. I was blushing by this time. Did "none" mean I was rejecting my heritage out of Anglo-Celtic self-hate? Or was I revealing a hidden ethnic chauvinism in which the Britannically derived serve as a kind of neutral standard compared with the ethnic "others"?

Throughout the 1960's and 70's I watched one group after another—African Americans, Latinos, Native Americans—stand up and proudly reclaim their roots while I just sank back ever deeper into my seat. All this excitement over ethnicity stemmed, I uneasily sensed, from a past in which *their* ancestors had been trampled upon by *my* ancestors, or at least by people who looked very much like them. In addition, it had begun to seem almost un-American not to have some sort of hyphen at hand, linking one to more venerable times and locales.

But the truth is I was raised with none. We'd eaten ethnic foods in my childhood home, but these were all borrowed, like the pastries, or Cornish meat pies, my father had picked up from his fellow miners in Butte, Montana. If my mother had one rule, it was militant ecumenism in all matters of food and experience. "Try new things," she would say, meaning anything from sweetbreads to clams, with an emphasis on the "new."

As a child, I briefly nourished a craving for tradition and roots. I   5
immersed myself in the works of Sir Walter Scott. I pretended to believe that the bagpipe was a musical instrument. I was fascinated to learn from my grandmother that we were descended from certain Highland clans and longed for a pleated skirt in one of their distinctive tartans.

But in *Ivanhoe*, it was the dark-eyed "Jewess" Rebecca I identified with, not the flaxen-haired bimbo Rowena. As for clans: Why not call them "tribes," those bands of half-clad peasants and warriors whose idea of cuisine was stuffed sheep gut washed down with whisky? And then in my early teens I was stung by Disraeli's[1] remark to the effect that his ancestors had been leading orderly, literate lives when my ancestors were still rampaging through the highlands daubing themselves with blue paint.

Motherhood put the screws on me, ethnicity-wise. I had hoped that by marrying a man of Eastern European-Jewish ancestry I would acquire for my descendants the ethnic genes that my own forebears so sadly lacked. At one point, I even subjected the children to a Passover seder[2] of my own design, which included a little talk about the flight from Egypt and its relevance to modern social issues. But the kids insisted on buttering their matzohs and snickering through my talk. "Give me a break, Mom," the older one said. "You don't even believe in God."

After the tiny pagans had been put to bed, I sat down to brood over Elijah's wine.[3] What had I been thinking? The kids knew that their Jewish grandparents were secular folks who didn't hold seders themselves. And if ethnicity eluded me, how could I expect it to take root in my children, who are not only Scottish-English-Irish, but Hungarian-Polish-Russian to boot?

But, then, on the fumes of Manischewitz,[4] a great insight took form in my mind. It was true, as the kids said, that I didn't "believe in God." But this could be taken as something very different from an accusation—a reminder of a genuine heritage. My parents had not believed in God either, nor had my grandparents or any other progenitors going back to the great-great level. They had become disillusioned with Christianity generations ago—just as, on the in-law side, my children's other ancestors had shaken off their Orthodox Judaism. This

---

[1] Benjamin Disraeli (1804–81), British prime minister in 1868 and from 1874 to 1880 and the only Jew to hold that office.

[2] A ceremonial dinner held to commemorate the exodus of the Jews from Egypt.

[3] At a seder, a portion of wine set aside as "Elijah's cup."

[4] A kosher brand of sweet red wine, common at seders.

insight did not exactly furnish me with an "identity," but it was at least something to work with: we are the kind of people, I realized—whatever our distant ancestors' religions—who do *not* believe, who do not carry on traditions, who do not do things just because someone has done them before.

The epiphany went on: I recalled that my mother never introduced 10 a procedure for cooking or cleaning by telling me, "Grandma did it this way." What did Grandma know, living in the days before vacuum cleaners and disposable toilet mops? In my parents' general view, new things were better than old, and the very fact that some ritual had been performed in the past was a good reason for abandoning it now. Because what was the past, as our forebears knew it? Nothing but poverty, superstition, and grief. "Think for yourself," Dad used to say. "Always ask why."

In fact, this may have been the ideal cultural heritage for my particular ethnic strain—bounced as it was from the Highlands of Scotland across the sea, out to the Rockies, down into the mines and finally spewed out into high-tech, suburban America. What better philosophy, for a race of migrants, than "think for yourself"? What better maxim, for a people whose whole world was rudely inverted every thirty years or so, than "try new things"?

The more tradition minded, the newly enthusiastic celebrants of Purim and Kwanzaa and Solstice,[5] may see little point to survival if the survivors carry no cultural freight—religion, for example, or ethnic tradition. To which I would say that skepticism, curiosity, and wide-eyed ecumenical tolerance are also worthy elements of the human tradition and are at least as old as such notions as "Serbian" or "Croatian," "Scottish," or "Jewish." I make no claims for my personal line of progenitors except that they remained loyal to the values that may have induced all of our ancestors, long, long ago, to climb down from the trees and make their way into the open plains.

A few weeks ago, I cleared my throat and asked the children, now mostly grown and fearsomely smart, whether they felt any stirrings of

[5]Holidays celebrated by, respectively, Jewish groups, African American groups, and so-called "Neopagans."

ethnic or religious identity, etc., which might have been, ahem, insufficiently nourished at home. "None," they said, adding firmly, "and the world would be a better place if nobody else did, either." My chest swelled with pride, as would my mother's, to know that the race of "none" marches on.

STUDY QUESTIONS

1. What epiphany did Ehrenreich have about her heritage? Explain.

2. Ehrenreich frames her essay with the word "none," which appears very early and returns at the end. What does "none" refer to in each place? How does she use language to convey her pride? Cite specific words and phrases in your response.

3. *For Writing.* Ehrenreich explores the opposition many of us experience between the desire to be true to our ancestry and the desire to think for ourselves. Write an essay about a cultural value or tradition that you have been strongly encouraged to accept. Be sure to examine how you have negotiated the tension between accepting tradition and thinking for yourself, and its effect on you.

LINDA HASSELSTROM   { *Why One Peaceful Woman*

Carries a Pistol

LINDA HASSELSTROM (b. 1943) lives on a farm near the Black Hills in
South Dakota. She earned degrees in English and journalism from the
University of South Dakota and completed her MA in American literature
at the University of Missouri. Hasselstrom writes from a profound connection to the land: her first collection of essays, *Windbreak: A Woman Rancher
on the Northern Plains* (1987), based on the journals she has kept all her
life, was enthusiastically received by a national audience. She is particularly
interested in women's relationship to the West—she invites women to write
at her ranch, Windbreak House, and coedited *Leaning into the Wind:
Women Write from the Heart of the West* (1997), the first in a series of three
anthologies of works about the West written by women. Her books of poetry
include *Caught by One Wing* (1984), *Roadkill* (1987), and *Dakota Bones*
(1993). Her nonfiction works include *Land Circle: Writings Collected from
the Land* (1991) and *Between Grass and Sky: Where I Live and Work* (2002).

In "Why One Peaceful Woman Carries a Pistol," Hasselstrom recounts
how she came to carry a handgun for her own safety and argues that handguns are one good way for women to protect themselves. Through personal
anecdotes and cultural examples, Hasselstrom responds to the question
suggested by her title. How persuasive is her argument in favor of carrying
a handgun? Is it necessary for women to protect themselves with guns?
Why or why not?

I'M A PEACE-LOVING WOMAN. I also carry a pistol. For years, I've
written about my decision in an effort to help other women make intelligent choices about gun ownership, but editors rejected the arti-

cles. Between 1983 and 1986, however, when gun sales to men held steady, gun ownership among women rose fifty-three percent, to more than twelve million. We learned that any female over the age of twelve can expect to be criminally assaulted some time in her life, that women aged thirty have a fifty-fifty chance of being raped, robbed, or attacked, and that many police officials say flatly that they cannot protect citizens from crime. During the same period, the number of women considering gun ownership quadrupled to nearly two million. Manufacturers began showing lightweight weapons with small grips, and purses with built-in holsters. A new magazine is called *Guns and Women*, and more than eight thousand copies of the video *A Woman's Guide to Firearms* were sold by 1988. Experts say female gun buyers are not limited to any particular age group, profession, social class, or area of the country, and most are buying guns to protect themselves. Shooting instructors say women view guns with more caution than do men, and may make better shots.

I decided to buy a handgun for several reasons. During one four-year period, I drove more than a hundred thousand miles alone, giving speeches, readings, and workshops. A woman is advised, usually by men, to protect herself by avoiding bars, by approaching her car like an Indian scout, by locking doors and windows. But these precautions aren't always enough. And the logic angers me: *because* I am female, it is my responsibility to be extra careful.

As a responsible environmentalist, I choose to recycle, avoid chemicals on my land, minimize waste. As an informed woman alone, I choose to be as responsible for my own safety as possible: I keep my car running well, use caution in where I go and what I do. And I learned about self-protection—not an easy or quick decision. I developed a strategy of protection that includes handgun possession. The following incidents, chosen from a larger number because I think they could happen to anyone, helped make up my mind.

When I camped with another woman for several weeks, she didn't want to carry a pistol, and police told us Mace was illegal. We tucked spray deodorant into our sleeping bags, theorizing that any man crawling into our tent at night would be nervous anyway; anything sprayed in his face would slow him down until we could hit him with a frying pan, or escape. We never used our improvised weapon, because we were lucky enough to camp beside people who came to our aid when we needed them. I returned from that trip determined to reconsider.

At that time, I lived alone and taught night classes in town. Along a city street I often traveled, a woman had a flat tire, called for help on her CB, and got a rapist; he didn't fix the tire either. She was afraid to call for help again and stayed in her car until morning. Also, CBs work best along line-of-sight; I ruled them out.

As I drove home one night, a car followed me, lights bright. It passed on a narrow bridge, while a passenger flashed a spotlight in my face, blinding me. I braked sharply. The car stopped, angled across the bridge, and four men jumped out. I realized the locked doors were useless if they broke my car windows. I started forward, hoping to knock their car aside so I could pass. Just then, another car appeared, and the men got back in their car, but continued to follow me, passing and repassing. I dared not go home. I passed no lighted houses. Finally, they pulled to the roadside, and I decided to use their tactic: fear. I roared past them inches away, horn blaring. It worked; they turned off the highway. But it was desperate and foolish, and I was frightened and angry. Even in my vehicle I was too vulnerable.

Other incidents followed. One day I saw a man in the field near my house, carrying a shotgun and heading for a pond full of ducks. I drove to meet him, and politely explained that the land was posted. He stared at me, and the muzzle of his shotgun rose. I realized that if he simply shot me and drove away, I would be a statistic. The moment passed; the man left.

One night, I returned home from class to find deep tire ruts on the lawn, a large gas tank empty, garbage in the driveway. A light shone in the house; I couldn't remember leaving it on. I was too embarrassed to wake the neighbors. An hour of cautious exploration convinced me the house was safe, but once inside, with the doors locked, I was still afraid. I put a .22 rifle by my bed, but I kept thinking of how naked I felt, prowling around my own house in the dark.

It was time to consider self-defense. I took a kung fu class and learned to define the distance to maintain between myself and a stranger. Once someone enters that space without permission, kung fu teaches appro-

priate evasive or protective action. I learned to move confidently, scanning for possible attack. I learned how to assess danger, and techniques
for avoiding it without combat.

I also learned that one must practice several hours every day to be   10
good at kung fu. By that time I had married George; when I practiced
with him, I learned how *close* you must be to your attacker to use
martial arts, and decided a 120-pound woman dare not let a six-foot,
220-pound attacker get that close unless she is very, very good at self-
defense. Some women who are well trained in martial arts have been
raped and beaten anyway.

Reluctantly I decided to carry a pistol. George helped me practice
with his .357 and .22. I disliked the .357's recoil, though I later became
comfortable with it. I bought a .22 at a pawn shop. A standard .22 bullet, fired at close range, can kill, but news reports tell of attackers advancing with five such bullets in them. I bought magnum shells, with
more power, and practiced until I could hit someone close enough to
endanger me. Then I bought a license making it legal for me to carry the
gun concealed.

George taught me that the most important preparation was mental:
convincing myself I could shoot someone. Few of us really wish to hurt
or kill another human being. But there is no point in having a gun—in
fact, gun possession might increase your danger—unless you know
you can use it against another human being. A good training course
includes mental preparation, as well as training in safety. As I drive
or walk, I often rehearse the conditions which would cause me to
shoot. Men grow up handling firearms, and learn controlled violence
in contact sports, but women grow up learning to be subservient and
vulnerable. To make ourselves comfortable with the idea that we are
capable of protecting ourselves requires effort. But it need not turn us
into macho, gun-fighting broads. We must simply learn to do as men
do from an early age: believe in, and rely on, *ourselves* for protection.
The pistol only adds an extra edge, an attention-getter; it is a weapon
of last resort.

Because shooting at another person means shooting to kill. It's impossible even for seasoned police officers to be sure of only wounding
an assailant. If I shot an attacking man, I would aim at the largest tar-

get, the chest. This is not an easy choice, but for me it would be better than rape.

In my car, my pistol is within instant reach. When I enter a deserted rest stop at night, it's in my purse, my hand on the grip. When I walk from a dark parking lot into a motel, it's in my hand, under a coat. When I walk my dog in the deserted lots around most motels, the pistol is in a shoulder holster, and I am always aware of my surroundings. In my motel room, it lies on the bedside table. At home, it's on the headboard.

Just carrying a pistol is not protection. Avoidance is still the best approach to trouble; watch for danger signs, and practice avoiding them. Develop your instinct for danger.   15

One day while driving to the highway mailbox, I saw a vehicle parked about halfway to the house. Several men were standing in the ditch, relieving themselves. I have no objection to emergency urination; we always need moisture. But they'd also dumped several dozen beer cans, which blow into pastures and can slash a cow's legs or stomach.

As I slowly drove closer, the men zipped their trousers ostentatiously while walking toward me. Four men gathered around my small foreign car, making remarks they wouldn't make to their mothers, and one of them demanded what the hell I wanted.

"This is private land; I'd like you to pick up the beer cans."

"What beer cans?" said the belligerent one, putting both hands on the car door, and leaning in my window. His face was inches from mine, the beer fumes were strong, and he looked angry. The others laughed. One tried the passenger door, locked; another put his foot on the hood and rocked the car. They circled, lightly thumping the roof, discussing my good fortune in meeting them, and the benefits they were likely to bestow upon me. I felt small and trapped; they knew it.

"The ones you just threw out," I said politely.   20

"I don't see no beer cans. Why don't you get out here and show them to me, honey?" said the belligerent one, reaching for the handle inside my door.

"Right over there," I said, still being polite, "there and over there." I pointed with the pistol, which had been under my thigh. Within one minute the cans and the men were back in the car, and headed down the road.

I believe this small incident illustrates several principles. The men were trespassing and knew it; their judgment may have been impaired by alcohol. Their response to the polite request of a woman alone was to use their size and numbers to inspire fear. The pistol was a response in the same language. Politeness didn't work; I couldn't intimidate them. Out of the car, I'd have been more vulnerable. The pistol just changed the balance of power.

My husband, George, asked one question when I told him. "What would you have done if he'd grabbed for the pistol?"

"I had the car in reverse; I'd have hit the accelerator, and backed up; 25 if he'd kept coming, I'd have fired straight at him." He nodded.

In fact, the sight of the pistol made the man straighten up; he cracked his head on the door frame. He and the two in front of the car stepped backward, catching the attention of the fourth, who joined them. They were all in front of me then, and as the car was still running and in reverse gear, my options had multiplied. If they'd advanced again, I'd have backed away, turning to keep the open window toward them. Given time, I'd have put the first shot into the ground in front of them, the second into the belligerent leader. It might have been better to wait until they were gone, pick up the beer cans, and avoid confrontation, but I believed it was reasonable and my right to make a polite request to strangers littering my property. Showing the pistol worked on another occasion when I was driving in a desolate part of Wyoming. A man played cat-and-mouse with me for thirty miles, ultimately trying to run my car off the road. When his car was only two inches from mine, I pointed my pistol at him, and he disappeared.

I believe that a handgun is like a car; both are tools for specific purposes; both can be lethal if used improperly. Both require a license, training, and alertness. Both require you to be aware of what is happening before and behind you. Driving becomes almost instinctive; so does handgun use. When I've drawn my gun for protection, I simply found it in my hand. Instinct told me a situation was dangerous before my conscious mind reacted; I've felt the same while driving. Most good drivers react to emergencies by instinct.

Knives are another useful tool often misunderstood and misused; some people acquire knives mostly for display, either on a wall or on a belt, and such knives are often so large as to serve no useful purpose. My pocket knives are always razor sharp, because a small, sharp knife will do most jobs. Skinning blades serve for cutting meat and splitting small kindling in camp. A *sgian dubh*, a four-inch flat blade in a wooden sheath, was easily concealed inside a Scotsman's high socks, and slips into my dress or work boots as well. Some buckskinners keep what they call a "grace knife" on a thong around their necks; the name may derive from *coup de grâce*, the welcome throat-slash a wounded knight asked from his closest friend, to keep him from falling alive into the hands of his enemies. I also have a push dagger, with a blade only three inches long, attached to a handle that fits into the fist so well that the knife would be hard to lose even in hand-to-hand combat. When I first showed it, without explanation, to an older woman who would never consider carrying a knife, she took one look and said, "Why, you could push that right into someone's stomach," and demonstrated with a flourish. That's what it's for. I wear it for decoration, because it was handmade by Jerry and fits my hand perfectly, but I am intently aware of its purpose. I like my knives, not because they are weapons, but because they are well designed, and beautiful, and because each is a tool with a specific purpose.

Women didn't always have jobs, or drive cars or heavy equipment, though western women did many of those things almost as soon as they arrived here. Men in authority argued that their attempt to do so would unravel the fabric of society. Women, they said, would become less feminine; they hadn't the intelligence to cope with the mechanics of a car, or the judgment to cope with emergencies. Since these ideas were so wrong, perhaps it is time women brought a new dimension to the wise use of handguns as well.

We can and should educate ourselves in how to travel safely, take 30 self-defense courses, reason, plead, or avoid trouble in other ways. But some men cannot be stopped by those methods; they understand only power. A man who is committing an attack already knows he's breaking laws; he has no concern for someone else's rights. A pistol is a woman's answer to his greater power. It makes her equally frightening. I have thought of revising the old Colt slogan: "God made man, but Sam Colt made them equal" to read "God made men *and women* but Sam Colt made them equal." Recently I have seen an ad for a popular gunmaker with a similar sentiment; perhaps this is an idea whose time has come, though the pacifist inside me will be saddened if the only way women can achieve equality is by carrying a weapon.

As a society, we were shocked in early 1989 when a female jogger in New York's Central Park was beaten and raped savagely and left in a coma. I was even more shocked when reporters interviewed children who lived near the victim and quoted a twelve-year-old as saying, "She had nothing to guard herself; she didn't have no man with her; she didn't have no Mace." And another sixth-grader said, "It is like she committed suicide." Surely this is not a majority opinion, but I think it is not so unusual, either, even in this liberated age. Yet there is no city or county in the nation where law officers can relax because all the criminals are in jail. Some authorities say citizens armed with handguns stop almost as many crimes annually as armed criminals succeed in committing, and that people defending themselves kill three times more attackers and robbers than police do. I don't suggest all criminals should be killed, but some can be stopped only by death or permanent incarceration. Law enforcement officials can't prevent crimes; later punishment may be of little comfort to the victim. A society so controlled that no crime existed would probably be too confined for most of us, and is not likely to exist any time soon. Therefore, many of us should be ready and able to protect ourselves, and the intelligent use of firearms is one way.

We must treat a firearm's power with caution. "Power tends to corrupt, and absolute power corrupts absolutely," as a man (Lord Acton) once said. A pistol is not the only way to avoid being raped or murdered in today's world, but a firearm, intelligently wielded, can shift the balance and provide a measure of safety.

STUDY QUESTIONS

1. How does Hasselstrom answer the question suggested by her title? Why *does* this peaceful woman carry a pistol?

2. As Hasselstrom EXPLAINS THE PROCESS of how she came to carry a firearm, she also ARGUES that guns are a good way for women to protect themselves. What EVIDENCE does she use to support this CLAIM? How effective is her evidence? Explain.

3. *For Writing.* This essay was written more than a decade ago. In an essay of your own, ANALYZE whether Hasselstrom's ARGUMENT is still relevant. How has the cultural context changed? (Or has it?) Is the need for a pistol more or less urgent today than it was when the essay was written?

MARTIN LUTHER KING JR. { *I Have a Dream*

MARTIN LUTHER KING JR. (1929–1968), civil rights leader and minister, was an advocate of civil disobedience, boycotts, and peaceful protest marches as ways of gaining equal rights for African Americans. His activism was grounded in his religious training and the philosophical teachings of passive resistance of both Jesus and Mahatma Gandhi. For his work to promote equality without the use of violence for African Americans, King received the 1964 Nobel Peace Prize. In August 1963, King and several labor and civil rights leaders organized the March on Washington for Jobs and Freedom, a political rally that influenced later policy, including the Civil Rights Act of 1964 and the National Voting Rights Act of 1965. King was assassinated in Memphis, Tennessee, in 1968.

King's speech "I Have a Dream," delivered from the steps of the Lincoln Memorial at the March on Washington, carries a message of hope for a people who had long been disenfranchised in America. As you read this speech, think about how it was crafted to be heard, not read; look for techniques such as repetition and rhythm that would have captured and held the attention of King's audience and that helped make this one of history's best-remembered speeches.

I AM HAPPY TO JOIN with you today in what will go down in history as the greatest demonstration for freedom in the history of our nation.

Five score years ago, a great American, in whose symbolic shadow we stand today, signed the Emancipation Proclamation.[1] This momen-

---

[1] President Abraham Lincoln issued the Emancipation Proclamation on September 22, 1862, declaring that all slaves were henceforth free.

"I Have a Dream". Reprinted by arrangement with The Heirs to the Estate of Martin Luther King Jr., c/o Writers House as agent for the proprietor New York, NY.

tous decree came as a great beacon light of hope to millions of Negro slaves who had been seared in the flames of withering injustice. It came as a joyous daybreak to end the long night of their captivity.

But one hundred years later, the Negro still is not free. One hundred years later, the life of the Negro is still sadly crippled by the manacles of segregation and the chains of discrimination. One hundred years later, the Negro lives on a lonely island of poverty in the midst of a vast ocean of material prosperity. One hundred years later, the Negro is still languished in the corners of American society and finds himself an exile in his own land. And so we've come here today to dramatize a shameful condition.

In a sense we've come to our nation's capital to cash a check. When the architects of our republic wrote the magnificent words of the Constitution and the Declaration of Independence, they were signing a promissory note to which every American was to fall heir. This note was a promise that all men, yes, black men as well as white men, would be guaranteed the "unalienable Rights" of "Life, Liberty and the pursuit of Happiness." It is obvious today that America has defaulted on this promissory note, insofar as her citizens of color are concerned. Instead of honoring this sacred obligation, America has given the Negro people a bad check, a check which has come back marked "insufficient funds."

But we refuse to believe that the bank of justice is bankrupt. We 5 refuse to believe that there are insufficient funds in the great vaults of opportunity of this nation. And so, we've come to cash this check, a check that will give us upon demand the riches of freedom and the security of justice.

We have also come to this hallowed spot to remind America of the fierce urgency of Now. This is no time to engage in the luxury of cooling off or to take the tranquilizing drug of gradualism. Now is the time to make real the promises of democracy. Now is the time to rise from the dark and desolate valley of segregation to the sunlit path of racial justice. Now is the time to lift our nation from the quicksands of racial injustice to the solid rock of brotherhood. Now is the time to make justice a reality for all of God's children.

It would be fatal for the nation to overlook the urgency of the moment. This sweltering summer of the Negro's legitimate discontent[2] will not pass until there is an invigorating autumn of freedom and equality. Nineteen sixty-three is not an end, but a beginning. And those who hope that the Negro needed to blow off steam and will now be content will have a rude awakening if the nation returns to business as usual. And there will be neither rest nor tranquility in America until the Negro is granted his citizenship rights. The whirlwinds of revolt will continue to shake the foundations of our nation until the bright day of justice emerges.

But there is something that I must say to my people, who stand on the warm threshold which leads into the palace of justice: In the process of gaining our rightful place, we must not be guilty of wrongful deeds. Let us not seek to satisfy our thirst for freedom by drinking from the cup of bitterness and hatred. We must forever conduct our struggle on the high plane of dignity and discipline. We must not allow our creative protest to degenerate into physical violence. Again and again, we must rise to the majestic heights of meeting physical force with soul force.

The marvelous new militancy which has engulfed the Negro community must not lead us to distrust of all white people, for many of our white brothers, as evidenced by their presence here today, have come to realize that their destiny is tied up with our destiny. And they have come to realize that their freedom is inextricably bound to our freedom.

We cannot walk alone.   10

And as we walk, we must make the pledge that we shall always march ahead.

We cannot turn back.

There are those who are asking the devotees of civil rights, "When will you be satisfied?" We can never be satisfied as long as the Negro is the victim of the unspeakable horrors of police brutality. We can never

---

[2]An allusion to the opening line of Shakespeare's *Richard III*: "Now is the winter of our discontent."

be satisfied as long as our bodies, heavy with the fatigue of travel, cannot gain lodging in the motels of the highways and the hotels of the cities. We cannot be satisfied as long as the Negro's basic mobility is from a smaller ghetto to a larger one. We can never be satisfied as long as our children are stripped of their self-hood and robbed of their dignity by signs stating: "For Whites Only." We cannot be satisfied as long as a Negro in Mississippi cannot vote and a Negro in New York believes he has nothing for which to vote. No, no, we are not satisfied, and we will not be satisfied until "justice rolls down like waters, and righteousness like a mighty stream."[3]

I am not unmindful that some of you have come here out of great trials and tribulations. Some of you have come fresh from narrow jail cells. And some of you have come from areas where your quest for freedom left you battered by the storms of persecution and staggered by the winds of police brutality. You have been the veterans of creative suffering. Continue to work with the faith that unearned suffering is redemptive. Go back to Mississippi, go back to Alabama, go back to South Carolina, go back to Georgia, go back to Louisiana, go back to the slums and ghettos of our northern cities, knowing that somehow this situation can and will be changed.

Let us not wallow in the valley of despair. I say to you today, my 15
friends.

And so even though we face the difficulties of today and tomorrow, I still have a dream. It is a dream deeply rooted in the American dream.

I have a dream that one day this nation will rise up and live out the true meaning of its creed: "We hold these truths to be self-evident, that all men are created equal."

I have a dream that one day on the red hills of Georgia, the sons of former slaves and the sons of former slave owners will be able to sit down together at the table of brotherhood.

I have a dream that one day even the state of Mississippi, a state sweltering with the heat of injustice, sweltering with the heat of oppression, will be transformed into an oasis of freedom and justice.

I have a dream that my four little children will one day live in a 20

[3]Amos 5:24.

nation where they will not be judged by the color of their skin but by the content of their character.

I have a *dream* today!

I have a dream that one day, down in Alabama, with its vicious racists, with its governor having his lips dripping with the words of "interposition" and "nullification"[4]—one day right there in Alabama little black boys and black girls will be able to join hands with little white boys and white girls as sisters and brothers.

I have a *dream* today!

I have a dream that one day every valley shall be exalted, every hill and mountain shall be made low, the rough places will be made plain, and the crooked places will be made straight; "and the glory of the Lord shall be revealed, and all flesh shall see it together."[5]

This is our hope, and this is the faith that I go back to the South 25 with.

With this faith, we will be able to hew out of the mountain of despair a stone of hope. With this faith, we will be able to transform the jangling discords of our nation into a beautiful symphony of brotherhood. With this faith, we will be able to work together, to pray together, to struggle together, to go to jail together, to stand up for freedom together, knowing that we will be free one day.

And this will be the day—this will be the day when all of God's children will be able to sing with new meaning:

> My country, 'tis of thee, sweet land of liberty, of thee I sing.
> Land where my fathers died, land of the pilgrim's pride,
> From every mountainside, let freedom ring.

And if America is to be a great nation, this must become true.

And so let freedom ring from the prodigious hilltops of New Hampshire.

Let freedom ring from the mighty mountains of New York. 30

---

[4]A reference to the legalisms employed by then–Alabama governor George Wallace (1919–98) in his efforts to prevent integration at the University of Alabama.

[5]Isaiah 40:5.

Let freedom ring from the heightening Alleghenies of Pennsylvania.

Let freedom ring from the snowcapped Rockies of Colorado.

Let freedom ring from the curvaceous slopes of California.

But not only that:

Let freedom ring from Stone Mountain of Georgia.[6]

Let freedom ring from Lookout Mountain of Tennessee.[7]

Let freedom ring from every hill and molehill of Mississippi.

From every mountainside, let freedom ring.

And when this happens, when we allow freedom ring, when we let 35 it ring from every village and every hamlet, from every state and every city, we will be able to speed up that day when *all* of God's children, black men and white men, Jews and Gentiles, Protestants and Catholics, will be able to join hands and sing in the words of the old Negro spiritual:

Free at last! Free at last!

Thank God Almighty, we are free at last!

---

[6]Site of memorial to Confederate soldiers.

[7]Site of Civil War battleground.

STUDY QUESTIONS

1. Martin Luther King Jr. was a minister quite familiar with giving sermons. The "I Have a Dream" speech is structured like a sermon with one predominant characteristic: repetition. Identify two different examples of repeated phrases and discuss the effect they have on you.

2. Many sermons have three parts: they begin with a scriptural passage or an introduction to a commonplace thought or idea, move to an explanation of the TOPIC, and conclude with an application to daily life. King's speech follows this tripartite structure. Analyze the speech and explain where you think each part begins and ends. Provide a rationale for your choices.

3. King argues not only from personal and historical experience, but also through allusions to such well-known sources as Abraham Lincoln's "Gettysburg Address," William Shakespeare's play *Richard III,* and the Bible to support his ARGUMENT. Reread the speech, determine its THESIS, and select two allusions King uses that you believe are most effective in supporting his thesis. Explain why these allusions are effective.

4. *For Writing.* King wrote this speech knowing that his AUDIENCE would be composed of a wide range of listeners from the general public. Rewrite his speech without changing the PURPOSE or structure but aiming at a different audience, possibly Congress, the United Nations, or a group of business leaders.

HORACE MINER { *Body Ritual among*
the Nacirema

HORACE MINER (1912–1993) was born in St. Paul, Minnesota, and grew
up in Lexington, Kentucky. He received his PhD in anthropology from the
University of Chicago in 1937. Miner taught sociology and anthropology at
a number of universities in the United States, including Wayne State
University and the University of Michigan. Although he published many
books, including *Culture and Agriculture* (1949) and *City in Modern Africa*
(1967), he may be best known for his humorous study "Body Ritual among
the Nacirema."

At first glance, this ostensibly serious report explores the different cultural rituals that the Nacirema undergo daily—rituals that should begin to
sound familiar as you read. Note how Miner describes everyday activities
with the impartial language of an academic observer. Look for markers of
academic writing. What is the effect of the familiar being rendered in this
manner?

THE ANTHROPOLOGIST HAS BECOME SO familiar with the diversity of
ways in which different peoples behave in similar situations that he is
not apt to be surprised by even the most exotic customs. In fact, if all
of the logically possible combinations of behavior have not been found
somewhere in the world, he is apt to suspect that they must be present
in some yet undescribed tribe. This point has, in fact, been expressed
with respect to clan organization by Murdock (1949:71). In this light,
the magical beliefs and practices of the Nacirema present such unusual
aspects that it seems desirable to describe them as an example of the
extremes to which human behavior can go.

"Body Ritual among the Nacirema" by Horace Miner. *American Anthropologist*. Volume
58 (3), 1956: pp. 503–507.

Professor Linton first brought the ritual of the Nacirema to the attention of anthropologists twenty years ago (1936:326), but the culture of this people is still very poorly understood. They are a North American group living in the territory between the Canadian Cree, the Yaqui and Tarahumare of Mexico, and the Carib and Arawak of the Antilles. Little is known of their origin, although tradition states that they came from the east. According to Nacirema mythology, their nation was originated by a culture hero, Notgnihsaw, who is otherwise known for two great feats of strength—the throwing of a piece of wampum across the river Pa-To-Mac and the chopping down of a cherry tree in which the Spirit of Truth resided.

Nacirema culture is characterized by a highly developed market economy which has evolved in a rich natural habitat. While much of the people's time is devoted to economic pursuits, a large part of the fruits of these labors and a considerable portion of the day are spent in ritual activity. The focus of this activity is the human body, the appearance and health of which loom as a dominant concern in the ethos of the people. While such a concern is certainly not unusual, its ceremonial aspects and associated philosophy are unique.

The fundamental belief underlying the whole system appears to be that the human body is ugly and that its natural tendency is to debility and disease. Incarcerated in such a body, man's only hope is to avert these characteristics through the use of the powerful influences of ritual and ceremony. Every household has one or more shrines devoted to this purpose. The more powerful individuals in the society have several shrines in their houses and, in fact, the opulence of a house is often referred to in terms of the number of such ritual centers it possesses. Most houses are of wattle and daub construction, but the shrine rooms of the more wealthy are walled with stone. Poorer families imitate the rich by applying pottery plaques to their shrine walls.

While each family has at least one such shrine, the rituals associated with it are not family ceremonies but are private and secret. The rites are normally only discussed with children, and then only during the period when they are being initiated into these mysteries. I was able, however, to establish sufficient rapport with the natives to examine these shrines and to have the rituals described to me.

5

The focal point of the shrine is a box or chest which is built into the wall. In this chest are kept the many charms and magical potions without which no native believes he could live. These preparations are secured from a variety of specialized practitioners. The most powerful of these are the medicine men, whose assistance must be rewarded with substantial gifts. However, the medicine men do not provide the curative potions for their clients, but decide what the ingredients should be and then write them down in an ancient and secret language. This writing is understood only by the medicine men and by the herbalists who, for another gift, provide the required charm.

The charm is not disposed of after it has served its purpose, but is placed in the charm-box of the household shrine. As these magical materials are specific for certain ills, and the real or imagined maladies of the people are many, the charm-box is usually full to overflowing. The magical packets are so numerous that people forget what their purposes were and fear to use them again. While the natives are very vague on this point, we can only assume that the idea in retaining all the old magical materials is that their presence in the charm-box, before which the body rituals are conducted, will in some way protect the worshipper.

Beneath the charm-box is a small font. Each day every member of the family, in succession, enters the shrine room, bows his head before the charm-box, mingles different sorts of holy water in the font, and proceeds with a brief rite of ablution. The holy waters are secured from the Water Temple of the community, where the priests conduct elaborate ceremonies to make the liquid ritually pure.

In the hierarchy of magical practitioners, and below the medicine men in prestige, are specialists whose designation is best translated "holy-mouth-men." The Nacirema have an almost pathological horror of and fascination with the mouth, the condition of which is believed to have a supernatural influence on all social relationships. Were it not for the rituals of the mouth, they believe that their teeth would fall out, their gums bleed, their jaws shrink, their friends desert them, and their lovers reject them. They also believe that a strong relationship exists between oral and moral characteristics. For example, there is a ritual ablution of the mouth for children which is supposed to improve their moral fiber.

The daily body ritual performed by everyone includes a mouth-rite. 10 Despite the fact that these people are so punctilious about care of the mouth, this rite involves a practice which strikes the uninitiated stranger as revolting. It was reported to me that the ritual consists of inserting a small bundle of hog hairs into the mouth, along with certain magical powders, and then moving the bundle in a highly formalized series of gestures.

In addition to the private mouth-rite, the people seek out a holy-mouth-man once or twice a year. These practitioners have an impressive set of paraphernalia, consisting of a variety of augers, awls, probes, and prods. The use of these objects in the exorcism of the evils of the mouth involves almost unbelievable ritual torture of the client. The holy-mouth-man opens the client's mouth and, using the above mentioned tools, enlarges any holes which decay may have created in the teeth. Magical materials are put into these holes. If there are no naturally occurring holes in the teeth, large sections of one or more teeth are gouged out so that the supernatural substance can be applied. In the client's view, the purpose of these ministrations is to arrest decay and to draw friends. The extremely sacred and traditional character of the rite is evident in the fact that the natives return to the holy-mouth-men year after year, despite the fact that their teeth continue to decay.

It is to be hoped that, when a thorough study of the Nacirema is made, there will be careful inquiry into the personality structure of these people. One has but to watch the gleam in the eye of a holy-mouth-man, as he jabs an awl into an exposed nerve, to suspect that a certain amount of sadism is involved. If this can be established, a very interesting pattern emerges, for most of the population shows definite masochistic tendencies. It was to these that Professor Linton referred in discussing a distinctive part of the daily body ritual which is performed only by men. This part of the rite involves scraping and lacerating the surface of the face with a sharp instrument. Special women's rites are performed only four times during each lunar month, but what they lack in frequency is made up in barbarity. As part of this ceremony, women bake their heads in small ovens for about an hour. The theoretically interesting point is that what seems to be a preponderantly masochistic people have developed sadistic specialists.

The medicine men have an imposing temple, or *latipso*, in every community of any size. The more elaborate ceremonies required to treat very sick patients can only be performed at this temple. These ceremonies involve not only the thaumaturge but a permanent group of vestal maidens who move sedately about the temple chambers in distinctive costume and headdress.

The *latipso* ceremonies are so harsh that it is phenomenal that a fair proportion of the really sick natives who enter the temple ever recover. Small children whose indoctrination is still incomplete have been known to resist attempts to take them to the temple because "that is where you go to die." Despite this fact, sick adults are not only willing but eager to undergo the protracted ritual purification, if they can afford to do so. No matter how ill the supplicant or how grave the emergency, the guardians of many temples will not admit a client if he cannot give a rich gift to the custodian. Even after one has gained admission and survived the ceremonies, the guardians will not permit the neophyte to leave until he makes still another gift.

The supplicant entering the temple is first stripped of all his or her clothes. In every-day life the Nacirema avoids exposure of his body and its natural functions. Bathing and excretory acts are performed only in the secrecy of the household shrine, where they are ritualized as part of the body-rites. Psychological shock results from the fact that body secrecy is suddenly lost upon entry into the *latipso*. A man, whose own wife has never seen him in an excretory act, suddenly finds himself naked and assisted by a vestal maiden while he performs his natural functions into a sacred vessel. This sort of ceremonial treatment is necessitated by the fact that the excreta are used by a diviner to ascertain the course and nature of the client's sickness. Female clients, on the other hand, find their naked bodies are subjected to the scrutiny, manipulation and prodding of the medicine men.

Few supplicants in the temple are well enough to do anything but lie on their hard beds. The daily ceremonies, like the rites of the holy-mouth-men, involve discomfort and torture. With ritual precision, the vestals awaken their miserable charges each dawn and roll them about on their beds of pain while performing ablutions, in the formal movements of which the maidens are highly trained. At other times they

15

insert magic wands in the supplicant's mouth or force him to eat substances which are supposed to be healing. From time to time the medicine men come to their clients and jab magically treated needles into
their flesh. The fact that these temple ceremonies may not cure, and
may even kill the neophyte, in no way decreases the people's faith in
the medicine men.

There remains one other kind of practitioner, known as a "listener."
This witch-doctor has the power to exorcise the devils that lodge in
the heads of people who have been bewitched. The Nacirema believe
that parents bewitch their own children. Mothers are particularly suspected of putting a curse on children while teaching them the secret
body rituals. The counter-magic of the witch-doctor is unusual in its
lack of ritual. The patient simply tells the "listener" all his troubles and
fears, beginning with the earliest difficulties he can remember. The
memory displayed by the Nacirema in these exorcism sessions is truly
remarkable. It is not uncommon for the patient to bemoan the rejection
he felt upon being weaned as a babe, and a few individuals even see
their troubles going back to the traumatic effects of their own birth.

In conclusion, mention must be made of certain practices which
have their base in native esthetics but which depend upon the pervasive aversion to the natural body and its functions. There are ritual
fasts to make fat people thin and ceremonial feasts to make thin people
fat. Still other rites are used to make women's breasts larger if they are
small, and smaller if they are large. General dissatisfaction with breast
shape is symbolized in the fact that the ideal form is virtually outside
the range of human variation. A few women afflicted with almost inhuman hypermammary development are so idolized that they make a
handsome living by simply going from village to village and permitting
the natives to stare at them for a fee.

Reference has already been made to the fact that excretory functions
are ritualized, routinized, and relegated to secrecy. Natural reproductive functions are similarly distorted. Intercourse is taboo as a topic
and scheduled as an act. Efforts are made to avoid pregnancy by the
use of magical materials or by limiting intercourse to certain phases of
the moon. Conception is actually very infrequent. When pregnant,
women dress so as to hide their condition. Parturition takes place in

secret, without friends or relatives to assist, and the majority of women do not nurse their infants.

Our review of the ritual life of the Nacirema has certainly shown 20 them to be a magic-ridden people. It is hard to understand how they have managed to exist so long under the burdens which they have imposed upon themselves. But even such exotic customs as these take on real meaning when they are viewed with the insight provided by Malinowski when he wrote (1948:70):

> Looking from far and above, from our high places of safety in the developed civilization, it is easy to see all the crudity and irrelevance of magic. But without its power and guidance early man could not have mastered his practical difficulties as he has done, nor could man have advanced to the higher stages of civilization.

REFERENCES CITED

Linton, Ralph. 1936. *The Study of Man.* New York, D. Appleton-Century Co.

Malinowski, Bronislaw. 1948. *Magic, Science, and Religion.* Glencoe, The Free Press.

Murdock, George P. 1949. *Social Structure.* New York, The Macmillan Co.

STUDY QUESTIONS

1. Who are the Nacirema? What are the real names of the rituals that Miner describes?

2. In ANALYZING THE PROCESS of the Nacirema body rituals, what STRATEGIES does Miner employ to defamiliarize the familiar? How does he use humor throughout this ostensibly serious piece?

3. *For Writing.* Choose another everyday process to analyze—perhaps the process of sending and receiving information, playing a sport, or eating at your college cafeteria. Write an essay in which you analyze this familiar process from the perspective of an anthropologist encountering it for the first time.

ANNA QUINDLEN ⎰ *Homeless*

ANNA QUINDLEN (b. 1952), journalist and novelist, was born in
Philadelphia, Pennsylvania. After graduating from Barnard College in 1974,
Quindlen began her career as a journalist at *The New York Post*. Three years
later she moved to the *New York Times*, where she remained for eighteen
years, winning the Pulitzer Prize for Commentary in 1992. Quindlen left
journalism in 1995 to write fiction full time, but she returned four years
later as contributing editor at *Newsweek*, where she wrote a biweekly column
until 2009. Quindlen has published two children's books, numerous essay
collections, and five novels, including *One True Thing* (1994) and *Blessings*
(2002). She holds honorary doctorates from Dartmouth College and Mount
Holyoke College, among others, and she was awarded the University Medal
of Excellence from Columbia University.

In "Homeless," Quindlen writes about meeting a woman named Ann in
New York City's Port Authority Bus Terminal. When Ann produces a
photograph of a yellow house—presumably where she used to live—
Quindlen reflects on the importance of having a home, in ways both obvious
and surprising. Unlike many other essays on homelessness, Quindlen does
not provide statistics, consider causes, or argue for specific action; instead,
she argues simply that having a home "is everything." As you read, consider
how and why Quindlen personalizes the issue of homelessness.

———————

HER NAME WAS ANN, AND we met in the Port Authority Bus Terminal
several Januarys ago. I was doing a story on homeless people. She said
I was wasting my time talking to her; she was just passing through, al-

though she'd been passing through for more than two weeks. To impress me with her bona fides, she rummaged through a tote bag and a manila envelope and finally unfolded a sheet of typing paper and brought out her photographs.

They were not pictures of family, or friends, or even a dog or cat, its eyes brown-red in the flashbulb's light. They were pictures of a house. It was like a thousand houses in a hundred towns, not suburb, not city, but somewhere in between, with aluminum siding and a chain-link fence, a narrow driveway running up to a one-car garage and a patch of backyard. The house was yellow. I looked on the back for a date or a name, but neither was there.

There was no need for discussion. I knew what she was trying to tell me, for it was something I had often felt. She was not adrift, alone, anonymous, although her bags and her raincoat with the grime shadowing its creases had made me believe she was. She had a house, or at least once upon a time had had one. Inside were curtains, a couch, a stove, potholders. You are where you live. She was somebody.

I've never been very good at looking at the big picture, taking the global view, and I've always been a person with an overactive sense of place, the legacy of an Irish grandfather. So it is natural that the thing that seems most wrong with the world to me right now is that there are so many people with no homes. I'm not simply talking about shelter from the elements, or three square meals a day or a mailing address to which the welfare people can send the check—although I know that all these are important for survival. I'm talking about a home, about precisely those kinds of feelings that have wound up in cross-stitch and French knots on samplers over the years. Home is where the heart is. There's no place like it. I love my home with a ferocity totally out of proportion to its appearance or location. I love dumb things about it: the hot-water heater, the plastic thing you drain dishes in, the roof over my head, which occasionally leaks. And yet it is precisely those dumb things that make it what it is—a place of certainty, stability, predictability, privacy, for me and for my family. It is where I live. What more can you say about a place than that? That is everything.

Yet it is something that we have been edging away from gradually 5 during my lifetime and the lifetimes of my parents and grandparents. There was a time when where you lived often was where you worked and where you grew the food you ate and even where you were buried. When that era passed, where you lived at least was where your parents had lived and where you would live with your children when you became enfeebled. Then, suddenly, where you lived was where you lived for three years, until you could move on to something else and something else again.

And so we have come to something else again, to children who do not understand what it means to go to their rooms because they have never had a room, to men and women whose fantasy is a wall they can paint a color of their own choosing, to old people reduced to sitting on molded plastic chairs, their skin blue-white in the lights of a bus station, and pulling pictures of houses out of their bags. Homes have stopped being homes. Now they are real estate.

People find it curious that those without homes would rather sleep sitting up on benches or huddled in doorways than go to shelters. Certainly some prefer to do so because they are emotionally ill, because they have been locked in before and they are damned if they will be locked in again. Others are afraid of the violence and trouble they may find there. But some seem to want something that is not available in shelters, and they will not compromise, not for a cot, or oatmeal or a shower with special soap that kills the bugs. "One room," a woman with a baby who was sleeping on her sister's floor, once told me, "painted blue." That was the crux of it; not size or location, but pride of ownership. Painted blue.

This is a difficult problem, and some wise and compassionate people are working hard at it. But in the main I think we work around it, just as we walk around it when it is lying on the sidewalk or sitting in the bus terminal—the problem, that is. It has been customary to take people's pain and lessen our own participation in it by turning it into an issue, not a collection of human beings. We turn an adjective into a noun: the poor, not poor people; the homeless, not Ann or the man who lives in the box or the woman who sleeps on the subway grate.

Sometimes I think we would be better off if we forgot about the broad strokes and concentrated on the details. Here is a woman without a bureau. There is a man with no mirror, no wall to hang it on. They are not the homeless. They are people who have no homes. No drawer that holds the spoons. No window to look out upon the world. My God. That is everything.

STUDY QUESTIONS

1. Explain the distinction Quindlen makes in her final paragraph between "the homeless" and "people who have no homes."

2. Who is Ann? Why does Quindlen tell her story? What is the effect on the reader of focusing on just one person?

3. What larger conversation is Quindlen joining in "Homeless"? What is her contribution to this conversation? What is she asking of her readers?

4. *For Writing.* Quindlen writes, "Homes have stopped being homes. Now they are real estate." Write an essay that examines your relationships with the home you have now and other homes you've lived in. Consider your own identity as a function of that relationship. How have you felt about the home(s) in which you have lived? How much of who you are now is DEFINED by where you live or have lived?

BRENT STAPLES { *Just Walk on By:*
Black Men and Public Space

BRENT STAPLES (b. 1951) grew up in Chester, Pennsylvania, remaining there to attend college after a faculty member encouraged him to apply to Widener University, where he studied behavioral science before going on to earn a PhD in psychology from the University of Chicago. After teaching briefly at Widener, he worked as a reporter for the *Chicago Sun-Times* and then joined the *New York Times* in 1985. Five years later, he was appointed to the *Times* editorial board, and he continues to write for that paper and for other publications, frequently focusing on politics and race in American culture. His memoir, *Parallel Time: Growing Up in Black and White* (1994), details his childhood in Chester and the death of his younger brother.

In this selection, Staples, who is African American, tells of the ways he has been perceived as dangerous because of his appearance. First published in *Ms.* magazine, a periodical read by just the type of middle-class, white woman the author describes in his first paragraph, the essay has become a mainstay in textbooks for freshman composition. As you read, think about the tone Staples adopts in his essay and how it helps to shape your reaction as a reader.

MY FIRST VICTIM WAS A woman—white, well dressed, probably in her early twenties. I came upon her late one evening on a deserted street in Hyde Park, a relatively affluent neighborhood in an otherwise mean, impoverished section of Chicago. As I swung onto the avenue behind her, there seemed to be a discreet, uninflammatory distance between us. Not so. She cast back a worried glance. To her, the youngish black man—a broad six feet two inches with a beard and billowing hair, both

"Just Walk on By: Black Men and Public Space" originally published in *Ms. Magazine*, September 1986. Reprinted with permission of the author.

hands shoved into the pockets of a bulky military jacket—seemed menacingly close. After a few more quick glimpses, she picked up her pace and was soon running in earnest. Within seconds she disappeared into a cross street.

That was more than a decade ago, I was twenty-two years old, a graduate student newly arrived at the University of Chicago. It was in the echo of that terrified woman's footfalls that I first began to know the unwieldy inheritance I'd come into—the ability to alter public space in ugly ways. It was clear that she thought herself the quarry of a mugger, a rapist, or worse. Suffering a bout of insomnia, however, I was stalking sleep, not defenseless wayfarers. As a softy who is scarcely able to take a knife to a raw chicken—let alone hold one to a person's throat—I was surprised, embarrassed, and dismayed all at once. Her flight made me feel like an accomplice in tyranny. It also made it clear that I was indistinguishable from the muggers who occasionally seeped into the area from the surrounding ghetto. That first encounter, and those that followed, signified that a vast, unnerving gulf lay between nighttime pedestrians—particularly women—and me. And I soon gathered that being perceived as dangerous is a hazard in itself. I only needed to turn a corner into a dicey situation, or crowd some frightened, armed person in a foyer somewhere, or make an errant move after being pulled over by a policeman. Where fear and weapons meet—and they often do in urban America—there is always the possibility of death.

In that first year, my first away from my hometown, I was to become thoroughly familiar with the language of fear. At dark, shadowy intersections, I could cross in front of a car stopped at a traffic light and elicit the *thunk, thunk, thunk, thunk* of the driver—black, white, male, or female—hammering down the door locks. On less traveled streets after dark, I grew accustomed to but never comfortable with people crossing to the other side of the street rather than pass me. Then there were the standard unpleasantries with policemen, doormen, bouncers, cabdrivers, and others whose business it is to screen out troublesome individuals *before* there is any nastiness.

I moved to New York nearly two years ago and I have remained an avid night walker. In central Manhattan, the near-constant crowd cover minimizes tense one-on-one street encounters. Elsewhere—in SoHo, for example, where sidewalks are narrow and tightly spaced buildings shut out the sky—things can get very taut indeed.

After dark, on the warrenlike streets of Brooklyn where I live, I often 5 see women who fear the worst from me. They seem to have set their faces on neutral, and with their purse straps strung across their chests bandolier-style, they forge ahead as though bracing themselves against being tackled. I understand, of course, that the danger they perceive is not a hallucination. Women are particularly vulnerable to street violence, and young black males are drastically overrepresented among the perpetrators of that violence. Yet these truths are no solace against the kind of alienation that comes of being ever the suspect, a fearsome entity with whom pedestrians avoid making eye contact.

It is not altogether clear to me how I reached the ripe old age of twenty-two without being conscious of the lethality nighttime pedestrians attributed to me. Perhaps it was because in Chester, Pennsylvania, the small, angry industrial town where I came of age in the 1960s, I was scarcely noticeable against a backdrop of gang warfare, street knifings, and murders. I grew up one of the good boys, had perhaps a half-dozen fistfights. In retrospect, my shyness of combat has clear sources.

As a boy, I saw countless tough guys locked away; I have since buried several, too. They were babies, really—a teenage cousin, a brother of twenty-two, a childhood friend in his mid-twenties—all gone down in episodes of bravado played out in the streets. I came to doubt the virtues of intimidation early on. I chose, perhaps unconsciously, to remain a shadow—timid, but a survivor.

The fearsomeness mistakenly attributed to me in public places often has a perilous flavor. The most frightening of these confusions occurred in the late 1970s and early 1980s, when I worked as a journalist in Chicago. One day, rushing into the office of a magazine I was writing for with a deadline story in hand, I was mistaken for a burglar. The office manager called security and, with an ad hoc posse, pursued me through the labyrinthine halls, nearly to my editor's door. I had no way of proving who I was. I could only move briskly toward the company of someone who knew me.

Another time I was on assignment for a local paper and killing time before an interview. I entered a jewelry store on the city's affluent Near North Side. The proprietor excused herself and returned with an enormous red Doberman pinscher straining at the end of a leash. She stood, the dog extended toward me, silent to my questions, her eyes bulging nearly out of her head. I took a cursory look around, nodded, and bade her good night.

Relatively speaking, however, I never fared as badly as another black   10
male journalist. He went to nearby Waukegan, Illinois, a couple of summers ago to work on a story about a murderer who was born there. Mistaking the reporter for the killer, police officers hauled him from his car at gunpoint and but for his press credentials would probably have tried to book him. Such episodes are not uncommon. Black men trade tales like this all the time.

Over the years, I learned to smother the rage I felt at so often being taken for a criminal. Not to do so would surely have led to madness. I now take precautions to make myself less threatening. I move about with care, particularly late in the evening. I give a wide berth to nervous people on subway platforms during the wee hours, particularly when I have exchanged business clothes for jeans. If I happen to be entering a building behind some people who appear skittish, I may walk by, letting them clear the lobby before I return, so as not to seem to be following them. I have been calm and extremely congenial on those rare occasions when I've been pulled over by the police.

And on late-evening constitutionals I employ what has proved to be an excellent tension-reducing measure: I whistle melodies from Beethoven and Vivaldi and the more popular classical composers. Even steely New Yorkers hunching toward nighttime destinations seem to relax, and occasionally they even join in the tune. Virtually everybody seems to sense that a mugger wouldn't be warbling bright, sunny selections from Vivaldi's *Four Seasons*. It is my equivalent of the cowbell that hikers wear when they know they are in bear country.

STUDY QUESTIONS

1. What is one "precaution" Staples takes to make himself "less threatening"?

2. What is Staples's ETHOS in this essay? Find specific passages to support your RESPONSE.

3. What rhetorical strategies does Staples use in his introductory paragraph to catch his readers' attention and draw them into the essay? How effective do you find them to be?

4. *For Writing.* Although this essay was published over two decades ago, the issues Staples presents in it continue to be topics of discussion. Have you had an experience where someone else's reaction to your appearance caused you to behave differently? Alternately, do you know of any events on your campus or in your community where people have drawn conclusions about someone because of his or her appearance? In an essay, NARRATE the event itself and then draw conclusions about it.

FRANCIS BACON { *Of Studies*

FRANCIS BACON (1561–1626), English politician, essayist, and scientist, was born in London and was educated at Trinity College, Cambridge. As a young man he traveled with the English ambassador to Paris, where he engaged in diplomatic work and studied law. A three-time member of Parliament, Bacon worked as a lawyer for many years. He was knighted by King James I in 1603 and was appointed attorney general in 1613 and lord chancellor in 1618. However, following a charge of corruption in 1621 and a brief stay in jail in the Tower of London, Bacon was barred from parliamentary or government work. A well-known essayist, Bacon published numerous works throughout his life, including *Essays* (1597); *Novum Organum* (1620), which proposed a new system of logic to replace the one invented by Aristotle; and *The New Atlantis* (1627), a utopian vision.

In "Of Studies," Bacon tells his readers why one should engage in scholarly study—and why one should not. Bacon praises variety in learning and details reasons to study widely. He points out that we can study different texts at different depths, depending on our purpose, and can also learn from discussion and writing. As he argues his case, consider how his perspective, more than three centuries old, could be relevant to a contemporary reader. What about education has changed? What hasn't?

STUDIES SERVE FOR DELIGHT, FOR ornament, and for ability. Their chief use for delight, is in privateness and retiring; for ornament, is in discourse; and for ability, is in the judgment, and disposition of business. For expert men can execute, and perhaps judge of particulars, one by one; but the general counsels, and the plots and marshalling of affairs, come best, from those that are learned. To spend too much time in studies is sloth; to use them too much for ornament, is affectation; to make judgment wholly by their rules, is the humor of a scholar. They perfect nature, and are perfected by experience: for natural abilities are like natural plants, that need proyning,[1] by study; and studies themselves, do give forth directions too much at large, except they be bounded in by experience. Crafty men contemn studies, simple men admire them, and wise men use them; for they teach not their own use; but that is a wisdom without them, and above them, won by observation. Read not to contradict and confute; nor to believe and take for granted; nor to find talk and discourse; but to weigh and consider. Some books are to be tasted, others to be swallowed, and some few to be chewed and digested; that is, some books are to be read only in parts; others to be read, but not curiously; and some few to be read wholly, and with diligence and attention. Some books also may be read by deputy, and extracts made of them by others; but that would be only in the less important arguments, and the meaner sort of books, else distilled books are like common distilled waters, flashy things. Reading maketh a full man; conference a ready man; and writing an exact man. And therefore, if a man write little, he had need have a great memory; if he confer little, he had need have a present wit: and if he read little, he had need have much cunning, to seem to know, that he doth not. Histories make men wise; poets witty; the mathematics subtile; natural philosophy deep; moral grave; logic and rhetoric able to contend. *Abeunt studia in mores.*[2] Nay, there is no *stond*[3] or impediment in the wit, but may be wrought out by fit studies; like as diseases of the body, may have appropriate exercises. Bowling is good for the stone and reins; shooting for the lungs and breast; gentle walking for the stomach; riding for the head; and the like. So if a man's wit be wandering, let him study the mathematics; for in demonstrations, if his wit be called away never so little, he must begin again. If his wit

[1]Pruning.
[2]Practices zealously pursued pass into habits (Latin).
[3]Stop.

be not apt to distinguish or find differences, let him study the School-men; for they are *cymini sectores*.[4] If he be not apt to beat over matters, and to call up one thing to prove and illustrate another, let him study the lawyers' cases. So every defect of the mind, may have a special receipt.

---

[4]Splitters of hairs (Latin). The "Schoolmen" were Medieval theologians known for meticulous teaching and learning.

STUDY QUESTIONS

1. According to Bacon, what are the benefits of studies? The limitations?

2. How does Bacon DIVIDE reading. Which type would he CLASSIFY as optimal?

3. How does Bacon attempt to convince the reader that studies are worthwhile? How effective is his logic? Explain.

4. *For Writing.* For many reasons, Bacon ARGUES for liberal arts education. RESEARCH the elements of a liberal arts education and write an essay in which you argue for or against it in our current society.

TANYA BARRIENTOS { *Se Habla Español*

TANYA BARRIENTOS (b. 1960) holds a bachelor's degree in journalism from the University of Missouri, Columbia, and has worked as a reporter, editor, and columnist for the *Philadelphia Inquirer* for more than twenty years. In addition, she has contributed commentary to National Public Radio and published two novels, *Family Resemblance* (2002) and *Frontera Street* (2003). She is the recipient of a fellowship from the Pennsylvania Council of the Arts and the Pew Fellowship of the Arts.

A version of Barrientos's essay "Se Habla Español" appeared in *Border-Line Personalities: A New Generation of Latinas Dish on Sex, Sass, and Cultural Shifting* (2004). In it, Barrientos discusses why she did not learn Spanish as a child and why she wants to learn the language as an adult. In both cases, the reasons relate closely to questions of identity—speaking only English made her feel like a "true" young American, but as she grew older, Barrientos came to believe that learning Spanish connected her to her family's Guatemalan heritage. As you read, note how Barrientos argues that her changing thoughts on language reflect changing ideas of what it means to be an American, while at the same time acknowledging our roots.

THE MAN ON THE OTHER end of the phone line is telling me the classes I've called about are first-rate: native speakers in charge, no more than six students per group. I tell him that will be fine and yes, I've studied a bit of Spanish in the past. He asks for my name and I supply it, rolling the double "r" in "Barrientos" like a pro. That's when I hear the silent snag, the momentary hesitation I've come to expect at this part of the exchange. Should I go into it again? Should I explain, the way I have to half-a-dozen others, that I am Guatemalan by birth but *pura gringa* by circumstance?

This will be the sixth time I've signed up to learn the language my parents speak to each other. It will be the sixth time I've bought workbooks and notebooks and textbooks listing 501 conjugated verbs in alphabetical order, in hopes that the subjunctive tense will finally take root in my mind. In class I will sit across a table from the "native speaker," who will wonder what to make of me. "Look," I'll want to say (but never do). "Forget the dark skin. Ignore the obsidian eyes. Pretend I'm a pink-cheeked, blue-eyed blonde whose name tag says 'Shannon.'" Because that is what a person who doesn't innately know the difference between *corre, corra,* and *corrí* is supposed to look like, isn't it?

I came to the United States in 1963 at age three with my family and immediately stopped speaking Spanish. College-educated and seamlessly bilingual when they settled in west Texas, my parents (a psychology professor and an artist) wholeheartedly embraced the notion of the American melting pot. They declared that their two children would speak nothing but *inglés*. They'd read in English, write in English, and fit into Anglo society beautifully.

It sounds politically incorrect now. But America was not a hyphenated nation back then. People who called themselves Mexican Americans or Afro-Americans were considered dangerous radicals, while law-abiding citizens were expected to drop their cultural baggage at the border and erase any lingering ethnic traits.

To be honest, for most of my childhood I liked being the brown girl 5
who defied expectations. When I was seven, my mother returned my older brother and me to elementary school one week after the school year had already begun. We'd been on vacation in Washington, D.C., visiting the Smithsonian, the Capitol, and the home of Edgar Allan Poe. In the Volkswagen on the way home, I'd memorized "The Raven," and I would recite it with melodramatic flair to any poor soul duped into sitting through my performance. At the school's office, the registrar frowned when we arrived.

"You people. Your children are always behind, and you have the nerve to bring them in late?"

"My children," my mother answered in a clear, curt tone, "will be at the top of their classes in two weeks."

The registrar filed our cards, shaking her head.

I did not live in a neighborhood with other Latinos, and the public school I attended attracted very few. I saw the world through the clear, cruel vision of a child. To me, speaking Spanish translated into being poor. It meant waiting tables and cleaning hotel rooms. It meant being left off the cheerleading squad and receiving a condescending smile from the guidance counselor when you said you planned on becoming a lawyer or a doctor. My best friends' names were Heidi and Leslie and Kim. They told me I didn't seem "Mexican" to them, and I took it as a compliment. I enjoyed looking into the faces of Latino store clerks and waitresses and, yes, even our maid and saying, "*Yo no hablo español.*" It made me feel superior. It made me feel American. It made me feel white. I thought that if I stayed away from Spanish, stereotypes would stay away from me.

Then came the backlash. During the two decades when I'd worked 10 hard to isolate myself from the stereotype I'd constructed in my own head, society shifted. The nation changed its views on ethnic identity. College professors started teaching history through African American and Native American eyes. Children were told to forget about the melting pot and picture America as a multicolored quilt instead. Hyphens suddenly had muscle, and I was left wondering where I fit in.

The Spanish language was supposedly the glue that held the new Latino community together. But in my case it was what kept me apart. I felt awkward among groups whose conversations flowed in and out of Spanish. I'd be asked a question in Spanish and I'd have to answer in English, knowing this raised a mountain of questions. I wanted to call myself Latina, to finally take pride, but it felt like a lie. So I set out to learn the language that people assumed I already knew.

After my first set of lessons, I could function in the present tense. "*Hola, Paco. ¿Qué tal? ¿Qué color es tu cuaderno? El mío es azul.*" My vocabulary built quickly, but when I spoke, my tongue felt thick inside my mouth—and if I needed to deal with anything in the future or the past, I was sunk. I enrolled in a three-month submersion program in Mexico and emerged able to speak like a sixth-grader with a solid C average. I could read Gabriel García Márquez with a Spanish-English dictionary at my elbow, and I could follow 90 percent of the melo-drama on any given telenovela. But true speakers discover my limita-tions the moment I stumble over a difficult construction, and that is when I get the look. The one that raises the wall between us. The one that makes me think I'll never really belong. Spanish has become a litmus test showing how far from your roots you've strayed.

My bilingual friends say I make too much of it. They tell me that my Guatemalan heritage and unmistakable Mayan features are enough to legitimize my membership in the Latin American club. After all, not all Poles speak Polish. Not all Italians speak Italian. And as this nation grows more and more Hispanic, not all Latinos will share one lan-guage. But I don't believe them.

There must be other Latinas like me. But I haven't met any. Or, I should say, I haven't met any who have fessed up. Maybe they are secretly struggling to fit in, the same way I am. Maybe they are hiring tutors and listening to tapes behind locked doors, just like me. I wish we all had the courage to come out of our hiding places and claim our rightful spot in the broad Latino spectrum. Without being called hopeless gringas. Without having to offer apologies or show remorse.

If it will help, I will go first. 15

Aquí estoy. Spanish-challenged and *pura* Latina.

STUDY QUESTIONS

1. Tanya Barrientos describes how her STANCE toward Spanish has changed over time. What did the Spanish language mean to her as a young person, and what does it mean to her as an adult? What provoked this change in attitude?

2. Even though she claims that she does not speak Spanish well, Barrientos uses Spanish words and phrases in the essay and in its title. Why do you think she makes these shifts in VOICE instead of writing exclusively in English?

3. How would you characterize the STEREOTYPES that led Barrientos to avoid Spanish? What other stereotypes, if any, are represented in the essay?

4. *For Writing.* Think about your own relationship with language in different environments. Do you speak and write differently at home than when you are at school or with your friends? If so, what are some differences that you notice, and do you see yourself differently as a person when you speak and write in different ways? Turn your reflections into a LITERACY NARRATIVE.

RACHEL CARSON { *A Fable for Tomorrow*

RACHEL CARSON (1907–1964) was born in Springdale, Pennsylvania, where her mother instilled in her a love of nature. As a writer, she expressed this love first in works about the sea: *Under the Sea Wind* (1941), *The Sea Around Us* (1952), and *The Edge of the Sea* (1955). Turning her attention to the synthetic chemicals being produced by the government as well as by the chemical industry, she began investigating the use of agricultural pesticides. Her discoveries resulted in her seminal work, *Silent Spring* (1962), which challenged the short-sightedness of scientists and the government, and is widely acknowledged to have launched the contemporary environmental movement.

The selection reprinted here is the first chapter of *Silent Spring*, in which Carson describes a town suddenly made desolate by the mysterious loss of animals, birds, fish, and even humans. She captures the attention of the reader with this apocalyptic view of mysterious environmental degradation. However, rather than give the audience a quick solution to that mystery, she ends the first chapter with a rhetorical question to pull the reader into the text.

━━━━━━━━━━━━━

THERE WAS ONCE A TOWN in the heart of America where all life seemed to live in harmony with its surroundings. The town lay in the midst of a checkerboard of prosperous farms, with fields of grain and hillsides of orchards where, in spring, white clouds of bloom drifted above the green fields. In autumn, oak and maple and birch set up a blaze of color that flamed and flickered across a backdrop of pines.

Then foxes barked in the hills and deer silently crossed the fields, half hidden in the mists of the fall mornings.

Along the roads, laurel, viburnum and alder, great ferns and wild-flowers delighted the traveler's eye through much of the year. Even in winter the roadsides were places of beauty, where countless birds came to feed on the berries and on the seed heads of the dried weeds rising above the snow. The countryside was, in fact, famous for the abundance and variety of its bird life, and when the flood of migrants was pouring through in spring and fall people traveled from great distances to observe them. Others came to fish the streams, which flowed clear and cold out of the hills and contained shady pools where trout lay. So it had been from the days many years ago when the first settlers raised their houses, sank their wells, and built their barns.

Then a strange blight crept over the area and everything began to change. Some evil spell had settled on the community: mysterious maladies swept the flocks of chickens; the cattle and sheep sickened and died. Everywhere was a shadow of death. The farmers spoke of much illness among their families. In the town the doctors had become more and more puzzled by new kinds of sickness appearing among their patients. There had been several sudden and unexplained deaths, not only among adults but even among children, who would be stricken suddenly while at play and die within a few hours.

There was a strange stillness. The birds, for example—where had they gone? Many people spoke of them, puzzled and disturbed. The feeding stations in the backyards were deserted. The few birds seen anywhere were moribund; they trembled violently and could not fly. It was a spring without voices. On the mornings that had once throbbed with the dawn chorus of robins, catbirds, doves, jays, wrens, and scores of other bird voices there was now no sound; only silence lay over the fields and woods and marsh.

On the farms the hens brooded, but no chicks hatched. The farmers 5
complained that they were unable to raise any pigs—the litters were small and the young survived only a few days. The apple trees were coming into bloom but no bees droned among the blossoms, so there was no pollination and there would be no fruit.

The roadsides, once so attractive, were now lined with browned and withered vegetation as though swept by fire. These, too, were silent, deserted by all living things. Even the streams were now lifeless. Anglers no longer visited them, for all the fish had died.

In the gutters under the eaves and between the shingles of the roofs, a white granular powder still showed a few patches; some weeks before it had fallen like snow upon the roofs and the lawns, the fields and streams.

No witchcraft, no enemy action had silenced the rebirth of new life in this stricken world. The people had done it themselves.

● ○ ●

This town does not actually exist, but it might easily have a thousand counterparts in America or elsewhere in the world. I know of no community that has experienced all the misfortunes I describe. Yet every one of these disasters has actually happened somewhere, and many real communities have already suffered a substantial number of them. A grim specter has crept upon us almost unnoticed, and this imagined tragedy may easily become a stark reality we all shall know.

What has already silenced the voices of spring in countless towns in 10 America?

STUDY QUESTIONS

1. A FABLE tells a story with a lesson to be learned. What lesson is Carson attempting to teach?

2. Carson uses a RHETORICAL QUESTION at the end of the chapter to entice the AUDIENCE to continue reading. Has she already answered the question in the fable that precedes it? Explain.

3. DESCRIPTIONS of widespread death and destruction, as in "A Fable for Tomorrow," are used in countless stories to warn us that something about our way of life holds the seed of disaster. Consider a familiar story or film that uses such death and destruction to warn us of dangers, and analyze it. What is the writer's or filmmaker's intent? How persuasive do you find it, and why? Be sure to refer to and describe specific scenes.

4. *For Writing.* Go home when you finish classes today and look through your cabinets for all the chemical products in your house or apartment—chemicals to clean your toilet bowl, to wipe your counters, to dye your hair, to wash your clothes, and so forth. Find at least five different household products that you buy and use regularly. Read their labels for the ingredients they contain and the warnings they give. Do any of them warn that they might contain carcinogens? Might any of them harm the environment? Might any of them be dangerous on contact with your skin? Write a letter to the manufacturer of one of the more dangerous products that you use, taking a POSITION about the chemicals to which the manufacturer is exposing you and the environment.

SHELBY STEELE { *I'm Black, You're White, Who's Innocent?*

SHELBY STEELE (b. 1946), who describes himself as a black conservative, writes extensively about race relations, multiculturalism, and affirmative action. A contributing editor to *Harper's* magazine and a frequent guest on news programs such as *Nightline* and *60 Minutes*, Steele holds degrees in political science, sociology, and English. In 1990 he received the Book Critics Circle Award in general nonfiction for his study *The Content of Our Character*. Following a long tenure as an English professor at San Jose State University in California, he is presently a research fellow at the Hoover Institute at Stanford University, where he focuses on issues of race in the United States.

In the following 1988 essay, Steele begins by telling an anecdote that illustrates the difficulty of talking about race in a mixed-race setting and goes on to argue that American society is driven by a racial power struggle in which both blacks and whites lay claim to the moral authority that comes with innocence, or essential goodness: for blacks, innocence lies in the history of their victimization, while for whites it lies in making claims that they are color-blind in matters of race. Real progress toward equality, he concludes, can come about only when power is apportioned according to moral principles, not demands that one race acknowledge the innocence (or guilt) of the other. What does the concept of racial innocence mean to you? How does it factor into your life?

═══════════════

IT IS A WARM, WINDLESS California evening, and the dying light that covers the redbrick patio is tinted pale orange by the day's smog. Eight of us, not close friends, sit in lawn chairs sipping chardonnay. A black engineer and I (we had never met before) integrate the group. A psychologist is also among us, and her presence encourages a surprising openness. But not until well after the lovely twilight dinner has been served, when the sky has turned to deep black and the drinks have long since changed to scotch, does the subject of race spring awkwardly upon us. Out of nowhere the engineer announces, with a coloring of accusation in his voice, that it bothers him to send his daughter to a school where she is one of only three black children. "I didn't realize my ambition to get ahead would pull me into a world where my daughter would lose touch with her blackness," he says.

Over the course of the evening we have talked about money, infidelity, past and present addictions, child abuse, even politics. Intimacies have been revealed, fears named. But this subject, race, sinks us into one of those shaming silences where eye contact terrorizes. Our host looks for something in the bottom of his glass. Two women stare into the black sky as if to locate the Big Dipper and point it out to us. Finally, the psychologist seems to gather herself for a challenge, but it is too late. "Oh, I'm sure she'll be just fine," says our hostess, rising from her chair. When she excuses herself to get the coffee, the two sky gazers offer to help.

With three of us now gone, I am surprised to see the engineer still silently holding his ground. There is a willfulness in his eyes, an inner pride. He knows he has said something awkward, but he is determined not to give a damn. His unwavering eyes intimidate me. At last the host's head snaps erect. He has an idea. "The hell with coffee," he says. "How about some of the smoothest brandy you ever tasted?" An idea made exciting by the escape it offers. Gratefully we follow him back into the house, quickly drink his brandy, and say our good-byes.

An autopsy of this party might read: death induced by an abrupt and lethal injection of the American race issue. An accurate if superficial assessment. Since it has been my fate to live a rather integrated life, I have often witnessed sudden deaths like this. The threat of them, if not the reality, is a part of the texture of integration. In the late 1960s, when I was just out of college, I took a delinquent's delight in playing the engineer's role, and actually developed a small reputation for playing it well. Those were the days of flagellatory white guilt; it was such great fun to pinion some professor or housewife or, best of all, a large group of remorseful whites, with the knowledge of both their racism and their denial of it. The adolescent impulse to sneer at convention, to startle the middle-aged with doubt, could be indulged under the guise of racial indignation. And how could I lose? My victims—earnest liberals for the most part—could no more crawl out from under my accusations than Joseph K. in Kafka's *Trial*[1] could escape the amorphous charges brought against him. At this odd moment in history the world was aligned to facilitate my immaturity.

About a year of this was enough: the guilt that follows most cheap thrills caught up to me, and I put myself in check. But the impulse to do it faded more slowly. It was one of those petty talents that is tied to vanity, and when there were ebbs in my self-esteem the impulse to use it would come alive again. In integrated situations I can still feel the faint itch. But then there are many youthful impulses that still itch, and now, just inside the door of mid-life, this one is least precious to me.

In the literature classes I teach, I often see how the presence of whites all but seduces some black students into provocation. When we come to a novel by a black writer, say Toni Morrison,[2] the white students can easily discuss the human motivations of the black characters. But, inevitably, a black student, as if by reflex, will begin to set in relief the various racial problems that are the background of these characters' lives. This student's tone will carry a reprimand: the class is afraid to confront the reality of racism. Classes cannot be allowed to die like dinner parties, however. My latest strategy is to thank that student for his or her moral vigilance, and then appoint the young man or woman as the class's official racism monitor. But even if I get a laugh—I usually do, but sometimes the student is particularly indignant, and it gets uncomfortable—the strategy never quite works. Our racial division is suddenly drawn in neon. Overcaution spreads like spilled paint. And, in fact, the black student who started it all does become a kind of monitor. The very presence of this student imposes a new accountability on the class.

I think those who provoke this sort of awkwardness are operating

---

[1]Novel written in 1924 by German author Franz Kafka (1883–1924). In it, the main character is put on trial for an unspecified crime.

[2]American novelist (b. 1931), author of the Pulitzer Prize-winning *Beloved* (1987) and winner of the Nobel Prize in Literature in 1993.

out of a black identity that obliges them to badger white people about race almost on principle. Content hardly matters. (For example, it made no sense for the engineer to expect white people to sympathize with his anguish over sending his daughter to school with *white* children.) Race indeed remains a source of white shame; the goal of these provocations is to put whites, no matter how indirectly, in touch with this collective guilt. In other words, these provocations I speak of are *power* moves, little shows of power that try to freeze the "enemy" in self-consciousness. They gratify and inflate the provocateur. They are the underdog's bite. And whites, far more secure in their power, respond with a self-contained and tolerant silence that is, itself, a show of power. What greater power than that of non-response, the power to let a small enemy sizzle in his own juices, to even feel a little sad at his frustration just as one is also complimented by it. Black anger always, in a way, flatters white power. In America, to know that one is not black is to feel an extra grace, a little boost of impunity.

I think the real trouble between the races in America is that the races are not just races but competing power groups—a fact that is easily minimized perhaps because it is so obvious. What is not so obvious is that this is true quite apart from the issue of class. Even the well-situated middle-class (or wealthy) black is never completely immune to that peculiar contest of power that his skin color subjects him to. Race is a separate reality in American society, an entity that carries its own potential for power, a mark of fate that class can soften considerably but not eradicate.

The distinction of race has always been used in American life to sanction each race's pursuit of power in relation to the other. The allure of race as a human delineation is the very shallowness of the delineation it makes. Onto this shallowness—mere skin and hair—men can project a false depth, a system of dismal attributions, a series of malevolent or ignoble stereotypes that skin and hair lack the substance to contradict. These dark projections then rationalize the pursuit of power. Your difference from me makes you bad, and your badness justifies, even demands, my pursuit of power over you—the oldest formula for aggression known to man. Whenever much importance is given to race, power is the primary motive.

But the human animal almost never pursues power without first 10
convincing himself that he is *entitled* to it. And this feeling of entitlement has its own precondition: to be entitled one must first believe in
one's innocence, at least in the area where one wishes to be entitled. By
innocence I mean a feeling of essential goodness in relation to others
and, therefore, superiority to others. Our innocence always inflates us
and deflates those we seek power over. Once inflated we are entitled;
we are in fact licensed to go after the power our innocence tells us we
deserve. In this sense, *innocence is power.* Of course, innocence need
not be genuine or real in any objective sense, as the Nazis demonstrated not long ago. Its only test is whether or not we can convince
ourselves of it.

I think the racial struggle in America has always been primarily a
struggle for innocence. White racism from the beginning has been a
claim of white innocence and, therefore, of white entitlement to subju-
gate blacks. And in the '60s, as went innocence so went power. Blacks
used the innocence that grew out of their long subjugation to seize
more power, while whites lost some of their innocence and so lost a
degree of power over blacks. Both races instinctively understand that
to lose innocence is to lose power (in relation to each other). Now to
be innocent someone else must be guilty, a natural law that leads the
races to forge their innocence on each other's backs. The inferiority of
the black always makes the white man superior; the evil might of
whites makes blacks good. This pattern means that both races have
a hidden investment in racism and racial disharmony, despite their
good intentions to the contrary. Power defines their relations, and
power requires innocence, which, in turn, requires racism and racial
division.

I believe it was this hidden investment that the engineer was protecting when he made his remark—the white "evil" he saw in a white
school "depriving" his daughter of her black heritage confirmed his
innocence. Only the logic of power explained this—he bent reality to
show that he was once again a victim of the white world and, as a
victim, innocent. His determined eyes insisted on this. And the whites,
in their silence, no doubt protected their innocence by seeing him as

an ungracious troublemaker—his bad behavior underscoring their goodness. I can only guess how he was talked about after the party. But it isn't hard to imagine that his blunder gave everyone a lift. What none of us saw was the underlying game of power and innocence we were trapped in, or how much we needed a racial impasse to play that game.

When I was a boy of about twelve, a white friend of mine told me one day that his uncle, who would be arriving the next day for a visit, was a racist. Excited by the prospect of seeing such a man, I spent the following afternoon hanging around the alley behind my friend's house, watching from a distance as this uncle worked on the engine of his Buick. Yes, here was evil and I was compelled to look upon it. And I saw evil in the sharp angle of his elbow as he pumped his wrench to tighten nuts, I saw it in the blade-sharp crease of his chinos, in the pack of Lucky Strikes that threatened to slip from his shirt pocket as he bent, and in the way his concentration seemed to shut out the human world. He worked neatly and efficiently, wiping his hands constantly, and I decided that evil worked like this.

I felt a compulsion to have this man look upon me so that I could see evil—so that I could see the face of it. But when he noticed me standing beside his toolbox, he said only, "If you're looking for Bobby, I think he went up to the school to play baseball." He smiled nicely and went back to work. I was stunned for a moment, but then I realized that evil could be sly as well, could smile when it wanted to trick you.

Need, especially hidden need, puts a strong pressure on perception, 15 and my need to have this man embody white evil was stronger than any contravening evidence. As a black person you always hear about racists but never meet any. And I needed to incarnate this odious category of humanity, those people who hated Martin Luther King Jr. and thought blacks should "go slow" or not at all. So, in my mental dictionary, behind the term "white racist," I inserted this man's likeness. I would think of him and say to myself, "There is no reason for him to hate black people. Only evil explains unmotivated hatred." And this thought soothed me; I felt innocent. If I hated white people, which I did not, at least I had a reason. His evil commanded me to assert in the world the goodness he made me confident of in myself.

In looking at this man I was *seeing for innocence*—a form of seeing that has more to do with one's hidden need for innocence (and power) than with the person or group one is looking at. It is quite possible, for example, that the man I saw that day was not a racist. He did absolutely nothing in my presence to indicate that he was. I invested an entire afternoon in seeing not the man but in seeing my innocence through the man. *Seeing for innocence* is, in this way, the essence of racism—the use of others as a means to our own goodness and superiority.

The loss of innocence has always to do with guilt, Kierkegaard[3] tells us, and it has never been easy for whites to avoid guilt where blacks are concerned. For whites, *seeing for innocence* means seeing themselves and blacks in ways that minimize white guilt. Often this amounts to a kind of white revisionism, as when President Reagan declares himself "color-blind" in matters of race. The president, like many of us, may aspire to racial color blindness, but few would grant that he has yet reached this sublimely guiltless state. The statement clearly revises reality, moves it forward into some heretofore unknown America where all racial determinism will have vanished. I do not think that Ronald Reagan is a racist, as that term is commonly used, but neither do I think that he is capable of seeing color without making attributions, some of which may be negative—nor am I, or anyone else I've ever met.

So why make such a statement? I think Reagan's claim of color blindness with regard to race is really a claim of racial innocence and guiltlessness—the preconditions for entitlement and power. This was the claim that grounded Reagan's campaign against special entitlement programs—affirmative action, racial quotas, and so on—that black power had won in the '60s. Color blindness was a strategic assumption of innocence that licensed Reagan's use of government power against black power.

[3]Søren Kierkegaard (1813–55), Danish philosopher and theologian best known for his attacks on the hypocrisy and complacency of the established Christian church.

I do not object to Reagan's goals in this so much as the presumption of innocence by which he rationalized them. I, too, am strained to defend racial quotas and any affirmative action that supersedes merit. And I believe there is much that Reagan has to offer blacks. His emphasis on traditional American values—individual initiative, self-sufficiency, strong families—offers what I think is the most enduring solution to the demoralization and poverty that continue to widen the gap between blacks and whites in America. Even his de-emphasis of race is reasonable in a society where race only divides. But Reagan's posture of innocence undermines any beneficial interaction he might have with blacks. For blacks instinctively sense that a claim of racial innocence always precedes a power move against them. Reagan's pretense of innocence makes him an adversary, and makes his quite reasonable message seem vindictive. You cannot be innocent of a man's problem and expect him to listen.

I'm convinced that the secret of Reagan's "teflon" coating, his personal popularity apart from his policies and actions, has been his ability to offer mainstream America a vision of itself as innocent and entitled (unlike Jimmy Carter, who seemed to offer only guilt and obligation). Probably his most far-reaching accomplishment has been to reverse somewhat the pattern by which innocence came to be distributed in the '60s, when outsiders were innocent and insiders were guilty. Corporations, the middle class, entrepreneurs, the military—all villains in the '60s—either took on a new innocence in Reagan's vision or were designated as protectors of innocence. But again, for one man to be innocent another man must be bad or guilty. Innocence imposes, *demands,* division and conflict, a right/wrong view of the world. And this, I feel, has led to the underside of Reagan's achievement. His posture of innocence draws him into a partisanship that undermines the universality of his values. He can't sell these values to blacks and others because he has made blacks into the bad guys and outsiders who justify his power. It is humiliating for a black person to like Reagan because Reagan's power is so clearly derived from a distribution of innocence that leaves a black with less of it, and the white man with more.

20

• ○ •

Black Americans have always had to find a way to handle white society's presumption of racial innocence whenever they have sought to enter the American mainstream. Louis Armstrong's[4] exaggerated smile honored the presumed innocence of white society—I will not bring you your racial guilt if you will let me play my music. Ralph Ellison[5] calls this "masking"; I call it bargaining. But whatever it's called, it points to the power of white society to enforce its innocence. I believe this power is greatly diminished today. Society has reformed and transformed—Miles Davis[6] never smiles. Nevertheless, this power has not faded altogether; blacks must still contend with it.

Historically, blacks have handled white society's presumption of innocence in two ways: they have bargained with it, granting white society its innocence in exchange for entry into the mainstream; or they have challenged it, holding that innocence hostage until their demand for entry (or other concessions) was met. A bargainer says, *I already believe you are innocent (good, fair-minded) and have faith that you will prove it.* A challenger says, *If you are innocent, then prove it.* Bargainers *give* in hope of receiving; challengers *withhold* until they receive. Of course, there is risk in both approaches, but in each case the black is negotiating his own self-interest against the presumed racial innocence of the larger society.

Clearly the most visible black bargainer on the American scene today is Bill Cosby.[7] His television show is a perfect formula for black bargaining in the '80s. The remarkable Huxtable family—with its doctor/lawyer parent combination, its drug-free, college-bound children, and its wise yet youthful grandparents—is a blackface version of the American dream. Cosby is a subscriber to the American identity, and his subscription confirms his belief in its fair-mindedness. His vast

---

[4]African American jazz trumpeter and singer (1901–71).

[5]African American author (1914–94) of the National Book Award–winning *Invisible Man* (1953).

[6]African American jazz trumpeter and composer (1926–91).

[7]African American comedian, writer, activist, and television star (b. 1937). His long-running sitcom *The Cosby Show* (1984–92) depicted the Huxtables, an upper-middle-class black family living in Brooklyn, New York.

audience knows this, knows that Cosby will never assault their innocence with racial guilt. Racial controversy is all but banished from the
show. The Huxtable family never discusses affirmative action.

The bargain Cosby offers his white viewers—I will confirm your
racial innocence if you accept me—is a good deal for all concerned.
Not only does it allow whites to enjoy Cosby's humor with no loss of
innocence, but it actually enhances their innocence by implying that
race is not the serious problem for blacks that it once was. If anything,
the success of this handsome, affluent black family points to the fair-
mindedness of whites who, out of their essential goodness, changed
society so that black families like the Huxtables could succeed. Whites
can watch *The Cosby Show* and feel complimented on a job well done.

The power that black bargainers wield is the power of absolution.   25
On Thursday nights, Cosby, like a priest, absolves his white viewers,
forgives and forgets the sins of the past. (Interestingly, Cosby was one
of the first blacks last winter to publicly absolve Jimmy the Greek[8] for
his well-publicized faux pas about black athletes.) And for this he is
rewarded with an almost sacrosanct status. Cosby benefits from what
might be called a gratitude factor. His continued number-one rating
may have something to do with the (white) public's gratitude at being
offered a commodity so rare in our time; he tells his white viewers each
week that they are okay, and that this black man is not going to challenge them.

When a black bargains, he may invoke the gratitude factor and find
himself cherished beyond the measure of his achievement; when he
challenges, he may draw the dark projections of whites and become a
source of irritation to them. If he moves back and forth between these
two options, as I think many blacks do today, he will likely baffle
whites. It is difficult for whites to either accept or reject such blacks. It
seems to me that Jesse Jackson[1] is such a figure—many whites see

[9]Jimmy Snyder (1919–96), a Greek American sports commentator who was fired by the
CBS network in 1988 (shortly before this essay first appeared) after he made inappropriate
on-air comments about what he considered to be the physical superiority of African
American athletes.

[1]African American Baptist minister, civil rights activist, and candidate for the Democratic
Party's presidential nomination in 1984 and 1988 (b. 1941).

Jackson as a challenger by instinct and a bargainer by political ambition. They are uneasy with him, more than a little suspicious. His powerful speech at the 1984 Democratic convention was a masterpiece of bargaining. In it he offered a Kinglike vision of what America could be, a vision that presupposed Americans had the fair-mindedness to achieve full equality—an offer in hope of a return. A few days after this speech, looking for rest and privacy at a lodge in Big Sur, he and his wife were greeted with standing ovations three times a day when they entered the dining room for meals. So much about Jackson is deeply American—his underdog striving, his irrepressible faith in himself, the daring of his ambition, and even his stubbornness. These qualities point to his underlying faith that Americans can respond to him despite his race, and this faith is a compliment to Americans, an offer of innocence.

But Jackson does not always stick to the terms of his bargain—he is not like Cosby on TV. When he hugs Arafat, smokes cigars with Castro, refuses to repudiate Farrakhan,[2] threatens a boycott of major league baseball, or, more recently, talks of "corporate barracudas," "pension-fund socialism," and "economic violence," he looks like a challenger in bargainer's clothing, and his positions on the issues look like familiar protests dressed in white-paper formality. At these times he appears to be revoking the innocence so much else about him seems to offer. The old activist seems to come out of hiding once again to take white innocence hostage until whites prove they deserve to have it. In his candidacy there is a suggestion of protest, a fierce insistence on his *right* to run, that sends whites a message that he may secretly see them as a good bit less than innocent. His dilemma is to appear the bargainer while his campaign itself seems to be a challenge.

There are, of course, other problems that hamper Jackson's bid for the Democratic presidential nomination. He has held no elective office, he is thought too flamboyant and opportunistic by many, there are rather loud whispers of "character" problems. As an individual

---

[2]Louis Farrakhan (b. 1933), African American national representative for the Nation of Islam. *Yasser Arafat*: chairman of the Palestine Liberation Organization (1929–2004) who fought for Palestine's independence from Israel. *Fidel Castro*: Cuban revolutionary leader and president of that country until his resignation in February 2008 (b. 1926).

he may not be the best test of a black man's chances for winning so high an office. Still, I believe it is the aura of challenge surrounding him that hurts him most. Whether it is right or wrong, fair or unfair, I think no black candidate will have a serious chance at his party's nomination, much less the presidency, until he can convince white Americans that he can be trusted to preserve *their* sense of racial innocence. Such a candidate will have to use his power of absolution; he will have to flatly forgive and forget. He will have to bargain with white innocence out of a genuine belief that it really exists. There can be no faking it. He will have to offer a vision that is passionately raceless, a vision that strongly condemns any form of racial politics. This will require the most courageous kind of leadership, leadership that asks all the people to meet a new standard.

Now the other side of America's racial impasse: How do blacks lay claim to their racial innocence?

The most obvious and unarguable source of black innocence is the victimization that blacks endured for centuries at the hands of a race that insisted on black inferiority as a means to its own innocence and power. Like all victims, what blacks lost in power they gained in innocence—innocence that, in turn, entitled them to pursue power. This was the innocence that fueled the civil rights movement of the '60s, and that gave blacks their first real power in American life—victimization metamorphosed into power via innocence. But this formula carries a drawback that I believe is virtually as devastating to blacks today as victimization once was. It is a formula that binds the victim to his victimization by linking his power to his status as a victim. And this, I'm convinced, is the tragedy of black power in America today. It is primarily a victim's power, grounded too deeply in the entitlement derived from past injustice and in the innocence that Western/Christian tradition has always associated with poverty.

Whatever gains this power brings in the short run through political action, it undermines in the long run. Social victims may be collectively entitled, but they are all too often individually demoralized. Since the social victim has been oppressed by society, he comes to feel that his individual life will be improved more by changes *in* society than by his own initiative. Without realizing it, he makes society rather than himself the agent of change. The power he finds in his victimization may lead him to collective action against society, but it also encourages passivity within the sphere of his personal life.

This past summer I saw a television documentary that examined life in Detroit's inner city on the twentieth anniversary of the riots there in which forty-three people were killed. A comparison of the inner city then and now showed a decline in the quality of life. Residents feel less safe than they did twenty years ago, drug trafficking is far worse, crimes by blacks against blacks are more frequent, housing remains substandard, and the teenage pregnancy rate has skyrocketed. Twenty years of decline and demoralization, even as opportunities for blacks to better themselves have increased. This paradox is not peculiar to Detroit. By many measures, the majority of blacks—those not yet in the middle class—are further behind whites today than before the victories of the civil rights movement. But there is a reluctance among blacks to examine this paradox, I think, because it suggests that racial victimization is not our real problem. If conditions have worsened for most of us as racism has receded, then much of the problem must be of our own making. But to fully admit this would cause us to lose the innocence we derive from our victimization. And we would jeopardize the entitlement we've always had to challenge society. We are in the odd and self-defeating position where taking responsibility for bettering ourselves feels like a surrender to white power.

So we have a hidden investment in victimization and poverty. These distressing conditions have been the source of our only real power, and there is an unconscious sort of gravitation toward them, a complaining celebration of them. One sees evidence of this in the near happiness with which certain black leaders recount the horror of Howard Beach[3] and other recent (and I think over-celebrated) instances of racial tension. As one is saddened by these tragic events, one is also repelled at the way some black leaders—agitated to near hysteria by the scent of victim-power inherent in them—leap forward to exploit them as evi-

[3]On December 20, 1986, three young African American men were brutally beaten when their car broke down while they were driving through the predominantly white neighborhood of Howard Beach, Queens, in New York City. The African American community responded with protest marches in the neighborhood; crowds numbered five thousand.

dence of black innocence and white guilt. It is as though they sense the decline of black victimization as a loss of standing and dive into the middle of these incidents as if they were reservoirs of pure black innocence swollen with potential power.

Seeing for innocence pressures blacks to focus on racism and to neglect the individual initiative that would deliver them from poverty—the only thing that finally delivers anyone from poverty. With our eyes on innocence we see racism everywhere and miss opportunity even as we stumble over it. About 70 percent of black students at my university drop out before graduating—a flight from opportunity that racism cannot explain. It is an injustice that whites can *see for innocence* with more impunity than blacks can. The price whites pay is a certain blindness to themselves. Moreover, for whites *seeing for innocence* continues to engender the bad faith of a long-disgruntled minority. But the price blacks pay is an ever-escalating poverty that threatens to make the worst off of them a permanent underclass. Not fair, but real.

Challenging works best for the collective, while bargaining is more 35
the individual's suit. From this point on, the race's advancement will come from the efforts of its individuals. True, some challenging will be necessary for a long time to come. But bargaining is now—today—a way for the black individual to *join* the larger society, to make a place for himself or herself.

"Innocence is ignorance," Kierkegaard says, and if this is so, the claim of innocence amounts to an insistence on ignorance, a refusal to know. In their assertions of innocence both races carve out very functional areas of ignorance for themselves—territories of blindness that license a misguided pursuit of power. Whites gain superiority by *not* knowing blacks; blacks gain entitlement by *not* seeing their own responsibility for bettering themselves. The power each race seeks in relation to the other is grounded in a double-edged ignorance, ignorance of the self as well as the other.

The original sin that brought us to an impasse at the dinner party I mentioned at the outset occurred centuries ago, when it was first decided to exploit racial difference as a means to power. It was the determinism[4] that flowed karmically from this sin that dropped over us like a net that night. What bothered me most was our helplessness. Even the engineer did not know how to go forward. His challenge hadn't worked, and he'd lost the option to bargain. The marriage of race and power depersonalized us, changed us from eight people to six whites and two blacks. The easiest thing was to let silence blanket our situation, our impasse.

I think the civil rights movement in its early and middle years offered the best way out of America's racial impasse: in this society, race must not be a source of advantage or disadvantage for anyone. This is fundamentally a *moral* position, one that seeks to breach the corrupt union of race and power with principles of fairness and human equality: if all men are created equal, then racial difference cannot sanction power. The civil rights movement was conceived for no other reason than to redress that corrupt union, and its guiding insight was that only a moral power based on enduring principles of justice, equality, and freedom could offset the lower impulse in man to exploit race as a means to power. Three hundred years of suffering had driven the point home, and in Montgomery, Little Rock, and Selma,[5] racial power was the enemy and moral power the weapon.

An important difference between genuine and presumed innocence, I believe, is that the former must be earned through sacrifice, while the latter is unearned and only veils the quest for privilege. And there was much sacrifice in the early civil rights movement. The Gandhian principle of non-violent resistance that gave the movement a spiritual center as well as method of protest demanded sacrifice, a passive offering of the self in the name of justice. A price was paid in terror and lost life, and from this sacrifice came a hard-earned innocence and a credible moral power.

[4]The belief that behaviors and events are the predetermined result of prior events or conditions such as genetic inheritance; in this case, the belief that race determines an individual's behavior and fate.

[5]In the early days of the civil rights movement, each of these cities (in Alabama, Arkansas, and Alabama, respectively) was the scene of racial strife followed by a major peaceful demonstration led by Dr. Martin Luther King Jr.

Non-violent passive resistance is a bargainer's strategy. It assumes 40
the power that is the object of the protest has the genuine innocence to
morally respond, and puts the protesters at the mercy of that innocence. I think this movement won so many concessions precisely
because of its belief in the capacity of whites to be moral. It did not so
much demand that whites change as offer them relentlessly the opportunity to live by their own morality—to attain a true innocence based
on the sacrifice of their racial privilege, rather than a false innocence
based on presumed racial superiority. Blacks always bargain with or
challenge the larger society; but I believe that in the early civil rights
years, these forms of negotiation achieved a degree of integrity and
genuineness never seen before or since.

In the mid-'60s all this changed. Suddenly a sharp *racial* consciousness emerged to compete with the moral consciousness that had
defined the movement to that point. Whites were no longer welcome
in the movement, and a vocal "black power" minority gained dramatic
visibility. Increasingly, the movement began to seek racial as well as
moral power, and thus it fell into a fundamental contradiction that
plagues it to this day. Moral power precludes racial power by denounc-
ing race as a means to power. Now suddenly the movement itself was
using race as a means to power, and thereby affirming the very union
of race and power it was born to redress. In the end, black power can
claim no higher moral standing than white power.

It makes no sense to say this shouldn't have happened. The sacrifices that moral power demands are difficult to sustain, and it was
inevitable that blacks would tire of these sacrifices and seek a more
earthly power. Nevertheless, a loss of genuine innocence and moral
power followed. The movement, splintered by a burst of racial militancy in the late '60s, lost its hold on the American conscience and
descended more and more to the level of secular, interest-group politics. Bargaining and challenging once again became racial rather than
moral negotiations.

You hear it asked, why are there no Martin Luther Kings around
today? I think one reason is that there are no black leaders willing to
resist the seductions of racial power, or to make the sacrifices moral
power requires. King understood that racial power subverts moral

power, and he pushed the principles of fairness and equality rather than black power because he believed those principles would bring blacks their most complete liberation. He sacrificed race for morality, and his innocence was made genuine by that sacrifice. What made King the most powerful and extraordinary black leader of this century was not his race but his morality.

Black power is a challenge. It grants whites no innocence; it denies their moral capacity and then demands that they be moral. No power can long insist on itself without evoking an opposing power. Doesn't an insistence on black power call up white power? (And could this have something to do with what many are now calling a resurgence of white racism?) I believe that what divided the races at the dinner party I attended, and what divides them in the nation, can only be bridged by an adherence to those moral principles that disallow race as a source of power, privilege, status, or entitlement of any kind. In our age, principles like fairness and equality are ill-defined and all but drowned in relativity. But this is the fault of people, not principles. We keep them muddied because they are the greatest threat to our presumed innocence and our selective ignorance. Moral principles, even when somewhat ambiguous, have the power to assign responsibility and therefore to provide us with knowledge. At the dinner party we were afraid of so severe an accountability.

What both black and white Americans fear are the sacrifices and risks 45 that true racial harmony demands. This fear is the measure of our racial chasm. And though fear always seeks a thousand justifications, none is ever good enough, and the problems we run from only remain to haunt us. It would be right to suggest courage as an antidote to fear, but the glory of the word might only intimidate us into more fear. I prefer the word effort—relentless effort, moral effort. What I like most about this word are its connotations of everydayness, earnestness, and practical sacrifice. No matter how badly it might have gone for us that warm summer night, we should have talked. We should have made the effort.

STUDY QUESTIONS

1. What does Steele mean by "racial innocence"? On what basis do white Americans claim such innocence? On what basis do black Americans claim it? What, according to Steele, is the connection between innocence and power?

2. How does Steele SUPPORT his CLAIM that the racial struggle in America has been primarily a struggle for innocence? Consider how he offers figures such as Bill Cosby and Jesse Jackson as examples to illustrate his assertions. How does Steele suggest that this struggle might be resolved?

3. How does Steele DEFINE "bargainers" and "challengers"? How does each type of person approach race relations? Which kind does Steele say was most prevalent in 1988, when he wrote this essay? Which kind do you think is most prevalent today, and why?

4. *For Writing.* Twenty years after Steele wrote this essay, Barack Obama—like Steele, the son of a black father and a white mother—was elected the first African American president of the United States. In an essay, ANALYZE how the election of President Obama either refutes or upholds Steele's concepts of racial innocence and power. (How does it reflect on Steele's 1988 thesis that in January 2008 he published a short book called *A Bound Man: Why We Are Excited about Obama and Why He Can't Win*?)

E. B. WHITE { *Once More to the Lake*

ELWYN BROOKS WHITE (1899–1985) was born in Mount Vernon, New York. After serving in the army, White attended Cornell University, where he wrote for the *Cornell Daily Sun*. He graduated in 1921 and moved to Seattle to work as a reporter. He joined the staff of *The New Yorker* magazine, where he remained a regular contributor for almost sixty years, in 1927, and he wrote for *Harper's* between 1938 and 1943. In addition to being a celebrated writer for adults, White is also known for his children's classics *Stuart Little* (1945) and *Charlotte's Web* (1952). In 1959, White revised and updated *The Elements of Style*, a classic handbook and style manual originally written in 1918 by one of his Cornell professors, William Strunk Jr. In 1978, White received a special Pulitzer Prize.

"Once More to the Lake" was originally published in *Harper's* in 1941. In this often-reprinted essay, White describes a week-long trip he took with his son to the same lake in Maine that White's father took him to almost forty years earlier. Written in the early years of World War II, White's meditation on memory and the passage of time is rich with detailed description that evokes a rural America still familiar to many. As you read, pay particular attention to the precise language White uses to describe a scene and create a particular mood.

ONE SUMMER, ALONG ABOUT 1904, my father rented a camp on a lake in Maine and took us all there for the month of August. We all got ringworm from some kittens and had to rub Pond's Extract on our arms and legs night and morning, and my father rolled over in a canoe with all his clothes on; but outside of that the vacation was a success and from then on none of us ever thought there was any place in the world like that lake in Maine. We returned summer after summer—always on August 1st for one month. I have since become a salt-water man, but sometimes in summer there are days when the restlessness of the tides and the fearful cold of the sea water and the incessant wind which blows across the afternoon and into the evening make me wish for the placidity of a lake in the woods. A few weeks ago this feeling got so strong I bought myself a couple of bass hooks and a spinner and returned to the lake where we used to go, for a week's fishing and to revisit old haunts.

I took along my son, who had never had any fresh water up his nose and who had seen lily pads only from train windows. On the journey over to the lake I began to wonder what it would be like. I wondered how time would have marred this unique, this holy spot—the coves and streams, the hills that the sun set behind, the camps and the paths behind the camps. I was sure that the tarred road would have found it out and I wondered in what other ways it would be desolated. It is strange how much you can remember about places like that once you allow your mind to return into the grooves which lead back. You remember one thing, and that suddenly reminds you of another thing. I guess I remembered clearest of all the early mornings, when the lake was cool and motionless, remembered how the bedroom smelled of the lumber it was made of and of the wet woods whose scent entered through the screen. The partitions in the camp were thin and did not extend clear to the top of the rooms, and as I was always the first up I would dress softly so as not to wake the others, and sneak out into the sweet outdoors and start out in the canoe, keeping close along the shore in the long shadows of the pines. I remembered being very careful never to rub my paddle against the gunwale for fear of disturbing the stillness of the cathedral.

The lake had never been what you would call a wild lake. There were cottages sprinkled around the shores, and it was in farming country although the shores of the lake were quite heavily wooded. Some of the cottages were owned by nearby farmers, and you would live at the shore and eat your meals at the farmhouse. That's what our family did.

But although it wasn't wild, it was a fairly large and undisturbed lake and there were places in it which, to a child at least, seemed infinitely remote and primeval.

I was right about the tar: it led to within half a mile of the shore. But when I got back there, with my boy, and we settled into a camp near a farmhouse and into the kind of summertime I had known, I could tell that it was going to be pretty much the same as it had been before—I knew it, lying in bed the first morning, smelling the bedroom, and hearing the boy sneak quietly out and go off along the shore in a boat. I began to sustain the illusion that he was I, and therefore, by simple transposition, that I was my father. This sensation persisted, kept cropping up all the time we were there. It was not an entirely new feeling, but in this setting it grew much stronger. I seemed to be living a dual existence. I would be in the middle of some simple act, I would be picking up a bait box or laying down a table fork, or I would be saying something, and suddenly it would be not I but my father who was saying the words or making the gesture. It gave me a creepy sensation.

We went fishing the first morning. I felt the same damp moss covering the worms in the bait can, and saw the dragonfly alight on the tip of my rod as it hovered a few inches from the surface of the water. It was the arrival of this fly that convinced me beyond any doubt that everything was as it always had been, that the years were a mirage and there had been no years. The small waves were the same, chucking the rowboat under the chin as we fished at anchor, and the boat was the same boat, the same color green and the ribs broken in the same places, and under the floor-boards the same fresh-water leavings and débris— the dead hellgrammite, the wisps of moss, the rusty discarded fish-hook, the dried blood from yesterday's catch. We stared silently at the tips of our rods, at the dragonflies that came and went. I lowered the tip of mine into the water, tentatively, pensively dislodging the fly, which darted two feet away, poised, darted two feet back, and came to rest again a little farther up the rod. There had been no years between the ducking of this dragonfly and the other one—the one that was part of memory. I looked at the boy, who was silently watching his fly, and it was my hands that held his rod, my eyes watching. I felt dizzy and didn't know which rod I was at the end of.

We caught two bass, hauling them in briskly as though they were mackerel, pulling them over the side of the boat in a businesslike manner without any landing net, and stunning them with a blow on the back of the head. When we got back for a swim before lunch, the lake was exactly where we had left it, the same number of inches from the dock, and there was only the merest suggestion of a breeze. This seemed an utterly enchanted sea, this lake you could leave to its own devices for a few hours and come back to, and find that it had not stirred, this constant and trustworthy body of water. In the shallows, the dark, water-soaked sticks and twigs, smooth and old, were undulating in clusters on the bottom against the clean ribbed sand, and the track of the mussel was plain. A school of minnows swam by, each minnow with its small individual shadow, doubling the attendance, so clear and sharp in the sunlight. Some of the other campers were in swimming, along the shore, one of them with a cake of soap, and the water felt thin and clear and unsubstantial. Over the years there had been this person with the cake of soap, this cultist, and here he was. There had been no years.

Up to the farmhouse to dinner through the teeming, dusty field, the road under our sneakers was only a two-track road. The middle track was missing, the one with the marks of the hooves and the splotches of dried, flaky manure. There had always been three tracks to choose from in choosing which track to walk in; now the choice was narrowed down to two. For a moment I missed terribly the middle alternative. But the way led past the tennis court, and something about the way it lay there in the sun reassured me; the tape had loosened along the backline, the alleys were green with plantains and other weeds, and the net (installed in June and removed in September) sagged in the dry noon, and the whole place steamed with midday heat and hunger and emptiness. There was a choice of pie for dessert, and one was blueberry and one was apple, and the waitresses were the same country girls, there having been no passage of time, only the illusion of it as in a dropped curtain—the waitresses were still fifteen; their hair had been washed, that was the only difference—they had been to the movies and seen the pretty girls with the clean hair.

Summertime, oh summertime, pattern of life indelible, the fade-proof lake, the woods unshatterable, the pasture with the sweet fern and the juniper forever and ever, summer without end; this was the background, and the life along the shore was the design, the cottages with their innocent and tranquil design, their tiny docks with the flagpole and the American flag floating against the white clouds in the blue sky, the little paths over the roots of the trees leading from camp to camp and the paths leading back to the outhouses and the can of lime for sprinkling, and at the souvenir counters at the store the miniature birch-bark canoes and the post cards that showed things looking a little better than they looked. This was the American family at play, escaping the city heat, wondering whether the newcomers in the camp at the head of the cove were "common" or "nice," wondering whether it was true that the people who drove up for Sunday dinner at the farmhouse were turned away because there wasn't enough chicken.

It seemed to me, as I kept remembering all this, that those times and those summers had been infinitely precious and worth saving. There had been jollity and peace and goodness. The arriving (at the beginning of August) had been so big a business in itself, at the railway station the farm wagon drawn up, the first smell of the pine-laden air, the first glimpse of the smiling farmer, and the great importance of the trunks and your father's enormous authority in such matters, and the feel of the wagon under you for the long ten-mile haul, and at the top of the last long hill catching the first view of the lake after eleven months of not seeing this cherished body of water. The shouts and cries of the other campers when they saw you, and the trunks to be unpacked, to give up their rich burden. (Arriving was less exciting nowadays, when you sneaked up in your car and parked it under a tree near the camp and took out the bags and in five minutes it was all over, no fuss, no loud wonderful fuss about trunks.)

Peace and goodness and jollity. The only thing that was wrong now, really, was the sound of the place, an unfamiliar nervous sound of the outboard motors. This was the note that jarred, the one thing that would sometimes break the illusion and set the years moving. In those other summertimes all motors were inboard; and when they were at a little distance, the noise they made was a sedative, an ingredient of summer sleep. They were one-cylinder and two-cylinder engines, and some were make-and-break and some were jump-spark, but they all

10

made a sleepy sound across the lake. The one-lungers throbbed and fluttered, and the twin-cylinder ones purred and purred, and that was a quiet sound too. But now the campers all had outboards. In the daytime, in the hot mornings, these motors made a petulant, irritable sound; at night, in the still evening when the afterglow lit the water, they whined about one's ears like mosquitoes. My boy loved our rented outboard, and his great desire was to achieve singlehanded mastery over it, and authority, and he soon learned the trick of choking it a little (but not too much), and the adjustment of the needle valve. Watching him I would remember the things you could do with the old one-cylinder engine with the heavy flywheel, how you could have it eating out of your hand if you got really close to it spiritually. Motor boats in those days didn't have clutches, and you would make a landing by shutting off the motor at the proper time and coasting in with a dead rudder. But there was a way of reversing them, if you learned the trick, by cutting the switch and putting it on again exactly on the final dying revolution of the flywheel, so that it would kick back against compression and begin reversing. Approaching a dock in a strong following breeze, it was difficult to slow up sufficiently by the ordinary coasting method, and if a boy felt he had complete mastery over his motor, he was tempted to keep it running beyond its time and then reverse it a few feet from the dock. It took a cool nerve, because if you threw the switch a twentieth of a second too soon you would catch the flywheel when it still had speed enough to go up past center, and the boat would leap ahead, charging bull-fashion at the dock.

We had a good week at the camp. The bass were biting well and the sun shone endlessly, day after day. We would be tired at night and lie down in the accumulated heat of the little bedrooms after the long hot day and the breeze would stir almost imperceptibly outside and the smell of the swamp drift in through the rusty screens. Sleep would come easily and in the morning the red squirrel would be on the roof, tapping out his gay routine. I kept remembering everything, lying in bed in the mornings—the small steamboat that had a long rounded stern like the lip of a Ubangi, and how quietly she ran on the moonlight sails, when the older boys played their mandolins and the girls sang and we ate doughnuts dipped in sugar, and how sweet the music was on the water in the shining night, and what it had felt like to think about girls then. After breakfast we would go up to the store and the things were in the same place—the minnows in a bottle, the plugs and spinners disarranged and pawed over by the youngsters from the boys' camp, the fig newtons and the Beeman's gum. Outside, the road was tarred and cars stood in front of the store. Inside, all was just as it had always been, except there was more Coca Cola and not so much Moxie and root beer and birch beer and sarsaparilla. We would walk out with a bottle of pop apiece and sometimes the pop would backfire up our noses and hurt. We explored the streams, quietly, where the turtles slid off the sunny logs and dug their way into the soft bottom; and we lay on the town wharf and fed worms to the tame bass. Everywhere we went I had trouble making out which was I, the one walking at my side, the one walking in my pants.

One afternoon while we were there at that lake a thunderstorm came up. It was like the revival of an old melodrama that I had seen long ago with childish awe. The second-act climax of the drama of the electrical disturbance over a lake in America had not changed in any important respect. This was the big scene, still the big scene. The whole thing was so familiar, the first feeling of oppression and heat and a general air around camp of not wanting to go very far away. In midafternoon (it was all the same) a curious darkening of the sky, and a lull in everything that had made life tick; and then the way the boats suddenly swung the other way at their moorings with the coming of a breeze out of the new quarter, and the premonitory rumble. Then the kettle drum, then the snare, then the bass drum and cymbals, then crackling light against the dark, and the gods grinning and licking their chops in the hills. Afterward the calm, the rain steadily rustling in the calm lake, the return of light and hope and spirits, and the campers running out in joy and relief to go swimming in the rain, their bright cries perpetuating the deathless joke about how they were getting simply drenched, and the children screaming with delight at the new sensation of bathing in the rain, and the joke about getting drenched linking the generations in a strong indestructible chain. And the comedian who waded in carrying an umbrella.

When the others went swimming my son said he was going in too.

He pulled his dripping trunks from the line where they had hung all through the shower, and wrung them out. Languidly, and with no thought of going in, I watched him, his hard little body, skinny and bare, saw him wince slightly as he pulled up around his vitals the small, soggy, icy garment. As he buckled the swollen belt suddenly my groin felt the chill of death.

STUDY QUESTIONS

1. Which of White's observations seem to confirm that "everything was as it always had been, that the years were a mirage and there had been no years"? Which observations "set the years moving"?

2. Identify the passages in which White is unable to distinguish between his son and himself as a boy. After clearly identifying so strongly with his son, what is it that leads White to recognize his own mortality as expressed in the final line: "As he buckled the swollen belt suddenly my groin felt the chill of death"?

3. Reread White's DESCRIPTION of the thunderstorm (paragraph 12). What language is most effective in evoking the sound and feel of a storm? Why?

4. *For Writing.* White explores the passage of time by juxtaposing a lake, which has changed little in forty years, and himself, who has changed considerably. Write an essay that explores the passage of time in your own life by adopting a strategy similar to White's. Begin by choosing an object or place that has been part of your life for many years, one that in many ways seems immune to time. Write about your relationship with that place or object, describing how it has changed and how you have changed.

PAULA GUNN ALLEN   { *Deer Woman*

PAULA GUNN ALLEN (1939–2008) was born in Albuquerque, the
daughter of a Lebanese American father and a Scottish-Sioux-Laguna
mother. She grew up in Cubero, New Mexico, on the border of the
Laguna Pueblo Indian reservation, and attended the University of
Oregon for both her BA in English (1966) and her MFA in creative
writing (1968). She continued her graduate studies at the University of
New Mexico, where she earned her PhD in American studies in 1976.
Allen taught at a variety of colleges, including San Francisco State
University and the University of New Mexico, before becoming a
professor of Native American and ethnic studies at the University of
California, Berkeley, and UCLA. She published six volumes of poetry,
four novels, and several works of academic criticism, including the
influential *The Sacred Hoop: Recovering the Feminine in American
Indian Traditions* (1986); she also edited collections of Native American
works such as *Spider Woman's Granddaughters: Traditional Tales and
Contemporary Writing by Native American Women* (1989). Her biography *Pocahontas: Medicine Woman, Spy, Entrepreneur, Diplomat* (2004)
was nominated for a Pulitzer Prize.

"Deer Woman" recounts a tale that turns the tables on two men
looking for an evening of female companionship. When they meet Linda
and Junella, the men are captivated not only by the women's beauty, but
also by the extraordinary world the women lead them to. As you read,
notice how Gunn imbues nature with a sense of the supernatural.

Two young men were out "snagging"—chasing girls—one afternoon. They rode around in their pickup, their Indian Cadillac, cruising up this road and down that one through steamy green countryside,
stopping by friends' places here and there to lift a few. The day was
sultry as summer days in Oklahoma get, hot as a sweat.[1]

Long after dark, they stopped at a tavern twenty or thirty miles
outside of Anadarko,[2] and joined some skins gathered around several tables. After the muggy heat outside, the slowly turning fan inside
felt cool. When they'd been there a while, one of the men at their table
asked them if they were headed to the stomp dance. "Sure," they said,
though truth to tell, they hadn't known there was a stomp dance that
night. The three headed out to the pickup.

They drove for some distance along narrow country roads, turning
occasionally at unmarked crossings, bumping across cattle guards,
until at length they saw the light of the bonfire. Several unshaded
lights hung from small huts that ringed the danceground, and head-
lights shone from a couple of parking cars.

They pulled into a spot in the midst of a new Winnebago, a Dodge
van, two Toyotas, and a small herd of more battered models, and made
their way to the danceground. The dance was going strong, and the
sound of turtle shell and aluminum can rattles and singing, mixed
with occasional laughter and bits of talk, reached their ears. "Alright!"
exclaimed Ray, the taller and heavier of the two, slapping his buddy's
raised hand in glee. "Yeah!" his pal Jackie responded, and they grinned
at each other in the unsteady light. Slapping the man who'd ridden
along with them on the back, the taller one said, "Man, let's go find us
some snags!"

They hung out all night, occasionally starting a conversation with   5
one good-looking woman or another, but though the brother who'd
accompanied them soon disappeared with a long-legged beauty
named Lurine, the two anxious friends didn't score. They were not the
sort to feel disheartened, though. They kept up their spirits, dancing
well and singing even better. They didn't really care so much about

---

[1]That is, as hot as a traditional Indian sweat lodge, a kind of sauna.
[2]Small town in southwestern Oklahoma.

snagging. It simply gave them something to think about while they filled the day and night with interesting activity. They were among their own people, and they were satisfied with their lives and themselves.

Toward morning, though, Ray spotted two strikingly beautiful young women stepping onto the danceground. Their long hair flowed like black rivers down their backs. They were dressed in traditional clothes, and something about them—some elusive something—made Ray shiver with what felt almost like recognition and, at the same time, like dread. "Who are they?" he asked his friend, but the smaller man shrugged silently. Ray could see his eyes shining for a moment as the fire near them flared up suddenly.

At the same moment, they both saw the young women looking at them out of the corners of their eyes as they danced modestly and almost gravely past. Jackie nudged Ray and let out a long slow sigh. "Alright," he said in a low, almost reverent voice. "Alright!"

When the dance was ended, the young women made their way to where the two youths were standing. One of them said, "My friend and I need a ride to Anadarko, and they told us you were coming from there." As she said that, she gestured with her chin over her left shoulder toward a vaguely visible group standing on the other side of the danceground.

"What's your friend's name?" Ray countered.

"Linda," the other woman said. "Hers is Junella." 10

"My friend's name's Jackie," Ray said, grinning. "When do you want to take off?"

"We'll go whenever you do," Junella answered. She held his eyes with hers. "Where are you parked?"

They made their way to the pickup and got in. It was a tight fit, but nobody seemed to mind. Ray drove, backing the pickup carefully to thread among the haphazardly parked vehicles. As he did, he glanced down for a second, and he thought he saw the feet of both women as deer hooves. "Man," he thought, "I gotta lay off the weed." He didn't remember he'd quit smoking it months before, and he hadn't had even a beer since they'd left the tavern hours before. The women tucked their feet under their bags, and in the darkness he didn't see them anymore. Besides, he had more engaging things on his mind.

They drove companionably for some time, joking around, telling a bit about themselves, their tastes in music, where they'd gone to school, when they'd graduated. Linda kept fiddling with the dial, reaching across Junella to get to the knob. Her taste seemed to run to either hard-core country-and-western or what Ray privately thought of as "space" music.

She and Junella occasionally lapsed into what seemed like a private 15 conversation or joke, Ray couldn't be sure which; then, as though remembering themselves, they'd laugh and engage the men in conversation again.

After they'd traveled for an hour or so, Linda suddenly pointed to a road that intersected the one they were on. "Take a left," she said, and Ray complied. He didn't even think about it or protest that they were on the road to Anadarko already. A few hundred yards further she said, "Take a right." Again he complied, putting the brake on suddenly as he went into the turn, spilling Junella hard against him. He finished shifting quickly and put his arm around her. She leaned into him, saying nothing.

The road they had turned onto soon became gravel, and by the time they'd gone less than a quarter mile turned into hard-packed dirt. Ray could smell water nearby. He saw some trees standing low on the horizon and realized it was coming light.

"Let's go to the water," Linda said. "Junella and I are traditional, and we try to wash in fresh running water every morning."

"Yeah," Junella murmured. "We were raised by our mother's grandmother, and the old lady was real strict about some things. She always made sure we prayed to Long Man[3] every day." Jackie and Ray climbed out of the truck, the women following. They made their way through the thickest of scrub oak and bushes and clambered down the short bank to the stream, the men leading the way. They stopped at the edge of the water, but the young women stepped right in, though still dressed in their dance clothes. They bent and splashed water on their faces, speaking the old tongue softly as they did so. The men removed their

---

[3]Cherokee river spirit.

tennis shoes and followed suit, tucking their caps in the hip pockets of their jeans.

After a suitable silence, Junella pointed to the opposite bank with her uplifted chin. "See that path," she asked the men. "I think it goes to our old house. Let's go up there and see." 20

"Yes," Linda said, "I thought it felt familiar around here. I bet it is our old place." As the women didn't move to cross the shallow river and go up the path, the men took the lead again. Ray briefly wondered at his untypical pliability, but he banished the thought almost as it arose. He raised his head just as he reached the far bank and saw that the small trees and brush were backed by a stone bluff that rose steeply above them. As he tilted his head back to spot the top of the bluff, he had a flashing picture of the small round feet he'd thought he'd seen set against the floorboard of the truck. But as the image flashed into his mind, the sun blazed out over the bluff; the thought faded as quickly as it had come, leaving him with a slightly dazed feeling and a tingling that climbed rapidly up his spine. He put on his cap.

Jackie led the way through the thicket, walking as quickly as the low branches would allow, bending almost double in places. Ray followed him, and the women came after. Shortly they emerged from the trees onto a rocky area that ran along the foot of the bluff like a narrow path. When he reached it, Jackie stopped and waited while the others caught up. "Do you still think this is the old homestead?" he quipped. The women laughed sharply, then fell into animated conversation in the old language.

Neither Ray nor Jackie could speak it, so they stood waiting, admiring the beauty of the morning, feeling the cool dawn air on their cheeks and the water still making their jeans cling to their ankles. At least their feet were dry, and so were the tennies they'd replaced after leaving the river.

After a few animated exchanges, the women started up the path, the men following. "She says it's this way," Linda said over her shoulder. "It can't be far." They trudged along for what seemed a long time, following the line of the bluff that seemed to grow even higher. After a time, Junella turned into a narrow break in the rock and began to trudge up its gradual slope, which soon became a steep rise.

"I bet we're not going to grandma's house," Jackie said in quiet 25 tones to his friend. "I didn't know this bluff was even here," Ray replied. "It's not much farther," Junella said cheerfully. "What's the matter, you dudes out of shape or something?"

"Well, I used to say I'd walk a mile for a Camel," Jackie said wryly, "but I didn't say anything about snags!" He and Ray laughed, perhaps more heartily than the joke warranted.

"This is the only time I've heard of Little Red Riding Hood leading the wolves to grandma's," Ray muttered. "Yah," Linda responded brightly. "And wait'll you see what I'm carrying in my basket of goodies." The women glanced at each other, amused, and Jackie laughed abashedly.

"Here's the little creek I was looking for," Junella said suddenly. "Let's walk in it for a while." Ray looked at Jackie quizzically.

"I don't want to walk in that," Jackie said quickly. "I just got dry from the last dip." The women were already in the water walking upstream. "Not to worry," Junella said. "It's not wet—it's the path to the old house."

"Yeah, right," Ray mumbled, stepping into the water with a sigh. 30 Jackie followed him, falling suddenly silent. As they stepped into what they thought was a fast-running stream, their feet touched down on soft grass. "Hey!" Ray exclaimed. "What's happening?" He stopped abruptly, and Jackie ploughed into him. "Watch it, man," the smaller man said shortly. He brushed past Ray and made after the women, who were disappearing around a sharp turn. Ray stood rooted a moment, then hurried after him. "Wait up," he called. His voice sounded loudly against the cliff and came back to him with a crack.

As he turned the corner, he saw Linda reaching upward along the cliff where a tall rock slab leaned against it. She grasped the edge of the slab and pulled. To the men's astonishment, it swung open, for all the world like an ordinary door. The women stepped through.

Ray and Jackie regarded each other for long moments. Finally Ray shrugged, and Jackie gestured with his outspread arm at the opening in the cliff. They followed the women inside.

Within, they were greeted with an astonishing scene. Scores of people, upward of two hundred, stood or walked about a green land.

Houses stood scattered in the near distance, and smoke arose from a few chimneys. There were tables spread under some large trees, syca-more or elm, Ray thought, and upon them food was spread in large quantities and tantalizing variety. Suddenly aware they hadn't eaten since early the day before, the men started forward. But before they'd taken more than a few steps, Linda and Junella took their arms and led them away from the feast toward the doorway of one of the houses.

There sat a man who seemed ancient to the young men. His age wasn't so much in his hair, though it hung in waist-long white strands. It wasn't even so much in his skin, wrinkled and weathered though his face was beneath the tall crowned hat he wore. It was just that he seemed to be age personified. He seemed to be older than the bluff, than the river, than even the sky.

Next to him lay two large mastiffs, their long, lean bodies relaxed, their heads raised, their eyes alert and full of intelligence. "So," the old one said to the women, "I see you've snagged two strong young men." He shot an amused glance in the young men's direction. "Go, get ready," he directed the women, and at his words they slipped into the house, closing the door softly behind them.

The young men stood uneasily beside the old one, who disregarded them completely, lost in his own thoughts as he gazed steadily at some point directly before him.

After half an hour or more had passed, the old man addressed the young men again. "It was a good thing that you did," he mused, "fol-lowing my nieces here. I wonder that you didn't give up or get lost along the way." He chuckled quietly as at a private joke. "Maybe you two are intelligent men." He turned his head suddenly and gave them an appraising look. Each of the young men shifted under that know-ing gaze uncomfortably. From somewhere, the ground, the sky, they didn't feel sure, they heard thunder rumbling. "I have told everybody that they did well for themselves by bringing you here."

Seeing the surprised look on their faces, he smiled. "Yes, you didn't hear me, I know. I guess we talk different here than you're used to where you come from. Maybe you'll be here long enough to get used to it," he added, "that is, if you like my nieces well enough. We'll feed you soon," he said. "But first there are some games I want you to join in." He pointed with pursed lips and chin in the direction of a low hill that rose just beyond the farthest dwelling. Again the thunder rumbled, louder than before.

A moment later the women appeared. Their long, flowing hair was gone, and their heads shone in the soft light that filled the area, allowing distant features to recede into its haze. The women wore soft clothing that completely covered their bodies, even their hands and feet. The bright, gleaming cloth reflected light at the same intensity as their bald heads. Their dark eyes seemed huge and luminous against skin that gave off a soft radiance. Seeing them, both men were nearly overcome with fear. "They have no hair at all," Ray thought. "Where is this place?" He glanced over at Jackie, whose face mirrored his own unease. Jackie shook his head almost imperceptibly, slowly moving it from side to side in a gesture that seemed mournful and at the same time oddly resigned.

Linda and Junella moved to the young men, each taking one by the 40 hand and drawing him toward the central area nearby. In a daze, Ray and Jackie allowed themselves to be led into the center of the area ringed by heavily laden tables, barely aware that the old man had risen from his place and with his dogs was following behind them. They were joined by a number of other young men, all wearing caps like the ones Ray and Jackie wore. Two of the men carried bats, several wore gloves, and one was tossing a baseball in the air as he walked. Slowly the throng made their way past the tables and came to an open area where Jackie and Ray saw familiar shapes. They were bases, and the field that the soft light revealed to them was a baseball diamond.

The old man took his place behind home plate, and one of the young men crouched before him as a loud peal of thunder crashed around them. "Play ball!" the old man shouted, and the men took up their places as the women retired to some benches at the edge of the field.

The bewildered young men found their positions, and the game was on. It was a hard-played game, lasting some time. At length it reached a rowdy end, the team Jackie and Ray were on barely edging out the opposition in spite of a couple of questionable calls the old man made against them. Their victory was due in no small measure to the wiry

Jackie's superb pitching. He'd pitched two no-hit innings, and that had won them the game.

As they walked with the players back toward the houses, the old man came up to them. Slapping each in turn on the back a couple of times, he told them he thought they were good players. "Maybe that means you'll be ready for tomorrow's games," he said, watching Jackie sharply. "They're not what you're used to, I imagine, but you'll do alright."

They reached the tables and were helped to several large portions of food by people whose faces never seemed to come quite into focus but whose goodwill seemed unquestionable. They ate amid much laughter and good-natured joshing, only belatedly realizing that neither Linda nor Junella was among the revelers. Ray made his way to Jackie and asked him if he'd seen either woman. Replying in the negative, Jackie offered to go look around for them.

They both agreed to make a quick search and to rendezvous at the 45 large tree near the old man's house. But after a fruitless hour, Ray went to the front of the house and waited. His friend didn't come. At last, growing bored, he made his way back to the tables where a group had set up a drum and were singing lustily. A few of the younger people had formed a tight circle around the drummers and were slowly stepping round in it, their arms about each others' waists and shoulders. "Alright!" Ray thought, "49's!"[4] He was cheered at the anticipation of the close social-bond dancing, drumming, and singing, the joking and relaxation the social signified. He joined the circle between two women he hadn't seen before who easily made way for him and smoothly closed about him, each wrapping an arm around his waist. He forgot all about his friend.

When Ray awoke, the sun was beating down on his head. He sat up and realized he was lying near the river's edge, his legs in the thicket, his head and half-turned face unshielded from the sun. It was about a third of the way up in a clear sky. As he looked groggily around, he discovered Junella sitting quietly a few yards away on a large stone. "Hey," she said, smiling.

---

[4]That is, songs combining English and Native American lyrics, commonly sung at pow-wow events following the dancing.

"How'd I get here?" Ray asked. He stood and stretched, surreptitiously feeling to see if everything worked. His memory seemed hesitant to return, but he had half-formed impressions of a baseball game and eating and then the 49. He looked around. "Where's Jackie, and, uh—"

"Linda?" Junella supplied as he paused. "Yeah, Linda," he finished.

"Jackie is staying there," she told him calmly. She reached into her bag and brought out a man's wristwatch. "He said to give you this," she said, holding it out to him.

Ray felt suddenly dizzy. He swayed for a moment while strange 50 images swept through him. Junella with no hair and that eerie light— that pale tan but with spots or a pattern of soft grey dots that sort of fuzzed out at the edges to blend into the tan. The old man.

He took a step in her direction. "Hey," he began. "What the hell's—" He broke off. The rock where she sat was empty. On the ground next to it lay Jackie's watch.

When he told me the story, about fifteen months afterward, Ray had heard that Jackie had showed up at his folks' place. They lived out in the country, a mile or so beyond one of the numerous small towns that dot the Oklahoma landscape. The woman who told him about Jackie's return, Jackie's cousin Ruth Ann, said he had come home with a strange woman who was a real fox. At thirteen, Ruth Ann had developed an eye for good looks and thought herself quite a judge of women's appearance. They hadn't stayed long, he'd heard. They packed up some of Jackie's things and visited with his family. Ray had been in Tulsa and hadn't heard Jackie was back. None of their friends had seen him either. There had been a child with them, he said, maybe two or so, Ruth Ann had thought, because she could walk by herself.

"You know," he'd said thoughtfully, turning a Calistoga[5] slowly between his big hands. The gesture made him seem very young and somehow vulnerable. "One of my grandma's brothers, old Jess, used to talk about the little people a lot. He used to tell stories about strange things happening around the countryside here. I never paid much

[5] A brand of mineral water.

attention. You know how it is, I just thought he was putting me on, or maybe he was pining away for the old days. He said Deer Woman would come to dances sometimes, and if you weren't careful she'd put her spell on you and take you inside the mountain to meet her uncle. He said her uncle was Thunder, one of the old gods or supernaturals, whatever the traditionals call them."

He finished his drink in a couple of swallows, pushing away from the table where we sat. "I dunno," and he gave me a look that I still haven't forgotten, a look somehow wounded and yet with a kind of wild hope mixed in. "Maybe those old guys know something, eh?"

It was a few years before I saw Ray again. Then I ran into him unex- 55 pectedly in San Francisco a couple of years ago. We talked for a while, standing on the street near the Mission BART station.[6] He started to leave when my curiosity got the better of my manners. I asked if he'd ever found out what happened to Jackie.

Well, he said that he'd heard that Jackie came home off and on, but the woman—probably Linda, though he wasn't sure—was never with him. Then he'd heard that someone had run into him, or a guy they thought sure was him, up in Seattle. He'd gone alcoholic. They'd heard he'd died. "But the weird thing is that he'd evidently been telling someone all about that time inside the mountain, and that he'd married her, and about some other stuff, stuff I guess he wasn't supposed to tell." Another guy down on his luck, he guessed. "Remember how I was telling you about my crazy uncle, the one who used to tell about Deer Woman? Until I heard about Jackie, I'd forgotten that the old man used to say that the ones who stayed there were never supposed to talk about it. If they did, they died in short order."

After that there didn't seem to be much more to say. Last time I saw Ray, he was heading down the steps to catch BART. He was on his way to a meeting, and he was running late.

---

[6]That is, the Mission Street station of the Bay Area Rapid Transit, a light-rail subway system.

STUDY QUESTIONS

1. What is Ray and Jackie's attitude at the beginning of the story? How are the two men transformed throughout their encounter with the Deer Women?

2. How does the landscape change for the two men as the story progresses? How does the change in landscape SYMBOLIZE their internal journey? What is the place of the Deer Woman in both the artificial and the natural landscape?

3. This story begins in the third-person POINT OF VIEW and ends in the first person. What is the effect of this change in narrative VOICE?

4. *For Writing.* In many ways, Allen's story is an updated version of an Indian captivity narrative. Research the characteristics of the classic captivity narrative and then write an essay in which you ANALYZE how Allen's story both draws upon and departs from that genre.

MAYA ANGELOU { *Champion of the World*

MAYA ANGELOU (b. 1928), African American poet, playwright, essayist, and lecturer, was born in St. Louis, Missouri. A successful singer and dancer early in her career, Angelou was inspired to start writing by her friend James Baldwin during the Civil Rights Movement of the 1960s. In 1993, Angelou became the first African American to read at a presidential inauguration—the second poet in history to do so—when she read her poem "On the Pulse of Morning" for the inauguration of President Bill Clinton. Angelou's many works include a multivolume autobiography that begins with *I Know Why the Caged Bird Sings* (1970), from which the following excerpt was taken.

In "Champion of the World," Angelou tells of the 1935 Joe Louis versus Primo Carnera boxing match, which her friends and family had listened to on the radio. Louis was the heavyweight champion of the world at the time, and Carnera was a white challenger who outweighed Louis by sixty-five pounds. To Angelou's friends and family, this fight symbolized the struggle of all African Americans: Louis's falling "was our people falling." As you read, notice how Angelou weaves the words of the radio announcer with her own commentary as she interprets the significance of this event.

THE LAST INCH OF SPACE was filled, yet people continued to wedge themselves along the walls of the Store. Uncle Willie had turned the radio up to its last notch so that youngsters on the porch wouldn't miss a word. Women sat on kitchen chairs, dining-room chairs, stools, and upturned wooden boxes. Small children and babies perched on every lap available and men leaned on the shelves or on each other.

The apprehensive mood was shot through with shafts of gaiety, as a black sky is streaked with lightning.

"I ain't worried 'bout this fight. Joe's gonna whip that cracker like it's open season."

"He gone whip him till that white boy call him Momma."

At last the talking was finished and the string-along songs about   5
razor blades were over and the fight began.

"A quick jab to the head." In the Store the crowd grunted. "A left to the head and a right and another left." One of the listeners cackled like a hen and was quieted.

"They're in a clench, Louis is trying to fight his way out."

Some bitter comedian on the porch said, "That white man don't mind hugging that niggah now, I betcha."

"The referee is moving in to break them up, but Louis finally pushed the contender away and it's an uppercut to the chin. The contender is hanging on, now he's backing away. Louis catches him with a short left to the jaw."

A tide of murmuring assent poured out the doors and into the yard.   10

"Another left and another left. Louis is saving that mighty right . . ." The mutter in the Store had grown into a baby roar and it was pierced by the clang of a bell and the announcer's "That's the bell for round three, ladies and gentlemen."

As I pushed my way into the Store I wondered if the announcer gave any thought to the fact that he was addressing as "ladies and gentlemen" all the Negroes around the world who sat sweating and praying, glued to their "master's voice."[1]

There were only a few calls for R. C. Colas, Dr. Peppers, and Hire's root beer. The real festivities would begin after the fight. Then even the old Christian ladies who taught their children and tried themselves to practice turning the other cheek would buy soft drinks, and if the

---

[1] An allusion to the slogan of the Radio Corporation of America (RCA).

Brown Bomber's[2] victory was a particularly bloody one they would order peanut patties and Baby Ruths also.

Bailey and I lay the coins on top of the cash register. Uncle Willie didn't allow us to ring up sales during a fight. It was too noisy and might shake up the atmosphere. When the gong rang for the next round we pushed through the near-sacred quiet to the herd of children outside.

"He's got Louis against the ropes and now it's a left to the body and   15
a right to the ribs. Another right to the body, it looks like it was low . . .
Yes, ladies and gentlemen, the referee is signaling but the contender keeps raining the blows on Louis. It's another to the body, and it looks like Louis is going down."

My race groaned. It was our people falling. It was another lynching, yet another Black man hanging on a tree. One more woman ambushed and raped. A Black boy whipped and maimed. It was hounds on the trail of a man running through slimy swamps. It was a white woman slapping her maid for being forgetful.

The men in the Store stood away from the walls and at attention. Women greedily clutched the babes on their laps while on the porch the shufflings and smiles, flirtings and pinching of a few minutes before were gone. This might be the end of the world. If Joe lost we were back in slavery and beyond help. It would all be true, the accusations that we were lower types of human beings. Only a little higher than the apes. True that we were stupid and ugly and lazy and dirty and, unlucky and worst of all, that God Himself hated us and ordained us to be hewers of wood and drawers of water, forever and ever, world without end.

We didn't breathe. We didn't hope. We waited.

"He's off the ropes, ladies and gentlemen. He's moving towards the center of the ring." There was no time to be relieved. The worst might still happen.

"And now it looks like Joe is mad. He's caught Carnera[3] with a left   20

[2]Nickname for heavyweight boxer Joe Louis (1914–81).
[3]Italian boxer Primo Carnera (1906–67), World Heavyweight Champion from 1933 to 1934.

hook to the head and a right to the head. It's a left jab to the body and another left to the head. There's a left cross and a right to the head. The contender's right eye is bleeding and he can't seem to keep his block up. Louis is penetrating every block. The referee is moving in, but Louis sends a left to the body and it's the uppercut to the chin and the contender is dropping. He's on the canvas, ladies and gentlemen."

Babies slid to the floor as women stood up and men leaned toward the radio.

"Here's the referee. He's counting. One, two, three, four, five, six, seven . . . Is the contender trying to get up again?"

All the men in the store shouted, "NO."

"—eight, nine, ten." There were a few sounds from the audience, but they seemed to be holding themselves in against tremendous pressure.

"The fight is all over, ladies and gentlemen. Let's get the micro-25 phone over to the referee . . . Here he is. He's got the Brown Bomber's hand, he's holding it up . . . Here he is . . ."

Then the voice, husky and familiar, came to wash over us—"The winnah, and still heavyweight champeen of the world . . . Joe Louis."

Champion of the world. A Black boy. Some Black mother's son. He was the strongest man in the world. People drank Coca-Colas like ambrosia and ate candy bars like Christmas. Some of the men went behind the Store and poured white lightning in their soft-drink bottles, and a few of the bigger boys followed them. Those who were not chased away came back blowing their breath in front of themselves like proud smokers.

It would take an hour or more before the people would leave the Store and head for home. Those who lived too far had made arrangements to stay in town. It wouldn't do for a Black man and his family to be caught on a lonely country road on a night when Joe Louis had proved that we were the strongest people in the world.

STUDY QUESTIONS

1. What is Angelou's PURPOSE in telling this story? Does she state her purpose explicitly or is it implied? Use specific passages from the story to support your view.

2. To some, this boxing match was just another sporting event, but to Angelou's friends and family, it was much more. What is the significance of this event, and how does she convey it?

3. *For Writing.* Write an essay DESCRIBING an event in your life that seemed ordinary on one level but was richly SYMBOLIC on another. Be sure to establish a context for the event by describing the scene and providing background information. Then, include passages that explore the symbolic importance of this event.

CECILIA BALLÍ { *Ciudad de la Muerte*

CECILIA BALLÍ (b. 1976), an anthropology professor at the University of
Texas at Austin, has written articles for *Harper's Monthly*, the *San Antonio
Express-News*, and the *Los Angeles Times*, serving as the Washington, DC,
correspondent for the *Times*. In addition to publishing scholarly articles,
she serves as a senior editor at *Texas Monthly* magazine, contributing
investigative stories about gender and violence, immigration, crime, and
music in the U.S.–Mexico borderlands.

"Ciudad de la Muerte" ("City of Death") explores the numerous brutal
murders of young Mexican women that have continued unabated since the
early 1990s in Ciudad Juárez, Mexico, a city of 1.5 million across the Rio
Grande from El Paso, Texas. In 2009 the city witnessed more than two
thousand murders, most of which were unsolved, leading one of Juárez's
newspapers to declare, "This is the most violent zone in the world outside
of declared war zones." Ballí's article puts readers in this "zone," narrating
her own visits to Juárez and offering insights about the mysterious killings
and the dangers of a city she so clearly associates with death. As you read,
note how Ballí uses techniques borrowed from fiction to create vivid scenes
and moments of suspense.

DO YOU KNOW WHAT HAPPENS to a human body in the desert? If it's
fresh, the intestines eat themselves out. The body swells, the lungs
ooze fluids through the nostrils and mouth, and the decaying organs
let out a cocktail of nauseating gases. Sometimes, scavengers leave
their mark: a gnawed leg, a missing shoulder. Eventually, all that is left
is a pile of white bones. But there is a cruel trick the dry weather will

sometimes play on a corpse. It will dehydrate the skin before the bacteria can get to it, producing a mummy—a blackened girl with skin dry as cardboard, baring her teeth like a frightened animal.

• ○ •

In February 1996 a seventeen-year-old girl named María Guadalupe del Rio Vázquez went shopping in downtown Ciudad Juárez and vanished into thin air. Days later, her body was found in the desolate mountains of the Chihuahuan Desert—raped, strangled, her left breast mutilated. As girls continued to disappear, residents of the city formed bands and scoured the mountains for more bodies. The state police picked up the corpses—seventeen in all, an epidemic of murder—and quickly scurried away, leaving behind clothing, locks of hair, shoes curled like orange peels. The girls' hands were bound with their own shoelaces. All of the victims resembled each other: pretty, slim, medium to dark skin, long, straight dark hair. In a country that privileges men, whiteness, and wealth, these victims were female, brown, and poor. In a city that resents immigration and anything else from central and southern Mexico, these young women who had come to the northern border hoping to find work were social outcasts, strangers without names—especially now that they lay in silence in the sand, looking just like the ones before and the ones who would follow.

The deaths in the mountainous desert region known as Lomas de Poleo confirmed the worst fears of the women of Juárez: that something sinister had overcome their city. Beginning in 1993, there had been an unusual number of news reports in Juárez about the abduction and murder of women, an anomaly in Mexico. The grisly discoveries in the desert signaled that the worst crime wave in modern Mexican history had entered a new and more intense phase. Today, the toll of women who have been murdered in the past ten years is more than three hundred, staining the reputation of the country's fourth-largest city worldwide. Some of the women were murdered by their husbands and boyfriends. Other killings seemed to be random acts of violence. Around a third of the victims, however, were teenage girls whose deaths appear to be connected to a cryptic and chilling kind of serial killing. This crime is indisputably solvable: Evidence has been scattered like bread crumbs all over the crime scenes, but the state authorities have jailed no one who truly seems responsible. Be it incompetence or a cover-up, the lack of credible prosecution in these cases is perhaps the most blatant—and certainly the most baffling—illustration of the nearly flawless record of impunity that characterizes the Mexican justice system.

Who would commit such crimes? Juárez brims with rumor and suspicion. A serial killer with government protection is an obvious possibility. The indifference of the authorities charged with investigating the murders has focused suspicion on themselves. Maybe it's the Juárez police, some people say. They drive those white pickups with the campers, where they could easily hide a rotting body or a pile of bones, and they're always prowling around the shantytown of Anapra, on the edge of the desert, peering out their windows. The Chihuahua state police zoom about in sleek, unmarked SUVs capable of navigating the rugged desert terrain. Recently, federal investigators speculated that fourteen of the killings might be linked to an organ-smuggling ring.

Or maybe it's the drug dealers. The desert is, after all, their country, a frontier on the fringe of globalization. Between dips in the mountains, you glimpse El Paso to the north, its downtown towers gleaming like teeth. The Rio Grande cut through the mountains and created a valley that would in time birth the most densely populated border region in the world. But in Lomas de Poleo, there is only the sand and the desert scrub and a sea of trash—empty jugs, shabby toys, broken toilets, an unwound cassette of English lessons, plastic bags clinging to the brush like confetti. A frail man picks his way through a dumpster. An occasional small truck rattles off into the distance. They say that at night, this becomes the realm of gang members and drug runners, an army of men hauling their illicit goods into the United States. Rumor has it that if you wander far enough into the disorienting maze of primitive roads that have been scratched out of the sand, you will come upon a crude runway and a marvelous ranch with a swimming pool. If anybody sees you there, you should say you got lost and quickly turn around.

The obvious questions—who, why, how—remain unanswered. The abductions occur in mysterious moments, in quick, ghastly twists of fate that nobody seems—or at least wants to admit—to have witnessed. Most recently, they have transpired in the heart of the city in broad daylight. Some people believe the girls are taken by force, while others think it is more likely that the victims are lured by a seemingly innocent offer. A few mothers have said that their daughters disappeared a day or two after being approached about a job. Only one thing can be said with certainty, and it's that in Juárez, Mexico, the most barbarous things are possible.

• o •

The sun shimmers over downtown Juárez like white linen, but I have learned to march down its streets staring at the ground or ahead with icy, distant eyes. To do anything else is to acknowledge the lusty stares from men of all ages who stand at the corners of the city's busy thoroughfares waiting for nothing to happen. So begins the taunting. A skinny man with red eyes lets out a slow whistle through clenched teeth. Two young boys look at me, look at each other, and nod with a dirty grin. From among a group of men huddled on the steps of a shop, one calls out, "*¡Una como esa!*"—One like her!—and the rest burst out laughing, their mustaches spreading gleefully across their faces as they watch me walk by. This is everywhere in urban Mexico, I remind myself, but knowing what I do about the fate of women in Juárez, their glares begin to feel more predatory. I watch my feet skitter on the pavement and, with every step, wish I could shed these hips, this chest, this hair. To walk through downtown Juárez is to know and deeply regret that you are a young woman.

Juárez, though, is a city of young women. They run its shops; they keep its hundreds of factories humming. In 1964 the United States terminated the Bracero guest-worker program[1] with Mexico and deported many of its laborers, dumping thousands of men along the Mexican side of the border. In an effort to reemploy them, the Mexican government launched the Border Industrialization Program, which

---

[1] Diplomatic agreement starting in 1942 that allowed temporary contract laborers from Mexico to work in the U.S. in order to meet labor shortages caused by World War II. After the war, workers in the program primarily filled low-wage positions in the agriculture industry.

prodded American manufacturers to assemble their products in northern Mexico using cheap labor. The plan succeeded, but its main beneficiaries turned out to be women, who, it was determined, would make better workers for the new factories, or *maquiladoras*, because of their presumed superior manual dexterity. Word spread throughout Mexico that thousands of assembly-line jobs were cropping up in Juárez, and the nation's north quickly became the emblem of modernity and economic opportunity. In the seventies, factory-sponsored buses rumbled into the heartland and along the coasts and returned with thousands of hungry laborers. Among them were many single women with children in tow, who, aside from landing their own jobs in the *maquilas*,[2] began to staff the throngs of stores and restaurants that proliferated to satisfy the new consumerism of Juárez's formerly cash-strapped population.

And so, if the working women of this border city had once earned reputations as prostitutes or bartenders, they now earned paychecks as factory workers, saleswomen, police officers, teachers—a few even as managers and engineers in the concrete tilt-ups[3] that were constructed all around town to house around four hundred maquiladoras. For anywhere from $4 to $7 a day, they assembled automotive parts and electronic components and made clothing. Of the girls who couldn't afford to go to college—which is to say, the vast majority—some took computer classes, where they learned to use Microsoft Word and Excel so that they might become secretaries and administrative assistants. Juárez, after all, is a city that places a high premium on skills such as knowing how to use computers and speak English. Even in its most impoverished desert neighborhood, a dazed collection of impromptu homes stitched together from wood pallets, mattresses, cardboard boxes, and baling wire, I saw a tiny brick shack with a dozen mismatched chairs planted outside and a hand-painted sign that promised "*Clases de inglés*."[4]

But the migration was too fast, too disorganized. The population 10 shot up to an estimated 1.5 million. Gone was the charm Juárez had

---

[2] Factories (Spanish).

[3] That is, factories built cheaply and quickly with prefabricated concrete walls.

[4] English classes (Spanish).

possessed in the thirties, when its valley bore succulent grapes, or in the forties, when the music of Glenn Miller and Agustín Lara never stopped playing on Juárez Avenue, even as its neighboring country went to war. It was one of Mexico's biggest blunders to have planted its largest industrial experiment in the desert, in a city separated from the rest of the country not only symbolically, by its distinctly North American feel, but also physically, by the stunning but unforgiving Juárez Mountains. Cardboard shanties began to dot the landscape. Sewage spilled onto the streets. Power lines reproduced like parasites. Today, radio talk-show hosts ramble on about the ways in which immigrants ruined their beautiful community. I asked a well-bred young man what he felt were the virtues of his hometown, and despite a genuine effort, all he could name were the swank, cavernous clubs where the rich kids spend their weekends consuming alcohol by the bottle.

Even as the maquiladoras have begun relocating to China in the past two years, the reputation of Juárez as a city of opportunity lingers in impoverished rural Mexico. Inside the city, however, Mexico's economic vulnerability is exposed like raw flesh. The city is filled with broken people who crack open with the most innocent of questions. I met a woman from Zacatecas who lives in Anapra with her husband and three daughters in a minuscule house that they built out of wood pallets and thatched with black roofing material. They possess one bed, no refrigerator, and a tin washtub for bathing. State officials offered them this sliver of land, but the sliver is in the desert mountains, where life is not "beautiful," as the woman's brother had sent word home; it's shivery cold and always covered in a thin film of orange dirt. When I asked her how she liked living in this *colonia*[5] along the city's northwestern frontier, the woman's smile quivered and a puddle of tears instantly dribbled to her chin.

Still, the worst part about Juárez, she told me, is the threat of violence that hangs over the sprawling city like a veil of terror. For just a short distance from her home, the bodies of girls who resemble her

---

[5] Literally, colony (Spanish), colonias are low-income rural settlements along the U.S.-Mexico border, characterized by makeshift housing and lack of social, political, and physical infrastructures.

own sixteen-year-old Ana have appeared in the desert. Lured to their deaths—perhaps by promises of a job?—they lie abandoned like the heaps of trash that fleck this interminable sea of sand.

• ○ •

"*Disculpe, señorita . . .*"[6]

I turned toward the male voice that came from behind me and saw a dark-skinned, round-faced man in his thirties striding in my direction with a large basket of candies wedged between his neck and shoulder. He was heavyset, clad in light-brown slacks, a white, long-sleeved shirt with blue pinstripes, and a green windbreaker.

It was lunchtime, and I had walked out of a restaurant to return a call 15 to a source on my cell phone, leaving behind three journalists with whom I'd been roaming the city. Diana Washington Valdez, an *El Paso Times* reporter who has been chronicling the Juárez women's deaths, had thought I should meet an attorney who is defending one of the government's scapegoats for the murders. But when we had rattled the wrought-iron gates of his office, there had been no reply. We had decided to wait at a small restaurant next door, and since a peal of music was issuing from a nearby television, I had gone outside to return the call. After I'd finished, I'd dialed my sister's number.

He looked rather humble, and this, I thought, was confirmed by the apologetic smile he wore, as if he were sorry to be intruding for something as mundane as the time or how to find a street. I half-smiled at him. "Hold on," I told my sister. I was about to save him the trouble of asking by telling him that I was not from around here when he spoke once more.

"Are you looking for work?"

• ○ •

Journalists and activists and sociologists trying to explain the loss of hundreds of women in such violent ways have constructed a common narrative. The story tells that when the immigrants came to Juárez from the countryside, they brought with them traditional

---

[6] "Excuse me, Miss" (Spanish).

Mexican ideas about gender. Women were to stay home, obey their husbands, and raise their children. But when wives and girlfriends and daughters began earning their own paychecks, they tasted a new independence and savored it. They bought nice things for themselves. They went dancing. They decided when bad relationships needed ending. In many cases, because unemployment rates for men were higher, women even took on the role of breadwinner in their families. The men saw their masculinity challenged and lashed out. Their resentment, uncontained by weakened religious and community bonds, turned violent, into a rage that manifested itself in the ruthless killing of women. This story has become so popular that when I interviewed the director of the Juárez Association of Maquiladoras, he recited it for me almost as though he were delivering a pitch at a business convention.

Yet the violence in Juárez—against men as well as women—is at its barest a criminal act and the direct by-product of the lack of rule of law in the Mexican justice system. Killers know that the odds are overwhelming that they can get away with murder. Nationally, only two in every one hundred crimes are ever solved, including cases that are closed by throwing a scapegoat in jail. There are no jury trials, and it is easy to influence a judge with money. If not one of the Juárez girls' cases has been properly resolved in ten years, only two explanations are possible: Law enforcement is either inept or corrupt. Most people believe both are true.

"I got to witness the inefficiency," says Oscar Maynez, the chief of 20 forensics in Juárez from 1999 to 2002. Maynez has been involved in the cases of the murdered women of Juárez from the beginning. In 1993, as an instructor at the state police academy, he was skimming criminal files to use in his class when something disturbing grabbed his attention: In three separate cases, it appeared that three young women had been raped and strangled. Fearing that a serial killer might be on the loose, he created a psychological profile of the killer. When he approached his superiors with the report, however, every one of them, including the Juárez police chief and the deputy attorney general in the state capital of Chihuahua, dismissed its importance.

Maynez left his job a year later to pursue a master's degree in Washington, D.C. When he returned to reorganize the state crime lab, in

New graves fill cemeteries on the edge of a stark and empty land.

1999, he was greeted by a growing pile of women's remains, along with case records and forensic evidence, all of it hopelessly confused. Though some of the bodies still had vital clues embedded, the lab had never done any follow-up on those that had appeared between 1993 and 1999, including DNA analyses of the rapists' semen. Maynez was certain now—and the thought enraged him—that either a serial killer or a well-funded criminal ring was systematically target-ing Juárez's youngest and poorest women. And yet, six years after his initial findings, neither the local nor the state authorities had made an effort to pursue an investigation according to Maynez's profile.

In early November 2001 eight female bodies were found in a cotton field across a busy street from the maquiladora association's air-conditioned offices. Five of them had been dumped in an old sewage canal, the other three in an irrigation ditch. Most followed a similar modus operandi: hands bound, apparently raped and strangled. Two days after the first corpses were found, Maynez and his crew began their work, dusting for evidence with tiny paintbrushes. As they did so, a man drove up in a bulldozer, saying that he'd been ordered by the attorney general's office to dig up the area to search for more bodies. Maynez sent him off to work elsewhere, preserving the crime scene.

Just a few days later, the police presented an edited videotape con-fession of two bus drivers who said they had killed the women, naming each of the eight. It seemed odd that the murderers would know the complete names of their victims—middle names, maternal and pater-nal names. When the accused were admitted to the city jail, it became obvious that they were scapegoats and had been forced to confess, for they showed multiple signs of torture, including electrical burns on their genitals. The cost of defending them turned out to be quite high. In February 2002 one of the two lawyers who was representing the drivers was shot and killed by state police officers as he drove his car; they say they mistook him for a fugitive. (An investigation was con-ducted, but the officers were never charged.) And a few days after the national human rights commission agreed to hear the drivers' cases, one of them mysteriously died in custody while undergoing an unau-thorized surgery based on forged documents for a hernia that he had developed from the torture.

To date, eighteen people have been arrested in connection with the murders, including an Egyptian chemist named Abdel Latif Sharif Sharif, who arrived in Juárez by way of the United States, where he had lived for 25 years. He had accumulated two convictions for sexual battery in Florida. Sharif, who has been jailed in Mexico since October 1995, was accused by Chihuahua state prosecutors of several of the

Juárez murders but convicted of only one. Though the conviction was overturned in 2000, a state judge ruled in favor of the prosecution's appeal, and Sharif remains imprisoned in Chihuahua City.

Judging from the lack of evidence, none of those eighteen individuals 25 has been justly charged or convicted. The biggest testament to this is the fact that the murders continue unabated. At a press conference in jail in 1998, Sharif divulged information he had received from a police officer who claimed that the person behind the killings was Armando Martínez, the adopted son of a prominent Juárez bar owner. Sharif's source, Victor Valenzuela Rivera, said that he had overheard Martínez bragging about the murders at the Safari Club, one of his father's bars and a place frequented by police officers and *narcotraficantes*.[7] Valenzuela insisted that Martínez, who also goes by Alejandro Maynez, had said he was being protected by government officials and the police and that he had bragged about his involvement in the trafficking of drugs and jewelry. The following year, Valenzuela repeated this account before several federal legislators and reporters; again, there were bloody repercussions. After Irene Blanco, the woman who had defended Sharif in court, demanded that the press investigate the allegations against Martínez, her son was shot and nearly killed by unknown assailants. The police say the shooting was drug-related; others blame police officers themselves. Martínez's whereabouts are unknown.

Valenzuela's testimony was not the only suggestion that the murders might be linked to the drug world. In 1996 a group of civilians searching for women's remains in Lomas de Poleo came upon a wooden shack and inside it an eerie sight: red and white votive candles, female garments, traces of fresh blood, and a wooden panel with detailed sketches on it. On one side of the panel was a drawing of a scorpion—a symbol of the Juárez cartel—as well as depictions of three unclothed women with long hair and a fourth lying on the floor, eyes closed, looking sad. A handful of soldiers peered out from behind what looked like marijuana plants, and at the top there was an ace of spades. The other side showed similar sketches: two unclothed women with their legs spread, an ace of clubs, and a male figure that looked

---

[7] Drug traffickers (Spanish).

like a gang member in a trench coat and hat. The panel was handed over to Victoria Caraveo, a women's activist, who turned it in to state authorities. Though the incident was reported by the Mexican papers, today government officials refuse to acknowledge that the panel ever existed.

As Oscar Maynez sees it, the problem with the Mexican justice system begins with "a complete absence of scruples among the people at the top." The criminologist says that the state crime lab has become merely an office that signs death certificates. In the case of the eight girls' bodies discovered in 2001, Maynez told the *El Paso Times,* "We were asked to plant evidence against two bus drivers who were charged with the murders." Though the drivers were prosecuted, their evidence file, Maynez says, remained empty. Frustrated, he resigned in January 2002. Because it has become his life's mission to save Juárez—or at least reduce its death toll—he is still intent upon getting his job back some day. The only chance of this happening is if the National Action Party (PAN) retakes control of the state.

But the PAN-controlled federal government isn't doing much to solve the Juárez murders either. Some of Chihuahua's top leaders a decade ago now sit in the highest ranks of President Vicente Fox's administration. In December 2001 federal legislators formed a committee to investigate the issue; it has yet to release a report. The bad blood between political parties and the long history of turf wars between state and federal law enforcement groups have prevented any sort of interagency cooperation, a key to solving difficult crimes in the United States. (On one of my trips to Juárez, I watched news footage of a mob of men pummeling each other—it was the state and federal police, fighting over who was supposed to protect the governor of Chihuahua when he flew into the city.) Early this March, the federal attorney general finally sent his investigators to the border, and in May they announced their intention to reopen fourteen of the murder cases as part of an investigation into organ smuggling.

Activists in Juárez and El Paso believe that the only way the murders can ever be solved is for Mexican federal officials to invite the American FBI to investigate, but historically, neither side has seemed eager for this to occur. Nationalism runs high in Mexico, and the country's leaders do not want Americans meddling in their affairs. In El Paso, officials like outgoing mayor Ray Caballero hesitate to offend their peers in Chihuahua. Caballero, who has had little to say publicly about the murdered women, told me. "For me to come out and make one pronouncement does not solve the problem." Perhaps circumstances are changing. This spring his office announced the creation of a hotline that will allow people in Juárez to report information to the El Paso police, who will then turn it over to investigators in Chihuahua. In late April, two deputies of the Mexican federal attorney general asked the FBI to collaborate with them on their investigations of the Juárez murder cases and the Juárez drug cartel. FBI agents have also been training Mexican prosecutors and detectives in Juárez and El Paso.

• ○ •

"Are you looking for work?"   30

My heart stopped. I knew that line, knew it immediately. My eyes, frozen, terrified, locked onto his. "N-n-n-o," I believe I stuttered, but the man spoke again: "Where are you from?" His eyes crawled down my body and back up to my face. I was wearing leather boots, a black turtleneck, and fitted jeans—the last pair of clean pants I had managed to dig out of my suitcase that morning. And I regretted it immediately, because they might have been appropriate for trekking in mountains but not, I realized now, for walking around downtown. My heart was back, pounding furiously. Only then did I notice that as I had talked on the phone, I had absentmindedly paced half a block away from the restaurant's door. At that moment, there was nobody within sight, not even a single officer from the police station next door. I tried to envision the scenarios, tried to imagine some chance of safety. Would he ask me to follow him somewhere? Would someone drive up out of nowhere and force me into a vehicle? Did I have control of the situation or did he? If I darted toward the restaurant door, would I startle him, causing him to reach over and grab me? If I screamed, would my sister, who was now dangling by my thigh on the other end of a cell phone—listening, I hoped desperately, to this conversation—be able to help? Would Diana and the others inside the restaurant hear me over the music? If I was not able to escape, how much would I have to suffer before being killed? Was this it? Had I really—and the brief thought of this made me sad—gambled it all for a story?

For a few infinite seconds, nothing, and everything, was possible. But as my heart began to slow down and my mind sped up, I thought of another possibility. "I'm from El Paso," I said.

• ○ •

Irma Monrreal lives in a dust-tinged neighborhood known as Los Aztecas. The streets are unpaved, lined with tiny cement homes that peek out from behind clumsy cinder-block walls. Her home on Calle Grulla, which she bought on credit for $1,000, originally consisted of one room, in which she slept with seven children, but her eldest sons constructed another two rooms. Like so many immigrants in Juárez, Irma had hopped on a train and headed to the border with visions of prosperity flitting about in her head. In the fields of her state of Zacatecas, she had earned $3 a day hoeing beans and chiles. The big talk those days was of the factories in Juárez, where one could make nearly three times as much money. Since she and her husband had separated and her two eldest boys, who were thirteen and fourteen years old, would soon be needing jobs, she moved to Juárez and altered her sons' birth certificates so that they could immediately begin work in the maquiladoras.

Though Irma had a bundle of children to care for, she was closest to her third-youngest, Esmeralda, a blithe girl with a broad, round face and an unflinchingly optimistic attitude. At fifteen, she had completed middle school and was determined to keep studying so that someday she might work in a big place—like the airport, she told her mother— and earn lots of money. She was an excellent typist. She didn't date or spend much time with friends, but she was extremely close to her little sister Zulema, who was four years younger. The two pretended that they were television stars or models, and on special occasions they attended mass and treated themselves to lunch. When nighttime set in, they dreamed in bunk beds.

The only thing Esmeralda desired even more than an education 35 was to have a *quinceañera*[8] and to wear, like every other girl in Juárez

---

[8] Celebration of a girl's fifteenth birthday (Spanish).

who turns fifteen, a white gown to her rite-of-passage celebration. Her mother, who earns about $30 a week at a plastics factory, was saving up what she could to pay for the party, but Esmeralda felt the urge to pitch in. When an acquaintance asked Irma if she could borrow her teenage daughter to help around the house. Esmeralda pleaded with her hesitant mother to say yes, promising that she would work only up until the December 15 ceremony.

A week went by, and Esmeralda was excited, chatty. One evening she confided to her mom that a young man who was a few years older than she and who worked at the printshop where she had ordered her invitations had asked her out to lunch. She seemed deeply flattered that someone would notice her, but Irma admonished her not to take any offers from strangers. Her daughter promised that she wouldn't. A second week passed. Esmeralda would finish working at about four o'clock and head straight home, arriving well before Irma departed for her overnight shift at the maquiladora.

But a few days later, something went terribly wrong. At four-thirty, there was no sign of Esmeralda. Then it was five o'clock. Then six. At ten minutes to seven, Irma was forced to leave for work, but she asked her other children to watch for their sister. In the factory, she punched her time card and began talking to God silently.

The night dragged. When her shift was finally over, at seven in the morning, Irma rushed home to see her daughter's face, but her world imploded when her children opened the door: *Esmeralda no llegó.*[9] The girl had vanished.

During the following ten days, Irma sometimes wondered whether her mind hadn't just taken a crazy turn. *Her* Esmeralda. How could this be happening? At night, she was overwhelmed with terror as she speculated where the girl might be, what she might be going through at that very moment. To lose a family member and not know what has happened to her is to live an existential anguish of believing fiercely and at the same time losing all notion of truth. I spoke with a psychologist at a Juárez women's crisis center who said that she finds it almost impossible to help the relatives of disappeared people heal

[9] Esmeralda didn't come (Spanish).

© Dan Winters

Elegy for Esmerelda: Irma Monrreal mourns her daughter.

because they are unable to discount that their abducted family member is either dead or alive. In El Paso I met Jaime Hervella, a Juárez native who runs a small accounting and consulting business as well as an organization for relatives of the disappeared on both sides of the border. "It's the worst of tragedies," he said, motioning with his wax-like hands over a cluttered desk. Then his bifocals fogged up, and he wept suddenly. "I just can't handle talking to the little old women, the mothers. Morning comes and they implore God, the Virgin, the man who drives the dump truck. Nighttime falls and they are still asking themselves. 'Where could my child be?' And the hours pass in this way, and the sun begins to disappear."

As she scavenged her memory for clues, Irma recalled the young man who had invited her daughter to lunch and immediately sent her son to look for him. But the owner of the printshop said he'd left his job. He refused to give any more information. After several visits herself, Irma finally persuaded the shop owner's son to tell her where their former employee lived. She found the little house, but it was locked; she banged on the door, the windows, screaming loudly in case her daughter was inside, listening. Esmeralda had told her mother that the young man had asked her for her schedule and that he had wanted to know whether her mom always walked her home from work. As Irma circled the house, the man arrived. She explained who she was and asked if he knew anything about her daughter, but he brushed her away, saying that he was married.

A few days later, a co-worker at the maquiladora asked Irma if she'd heard the news: Eight bodies had been found in a couple of ditches at the intersection of Ejército Nacional and Paseo de la Victoria. Could one of them be Esmeralda? Next came the phone call from the state prosecutor's office, asking her to identify the body. At the morgue, however, Irma was told it was too gruesome to view. She would have to obtain signed permission from the prosecutor's office. They offered to bring out the blouse that was on the corpse when it was found; Irma's heart collapsed when she glimpsed the speckled yellow, pink, orange, and white. It was the blouse that Esmeralda's older sister Cecilia had sent from Colorado, where she had moved to with her husband.

Yet there was still that lingering doubt, so Irma requested the permit to see the body. Fearing the shock would be too great for their mother to bear, her two eldest sons insisted on identifying it themselves. When they arrived home from the morgue, they were silent, their heads hung low.

"So?" Irma asked anxiously. "Was it your sister?"

But the response was hesitant, brittle: "We don't know."

"What do you mean, you don't know?!" Irma sputtered.   45

"It's just that . . . she doesn't have a face."

The words shattered on the floor like a Christmas ornament. She burst: "But what about her hair—was it her hair?!"

"It's just that she doesn't have any hair," came the grief-stricken reply. "She doesn't have any ears. She doesn't have anything."

The corpse presumed to be Esmeralda's was one of the three found on November 6, a day before the other five were discovered a short distance away. All of the bodies were partially or wholly unclothed, some with their hands tied. But unlike the other girls, most of whom had been reduced to mere skeletal remains, Esmeralda's state of decomposition was particularly grisly and perplexing. She was missing most of the flesh from her collarbone up to her face. The authorities suggested that the rats in the fields had had their share, but Irma noted—and Oscar Maynez, the chief of forensics, concurred—that it would have made more sense for them to feast on the meatier parts of her body. The mystery deepened when the forensic workers took hair and blood from Esmeralda's mother and father and sent them to a laboratory in Mexico City. Even when DNA samples from the parents who had identified clothing were compared with those from the girls wearing the clothing, the results came back without a match. This opened up two possibilities: Either the samples had been grossly contaminated or, even more eerily, the murderers were switching clothes with other, as yet unfound, victims.

"Why?" Irma cried out as I sat with her one wintry afternoon in her   50
tidy home, which is crammed with curly-haired dolls and deflated balloons and stuffed animals her daughter had collected—the last traces of happiness left in her little house. "Do they want to drive me crazy or something? Is it her or isn't it?" In a silver frame on top of a brown armoire, Esmeralda sat squeezed into a strapless red top, her shoulder-length hair dyed a blondish brown. She was laughing irresistibly— cracking up—but across from the photo, Irma slumped in her chair in blue sweats and a denim shirt, her body heaving uncontrollably as I listened, speechless. "Why does God let the evil ones take the good

ones away? Why the poor, if we don't bring any harm on anybody? Nobody can imagine what this trauma is like. I go to work and I don't know if my children are going to be safe when I return. It's a terror that's lived day by day, hour by hour."

Like numerous stories I had heard from other victims' families, Irma's included the lament that her family has fallen apart as her children struggle to confront the tragedy of losing their sister and try to assign blame. Unable to channel their newfound hate, they have begun hating each other. Her eldest sons have stopped talking to her. Zulema, who refuses to sleep in her bunk bed now, attempted to kill herself and her eight-year-old brother with tranquilizers a doctor had prescribed for Irma. Defeated, the woman spoke with the shame of a child who has discovered that she has made an irrevocably wrong choice. She wished, with all her might, that she had never made that fateful decision to come to Juárez. "They've destroyed my life," she said with vacant eyes and a flat voice, once she had regained her composure. "I don't believe in anything anymore. There is a saying that one comes here in search of a better life, but those are nothing but illusions."

Irma eventually claimed the body, she says, so that she would "have somewhere to cry." Instead of determining whether more lab work needed to be done, the authorities instantly handed it over. They never interrogated the suspicious young man Irma had reported, and in a tasteless act of disregard for her daughter, they ruled that the cause of the young woman's death was "undetermined," even though it seemed apparent that she had been strangled. On November 16 Irma buried the corpse, using the quinceañera savings to pay for the $600 coffin.

●　○　●

"Soy de El Paso,"[1] I said to the man outside the restaurant. I held my breath. I remembered what Diana had told me when we first met to talk about the story: "They know who to leave alone. They leave the Americans alone. They leave the rich girls alone, because there might be trouble. The other girls? A dime a dozen." And yes, his interest

---

[1] I'm from El Paso (Spanish).

faded instantly. "I'm sorry," he said, still bearing his apologetic smile, though somewhat more sheepishly. "I—I just saw you holding that piece of paper so I thought maybe you were looking for a job. Sorry." He turned around and began to walk away.

I was still frightened, but now that I felt a little safer, the journalist in me began to return. "Why?" I called out nervously. "Do you know of a job?" He turned around and stared at me. "I hire girls to work at a grocery store," he said. His eyebrows crinkled. "Where are you from?" Shaking my head, I stammered. "Oh, no—I'm from El Paso. My friends are waiting for me inside this restaurant." I brushed past him in a hurry, skipping up the restaurant's steps and to the table where the rest of the group was finishing their meal. Diana was gone. I took my seat. My legs, my hands, trembled violently.

"You'll never guess what happened to me," I said in a shaky voice. 55 The others fell silent and looked at me with interest. "I just got offered a job." As the words spilled, one of the group nodded slowly. "You fit the profile," she said. When I described the man to her, she said that he had walked into the restaurant earlier, while I was on the phone. He had chatted with the woman who was cooking, taken some food, and left.

I jumped from my chair and stepped over to the counter. "Excuse me, *señora*," I said to the woman at the grill. "Do you know the man who just came in a few minutes ago?" "Not very well," she replied. "At night he guards the lawyer's office next door and by day he sells candies on the street."

At that moment, something blocked the light from the doorway. I turned around and found myself face to face with the same man from outside, this time without his basket. He looked nervous. "Let me buy you a Coke," he offered. "No, thanks," I replied firmly. Then I asked him, "Do you really have a store?"

"You're a journalist," he said, "aren't you?" His question caught me by surprise. I turned toward my table, then back to his intense gaze. "I—I'm here with some journalist friends," I stuttered. "No." he said forcefully, "but *you're* a journalist, aren't you?" It was obvious that he knew. "Well, yes, but I'm just here accompanying my friends, who are working on a story." His tone softened. "Come on, let's sit down. Let me buy you a drink. *En confianza.*[2] *You can trust me.* "No," I repeated, "I'm with my friends and we're leaving." I walked back to the table. Diana had returned, unaware of what had transpired. Later I would learn that she had gone to the lawyer's office, encountered the candy man, and told him she was with a group of journalists who wanted to see his boss. But with the man standing there, all I wanted to do was get away. We all gathered our belongings and hurried toward the door. "The lawyer says he'll be here tomorrow, if you want to see him," we heard the man call out to us. I never turned back.

That night, safe in El Paso, I stared at the ceiling in the darkness of my hotel room and replayed the afternoon's events over and over. My family had worried when I told them that I was going to write about the women of Juárez, even after I assured them that plenty of other journalists had done so safely. But *you*, they shot back, as if I'd missed the most obvious point, *you* look just like those girls. I thought of how much care I had taken not to go to Juárez alone, even if it had meant sacrificing my journalistic independence. And yet, in that one brief instant I had let my guard down, and I had been approached by someone mysterious. I will never know for sure if that was it—if, as I have told colleagues I felt at that moment, I really touched the story, my own life colliding with those of the girls whose lives I had been hoping to preserve. What I do know is this: that I had felt my heart beat, the way they must have felt it beat too.

As I thought this, warm tears spilled down the sides of my face and trickled into my ears. And I realized that I was crying not for myself, but for the women of Juárez—for the girls who had died and for the mothers who survived them. They say that whenever a new body is found, every grieving mother relives her pain. I was crying for the girls who had stayed on the other side of the border. For the ones who couldn't leave their reflections on paper and run far, far away, as I was going to do. I cried because I realized how easy it would have been to believe the man who approached me; because I understood that the girls were not naive, or careless, or as a former attorney general of Chihuahua once said, asking for it. They were simply women—poor

2. In private (Spanish).

women, brown women. Fighters, dreamers. And they weren't even dreaming of all that much, by our standards: a secretarial job, a bedroom set, a fifteenth-birthday party. A little chance to live.

I cried because of the absurdity of it all, because it was possible for a life to be worth less than a brief taste of power. I cried thinking of how we had failed them.

♦

STUDY QUESTIONS

1. The title of Ballí's article implies that Juárez is an extremely violent city, but none of the people she interviews there are the actual perpetrators of this violence. How would you characterize the various individuals that Ballí speaks to in Juárez—their different situations and social positions, as well as the emotional effects they create in you as a reader? Explain by referring to specific passages from the text.

2. "Ciudad de la Muerte" mixes different RHETORICAL STRATEGIES, or modes, including DESCRIPTION of places, NARRATION of Ballí's own experiences, ETHNOGRAPHIC observations of people, and historical background. How does each of these modes contribute to the sense of place, and how effective is this multimodal approach overall?

3. Ballí recounts several moments of discomfort and fear during her visit to Juárez. How do her own gender, age, and skin color influence her experiences in Juárez, her conversations with residents there, and her thoughts and feelings about the murders? In what ways might this article be different if researched and written by a man?

4. *For Writing.* Ballí concludes that, after returning to the safety of El Paso, "I cried because of the absurdity of it all, because it was possible for a life to be worth less than a brief taste of power. I cried thinking of how we had failed them." Whom exactly does Ballí implicate here as "we"—Ballí and her fellow journalists? Her American AUDIENCE? Write an essay that explores Ballí's sense of who might be responsible for the failure to protect the young women of Juárez. What are some ARGUMENTS for and against her implication that Americans bear part of this responsibility?

ANTHONY BOURDAIN { *Food Is Good*

ANTHONY BOURDAIN (b. 1956) was born in New York City. He
attended Vassar College and, in 1978, graduated from the Culinary
Institute of America. He is a well-known chef and television personality,
hosting *Anthony Bourdain: No Reservations* on the Travel Channel. He
has written several nonfiction books about food, including *The Nasty
Bits, Kitchen Confidential, A Cook's Tour,* and *Anthony Bourdain's Les
Halles Cookbook.* He has also written two crime novels: *Gone Bamboo*
and *Bone in the Throat.*

In this excerpt from Bourdain's memoir *Kitchen Confidential:
Adventures in the Culinary Underbelly* (2000), the author begins with
the moment he discovered that eating wasn't merely "like filling up at
a gas station," a realization that came when he first tasted vichyssoise,
a cold soup, on a family cruise to Europe. He goes on to share the
experiences that helped him understand the power of food and become
a more adventurous eater.

MY FIRST INDICATION THAT FOOD was something other than a substance one stuffed in one's face when hungry—like filling up at a gas
station—came after fourth-grade elementary school. It was on a family
vacation to Europe, on the *Queen Mary*, in the cabin-class dining room.
There's a picture somewhere: my mother in her Jackie O sunglasses, my
younger brother and I in our painfully cute cruisewear, boarding the
big Cunard[1] ocean liner, all of us excited about our first transatlantic
voyage, our first trip to my father's ancestral homeland, France.

[1]British-American ocean liner company.

It was the soup.

It was *cold*.

This was something of a discovery for a curious fourth-grader whose entire experience of soup to this point had consisted of Campbell's cream of tomato and chicken noodle. I'd eaten in restaurants before, sure, but this was the first food I really noticed. It was the first food I enjoyed and, more important, remembered enjoying. I asked our patient British waiter what this delightfully cool, tasty liquid was.

"Vichyssoise," came the reply, a word that to this day—even though   5
it's now a tired old warhorse of a menu selection and one I've prepared thousands of times—still has a magical ring to it. I remember everything about the experience: the way our waiter ladled it from a silver tureen into my bowl, the crunch of tiny chopped chives he spooned on as garnish, the rich, creamy taste of leek and potato, the pleasurable shock, the surprise that it was cold.

I don't remember much else about the passage across the Atlantic. I saw *Boeing Boeing* with Jerry Lewis and Tony Curtis in the *Queen*'s movie theater, and a Bardot flick.[2] The old liner shuddered and groaned and vibrated terribly the whole way—barnacles on the hull was the official explanation—and from New York to Cherbourg, it was like riding atop a giant lawnmower. My brother and I quickly became bored, and spent much of our time in the "Teen Lounge," listening to "House of the Rising Sun"[3] on the jukebox, or watching the water slosh around like a contained tidal wave in the below-deck salt-water pool.

But that cold soup stayed with me. It resonated, waking me up, making me aware of my tongue, and in some way, preparing me for future events.

My second pre-epiphany in my long climb to chefdom also came during that first trip to France. After docking, my mother, brother and I stayed with cousins in the small seaside town of Cherbourg, a bleak, chilly resort area in Normandy, on the English Channel. The sky was almost always cloudy; the water was inhospitably cold. All the neigh-

[2]That is, a movie starring French actress Brigitte Bardot (b. 1934).
[3]Folk song recorded as a pop hit by the English band The Animals in 1964.

borhood kids thought I knew Steve McQueen and John Wayne personally—as an American, it was assumed we were all pals, that we hung out together on the range, riding horses and gunning down miscreants—so I enjoyed a certain celebrity right away. The beaches, while no good for swimming, were studded with old Nazi block-houses and gun emplacements, many still bearing visible bullet scars and the scorch of flamethrowers, and there were tunnels under the dunes—all very cool for a little kid to explore. My little French friends were, I was astonished to find, allowed to have a cigarette on Sunday, were given watered *vin ordinaire*[4] at the dinner table, and best of all, they owned Velo Solex motorbikes. *This* was the way to raise kids, I recall thinking, unhappy that my mother did not agree.

So for my first few weeks in France, I explored underground passageways, looking for dead Nazis, played miniature golf, sneaked cigarettes, read a lot of Tintin and Asterix comics, scooted around on my friends' motorbikes and absorbed little life-lessons from observations that, for instance, the family friend Monsieur Dupont brought his mistress to some meals and his wife to others, his extended brood of children apparently indifferent to the switch.

I was largely unimpressed by the food.   10

The butter tasted strangely "cheesy" to my undeveloped palate. The milk—a staple, no, a mandatory ritual in '60s American kiddie life—was undrinkable here. Lunch seemed always to consist of sandwich au jambon or croque-monsieur.[5] Centuries of French cuisine had yet to make an impression. What I noticed about food, French style, was what they *didn't* have.

After a few weeks of this, we took a night train to Paris, where we met up with my father, and a spanking new Rover Sedan Mark III, our touring car. In Paris, we stayed at the Hôtel Lutétia, then a large, slightly shabby old pile on Boulevard Haussmann. The menu selections for my brother and me expanded somewhat, to include steak-frites and steak haché (hamburger). We did all the predictable touristy things: climbed the Tour Eiffel, picnicked in the Bois de Boulogne,

---

[4]Inexpensive red table wine; literally, ordinary wine (French).
[5]Respectively, ham sandwich and grilled ham and cheese (French).

marched past the Great Works at the Louvre, pushed toy sailboats around the fountain in the Jardin de Luxembourg—none of it much fun for a nine-year-old with an already developing criminal bent. My principal interest at this time was adding to my collection of English translations of Tintin adventures. Hergé's crisply drafted tales of drug-smuggling, ancient temples, and strange and faraway places and cultures were *real* exotica for me. I prevailed on my poor parents to buy hundreds of dollars-worth of these stories at W. H. Smith, the English bookstore, just to keep me from whining about the deprivations of France. With my little short-shorts a permanent affront, I was quickly becoming a sullen, moody, difficult little bastard. I fought constantly with my brother, carped about everything, and was in every possible way a drag on my mother's Glorious Expedition.

My parents did their best. They took us everywhere, from restaurant to restaurant, cringing, no doubt, every time we insisted on steak haché (with ketchup, no less) and a "Coca." They endured silently my gripes about cheesy butter, the seemingly endless amusement I took in advertisements for a popular soft drink of the time, Pschitt. "I want shit! I want shit!" They managed to ignore the eye-rolling and fidgeting when they spoke French, tried to encourage me to find something, anything, to enjoy.

And there came a time when, finally, they *didn't* take the kids along.

I remember it well, because it was such a slap in the face. It was a wake-up call that food could be important, a challenge to my natural belligerence. By being denied, a door opened. 15

The town's name was Vienne. We'd driven miles and miles of road to get there. My brother and I were fresh out of Tintins and cranky as hell. The French countryside, with its graceful, tree-lined roads, hedgerows, tilled fields and picture-book villages provided little distraction. My folks had by now endured weeks of relentless complaining through many tense and increasingly unpleasant meals. They'd dutifully ordered our steak haché, crudités variées,[6] sandwich au jambon and the like long enough. They'd put up with our grousing that the beds were too hard, the pillows too soft, the neck-rolls and toilets and plumbing too weird.

[6]Mixed raw vegetables (French).

They'd even allowed us a little watered wine, as it was clearly the French thing to do—but also, I think, to shut us up. They'd taken my brother and me, the two Ugliest Little Americans, everywhere.

Vienne was different.

They pulled the gleaming new Rover into the parking lot of a restaurant called, rather promisingly, La Pyramide, handed us what was apparently a hoarded stash of Tintins . . . *and then left us in the car!*

It was a hard blow. Little brother and I were left in that car for over three hours, an eternity for two miserable kids already bored out of their minds. I had plenty of time to wonder: *What could be so great inside those walls?* They were eating in there. I knew that. And it was certainly a Big Deal; even at a witless age nine, I could recognize the nervous anticipation, the excitement, the near-reverence with which my beleaguered parents had approached this hour. And I had the Vichyssoise Incident still fresh in my mind. Food, it appeared, could be *important*. It could be an event. It had secrets.

I know now, of course, that La Pyramide, even in 1966, was the center of the culinary universe. Bocuse, Troisgros,[7] *everybody* had done their time there, making their bones under the legendarily fearsome proprietor, Ferdinand Point. Point was the Grand Master of cuisine at the time, and La Pyramide was Mecca for foodies. This was a pilgrimage for my earnestly francophile parents. In some small way, I got that through my tiny, empty skull in the back of the sweltering parked car, even then.

Things changed. *I* changed after that.

First of all, I was furious. Spite, always a great motivating force in my life, caused me to become suddenly adventurous where food was concerned. I decided then and there to outdo my foodie parents. At the same time, I could gross out my still uninitiated little brother. I'd show *them* who the gourmet was!

Brains? Stinky, runny cheeses that smelled like dead man's feet? Horsemeat? Sweetbreads? Bring it on!! Whatever had the most shock value became my meal of choice. For the rest of that summer, and in the summers that followed, I ate *everything*. I scooped gooey Vacherin,

[7]Paul Bocuse (b. 1926) and Jean (b. 1926) and Pierre (b. 1928) Troisgros, prominent French chefs.

learned to love the cheesy, rich Normandy butter, especially slathered on baguettes and dipped in bitter hot chocolate. I sneaked red wine whenever possible, tried fritures—tiny whole fish, fried and eaten with persillade—loving that I was eating heads, eyes, bones and all. I ate ray in beurre noisette, saucisson à l'ail, tripes, rognons de veau (kidneys), boudin noir that squirted blood down my chin.

And I had my first oyster.

Now, *this* was a truly significant event. I remember it like I remember losing my virginity—and in many ways, more fondly.   25

August of that first summer was spent in La Teste sur Mer, a tiny oyster village on the Bassin d'Arcachon in the Gironde (Southwest France). We stayed with my aunt, Tante Jeanne, and my uncle, Oncle Gustav, in the same red tile-roofed, white stuccoed house where my father had summered as a boy. My Tante Jeanne was a frumpy, bespectacled, slightly smelly old woman, my Oncle Gustav, a geezer in coveralls and beret who smoked hand-rolled cigarettes until they disappeared onto the tip of his tongue. Little had changed about La Teste in the years since my father had vacationed there. The neighbors were still all oyster fishermen. Their families still raised rabbits and grew tomatoes in their backyards. Houses had two kitchens, an inside one and an outdoor "fish kitchen." There was a hand pump for drinking water from a well, and an outhouse by the rear of the garden. Lizards and snails were everywhere. The main tourist attractions were the nearby Dune of Pyla (Europe's Largest Sand Dune!) and the nearby resort town of Arcachon, where the French flocked in unison for *Les Grandes Vacances.*[8] Television was a Big Event. At seven o'clock, when the two national stations would come on the air, my Oncle Gustav would solemnly emerge from his room with a key chained to his hip and ceremoniously unlock the cabinet doors that covered the screen.

My brother and I were happier here. There was more to do. The beaches were warm, and closer in climate to what we knew back home, with the added attraction of the ubiquitous Nazi blockhouses. There were lizards to hunt down and exterminate with readily available

---

[8]The long vacation (French), usually July and August, when many French people take their vacations from work and school.

pétards, firecrackers which one could buy legally (!) over-the-counter. There was a forest within walking distance where an actual hermit lived, and my brother and I spent hours there, spying on him from the underbrush. By now I could read and enjoy comic books in French and of course I was eating—*really* eating. Murky brown soupe de poisson, tomato salad, moules marinières, poulet basquaise (we were only a few miles from the Basque country). We made day trips to Cap Ferret, a wild, deserted and breathtakingly magnificent Atlantic beach with big rolling waves, taking along baguettes and saucissons and wheels of cheese, wine and Evian (bottled water was at that time unheard of back home). A few miles west was Lac Cazeaux, a fresh-water lake where my brother and I could rent *pédalo* watercraft and pedal our way around the deep. We ate gaufres, delicious hot waffles, covered in whipped cream and powdered sugar. The two hot songs of that summer on the Cazeaux jukebox were "Whiter Shade of Pale" by Procol Harum, and "These Boots Were Made for Walkin'" by Nancy Sinatra. The French played those two songs over and over again, the music punctuated by the sonic booms from French air force jets which would swoop over the lake on their way to a nearby bombing range. With all the rock and roll, good stuff to eat and high-explosives at hand, I was reasonably happy.

So, when our neighbor, Monsieur Saint-Jour, the oyster fisherman, invited my family out on his *penas* (oyster boat), I was enthusiastic.

At six in the morning, we boarded Monsieur Saint-Jour's small wooden vessel with our picnic baskets and our sensible footwear. He was a crusty old bastard, dressed like my uncle in ancient denim coveralls, espadrilles and beret. He had a leathery, tanned and wind-blown face, hollow cheeks, and the tiny broken blood vessels on nose and cheeks that everyone seemed to have from drinking so much of the local Bordeaux. He hadn't fully briefed his guests on what was involved in these daily travails. We put-putted out to a buoy marking his underwater oyster *parc*, a fenced-off section of bay bottom, and we sat . . . and sat . . . and sat, in the roaring August sun, waiting for the tide to go out. The idea was to float the boat over the stockaded fence walls, then sit there until the boat slowly sank with the water level, until it rested on the *bassin* floor. At this point, Monsieur Saint-Jour, and his guests presumably, would rake the oysters, collect a few good

specimens for sale in port, and remove any parasites that might be
endangering his crop.

There was, I recall, still about two feet of water left to go before the   30
hull of the boat settled on dry ground and we could walk about the
parc. We'd already polished off the Brie and baguettes and downed
the Evian, but I was still hungry, and characteristically said so.

Monsieur Saint-Jour, on hearing this—as if challenging his American passengers—inquired in his thick Girondais accent, if any of us
would care to try an oyster.

My parents hesitated. I doubt they'd realized they might have actually to *eat* one of the raw, slimy things we were currently floating over.
My little brother recoiled in horror.

But I, in the proudest moment of my young life, stood up smartly,
grinning with defiance, and volunteered to be the first.

And in that unforgettably sweet moment in my personal history,
that one moment still more alive for me than so many of the other
"firsts" which followed—first pussy, first joint, first day in high school,
first published book, or any other thing—I attained glory. Monsieur
Saint-Jour beckoned me over to the gunwale, where he leaned over,
reached down until his head nearly disappeared underwater, and
emerged holding a single silt-encrusted oyster, huge and irregularly
shaped, in his rough, clawlike fist. With a snubby, rust-covered oyster
knife, he popped the thing open and handed it to me, everyone watching now, my little brother shrinking away from this glistening, vaguely
sexual-looking object, still dripping and nearly alive.

I took it in my hand, tilted the shell back into my mouth as instructed   35
by the by now beaming Monsieur Saint-Jour, and with one bite and a
slurp, wolfed it down. It tasted of seawater . . . of brine and flesh . . .
and somehow . . . of the future.

Everything was different now. Everything.

I'd not only survived—I'd *enjoyed.*

This, I knew, was the magic I had until now been only dimly and
spitefully aware of. I was hooked. My parents' shudders, my little
brother's expression of unrestrained revulsion and amazement only
reinforced the sense that I had, somehow, become a man. I had had an
adventure, tasted forbidden fruit, and everything that followed in my

life—the food, the long and often stupid and self-destructive chase for *the next thing*, whether it was drugs or sex or some other new sensation—would all stem from this moment.

I'd learned something. Viscerally, instinctively, spiritually—even in some small, precursive way, sexually—and there was no turning back. The genie was out of the bottle. My life as a cook, and as a chef, had begun.

Food had *power*.   40

It could inspire, astonish, shock, excite, delight and *impress*. It had the power to please me . . . and others. This was valuable information.

For the rest of that summer, and in later summers, I'd often slip off by myself to the little stands by the port, where one could buy brown paper bags of unwashed, black-covered oysters by the dozen. After a few lessons from my new soul-mate, blood brother and bestest buddy, Monsieur Saint-Jour—who was now sharing his after-work bowls of sugared *vin ordinaire* with me too—I could easily open the oysters by myself, coming in from behind with the knife and popping the hinge like it was Aladdin's cave.

I'd sit in the garden among the tomatoes and the lizards and eat my oysters and drink Kronenbourgs (France was a wonderland for under-age drinkers), happily reading *Modesty Blaise* and the *Katzenjammer Kids* and the lovely hard-bound *bandes dessinées*[9] in French, until the pictures swam in front of my eyes, smoking the occasional pilfered Gitane. And I still associate the taste of oysters with those heady, wonderful days of illicit late-afternoon buzzes. The smell of French cigarettes, the taste of beer, that unforgettable feeling of doing something I shouldn't be doing.

I had, as yet, no plans to cook professionally. But I frequently look back at my life, searching for that fork in the road, trying to figure out where, exactly, I *went bad* and became a thrill-seeking, pleasure-hungry sensualist, always looking to shock, amuse, terrify and manipulate, seeking to fill that empty spot in my soul with something new.

I like to think it was Monsieur Saint-Jour's fault. But of course, it   45 was me all along.

---

[9]Comic books (French).

STUDY QUESTIONS

1. List the experiences Bourdain recounts that most affected his childhood relationship with food. Which experience was most memorable to you as reader?

2. In this MEMOIR, Bourdain often COMPARES AND CONTRASTS his responses to specific foods with the responses of his family members. Explain the differences in Bourdain's and his parents' and brother's responses. What do those differences show about Bourdain?

3. Bourdain is known for his unapologetically direct, sometimes bawdy writing and speaking style. How would you characterize his ETHOS? What passages in this excerpt best EXEMPLIFY this ethos

4. *For Writing.* Think back to your most important childhood memories of food—of tasting something new. Write a four- to five-page MEMOIR in which you describe several early experiences with food, and reflect on what your response to those experiences says about you as a person.

SHIRLEY JACKSON { *The Lottery*

SHIRLEY JACKSON (1916–1965) was born in San Francisco, California, and grew up in the West Coast suburb of Burlingame. She attended the University of Rochester but graduated from Syracuse University with a BA in 1940. Jackson and her husband, literary critic Stanley Hyman, moved to Bennington, Vermont, where he taught at Bennington College and Jackson raised their four children and published novels and short stories. Although Jackson is best known for her dark and disturbing works, such as "The Lottery" (1948), *The Bird's Nest* (1954), and *The Haunting of Hill House* (1959), she also wrote comically about marriage and motherhood in *Life among the Savages* (1953) and *Raising Demons* (1957).

When "The Lottery" was first published in the *New Yorker*, the magazine received an unprecedented amount of mail from shocked readers. Jackson's best-known story follows the process of a yearly town lottery, beginning with a description of a traditional community ritual but ending quite differently. The author carefully sets the scene with details about the town and its residents, paving the way for the plot twist. As you read, try to find the point at which the process of the lottery changes into something unexpected.

THE MORNING OF JUNE 27TH was clear and sunny, with the fresh warmth of a full-summer day; the flowers were blossoming profusely and the grass was richly green. The people of the village began to gather in the square, between the post office and the bank, around ten o'clock; in some towns there were so many people that the lottery took two days and had to be started on June 26th, but in this village, where there were only about three hundred people, the whole lottery took less than two hours, so it could begin at ten o'clock in the morning and still be through in time to allow the villagers to get home for noon dinner.

The children assembled first, of course. School was recently over for the summer, and the feeling of liberty sat uneasily on most of them; they tended to gather together quietly for a while before they broke into boisterous play, and their talk was still of the classroom and the teacher, of books and reprimands. Bobby Martin had already stuffed his pockets full of stones, and the other boys soon followed his example, selecting the smoothest and roundest stones; Bobby and Harry Jones and Dickie Delacroix—the villagers pronounced this name "Dellacroy"—eventually made a great pile of stones in one corner of the square and guarded it against the raids of the other boys. The girls stood aside, talking among themselves, looking over their shoulders at the boys, and the very small children rolled in the dust or clung to the hands of their older brothers or sisters.

Soon the men began to gather, surveying their own children, speaking of planting and rain, tractors and taxes. They stood together, away from the pile of stones in the corner, and their jokes were quiet and they smiled rather than laughed. The women, wearing faded house dresses and sweaters, came shortly after their menfolk. They greeted one another and exchanged bits of gossip as they went to join their husbands. Soon the women, standing by their husbands, began to call to their children, and the children came reluctantly, having to be called four or five times. Bobby Martin ducked under his mother's grasping hand and ran, laughing, back to the pile of stones. His father spoke up sharply, and Bobby came quickly and took his place between his father and his oldest brother.

The lottery was conducted—as were the square dances, the teenage club, the Halloween program—by Mr. Summers, who had time and energy to devote to civic activities. He was a round-faced, jovial man and he ran the coal business, and people were sorry for him, because he had no children and his wife was a scold. When he arrived in the square, carrying the black wooden box, there was a murmur of conversation among the villagers, and he waved and called, "Little late today, folks." The postmaster, Mr. Graves, followed him, carrying a three-legged stool, and the stool was put in the center of the square and Mr. Summers set the black box down on it. The villagers kept their distance, leaving a space between themselves and the stool, and when Mr. Summers said, "Some of you fellows want to give me a hand?" there was a hesitation before two men, Mr. Martin and his oldest son, Baxter, came forward to hold the box steady on the stool while Mr. Summers stirred up the papers inside it.

The original paraphernalia for the lottery had been lost long ago, and 5 the black box now resting on the stool had been put into use even before Old Man Warner, the oldest man in town, was born. Mr. Summers spoke frequently to the villagers about making a new box, but no one liked to upset even as much tradition as was represented by the black box. There was a story that the present box had been made with some pieces of the box that had preceded it, the one that had been constructed when the first people settled down to make a village here. Every year, after the lottery, Mr. Summers began talking again about a new box, but every year the subject was allowed to fade off without anything's being done. The black box grew shabbier each year; by now it was no longer completely black but splintered badly along one side to show the original wood color, and in some places faded or stained.

Mr. Martin and his oldest son, Baxter, held the black box securely on the stool until Mr. Summers had stirred the papers thoroughly with his hand. Because so much of the ritual had been forgotten or discarded, Mr. Summers had been successful in having slips of paper substituted for the chips of wood that had been used for generations. Chips of wood, Mr. Summers had argued, had been all very well when the village was tiny, but now that the population was more than three hundred and likely to keep on growing, it was necessary to use something that would fit more easily into the black box. The night before the lottery, Mr. Summers and Mr. Graves made up the slips of paper and put them in the box, and it was then taken to the safe of Mr. Summers's coal company and locked up until Mr. Summers was ready to take it to the square next morning. The rest of the year, the box was put away, sometimes one place, sometimes another; it had spent one year in Mr. Graves's barn and another year underfoot in the post office, and sometimes it was set on a shelf in the Martin grocery and left there.

There was a great deal of fussing to be done before Mr. Summers declared the lottery open. There were the lists to make up—of heads of families, heads of households in each family, members of each household in each family. There was the proper swearing-in of Mr. Summers by the postmaster, as the official of the lottery; at one time, some people remembered, there had been a recital of some sort, performed by the official of the lottery, a perfunctory, tuneless chant that had been rattled off duly each year; some people believed that the official of the lottery used to stand just so when he said or sang it, others believed that he was supposed to walk among the people, but years and years ago this part of the ritual had been allowed to lapse. There had been, also, a ritual salute, which the official of the lottery had had to use in addressing each person who came up to draw from the box, but this also had changed with time, until now it was felt necessary only for the official to speak to each person approaching. Mr. Summers was very good at all this; in his clean white shirt and blue jeans, with one hand resting carelessly on the black box, he seemed very proper and important as he talked interminably to Mr. Graves and the Martins.

Just as Mr. Summers finally left off talking and turned to the assembled villagers, Mrs. Hutchinson came hurriedly along the path to the square, her sweater thrown over her shoulders, and slid into place in the back of the crowd. "Clean forgot what day it was," she said to Mrs. Delacroix, who stood next to her, and they both laughed softly. "Thought my old man was out back stacking wood," Mrs. Hutchinson went on, "and then I looked out the window and the kids was gone, and then I remembered it was the twenty-seventh and came a-running." She dried her hands on her apron, and Mrs. Delacroix said, "You're in time, though. They're still talking away up there."

Mrs. Hutchinson craned her neck to see through the crowd and found her husband and children standing near the front. She tapped Mrs. Delacroix on the arm as a farewell and began to make her way through the crowd. The people separated good-humoredly to let her through; two or three people said, in voices just loud enough to be heard across the crowd, "Here comes your Missus, Hutchinson," and "Bill, she made it after all." Mrs. Hutchinson reached her husband, and Mr. Summers, who had been waiting, said cheerfully, "Thought we were going to have to get on without you, Tessie." Mrs. Hutchinson said, grinning, "Wouldn't have me leave m'dishes in the sink, now, would you, Joe?," and soft laughter ran through the crowd as the people stirred back into position after Mrs. Hutchinson's arrival.

"Well, now," Mr. Summers said soberly, "guess we better get started, get this over with, so's we can go back to work. Anybody ain't here?"   10

"Dunbar," several people said, "Dunbar, Dunbar."

Mr. Summers consulted his list. "Clyde Dunbar," he said. "That's right. He's broke his leg, hasn't he? Who's drawing for him?"

"Me, I guess," a woman said, and Mr. Summers turned to look at her. "Wife draws for her husband," Mr. Summers said. "Don't you have a grown boy to do it for you, Janey?" Although Mr. Summers and everyone else in the village knew the answer perfectly well, it was the business of the official of the lottery to ask such questions formally. Mr. Summers waited with an expression of polite interest while Mrs. Dunbar answered.

"Horace's not but sixteen yet," Mrs. Dunbar said regretfully. "Guess I gotta fill in for the old man this year."

"Right," Mr. Summers said. He made a note on the list he was holding. Then he asked, "Watson boy drawing this year?"   15

A tall boy in the crowd raised his hand. "Here," he said. "I'm drawing for m'mother and me." He blinked his eyes nervously and ducked his head as several voices in the crowd said things like "Good fellow, Jack," and "Glad to see your mother's got a man to do it."

"Well," Mr. Summers said, "guess that's everyone. Old Man Warner make it?"

"Here," a voice said, and Mr. Summers nodded.

A sudden hush fell on the crowd as Mr. Summers cleared his throat and looked at the list. "All ready?" he called. "Now, I'll read the names—heads of families first—and the men come up and take a paper out of the box. Keep the paper folded in your hand without looking at it until everyone has had a turn. Everything clear?"

The people had done it so many times that they only half listened to the directions; most of them were quiet, wetting their lips, not looking   20
around. Then Mr. Summers raised one hand high and said, "Adams." A man disengaged himself from the crowd and came forward. "Hi, Steve," Mr. Summers said, and Mr. Adams said, "Hi, Joe." They grinned at one

another humorlessly and nervously. Then Mr. Adams reached into the black box and took out a folded paper. He held it firmly by one corner as he turned and went hastily back to his place in the crowd, where he stood a little apart from his family, not looking down at his hand.

"Allen," Mr. Summers said. "Anderson. . . . Bentham."

"Seems like there's no time at all between lotteries any more," Mrs. Delacroix said to Mrs. Graves in the back row. "Seems like we got through with the last one only last week."

"Time sure goes fast," Mrs. Graves said.

"Clark. . . . Delacroix."

"There goes my old man," Mrs. Delacroix said. She held her breath   25 while her husband went forward.

"Dunbar," Mr. Summers said, and Mrs. Dunbar went steadily to the box while one of the women said, "Go on, Janey," and another said, "There she goes."

"We're next," Mrs. Graves said. She watched while Mr. Graves came around from the side of the box, greeted Mr. Summers gravely, and selected a slip of paper from the box. By now, all through the crowd there were men holding the small folded papers in their large hands, turning them over and over nervously. Mrs. Dunbar and her two sons stood together, Mrs. Dunbar holding the slip of paper.

"Harburt. . . . Hutchinson."

"Get up there, Bill," Mrs. Hutchinson said, and the people near her laughed.

"Jones."   30

"They do say," Mr. Adams said to Old Man Warner, who stood next to him, "that over in the north village they're talking of giving up the lottery."

Old Man Warner snorted. "Pack of crazy fools," he said. "Listening to the young folks, nothing's good enough for *them*. Next thing you know, they'll be wanting to go back to living in caves, nobody work any more, live *that* way for a while. Used to be a saying about 'Lottery in June, corn be heavy soon.' First thing you know, we'd all be eating stewed chickweed and acorns. There's *always* been a lottery," he added petulantly. "Bad enough to see young Joe Summers up there joking with everybody."

"Some places have already quit lotteries," Mrs. Adams said.

"Nothing but trouble in *that*," Old Man Warner said stoutly. "Pack of young fools."

"Martin." And Bobby Martin watched his father go forward. 35 "Overdyke.... Percy."

"I wish they'd hurry," Mrs. Dunbar said to her older son. "I wish they'd hurry."

"They're almost through," her son said.

"You get ready to run tell Dad," Mrs. Dunbar said.

Mr. Summers called his own name and then stepped forward precisely and selected a slip from the box. Then he called, "Warner."

"Seventy-seventh year I been in the lottery," Old Man Warner said 40 as he went through the crowd. "Seventy-seventh time."

"Watson." The tall boy came awkwardly through the crowd. Someone said, "Don't be nervous, Jack," and Mr. Summers said, "Take your time, son."

"Zanini."

After that, there was a long pause, a breathless pause, until Mr. Summers, holding his slip of paper in the air, said, "All right, fellows." For a minute, no one moved, and then all the slips of paper were opened. Suddenly, all the women began to speak at once, saying, "Who is it?," "Who's got it?," "Is it the Dunbars?," "Is it the Watsons?" Then the voices began to say, "It's Hutchinson. It's Bill," "Bill Hutchinson's got it."

"Go tell your father," Mrs. Dunbar said to her older son.

People began to look around to see the Hutchinsons. Bill Hutchinson 45 son was standing quiet staring down at the paper in his hand. Suddenly, Tessie Hutchinson shouted to Mr. Summers, "You didn't give him time enough to take any paper he wanted. I saw you. It wasn't fair."

"Be a good sport, Tessie," Mrs. Delacroix called, and Mrs. Graves said, "All of us took the same chance."

"Shut up, Tessie," Bill Hutchinson said.

"Well, everyone," Mr. Summers said, "that was done pretty fast, and now we've got to be hurrying a little more to get done in time." He consulted his next list. "Bill," he said, "you draw for the Hutchinson family. You got any other households in the Hutchinsons?"

"There's Don and Eva," Mrs. Hutchinson yelled. "Make *them* take their chance!"

"Daughters draw for their husbands' families, Tessie," Mr. Summers 50 said gently. "You know that as well as anyone else."

"It wasn't *fair*," Tessie said.

"I guess not, Joe," Bill Hutchinson said regretfully. "My daughter draws with her husband's family, that's only fair. And I've got no other family except the kids."

"Then, as far as drawing for families is concerned, it's you," Mr. Summers said in explanation, "and as far as drawing for households is concerned, that's you, too. Right?"

"Right," Bill Hutchinson said.

"How many kids, Bill?" Mr. Summers asked formally. 55

"Three," Bill Hutchinson said. "There's Bill, Jr., and Nancy, and little Dave. And Tessie and me."

"All right, then," Mr. Summers said. "Harry, you got their tickets back?"

Mr. Graves nodded and held up the slips of paper. "Put them in the box, then," Mr. Summers directed. "Take Bill's and put it in."

"I think we ought to start over," Mrs. Hutchinson said, as quietly as she could, "I tell you it wasn't *fair*. You didn't give him time enough to choose. *Every*body saw that."

Mr. Graves had selected the five slips and put them in the box, and 60 he dropped all the papers but those onto the ground, where the breeze caught them and lifted them off.

"Listen, everybody," Mrs. Hutchinson was saying to the people around her.

"Ready, Bill?" Mr. Summers asked, and Bill Hutchinson, with one quick glance around at his wife and children, nodded.

"Remember," Mr. Summers said, "take the slips and keep them folded until each person has taken one. Harry, you help little Dave." Mr. Graves took the hand of the little boy, who came willingly with him up to the box. "Take a paper out of the box, Davy," Mr. Summers said. Davy put his hand into the box and laughed. "Take just *one* paper," Mr. Summers said. "Harry, you hold it for him." Mr. Graves took the child's hand and removed the folded paper from the tight fist and held it while little Dave stood next to him and looked up at him wonderingly.

"Nancy next," Mr. Summers said. Nancy was twelve, and her school friends breathed heavily as she went forward, switching her skirt, and took a slip daintily from the box. "Bill, Jr.," Mr. Summers said, and Billy, his face red and his feet over-large, nearly knocked the box over as he got a paper out. "Tessie," Mr. Summers said. She hesitated for a minute, looking around defiantly, and then set her lips and went up to the box. She snatched a paper out and held it behind her.

"Bill," Mr. Summers said, and Bill Hutchinson reached into the box   65
and felt around, bringing his hand out at last with the slip of paper in it.

The crowd was quiet. A girl whispered, "I hope it's not Nancy," and the sound of the whisper reached the edges of the crowd.

"It's not the way it used to be," Old Man Warner said clearly. "People ain't the way they used to be."

"All right," Mr. Summers said. "Open the papers. Harry, you open little Dave's."

Mr. Graves opened the slip of paper and there was a general sigh through the crowd as he held it up and everyone could see that it was blank. Nancy and Bill, Jr., opened theirs at the same time, and both beamed and laughed, turning around to the crowd and holding their slips of paper above their heads.

"Tessie," Mr. Summers said. There was a pause, and then Mr. Summers   70
looked at Bill Hutchinson, and Bill unfolded his paper and showed it. It was blank.

"It's Tessie," Mr. Summers said, and his voice was hushed. "Show us her paper, Bill."

Bill Hutchinson went over to his wife and forced the slip of paper out of her hand. It had a black spot on it, the black spot Mr. Summers had made the night before with the heavy pencil in the coal-company office. Bill Hutchinson held it up, and there was a stir in the crowd.

"All right, folks," Mr. Summers said. "Let's finish quickly."

Although the villagers had forgotten the ritual and lost the original black box, they still remembered to use stones. The pile of stones the boys had made earlier was ready; there were stones on the ground with the blowing scraps of paper that had come out of the box. Mrs. Delacroix selected a stone so large she had to pick it up with both hands and turned to Mrs. Dunbar. "Come on," she said. "Hurry up."

Mrs. Dunbar had small stones in both hands, and she said, gasping for breath, "I can't run at all. You'll have to go ahead and I'll catch up with you."

The children had stones already, and someone gave little Davy Hutchinson a few pebbles.

Tessie Hutchinson was in the center of a cleared space by now, and she held her hands out desperately as the villagers moved in on her. "It isn't fair," she said. A stone hit her on the side of the head.

Old Man Warner was saying, "Come on, come on, everyone." Steve Adams was in the front of the crowd of villagers, with Mrs. Graves beside him.

"It isn't fair, it isn't right," Mrs. Hutchinson screamed, and then they were upon her.

STUDY QUESTIONS

1. Who wins the lottery in this story, and what happens to him or her?

2. What is the significance of the story's SETTING? Consider the mood of the gathering and how it relates to the events that are taking place. How does it contrast with and complement what is happening?

3. Why is the end of this story so shocking? Read the story again to see whether Jackson includes any hints that might foreshadow what happens in the yearly ritual.

4. *For Writing.* Winners of a lottery typically receive a desirable prize— entry into a particular school or a sum of money, for example. In an essay, REFLECT on how Jackson turns our understanding of a lottery upside down. What rhetorical STRATEGIES does she use, and to what effect? What larger point do you think she is trying to make? Support your ARGUMENT with examples and QUOTATIONS from the story.

RANDY PAUSCH ⎱ *I Never Made It*
⎰ *to the NFL*

RANDY PAUSCH (1960–2008), professor of computer science and pioneer
in the field of virtual reality, was born and raised in Maryland. He earned
two degrees in computer science, a bachelor's at Brown University in 1982
and a PhD at Carnegie Mellon University in 1988. As a professor at
Carnegie Mellon University, he developed the computer language Alice,
which helps teach young people computer programming. In addition to
publishing more than seventy scholarly articles and books, Pausch wrote
The Last Lecture (2008), an expanded version of his inspirational speech
delivered at Carnegie Mellon on September 18, 2007, as part of the "Last
Lecture" series—a series in which top academics give a talk that captures the
wisdom they would like to impart. Pausch's was especially poignant: he had
been diagnosed with terminal pancreatic cancer a month earlier and had less
than a year to live.

In this selection from the book, Pausch explains what he learned from
playing youth football. Children who play sports, according to Pausch, learn
far more than the skills and rules of the game. As you read, consider the role
of Coach Graham in helping Pausch learn these important lessons.

———————————

I LOVE FOOTBALL. *TACKLE* FOOTBALL. I started playing when I was
nine years old, and football got me through. It helped make me who
I am today. And even though I did not reach the National Football League, I sometimes think I got more from pursuing that dream,
and *not* accomplishing it, than I did from many of the ones I did
accomplish.

My romance with football started when my dad dragged me, kicking and screaming, to join a league. I had no desire to be there. I was naturally wimpy, and the smallest kid by far. Fear turned to awe when I met my coach, Jim Graham, a hulking, six-foot-four wall-of-a-guy. He had been a linebacker at Penn State, and was seriously old-school. I mean, *really* old-school; like he thought the forward pass was a trick play.[1]

On the first day of practice, we were all scared to death. Plus he hadn't brought along any footballs. One kid finally spoke up for all of us. "Excuse me, Coach. There are no footballs."

And Coach Graham responded, "We don't need any footballs."

There was a silence, while we thought about that . . .   5

"How many men are on the football field at a time?" he asked us.

Eleven on a team, we answered. So that makes twenty-two.

"And how many people are touching the football at any given time?" One of them.

"Right!" he said. "So we're going to work on what those *other*   10 twenty-one guys are doing."

Fundamentals. That was a great gift Coach Graham gave us. Fundamentals, fundamentals, fundamentals. As a college professor, I've seen this as one lesson so many kids ignore, always to their detriment: You've *got* to get the fundamentals down, because otherwise the fancy stuff is not going to work.

● ○ ●

Coach Graham used to ride me hard. I remember one practice in particular. "You're doing it all wrong, Pausch. Go back! Do it again!" I tried to do what he wanted. It wasn't enough. "You owe me, Pausch! You're doing push-ups after practice."

When I was finally dismissed, one of the assistant coaches came over to reassure me. "Coach Graham rode you pretty hard, didn't he?" he said.

I could barely muster a "yeah."

"That's a good thing," the assistant told me. "When you're screw-   15

---

[1]Football's forward pass become legal in 1906.

ing up and nobody says anything to you anymore, that means they've given up on you."

That lesson has stuck with me my whole life. When you see yourself doing something badly and nobody's bothering to tell you anymore, that's a bad place to be. You may not want to hear it, but your critics are often the ones telling you they still love you and care about you, and want to make you better.

There's a lot of talk these days about giving children self-esteem. It's not something you can *give;* it's something they have to build. Coach Graham worked in a no-coddling zone. Self-esteem? He knew there was really only one way to teach kids how to develop it: You give them something they can't do, they work hard until they find they can do it, and you just keep repeating the process.

When Coach Graham first got hold of me, I was this wimpy kid with no skills, no physical strength, and no conditioning. But he made me realize that if I work hard enough, there will be things I can do tomorrow that I can't do today. Even now, having just turned forty-seven, I can give you a three-point stance that any NFL lineman would be proud of.

I realize that, these days, a guy like Coach Graham might get thrown out of a youth sports league. He'd be too tough. Parents would complain.

I remember one game when our team was playing terribly. At half-time, in our rush for water, we almost knocked over the water bucket. Coach Graham was livid: "Jeez! That's the most I've seen you boys move since this game started!" We were eleven years old, just standing there, afraid he'd pick us up one by one and break us with his bare hands. "Water?" he barked. "You boys want water?" He lifted the bucket and dumped all the water on the ground.

We watched him walk away and heard him mutter to an assistant coach: "You can give water to the first-string defense. They played OK."

Now let me be clear. Coach Graham would never endanger any kid. One reason he worked so hard on conditioning was he knew it reduces injuries. However, it was a chilly day, we'd all had access to water during the first half, and the dash to the water bucket was more about us being a bunch of brats than really needing hydration.

20

Even so, if that kind of incident happened today, parents on the sidelines would be pulling out their cell phones to call the league commissioner, or maybe their lawyer.

It saddens me that many kids today are so coddled. I think back to how I felt during that halftime rant. Yes, I was thirsty. But more than that, I felt humiliated. We had all let down Coach Graham, and he let us know it in a way we'd never forget. He was right. We had shown more energy at the water bucket than we had in the damn game. And getting chewed out by him meant something to us. During the second half, we went back on the field, and gave it our all.

I haven't seen Coach Graham since I was a teen, but he just keeps showing up in my head, forcing me to work harder whenever I feel like quitting, forcing me to be better. He gave me a feedback loop for life.

• ○ •

When we send our kids to play organized sports—football, soccer, swimming, whatever—for most of us, it's not because we're desperate for them to learn the intricacies of the sport.

What we really want them to learn is far more important: teamwork, perseverance, sportsmanship, the value of hard work, an ability to deal with adversity. This kind of indirect learning is what some of us like to call a "head fake."

There are two kinds of head fakes. The first is literal. On a football field, a player will move his head one way so you'll think he's going in that direction. Then he goes the opposite way. It's like a magician using misdirection. Coach Graham used to tell us to watch a player's waist. "Where his belly button goes, his body goes," he'd say.

The second kind of head fake is the *really* important one—the one that teaches people things they don't realize they're learning until well into the process. If you're a head-fake specialist, your hidden objective is to get them to learn something you want them to learn.

This kind of head-fake learning is absolutely vital. And Coach Graham was the master.

STUDY QUESTIONS

1. What does the term "head fake" refer to in its original, literal sense? What does Pausch mean when he uses the term figuratively? How is this essay a "head fake"?

2. Notice how Pausch breaks this chapter into three sections. What is the main point of each section?

3. List some of Coach Graham's physical characteristics. Describe his personality. In what ways does Pausch create a DOMINANT IMPRESSION of his coach?

4. *For Writing.* What lessons have you learned that might be of value to others? Write an essay in which you use one or more ANECDOTES to illustrate how you learned a particular lesson. Be sure to include both specific details and the broader implications of your experience.

AUDREY WICK { *The Siren Call of the Bingo Hall*

AUDREY WICK is an American teacher and writer who works as a professor at Blinn College in Texas, having earned degrees in English and speech communication from Sam Houston State University. Her writing has appeared in a number of newspapers and magazines in Texas and on various Web sites, covering topics including education, politics, literature, and history. She is the co-editor of the book *Schulenburg: Halfway to Everywhere* (2007).

Wick's essay "The Siren Call of the Bingo Hall" was first published in *Texas Magazine* in 2003, and has since been reprinted in a number of publications. In it, Wick describes a trip she took with her family to a local church bingo game. She writes that playing bingo in such a setting is a complicated endeavor that requires stamina, skill, attention, and a good amount of social awareness; for this community of bingo players, observing the rules of behavior is almost as important as being able to play the game well. As you read, note how Wick creates a sense of suspense as she charts her evolving understanding of the game and her fellow players, and the tone with which she narrates the experience of being both an observer and a participant in the game.

IN CENTRAL TEXAS, PEPPERED AMONG the beer joints, riverside parks and kolache bakeries are makeshift bingo halls organized by small country churches. On any given evening, people can be seen flooding into local Catholic church centers and Knights of Columbus halls,

Audrey A. Wick is an English professor at Blinn College. This narrative essay about her experience playing bingo uses humor and an unlikely ending. It was originally published in 2003 in Texas magazine, a weekly supplement to the Houston Chronicle newspaper. Reprinted by permission of the author.

bingo tools in hand, eager to win not only a cash prize but also societal bragging rights until the next event.

Bingo is not a game; it is a sport. Competition, endurance and raw determination are needed to withstand this three-hour ordeal and to emerge with grace, regardless of the outcome.

My father, my 18-year-old brother and I had no idea what we were in for when we stepped virginally into bingo central. We were not warmly welcomed. We had never played bingo here and were immediately recognized as outsiders. Old women shook their canes at us for holding up the entrance line. The woman taking money sighed continuously when we asked her to explain the rules. Someone said, "I don't know how you can explain bingo. Just pay your money and sit down!"

We were definitely out of our element.

Bingo is an expensive habit, and "habit" is the word to describe it. Just as some people need cigarettes or alcohol, some need their weekly dose of bingo. I've seen wedding receptions, heck, even country fairs, with fewer people than were at the bingo hall that Monday night. Everything was meticulously organized. Tables were arranged to allow for maximum coverage by bingo personnel with minimal movement. Rules of conduct were posted, and the bingo caller was surrounded by bottles of spring water, lozenges and a backup microphone.

We had a hard time establishing our central post, because we did not want to invade anyone's bingo station. When we finally did sit down, we were overwhelmed by the three-card-per-game minimum that we were required to play and by trying to figure out how to use the bingo markers we were required to buy. No sharing allowed.

A man across the row from us was playing 21 cards at a time, staking them side-by-side, one paper sheet on top of the other so as not to crowd his neighbors' space. If he could manage those, we certainly could manage our trifling three.

We had arrived before the scheduled start time to get in on the advertised early-bird special. It was anything but "special." Enthusiasts are required to pay an additional fee for certain games before the actual regular bingo begins, with players vying for the pot accumulated from all participating players. To blend in with the crowd, we eagerly flashed our cash and confidently participated in the early-bird games. Each game was over as fast as the money could be dealt from player to official. We were getting a pretty sour taste of our anticipated bingo bliss.

Then the actual bingo games began. We tried to speak softly among ourselves to make sense of the chaos around us, but even that was greeted with sharp looks of disdain from our neighbors.

I barely had time to go to the bathroom because bingo was played during intermission, too. My father's stomach was one loud grumble the whole night. No one told us the menu was bring your own or starve.

After a while, the numbers, colors and lights were getting to be too much. My brother and I were thinking of bowing out for a game, just to get a break, but there was no polite, discreet way to do so.

The last game, blackout, was what everyone was waiting for. A fortune was on the line - $500 - as well as tri-county fame, if only for a week. Our hopes, as well as our bingo markers, were quickly running dry. The particulars of that game are a blur. All I clearly remember are the events that transpired after call No. 52.

When my dad elbowed me and indistinguishably grunted, my cards were a bloody mess of passion purple. I was having a hard time understanding the difference between numbers and letters. His grunt was persistent, however, and my brother, sitting across the table, raised his head from his own cards and focused on my father's third card, wide-eyed. The announcement of G-49 would cement a blackout win. One number passed, then two, then three, during which whispered gasps of "I only need one more number!" could be heard throughout the hall. For whatever reason, the pagan gods of gaming prosperity were shining down on my father that night. When his number was called, all he could do was calmly mark it, and then present a glazed look of distress.

"Should I say it?" he asked me. " I think I marked everything, but I can't be for sure."

My brother and I had no advice. A false call would mean certain condemnation. A false caller is forever branded as such and can never be trusted in a hall again. But a correct call would mean an end to the evening and any smidgen of hope held by everyone else.

"I guess it's do or die," my father breathed. "BINGO!"

With so much money at stake, I expected people to wait for verification, surely suspicious that my father, an outsider, had marked his card incorrectly. But after a few expletives here and there, the enthusiasts just destroyed their cards. While an official was checking the card for accuracy, I was getting my keys ready, and my brother was plotting how to make a quick getaway in case the marks were incorrect.

Much to our relief, they were correct, and the $500 prize was ours (minus, of course, $25 for church taxes). Beginners' luck, some said. Others offered sly congratulatory smirks, while still others gingerly expressed, "Good job," though secretly cursing our good fortune under their breath. With grins from ear to ear and pockets that had become much heavier from our good fortune, we were ready to part for the evening.

Leaving should have been much easier than arriving, but exiting a bingo hall as a winner is much messier in practice than in theory.

There was a final, winner-take-all game, in which players were again vying for a pot. We were the only people in the hall who did not take part in that game. We didn't realize it at the time, but that was a huge social faux pas. By not participating, we were hoarding our winnings. It would have been an even bigger social faux pas had we exited in the middle of the game (as we would have liked), because our departure would have been quite distracting.

When we did finally leave, after 10 uncomfortable minutes, we could not do so inconspicuously. People stopped to talk, wanting to know the secret of the big win.

"What color marker were you using? What time did you get here? Did you say any particular prayers?"

There also were some sore losers, the frowning ones who passed by us quickly.

We did not go to win. We were just looking for some good old-fashioned country fun, but I sensed a different motive for many that night - compulsion. They come to play, rain or shine, every Monday of the year.

From an outsider's view, it is a disturbing sight to behold, with fun taking a back seat - for some, not all.

Most disturbing for me is the fact that my father has returned every Monday since his inaugural visit, with no wins to add to his original $500 kismet.

Perhaps others, like him, were once winners who wore the tri-county crown of credit for a week. Now he has become one of them, clutching his several markers and a couple of sandwiches, pushing his worldly cares aside for three hours every week, hoping that "maybe tonight will be my night."

STUDY QUESTIONS

1. What are Wick's assumptions about bingo at the beginning of her trip to the bingo hall, and how does the evening change these assumptions?

2. What unwritten rules of bingo do Wick and her family have to master in order to establish their ETHOS with the community?

3. What DOMINANT TONE does Wick establish when writing about her evening in the bingo hall?

4. *For Writing.* Think of a time when you found yourself in an unfamiliar environment. In a short essay, describe the environment and explain how you figured out the best way to conduct yourself in it.

MORTIMER J. ADLER   {   *How to Mark a Book*

MORTIMER J. ADLER (1902–2001), a native of New York City, dropped out of school at fourteen, to embark on a career in journalism. He began taking night courses at Columbia University to develop his writing skills and discovered a love of philosophy. By the late 1920s Adler was teaching at Columbia while pursuing his doctorate and writing his first book, *Dialectic* (1927). Along with Max Weismann, Adler founded The Center for the Study of Great Ideas to investigate such philosophical questions as "What ought we seek in life?" and "How ought we seek it?"

In "How to Mark a Book," Adler explains not only *how* to mark a book, but also *why* we should mark our books. Adler uses a range of rhetorical strategies—process analysis, description, definition, division and classification, and exemplification—to develop his ideas. Real ownership of books, Adler advises, comes from truly possessing the ideas, not just the pages, between the covers, and the point of reading is not to get through books but to get them through you.

YOU KNOW YOU HAVE TO read "between the lines" to get the most out of anything. I want to persuade you to do something equally important in the course of your reading. I want to persuade you to write between the lines. Unless you do, you are not likely to do the most efficient kind of reading.

I contend, quite bluntly, that marking up a book is not an act of mutilation but of love. You shouldn't mark up a book which isn't yours.

"How to Mark a Book" by Mortimer Adler. Reprinted by permission of the Estate of Mortimer Adler.

Librarians (or your friends) who lend you books expect you to keep them clean, and you should. If you decide that I am right about the usefulness of marking books, you will have to buy them. Most of the world's great books are available today, in reprint editions.

There are two ways in which one can own a book. The first is the property right you establish by paying for it, just as you pay for clothes and furniture. But this act of purchase is only the prelude to possession. Full ownership comes only when you have made it a part of yourself, and the best way to make yourself a part of it is by writing in it. An illustration may make the point clear. You buy a beefsteak and transfer it from the butcher's icebox to your own. But you do not own the beefsteak in the most important sense until you consume it and get it into your bloodstream. I am arguing that books, too, must be absorbed in your bloodstream to do you any good.

Confusion about what it means to "own" a book leads people to a 5 false reverence for paper, binding, and type—a respect for the physical thing—the craft of the printer rather than the genius of the author. They forget that it is possible for a man to acquire the idea, to possess the beauty, which a great book contains, without staking his claim by pasting his bookplate inside the cover. Having a fine library doesn't prove that its owner has a mind enriched by books; it proves nothing more than that he, his father, or his wife, was rich enough to buy them.

There are three kinds of book owners. The first has all the standard sets and best sellers—unread, untouched. (This deluded individual owns woodpulp and ink, not books.) The second has a great many books—a few of them read through, most of them dipped into, but all of them as clean and shiny as the day they were bought. (This person would probably like to make books his own, but is restrained by a false respect for their physical appearance.) The third has a few books or many—every one of them dog-eared and dilapidated, shaken and loosened by continual use, marked and scribbled in from front to back. (This man owns books.)

Is it false respect, you may ask, to preserve intact and unblemished a beautifully printed book, an elegantly bound edition? Of course not. I'd no more scribble all over a first edition of *Paradise Lost* than I'd give my baby a set of crayons and an original Rembrandt. I

wouldn't mark up a painting or a statue. Its soul, so to speak, is insep-
arable from its body. And the beauty of a rare edition or of a richly
manufactured volume is like that of a painting or a statue.

But the soul of a book "can" be separate from its body. A book is
more like the score of a piece of music than it is like a painting. No
great musician confuses a symphony with the printed sheets of music.
Arturo Toscanini reveres Brahms,[1] but Toscanini's score of the G
minor Symphony is so thoroughly marked up that no one but the mae-
stro himself can read it. The reason why a great conductor makes nota-
tions on his musical scores—marks them up again and again each time
he returns to study them—is the reason why you should mark your
books. If your respect for magnificent binding or typography gets in the
way, buy yourself a cheap edition and pay your respects to the author.

Why is marking up a book indispensable to reading? First, it keeps
you awake. (And I don't mean merely conscious; I mean awake.) In
the second place, reading, if it is active, is thinking, and thinking tends
to express itself in words, spoken or written. The marked book is usually the thought-through book. Finally, writing helps you remember the
thoughts you had, or the thoughts the author expressed. Let me develop
these three points.

If reading is to accomplish anything more than passing time, it   10
must be active. You can't let your eyes glide across the lines of a book
and come up with an understanding of what you have read. Now an
ordinary piece of light fiction, like, say, *Gone With the Wind*,[2] doesn't
require the most active kind of reading. The books you read for pleasure can be read in a state of relaxation, and nothing is lost. But a great
book, rich in ideas and beauty, a book that raises and tries to answer
great fundamental questions, demands the most active reading of which
you are capable. You don't absorb the ideas of John Dewey the way you
absorb the crooning of Mr. Vallée.[3] You have reach for them. That you
cannot do while you're asleep.

[1]German composer (1833–97) of the Romantic era. *Arturo Toscanini* (1867–1957): Italian musician considered one of history's greatest orchestral conductors.
[2]Popular novel (1937) of the Civil War by Margaret Mitchell (1900–49).
[3]Rudy Vallée (1901–86), American singer and bandleader. *John Dewey* (1859–1952):
American philosopher and educational reformer.

If, when you've finished reading a book, the pages are filled with your notes, you know that you read actively. The most famous "active" reader of great books I know is President Hutchins,[4] of the University of Chicago. He also has the hardest schedule of business activities of any man I know. He invariably reads with a pencil, and sometimes, when he picks up a book and pencil in the evening, he finds himself, instead of making intelligent notes, drawing what he calls "caviar factories" on the margins. When that happens, he puts the book down. He knows he's too tired to read, and he's just wasting time.

But, you may ask, why is writing necessary? Well, the physical act of writing, with your own hand, brings words and sentences more sharply before your mind and preserves them better in your memory. To set down your reaction to important words and sentences you have read, and the questions they have raised in your mind, is to preserve those reactions and sharpen those questions.

Even if you wrote on a scratch pad, and threw the paper away when you had finished writing, your grasp of the book would be surer. But you don't have to throw the paper away. The margins (top and bottom as well as side), the end-papers, the very space between the lines, are all available. They aren't sacred. And, best of all, your marks and notes become an integral part of the book and stay there forever. You can pick up the book the following week or year, and there are all your points of agreement, disagreement, doubt, and inquiry. It's like resuming an interrupted conversation with the advantage of being able to pick up where you left off.

And that is exactly what reading a book should be: a conversation between you and the author. Presumably he knows more about the subject than you do; naturally, you'll have the proper humility as you approach him. But don't let anybody tell you that a reader is supposed to be solely on the receiving end. Understanding is a two-way operation; learning doesn't consist in being an empty receptacle. The learner has to question himself and question the teacher. He even has to argue with the teacher, once he understands what the teacher is

[4]Robert Hutchins (1899–1977), educational philosopher and president of the University of Chicago, where he hired Mortimer Adler as a professor of the philosophy of law.

saying. And marking a book is literally an expression of differences, or agreements of opinion, with the author.

There are all kinds of devices for marking a book intelligently and 15 fruitfully. Here's the way I do it:

- **Underlining (or highlighting):** of major points, of important or forceful statements.

- **Vertical lines at the margin:** to emphasize a statement already underlined.

- **Star, asterisk, or other doo-dad at the margin:** to be used sparingly, to emphasize the ten or twenty most important statements in the book. (You may want to fold the bottom corner of each page on which you use such marks. It won't hurt the sturdy paper on which most modern books are printed, and you will be able take the book off the shelf at any time and, by opening it at the folded-corner page, refresh your recollection of the book.)

- **Numbers in the margin:** to indicate the sequence of points the author makes in developing a single argument.

- **Numbers of other pages in the margin:** to indicate where else in the book the author made points relevant to the point marked; to tie up the ideas in a book, which, though they may be separated by many pages, belong together.

- **Circling or highlighting of key words or phrases.**

- **Writing in the margin, or at the top or bottom of the page:** for the sake of recording questions (and perhaps answers) which a passage raised in your mind; reducing a complicated discussion to a simple statement; recording the sequence of major points right through the books. I use the end-papers at the back of the book to make a personal index of the author's points in the order of their appearance.

The front end-papers are to me the most important. Some people reserve them for a fancy bookplate. I reserve them for fancy thinking. After I have finished reading the book and making my personal index on the back end-papers, I turn to the front and try to outline the book, not page by page or point by point (I've already done that at the back), but as an integrated structure, with a basic unity and an order of parts. This outline is, to me, the measure of my understanding of the work.

If you're a die-hard anti-book-marker, you may object that the margins, the space between the lines, and the end-papers don't give you room enough. All right. How about using a scratch pad slightly smaller than the page-size of the book—so that the edges of the sheets won't protrude? Make your index, outlines, and even your notes on the pad, and then insert these sheets permanently inside the front and back covers of the book.

Or, you may say that this business of marking books is going to slow up your reading. It probably will. That's one of the reasons for doing it. Most of us have been taken in by the notion that speed of reading is a measure of our intelligence. There is no such thing as the right speed for intelligent reading. Some things should be read quickly and effortlessly and some should be read slowly and even laboriously. The sign of intelligence in reading is the ability to read different things differently according to their worth. In the case of good books, the point is not to see how many of them you can get through, but rather how many can get through you—how many you can make your own. A few friends are better than a thousand acquaintances. If this be your aim, as it should be, you will not be impatient if it takes more time and effort to read a great book than it does a newspaper.

You may have one final objection to marking books. You can't lend them to your friends because nobody else can read them without being distracted by your notes. Furthermore, you won't want to lend them because a marked copy is kind of intellectual diary, and lending it is almost like giving your mind away.

If your friend wishes to read your *Plutarch's Lives, Shakespeare,* or 20 *The Federalist Papers,* tell him gently but firmly to buy a copy. You will lend him your car or your coat—but your books are as much a part of you as your head or your heart.

STUDY QUESTIONS

1. Why does Adler advise against lending books to friends? What comparison does he use to explore the idea of owning a book, and how effective is it?

2. Numbering items in an essay is a rhetorical technique that can help guide readers through the development of an idea. Adler uses this TRANSITION technique several times in his article. Find these passages and explain what he enumerates. Does the strategy help you to follow his reasoning? Why or why not?

3. The "how to" in Adler's title indicates that he will present a process. Look carefully for the way Adler structures the process of marking a book. Find each step in the process and number them in the order in which they occur. Are there enough to guide someone through the process? Explain.

4. *For Writing.* Adler clearly cares very much about reading books and absorbing their content. Choose an activity for which you have a similar passion, and write a PROCESS ANALYSIS essay describing how best to enjoy that activity. Reread Adler's essay and make sure your essay covers all relevant aspects of participating in the activity, answers possible objections to doing it your way, and provides signposts and transitions for your reader to follow, as Adler's does.

FREDERICK DOUGLASS ⎰ *Learning to Read*

FREDERICK DOUGLASS (ca. 1818–1895) was born a slave in
Maryland to an African American mother and an unknown father
whom he believed to be white. He lived with his grandmother until her
death; he was then sent to Baltimore, at the age of seven, to live with
Hugh and Sophia Auld, who hired him out to work. In 1838 Douglass
escaped slavery by dressing as a sailor, holding another sailor's
freeman papers, and taking a twenty-four-hour journey by train and
boat to New York. He continued on from there to Massachusetts,
where he became an acclaimed abolitionist speaker. His autobiography, *Narrative of the Life of Frederick Douglass, an American Slave*,
was published in 1845.

This selection from the *Narrative* shows Douglass's creativity and
perseverance as he finds ways to learn how to read and write in an
environment that is hostile to his ambitions. Pay attention not only to the
process that Douglass goes through but also to what he learns when he
can read—education, for him, brings painful awareness. What place
does reading have in your daily life? Do you read books, newspapers,
information online, text messages? How has your reading education
been different from that of Douglass? Do you think reading ultimately
did liberate Douglass?

━━━━━━━━━━━━

I LIVED IN MASTER HUGH'S family about seven years. During this time,
I succeeded in learning to read and write. In accomplishing this, I was
compelled to resort to various stratagems. I had no regular teacher. My
mistress, who had kindly commenced to instruct me, had, in compliance with the advice and direction of her husband, not only ceased to

instruct, but had set her face against my being instructed by any one else. It is due, however, to my mistress to say of her, that she did not adopt this course of treatment immediately. She at first lacked the depravity indispensable to shutting me up in mental darkness. It was at least necessary for her to have some training in the exercise of irresponsible power, to make her equal to the task of treating me as though I were a brute.

My mistress was, as I have said, a kind and tender-hearted woman; and in the simplicity of her soul she commenced, when I first went to live with her, to treat me as she supposed one human being ought to treat another. In entering upon the duties of a slaveholder, she did not seem to perceive that I sustained to her the relation of a mere chattel, and that for her to treat me as a human being was not only wrong, but dangerously so. Slavery proved as injurious to her as it did to me. When I went there, she was a pious, warm, and tender-hearted woman. There was no sorrow or suffering for which she had not a tear. She had bread for the hungry, clothes for the naked, and comfort for every mourner that came within her reach. Slavery soon proved its ability to divest her of these heavenly qualities. Under its influence, the tender heart became stone, and the lamblike disposition gave way to one of tiger-like fierceness. The first step in her downward course was in her ceasing to instruct me. She now commenced to practise her husband's precepts. She finally became even more violent in her opposition than her husband himself. She was not satisfied with simply doing as well as he had commanded; she seemed anxious to do better. Nothing seemed to make her more angry than to see me with a newspaper. She seemed to think that here lay the danger. I have had her rush at me with a face made all up of fury, and snatch from me a newspaper, in a manner that fully revealed her apprehension. She was an apt woman; and a little experience soon demonstrated, to her satisfaction, that education and slavery were incompatible with each other.

From this time I was most narrowly watched. If I was in a separate room any considerable length of time, I was sure to be suspected of having a book, and was at once called to give an account of myself. All this, however, was too late. The first step had been taken. Mistress, in teaching me the alphabet, had given me the *inch*, and no precaution could prevent me from taking the *ell*.[1]

The plan which I adopted, and the one by which I was most successful, was that of making friends of all the little white boys whom I met in the street. As many of these as I could, I converted into teachers. With their kindly aid, obtained at different times and in different places, I finally succeeded in learning to read. When I was sent of errands, I always took my book with me, and by going one part of my errand quickly, I found time to get a lesson before my return. I used also to carry bread with me, enough of which was always in the house, and to which I was always welcome; for I was much better off in this regard than many of the poor white children in our neighborhood. This bread I used to bestow upon the hungry little urchins, who, in return, would give me that more valuable bread of knowledge. I am strongly tempted to give the names of two or three of those little boys, as a testimonial of the gratitude and affection I bear them; but prudence forbids;—not that it would injure me, but it might embarrass them; for it is almost an unpardonable offence to teach slaves to read in this Christian country. It is enough to say of the dear little fellows, that they lived on Philpot Street, very near Durgin and Bailey's shipyard. I used to talk this matter of slavery over with them. I would sometimes say to them, I wished I could be as free as they would be when they got to be men. "You will be free as soon as you are twenty-one, *but I am a slave for life!* Have not I as good a right to be free as you have?" These words used to trouble them; they would express for me the liveliest sympathy, and console me with the hope that something would occur by which I might be free.

I was now about twelve years old, and the thought of being *a slave for life* began to bear heavily upon my heart. Just about this time, I got hold of a book entitled "The Columbian Orator."[2] Every opportunity I got, I used to read this book. Among much of other interesting matter, I found in it a dialogue between a master and his slave. The slave was

---

[1] An archaic unit of measurement equal to forty-five inches.
[2] First published in 1797, this anthology was used to teach rhetorical skills.

represented as having run away from his master three times. The dialogue represented the conversation which took place between them, when the slave was retaken the third time. In this dialogue, the whole argument in behalf of slavery was brought forward by the master, all of which was disposed of by the slave. The slave was made to say some very smart as well as impressive things in reply to his master—things which had the desired though unexpected effect; for the conversation resulted in the voluntary emancipation of the slave on the part of the master.

In the same book, I met with one of Sheridan's mighty speeches on and in behalf of Catholic emancipation.[3] These were choice documents to me. I read them over and over again with unabated interest. They gave tongue to interesting thoughts of my own soul, which had frequently flashed through my mind, and died away for want of utterance. The moral which I gained from the dialogue was the power of truth over the conscience of even a slaveholder. What I got from Sheridan was a bold denunciation of slavery, and a powerful vindication of human rights. The reading of these documents enabled me to utter my thoughts, and to meet the arguments brought forward to sustain slavery; but while they relieved me of one difficulty, they brought on another even more painful than the one of which I was relieved. The more I read, the more I was led to abhor and detest my enslavers. I could regard them in no other light than a band of successful robbers, who had left their homes, and gone to Africa, and stolen us from our homes, and in a strange land reduced us to slavery. I loathed them as being the meanest as well as the most wicked of men. As I read and contemplated the subject, behold! that very discontentment which Master Hugh had predicted would follow my learning to read had already come, to torment and sting my soul to unutterable anguish. As I writhed under it, I would at times feel that learning to read had been a curse rather than a blessing. It had given me a view of my wretched condition, without the remedy. It opened my eyes to the horrible pit, but to no ladder upon which to get out. In moments of agony, I envied my fellow-

---

[3]Richard Brinsley Sheridan (1751–1815), Irish playwright and political leader. The speech is by Arthur O'Connor, an Irish politician.

slaves for their stupidity. I have often wished myself a beast. I preferred the condition of the meanest reptile to my own. Any thing, no matter what, to get rid of thinking! It was this everlasting thinking of my condition that tormented me. There was no getting rid of it. It was pressed upon me by every object within sight or hearing, animate or inanimate. The silver trump of freedom had roused my soul to eternal wakefulness. Freedom now appeared, to disappear no more forever. It was heard in every sound, and seen in every thing. It was ever present to torment me with a sense of my wretched condition. I saw nothing without seeing it, I heard nothing without hearing it, and felt nothing without feeling it. It looked from every star, it smiled in every calm, breathed in every wind, and moved in every storm.

I often found myself regretting my own existence, and wishing myself dead; and but for the hope of being free, I have no doubt but that I should have killed myself, or done something for which I should have been killed. While in this state of mind, I was eager to hear any one speak of slavery. I was a ready listener. Every little while, I could hear something about the abolitionists. It was some time before I found what the word meant. It was always used in such connections as to make it an interesting word to me. If a slave ran away and succeeded in getting clear, or if a slave killed his master, set fire to a barn, or did any thing very wrong in the mind of a slaveholder, it was spoken of as the fruit of *abolition*. Hearing the word in this connection very often, I set about learning what it meant. The dictionary afforded me little or no help. I found it was "the act of abolishing"; but then I did not know what was to be abolished. Here I was perplexed. I did not dare to ask any one about its meaning, for I was satisfied that it was something they wanted me to know very little about. After a patient waiting, I got one of our city papers, containing an account of the number of petitions from the north, praying for the abolition of slavery in the District of Columbia, and of the slave trade between the States. From this time I understood the words *abolition* and *abolitionist*, and always drew near when that word was spoken, expecting to hear something of importance to myself and fellow-slaves. The light broke in upon me by degrees. I went one day down on the wharf of Mr. Waters; and seeing two Irishmen unloading a scow of stone, I went, unasked, and helped them.

When we had finished, one of them came to me and asked me if I were a slave. I told him I was. He asked, "Are ye a slave for life?" I told him that I was. The good Irishman seemed to be deeply affected by the statement. He said to the other that it was a pity so fine a little fellow as myself should be a slave for life. He said it was a shame to hold me. They both advised me to run away to the north; that I should find friends there, and that I should be free. I pretended not to be interested in what they said, and treated them as if I did not understand them; for I feared they might be treacherous. White men have been known to encourage slaves to escape, and then, to get the reward, catch them and return them to their masters. I was afraid that these seemingly good men might use me so; but I nevertheless remembered their advice, and from that time I resolved to run away. I looked forward to a time at which it would be safe for me to escape. I was too young to think of doing so immediately; besides, I wished to learn how to write, as I might have occasion to write my own pass. I consoled myself with the hope that I should one day find a good chance. Meanwhile, I would learn to write.

The idea as to how I might learn to write was suggested to me by being in Durgin and Bailey's ship-yard, and frequently seeing the ship carpenters, after hewing, and getting a piece of timber ready for use, write on the timber the name of that part of the ship for which it was intended. When a piece of timber was intended for the larboard side, it would be marked thus—"L." When a piece was for the starboard side it would be marked thus—"S." A piece for the larboard side forward, would be marked thus—"L. F." When a piece was for starboard side forward, it would be marked thus—"S. F." For larboard aft, it would be marked thus—"L. A." For starboard aft, it would be marked thus— "S. A." I soon learned the names of these letters, and for what they were intended when placed upon a piece of timber in the shipyard. I immediately commenced copying them, and in a short time was able to make the four letters named. After that, when I met with any boy who I knew could write, I would tell him I could write as well as he. The next word would be, "I don't believe you. Let me see you try it." I would then make the letters which I had been so fortunate as to learn, and ask him to beat that. In this way I got a good many lessons in writing, which it is quite possible I should never have gotten in any other way. During this time, my copy-book was the board fence, brick wall, and pavement; my pen and ink was a lump of chalk. With these, I learned mainly how to write. I then commenced and continued copying the Italics in Webster's Spelling Book,[4] until I could make them all without looking on the book. By this time, my little Master Thomas had gone to school, and learned how to write, and had written over a number of copy-books. These had been brought home, and shown to some of our near neighbors, and then laid aside. My mistress used to go to class meeting at the Wilk Street meetinghouse every Monday afternoon, and leave me to take care of the house. When left thus, I used to spend the time in writing in the spaces left in Master Thomas's copy-book, copying what he had written. I continued to do this until I could write a hand very similar to that of Master Thomas. Thus, after a long, tedious effort for years, I finally succeeded in learning how to write.

---

[4]*The American Spelling Book* (1783) by Noah Webster (1758–1843).

STUDY QUESTIONS

1. Why does Douglass's first teacher abandon his lessons? Why does reading become a curse, rather than a blessing, to him?

2. EXPLAIN THE PROCESS of how Douglass learns to read. Which methods seem most effective? How does Douglass CHARACTERIZE himself throughout the process? How does his CHARACTER change as he learns to read?

3. *For Writing.* Compose your own LITERACY NARRATIVE, in which you analyze the process of doing something literary—perhaps reading a challenging novel, writing an essay, teaching someone else to read. Your narrative does not have to end in triumph, but it should attempt to tease out the nuances of the situation.

LARS EIGHNER ⟩ *On Dumpster Diving*

LARS EIGHNER (b. 1948) grew up in Corpus Christi, Texas, and received his education at The University of Texas at Austin. He has written several books—*Travels with Lizbeth* (1993), *Elements of Arousal* (1994), and *Pawn to Queen Four* (1995). He has published numerous essays and maintains a blog. In addition to writing, he has worked in hospitals and counseled substance abusers.

In this chapter from *Travels with Lizbeth,* a memoir of the three years he and his dog were homeless, Eighner describes a realistic step-by-step process of becoming a scavenger, based on his own experiences. He uses various modes of writing not only to convey instructions for mastering the art of scrounging for food, but also to provide insight into how others feel about scavengers and how scavengers work through their feelings about themselves as they begin this way of life.

This chapter was composed while the author was homeless. The present tense has been preserved.

LONG BEFORE I BEGAN DUMPSTER diving I was impressed with Dumpsters, enough so that I wrote the Merriam-Webster research service to discover what I could about the word *Dumpster.* I learned from them that it is a proprietary word belonging to the Dempster Dumpster company. Since then I have dutifully capitalized the word, although it was lowercased in almost all the citations Merriam-Webster photocopied for me. Dempster's word is too apt. I have never heard these things called anything but Dumpsters. I do not know anyone who knows the generic name for these objects. From time to time I have heard a wino or hobo give some corrupted credit to the original and call them Dipsy Dumpsters.

I began Dumpster diving about a year before I became homeless.

I prefer the word *scavenging* and use the word *scrounging* when I mean to be obscure. I have heard people, evidently meaning to be polite, use the word *foraging,* but I prefer to reserve that word for gathering nuts and berries and such, which I do also according to the season and the opportunity. *Dumpster diving* seems to me to be a little too cute and, in my case, inaccurate because I lack the athletic ability to lower myself into the Dumpsters as the true divers do, much to their increased profit.

I like the frankess of the word *scavenging,* which I can hardly think of without picturing a big black snail on an aquarium wall. I live from the refuse of others. I am a scavenger. I think it a sound and honorable niche, although if I could I would naturally prefer to live the comfortable consumer life, perhaps—and only perhaps as a slightly less wasteful consumer, owing to what I have learned as a scavenger.

While Lizbeth and I were still living in the shack on Avenue B[1] as   5
my savings ran out, I put almost all my sporadic income into rent. The necessities of daily life I began to extract from Dumpsters. Yes, we ate from them. Except for jeans, all my clothes came from Dumpsters. Boom boxes, candles, bedding, toilet paper, a virgin male love doll, medicine, books, a typewriter, dishes, furnishings, and change, sometimes amounting to many dollars—

I acquired many things from the Dumpsters. I have learned much as a scavenger. I mean to put some of what I have learned down here, beginning with the practical art of Dumpster diving and proceeding to the abstract.

●   ○   ●

What is safe to eat?

After all, the finding of objects is becoming something of an urban

---

[1]In Austin, Texas.

art. Even respectable employed people will sometimes find something tempting sticking out of a Dumpster or standing beside one. Quite a number of people, not all of them of the bohemian type, are willing to brag that they found this or that piece in the trash. But eating from Dumpsters is what separates the dilettanti from the professionals. Eating safely from the Dumpsters involves three principles: using the senses and common sense to evaluate the condition of the found materials, knowing the Dumpsters of a given area and checking them regularly, and seeking always to answer the question "Why was this discarded?"

Perhaps everyone who has a kitchen and a regular supply of groceries has, at one time or another, made a sandwich and eaten half of it before discovering mold on the bread or got a mouthful of milk before realizing the milk had turned. Nothing of the sort is likely to happen to a Dumpster diver because he is constantly reminded that most food is discarded for a reason. Yet a lot of perfectly good food can be found in Dumpsters.

Canned goods, for example, turn up fairly often in the Dumpsters 10 I frequent. All except the most phobic people would be willing to eat from a can, even if it came from a Dumpster. Canned goods are among the safest of foods to be found in Dumpsters but are not utterly foolproof.

Although very rare with modern canning methods, botulism is a possibility. Most other forms of food poisoning seldom do lasting harm to a healthy person, but botulism is almost certainly fatal and often the first symptom is death. Except for carbonated beverages, all canned goods should contain a slight vacuum and suck air when first punctured. Bulging, rusty, and dented cans and cans that spew when punctured should be avoided, especially when the contents are not very acidic or syrupy.

Heat can break down the botulin, but this requires much more cooking than most people do to canned goods. To the extent that botulism occurs at all, of course, it can occur in cans on pantry shelves as well as in cans from Dumpsters. Need I say that home-canned goods are simply too risky to be recommended?

From time to time one of my companions, aware of the source of my provisions, will ask, "Do you think these crackers are really safe to eat?" For some reason it is most often the crackers they ask about.

This question has always made me angry. Of course I would not offer my companion anything I had doubts about. But more than that, I wonder why he cannot evaluate the condition of the crackers for himself. I have no special knowledge and I have been wrong before. Since he knows where the food comes from, it seems to me he ought to assume some of the responsibility for deciding what he will put in his mouth. For myself I have few qualms about dry foods such as crackers, cookies, cereal, chips, and pasta if they are free of visible contaminates and still dry and crisp. Most often such things are found in the original packaging, which is not so much a positive sign as it is the absence of a negative one.

Raw fruits and vegetables with intact skins seem perfectly safe to   15
me, excluding of course the obviously rotten. Many are discarded for minor imperfections that can be pared away. Leafy vegetables, grapes, cauliflower, broccoli, and similar things may be contaminated by liquids and may be impractical to wash.

Candy, especially hard candy, is usually safe if it has not drawn ants. Chocolate is often discarded only because it has become discolored as the cocoa butter de-emulsified. Candying, after all, is one method of food preservation because pathogens do not like very sugary substances.

All of these foods might be found in any Dumpster and can be evaluated with some confidence largely on the basis of appearance. Beyond these are foods that cannot be correctly evaluated without additional information.

I began scavenging by pulling pizzas out of the Dumpster behind a pizza delivery shop. In general, prepared food requires caution, but in this case I knew when the shop closed and went to the Dumpster as soon as the last of the help left.

Such shops often get prank orders; both the orders and the products made to fill them are called *bogus*. Because help seldom stays long at these places, pizzas are often made with the wrong topping, refused on delivery for being cold, or baked incorrectly. The products to be discarded are boxed up because inventory is kept by counting boxes: A boxed pizza can be written off; an unboxed pizza does not exist.

I never placed a bogus order to increase the supply of pizzas and I   20
believe no one else was scavenging in this Dumpster. But the people in
the shop became suspicious and began to retain their garbage in the
shop overnight. While it lasted I had a steady supply of fresh, sometimes warm pizza. Because I knew the Dumpster I knew the source of
the pizza, and because I visited the Dumpster regularly I knew what
was fresh and what was yesterday's.

The area I frequent is inhabited by many affluent college students. I am
not here by chance; the Dumpsters in this area are very rich. Students
throw out many good things, including food. In particular they tend to
throw everything out when they move at the end of a semester, before and
after breaks, and around midterm, when many of them despair of college.
So I find it advantageous to keep an eye on the academic calendar.

Students throw food away around breaks because they do not know
whether it has spoiled or will spoil before they return. A typical discard
is a half jar of peanut butter. In fact, nonorganic peanut butter does not
require refrigeration and is unlikely to spoil in any reasonable time. The
student does not know that, and since it is Daddy's money, the student
decides not to take a chance. Opened containers require caution and
some attention to the question "Why was this discarded?" But in the
case of discards from student apartments, the answer may be that the
item was thrown out through carelessness, ignorance, or wastefulness.
This can sometimes be deduced when the item is found with many others, including some that are obviously perfectly good.

Some students, and others, approach defrosting a freezer by chucking out the whole lot. Not only do the circumstances of such a find tell
the story, but also the mass of frozen good stays cold for a long time and
items may be found still frozen or freshly thawed.

Yogurt, cheese, and sour cream are items that are often thrown out
while they are still good. Occasionally I find a cheese with a spot of
mold, which of course I just pare off, and because it is obvious why
such a cheese was discarded, I treat it with less suspicion than an
apparently perfect cheese found in similar circumstances. Yogurt is
often discarded, still sealed, only because the expiration date on the
carton had passed. This is one of my favorite finds because yogurt will
keep for several days, even in warm weather.

Students throw out canned goods and staples at the end of   25
semesters and when they give up college at midterm. Drugs, pornogra-
phy, spirits, and the like are often discarded when parents are expected—Dad's Day, for example. And spirits also turn up after big party
weekends, presumably discarded by the newly reformed. Wine and
spirits, of course, keep perfectly well even once opened, but the same
cannot be said of beer.

My test for carbonated soft drinks is whether they still fizz
vigorously. Many juices or other beverages are too acidic or too syrupy
to cause much concern, provided they are not visibly contaminated. I
have discovered nasty molds in vegetable juices, even when the product was found under its original seal; I recommend that such products
be decanted slowly into a clear glass. Liquids always require some
care. One hot day I found a large jug of Pat O'Brien's Hurricane mix.
The jug had been opened but was still ice cold. I drank three
large glasses before it became apparent to me that someone had added
the rum to the mix, and not a little rum. I never tasted the rum, and by
the time I began to feel the effects I had already ingested a very large
quantity of the beverage. Some divers would have considered this a
boon, but being suddenly intoxicated in a public place in the early
afternoon is not my idea of a good time.

I have heard of people maliciously contaminating discarded food
and even handouts, but mostly I have heard of this from people with
vivid imaginations who have had no experience with the Dumpsters
themselves. Just before the pizza shop stopped discarding its garbage
at night, jalapeños began showing up on most of the thrown-out pizzas. If indeed this was meant to discourage me, it was a wasted effort
because I am a native Texan.

For myself, I avoid game, poultry, pork, and egg-based foods,
whether I find them raw or cooked. I seldom have the means to
cook what I find, but when I do I avail myself of plentiful supplies of
beef, which is often in very good condition. I suppose fish becomes
disagreeable before it becomes dangerous. Lizbeth is happy to have
any such thing that is past its prime and, in fact, does not recognize fish
as food until it is quite strong.

Home leftovers, as opposed to surpluses from restaurants, are very often bad. Evidently, especially among students, there is a common type of personality that carefully wraps up even the smallest leftover and shoves it into the back of the refrigerator for six months or so before discarding it. Characteristic of this type are the reused jars and margarine tubs to which the remains are committed. I avoid ethnic foods I am unfamiliar with. If I do not know what it is supposed to look like when it is good, I cannot be certain I will be able to tell if it is bad.

No matter how careful I am I still get dysentery at least once a 30 month, oftener in warm weather. I do not want to paint too romantic a picture. Dumpster diving has serious drawbacks as a way of life.

•   ○   •

I learned to scavenge gradually, on my own. Since then I have initiated several companions into the trade. I have learned that there is a predictable series of stages a person goes through in learning to scavenge.

At first the new scavenger is filled with disgust and self-loathing. He is ashamed of being seen and may lurk around, trying to duck behind things, or he may try to dive at night. (In fact, most people instinctively look away from a scavenger. By skulking around, the novice calls attention to himself and arouses suspicion. Diving at night is ineffective and needlessly messy.)

Every grain of rice seems to be a maggot. Everything seems to stink. He can wipe the egg yolk off the found can, but he cannot erase from his mind the stigma of eating garbage.

That stage passes with experience. The scavenger finds a pair of running shoes that fit and look and smell brand-new. He finds a pocket calculator in perfect working order. He finds pristine ice cream, still frozen, more than he can eat or keep. He begins to understand: People throw away perfectly good stuff, a lot of perfectly good stuff.

At this stage, Dumpster shyness begins to dissipate. The diver, after 35 all, has the last laugh. He is finding all manner of good things that are his for the taking. Those who disparage his profession are the fools, not he.

He may begin to hang on to some perfectly good things for which he has neither a use nor a market. Then he begins to take note of the things that are not perfectly good but are nearly so. He mates a

Walkman with broken earphones and one that is missing a battery cover. He picks up things that he can repair.

At this stage he may become lost and never recover. Dumpsters are full of things of some potential value to someone and also of things that never have much intrinsic value but are interesting. All the Dumpster divers I have known come to the point of trying to acquire everything they touch. Why not take it, they reason, since it is all free? This is, of course, hopeless. Most divers come to realize that they must restrict themselves to items of relatively immediate utility. But in some cases the diver simply cannot control himself. I have met several of these pack-rat types. Their ideas of the values of various pieces of junk verge on the psychotic. Every bit of glass may be a diamond, they think, and all that glisters, gold.[2]

I tend to gain weight when I am scavenging. Partly this is because I always find far more pizza and doughnuts than water-packed tuna, nonfat yogurt, and fresh vegetables. Also I have not developed much faith in the reliability of Dumpsters as a food source, although it has been proven to me many times. I tend to eat as if I have no idea where my next meal is coming from. But mostly I just hate to see food go to waste and so I eat much more than I should. Something like this drives the obsession to collect junk.

As for collecting objects, I usually restrict myself to collecting one kind of small object at a time, such as pocket calculators, sunglasses, or campaign buttons. To live on the street I must anticipate my needs to a certain extent: I must pick up and save warm bedding I find in August because it will not be found in Dumpsters in November. As I have no access to health care, I often hoard essential drugs, such as antibiotics and antihistamines. (This course can be recommended only to those with some grounding in pharmacology. Antibiotics, for example, even when indicated are worse than useless if taken in insufficient amounts.) But even if I had a home with extensive storage space, I could not save everything that might be valuable in some contingency.

I have proprietary feelings about my Dumpsters. As I have men- 40

---

[2] An allusion to Shakespeare's *The Merchant of Venice:* "All that glisters is not gold" (2.7.65).

tioned, it is no accident that I scavenge from ones where good finds are common. But my limited experience with Dumpsters in other areas suggests to me that even in poorer areas, Dumpsters, if attended with sufficient diligence, can be made to yield a livelihood. The rich students discard perfectly good kiwifruit; poorer people discard perfectly good apples. Slacks and Polo shirts are found in the one place; jeans and T-shirts in the other. The population of competitors rather than the affluence of the dumpers most affects the feasibility of survival by scavenging. The large number of competitors is what puts me off the idea of trying to scavenge in places like Los Angeles.

Curiously, I do not mind my direct competition, other scavengers, so much as I hate the can scroungers.

People scrounge cans because they have to have a little cash. I have tried scrounging cans with an able-bodied companion. Afoot a can scrounger simply cannot make more than a few dollars a day. One can extract the necessities of life from the Dumpsters directly with far less effort than would be required to accumulate the equivalent value in cans. (These observations may not hold in places with container redemption laws.)

Can scroungers, then, are people who must have small amounts of cash. These are drug addicts and winos, mostly the latter because the amounts of cash are so small. Spirits and drugs do, like all other commodities, turn up in Dumpsters and the scavenger will from time to time have a half bottle of a rather good wine with his dinner. But the wino cannot survive on these occasional finds; he must have his daily dose to stave off the DTs.[3] All the cans he can carry will buy about three bottles of Wild Irish Rose.

I do not begrudge them the cans, but can scroungers tend to tear up the Dumpsters, mixing the contents and littering the area. They become so specialized that they can see only cans. They earn my contempt by passing up change, canned goods, and readily hockable items.

There are precious few courtesies among scavengers. But it is common practice to set aside surplus items: pairs of shoes, clothing, canned goods, and such. A true scavenger hates to see good stuff go

45

---

[3]Delirium tremens, a condition caused by withdrawal from alcohol.

to waste, and what he cannot use he leaves in good condition in plain sight.

Can scroungers lay waste to everything in their path and will stir one of a pair of good shoes to the bottom of a Dumpster, to be lost or ruined in the muck. Can scroungers will even go through individual garbage cans, something I have never seen a scavenger do.

Individual garbage cans are set out on the public easement only on garbage days. On other days going through them requires trespassing close to a dwelling. Going through individual garbage cans without scattering litter is almost impossible. Litter is likely to reduce the public's tolerance of scavenging. Individual cans are simply not as productive as Dumpsters; people in houses and duplexes do not move so often, and for some reason do not tend to discard as much useful material. Moreover, the time required to go through one garbage can that serves one household is not much less than the time required to go through a Dumpster that contains the refuse of twenty apartments.

But my strongest reservation about going through individual garbage cans is that this seems to me a very personal kind of invasion to which I would object if I were a householder. Although many things in Dumpsters are obviously meant never to come to light, a Dumpster is somehow less personal.

•   ○   •

I avoid trying to draw conclusions about the people who dump in the Dumpsters I frequent. I think it would be unethical to do so, although I know many people will find the idea of scavenger ethics too funny for words.

Dumpsters contain bank statements, correspondence, and other documents, just as anyone might expect. But there are also less obvious sources of information. Pill bottles, for example. The labels bear the name of the patient, the name of the doctor, and the name of the drug. AIDS drugs and antipsychotic medicines, to name but two groups, are specific and are seldom prescribed for any other disorders. The plastic compacts for birth-control pills usually have complete label information.

Despite all of this sensitive information, I have had only one apart-

50

ment resident object to my going through the Dumpster. In that case it turns out the resident was a university athlete who was taking bets and who was afraid I would turn up his wager slips.

Occasionally a find tells a story. I once found a small paper bag containing some unused condoms, several partial tubes of flavored sexual lubricants, a partially used compact of birth-control pills, and the torn pieces of a picture of a young man. Clearly she was through with him and planning to give up sex altogether.

Dumpster things are often sad—abandoned teddy bears, shredded wedding books, despaired-of sales kits. I find many pets lying in state in Dumpsters. Although I hope to get off the streets so that Lizbeth can have a long and comfortable old age, I know this hope is not very realistic. So I suppose when her time comes she too will go into a Dumpster. I will have no better place for her. And after all, it is fitting, since for most of her life her livelihood has come from the Dumpster. When she finds something I think is safe that has been spilled from a Dumpster, I let her have it. She already knows the route around the best ones. I like to think that if she survives me she will have a chance of evading the dog catcher and of finding her sustenance on the route.

Silly vanities also come to rest in the Dumpsters. I am a rather accomplished needleworker. I get a lot of material from the Dumpsters. Evidently sorority girls, hoping to impress someone, perhaps themselves, with their mastery of a womanly art, buy a lot of embroider-by-number kits, work a few stitches horribly, and eventually discard the whole mess. I pull out their stitches, turn the canvas over, and work an original design. Do not think I refrain from chuckling as I make gifts from these kits.

I find diaries and journals. I have often thought of compiling a book of literary found objects. And perhaps I will one day. But what I find is hopelessly commonplace and bad without being, even unconsciously, camp. College students also discard their papers. I am horrified to discover the kind of paper that now merits an A in an undergraduate course. I am grateful, however, for the number of good books and magazines the students throw out.

In the area I know best I have never discovered vermin in the

55

Dumpsters, but there are two kinds of kitty surprise. One is alley cats whom I meet as they leap, claws first, out of Dumpsters. This is especially thrilling when I have Lizbeth in tow. The other kind of kitty surprise is a plastic garbage bag filled with some ponderous, amorphous mass. This always proves to be used cat litter.

City bees harvest doughnut glaze and this makes the Dumpster at the doughnut shop more interesting. My faith in the instinctive wisdom of animals is always shaken whenever I see Lizbeth attempt to catch a bee in her mouth, which she does whenever bees are present. Evidently some birds find Dumpsters profitable, for birdie surprise is almost as common as kitty surprise of the first kind. In hunting season all kinds of small game turn up in Dumpstes, some of it, sadly, not entirely dead. Curiously, summer and winter, maggots are uncommon.

The worst of the living and near-living hazards of the Dumpsters are the fire ants. The food they claim is not much of a loss, but they are vicsious and aggressive. It is very easy to brush against some surface of the Dumpster and pick up half a dozen or more fire ants, usually in some sensitive area such as the underarm. One advantage of bringing Lizbeth along as I make Dumpster rounds is that, for obvious reasons, she is very alert to ground-based fire ants. When Lizbeth recognizes a fire-ant infestation around our feet, she does the Dance of the Zillion Fire Ants. I have learned not to ignore this warning from Lizbeth, whether I perceive the tiny ants or not, but to remove ourselves at Lizbeth's first pas de bourrée.[4] All the more so because the ants are the worst in the summer months when I wear flip-flops if I have them. (Perhaps someone will misunderstand this. Lizbeth does the Dance of the Zillion Fire Ants when she recognizes more fire ants than she cares to eat, not when she is being bitten. Since I have learned to react promptly, she does not get bitten at all. It is the isolated patrol of fire ants that falls in Lizbeth's range that deserves pity. She finds them quite tasty.)

By far the best way to go through a Dumpster is to lower yourself into it. Most of the good stuff tends to settle at the bottom because it is usually weightier than the rubbish. My more athletic companions have

---

[4]A three-step dance move (French).

often demonstrated to me that they can extract much good material from a Dumpster I have already been over.

To those psychologically or physically unprepared to enter a 60 Dumpster, I recommend a stout stick, preferably with some barb or hook at one end. The hook can be used to grab plastic garbage bags. When I find canned goods or other objects loose at the bottom of a Dumpster, I lower a bag into it, roll the desired object into the bag, and then hoist the bag out—a procedure more easily described than executed. Much Dumpster diving is a matter of experience for which nothing will do except practice.

Dumpster diving is outdoor work, often surprisingly pleasant. It is not entirely predictable; things of interest turn up every day and some days there are finds of great value. I am always very pleased when I can turn up exactly the thing I most wanted to find. Yet in spite of the element of chance, scavenging more than most other pursuits tends to yield returns in some proportion to the effort and intelligence brought to bear. It is very sweet to turn up a few dollars in change from a Dumpster that has just been gone over by a wino.

The land is now covered with cities. The cities are full of Dumpsters. If a member of the canine race is ever able to know what it is doing, then Lizbeth knows that when we go around to the Dumpsters, we are hunting. I think of scavenging as a modern form of self-reliance. In any event, after having survived nearly ten years of government services, where everything is geared to the lowest common denominator, I find it refreshing to have work that rewards initiative and effort. Certainly I would be happy to have a sinecure again, but I am no longer heartbroken that I left one.

I find from the experience of scavenging two rather deep lessons. The first is to take what you can use and let the rest go by. I have come to think that there is no value in the abstract. A thing I cannot use or make useful, perhaps by trading, has no value however rare or fine it may be. I mean useful in a broad sense—some art I would find useful and some otherwise.

I was shocked to realize that some things are not worth acquiring, but now I think it is so. Some material things are white elephants that eat up the possessor's substance. The second lesson is the transience of material being. This has not quite converted me to a dualist,[5] but it has made some headway in that direction. I do not suppose that ideas are immortal, but certainly mental things are longer lived than other material things.

Once I was the sort of person who invests objects with sentimen- 65 tal value. Now I no longer have those objects, but I have the sentiments yet.

Many times in our travels I have lost everything but the clothes I was wearing and Lizbeth. The things I find in Dumpsters, the love letters and rag dolls of so many lives, remind me of this lesson. Now I hardly pick up a thing without envisioning the time I will cast it aside. This I think is a healthy state of mind. Almost everything I have now has already been cast out at least once, proving that what I own is valueless to someone.

Anyway, I find my desire to grab for the gaudy bauble has been largely sated. I think this is an attitude I share with the very wealthy— we both know there is plenty more where what we have came from. Between us are the rat-race millions who nightly scavenge the cable channels looking for they know not what.

I am sorry for them.

---

[5]Dualism is the philosophy that holds that mind and matter are irreducibly separate categories.

STUDY QUESTIONS

1. In this PROCESS essay, Eighner tells readers how he became a scavenger. Why did he start scavenging? Who is his companion?

2. Eighner divides his essay into four sections within which he uses several modes of writing to develop his essay: DEFINITION, DESCRIPTION, PROCESS, and DIVISION AND CLASSIFICATION. As you reread the essay, find examples of each mode in each section. How effective is he in using them? Who do you think his AUDIENCE is? Explain.

3. Identify Eighner's THESIS. Find two examples of each part of the thesis within the body of the essay. How does he support his thesis? Explain.

4. *For Writing.* In the third section of his essay, Eighner describes the stages that a scavenger goes through when he begins this activity. Think of an activity you learned to do and the stages you went through until you became comfortable with the process. For example, you might have learned to play a musical instrument, speak another language, cook, and so forth. Write a personal essay that explains the stages you experienced as you learned to do something new. How did you feel as you passed through these stages? Decide who your audience is for this essay before you begin, and keep them in mind as you write.

TEMPLE GRANDIN $\Big\{$ *My Mind Is a Web Browser:*
How People with Autism Think

TEMPLE GRANDIN (b. 1947) was born in Boston, Massachusetts, and
was diagnosed with autism when she was three years old. She did not
begin to speak until she was four, but later attended a boarding school
for gifted children in New Hampshire, graduating in 1966. She earned
a BS in psychology from Franklin Pierce College in 1970, an MS in
animal science from Arizona State University in 1975, and a PhD in
animal science from the University of Illinois at Urbana-Champaign in
1989. A professor at Colorado State University, Grandin designs
livestock-handling facilities and is an advocate for animal welfare. She
also advocates for autism rights and has been outspoken about this issue
in the media. HBO made a dramatic film about her life, released in 2010,
starring Claire Danes, which won five Emmys.

"My Mind Is a Web Browser: How People with Autism Think" analyzes
Grandin's thought process: she thinks in images, not words; indeed, she
has said that words are her second language. As you read, consider your
own thought process. How do you think in words, images, or both?

─────────────

SINCE WRITING *THINKING IN PICTURES*, which described my visual
way of thinking, I have gained further insights into how my thought
processes are different when compared to those of people who think
in language. At autism meetings, I am often asked, "How can you be
effective at public speaking when you think in pictures that are like
video tapes in your imagination?" It is almost as though I have two
levels of consciousness that operate separately. Only by interviewing

people did I learn that many of them think primarily in words, and that their thoughts are linked to emotion. In my brain, words act as a narrator for the visual images in my imagination. I can see the pictures in my memory files.

To use a computer analogy: The language part of my brain is the computer operator, and the rest of my brain is the computer. In most people, the brain's computer operator and the computer are merged into one seamless consciousness; but in me they are separate. I hypothesize that the frontal cortex of my brain is the operator and the rest of my brain is the computer.

When I lecture, the language itself is mostly "downloaded" out of memory from files that are like tape recordings. I use slides or notes to trigger opening the different files. When I am talking about something for the first time, I look at the visual images on the "computer monitor" in my imagination, then the language part of me describes those images. After I have given the lecture several times, the new material in language is switched over into "audio tape-recording files." When I was in high school, other kids called me "tape recorder."

Non-autistic people seem to have a whole upper layer of verbal thinking that is merged with their emotions. By contrast, unless I panic, I use logic to make all decisions; my thinking can be done independently of emotion. In fact, I seem to lack a higher consciousness composed of abstract verbal thoughts that are merged with emotion. Researchers have learned that people with autism have a decreased metabolism in the area in the frontal cortex that connects the brain's emotional centers with higher thinking (the anterior cingulate).[1] The frontal cortex is the brain's senior executive, like the CEO of a corporation. Brain scans indicate that people with autism use problem-solving circuits in social situations. Unlike non-autistic people, the emotion center in their amygdala is not activated, for example, when they judge expressions in another person's eyes.[2]

[1]Haznedar MM, Buchsbaum MS, Metzer M, et al. Anterior cingulate gyrus volume and glucose metabolism in autistic disorder. *American Journal of Psychiatry.* 1997: 154:1047–1050.

[2]Baron-Cohen S, Ring HA, Wheelwright S. Social intelligence in the normal and autistic brain: an FMRI study. *European Journal of Neuroscience.* 1999: 11:1891–1898.

MY MIND IS A WEB BROWSER

Now let me explain how the language part of my brain and the "think- 5
ing in pictures" part of my brain seem to interact. My mind works just
like an Internet Web browser. A Web browser finds specific words; by
analogy, my mind looks for picture memories that are associated with
a word. It can also go off on a tangent in the same way as a Web browser,
because visual thinking is non-linear, associative thinking.

To demonstrate how my mind works, at an autism meeting I asked
a member of the audience to name a thing for me to invent. I wanted to
show how the visual part of my brain and the language part worked
separately. Somebody said, "invent a better paper clip." The language part of my brain said, "I can do that," and pictures immediately
started flashing into my imagination of all kinds of paper clips I have
seen. My "Web browser" searched the picture memory files; many
paper clip pictures flashed through my imagination like slides. I could
stop on any one picture and study it. I saw an odd, plastic paper clip
that was on a scientific paper from Europe. At this point, I got off the
subject and saw pictures of the first scientific meeting I had attended
in Spain. The language voice inside me said: "Get back on the subject
of paper clips." The language part of me is a manager who uses simple
non-descriptive language to tell the rest of my brain what to do.

Often, the best ideas for inventing things come just as I am drifting
off to sleep. The pictures are clearer then. It is as though I can access
the most concrete, vivid memory files with the most detailed images.
The language part of my brain is completely shut off at night.

To get ideas for new paper clip designs, I can pull up pictures
of clothes pins and other clip-like things, such as mouse traps and C
clamps used in woodworking. I start thinking that inventing a better
clip for holding a thick pile of papers together might be more marketable than a new paper clip design. Existing spring binder clips tend to
rip envelopes when papers are mailed, because the clips have protruding edges. When I think about this, I see ripped envelopes. The
language part of my mind says, "Design a flat binder clip for thick documents." When I say this, I see a mailed document in an undamaged
envelope. My visual imagination then sees a large plastic clip that

I saw in Japan. Japanese apartment dwellers who do not have clothes driers use large, plastic clips to hold blankets and other laundry on balcony railings. A small version of the Japanese balcony clip may make a better paper clip for holding many pages.

When I was responding to the paper clip inquiry, I knew that I could visually associate all day about paper clips. The language part of my mind then said, "That is enough," and I resumed my lecture. But as I corrected the first draft of this article, I saw a one-piece molded plastic binder clip that would lay flat on a thick bunch of papers.

I do have the ability to control the rate at which pictures come onto the "computer screen" in my imagination. Some people with autism are not able to do this. One person with autism told me that images explode into a web of a pictures that are interrelated. The decision-making process can become "locked up" and overloaded with pictures coming in all at once.

UNMASKING TALENT

I have been fascinated with research indicating that the detailed, realistic pictures that autistic savants—autistic individuals with extraordinary talent in a specific area—make may be created by directly accessing primary memory areas deep in the brain. Researchers in Australia hypothesize that autistic savants may have privileged access to lower levels of information.[3] A study with a non-autistic "human calculator," who could solve multiplication problems twice as quickly as a normal person, indicated that his brain had enhanced low-level processing.[4] EEG recordings of his brain waves showed that brain activity was greatest, as compared with a normal person, when the multiplication problem was first flashed on the screen.

I hypothesize that I am able to access primary visual files in my brain. When designing livestock equipment in my business, I can do three-dimensional, full-motion videos of equipment and can test-run

[3]Snyder AW, Mitchell JD. Is integer arithmetic fundamental to mental processing? The mind's secret arithmetic. *Proceedings of the Royal Society of London*. 1999:266: 587–592.
[4]Birbaumer N. Rain Man's revelations. *Nature*. 1999:399:211–212.

the equipment in my imagination. I can walk around it or fly over it. My ability to rotate the image is slow. I move my mind's eye around or over the image.

When I read an article in *Neurology* about frontal temporal lobe dementia, I became extremely excited. It provided a scientific foundation for the idea of hidden visual thinking under a layer of verbal thinking. Research on frontal temporal lobe dementia, an Alzheimer's-like condition that destroys language and social areas in the brain, demonstrated that, as the condition progressed, visual skills in art emerged in people who had no interest in art.[5] The increase in creativity was always visual, never verbal. Brain scans found the highest activity in the visual cortex. As the patient's cognitive abilities deteriorated, the art became more photo realistic. Artwork published with the journal article looks like the art of autistic savants.

I SEE THE DECISION PROCESS

I see the decision-making process in my mind in a way most people do not. When I tried to explain this to a person who thinks in language, he just didn't get it. How my decision-making works is most clearly seen in an emergency.

On a bright, sunny day, I was driving to the airport when an elk ran   15 into the highway just ahead of my car. I had only three or four seconds to react. During those few seconds, I saw images of my choices. The first image was of a car rear-ending me. This is what would have happened if I had made the instinctive panic response and slammed on the brakes. The second image was of an elk smashing through my windshield. This is what would have happened if I had swerved. The last image showed the elk passing by in front of my car. The last choice was the one I could make if I inhibited the panic response and braked just a little to slow the car. I mentally "clicked" on slowing down and avoided an accident. It was like clicking a computer mouse on the desired picture.

[5]Miller BL, Cummings J, Mishkin F. Emergence of artistic talent in froniotemporal dementia. *Neurology.* 1998:51:978–982.

ANIMAL DECISION MAKING

I speculate that the decision-making process I used to avoid the accident may be similar to the process animals use. From my work with animals, I've come to believe that consciousness originally arose from the orienting response. When a deer sees a person, it will often freeze and look at him. This is the deer's orienting response. During this time, it decides either to run away or to keep grazing. It does not act as a programmed robot, governed by instinct or reflexes; it has the flexibility to make a decision. One of the things that has helped me to understand animals is that, more than most people, I think and feel like one. The more "animal" parts of the normal human brain may be covered by layers of language-based thinking.

THINKING IN AUDIO TAPES

In connection with my lectures, I have talked with autistic people who are not visual thinkers. They seem to think in audio tape clips. Audio tape thinking does not have to involve language; instead of using visual images to form memories, these people store very specific audio clips. I suspect that, for them, hearing is easier than seeing. Dr. John Stein and his colleagues at Oxford University have discovered that some people have difficulty seeing rapidly changing visual scenes. They find reading is difficult because the print appears jumbled.[6] This results from defects in brain circuits that process motion.[7] The eye is fine; the circuits between brain and eyes malfunction.

One person I know who is expert at training animals told me that she hears the animal's behavior instead of seeing it. She has audio tapes in her memory with little sound details. For example, she knows that the animal is relaxed or agitated by listening to its breathing or footsteps. She reads audio signals instead of body posture.

[6]Clayton J. Lost for Words. *New Scientist.* April 24, 1999. pp. 27–30.
[7]Eden GF, Van Meter JW, Ramsey J, et al. Abnormal processing of artistic talent in dyslexia revealed by functional brain imaging. *Nature.* 1996:382:66–69.

PIECING THE DETAILS TOGETHER

People with autism, and animals as well, pay more attention to details. As I described in *Thinking in Pictures*, all my thinking goes from the specific to the general. I look at lots of little details and piece them together to make a concept. The first step in forming an idea is to make categories. For example, the most primary level is sorting objects by color or shape. The next step is sorting things by less obvious features, as when we categorize cats and dogs. When I was five years old, I figured out that a miniature dachshund was not a cat because it had a dog's nose; all dogs had certain features that were visually recognizable.

My mind seeks these categories amidst an array of little details. In   20
problem solving, my thinking process is like that of an epidemiologist tracking down a disease. The epidemiologist collects lots of little pieces of information and finally figures out the common factor that caused certain people to fall ill. For example, they may all have eaten strawberries from a certain place.

Also, I understand concepts visually. For example, all objects classified as keys will open locks. I realize that the word "key" can also be used metaphorically, when we say, "the key to success is positive thinking." When I think about that phrase, I see Norman Vincent Peale's book, *The Power of Positive Thinking*, and I see myself back at my aunt's ranch reading it. I then see a stage where a person is getting an award and I see a large cardboard key. Even in this situation, the key still unlocks the door to success. The ability to form categories is the beginning of the ability to form concepts. Keys in their physical form open physical locks but abstract keys can open many things, such as a scientific discovery or career success.

In teaching people to understand animal behavior, I have to help them to learn how to observe details that seem insignificant. Animals notice details in their environment that most people do not see, such as a branch that moves slightly or a shadow. In my work with livestock facilities, I try to get the language-based thinkers of the world to be more observant of little details that spook cattle. A cow may balk at entering a vaccinating chute because it sees a piece of jiggling chain that most people ignore, but which is significant in the cow's environment.

That little chain attracts the cow's attention because it moves quickly. Rapid movement activates the amygdala, the brain's emotion center.[8] In a prey species such as cattle, rapid movement elevates fear because, in the wild, things that move rapidly are often dangerous. Something moving quickly in the bushes may be a lion. On the other hand, a predatory animal, such as a dog, is attracted to rapid movement. This may explain why some dogs attack joggers. Rapid movement triggers chasing and attacking in a predatory animal, but it triggers flight in a prey species such as deer or cattle.

Objects that move rapidly also attract the attention of people with autism. When I was younger, I liked to play with automatic doors at supermarkets. I enjoyed watching the rapid opening movement. Elevator doors were not interesting; they did not move fast enough to be pleasurable to watch. Tests of my visual tracking indicate that I have a slight abnormality in my eye's ability to track a moving object. Children and adults with autism who never learn to speak have graver defects in their nervous system. The automatic doors that I liked to watch cause many nonverbal autistics to put their hands over their eyes. The rapid movement of the doors hurts their eyes. Possibly, a small defect in eye tracking makes rapidly moving things attractive to me, while a more serious neurological defect makes them unpleasant to other autistics. As a child, my favorite things all made rapid movements. I liked flapping flags, kites, and model airplanes that flew.

DISTURBING SOUNDS

I have always felt that my senses were more like those of an animal. 25 Does my brain have deeper access to the ancient anti-predator circuits that humans share with animals? At night, I cannot get to sleep if I hear high-pitched, intermittent noise such as a backup alarm on a truck or children yelling in the next hotel room; they make my heart race. Thunder or airport noise does not bother me, but the little high-

[8]LeDoux J. *The Emotional Brain*. Simon and Schuster; 1996.

pitched noises cannot be shut out. Recent research with pigs has confirmed that intermittent sounds are more disturbing to them than steady sounds.[9]

Why are high-pitched sounds disturbing to animals (and to me), while airport noises and thunder are not? I speculate that in nature the rumble of thunder is not dangerous but a high-pitched noise would be an animal's distress call. Beeping backup alarms and car alarms are electronic distress calls, which activate my nervous system even though I know they are harmless. It is almost as though these animal circuits in my brain have been laid bare.

PROPORTIONAL THINKING

A recent report in *Science* indicated that activities involving numbers are processed in at least two different parts of the brain.[1] Precise calculations are dependent on language and are processed in the frontal areas; proportional figuring is processed in visual areas. Proportional thinking is figuring out if one object is less or more than another. For example, three marbles are more than one marble. Animals can do proportional thinking. They can easily determine that 10 pieces of food are more than two. It is likely that proportional thinking is the kind of number processing that humans share with animals.

In school, math was a tough subject for me. Finding the precisely correct answer is difficult because I mix up numbers. On the other hand, I am very good at proportional thinking, coming up with an accurate approximate answer. In my scientific work, I often convert numerical differences between my control and experimental groups to percentage differences. Percentage differences can be visualized on a pie chart. When I present data, I like to use charts and graphs so I can see the proportional differences between different sets of data.

When I did cost estimating for cattle industry construction projects, I never tried to calculate projects to the penny. Instead, I estimated

[9]Talling JC, Waran NK, Wathes CM. Sound avoidance by domestic pigs depends on the characteristics of the signal. *Applied Animal Behavior Science.* 1998: 58: 255–266.

[1]Dehaene S, Spelke E, Pinel P, Stanescu R, Tsivkin S. Sources of mathematical thinking: Behavioral and brain imaging evidence. *Science.* 1999: 284:970–973.

the cost of a new job by figuring out its proportional cost in relation to other finished projects. This was mainly a visual process. I would look at the drawing and build the entire project in my imagination. I then would put it up on the video screen in my imagination and compare it in size to other completed projects that had complete cost figures. In my mind, I could compare four or five completed projects with the drawing I was estimating. The project being estimated might be equal to two-thirds of a cattle-handling facility that I designed at Red River Feedlot and about 25 percent bigger than a corral I designed for Lone Mountain Ranch.

For money to have meaning to me, it must be related to something I can buy with it, otherwise it is too abstract. For example, $3 is equal to lunch at McDonald's, $20 is a tank of gas, and $1000 can buy a computer. Big tables full of figures make little sense to me. Some more severely autistic people do not understand money at all. For me to understand a billion dollars, I have to have a picture in my mind of something that cost a billion dollars. One billion is one quarter of the cost of the new Denver Airport. When President Clinton announced part way through the war in Kosovo that it had cost $2 billion, I figured that half a Denver Airport worth of money had been spent. Different amounts of money have different visual values. It is interesting that proportional thinking for numbers is in the visual parts of the brain.

In proportional thinking, as in creating something new, making a decision, and forming concepts, my thinking relies on more direct access to the primary visual memory areas in my brain. There is a whole higher level of abstract thinking seamlessly linked to emotion that I do not have.

STUDY QUESTIONS

1. What is the difference between a verbal and a visual way of thinking? What role does emotion play in each? Why?

2. How effective is the METAPHOR of the web browser that Grandin uses for describing how her mind works?

3. What is the function of the subheadings in this essay? Are the subheadings effective? What other ways might Grandin have supplied TRANSITIONS and other signposts to the reader?

4. How does Grandin think in pictures? ANALYZE THE PROCESS of her "visual way of thinking."

5. *For Writing.* Consider your thought process by testing two of Grandin's examples. How would you go about designing a paper clip? How would you deal with an elk that suddenly entered your path? In an essay, explore the way that you would come to a solution. What does your process say about you?

JON KRAKAUER { *The Alaska Interior*

JON KRAKAUER (b. 1954) was raised in Oregon, where he began climbing mountains at the age of eight. He graduated from Hampshire College with a BS in 1976 and took to the outdoors, working in Colorado, Alaska, and the Pacific Northwest as a carpenter and salmon fisherman. In 1996 he climbed Mt. Everest; the expedition was struck by a severe storm and claimed the lives of four of his five fellow climbers. Krakauer wrote an award-winning article about the ordeal for *Outside* magazine. The article became the basis for his book *Into Thin Air* (1998), which was a finalist for the Pulitzer Prize. Krakauer specializes in nonfiction accounts of extreme situations: *Into the Wild* (1996) documents the perilous journey that a naïve, idealistic college graduate took to Alaska; *Under the Banner of Heaven: A Story of Violent Faith* (2003) explores violent acts committed in the name of Mormon fundamentalism. Krakauer's work has appeared in many periodicals, including *Rolling Stone, Time*, the *Washington Post*, and *National Geographic*. He is the editor of the Modern Library Exploration series.

In this chapter from *Into the Wild*, Krakauer tells the story of Chris McCandless's travel to the interior of Alaska and his struggle to survive there alone for four months. As you read, notice how Krakauer uses dates, locations, and detailed descriptions to establish the narrative in a specific time and place, a setting that is crucial to the events of the narrative.

> *I wished to acquire the simplicity, native feelings, and virtues of savage life; to divest myself of the factitious habits, prejudices and imperfections of civilization; . . . and to find, amidst the solitude and grandeur of the western wilds, more correct*

views of human nature and of the true interests of man. The
season of snows was preferred, that I might experience the
pleasure of suffering, and the novelty of danger.

—ESTWICK EVANS,
A Pedestrious Tour, of Four Thousand Miles,
Through the Western States and Territories,
During the Winter and Spring of 1818

Wilderness appealed to those bored or disgusted with man and
his works. It not only offered an escape from society but also
was an ideal stage for the Romantic individual to exercise
the cult that he frequently made of his own soul. The solitude
and total freedom of the wilderness created a perfect setting
for either melancholy or exultation.

—RODERICK NASH,
Wilderness and the American Mind

ON APRIL 15, 1992, CHRIS McCandless departed Carthage, South
Dakota, in the cab of a Mack truck hauling a load of sunflower seeds:
His "great Alaskan odyssey" was under way. Three days later he
crossed the Canadian border at Roosville, British Columbia, and
thumbed north through Skookumchuck and Radium Junction, Lake
Louise and Jasper, Prince George and Dawson Creek—where, in the
town center, he took a snapshot of the signpost marking the official
start of the Alaska Highway. MILE "0," the sign reads, FAIRBANKS 1,523
MILES.

Hitchhiking tends to be difficult on the Alaska Highway. It's not
unusual, on the outskirts of Dawson Creek, to see a dozen or more
doleful-looking men and women standing along the shoulder with
extended thumbs. Some of them may wait a week or more between
rides. But McCandless experienced no such delay. On April 21, just
six days out of Carthage, he arrived at Liard River Hotsprings, at the
threshold of the Yukon Territory.

There is a public campground at Liard River, from which a boardwalk leads half a mile across a marsh to a series of natural thermal
pools. It is the most popular way-stop on the Alaska Highway, and
McCandless decided to pause there for a soak in the soothing waters.

When he finished bathing and attempted to catch another ride north, however, he discovered that his luck had changed. Nobody would pick him up. Two days after arriving, he was still at Liard River, impatiently going nowhere.

At six-thirty on a brisk Thursday morning, the ground still frozen hard, Gaylord Stuckey walked out on the boardwalk to the largest of the pools, expecting to have the place to himself. He was surprised, therefore, to find someone already in the steaming water, a young man who introduced himself as Alex.

Stuckey—bald and cheerful, a ham-faced sixty-three-year-old Hoosier—was en route from Indiana to Alaska to deliver a new motor home to a Fairbanks RV dealer, a part-time line of work in which he'd dabbled since retiring after forty years in the restaurant business. When he told McCandless his destination, the boy exclaimed, "Hey, that's where I'm going, too! But I've been stuck here for a couple of days now, trying to get a lift. You mind if I ride with you?"

"Oh, jiminy," Stuckey replied. "I'd love to, son, but I can't. The company I work for has a strict rule against picking up hitchhikers. It could get me canned." As he chatted with McCandless through the sulfurous mist, though, Stuckey began to reconsider: "Alex was clean-shaven and had short hair, and I could tell by the language he used that he was a real sharp fella. He wasn't what you'd call a typical hitchhiker. I'm usually leery of 'em. I figure there's probably something wrong with a guy if he can't even afford a bus ticket. So anyway, after about half an hour I said, 'I tell you what, Alex: Liard is a thousand miles from Fairbanks. I'll take you five hundred miles, as far as Whitehorse; you'll be able to get a ride the rest of the way from there.' "

A day and a half later, however, when they arrived in Whitehorse—the capital of the Yukon Territory and the largest, most cosmopolitan town on the Alaska Highway—Stuckey had come to enjoy McCandless's company so much that he changed his mind and agreed to drive the boy the entire distance. "Alex didn't come out and say too much at first," Stuckey reports. "But it's a long, slow drive. We spent a total of three days together on those washboard roads, and by the end he kind of let his guard down. I tell you what: He was a dandy kid. Real courteous, and he didn't cuss or use a lot of that there slang. You could tell he came from a nice family. Mostly he talked about his sister. He didn't get along with his folks too good, I guess. Told me his dad was a genius, a NASA rocket scientist, but he'd been a bigamist at one time—and that kind of went against Alex's grain. Said he hadn't seen his parents in a couple of years, since his college graduation."

McCandless was candid with Stuckey about his intent to spend the summer alone in the bush, living off the land. "He said it was something he'd wanted to do since he was little," says Stuckey. "Said he didn't want to see a single person, no airplanes, no sign of civilization. He wanted to prove to himself that he could make it on his own, without anybody else's help."

Stuckey and McCandless arrived in Fairbanks on the afternoon of April 25. The older man took the boy to a grocery store, where he bought a big bag of rice, "and then Alex said he wanted to go out to the university to study up on what kind of plants he could eat. Berries and things like that. I told him, 'Alex, you're too early. There's still two foot, three foot of snow on the ground. There's nothing growing yet.' But his mind was pretty well made up. He was champing at the bit to get out there and start hiking." Stuckey drove to the University of Alaska campus, on the west end of Fairbanks, and dropped McCandless off at 5:30 P.M.

"Before I let him out," Stuckey says, "I told him, 'Alex, I've driven 10 you a thousand miles. I've fed you and fed you for three straight days. The least you can do is send me a letter when you get back from Alaska.' And he promised he would.

"I also begged and pleaded with him to call his parents. I can't imagine anything worse than having a son out there and not knowing where he's at for years and years, not knowing whether he's living or dead. 'Here's my credit card number,' I told him. '*Please* call them!' But all he said was 'Maybe I will and maybe I won't.' After he left, I thought, 'Oh, why didn't I get his parents' phone number and call them myself?' But everything just kind of happened so quick."

After dropping McCandless at the university, Stuckey drove into town to deliver the RV to the appointed dealer, only to be told that the person responsible for checking in new vehicles had already gone home for the day and wouldn't be back until Monday morning, leaving Stuckey with two days to kill in Fairbanks before he could fly home to Indiana. On Sunday morning, with time on his hands, he returned to the campus. "I hoped to find Alex and spend another day with him, take him sightseeing or something. I looked for a couple of hours, drove all over the place, but didn't see hide or hair of him. He was already gone."

After taking his leave of Stuckey on Saturday evening, McCandless spent two days and three nights in the vicinity of Fairbanks, mostly at the university. In the campus book store, tucked away on the bottom shelf of the Alaska section, he came across a scholarly, exhaustively researched field guide to the region's edible plants, *Tanaina Plantlore/Dena'ina K'et'una: An Ethnobotany of the Dena'ina Indians of Southcentral Alaska* by Priscilla Russell Kari. From a postcard rack near the cash register, he picked out two cards of a polar bear, on which he sent his final messages to Wayne Westerberg and Jan Burres[1] from the university post office.

Perusing the classified ads, McCandless found a used gun to buy, a semiautomatic .22-caliber Remington with a 4-×-20 scope and a plastic stock. A model called the Nylon 66, no longer in production, it was a favorite of Alaska trappers because of its light weight and reliability. He closed the deal in a parking lot, probably paying about $125 for the weapon, and then purchased four one-hundred-round boxes of hollow-point long-rifle shells from a nearby gun shop.

At the conclusion of his preparations in Fairbanks, McCandless loaded up his pack and started hiking west from the university. Leaving the campus, he walked past the Geophysical Institute, a tall glass-and-concrete building capped with a large satellite dish. The dish, one of the most distinctive landmarks on the Fairbanks skyline, had been erected to collect data from satellites equipped with synthetic aperture radar of Walt McCandless's design. Walt had in fact visited Fairbanks during the start-up of the receiving station and had written some of the software crucial to its operation. If the Geophysical Institute prompted Chris to think of his father as he tramped by, the boy left no record of it.

15

---

[1]Friends McCandless had made earlier in his travels.

Four miles west of town, in the evening's deepening chill, McCandless pitched his tent on a patch of hard-frozen ground surrounded by birch trees, not far from the crest of a bluff overlooking Gold Hill Gas & Liquor. Fifty yards from his camp was the terraced road cut of the George Parks Highway, the road that would take him to the Stampede Trail. He woke early on the morning of April 28, walked down to the highway in the predawn gloaming, and was pleasantly surprised when the first vehicle to come along pulled over to give him a lift. It was a gray Ford pickup with a bumper sticker on the back that declared, I FISH THEREFORE I AM. PETERSBURG, ALASKA. The driver of the truck, an electrician on his way to Anchorage, wasn't much older than McCandless. He said his name was Jim Gallien.

Three hours later Gallien turned his truck west off the highway and drove as far as he could down an unplowed side road. When he dropped McCandless off on the Stampede Trail, the temperature was in the low thirties—it would drop into the low teens at night—and a foot and a half of crusty spring snow covered the ground. The boy could hardly contain his excitement. He was, at long last, about to be alone in the vast Alaska wilds.

As he trudged expectantly down the trail in a fake-fur parka, his rifle slung over one shoulder, the only food McCandless carried was a ten-pound bag of long-grained rice—and the two sandwiches and bag of corn chips that Gallien had contributed. A year earlier he'd subsisted for more than a month beside the Gulf of California on five pounds of rice and a bounty of fish caught with a cheap rod and reel, an experience that made him confident he could harvest enough food to survive an extended stay in the Alaska wilderness, too.

The heaviest item in McCandless's half-full backpack was his library: nine or ten paperbound books, most of which had been given to him by Jan Burres in Niland. Among these volumes were titles by Thoreau and Tolstoy and Gogol,[1] but McCandless was no literary snob: He simply carried what he thought he might enjoy reading,

[1]Henry David Thoreau (1817–62), American transcendentalist philosopher and author of *Walden*, who advocated living simply; Leo Tolstoy (1828–1910), Russian author of epic novels such as *War and Peace* as well as philosophical short stories such as "Family Happiness"; Nikolai Gogol (1809–52), Ukranian-Russian author of *Dead Souls*.

including mass-market books by Michael Crichton, Robert Pirsig, and Louis L'Amour.[2] Having neglected to pack writing paper, he began a laconic journal on some blank pages in the back of *Tanaina Plantlore*.

The Healy terminus of the Stampede Trail is traveled by a handful of dog mushers, ski tourers, and snow-machine enthusiasts during the winter months, but only until the frozen rivers begin to break up, in late March or early April. By the time McCandless headed into the bush, there was open water flowing on most of the larger streams, and nobody had been very far down the trail for two or three weeks; only the faint remnants of a packed snow-machine track remained for him to follow. 20

McCandless reached the Teklanika River his second day out. Although the banks were lined with a jagged shelf of frozen overflow, no ice bridges spanned the channel of open water, so he was forced to wade. There had been a big thaw in early April, and breakup had come early in 1992, but the weather had turned cold again, so the river's volume was quite low when McCandless crossed—probably thigh-deep at most—allowing him to splash to the other side without difficulty. He never suspected that in so doing, he was crossing his Rubicon.[3] To McCandless's inexperienced eye, there was nothing to suggest that two months hence, as the glaciers and snowfields at the Teklanika's headwater thawed in the summer heat, its discharge would multiply nine or ten times in volume, transforming the river into a deep, violent torrent that bore no resemblance to the gentle brook he'd blithely waded across in April.

From his journal we know that on April 29, McCandless fell through the ice somewhere. It probably happened as he traversed a series of melting beaver ponds just beyond the Teklanika's western bank, but there is nothing to indicate that he suffered any harm in the mishap. A day later, as the trail crested a ridge, he got his first glimpse

---

[2]Michael Crichton (1942–2008), American author of popular novels such as *The Andromeda Strain* and *Jurassic Park*; Robert Pirsig (b. 1928), American author of *Zen and the Art of Motorcycle Maintenance*; Louis L'Amour (1903–88), American writer of western or frontier fiction.

[3]That is, taking a step from which there is no turning back. The Rubicon is a river in northern Italy; when Julius Caesar's army crossed it in 49 BCE the Roman Senate regarded it as an irrevocable act of war.

of Mt. McKinley's high, blinding-white bulwarks, and a day after that, May 1, some twenty miles down the trail from where he was dropped by Gallien, he stumbled upon the old bus beside the Sushana River. It was outfitted with a bunk and a barrel stove, and previous visitors had left the improvised shelter stocked with matches, bug dope, and other essentials. "Magic Bus Day," he wrote in his journal. He decided to lay over for a while in the vehicle and take advantage of its crude comforts.

He was elated to be there. Inside the bus, on a sheet of weathered plywood spanning a broken window, McCandless scrawled an exultant declaration of independence:

> *TWO YEARS HE WALKS THE EARTH, NO PHONE, NO POOL, NO PETS, NO CIGA-*
> *RETTES. ULTIMATE FREEDOM. AN EXTREMIST. AN AESTHETIC VOYAGER WHOSE*
> *HOME IS <u>THE ROAD.</u> ESCAPED FROM ATLANTA. THOU SHALT NOT RETURN,*
> *'CAUSE "THE WEST <u>IS</u> THE BEST." AND NOW AFTER TWO RAMBLING YEARS*
> *COMES THE FINAL AND GREATEST ADVENTURE. THE CLIMACTIC BATTLE TO*
> *KILL THE FALSE BEING WITHIN AND VICTORIOUSLY CONCLUDE THE SPIRITUAL*
> *REVOLUTION. TEN DAYS AND NIGHTS OF FREIGHT TRAINS AND HITCHHIKING*
> *BRING HIM TO THE GREAT WHITE NORTH. NO LONGER TO BE POISONED BY*
> *CIVILIZATION HE FLEES, AND WALKS ALONE UPON THE LAND TO BECOME <u>LOST</u>*
> *<u>IN THE WILD.</u>*
>
> *ALEXANDER SUPERTRAMP*
> *MAY 1992*

Reality, however, was quick to intrude on McCandless's reverie. He had difficulty killing game, and the daily journal entries during his first week in the bush include "Weakness," "Snowed in," and "Disaster." He saw but did not shoot a grizzly on May 2, shot at but missed some ducks on May 4, and finally killed and ate a spruce grouse on May 5; but he didn't shoot anything else until May 9, when he bagged a single small squirrel, by which point he'd written "4th day famine" in the journal.

But soon thereafter his fortunes took a sharp turn for the better. By mid-May the sun was circling high in the heavens, flooding the taiga with light. The sun dipped below the northern horizon for fewer than four hours out of every twenty-four, and at midnight the sky was still bright enough to read by. Everywhere but on the north-facing slopes and in the shadowy ravines, the snowpack had melted down to bare ground, exposing the previous season's rose hips and lingonberries, which McCandless gathered and ate in great quantity.

He also became much more successful at hunting game and for the next six weeks feasted regularly on squirrel, spruce grouse, duck, goose, and porcupine. On May 22, a crown fell off one of his molars, but the event didn't seem to dampen his spirits much, because the following day he scrambled up the nameless, humplike, three-thousand-foot butte that rises directly north of the bus, giving him a view of the whole icy sweep of the Alaska Range and mile after mile of uninhabited country. His journal entry for the day is characteristically terse but unmistakably joyous: "CLIMB MOUNTAIN!"

McCandless had told Gallien that he intended to remain on the move during his stay in the bush. "I'm just going to take off and keep walking west," he'd said. "I might walk all the way to the Bering Sea." On May 5, after pausing for four days at the bus, he resumed his per-ambulation. From the snapshots recovered with his Minolta, it appears that McCandless lost (or intentionally left) the by-now-indistinct Stampede Trail and headed west and north through the hills above the Sushana River, hunting game as he went.

It was slow going. In order to feed himself, he had to devote a large part of each day to stalking animals. Moreover, as the ground thawed, his route turned into a gauntlet of boggy muskeg and impenetrable alder, and McCandless belatedly came to appreciate one of the funda-mental (if counterintuitive) axioms of the North: winter, not summer, is the preferred season for traveling overland through the bush.

Faced with the obvious folly of his original ambition, to walk five hundred miles to tidewater, he reconsidered his plans. On May 19, having traveled no farther west than the Toklat River—less than fifteen miles beyond the bus—he turned around. A week later he was back at the derelict vehicle, apparently without regret. He'd decided that the Sushana drainage was plenty wild to suit his purposes and that Fairbanks bus 142 would make a fine base camp for the remainder of the summer.

Ironically, the wilderness surrounding the bus—the patch of over-grown country where McCandless was determined "to become lost in 30 the wild"—scarcely qualifies as wilderness by Alaska standards. Less than thirty miles to the east is a major thoroughfare, the George Parks Highway. Just sixteen miles to the south, beyond an escarpment of the Outer Range, hundreds of tourists rumble daily into Denali Park over a road patrolled by the National Park Service. And unbeknownst to the Aesthetic Voyager, scattered within a six-mile radius of the bus are four cabins (although none happened to be occupied during the summer of 1992).

But despite the relative proximity of the bus to civilization, for all practical purposes McCandless was cut off from the rest of the world. He spent nearly four months in the bush all told, and during that period he didn't encounter another living soul. In the end the Sushana River site was sufficiently remote to cost him his life.

In the last week of May, after moving his few possessions into the bus, McCandless wrote a list of housekeeping chores on a parchment-like strip of birch bark: collect and store ice from the river for refrigerating meat, cover the vehicle's missing windows with plastic, lay in a supply of firewood, clean the accumulation of old ash from the stove. And under the heading "<u>LONG TERM</u>" he drew up a list of more ambitious tasks: map the area, improvise a bathtub, collect skins and feathers to sew into clothing, construct a bridge across a nearby creek, repair mess kit, blaze a network of hunting trails.

The diary entries following his return to the bus catalog a bounty of wild meat. May 28: "Gourmet Duck!" June 1: "5 Squirrel." June 2: "Porcupine, Ptarmigan, 4 Squirrel, Grey Bird." June 3: "Another Porcupine! 4 Squirrel, 2 Grey Bird, Ash Bird." June 4: "A THIRD PORCUPINE! Squirrel, Grey Bird." On June 5, he shot a Canada goose as big as a Christmas turkey. Then, on June 9, he bagged the biggest prize of all: "<u>MOOSE</u>!" he recorded in the journal. Overjoyed, the proud hunter took a photograph of himself kneeling over his trophy, rifle thrust triumphantly overhead, his features distorted in a rictus of ecstasy and amazement, like some unemployed janitor who'd gone to Reno and won a million-dollar jackpot.

Although McCandless was enough of a realist to know that hunting game was an unavoidable component of living off the land, he had always been ambivalent about killing animals. That ambivalence turned to remorse soon after he shot the moose. It was relatively small, weighing perhaps six hundred or seven hundred pounds, but it nevertheless amounted to a huge quantity of meat. Believing that it was morally indefensible to waste any part of an animal that has been shot for food, McCandless spent six days toiling to preserve what he had killed before it spoiled. He butchered the carcass under a thick cloud of flies and mosquitoes, boiled the organs into a stew, and then laboriously excavated a burrow in the face of the rocky stream bank directly below the bus, in which he tried to cure, by smoking, the immense slabs of purple flesh.

Alaskan hunters know that the easiest way to preserve meat in the 35 bush is to slice it into thin strips and then air-dry it on a makeshift rack. But McCandless, in his naïveté, relied on the advice of hunters he'd consulted in South Dakota, who advised him to smoke his meat, not an easy task under the circumstances. "Butchering extremely difficult," he wrote in the journal on June 10. "Fly and mosquito hordes. Remove intestines, liver, kidneys, one lung, steaks. Get hindquarters and leg to stream."

June 11: "Remove heart and other lung. Two front legs and head. Get rest to stream. Haul near cave. Try to protect with smoker."

June 12: "Remove half rib-cage and steaks. Can only work nights. Keep smokers going."

June 13: "Get remainder of rib-cage, shoulder and neck to cave. Start smoking."

June 14: "Maggots already! Smoking appears ineffective. Don't know, looks like disaster. I now wish I had never shot the moose. One of the greatest tragedies of my life."

At that point he gave up on preserving the bulk of the meat and 40 abandoned the carcass to the wolves. Although he castigated himself severely for this waste of a life he'd taken, a day later McCandless appeared to regain some perspective, for his journal notes, "henceforth will learn to accept my errors, however great they be."

Shortly after the moose episode McCandless began to read Thoreau's *Walden*. In the chapter titled "Higher Laws," in which

Thoreau ruminates on the morality of eating, McCandless highlighted, "when I had caught and cleaned and cooked and eaten my fish, they seemed not to have fed me essentially. It was insignificant and unnecessary, and cost more than it came to."

"THE MOOSE," McCandless wrote in the margin. And in the same passage he marked,

> *The repugnance to animal food is not the effect of experience, but is an instinct. It appeared more beautiful to live low and fare hard in many respects; and though I never did so, I went far enough to please my imagination. I believe that every man who has ever been earnest to preserve his higher or poetic faculties in the best condition has been particularly inclined to abstain from animal food, and from much food of any kind. . . .*
>
> *It is hard to provide and cook so simple and clean a diet as will not offend the imagination; but this, I think, is to be fed when we feed the body; they should both sit down at the same table. Yet perhaps this may be done. The fruits eaten temperately need not make us ashamed of our appetites, nor interrupt the worthiest pursuits. But put an extra condiment into your dish, and it will poison you.*

"YES," wrote McCandless and, two pages later, "<u>Consciousness</u> of food. Eat and cook with <u>concentration</u>. . . . Holy Food." On the back pages of the book that served as his journal, he declared:

> *I am reborn. This is my dawn. <u>Real</u> life has just begun.*
> <u>*Deliberate Living*</u>: *Conscious attention to the basics of life, and a constant attention to your immediate environment and its concerns, example→A job, a task, a book; anything requiring efficient concentration (Circumstance has no value. It is how one <u>relates</u> to a situation that has value. All true meaning resides in the personal relationship to a phenomenon, what it means to you).*
> *The Great Holiness of **FOOD**, the Vital Heat.*
> <u>*Positivism*</u>, *the Insurpassable Joy of the Life Aesthetic.*
> *Absolute Truth and Honesty.*
> *Reality.*
> *Independence.*
> *Finality—Stability—Consistency.*

As McCandless gradually stopped rebuking himself for the waste of the moose, the contentment that began in mid-May resumed and seemed to continue through early July. Then, in the midst of this idyll, came the first of two pivotal setbacks.

Satisfied, apparently, with what he had learned during his two 45 months of solitary life in the wild, McCandless decided to return to civilization: It was time to bring his "final and greatest adventure" to a close and get himself back to the world of men and women, where he could chug a beer, talk philosophy, enthrall strangers with tales of what he'd done. He seemed to have moved beyond his need to assert so adamantly his autonomy, his need to separate himself from his parents. Maybe he was prepared to forgive their imperfections; maybe he was even prepared to forgive some of his own. McCandless seemed ready, perhaps, to go home.

Or maybe not; we can do no more than speculate about what he intended to do after he walked out of the bush. There is no question, however, that he intended to walk out.

Writing on a piece of birch bark, he made a list of things to do before he departed: "Patch Jeans, Shave!, Organize pack. . . ." Shortly thereafter he propped his Minolta on an empty oil drum and took a snapshot of himself brandishing a yellow disposable razor and grinning at the camera, clean-shaven, with new patches cut from an army blanket stitched onto the knees of his filthy jeans. He looks healthy but alarmingly gaunt. Already his cheeks are sunken. The tendons in his neck stand out like taut cables.

On July 2, McCandless finished reading Tolstoy's "Family Happiness," having marked several passages that moved him:

> He was right in saying that the only certain happiness in life is to live for others. . . . I have lived through much, and now I think I have found what is needed for happiness. A quiet secluded life in the country, with the possibility of being useful to people to whom it is easy to do good, and who are not accustomed to have it done to them; then work which one hopes may be of some use; then rest, nature, books, music, love for one's neighbor—such is my idea of happiness. And

then, on top of all that, you for a mate, and children, perhaps— what more can the heart of a man desire?

Then, on July 3, he shouldered his backpack and began the twenty-mile hike to the improved road. Two days later, halfway there, he arrived in heavy rain at the beaver ponds that blocked access to the west bank of the Teklanika River. In April they'd been frozen over and hadn't presented an obstacle. Now he must have been alarmed to find a three-acre lake covering the trail. To avoid having to wade through the murky chest-deep water, he scrambled up a steep hillside, bypassed the ponds on the north, and then dropped back down to the river at the mouth of the gorge.

When he'd first crossed the river, sixty-seven days earlier in the 50 freezing temperatures of April, it had been an icy but gentle knee-deep creek, and he'd simply strolled across it. On July 5, however, the Teklanika was at full flood, swollen with rain and snowmelt from glaciers high in the Alaska Range, running cold and fast.

If he could reach the far shore, the remainder of the hike to the highway would be easy, but to get there he would have to negotiate a channel some one hundred feet wide. The water, opaque with glacial sediment and only a few degrees warmer than the ice it had so recently been, was the color of wet concrete. Too deep to wade, it rumbled like a freight train. The powerful current would quickly knock him off his feet and carry him away.

McCandless was a weak swimmer and had confessed to several people that he was in fact afraid of the water. Attempting to swim the numbingly cold torrent or even to paddle some sort of improvised raft across seemed too risky to consider. Just downstream from where the trail met the river, the Teklanika erupted into a chaos of boiling whitewater as it accelerated through the narrow gorge. Long before he could swim or paddle to the far shore, he'd be pulled into these rapids and drowned.

In his journal he now wrote, "Disaster. . . . Rained in. River look impossible. Lonely, scared." He concluded, correctly, that he would probably be swept to his death if he attempted to cross the Teklanika at that place, in those conditions. It would be suicidal; it was simply not an option.

If McCandless had walked a mile or so upstream, he would have discovered that the river broadened into a maze of braided channels. If he'd scouted carefully, by trial and error he might have found a place where these braids were only chest-deep. As strong as the current was running, it would have certainly knocked him off his feet, but by dog-paddling and hopping along the bottom as he drifted downstream, he could conceivably have made it across before being carried into the gorge or succumbing to hypothermia.

But it would still have been a very risky proposition, and at that 55 point McCandless had no reason to take such a risk. He'd been fending for himself quite nicely in the country. He probably understood that if he was patient and waited, the river would eventually drop to a level where it could be safely forded. After weighing his options, therefore, he settled on the most prudent course. He turned around and began walking to the west, back toward the bus, back into the fickle heart of the bush.

STUDY QUESTIONS

1. How does Krakauer portray the Alaskan SETTING of this chapter? How does Chris McCandless interact with Alaska?

2. In this chapter, Krakauer ANALYZES the PROCESS that leads McCandless to put himself into greater and greater danger. Does Krakauer present Chris's actions as inevitably leading toward a single conclusion? Explain your answer.

3. What is the relationship between the epigraphs and McCandless's journey? How do the epigraphs comment on or reflect the situations that Krakauer DESCRIBES?

4. In what ways does Krakauer characterize McCandless's TONE in the latter's journal entries? What do these characterizations contribute to the NARRATIVE?

5. *For Writing.* McCandless went to Alaska to live deliberately and simply, like Thoreau, one of his heroes. How could you live more deliberately and simply, even without moving away from your present home? Write a PERSONAL ESSAY in which you analyze the process of removing extraneous elements from your life. Could it really be done? *Should* it be done?

JOSEPH WOOD KRUTCH { *The Most Dangerous Predator*

JOSEPH WOOD KRUTCH (1893–1970) was born in Knoxville, Tennessee, studied at the University of Tennessee, and received his PhD from Columbia University in 1923. After a stint as a theater critic for *The Nation,* he returned to Columbia to teach. He later moved to Arizona where his interest shifted from literature to the environment. His many books include *The Twelve Seasons* (1949) and *The Voice of the Desert: A Naturalist's Interpretation* (1955).

The following selection is a chapter from Krutch's book *The Forgotten Peninsula: A Naturalist in Baja California* (1961), in which the author reveals his extensive knowledge of other naturalists' research on the relationship between people and wildlife. Krutch also displays his literary training by citing the environmental concerns of authors such as Tennyson and Steinbeck. Literary allusion, scientific fact, and personal observation contribute to the development of the essay, showing how people tend to disrupt natural cycles by acting without regard for the balance of nature.

IN THE UNITED STATES THE slaughter of wild animals for fun is subject to certain restrictions fairly well enforced. In Mexico the laws are less strict and in many regions there is little or no machinery for enforcement. Hence an automobile club in southern California distributes to its members an outline map of Baja purporting to indicate in detail just where various large animals not yet quite extinct may be found by those eager to do their bit toward eliminating them completely. This map gives the impression that pronghorn antelopes, mountain sheep, and various other "game animals" abound.

In actual fact, the country can never have supported very many such and today the traveler accustomed to the open country of our own Southwest would be struck by the fact that, except for sea birds, sea mammals, and fish, wildlife of any kind is far scarcer than at home. This is no doubt due in part to American hunters but also in part to the fact that native inhabitants who once could not afford the cartridges to shoot anything they did not intend to eat now get relatively cheap ammunition from the United States and can indulge in what seems to be the almost universal human tendency to kill anything that moves.

Someday—probably a little too late—the promoters of Baja as a resort area will wake up to the fact that wildlife is a tourist attraction and that though any bird or beast can be observed or photographed an unlimited number of times it can be shot only once. The Mexican government is cooperating with the government of the United States in a successful effort to save the gray whale and the sea elephant but to date does not seem much interested in initiating its own measures of protection. As long ago as 1947, Lewis Wayne Walker[1] (who guided me on our innocent hunt for the boojum trees he had previously photographed) wrote for *Natural History Magazine* a survey of the situation, particularly as it concerns the pronghorn and the mountain sheep. A quarter of a century before, herds of antelope were to be found within thirty or forty miles of the United States border. But by 1933 they had all, so a rancher told him, been killed after a party of quail hunters had discovered them. In the roadless areas some bands of mountain sheep still existed (and doubtless do even today) but the water holes near traversable areas were already deserted by the midforties. All the large animals of a given region must come to drink at the only pool or spring for many miles around, hence a single party need only wait beside it to exterminate the entire population inhabiting that area. Though Walker had driven more than ten thousand miles on the Baja trails during the two years preceding the writing of his letter, he saw only one deer, no sheep, and no antelope. Despite the publicity given it, "Baja is," he wrote, "the poorest game area I have ever visited."

[1]American writer and naturalist, best known for *The Book of Owls* (1974).

The depredations of the hunter are not always the result of any fundamental blood lust. Perhaps he is only, more often than not, merely lacking in imagination. The exterminator of the noble animals likes the out-of-doors and thrills at the sight of something which suggests the world as it once was. But contemplation is not widely recognized as an end in itself. Having seen the antelope or the sheep, he must "do something about it." And the obvious thing to do is to shoot.

In the *Sea of Cortez* John Steinbeck[2] describes how a Mexican rancher invited his party to a sheep hunt. They were reluctant to accept until they realized that the rancher himself didn't really want to kill the animals—he merely didn't know what other excuse to give for seeking them out. When his Indians returned empty-handed he said with only mild regret: "If they had killed one we could have had our pictures taken with it." Then Steinbeck adds: "They had taught us the best of all ways to go hunting and we shall never use any other. We have, however, made one slight improvement on their method; we shall not take a gun, thereby obviating the last remote possibility of having the hunt cluttered up with game. We have never understood why men mount the heads of animals and hang them up to look down on their conquerors. Possibly it feels good to these men to be superior to animals but it does seem that if they were sure of it they would not have to prove it." Later, when one of the Indians brought back some droppings which he seemed to treasure and presented a portion of them to the white men, Steinbeck adds: "Where another man can say, 'there was an animal but because I am greater than he, he is dead and I am alive and there is his head to prove it' we can say, 'There was an animal, and for all we know there still is and here is proof of it. He was very healthy when we last heard of him.' "

• ○ •

"Very pretty," so the tough-minded will say, "but hardly realistic. Man is a predator, to be sure, but he isn't the only one. The mountain lion killed sheep long before even the Indian came to Baja. The law of life is also a law of death. Nature is red in tooth and claw. You can't get

[2]American author (1902–68) best known for his novel *The Grapes of Wrath*.

away from that simple fact and there is no use in trying. Whatever else he may be, man is an animal; and like the other animals he is the enemy of all other living things. You talk of 'the balance of nature' but we are an element in it. As we increase, the mountain sheep disappear. The fittest, you know, survive."

Until quite recent times this reply would have been at least a tenable one. Primitive man seems to have been a rather unsuccessful animal, few in numbers and near the ragged edge of extinction. But gradually the balance shifted. He held his own; then he increased in numbers; then he developed techniques of aggression as well as of protection incomparably more effective than any which nature herself had ever been able to devise before the human mind intervened. Up until then, animals had always been a match, one for another. But they were no match for him. The balance no longer worked. Though for another 500,000 years "coexistence" still seemed to be a *modus vivendi*[3] the time came, only a short while ago, when man's strength, his numers, and his skill made him master and tyrant. He now dominated the natural world of which he had once been only a part. Now for the first time he could exterminate, if he wished to do so, any other living creature—perhaps even (as we learned just yesterday) his fellow man.[4] What this means in a specific case; what the difference is between nature, however red she may be in tooth and claw, and the terrifying predator who is no longer subject to the limitations she once imposed, can readily be illustrated on the Baja peninsula. In neither case is the story a pretty one. Both involve a ruthless predator and the slaughter of innocents. But nature's far from simple plan does depend upon a coexistence. Man is, on the other hand, the only animal who habitually exhausts or exterminates what he has learned to exploit.

●　○　●

Let us, then, take first a typical dog-eat-dog story as nature tells it, year after year, on Rasa Island[5] where confinement to a small area keeps it

[3]Way of life (Latin).

[4]A reference to the Holocaust, the attempt by the German Nazis in the 1940s to exterminate the Jews of Europe.

[5]Located in the Sea of Cortez, east of Mexico's Baja California peninsula.

startlingly simple without any of those sub-plots which make nature's usual stories so endlessly complicated.

This tiny island—less than a mile square in area and barely one hundred feet above sea level at its highest point—lies in the Gulf fifteen or twenty miles away from the settlement at Los Angeles Bay. It is rarely visited because even in fair weather the waters round about it are treacherous. Currents up to eight knots create whirlpools between it and other small islands and there is a tide drop of twelve to thirty feet, depending upon the season. It is almost bare of vegetation except for a little of the salt weed or Salicornia which is found in so many of the saline sands in almost every climate. But it is the nesting place of thousands of Heermann gulls who, after the young are able to fend for themselves, migrate elsewhere—a few southward as far as Central America but most of them north to various points on the Pacific coast. A few of the latter take the shortest route across the Baja peninsula but most take what seems an absurd detour by going first some 450 miles south to the tip of Baja and then the eight hundred or a thousand miles up its west coast to the United States—perhaps, as seems to be the case in various other paradoxes of migration—because they are following some ancestral habit acquired when the climate or the lay of the land was quite different.

My travels in Baja are, I hope, not finished, and I intend someday to set foot on Rasa to see what goes on there for myself. So far, however, I have observed the huge concentration of birds only from a low-flying plane and what I have to describe is what Walker has told me and what he wrote some ten years ago in an illustrated account for the *National Geographic Magazine*.

In late April, when the breeding season is at its height, the ground is crowded with innumerable nests—in some places no more than a yard apart, nowhere with more than twenty feet between them. Because man has so seldom disturbed the gulls here they show little fear of him though once they have reached the northern shore they rise and fly out to sea at the first sight of a human being.

If this were all there was to tell, Rasa might seem to realize that idyllic state of nature of which man, far from idyllic though he has made his own society, often loves to dream. Though on occasion gulls are predators as well as scavengers they respect one another's eggs and off-spring on Rasa and live together in peace. But like most animals (and like most men) they are ruthless in their attitude toward other species though too utterly nature's children to rationalize as man does that ruthlessness. They know in their nerves and muscles without even thinking about it that the world was made for the exclusive use and convenience of gulls.

In the present case the victims of that egomania of the species are the two kinds of tern which share the island with them and have chosen to lay their eggs in a depression surrounded by gulls.

Here Walker had best tell his own story: "In the early morning of the second day a few eggs were seen under the terns but even as we watched, several were stolen by gulls. By late afternoon not an egg remained. Nightfall brought on an influx of layers, and morning found twice as many eggs dotting the ground. By dusk only a fraction of the number in the exact center of the plot had escaped the inroads of the egg-eating enemy.

"The new colony had now gained a permanent foothold. Accordion-like it expanded during the night, contracted by evening. Each twenty-four hour period showed a gain for the terns and a corresponding retreat in the waiting ranks of the killing gulls.

"By the end of a week the colony had expanded from nothing to approximately four hundred square feet of egg-spotted ground and it continued to spread. The gulls seemed to be losing their appetites. Like children sated with ice cream, they had found that a single diet can be over-done."

What an absurd—some would say what a horrid—story that is. How decisively it gives the lie to what the earliest idealizers of nature called her "social union." How difficult it makes it to believe that some all-good, omnipotent, conscious, and transcendental power consciously chose to set up a general plan of which this is a typical detail. How much more probable it makes it seem that any purpose that may exist in the universe is one emerging from a chaos rather than one which had deliberately created that chaos.

But a fact remains: one must recognize that the scheme works—for the terns as well as for the gulls. If it is no more than the mechanism which so many call it, then it is at least (to use the newly current terminology) a cybernetic or self-regulating mechanism. If the gulls destroyed so many eggs that the tern population began to decline, then the gulls, deprived of their usual food supply, would also decline in numbers and the terns would again increase until the balance had been reached. "How careful of the type she seems; how careless of the single life"—as Tennyson observed some years before Darwin made the same humanly disturbing fact a cornerstone of his theories.

Absurd as the situation on Rasa may seem, it has probably existed for thousands of years and may well continue for thousands more—if left to itself, undisturbed by the only predator who almost invariably renders the "cybernetic" system inoperable.

•   ∘   •

Consider now the case of the elephant seal, a great sea beast fourteen   20
to sixteen feet long and nearly three tons in weight. Hardly more than a century ago it bred in enormous numbers on the rocky coast and on the island from Point Reyes, just north of San Francisco, almost to the Magdalena Bay on the Pacific coast of Baja. Like the gray whale it was preyed upon by the ferocious killer whale which is, perhaps, the most formidable of all the predators of the sea. But a balance had been reached and the two coexisted in much the same fashion as the gulls and the terns of Rasa.

Unfortunately (at least for them) human enterprise presently discovered that sea elephants could become a source of oil second in importance to the whale alone. And against this new predator nature afforded no protection. The elephant seals had learned to be wary of the killer whale but they had known no enemy on land and they feared none. Because instinct is slow while the scheming human brain works fast, those who must depend upon instinct are lost before it can protect them gainst any new threat. Captain Scammon,[6] always clear, vivid, and businesslike, describes how easy and how profitable it was to bring the seals as near to extinction as the gray whales were brought at approximately the same time.

---

[6]Charles Scammon, author of *The Marine Mammals of the North-western Coast of North America* (1874).

691

"The mode of capturing them is thus; the sailors get between the herd and the water; then raising all possible noise by shouting, and at the same time flourishing clubs, guns, and lances, the party advances slowly towards the rookery, when the animals will retreat, appearing in a state of great alarm. Occasionally, an overgrown male will give battle, or attempt to escape; but a musket ball through the brain dispatches it; or someone checks its progress by thrusting a lance into the roof of its mouth, which causes it to settle on its haunches, when two men with heavy oaken clubs give the creature repeated blows about the head, until it is stunned or killed. After securing those that are disposed to showing resistance, the party rush on the main body. The onslaught creates such a panic among these peculiar creatues, that, losing all control of their actions, they climb, roll, and tumble over each other, when prevented from further retreat by the projecting cliffs. We recollect in one instance, where sixty-five were captured, that several were found showing no signs of having been either clubbed or lanced but were smothered by numbers of their kind heaped upon them. The whole flock, when attacked, manifested alarm by their peculiar roar, the sound of whch, among the largest males, is nearly as loud as the lowing of an ox, but more prolonged in one strain, accompanied by a rattling noise in the throat. The quantity of blood in this species of the seal tribe is supposed to be double that contained in an ox, in proportion to its size.

"After the capture, the flay begins. First, with a large knife, the skin is ripped along the upper side of the body its whole length, and then cut down as far as practicable, without rolling it over; then the coating of fat that lies between the skin and flesh—which may be from one to seven inches in thickness, according to the size and condition of the animal—is cut into 'horse pieces,' about eight inches wide and twelve to fifteen long, and a puncture is made in each piece sufficiently large to pass a rope through. After flensing the upper portion of the body, it is rolled over, and cut all around as above described. Then the 'horse pieces' are strung on a raft rope (a rope three fathoms long, with an eye splice in one end) and taken to the edge of the surf; a long line is made fast to it, the end of which is thrown to a boat lying just outside of the breakers; they are then hauled through the rollers and towed to the vessel, where the oil is tried out by boiling the blubber, or fat, in large pots set in a brick furnace. . . . The oil produced is superior to whale oil for lubricating purposes. Owing to the continual pursuit of the animals, they have become nearly if not quite extinct on the California coast, or the few remaining have fled to some unknown point for security."

Captain Scammon's account was first published in the *Overland Monthly* in 1870. A few members of the herds he had helped to slaughter must have survived because in 1884 the zoologist Charles Haskins Townsend accompanied a party of sealers who hunted for two months and succeeded in killing sixty. Then, eight years later, he found eight elephant seals on Guadalupe, the lonely lava-capped island twenty-two by seven miles in extent which lies 230 miles southwest of Ensenada in Baja and is the most westerly of Mexican possessions.

It seems to be a biological law that if a given species diminishes in 25 numbers, no matter how slowly, it presently reaches a point of no return from which even the most careful fostering cannot bring it back. Eight elephant seals would probably have been far too few to preserve the species; but there must have been others somewhere because when Townsend visited the islands again in 1911 he found 125, and in 1922 scientists from the Scripps Institution[7] and the California Academy of Sciences counted 264 males at a time of year when the females had already left the breeding grounds.

Had Guadalupe not happened to be one of the most remote and inaccessible islands in our part of the world, the few refugees could hardly have survived. By the time it became known that on Guadalupe they had not only survived but multiplied into the hundreds, sealers would almost certainly have sought them out again to finish the job of extermination had not the Mexican government agreed to make Guadalupe a closed area. Because the elephant seal has again no enemy except the killer whale it now occupies all the beaches of the island to which it fled and has established new colonies on various other small islands in the same Pacific area, espcially on the San Benitos group nearly two hundred miles to the east. By 1950 the total population was estimated at one thousand.

[7]Oceanographic research center located in La Jolla, California.

The earliest voyagers described Guadalupe, rising majestically from the sea to its four-thousand-foot summit, as a true island paradise and also, like other isolated islands, so rich in the unique forms of life which had been slowly evolved in isolation that half the birds and half the plants were unknown anywhere else. So far, I know it only by reputation and have not even seen it, as I have seen Rasa, from the air; but it is said to be a very far from a paradise today. Though inhabited only by a few officers of the Mexican Navy who operate a meteorological station, whalers had begun to visit it as early as 1700 and disastrously upset the balance of nature by intentionally introducing goats to provide food for subsequent visits and unintentionally allowing cats and rats to escape from their ships. Several thousand wild goats as well as innumerable cats and rats now manage to exist there, but it is said that almost nothing of the original flora and fauna remains. Most of the unique birds are extinct; the goats have nibbled the trees as high as they are able to reach, and have almost completely destroyed all other plant life. In the absence of the natural predators necessary to establish a tolerable balance, many of the goats are said to die of starvation every year for the simple reason that any animal population will ultimately destroy its own food supply unless multiplication is regulated by either natural or artificial means. Guadalupe is, in short, a perfect demonstration of three truths: (1) That nature left to herself establishes a *modus vivendi* which may be based upon tooth and claw but which nevertheless does permit a varied flora and fauna to live and flourish; (2) that man easily upsets the natural balance so quickly and drastically that nature herself cannot reestablish it in any fashion so generally satisfactory as that which prevailed before the balance was destroyed; (3) that man, if he wishes, can mitigate to some extent the destructive effects of his intervention by intervening again to save some individual species as he seems now to have saved the gray whale and the elephant seal.

• ○ •

How important is it that he should come to an adequate realization of these three truths? Of the second he must take some account if he is not, like the goats of Guadalupe, to come up against the fact that any species may become so "successful" that starvation is inevitable as the ultimate check upon its proliferation and that from this fate not even his technology can save him ultimately, because even those cakes of sewage-grown algae with which he is already experimenting could do no more than postpone a little longer the final day of reckoning. He has proved himself so much cleverer than nature that, once he has intervened, she can no longer protect him just as she could not protect either the life indigenous to Guadalupe or the goats man had introduced there. Having decided to go it alone, he needs for his survival to become more clever still and, especially, more farseeing.

On the other hand, and if he so wishes, he can, perhaps, disregard the other two laws that prevent the gradual disappearance of every area which illustrates the profusion and variety which nature achieves by her own methods and he may see no reason why he should preserve from extinction the elephant seal, which will probably never again be commercially valuable, or for that matter any other of the plants and animals which supply none of his physical needs. None of them may be necessary to his survival, all of them merely "beautiful" or "curious," rather than "useful."

Many arguments have been advanced by those who would persuade 30 him to take some thought before it is too late. But the result may depend less upon arguments than upon the attitudes which are essentially emotional and aesthetic.

Thoreau[8]—perhaps the most eloquent exponent we have ever had of the practical, the aesthetic, and the mystical goods which man can receive from the contemplation of the natural as opposed to the man-made or man-managed—once wrote as follows:

"When I consider that the nobler animals have been exterminated here—the cougar, the panther, lynx, wolverine, wolf, bear, moose, deer, the beaver, the turkey and so forth and so forth, I cannot but feel as if I lived in a tamed and, as it were, emasculated country. . . . Is it not a maimed and imperfect nature that I am conversing with? As if I were to study a tribe of Indians that had lost all its warriors. . . . I take infinite pains to know all the phenomena of the spring, for instance, think-

---

[8]Henry David Thoreau (1817–62), American author, naturalist, and political philosopher.

ing that I have here the entire poem, and then, to my chagrin, I hear that it is but an imperfect copy that I possess and have read, that my ancestors had torn out many of the first leaves and grandest passages, and mutilated it in many places. I should not like to think that some demigod had come before me and picked out some of the best of the stars. I wish to know an entire heaven and an entire earth."

To what proportion of the human race such a statement is, or could be made, meaningful I do not know. But upon the answer that time is already beginning to give will depend how much, if any, of the "poem" will be legible even a few generations hence.

Many of us now talk as if, until recently, there was no need to talk about "conservation." Probably there are today more men than ever before who could answer in the affirmative Emerson's question:

> Hast thou named all the birds without a gun?
> Loved the wild rose, and left it on its stalk?[9]

But in absolute rather than relative numbers there are vastly more 35 men today equipped with vastly more efficient instruments of destruction than there ever were before and many of them respect neither the bird nor the wild rose. As of this moment it is they who are winning against everything those of us who would like to preserve the poem are able to say or do.

[9]From the poem "Forbearance" by Ralph Waldo Emerson (1803–82), American essayist, poet, and leader of Transcendentalist movement.

STUDY QUESTIONS

1. Why does Krutch cite Steinbeck's *Sea of Cortez* (paragraph 5)? Explain how he uses this QUOTATION to further his own ARGUMENT. What other quotations and allusions does Krutch cite, and how do these function in the essay?

2. Identify Krutch's THESIS and list three ways he supports it. Does his conclusion adequately SUMMARIZE his thesis and essay? Explain.

3. *For Writing.* Select an animal who is currently on a protected species list and conduct RESEARCH about it—its primary habitat, its current population, the reason it is endangered, how long it has been on the list, and what is being done to protect it and help it repopulate. How do these efforts affect people, and how do people respond to these efforts? For instance, does protection of the species have either positive or adverse economic effects? Explain.

JESSICA MITFORD ⎰ *Behind the Formaldehyde Curtain*

JESSICA MITFORD (1917–1996) was born into an aristocratic English family and moved in 1939 to the United States, where she became a naturalized American citizen and pursued a career as an investigative reporter. A lifelong activist, Mitford worked on behalf of pacifism and civil rights; when she and her husband, Robert Treuhaft, a lawyer, became aware of funeral costs for working-class families in the San Francisco Bay Area, she published *The American Way of Death* (1963), which sold out on the day of publication. While the work provoked queasiness in some readers and outrage in others (mainly funeral directors), it has become a classic piece of expository prose, anthologized in more than fifty textbooks. Mitford is the author of several books, including *The American Way of Death Revisited* (1998).

This chapter from *The American Way of Death* presents a critical look at the process of embalming bodies and preparing them for burial. Mitford uses an ironically breezy tone to convey her attitude toward the way funerals are conducted in the United States as she describes the procedures used to embalm the fictitious "Mr. Jones." Despite her gruesome subject matter (or perhaps, for some readers, because of it), Mitford's understated sense of humor has made "Behind the Formaldehyde Curtain" enduringly popular.

THE DRAMA BEGINS TO UNFOLD with the arrival of the corpse at the mortuary.

Alas, poor Yorick![1] How surprised he would be to see how his counterpart of today is whisked off to a funeral parlor and is in short

---

[1]*Hamlet*, 5.1.171. Hamlet discovers the skull of an old friend in a graveyard.

order sprayed, sliced, pierced, pickled, trussed, trimmed, creamed, waxed, painted, rouged and neatly dressed—transformed from a common corpse into a Beautiful Memory Picture. This process is known in the trade as embalming and restorative art, and is so universally employed in the United States and Canada that the funeral director does it routinely, without consulting corpse or kin. He regards as eccentric those few who are hardy enough to suggest that it might be dispensed with. Yet no law requires embalming, no religious doctrine commends it, nor is it dictated by considerations of health, sanitation, or even of personal daintiness. In no part of the world but in Northern America is it widely used. The purpose of embalming is to make the corpse presentable for viewing in a suitably costly container; and here too the funeral director routinely, without first consulting the family, prepares the body for public display.

Is all this legal? The processes to which a dead body may be subjected are after all to some extent circumscribed by law. In most states, for instance, the signature of next of kin must be obtained before an autopsy may be performed, before the deceased may be cremated, before the body may be turned over to a medical school for research purposes; or such provision must be made in the decedent's will. In the case of embalming, no such permission is required nor is it ever sought. A textbook, *The Principles and Practices of Embalming*, comments on this: "There is some question regarding the legality of much that is done within the preparation room." The author points out that it would be most unusual for a responsible member of a bereaved family to instruct the mortician, in so many words, to *"embalm"* the body of a deceased relative. The very term "embalming" is so seldom used that the mortician must rely upon custom in the matter. The author concludes that unless the family specifies otherwise, the act of entrusting the body to the care of a funeral establishment carries with it an implied permission to go ahead and embalm.

Embalming is indeed a most extraordinary procedure, and one must wonder at the docility of Americans who each year pay hundreds of millions of dollars for its perpetuation, blissfully ignorant of what it is all about, what is done, how it is done. Not one in ten thousand has any idea of what actually takes place. Books on the subject are extremely hard to come by. They are not to be found in most libraries or bookshops.

In an era when huge television audiences watch surgical operations 5 in the comfort of their living rooms, when, thanks to the animated cartoon, the geography of the digestive system has become familiar territory even to the nursery school set, in a land where the satisfaction of curiosity about almost all matters is a national pastime, the secrecy surrounding embalming can, surely, hardly be attributed to the inherent gruesomeness of the subject. Custom in this regard has within this century suffered a complete reversal. In the early days of American embalming, when it was performed in the home of the deceased, it was almost mandatory for some relative to stay by the embalmer's side and witness the procedure. Today, family members who might wish to be in attendance would certainly be dissuaded by the funeral director. All others, except apprentices, are excluded by law from the preparation room.

A close look at what does actually take place may explain in large measure the undertaker's intractable reticence concerning a procedure that has become his major *raison d'être*. Is it possible he fears that public information about embalming might lead patrons to wonder if they really want this service? If the funeral men are loath to discuss the subject outside the trade, the reader may, understandably, be equally loath to go on reading at this point. For those who have the stomach for it, let us part the formaldehyde curtain. Others should skip to paragraph 20.

The body is first laid out in the undertaker's morgue—or rather, Mr. Jones is reposing in the preparation room—to be readied to bid the world farewell.

The preparation room in any of the better funeral establishments has the tiled and sterile look of a surgery, and indeed the embalmer-restorative artist who does his chores there is beginning to adopt the term "dermasurgeon" (appropriately corrupted by some mortician-writers as "demisurgeon") to describe his calling. His equipment, consisting of scalpels, scissors, augers, forceps, clamps, needles, pumps, tubes, bowls and basins, is crudely imitative of the surgeon's, as is his technique, acquired in a nine- or twelve-month post-high-school course in an embalming school. He is supplied by an advanced chemical industry with a bewildering array of fluids, sprays, pastes, oils, powders, creams, to fix or soften tissue, shrink or distend it as needed, dry it here, restore the moisture there. There are cosmetics, waxes and paints to fill and cover features, even plaster of Paris to replace entire limbs. There are ingenious aids to prop and stabilize the cadaver: a Vari-Pose Head Rest, the Edwards Arm and Hand Positioner, the Repose Block (to support the shoulders, during the embalming), and the Throop Foot Positioner, which resembles an old-fashioned stocks.

Mr. John H. Eckels, president of the Eckels College of Mortuary Science, thus describes the first part of the embalming procedure: "In the hands of a skilled practitioner, this work may be done in a comparatively short time and without mutilating the body other than by slight incision—so slight that it scarcely would cause serious inconvenience if made upon a living person. It is necessary to remove the blood, and doing this not only helps in the disinfecting, but removes the principal cause of disfigurements due to discoloration."

Another textbook discusses the all-important time element: "The 10 earlier this is done, the better, for every hour that elapses between death and embalming will add to the problems and complications encountered...." Just how soon should one get going on the embalming? The author tells us, "On the basis of such scanty information made available to this profession through its rudimentary and haphazard system of technical research, we must conclude that the best results are to be obtained if the subject is embalmed before life is completely extinct—that is, before cellular death has occurred. In the average case, this would mean within an hour after somatic death." For those who feel that there is something a little rudimentary, not to say haphazard, about this advice, a comforting thought is offered by another writer. Speaking of fears entertained in early days of premature burial, he points out, "One of the effects of embalming by chemical injection, however, has been to dispel fears of live burial." How true; once the blood is removed, chances of live burial are indeed remote.

To return to Mr. Jones, the blood is drained out through the veins and replaced by embalming fluid pumped in through the arteries. As noted in *The Principles and Practices of Embalming*, "every operator has a favorite injection and drainage point—a fact which becomes a handicap only if he fails or refuses to forsake his favorites when conditions demand it." Typical favorites are the carotid artery, femoral artery, jugular vein, subclavian vein. There are various choices of embalming fluid. If Flextone is used, it will produce a "mild, flexible rigidity. The skin retains a velvety softness, the tissues are rubbery and pliable. Ideal for women and children." It may be blended with B. and G. Products Company's Lyf-Lyk tint, which is guaranteed to reproduce "nature's own skin texture . . . the velvety appearance of living tissue." Suntone comes in three separate tints: Suntan; Special Cosmetic Tint, a pink shade "especially indicated for young female subjects"; and Regular Cosmetic Tint, moderately pink.

About three to six gallons of a dyed and perfumed solution of formaldehyde, glycerin, borax, phenol, alcohol and water is soon circulating through Mr. Jones, whose mouth has been sewn together with a "needle directed upward between the upper lip and gum and brought out through the left nostril," with the corners raised slightly "for a more pleasant expression." If he should be bucktoothed, his teeth are cleaned with Bon Ami and coated with colorless nail polish. His eyes, meanwhile, are closed with flesh-tinted eye caps and eye cement.

The next step is to have at Mr. Jones with a thing called a trocar. This is a long, hollow needle attached to a tube. It is jabbed into the abdomen, poked around the entrails and chest cavity, the contents of which are pumped out and replaced with "cavity fluid." This done, and the hole in the abdomen sewn up, Mr. Jones's face is heavily creamed (to protect the skin from burns which may be caused by leakage of the chemicals), and he is covered with a sheet and left unmolested for a while. But not for long—there is more, much more, in store for him. He has been embalmed, but not yet restored, and the best time to start the restorative work is eight to ten hours after embalming, when the tissues have become firm and dry.

The object of all this attention to the corpse, it must be remembered, is to make it presentable for viewing in an attitude of healthy repose. "Our customs require the presentation of our dead in the semblance of normality . . . unmarred by the ravages of illness, disease, or mutilation," says Mr. J. Sheridan Mayer in his *Restorative Art*. This is rather a large order since few people die in the full bloom of health, unravaged by illness and unmarked by some disfigurement. The funeral industry is equal to the challenge: "In some cases the gruesome appearance of a mutilated or disease-ridden subject may be quite discouraging. The task of restoration may seem impossible and shake the confidence of the embalmer. This is the time for intestinal fortitude and determination. Once the formative work is begun and affected tissues are cleaned or removed, all doubts of success vanish. It is surprising and gratifying to discover the results which may be obtained."

The embalmer, having allowed an appropriate interval to elapse, 15 returns to the attack, but now he brings into play the skill and equipment of sculptor and cosmetician. Is a hand missing? Casting one in plaster of Paris is a simple matter. "For replacement purposes, only a cast of the back of the hand is necessary; this is within the ability of the average operator and is quite adequate." If a lip or two, a nose or an ear should be missing, the embalmer has at hand a variety of restorative waxes with which to model replacements. Pores and skin texture are simulated by stippling with a little brush, and over this cosmetics are laid on. Head off? Decapitation cases are rather routinely handled. Ragged edges are trimmed, and head joined to torso with a series of splints, wires and sutures. It is a good idea to have a little something at the neck—a scarf or high collar—when time for viewing comes. Swollen mouth? Cut out tissue as needed from inside the lips. If too much is removed, the surface contour can easily be restored by padding with cotton. Swollen necks and cheeks are reduced by removing tissue through vertical incisions made down each side of the neck. "When the deceased is casketed, the pillow will hide the suture incisions . . . as an extra precaution against leakage, the suture may be painted with liquid sealer."

The opposite condition is more likely to present itself—that of emaciation. His hypodermic syringe now loaded with massage cream, the embalmer seeks out and fills the hollowed and sunken areas by injection. In this procedure the backs of the hands and fingers and the under-chin area should not be neglected.

Positioning the lips is a problem that recurrently challenges the ingenuity of the embalmer. Closed too tightly, they tend to give a stern, even disapproving expression. Ideally, embalmers feel, the lips should give the impression of being ever so slightly parted, the upper lip protruding slightly for a more youthful appearance. This takes some engineering, however, as the lips tend to drift apart. Lip drift can sometimes be remedied by pushing one or two straight pins through the inner margin of the lower lip and then inserting them between the two front upper teeth. If Mr. Jones happens to have no teeth, the pins can just as easily be anchored in his Armstrong Face Former and Denture Replacer. Another method to maintain lip closure is to dislocate the lower jaw, which is then held in its new position by a wire run through holes which have been drilled through the upper and lower jaws at the midline. As the French are fond of saying, *il faut souffrir pour être belle.*[2]

If Mr. Jones has died of jaundice, the embalming fluid will very likely turn him green. Does this deter the embalmer? Not if he has intestinal fortitude. Masking pastes and cosmetics are heavily laid on, burial garments and casket interiors are color-correlated with particular care, and Jones is displayed beneath rose-colored lights. Friends will say, "How *well* he looks." Death by carbon monoxide, on the other hand, can be rather a good thing from the embalmer's viewpoint: "One advantage is the fact that this type of discoloration is an exaggerated form of a natural pink coloration." This is nice because the healthy glow is already present and needs but little attention.

The patching and filling completed, Mr. Jones is now shaved, washed and dressed. Cream-based cosmetic, available in pink, flesh, suntan, brunette and blond, is applied to his hands and face, his hair is shampooed and combed (and, in the case of Mrs. Jones, set), his hands manicured. For the horny-handed son of toil special care must be taken; cream should be applied to remove ingrained grime, and the nails cleaned. "If he were not in the habit of having them manicured in

---

[2]In 1963 *Mortuary Management* reports a new development: "Natural Expression Formers," an invention of Funeral Directors Research Company. "They may be used to replace one or both artificial dentures, or over natural teeth; have 'bite-indicator' lines as a closure guide . . . Natural Expression Formers also offer more control of facial expression" [Author's note]. *Il faut souffrir pour être belle:* One must suffer to be beautiful (French).

life, trimming and shaping is advised for better appearance—never questioned by kin."

Jones is now ready for casketing (this is the present participle of 20 the verb "to casket"). In this operation his right shoulder should be depressed slightly "to turn the body a bit to the right and soften the appearance of lying flat on the back." Positioning the hands is a matter of importance, and special rubber positioning blocks may be used. The hands should be cupped slightly for a more lifelike, relaxed appearance. Proper placement of the body requires a delicate sense of balance. It should lie as high as possible in the casket, yet not so high that the lid, when lowered, will hit the nose. On the other hand, we are cautioned, placing the body too low "creates the impression that the body is in a box."

Jones is next wheeled into the appointed slumber room where a few last touches may be added—his favorite pipe placed in his hand or, if he was a great reader, a book propped into position. (In the case of little Master Jones a Teddy bear may be clutched.) Here he will hold open house for a few days, visiting hours 10 A.M. to 9 P.M.

All now being in readiness, the funeral director calls a staff conference to make sure that each assistant knows his precise duties. Mr. Wilber Krieger writes: "This makes your staff feel that they are a part of the team, with a definite assignment that must be properly carried out if the whole plan is to succeed. You never heard of a football coach who failed to talk to his entire team before they go on the field. They have drilled on the plays they are to execute for hours and days, and yet the successful coach knows the importance of making even the bench-warming third-string substitute feel that he is important if the game is to be won." The winning of *this* game is predicated upon glass-smooth handling of the logistics. The funeral director has notified the pallbearers whose names were furnished by the family, has arranged for the presence of clergyman, organist, and soloist, has provided transportation for everybody, has organized and listed the flowers sent by friends. In *Psychology of Funeral Service* Mr. Edward A. Martin points out: "He may not always do as much as the family thinks he is doing, but it is his helpful guidance that they appreciate in knowing they are proceeding as they should. . . . The important thing is how well his services can be used to make the family believe they are giving unlimited expression to their own sentiment."

The religious service may be held in a church or in the chapel of the funeral home; the funeral director vastly prefers the latter arrangement, for not only is it more convenient for him but it affords him the opportunity to show off his beautiful facilities to the gathered mourners. After the clergyman has had his say, the mourners queue up to file past the casket for a last look at the deceased. The family is *never* asked whether they want an open-casket ceremony; in the absence of their instruction to the contrary, this is taken for granted. Consequently well over 90 percent of all American funerals feature the open casket—a custom unknown in other parts of the world. Foreigners are astonished by it. An English woman living in San Francisco described her reaction in a letter to the writer:

> I myself have attended only one funeral here—that of an elderly fellow worker of mine. After the service I could not understand why everyone was walking towards the coffin (sorry, I mean casket), but thought I had better follow the crowd. It shook me rigid to get there and find the casket open and poor old Oscar lying there in his brown tweed suit, wearing a suntan makeup and just the wrong shade of lipstick. If I had not been extremely fond of the old boy, I have a horrible feeling that I might have giggled. Then and there I decided that I could never face another American funeral—even dead.

The casket (which has been resting throughout the service on a Classic Beauty Ultra Metal Casket Bier) is now transferred by a hydraulically operated device called Porto-Lift to a balloon-tired, Glide Easy casket carriage which will wheel it to yet another conveyance, the Cadillac Funeral Coach. This may be lavender, cream, light green—anything but black. Interiors, of course, are color-correlated, "for the man who cannot stop short of perfection."

At graveside, the casket is lowered into the earth. This office, once 25 the prerogative of friends of the deceased, is now performed by a patented mechanical lowering device. A "Lifetime Green" artificial grass mat is at the ready to conceal the sere earth, and overhead, to conceal the sky, is a portable Steril Chapel Tent ("resists the intense heat and humidity of summer and the terrific storms of winter . . . available in Silver Grey, Rose or Evergreen"). Now is the time for the ritual scattering of earth over the coffin, as the solemn words "earth to earth, ashes to ashes, dust to dust" are pronounced by the officiating cleric. This can today be accomplished "with a mere flick of the wrist with the Gordon Leak-Proof Earth Dispenser. No grasping of a handful of dirt, no soiled fingers. Simple, dignified, beautiful, reverent! The modern way!" The Gordon Earth Dispenser (at $5) is of nickel-plated brass construction. It is not only "attractive to the eye and long wearing"; it is also "one of the 'tools' for building better public relations" if presented as "an appropriate non-commercial gift" to the clergyman. It is shaped something like a saltshaker.

Untouched by human hand, the coffin and the earth are now united.

It is in the function of directing the participants through this maze of gadgetry that the funeral director has assigned to himself his relatively new role of "grief therapist." He has relieved the family of every detail, he has revamped the corpse to look like a living doll, he has arranged for it to nap for a few days in a slumber room, he has put on a well-oiled performance in which the concept of *death* has played no part whatsoever—unless it was inconsiderately mentioned by the clergyman who conducted the religious service. He has done everything in his power to make the funeral a real pleasure for everybody concerned. He and his team have given their all to score an upset victory over death.

STUDY QUESTIONS

1. In paragraph 6, Mitford invites the reader to "part the formaldehyde curtain." What does she mean? How is the formaldehyde curtain like the "Iron Curtain" that divided western and eastern Europe during the Cold War era?

2. Mitford writes a PROCESS essay about embalming. However, rather than simply list each step, she DESCRIBES and EXPLAINS each part of the process. Identify two steps that are fully explained and discuss your reaction to them. Does this kind of process essay help you better understand the subject? Explain.

3. Consider the TOPIC and the TONE of the article. Do you think the two are consistent? Describe the tone that Mitford uses to explain the process of embalming. Who is her intended AUDIENCE? Rewrite one or two steps using a different tone for a different audience.

4. *For Writing.* Consider a process that you are familiar with. Write a process essay that explains the steps to complete the activity. Use Mitford's essay as a model—don't just list the steps, explain the steps and DESCRIBE the equipment needed to perform the activity. Write the paper for two different audiences: one that is familiar with the process and one that is unfamiliar with it.

SAMUEL SCUDDER { *Look at Your Fish: In the Laboratory with Agassiz*

SAMUEL SCUDDER (1837–1911) the first North American insect paleontologist, was born in Boston, Massachusetts, and educated at both Williams
College, graduating in 1857, and Harvard University, graduating in 1862.
Well known for advocating firsthand observation as an indispensable part
of the scientific process, Scudder published extensively—more than seven
hundred articles during the course of his career. He was twice president
of the Boston Society of Natural History, cofounder of the Cambridge
Entomological Club's journal *Psyche*, and the first editor of the journal
Science.

In the following selection, Scudder recounts the story of his first
encounter with the famed paleontologist Louis Agassiz at Harvard
University. It tells of an impatient young biology student, bored after ten
minutes of looking at a dead fish, who discovers that he cannot really begin
to engage in science at all until he immerses himself in the process of observation, which can take days, even months, in order to understand something. Consider how well you think you know the physical structure or the
behavior of a family member, a pet, or even yourself. Do you think you
might learn something new with closer, longer observations?

IT WAS MORE THAN FIFTEEN years ago that I entered the laboratory of
Professor Agassiz, and told him I had enrolled my name in the scientific school as a student of natural history. He asked me a few questions
about my object in coming, my antecedents generally, the mode in
which I afterwards proposed to use the knowledge I might acquire,
and finally, whether I wished to study any special branch. To the latter
I replied that while I wished to be well grounded in all departments of
zoology, I purposed to devote myself specially to insects.

"When do you wish to begin?" he asked.

"Now," I replied.

This seemed to please him, and with an energetic "Very well," he reached from a shelf a huge jar of specimens in yellow alcohol.

"Take this *fish*," said he, "and look at it; we call it a Hæmulon; by and by I will ask what you have seen." 5

With that he left me, but in a moment returned with explicit instructions as to the care of the object entrusted to me.

"No man is fit to be a naturalist," said he, "who does not know how to take care of specimens."

I was to keep the fish before me in a tin tray, and occasionally moisten the surface with alcohol from the jar, always taking care to replace the stopper tightly. Those were not the days of ground glass stoppers, and elegantly shaped exhibition jars; all the old students will recall the huge, neckless glass bottles with their leaky, wax-besmeared corks, half eaten by insects and begrimed with cellar dust. Entomology was a cleaner science than ichthyology, but the example of the professor, who had unhesitatingly plunged to the bottom of the jar to produce the fish, was infectious; and though this alcohol had "a very ancient and fish-like smell," I really dared not show any aversion within these sacred precincts, and treated the alcohol as though it were pure water. Still I was conscious of a passing feeling of disappointment, for gazing at a fish did not commend itself to an ardent entomologist. My friends at home, too, were annoyed, when they discovered that no amount of eau de cologne would drown the perfume which haunted me like a shadow.

In ten minutes I had seen all that could be seen in that fish, and started in search of the professor, who had however left the museum; and when I returned, after lingering over some of the odd animals stored in the upper apartment, my specimen was dry all over. I dashed the fluid over the fish as if to resuscitate the beast from a fainting-fit, and looked with anxiety for a return of the normal, sloppy appearance. This little excitement over, nothing was to be done but return to a steadfast gaze at my mute companion. Half an hour passed,—an hour,—another hour; the fish began to look loathsome. I turned it over and around; looked it in the face,—ghastly; from behind, beneath, above, sideways, at a three quarters' view,—just as ghastly. I was in despair; at an early hour I concluded that lunch was necessary; so, with infinite relief, the fish was carefully replaced in the jar, and for an hour I was free.

On my return, I learned that Professor Agassiz had been at the museum, but had gone and would not return for several hours. My fellow-students were too busy to be disturbed by continued conversation. Slowly I drew forth that hideous fish, and with a feeling of desperation again looked at it. I might not use a magnifying glass; instruments of all kinds were interdicted. My two hands, my two eyes, and the fish; it seemed a most limited field. I pushed my finger down its throat to feel how sharp the teeth were. I began to count the scales in the different rows until I was convinced that that was nonsense. At last a happy thought struck me—I would draw the fish; and now with surprise I began to discover new features in the creature. Just then the professor returned.

"That is right," said he; "a pencil is one of the best of eyes. I am glad to notice, too, that you keep your specimen wet and your bottle corked."

With these encouraging words, he added,—

"Well, what is it like?"

He listened attentively to my brief rehearsal of the structure of parts whose names were still unknown to me: the fringed gill-arches and movable operculum; the pores of the head, fleshy lips, and lidless eyes; the lateral line, the spinous fins, and forked tail; the compressed and arched body. When I had finished, he waited as if expecting more, and then, with an air of disappointment,—

"You have not looked very carefully; why," he continued, more earnestly, "you haven't even seen one of the most conspicuous features of the animal, which is as plainly before your eyes as the fish itself; look again, look again!" and he left me to my misery.

I was piqued; I was mortified. Still more of that wretched fish! But now I set myself to my task with a will, and discovered one new thing after another, until I saw how just the professor's criticism had been. The afternoon passed quickly, and when, toward its close, the professor inquired,—

"Do you see it yet?"

"No," I replied, "I am certain I do not, but I see how little I saw before."

"That is next best," said he, earnestly, "but I won't hear you now; put away your fish and go home; perhaps you will be ready with a better answer in the morning. I will examine you before you look at the fish."

This was disconcerting; not only must I think of my fish all night, 20 studying, without the object before me, what this unknown but most visible feature might be; but also, without reviewing my new discoveries, I must give an exact account of them the next day. I had a bad memory; so I walked home by Charles River[1] in a distracted state, with my two perplexities.

The cordial greeting from the professor the next morning was reassuring; here was a man who seemed to be quite as anxious as I, that I should see for myself what he saw.

"Do you perhaps mean," I asked, "that the fish has symmetrical sides with paired organs?"

His thoroughly pleased, "Of course, of course!" repaid the wakeful hours of the previous night. After he had discoursed most happily and enthusiastically—as he always did—upon the importance of this point, I ventured to ask what I should do next.

"Oh, look at your fish!" he said, and left me again to my own devices. In a little more than an hour he returned and heard my new catalogue.

"That is good, that is good!" he repeated; "but that is not all; go on;" 25 and so for three long days he placed that fish before my eyes, forbidding me to look at anything else, or to use any artificial aid. "Look, look, look," was his repeated injunction.

This was the best entomological lesson I ever had,—a lesson, whose influence has extended to the details of every subsequent study; a legacy the professor has left to me, as he has left it to many others, of inestimable value, which we could not buy, with which we cannot part.

[1]Massachusetts river between Boston and Cambridge.

A year afterward, some of us were amusing ourselves with chalking outlandish beasts upon the museum blackboard. We drew prancing star-fishes; frogs in mortal combat; hydra-headed worms; stately craw-fishes, standing on their tails, bearing aloft umbrellas; and grotesque fishes with gaping mouths and staring eyes. The professor came in shortly after, and was as amused as any, at our experiments. He looked at the fishes.

"Hæmulons, every one of them," he said; "Mr. ——[2] drew them."

True; and to this day, if I attempt a fish, I can draw nothing but Hæmulons.

The fourth day, a second fish of the same group was placed beside 30 the first, and I was bidden to point out the resemblances and differences between the two; another and another followed, until the entire family lay before me, and a whole legion of jars covered the table and surrounding shelves; the odor had become a pleasant perfume; and even now, the sight of an old, six-inch, worm-eaten cork brings fragrant memories!

The whole group of Hæmulons was thus brought in review; and, whether engaged upon the dissection of the internal organs, the preparation and examination of the bony frame-work, or the description of the various parts, Agassiz' training in the method of observing facts and their orderly arrangement was ever accompanied by the urgent exhortation not to be content with them.

"Facts are stupid things," he would say, "until brought into connection with some general law."

At the end of eight months, it was almost with reluctance that I left these friends and turned to insects; but what I had gained by this outside experience has been of greater value than years of later investigation in my favorite groups.

[2]The article originally appeared anonymously—"BY A FORMER PUPIL."

STUDY QUESTIONS

1. What is the student's initial mindset regarding lab work? How does it change? What sensory details enliven Scudder's DESCRIPTION of his first days in the laboratory?

2. What kind of PROCESS does Professor Agassiz encourage? How is this process both challenging and helpful to the student?

3. What kind of ORGANIZATION does Scudder use to present the process of learning to observe? What other organization might he have used?

4. *For Writing.* Choose something to observe—perhaps an animal, a plant, or even yourself—and spend several days looking at it carefully. Then in an essay ANALYZE your process of observation and what it yielded. What did you learn and how did you learn it?